PRENTICE HALL

WORLD STUDIES

Don't miss these powerful teacher timesavers!

Teacher's Edition Step-by-step guide for teachers ensures that objectives are met, provides reading strategies, makes point-of-use suggestions for using resources, and offers differentiated instruction.

Teaching Resources

All-in-One Teaching Resources Everything you need to teach in one location—including lesson plans, worksheets, tests, and transparency planner—making it easy to find materials, prep for class, and teach exciting lessons.

PRENTICE HALL

TeacherEXPRESS™

Plan • Teach • Assess

TeacherExpress CD-ROM Powerful lesson planning, resource management, testing, and an interactive Teacher's Edition, all in one place, make class preparation quick and easy!

Teacher's Edition

PRENTICE HALL

WORLD STUDIES

EUROPE and RUSSIA

Geography • History • Culture

In association with
DK

DISCOVERY
CHANNEL
SCHOOL

PEARSON

Prentice
Hall

Needham, Massachusetts
Upper Saddle River, New Jersey

Program Consultants

Heidi Hayes Jacobs

Heidi Hayes Jacobs has served as an education consultant to more than 1,000 schools across the nation and abroad. Dr. Jacobs serves as an adjunct professor in the Department of Curriculum on Teaching at Teachers College, Columbia University. She has written two best-selling books and numerous articles on curriculum reform. She received an M.A. from the University of Massachusetts, Amherst, and completed her doctoral work at Columbia University's Teachers College in 1981. The core of Dr. Jacobs's experience comes from her years teaching high school, middle school, and elementary school students. As an educational consultant, she works with K–12 schools and districts on curriculum reform and strategic planning.

Michal L. LeVasseur

Michal L. LeVasseur is the Executive Director of the National Council for Geography Education. She is an instructor in the College of Education at Jacksonville State University and works with the Alabama Geographic Alliance. Her undergraduate and graduate work were in the fields of anthropology (B.A.), geography (M.A.), and science education (Ph.D.). Dr. LeVasseur's specialization has moved increasingly into the area of geography education. Since 1996 she has served as the Director of the National Geographic Society's Summer Geography Workshops. As an educational consultant, she has worked with the National Geographic Society as well as with schools and organizations to develop programs and curricula for geography.

Senior Reading Consultants

Kate Kinsella

Kate Kinsella, Ed.D., is a faculty member in the Department of Secondary Education at San Francisco State University. A specialist in second-language acquisition and adolescent literacy, she teaches coursework addressing language and literacy development across the secondary curricula. Dr. Kinsella earned her M.A. in TESOL from San Francisco State University, and her Ed.D. in Second Language Acquisition from the University of San Francisco.

Kevin Feldman

Kevin Feldman, Ed.D., is the Director of Reading and Early Intervention with the Sonoma County Office of Education (SCOE) and an independent educational consultant. At the SCOE, he develops, organizes, and monitors programs related to K–12 literacy. Dr. Feldman has an M.A. from the University of California, Riverside in Special Education, Learning Disabilities and Instructional Design. He earned his Ed.D. in Curriculum and Instruction from the University of San Francisco.

Acknowledgments appear on pages 248–9, which constitute an extension of this copyright page.

Copyright © 2005 by Pearson Education, Inc., publishing as Pearson Prentice Hall, Upper Saddle River, New Jersey 07458.
All rights reserved. Printed in the United States of America. This publication is protected by copyright, and permission should be obtained from the publisher prior to any prohibited reproduction, storage in a retrieval system, or transmission in any form or by any means, electronic, mechanical, photocopying, recording, or likewise. For information regarding permission(s), write to: Rights and Permissions Department.

MapMaster™ is a trademark of Pearson Education, Inc.
Pearson Prentice Hall™ is a trademark of Pearson Education, Inc.
Pearson® is a registered trademark of Pearson plc.
Prentice Hall® is a registered trademark of Pearson Education, Inc.
Discovery Channel School® is a registered trademark of Discovery Communications, Inc.
ExamView® is a trademark of FSCreations, Inc.

 is a registered trademark of Dorling Kindersley Limited. Prentice Hall World Studies is published in collaboration with DK Designs, Dorling Kindersley Limited, 80 Strand, London WC2R ORL. A Penguin Company.

ISBN 0-13-128008-2
12345678910   08 07 06 05 04

Cartography Consultant

 ## Andrew Heritage

Andrew Heritage has been publishing atlases and maps for some 25 years. In 1991, he joined the leading illustrated nonfiction publisher Dorling Kindersley (DK) with the task of building an international atlas list from scratch. The DK atlas list now includes some 10 titles, which are constantly updated and appear in new editions either annually or every other year.

Academic Reviewers

Africa
Barbara B. Brown, Ph.D.
African Studies Center
Boston University
Boston, Massachusetts

Ancient World
Evelyn DeLong Mangie, Ph.D.
Department of History
University of South Florida
Tampa, Florida

Central Asia and the Middle East
Pamela G. Sayre
History Department,
   Social Sciences Division
Henry Ford Community College
Dearborn, Michigan

East Asia
Huping Ling, Ph.D.
History Department
Truman State University
Kirksville, Missouri

Eastern Europe
Robert M. Jenkins
Center for Slavic, Eurasian and
   East European Studies
University of North Carolina
Chapel Hill, North Carolina

Latin America
Dan La Botz
Professor, History Department
Miami University
Oxford, Ohio

Medieval Times
James M. Murray
History Department
University of Cincinnati
Cincinnati, Ohio

North Africa
Barbara E. Petzen
Center for Middle Eastern Studies
Harvard University
Cambridge, Massachusetts

Religion
Charles H. Lippy, Ph.D.
Department of Philosophy
   and Religion
University of Tennessee
   at Chattanooga
Chattanooga, Tennessee

Russia
Janet Vaillant
Davis Center for Russian
   and Eurasian Studies
Harvard University
Cambridge, Massachusetts

South Asia
Robert J. Young
Professor Emeritus
History Department
West Chester University
West Chester, Pennsylvania

United States and Canada
Victoria Randlett
Geography Department
University of Nevada, Reno
Reno, Nevada

Western Europe
Ruth Mitchell-Pitts
Center for European Studies
University of North Carolina
   at Chapel Hill
Chapel Hill, North Carolina

Reviewers

Sean Brennan
Brecksville-Broadview Heights
   City School District
Broadview Heights, Ohio

Stephen Bullick
Mt. Lebanon School District
Pittsburgh, Pennsylvania

William R. Cranshaw, Ed.D.
Waycross Middle School
Waycross, Georgia

Dr. Louis P. De Angelo
Archdiocese of Philadelphia
Philadelphia, Pennsylvania

Paul Francis Durietz
Social Studies
   Curriculum Coordinator
Woodland District #50
Gurnee, Illinois

Gail Dwyer
Dickerson Middle School,
   Cobb County
Marietta, Georgia

Michal Howden
Social Studies Consultant
Zionsville, Indiana

Rosemary Kalloch
Springfield Public Schools
Springfield, Massachusetts

Deborah J. Miller
Office of Social Studies,
   Detroit Public Schools
Detroit, Michigan

Steven P. Missal
Newark Public Schools
Newark, New Jersey

Catherine Fish Petersen (Retired)
East Islip School District
Islip Terrace, New York

Joe Wieczorek
Social Studies Consultant
Baltimore, Maryland

Table of Contents

EUROPE and RUSSIA

Develop Skills

Use these pages to develop students' reading, writing, and geography skills.

Build a Regional Background

Introduce students to the geography, history, and culture of the region.

Focus on Countries

Create an understanding of the region by focusing on specific countries.

DISCOVERY CHANNEL SCHOOL

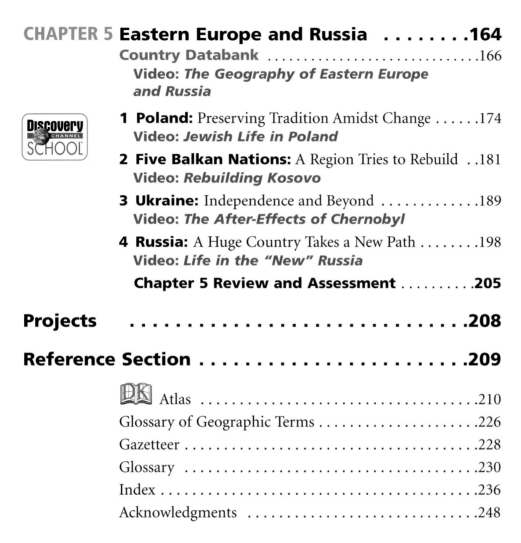

- Learn map skills with the MapMaster Skills Handbook.
- Practice your skills with every map in this book.
- Interact with every map online and on CD-ROM.

Maps and illustrations created by DK help build your understanding of the world. The DK World Desk Reference Online keeps you up to date.

Video/DVD

The World Studies Video Program takes you on field trips to study countries around the world.

The World Studies Interactive Textbook online and on CD-ROM uses interactive maps and other activities to help you learn.

COUNTRY DATABANK

Read about all the countries that make up Europe and Russia.

Literature

A selection by a European author brings social studies to life.

COUNTRY PROFILES

Theme-based maps and charts provide a closer look at countries, regions, and provinces.

Links

See the fascinating links between social studies and other disciplines.

Skills for Life

Teach skills that students will use throughout their lives.

Target Reading Skills

Chapter-by-chapter reading skills help students read and understand social studies concepts.

Citizen Heroes

Introduce people who have made a difference in their country.

DK Eyewitness Technology

Detailed drawings show how technology shapes places and societies.

Discovery Channel School Video/DVD

Explore the geography, history, and cultures of Russia and the countries of Europe.

MAP★MASTER™ Interactive

Go online to find an interactive version of every MapMaster™ map in this book. Use the Web Code provided to gain direct access to these maps.

How to Use Web Codes:

1. Go to **www.PHSchool.com**.

2. Enter the Web Code.

3. Click Go!

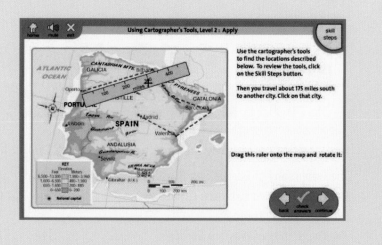

NCLB Implications for Social Studies

The No Child Left Behind (NCLB) legislation was a landmark in educational reform designed to improve student achievement and create a fundamental shift in American education. In the essay that follows, we will explore the implications of NCLB on social studies curriculum, instruction, assessment, and instructional programs.

Facts about NCLB

The No Child Left Behind Act of 2001 (NCLB) calls for sweeping educational reform, requiring all students to perform proficiently on standardized tests in reading, mathematics, and (soon to be added) science by the year 2014. Under NCLB, schools will be held accountable for students' academic progress. In exchange for this accountability, the law offers more flexibility to individual states and school districts to decide how best to use federal education funds. NCLB places an emphasis on implementing scientifically proven methods in teaching reading and mathematics, and promotes teacher quality. It also offers parental choice for students in failing schools.

Effects on Curriculum, Instruction, and Assessment

Since the primary focus of NCLB is on raising the achievement of students in reading and mathematics, some educators have wondered how it relates to social studies. Some teachers have expressed concerns that since NCLB does not require yearly testing of social studies, state and school districts may decide to shift resources and class time away from teaching social studies. However, NCLB considers the social studies areas of history, geography, economics, and government and civics to be core academic subjects. Many states are requiring middle grades social studies teachers to be highly qualified in history and geography in order to comply with the principle of improving teacher quality in NCLB.

NCLB sets the goal of having every child meet state-defined education standards. Since social studies educators have been leaders in the development of standards-based education and accountability through student testing over the past decade, many state and local districts have their own standards and assessments for social studies already in place. Assessment, including screening, diagnostic, progress-monitoring—including end-of-year, end-of-schooling, grade level, district, and state testing—and large-scale assessments, will continue to play a significant role in shaping social studies curriculum and instruction in the near future.

Integrating Reading into Social Studies Instruction

Due to the increased emphasis on reading and mathematics required by NCLB, social studies teachers may be called on to help improve their students' reading and math skills. For example, a teacher might use a graph about exports and imports to reinforce math skills, or a primary source about a historical event to improve reading skills. The connection between reading and social studies is especially important. Since many state and local assessments of reading require students to read and interpret informational texts, social studies passages are often used in the exams. Therefore, social studies teachers may assist in raising reading scores by integrating reading instruction into their teaching of social studies content.

Implications for Instructional Programs

The environment created by the NCLB legislation has implications for instructional programs. In keeping with the spirit of NCLB, social studies programs should clearly tie their content to state and local standards. Programs should also provide support so that all students can master these standards, ensuring that no child is left behind. An ideal instructional program is rooted in research, embeds reading instruction into the instructional design, and provides assessment tools that inform instruction—helping teachers focus on improving student performance.

Prentice Hall Response

We realize that raising the achievement level of all students is the number one challenge facing teachers today. To assist you in meeting this challenge, Prentice Hall enlisted a team of respected consultants who specialize in middle grades issues, reading in the content areas, and geographic education. This team created a middle grades world studies program that breaks new ground and meets the changing needs of you and your students.

With Prentice Hall, you can be confident that your students will not only be motivated, inspired, and excited to learn world studies, but they will also achieve the success needed in today's environment of the No Child Left Behind (NCLB) legislation and testing reform.

In the following pages, you will find the key elements woven throughout this World Studies program that truly set it apart and assure success for you and your students.

Teacher's Edition Contents in Brief

Research on Effective Reading Instruction

Why do many students have difficulty reading textbooks? How can we help students read to learn social studies? In the pages that follow, we examine the research on the challenge of reading textbooks; explain the direct, systematic, and explicit instruction needed to help students; and then show how Prentice Hall has responded to this research.

What is skilled reading?

Recent research (Snow et al., 2002) suggests that skillful and strategic reading is a long-term developmental process in which "readers learn how to simultaneously extract and construct meaning through interaction with written language." In other words, successful readers know how to decode all kinds of words, read with fluency and expression, have well-developed vocabularies, and possess various comprehension strategies such as note-taking and summarizing to employ as the academic reading task demands.

Many students lack reading skills

Sadly, many secondary students do not have solid reading skills. In the early years, students read mainly engaging and accessible narratives, such as stories, poems, and junior biographies. But in the upper elementary years, they shift toward conceptually dense and challenging nonfiction, or expository texts. It is no accident that the infamous "Fourth-Grade Slump" (Chall, 2003; Hirsch 2003)—a well-documented national trend of declining literacy after grade four—occurs during this time. The recent National Assessment of Educational Progress (NAEP, 2002) found that only 33 percent of eighth-grade students scored at or above the proficient level in reading.

Even students quite skilled in reading novels, short stories, and adolescent magazines typically come to middle school ill-equipped for the rigors of informational texts or reading to learn. They tend to dive right into a social studies chapter as if reading a recreational story. They don't first preview the material to create a mental outline and establish a reading purpose. They have not yet learned other basic strategies, including reading a section more than once, taking notes as they read, and reading to answer specific questions.

Dr. Kate Kinsella
Reading Consultant for *World Studies*
Department of Secondary Education
San Francisco State University, CA

Dr. Kevin Feldman
Reading Consultant for *World Studies*
Director of Reading and Early Intervention
Sonoma County, CA

"Even students quite skilled in reading novels, short stories, and adolescent magazines typically come to middle school ill-equipped for the rigors of informational texts or reading to learn."

The unique demands of textbooks

The differences between textbooks and the narratives students are used to reading are dramatic. The most distinctive challenges include dense conceptual content, heavy vocabulary load, unfamiliar paragraph and organizational patterns, and complex sentence structures. Academic texts present such a significant challenge to most students that linguists and language researchers liken them to learning a foreign language (Schleppegrell, 2002). In other words, most secondary students are second language learners: they are learning the academic language of informational texts!

Effective reading instruction

Research illustrates that virtually all students benefit from direct, systematic, and explicit instruction in reading informational texts (Baker & Gersten, 2000). There are three stages to the instructional process for content-area reading:

(1) before reading: instructional frontloading;

(2) during reading: guided instruction;

(3) after reading: reflection and study.

Before reading

Placing a major emphasis on preteaching, or "front-loading" your instruction—building vocabulary, setting a purpose for reading, and explicitly teaching students strategies for actively engaging with the text—helps you structure learning to ensure student success (see Strategies 1 and 2 on pages T32-T33). Frontloading strategies are especially critical in mixed-ability classrooms with English language learners, students with special needs, and other students performing below grade level in terms of literacy.

During reading

In guided instruction, the teacher models approaches for actively engaging with text to gain meaning. The teacher guides students through the first reading of the text using passage reading strategies (see Strategies 3-7 on pages T33-35), and then guides discussion about the content using participation strategies (see Strategies 8-11 on pages T35-T37). Finally, students record key information in a graphic organizer.

After reading

During the reflection and study phase, the teacher formally checks for student understanding, offers remediation if necessary, and provides activities that challenge students to apply content in a new way. To review the chapter, students recall content, analyze the reading as a whole, and study key vocabulary and information likely to be tested.

References

Baker, Scott and Russell Gersten. "What We Know About Effective Instructional Practices for English Language Learners." *Exceptional Children*, 66 (2000):454–470.

Chall, Jeanne S. and Vicki A. Jacobs. "Poor Children's Fourth-Grade Slump." *American Educator* (Spring 2003):14.

Donahue, P.L., et al. *The 1998 NAEP Reading Report Card for the Nation and the States* (NCES 1999-500). Washington, D.C.: U.S. Department of Education, Office of Education Research and Improvement, National Center for Education Statistics, 1999.

Grigg, W.S. et al. *The Nation's Report Card: Reading 2002* (NCES 2003-521). Washington, D.C.: U.S. Department of Education, Institute of Education Sciences, National Center for Education Statistics, 2003.

Hirsch, E.D., Jr. "Reading Comprehension Requires Knowledge—of Words and the World." *American Educator* (Spring 2003):10-29.

Kinsella, Kate, et al. *Teaching Guidebook for Universal Access.* Upper Saddle River, NJ: Prentice Hall, 2002.

Schleppegrell, M. "Linguistic Features of the Language of Schooling." *Linguistics and Education*, 12, no. 4 (2002): 431–459.

Snow, C., et al. *Reading for Understanding: Toward an R&D Program in Reading Comprehension.* Santa Monica, California: The Rand Corporation, 2002.

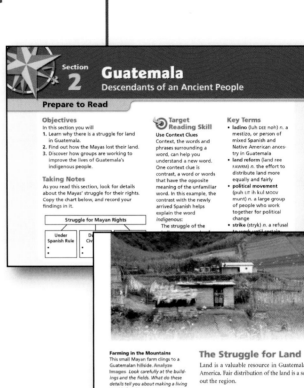

Reading Support

Putting Research Into Practice

Prentice Hall enlisted the assistance of Dr. Kate Kinsella and Dr. Kevin Feldman to ensure that the new middle grades world studies program would provide the direct, systematic, and explicit instruction needed to foster student success in reading informational texts. To help students rise to the challenge of reading an informational text, *World Studies* embedded reading support right into the student text.

Embedded Reading Support in the Student Text

Before students read

• **Objectives** set the purpose for what students will read.

• **Target Reading Skill** for the section is explained.

• **Key Terms** are defined up front with pronunciation and part of speech.

During the section

• **Target Reading Skill** is applied to help students read and understand the narrative.

• **Key Terms** are defined in context, with terms and definitions called out in blue type.

• **Reading Checks** reinforce students' understanding by slowing them down to review after every concept is discussed.

• **Caption Questions** draw students into the art and photos, helping them to connect the content to the images.

After students read

• **Section Assessment** revisits the **Key Terms**, provides an opportunity to master the **Target Reading Skill**, allows student to rehearse their understanding of the text through the **Writing Activity**.

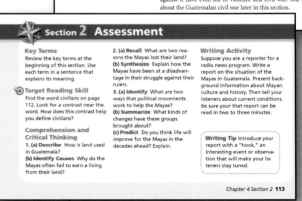

Putting Research Into Practice

World Studies offers teachers guidance in direct, systematic, and explicit reading instruction. The instructional sequence in the Teacher's Edition explicitly guides you in the use of effective strategies at each stage of the instructional process.

Reading Instruction in *World Studies* Teacher's Edition

Before Reading

Every lesson plan begins with suggestions that help you integrate frontloading strategies into your teaching. Build Background Knowledge activates and builds prior knowledge. Set a Purpose for Reading prompts students to predict and anticipate content and motivates students to engage with the text. Preview Key Terms helps students learn Key Terms to understand the text. Target Reading Skill models a reading strategy to help students gain meaning from the text. Vocabulary Builder gives teachers definitions and sample sentences to help teach high-use words.

During Reading

In the Instruct part of the lesson plan, you can use suggestions for getting students actively engaged in the text. Guided Instruction clarifies high-use words, applies a passage-reading strategy to promote text comprehension, and guides discussion to construct meaning. Independent Practice prompts students to reread and take notes in the graphic organizer provided to rehearse understanding.

After Reading

The lesson plan closes with specific strategies for the reflection and study phase after reading is completed. Monitor Progress checks students' note taking, and verifies students' prereading predictions. Assess and Reteach measures students' recall of content and provides additional instruction if needed. Review Chapter Content promotes retention of key concepts and vocabulary.

Integrated Reading Resources

The *World Studies* program provides instructional materials to support the reading instruction in the Teacher's Edition.

The **All-in-One Teaching Resources** provides reading instruction support worksheets, such as a Reading Readiness Guide, Word Knowledge, and Vocabulary Development.

Students can use the **Reading and Vocabulary Study Guide** (English and Spanish) to reinforce reading instruction and vocabulary development, and to review section summaries of every section of the student text.

Differentiated Instruction

Research on Differentiated Instruction

It's basic, but it's true—not all our students learn in the same manner and not all our students have the same academic background or abilities. As educators, we need to respond to this challenge through the development and utilization of instructional strategies that address the needs of diverse learners, or the number of children who "fall through the cracks" will continue to rise (Kame'enui & Carnine, 1998).

Providing universal access

Universal access happens when curriculum and instruction are provided in ways that allow all learners to participate and to achieve (Kinsella, et al., 2002). Teachers who teach in heterogeneous, inclusive classrooms can provide universal access by modifying their teaching to respond to the needs of typical learners, gifted learners, less proficient readers, English language learners, and special needs students. Many of these learner populations benefit from extensive reading support (see pages T14-T17).

It is also critical to properly match the difficulty level of tasks with the ability level of students. Giving students tasks that they perceive as too hard lowers their expectations of success. However, giving students assignments that they think are too easy, undermines their feelings of competence (Stipek, 1996). Therefore, it is important for a program to give teachers leveled activities that allow them to match tasks with the abilities of their individual students.

When students connect to and are engaged with the content, comprehension and understanding increase. Technology, such as online activities, can provide an ideal opportunity for such engagement. It also can be used to provide additional opportunities to access content. For example, a less proficient reader may reinforce understanding of a key concept through watching a video. A complete social studies program makes content available in a variety of formats, including text, audio, visuals, and interactivities.

"Universal access happens when curriculum and instruction are provided in ways that allow all learners to participate and to achieve (Kinsella, et al., 2002)."

Kame'enui, Edward and Douglas Carnine. *Effective Teaching Strategies that Accommodate Diverse Learners*. Upper Saddle River, NJ: Prentice Hall, 1998.

Kinsella, Kate, et al. *Teaching Guidebook for Universal Access*. Upper Saddle River, NJ: Prentice Hall, 2002.

Stipek, D.J. "Motivation and Instruction," in R.C. Clafee and D.C. Berlinger (Eds.), *Handbook of Educational Psychology*. New York: Macmillan, 1996.

Putting Research Into Practice

Prentice Hall recognizes that today's classrooms include students with diverse backgrounds and ability levels. Accordingly, the *World Studies* program was designed to provide access to the content for all students. The program provides both the instructional materials to meet the learning needs of all students and the guidance you need to accommodate these needs.

Differentiated Instruction in the Teacher's Edition

The Teacher's Edition was designed to make it easy for teachers to modify instruction for diverse learners. Teaching strategies, provided by Dr. Kate Kinsella and Dr. Kevin Feldman, to help you modify your teaching are incorporated into every lesson plan. Specific activities help you differentiate instruction for individual students in five categories—less proficient readers, advanced readers, special needs students, gifted and talented, and English language learners. Resources are identified as being appropriate for use by each of these categories. All resources are also assigned a level—basic, average, and above average—so you know exactly how to assign tasks of appropriate difficulty level.

All-in-One Teaching Resources

Everything you need to provide differentiated instruction for each lesson, including reading support, activities and projects, enrichment, and assessment—in one convenient location.

World Studies Video Program

Students will benefit from our custom-built video program—the result of an exclusive partnership with Discovery Channel School—making content accessible through dynamic footage and high-impact stories.

Student Edition on Audio CD

The complete narrative is read aloud, section by section, providing extra support for auditory learners, English language learners, and reluctant readers. Also available is the Guided Reading Audio CD (English/Spanish), containing section summaries read aloud.

Interactive Textbook—The Student Edition Online and on CD-ROM

The Interactive Textbook allows students to interact with the content, including reading aids, visual and interactive learning tools, and instant feedback assessments.

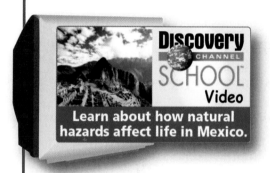

Research on Geographic Literacy

As the *Geography for Life: National Geography Standards* (1994) state, "There is now a widespread acceptance among the people of the United States that being literate in geography is essential if students are to leave school equipped to earn a decent living, enjoy the richness of life, and participate responsibly in local, national, and international affairs." A middle grades social studies program needs to help teachers produce students who are literate in geography.

Geographic literacy defined

Results for the 2001 National Assessment of Educational Progress (NAEP) Geography assessment show that the average scores of fourth- and eighth-grade students have improved since 1994. The average score of twelfth-grade students, however, has not changed significantly. In order to make the critical leap from basic geography skills to the kind of geographic literacy needed by the twelfth grade and beyond, a program must teach both geography content and geography skills, and then help students think critically. Geography content is made up of the essential knowledge that students need to know about the world. Geography skills are the ability to ask geographic questions, acquire and analyze geographic information, and answer these questions. To be truly literate in geography, students must be able to apply their knowledge and skills to understand the world.

Elements for success in middle grades

Students in the elementary grades don't always get enough training in geography. In order to help all students gain a base upon which to build middle grades geographic literacy, a program should introduce basic geography skills at the beginning of the school year.

The quality of maps is also vital to the success of a middle grades world studies program. Maps must be developmentally appropriate for middle grades students. They should be clean, clear, and accurate. Maps should be attractive and present subject matter in appealing ways, so that students *want* to use them to learn.

Another element that can lead to success is the incorporation of technology into the teaching and learning of geography, specifically the Internet. Research has shown that 8th grade students with high Internet usage scored higher in geography (NAEP, 2001).

U.S. Department of Education, Office of Educational Research and Improvement, National Center for Education Statistics, National Assessment of Educational Progress (NAEP), 2001 Geography Assessment.

Andrew Heritage
Head of Cartography
Dorling Kindersley (DK)

"Maps should be attractive and present subject matter in appealing ways, so that students *want* to use them to learn."

Putting Research Into Practice

Prentice Hall partnered with DK—internationally known for their dynamic atlases—to develop the *World Studies* program. DK's Andrew Heritage and his world-renowned cartography team designed all maps, resulting in stunning, high quality maps that are middle grades appropriate.

The MapMaster™ System

World Studies offers the first interactive geography instruction system available with a world studies textbook.

Introduce Basic Map Skills

The MapMaster™ Skills Handbook, a DK-designed introduction to the basics, brings students up to speed with a complete overview at the beginning of every book.

Build Geographic Literacy with Every Map

Scaffolded questions start with questions that require basic geography content and skills, and then ask students to demonstrate geographic literacy by thinking critically about the map.

Activate Learning Online

MapMaster™ Interactive—online and on CD-ROM—allows students to put their knowledge of geography skills and content into practice through interactivities.

Extend Learning with DK

- **DK World Desk Reference Online** is filled with up-to-date data, maps, and visuals that connect students to a wealth of information about the world's countries.

- **DK Compact Atlas of the World** with Map Master™ Teacher's Companion provides activities to introduce, develop, and master geography and map skills.

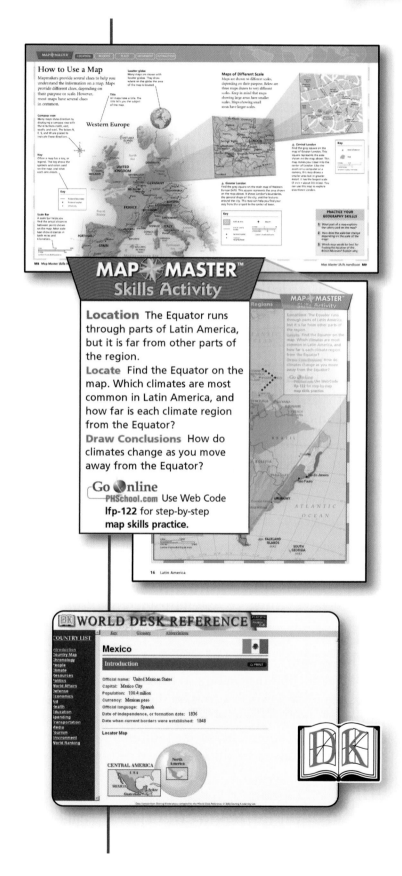

Research on Assessment

Meeting the NCLB challenge will necessitate an integrated approach to assessment with a variety of assessment tools. With the spotlight now on *improving* student performance, it is essential to use assessment results to inform instruction.

Assessments Tools for Informing Instruction

The key to success is using a variety of assessment tools coupled with data analysis and decision making. Teachers work with information coming from four kinds of assessment.

Screening assessments are brief procedures used to identify at-risk students who are not ready to work at grade level.

Diagnostic assessments provide a more in-depth analysis of strengths and weaknesses that can help teachers make instructional decisions and plan intervention strategies.

Progress-monitoring assessments (sometimes referred to as benchmark tests) provide an ongoing, longitudinal record of student achievement detailing individual student progress toward meeting end-of-year and end-of-schooling, grade level, district, or state standards.

Large-scale assessments, such as state tests and standardized tests, are used to determine whether individual students have met the expected standards and whether a school system has made adequate progress in improving its performance.

Ongoing Assessment

Daily assessment should be embedded in the program before, during, and after instruction in the core lessons. Legitimate test preparation experiences also should be embedded in the program. Test preparation involves teaching students strategies for taking tests, such as eliminating answers, reading comprehension, and writing extended response answers.

Eileen Depka
Supervisor of Standards and Assessment
Waukesha, WI

"Meeting the NCLB challenge will necessitate an integrated approach to assessment with a variety of assessment tools."

Putting Research Into Practice

Prentice Hall developed the *World Studies* program with a variety of assessment tools, including ongoing assessment in the student text.

Assessments for Informing Instruction

World Studies was designed to provide you with all four kinds of assessment.

- **Screening test** identifies students who are reading 2-3 years below grade level.

- **Diagnostic tests** focus on skills needed for success in social studies, including subtests in geographic literacy, visual analysis, critical thinking and reading, and communications skills, as well as vocabulary and writing.

- **Benchmark tests**, to be given six times throughout the year, monitor student progress in the course.

- **Outcome test**, to be administered at the end of the year, evaluates student mastery of social studies content standards.

Ongoing Assessment

- **Student Edition** offers section and chapter assessments with questions building from basic comprehension to critical thinking and writing.

- **Test Prep Workbook** and **Test-taking Strategies with Transparencies** develop students' test-taking skills and improve their scores on standardized tests.

- *ExamView® Test Bank CD-ROM* allows you to quickly and easily develop customized tests from a bank of thousands of questions.

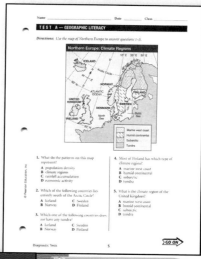

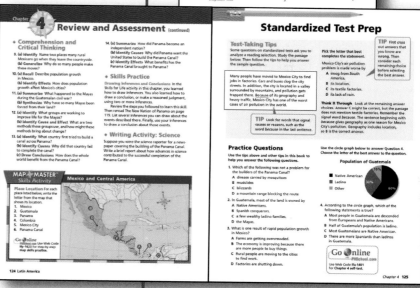

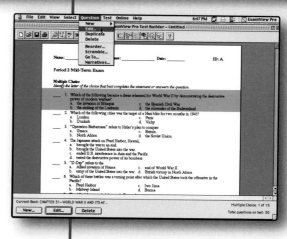

Europe and Russia Skills Scope and Sequence

Prentice Hall *World Studies* contains a comprehensive program of core skills. Each skill is taught in every book of the series. A Target Reading Skill is located at the beginning of each chapter and expanded upon in each section within the chapter. Core skills are also taught either in the "Skills for Life Activity" in the Student Edition, or in a "Skills Mini Lesson" in the Teacher's Edition. In addition, worksheets for the students' use in completing each skill are located in the All-in-One Teaching Resources. The chart below lists the skills covered in *Prentice Hall World Studies: Europe and Russia* and the page where each skill is taught.

Europe and Russia Analysis Skills	SE	TE
Analyzing Graphic Data		pp. 152–153
Analyzing Images		p. 41
Analyzing Primary Sources		p. 94
Clarifying Meaning	pp. 36, 38, 42, 45, 48, 53, 57, 61, 65, 70, 73	pp. 36b, 38, 45, 53, 70
Comparing and Contrasting	pp. 164, 174, 178, 181, 184, 189, 192, 198, 202	pp. 20, 164b, 174, 181, 189, 198
Decision Making		p. 143
Distinguishing Fact and Opinion		p. 104
Drawing Inferences and Conclusions		p. 157
Identifying Cause and Effect/Making Predictions		p. 48
Identifying Frame of Reference and Point of View	pp. 196–197	pp. 196–197
Identifying Main Ideas/Summarizing	pp. 82, 84, 87, 91, 93, 100, 102	pp. 73, 82b, 84, 91, 100
Making Valid Generalizations		p. 87
Problem Solving	pp. 60–61	pp. 60–61
Recognizing Bias and Propaganda		p. 200
Sequencing		p. 57
Supporting a Position	pp. 98–99	pp. 98–99
Synthesizing Information		p. 178
Transferring Information From One Medium to Another	pp. 152–153	pp. 124, 152–153
Using the Cartographer's Tools		p. 12
Using Context	pp. 110, 122, 125, 130, 136, 138, 142, 145, 146, 154, 158	pp. 110b, 122, 130, 138, 145, 154
Using the Reading Process	pp. 8, 10, 15, 17, 19, 26, 31	pp. 8b, 10, 17, 26
Using Reliable Information		p. 64
Using Special-Purpose Maps	pp. 24–25	pp. 24–25

Pacing Options

World Studies offers many aids to help you plan your instruction time, whether regular class periods or block scheduling. Section-by-section lesson plans for each chapter include suggested times, based on the 9-week course configuration below. Teacher Express CD-ROM will help you manage your time electronically.

PRENTICE HALL
TeacherEXPRESS™
Plan • Teach • Assess

Europe and Russia Pacing Options			9-week unit	12-week unit
Chapter 1	Section 1	Land and Water	3.5	6
	Section 2	Climate and Vegetation	2	3
	Section 3	Resources and Land Use	3.5	4
Chapter 2	Section 1	From Ancient Greece to the Middle Ages	1.5	2
	Section 2	Renaissance and the Age of Revolution	1	1.5
	Section 3	Industrial Revolution and Nationalism	2	3
	Section 4	Imperial Russia to the Soviet Union	1	1.5
	Section 5	The European Union	4	5
Chapter 3	Section 1	The Cultures of Western Europe	1	1.5
	Section 2	The Cultures of Eastern Europe	2	3
	Section 3	The Cultures of the Russian Federation	3	3.5
Chapter 4	Section 1	The United Kingdom: Democracy and Monarchy	2	3
	Section 2	France: Cultural Heritage and Diversity	1.5	2
	Section 3	Sweden: A Welfare State	1.5	2
	Section 4	Italy: Northern and Southern Divisions	2.5	3
	Section 5	Germany: A Unified Nation	3.5	4
Chapter 5	Section 1	Poland: Preserving Tradition Amidst Change	2	3
	Section 2	Five Balkan Nations: A Region Tries to Rebuild	1.5	2
	Section 3	Ukraine: Independence and Beyond	2.5	3
	Section 4	Russia: A Huge Country Takes a New Path	3.5	4
		Total Number of Days	**45**	**60**

Correlation to *Geography for Life,* the National Geography Standards

On the following pages, *Prentice Hall World Studies Europe and Russia* is correlated with *Geography for Life,* the National Geography Standards. These standards were prepared in response to the Goals 2000, Educate America Act, by the Geography Education Standards Project. Participating in the project were the American Geographical Society, the Association of American Geographers, the National Council for Geographic Education, and the National Geographic Society. Concepts and skills contained in the Geography Standards are incorporated throughout the program. This correlation displays places where the standards are directly addressed.

Standard	Europe and Russia
The World in Spatial Terms	
Standard 1 Use maps and other geographic representations, tools, and technologies to acquire, process, and report information from a spatial perspective.	MapMaster Skills Handbook, Regional Overview, 1:1–3, 2:1, 2:3, 2:4, 3:1, 3:2, 4:1–5, 5:1–4, Skills for Life: Ch. 1, Review and Assessment: Chs. 1–5
Standard 2 Use mental maps to organize information about people, places, and environments in a spatial context.	MapMaster Skills Handbook, Regional Overview, 1:2, 2:1, 2:2, 3:1, 3:2, 5:3, Review and Assessment: Chs. 1, 3, 4, 5
Standard 3 Analyze the spatial organization of people, places, and environments on Earth's surface.	MapMaster Skills Handbook, Regional Overview, 1:1–3, 3:1, 3:2, 4:1, 4:4, 5:2, Review and Assessment: Chs. 1, 2, 3
Places and Regions	
Standard 4 Understand the physical and human characteristics of places.	MapMaster Skills Handbook, Regional Overview, 1:1–3, 3:1–3, 4:1–5, 5:1, 5:4, Review and Assessment: Chs. 1–5
Standard 5 Understand that people create regions to interpret Earth's complexity.	MapMaster Skills Handbook, Regional Overview, 1:1, 3:2, 3:3, 4:1, 4:4, 4:5, 5:1, 5:3
Standard 6 Understand how culture and experience influence people's perception of places and regions.	MapMaster Skills Handbook, 2:5, 3:1–3, 4:1, 4:4, 4:5, 5:1–4, Review and Assessment: Chs. 3, 4, 5
Physical Systems	
Standard 7 Understand the physical processes that shape the patterns of Earth's surface.	Regional Overview, 1:1–3
Standard 8 Understand the characteristics and spatial distribution of ecosystems on Earth's surface.	MapMaster Skills Handbook, Regional Overview, 1:1–3, 5:4, Review and Assessment: Ch. 1

Correlation to *Geography for Life*, the National Geography Standards *(continued)*

Standard	Europe and Russia
Human Systems	
Standard 9 Understand the characteristics, distribution, and migration of human populations on Earth's surface.	MapMaster Skills Handbook, 1:1, 2:1–5, 3:1–3, 4:2, 4:5, 5: 1, 5:4, Review and Assessment: Chs. 1, 3
Standard 10 Understand the characteristics, distribution, and complexity of Earth's cultural mosaics.	MapMaster Skills Handbook, 2:1, 2:2, 2:4, 2:5, 3:1–3, 4:2, 4:4, 4:5, 5: 1–4, Review and Assessment: Chs. 2, 3, 4, 5
Standard 11 Understand the patterns and networks of economic interdependence on Earth's surface.	MapMaster Skills Handbook, 1:3, 2:2, 2:3, 2:4, 2:5, 3:1, 4:1–5, 5:1, 5:3, 5:4, Review and Assesment: Chs. 1, 2
Standard 12 Understand the processes, patterns, and functions of human settlement.	MapMaster Skills Handbook, Regional Overview, 1:1, 2:1, 2:3, 3:1, 3:2, 4:1, 5:2, Review and Assessment: Ch. 1
Standard 13 Understand how the forces of cooperation and conflict among people influence division and control of Earth's surface.	2:1–5, 3:1–3, 4:1, 4:4, 4:5, 5:1–4, Review and Assessment: Chs. 2, 3, 4, 5
Environment and Society	
Standard 14 Understand how human actions modify the physical environment.	1:1, 1:3, 5:1, 5:3, 5:4
Standard 15 Understand how physical systems affect human systems.	1:1–3, 5:1, 5:3, 5:4, Review and Assessment: Chs. 1, 5
Standard 16 Understand the changes that occur in the meaning, use, distribution, and importance of resources.	1:1, 1:3, 2:2, 2:3, 4:1, 4:3, 4:4, 5:3, Review and Assessment: Ch. 5
The Uses of Geography	
Standard 17 Understand how to apply geography to interpret the past.	MapMaster Skills Handbook, 2:1, 2:2, 2:3, 2:4, 3:2, 4:1, 4:4, 5:1, 5:3, 5:4
Standard 18 Understand how to apply geography to interpret the present and plan for the future.	2:3, 2:5, 3:3, 4:1, 4:3, 4:4, 4:5, 5:1–4, Review and Assessment: Chs. 2, 3, 4

Correlation to the NCSS Curriculum Standards

On the following pages *Prentice Hall World Studies Europe and Russia* is correlated with *Expectations of Excellence*, the Curriculum Standards for Social Studies. These standards were developed by the National Council for the Social Studies to address overall curriculum design and comprehensive student performance expectations.

Standard	Europe and Russia
Performance Expectations 1: Culture	
• compare similarities and differences in the ways groups, societies, and cultures meet human needs and concerns • explain how information and experiences may be interpreted by people from diverse cultural perspectives and frames of reference • explain and give examples of how language, literature, the arts, architecture, other artifacts, traditions, beliefs, values, and behaviors contribute to the development and transmission of culture • explain why individuals and groups respond differently to their physical and social environments and/or changes to them on the basis of shared assumptions, values, and beliefs • articulate the implications of cultural diversity, as well as cohesion, within and across groups	MapMaster Skills Handbook, 1:3, 2:2, 2:5, 3:1–3, 4:1–5, 5:1–4
Performance Expectations 2: Time, Continuity, and Change	
• demonstrate an understanding that different scholars may describe the same event or situation in different ways but must provide reasons or evidence for their view • identify and use key concepts such as chronology, causality, change, conflict, and complexity to explain, analyze, and show connections among patterns of historical change and continuity • identify and describe selected historical periods and patterns of change within and across cultures • identify and use processes important to reconstructing and reinterpreting the past • develop critical sensitivities regarding attitudes, values, and behaviors of people in different historical contexts • use knowledge of facts and concepts drawn from history, along with methods of historical inquiry, to inform decision-making about and action-taking on public issues	2:1–5, 3:1–3, 4:1, 4:3, 4:4, 4:5, 5:1–4
Performance Expectations 3: People, Places, and Environment	
• elaborate mental maps of locales, regions, and the world that demonstrate understanding of relative location, direction, size, and shape • create, interpret, use, and distinguish various representations of the earth • use appropriate resources, data sources, and geographic tools to generate, manipulate, and interpret information • estimate distance, calculate scale, and distinguish geographic relationships • locate and describe varying landforms and geographic features and explain their relationship with the ecosystem • describe physical system changes and identify geographic patterns associated with them • describe how people create places that reflect cultural values and ideals • examine, interpret, and analyze physical and cultural patterns and their interactions • describe ways that historical events have been influenced by, and have influenced, physical and human geographic factors in local, regional, national, and global settings • observe and speculate about social and economic effects of environmental changes and crises resulting from natural phenomena • propose, compare, and evaluate alternative uses of land and resources in communities, regions, nations, and the world	MapMaster Skills Handbook, Regional Overview, 1:1–3, 2:1–5, 3:1–3, 4:1–5, 5:4

Correlation to the NCSS Curriculum Standards *(continued)*

Standard	Europe and Russia
Performance Expectations 4: Individual Development and Identity	
• relate personal changes to social, cultural, and historical contexts • describe personal connections to place—as associated with community, nation, and world • describe the ways family, gender, ethnicity, nationality, and institutional affiliations contribute to personal identity • relate such factors as physical endowment and capabilities, learning, motivation, personality, perception, and behavior to individual development • identify and describe ways regional, ethnic, and national cultures influence individuals' daily lives • identify and describe the influence of perception, attitudes, values, and beliefs on personal identity • identify and interpret examples of stereotyping, conformity, and altruism • work independently and cooperatively to accomplish goals	3:1–3, 4:1–5, 5:1–4
Performance Expectations 5: Individuals, Groups, & Institutions	
• demonstrate an understanding of concepts such as role, status, and social class in describing interactions of individuals and social groups • analyze group and institutional influences on people, events, and elements of culture • describe the various forms institutions take and the interactions of people with institutions • identify and analyze examples of tensions between expressions of individuality and group or institutional efforts to promote social conformity • identify and describe examples of tensions between belief systems and government policies and laws • describe the role of institutions in furthering both continuity and change • apply knowledge of how groups and institutions work to meet individual needs and promote the common good	2:1–5, 3:1–3, 4:1–5, 5:1–4
Performance Expectations 6: Power, Authority, and Governance	
• examine persistent issues involving the rights, roles, and status of the individual in relation to general welfare • describe the purpose of government and how its powers are acquired, used, and justified • analyze and explain ideas and governmental mechanisms to meet needs and wants of citizens, regulate territory, manage conflict, and establish order and security • describe the ways nations and organizations respond to forces of unity and diversity affecting order and security • identify and describe the basic features of the political system in the United States, and identify representative leaders from various levels and branches of government • explain conditions, actions, and motivations that contribute to conflict and cooperation within and among nations • describe and analyze the role of technology as it contributes to or helps resolve conflicts • explain how power, role, status, and justice influence the examination of persistent issues and social problems • give examples and explain how governments attempt to achieve their stated ideals at home and abroad	2:1–5, 4:1–5, 5:1–4

Correlation to the NCSS Curriculum Standards *(continued)*

Standard	Europe and Russia
Performance Expectation 7: Production, Distribution, and Consumption	
• give examples of ways that economic systems structure choices about how goods and services are to be produced and distributed • describe the role that supply and demand, prices, incentives, and profits play in determining what is produced and distributed in a competitive market system • explain differences between private and public goods and services • describe a range of examples of the various institutions that make up economic systems • describe the role of specialization and exchange in the economic process • explain and illustrate how values and beliefs influence different economic decisions • differentiate among various forms of exchange and money • compare basic economic systems according to who determines what is produced, distributed, and consumed • use economic concepts to help explain historical and current events in local, national, or global concepts • use economic reasoning to compare different proposals for dealing with contemporary social issues	1:2, 1:3, 2:3, 4:1–5, 5:1–4
Performance Expectation 8: Science, Technology, and Society	
• examine and describe the influence of culture on scientific and technological choices and advancement • show through specific examples how science and technology have changed peoples' perceptions of their social and natural world • describe examples in which values, beliefs, and attitudes have been influenced by new scientific and technological knowledge • explain the need for laws and policies to govern scientific and technological applications • seek reasonable and ethical solutions to problems that arise when scientific advancements and social norms or values come into conflict	1:1–3, 2:2, 2:3, 4:1, 4:3, 5:1, 5:3, 5:4
Performance Expectation 9: Global Connections	
• describe instances in which language, art, music, and belief systems, and other cultural elements can facilitate global understanding or cause misunderstanding • analyze examples of conflict, cooperation, and interdependence among groups, societies, and nations • describe and analyze the effects of changing technologies on the global community • explore the causes, consequences, and possible solutions to persistent contemporary and emerging global interests • describe and explain the relationships and tensions between national sovereignty and global interests • demonstrate understanding of concerns, standards, issues, and conflicts related to universal human rights • identify and describe the roles of international and multinational organizations	2:3, 2:5, 4:1–5, 5:1–4

Correlation to the NCSS Curriculum Standards *(continued)*

Standard	Europe and Russia
Performance Expectation 10: Civic Ideals and Practices	
• examine the origins and continuing influence of key ideals of the democratic republican form of government, such as individual human dignity, liberty, justice, equality, and rule of law • identify and interpret sources and examples of the rights and responsibilities of citizens • locate, access, analyze, organize, and apply information about selected public issues—recognizing and explaining multiple points of view • practice forms of civic discussion and participation consistent with the ideals of citizens in a democratic republic • explain and analyze various forms of citizen action that influence public policy decisions • identify and explain the roles of formal and informal political actors in influencing and shaping public policy and decision-making • analyze the influence of diverse forms of public opinion on the development of public policy and decision-making • analyze the effectiveness of selected public policies and citizen behaviors in realizing the stated ideals of a democratic republican form of government • explain the relationship between policy statements and action plans used to address issues of public concern • examine strategies designed to strengthen the "common good," which consider a range of options for citizen action	2:1–5, 3:2, 3:3, 4:1, 4:3, 4:5, 5:1–4

Instructional Strategies for Improving Student Comprehension

In response to today's environment of the NCLB legislation and testing reform, Prentice Hall asked Dr. Kate Kinsella and Dr. Kevin Feldman to provide specific instructional strategies you can use to improve student comprehension. Their guidance informed the development of the *World Studies* Teacher's Edition. The lesson plans in this Teacher's Edition incorporate the following instructional strategies to enhance students' comprehension.

There is no single magical strategy that will solve all of the difficulties students encounter in reading challenging content area texts. Secondary students in mixed-ability classrooms depend on teachers to use a consistent set of research-informed and classroom-tested strategies in a patient and recursive manner—not the occasional or random use of different strategies. Students will not become skillful readers of content area texts in a week or two of instruction. However, when teachers engage students in the consistent use of a well-chosen set of content reading strategies appropriately matched to the demands of the text and the students' level of knowledge, their ability to comprehend difficult grade level texts will be dramatically enhanced.

Strategy 1: Set a Purpose for Reading

This program has two types of activities designed to help students set a purpose for reading: an Anticipation Guide and a KWL chart. The two types rotate by section.

A. Anticipation Guide

Purpose: To focus students' attention on key concepts, and guide them to interact with ideas in the text

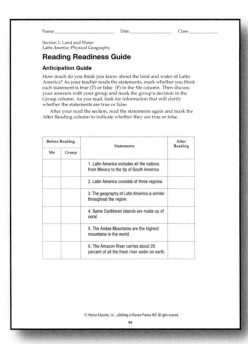

1. Distribute the *Reading Readiness Guide*. Read each statement aloud, and then ask students to react to the statements individually and in groups, marking their responses in the Before Reading column.

2. Use the worksheet as a springboard for discussing the section's key concepts as a unified class. Refrain from revealing the correct responses at this time, to avoid taking away the need for them to read the text.

3. Have students read the section with the purpose of finding evidence that confirms, disproves, or elaborates each statement in the *Reading Readiness Guide*.

4. After students finish reading, have them return to the statements and mark the After Reading column on their worksheets. Have them locate information from the text that supports or disproves each statement.

5. Discuss what the class has learned and probe for any lingering confusion about key concepts.

Instructional Strategies

B. KWL

Purpose: To engage students before, during, and after reading

The KWL worksheet guides students to recall what they **K**now, determine what they **W**ant to learn, and identify what they **L**earn as they read.

1. Distribute the *Reading Readiness Guide*. Brainstorm with the group about what they already know about the topic. List students' ideas on the board. Encourage students to generate questions at points of ambiguity.

2. Students then list pieces of information they already know and questions they want to answer in the first two columns of their worksheets.

3. As students read the section, ask them to note information that answers their questions or adds to what they know.

4. After reading, facilitate a class discussion about what the students have learned. Clarify any lingering confusion about key concepts.

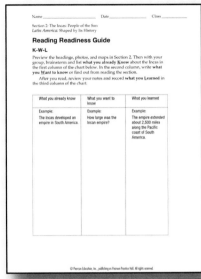

Strategy 2: Teach High-Use Academic Words

Purpose: To teach students words used often in academic texts, beyond the content-specific Key Terms

How to Do It

1. Have students rate how well they know each word on their *Word Knowledge* worksheets. Tell them there is no penalty for a low rating.

2. Survey students' ratings to decide which words need the most instruction.

3. Provide a brief definition or sample sentence for each word. (See Vocabulary Builder at the beginning of each section for definitions and sample sentences.) Rephrase your explanation, leaving out the word and asking students to substitute it aloud.

4. Work with students as they fill in the "Definition or Example" column of their *Word Knowledge* worksheets.

5. Point out each word in context as you read the chapters. Consider allowing students to earn extra credit if they use a word correctly in class discussion or assignments.

Strategy 3: Oral Cloze

Purpose: To help students read actively while the teacher reads aloud

How to Do It

1. Choose a passage and direct students to "read aloud silently using their inner voices." Be sure students understand reading is an active process, not simply a listening activity, and their job is to follow along—eyes riveted to each word, saying the words to themselves as you read aloud.

2. Tell students to be on their "reading toes," for you will be leaving out an occasional word and their task is to chorally supply the word.

3. The first few times you use the Oral Cloze, demonstrate by telling the students in advance what word you will be leaving out, directing them to read the word at the right time. Practice this a few times until they have the feel for the procedure. Leave out fewer words as students become more familiar with the Oral Cloze and require less direction to remain focused during teacher read alouds.

Instructional Strategies

Strategies for Improving Student Comprehension *(continued)*

Strategy 4: Choral Reading

Purpose: To have students attend to the text in a non-threatening atmosphere

How to Do It

1. Choose a relatively short passage.

2. Tell students that you will all read the text aloud at once. Direct students to "keep your voice with mine" as they read.

3. Read the passage slowly and clearly.

4. Have students read the text again silently.

Strategy 5: Structured Silent Reading

Purpose: To give students a task as they read silently to increase their attentiveness and accountability

How to Do It

1. Assign a section to read silently. Pose a question for the whole class to answer from their silent reading, such as the Reading Check question at the end of each subsection. Model how one thinks while reading to find answers to a question.

2. When students get used to reading to answer the Reading Check question, pose more in-depth questions, progressing from factual recall to questions that stimulate interpretive or applied thinking.

3. Teach students to ask and answer their own questions as they read. Model this process by reading a section aloud and asking and answering your own questions as you read.

4. After the students have finished reading, engage the class in a brief discussion to clarify questions, vocabulary, and key concepts.

Strategy 6: Paragraph Shrinking

Purpose: To increase comprehension during reading

How to Do It

1. Partner struggling students with more proficient students and assign a manageable portion of the text.

2. Ask one member of each pair to identify the "who or what" the paragraph is about and tell the other.

3. Have the other member of the pair identify important details about the "who or what" and tell the other.

4. Ask the first member to summarize the paragraph in fifteen to twenty words or less using the most important details. The second member of the pair monitors the number of words and says "Shrink it!" if the summary goes over twenty words.

5. Have the partners reverse roles and continue reading.

6. Discuss the reading as a class to make sure students' paragraphs have correctly hit upon the main ideas of the passage.

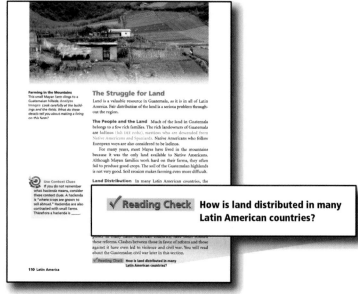

Strategy 7: ReQuest (Reciprocal Questioning)

Purpose: To ask and answer questions during reading to establish a purpose for reading and monitor one's own comprehension

How to Do It

1. Prepare students to read by doing the section's Build Background Knowledge, Set a Purpose for Reading, and Preview Key Terms activities.

2. Begin reading a brief portion of the text aloud. Ask and answer your own questions about the text, progressing from recall to critical thinking questions.

3. After modeling this question and response pattern with a brief passage, ask students to read the next section of the text. Tell students that they will be taking turns asking you questions about what they read, and you will answer their questions, just like you modeled for them.

4. Ask students to read the next section. Inform them that you will be asking them questions about the section and they will be answering your questions.

5. Continue to alternate between student-generated questions and teacher-generated questions until the entire designated passage has been read. As students become used to the strategy, they gradually assume more responsibility in the process.

6. When the students have read enough information to make predictions about the remainder of the assignment, stop the exchange of comprehension questions. Instead, ask prediction questions, such as, "What do you think will be discussed in the next section? Why do you think so?"

7. Assign the remaining portion for students to read silently. Then lead a wrap-up discussion of the material.

Strategy 8: Idea Wave

Purpose: To engage students in active class discussions

How to Do It

1. Pose a question or task.

2. Give students quiet time to consider what they know about the topic and record a number of responses.

3. Whip around the class in a fast-paced and structured manner (e.g. down rows, around tables), allowing as many students as possible to share an idea in 15 seconds or less.

4. After several contributions, if there tends to be repetition, ask students to point out similarities in responses rather than simply stating that their idea has already been mentioned.

Strategies for Improving Student Comprehension *(continued)*

Strategy 9: Numbered Heads

Purpose: To engage students in active class discussions

How to Do It

1. Seat students in groups of four and number off one through four (if possible, combine established partners to form groups of four).

2. After giving the discussion prompt, allow students to discuss possible responses for an established amount of time.

3. Remind students to pay close attention to the comments of each group member because you will be randomly selecting one student to represent the best thinking of the entire group.

4. Call a number (one through four), and ask all students with that number to raise their hands, ready to respond to the topic at hand in a teacher-directed, whole-class discussion.

5. Add comments, extend key ideas, ask follow-up questions, and make connections between individual student's comments to create a lively whole-class discussion.

6. Provide any summary comments required to ensure that all students understand critical points.

Strategy 10: Think-Write-Pair–Share

Purpose: To engage students in responding to instruction

How to Do It

1. **Think**—Students listen while the teacher poses a question or a task related to the reading or classroom discussion. The level of questions should vary from lower level literal to higher order inferential or analytical.

2. **Write**—Provide quiet thinking or writing time for students to deal with the question, and go back to the text or review notes. Have students record their ideas in their notebooks.

3. **Pair/Share**—Cue students to find a partner and discuss their responses, noting similarities and differences. Teach students to encourage one another to clarify and justify responses.

4. Randomly call on students to share during a unified class discussion after they have all rehearsed answers with their partners.

5. Invite any volunteers to contribute additional ideas and points of view to the discussion after calling on a reasonable number of students randomly.

6. Direct students to go back to notes and add any important information garnered during the partner and class discussions.

Strategy 11: Give One, Get One

Purpose: To foster independent reflection and peer interaction prior to a unified class discussion

How to Do It

1. Pose a thought-provoking question or a concrete task to the class.

2. Allow three to five minutes of quiet time for students to consider what they may already know about the topic and jot down a number of potential responses.

3. Ask students to place a check mark next to the two or three ideas that they perceive as their strongest and then draw a line after their final idea to separate their ideas from those that they will gather from classmates.

4. Give students a set amount of time (about eight to ten minutes) to get up from their seats and share ideas with classmates. After finding a partner, the two students exchange papers and first quietly read each other's ideas. They discuss the ideas briefly, then select one idea from their partner's list and add it to their own, making sure to accurately copy the idea alongside the partner's name.

5. When one exchange is completed, students move on to interact with a new partner.

6. At the end of the exchange period, facilitate a unified class discussion. Call on a volunteer to share one new idea acquired from a conversation partner. The student whose idea has just been reported then shares the next idea, gleaned from a different conversation partner.

Professional Development

For more information about these strategies, see the end of each chapter's Interleaf.

Objective

- Learn how to read nonfiction critically by analyzing an author's purpose, distinguishing between facts and opinions, identifying evidence, and evaluating credibility.

Prepare to Read

Build Background Knowledge **L2**

Write the phrase "Don't believe everything you read" on the board. Ask students to brainstorm examples that illustrate the saying. Provide a few simple examples to get them started (*tall tales, advertisements.*)

Instruct

Reading Informational Texts **L2**

Guided Instruction

- Tell students that they must actively evaluate the information in most of the nonfiction they read.

- Read the sample editorial on this page aloud. Tell students that an editorial usually expresses a person's opinion. Ask students to consider why the author wrote this editorial. (*The author expresses the opinion that the proposal to build the new shopping center should have been approved.*) Ask **How might this purpose affect what the editorial says?** (*The author may present information in the best possible light to prove his or her belief.*)

- Another important step in evaluating nonfiction is distinguishing between facts and opinions. Ask each student to write one fact and one opinion, on any subject, in their notebooks. Use the Idea Wave strategy (TE, p. T35) to get students to share their facts and opinions. If students have incorrectly categorized examples, help them to see why.

Reading Informational Texts

Reading a magazine, an Internet page, or a textbook is not the same as reading a novel. The purpose of reading nonfiction texts is to acquire new information. On page M18 you'll read about some **Target Reading Skills** that you'll have a chance to practice as you read this textbook. Here we'll focus on a few skills that will help you read nonfiction with a more critical eye.

Analyze the Author's Purpose

Different types of materials are written with different purposes in mind. For example, a textbook is written to teach students information about a subject. The purpose of a technical manual is to teach someone how to use something, such as a computer. A newspaper editorial might be written to persuade the reader to accept a particular point of view. A writer's purpose influences how the material is presented. Sometimes an author states his or her purpose directly. More often, the purpose is only suggested, and you must use clues to identify the author's purpose.

Distinguish Between Facts and Opinions

It's important when reading informational texts to read actively and to distinguish between fact and opinion. A fact can be proven or disproven. An opinion cannot—it is someone's personal viewpoint or evaluation.

For example, the editorial pages in a newspaper offer opinions on topics that are currently in the news. You need to read newspaper editorials with an eye for bias and faulty logic. For example, the newspaper editorial at the right shows factual statements in blue and opinion statements in red. The underlined words are examples of highly charged words. They reveal bias on the part of the writer.

> More than 5,000 people voted last week in favor of building a new shopping center, **but the opposition won out. The margin of victory is irrelevant.** Those radical voters who opposed the center are obviously self-serving elitists who do not care about anyone but themselves.
>
> This month's unemployment figure for our area is 10 percent, which represents an increase of about 5 percent over the figure for this time last year. **These figures mean unemployment is getting worse.** But the people who voted against the mall probably do not care about creating new jobs.

- Tell students that identifying evidence is another way to read nonfiction critically. Ask students to look again at the facts highlighted in the sample editorial. **Does the evidence presented in these facts convince you that building a new shopping center is a good idea?** (*The evidence is incomplete—the author has not shown that the new shopping center would solve the unemployment problem.*)

- Tell students that analyzing an author's purpose, distinguishing between facts and opinions, and identifying evidence are all ways to evaluate the credibility of the author. Tell students to look at the checklist for evaluating Web sites. Ask students to think about Web sites they have visited. Do those Web sites pass the checklist's test? Why or why not?

Identify Evidence

Before you accept an author's conclusion, you need to make sure that the author has based the conclusion on enough evidence and on the right kind of evidence. An author may present a series of facts to support a claim, but the facts may not tell the whole story. For example, what evidence does the author of the newspaper editorial on the previous page provide to support his claim that the new shopping center would create more jobs? Is it possible that the shopping center might have put many small local businesses out of business, thus increasing unemployment rather than decreasing it?

Evaluate Credibility

Whenever you read informational texts, you need to assess the credibility of the author. This is especially true of sites you may visit on the Internet. All Internet sources are not equally reliable. Here are some questions to ask yourself when evaluating the credibility of a Web site.

- ☐ Is the Web site created by a respected organization, a discussion group, or an individual?
- ☐ Does the Web site creator include his or her name as well as credentials and the sources he or she used to write the material?
- ☐ Is the information on the site balanced or biased?
- ☐ Can you verify the information using two other sources?
- ☐ Is there a date telling when the Web site was created or last updated?

Reading and Writing Handbook **RW1**

Independent Practice

Ask students to bring in an editorial from the local newspaper, or distribute copies of an appropriate editorial. Ask students to critically assess their editorial by analyzing the author's purpose; underlining facts and circling opinions in the text of the editorial; summarizing the evidence presented in the editorial; and finally drawing a conclusion about the credibility of the editorial.

Monitor Progress

Pair students and have them share their editorial assessments. Ask them to explain the reasoning behind the conclusions they drew about the editorial's credibility. Circulate and offer assistance as needed.

Assess and Reteach

Assess Progress L2

Collect students' papers and review their assessments.

Reteach L1

If students are struggling, tell them to approach the task by asking themselves the following questions as they read a piece of nonfiction: **Why** did the author write this? **How** has the author made his or her points, using facts or opinions? **What** evidence has the author used to support the main idea? **Who** is the author, and what sources has he or she used?

Extend L3

To extend this lesson, tell students to turn to the Table of Contents in the Student Edition and pick a chapter name that intrigues them. Then, ask them to search the Internet and find two Web sites about the chapter's topic. Finally, ask them to use the checklist on this page to evaluate each Web site and compare the two in terms of credibility.

Differentiated Instruction

For Advanced Readers L3
Draw students' attention to the checklist under the heading "Evaluate Credibility." Ask students to create a similar checklist for analyzing an author's purpose, distinguishing between fact and opinion, and identifying evidence.

For Special Needs Students L1
If special needs students are having trouble making the distinction between facts and opinions, partner them with more proficient students to do the *Distinguishing Fact and Opinion* lesson on the Social Studies Skill Tutor CD-ROM.

⊙ *Distinguishing Fact and Opinion*, **Social Studies Skill Tutor CD-ROM**

Objective

- Use a systematic approach to write narrative, persuasive, expository, and research essays.

Prepare to Read

Build Background Knowledge **L2**

As a group, brainstorm all the ways that people use writing to communicate. Start them with these examples: labeling a folder or writing an email. Conduct an Idea Wave (TE, p. T35) and write students' responses on the board. Tell them that people often write to express ideas or information. Give them *Four Purposes for Writing* and tell them to keep it in their notebooks for future reference.

All in One Europe and Russia Teaching Resources, *Four Purposes for Writing,* p. 7

Instruct

Narrative Essays **L2**

Guided Instruction

- Tell students that narrative essays tell a story about their own experiences. Discuss the steps listed in the Student Edition.

- Choose an event in your own life (or invent one) such as visiting friends in another city. Write your topic on the board and model how to list details *(what the trip was like, what you did while you were there, what your friends are like.)* Cross out the least interesting details.

- Think aloud as your form your topic into a sentence that conveys the main idea of your essay.

- Tell students that you will go on to flesh out the details into a colorful story.

Independent Practice

- Tell students to write a narrative essay about a recent positive experience. Have student pairs brainstorm topics.

Writing for Social Studies

Writing is one of the most powerful communication tools you will ever use. You will use it to share your thoughts and ideas with others. Research shows that writing about what you read actually helps you learn new information and ideas. A systematic approach to writing—including prewriting, drafting, revising, and proofing—can help you write better, whether you're writing an essay or a research report.

Narrative Essays

Writing that tells a story about a personal experience

① Select and Narrow Your Topic

A narrative is a story. In social studies, it might be a narrative essay about how an event affected you or your family.

② Gather Details

Brainstorm a list of details you'd like to include in your narrative.

③ Write a First Draft

Start by writing a simple opening sentence that conveys the main idea of your essay. Continue by writing a colorful story that has interesting details. Write a conclusion that sums up the significance of the event or situation described in your essay.

④ Revise and Proofread

Check to make sure you have not begun too many sentences with the word *I*. Replace general words with more colorful ones.

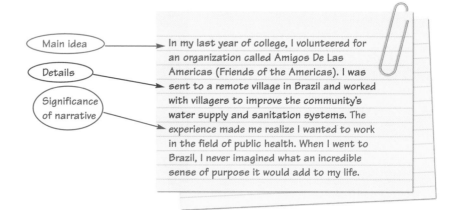

Main idea
Details
Significance of narrative

In my last year of college, I volunteered for an organization called Amigos De Las Americas (Friends of the Americas). I was sent to a remote village in Brazil and worked with villagers to improve the community's water supply and sanitation systems. The experience made me realize I wanted to work in the field of public health. When I went to Brazil, I never imagined what an incredible sense of purpose it would add to my life.

- Give students *Writing to Describe* to help them write their essays. After they have written the body of their essay, give them *Writing the Conclusion* to help them complete it.

All in One Europe and Russia Teaching Resources, *Writing to Describe,* p. 8; *Writing the Conclusion,* p. 9

Monitor Progress

Have students share their drafts with their partners. Give them *Using the Revision Checklist* and ask them to review their partners' papers. Urge them to provide constructive criticism and suggestions for improvement.

All in One Europe and Russia Teaching Resources, *Using the Revision Checklist,* p. 10

Persuasive Essays

Writing that supports an opinion or position

1 Select and Narrow Your Topic

Choose a topic that provokes an argument and has at least two sides. Choose a side. Decide which argument will appeal most to your audience and persuade it to understand your point of view.

2 Gather Evidence

Create a chart that states your position at the top and then lists the pros and cons for your position below, in two columns. Predict and address the strongest arguments against your stand.

3 Write a First Draft

Write a strong thesis statement that clearly states your position. Continue by presenting the strongest arguments in favor of your position and acknowledging and refuting opposing arguments.

4 Revise and Proofread

Check to make sure you have made a logical argument and that you have not oversimplified the argument.

Main Idea → It is vital to vote in elections. When people
Supporting (pro) argument → vote, they tell public officials how to run the government. Not every proposal is carried
Opposing (con) argument → out; however, politicians do their best to listen to what the majority of people want.
Transition words → Therefore, every vote is important.

Reading and Writing Handbook **RW3**

Guided Instruction

- Tell students that the purpose of writing a persuasive essay is to convince other people to believe your point of view. However, you must use solid, reliable evidence and arguments to make your points.

- Model the thought process by pointing out how the writer presents his or her argument in the paragraph on this page.

Independent Practice

- Tell students to write a persuasive essay about a topic that is important to them. Have students form pairs. One student in each pair should state his or her position. The other student then shares opposing arguments, which the first student should refute in his or her essay. Then the pairs switch roles.

- Give students *Writing to Persuade* to help them write their essays.

  All in One **Europe and Russia Teaching Resources,** *Writing to Persuade,* p. 11

Monitor Progress

If students are having trouble structuring their paragraphs, give them *Structuring Paragraphs* and *Creating Paragraph Outlines* to provide a framework.

  All in One **Europe and Russia Teaching Resources,** *Structuring Paragraphs,* p. 12; *Creating Paragraph Outlines,* p. 13

Differentiated Instruction

For Less Proficient Readers   L1

Tell students to use looping to help them focus on a topic. Have them follow these steps: Write freely on your topic for about five minutes. Read what you have written and circle the most important idea. Write for five minutes on the circled idea. Repeat the process until you isolate a topic narrow enough to cover well in a short essay.

Expository Essays ▪️L2

Guided Instruction
- Read the steps for writing expository essays with students.
- Tell students that the graphic organizer example given on the Student Edition page is for a cause-and-effect expository essay. They might use a Venn diagram for a compare-and-contrast essay and a flowchart for a problem-and-solution essay.
- Model how to create a topic sentence from the information in the cause-and-effect graphic organizer. (*Sample topic sentence: In Mexico, several factors are causing rural families to move from the countryside to the city.*)
- Create a brief outline showing how you will organize the paragraphs in your essay.

Independent Practice
Tell students to write an expository essay based on a recent current event. Have them brainstorm ideas with a partner, then choose which type of essay best suits their topic (cause and effect, compare and contrast, or problem and solution.) Give them *Writing to Inform and Explain* and *Gathering Details* to help them start drafting their essays.

All in One Europe and Russia Teaching Resources, *Writing to Inform and Explain,* p. 14; *Gathering Details,* p. 15

Monitor Progress
If students are struggling with their essays, give them *Writing a Cause-and-Effect Essay* or *Writing a Problem-and-Solution Essay.*

All in One Europe and Russia Teaching Resources, *Writing a Cause-and-Effect Essay,* p. 16; *Writing a Problem-and-Solution Essay,* p. 17

Research Papers ▪️L2

Guided Instruction
Go over the steps for writing a research paper carefully. Ask students to share questions about the process, using the Idea Wave strategy (TE, p. T35). Answer any questions they might have.

Reading and Writing Handbook

Expository Essays

Writing that explains a process, compares and contrasts, explains causes and effects, or explores solutions to a problem

1 Identify and Narrow Your Topic
Expository writing is writing that explains something in detail. It might explain the similarities and differences between two or more subjects (compare and contrast). It might explain how one event causes another (cause and effect). Or it might explain a problem and describe a solution.

2 Gather Evidence
Create a graphic organizer that identifies details to include in your essay.

Cause 1	Cause 2	Cause 3
Most people in the Mexican countryside work on farms.	The population in Mexico is growing at one of the highest rates in the world.	There is not enough farm work for so many people.

Effect
As a result, many rural families are moving from the countryside to live in Mexico City.

3 Write Your First Draft
Write a topic sentence and then organize the essay around your similarities and differences, causes and effects, or problem and solutions. Be sure to include convincing details, facts, and examples.

4 Revise and Proofread

Research Papers
Writing that presents research about a topic

1 Narrow Your Topic
Choose a topic you're interested in and make sure that it is not too broad. For example, instead of writing a report on Panama, write about the construction of the Panama Canal.

2 Acquire Information
Locate several sources of information about the topic from the library or the Internet. For each resource, create a source index card like the one at the right. Then take notes using an index card for each detail or subtopic. On the card, note which source the information was taken from. Use quotation marks when you copy the exact words from a source.

> Source #1
> McCullough, David. *The Path Between the Seas: The Creation of the Panama Canal, 1870–1914.* N.Y., Simon and Schuster, 1977.

3 Make an Outline
Use an outline to decide how to organize your report. Sort your index cards into the same order.

> Outline
> I. Introduction
> II. Why the canal was built
> III. How the canal was built
>   A. Physical challenges
>   B. Medical challenges
> IV. Conclusion

Differentiated Instruction

For Gifted and Talented ▪️L3
Tell students that a verb is in active voice when the subject performs the action named by the verb. A verb is in passive voice when the subject undergoes the action named by the verb.

Give these examples:

Passive voice: The house is being painted by my sister and me.

Active voice: My sister and I are painting the house.

Tell students that using the active voice whenever possible will make their writing more dynamic and concise.

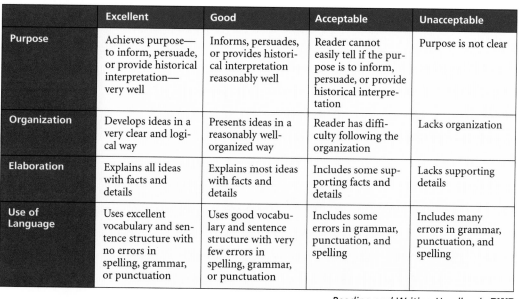

Introduction

Building the Panama Canal
Ever since Christopher Columbus first explored the Isthmus of Panama, the Spanish had been looking for a water route through it. They wanted to be able to sail west from Spain to Asia without sailing around South America. However, it was not until 1914 that the dream became a reality.

Conclusion

It took eight years and more than 70,000 workers to build the Panama Canal. It remains one of the greatest engineering feats of modern times.

④ Write a First Draft
Write an introduction, a body, and a conclusion. Leave plenty of space between lines so you can go back and add details that you may have left out.

⑤ Revise and Proofread
Be sure to include transition words between sentences and paragraphs. Here are some examples:

To show a contrast—*however, although, despite.*

To point out a reason—*since, because, if.*

To signal a conclusion—*therefore, consequently, so, then.*

Evaluating Your Writing
Use this table to help you evaluate your writing.

	Excellent	Good	Acceptable	Unacceptable
Purpose	Achieves purpose—to inform, persuade, or provide historical interpretation—very well	Informs, persuades, or provides historical interpretation reasonably well	Reader cannot easily tell if the purpose is to inform, persuade, or provide historical interpretation	Purpose is not clear
Organization	Develops ideas in a very clear and logical way	Presents ideas in a reasonably well-organized way	Reader has difficulty following the organization	Lacks organization
Elaboration	Explains all ideas with facts and details	Explains most ideas with facts and details	Includes some supporting facts and details	Lacks supporting details
Use of Language	Uses excellent vocabulary and sentence structure with no errors in spelling, grammar, or punctuation	Uses good vocabulary and sentence structure with very few errors in spelling, grammar, or punctuation	Includes some errors in grammar, punctuation, and spelling	Includes many errors in grammar, punctuation, and spelling

Reading and Writing Handbook **RW5**

Differentiated Instruction

For English Language Learners   L2
To help students understand the tasks you have given them, provide them with an example of a well-executed essay from a different class or a previous year. The example essay should be well written and organized but not above grade level. You could look for and save good examples each year you teach.

Independent Practice
- Have students consider topics for a research paper. Give them *Choosing a Topic* to help them learn how to evaluate potential topics.

  All in One Europe and Russia Teaching Resources, *Choosing a Topic,* p. 18

- Once students have selected a topic, tell them they will need facts to support their ideas. Give them *Using the Library, Summarizing and Taking Notes,* and *Preparing Note Cards* to help them start their research.

  All in One Europe and Russia Teaching Resources, *Using the Library,* p. 19; *Summarizing and Taking Notes,* p. 20; *Preparing Note Cards,* p. 21

Monitor Progress
Give students *Writing an Introduction* and *Writing the Body of an Essay* to help them write their essays.

All in One Europe and Russia Teaching Resources, *Writing an Introduction,* p. 22; *Writing the Body of an Essay,* p. 23

Assess and Reteach

Assess Progress   L2
Ask students to pick the best essay they have written so far and evaluate it using the rubric on this page.

Reteach   L1
Collect students' essays and self-evaluations. Meet with students to go over good points and areas for improvement. Revisit each type of essay as needed with the whole class.

Extend   L3
To extend this lesson, tell students there are many other different types of writing. Have them complete *Writing for Assessment* and *Writing a Letter* to learn about two more types of writing.

All in One Europe and Russia Teaching Resources, *Writing for Assessment,* p. 24; *Writing a Letter,* p. 25

Objective

- Identify and define the five themes of geography.

Prepare to Read

Build Background Knowledge L2

Assign students to small groups and give them five minutes to write a definition of geography. Then write the five themes of geography on the board. Remind students that a theme is an important underlying idea. As a class, decide which parts of their definitions go under each of the geography themes. For example, "landforms" would fall under the theme of place.

Instruct

Five Themes of Geography L2

Guided Instruction

- Divide the text using the headings and ask students to read the pages using the Structured Silent Reading technique (TE, p. T34). Clarify the meanings of any unfamiliar words.

- Ask students to give the relative locations of their homes.

- Mention the popularity of different kinds of ethnic foods in the United States. Ask **What theme of geography are these foods a good example of?** *(movement)* Encourage students to name other examples of the movement of cultural traditions from one region to another.

- Discuss the climate in your area. Ask **How does the environment affect how we live?** *(affects dress, travel, sports and other recreational activities, the way homes are built)*

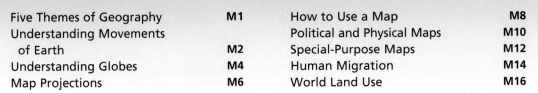

CONTENTS

 Use Web Code **lap-0000** for all of the maps in this handbook.

Five Themes of Geography

Studying the geography of the entire world is a huge task. You can make that task easier by using the five themes of geography: location, regions, place, movement, and human-environment interaction. The themes are tools you can use to organize information and to answer the where, why, and how of geography.

LOCATION

1 Location answers the question, "Where is it?" You can think of the location of a continent or a country as its address. You might give an absolute location such as 22 South Lake Street or 40° N and 80° W. You might also use a relative address, telling where one place is by referring to another place. *Between school and the mall* and *eight miles east of Pleasant City* are examples of relative locations.

▲ **Location**
This museum in England has a line running through it. The line marks its location at 0° longitude.

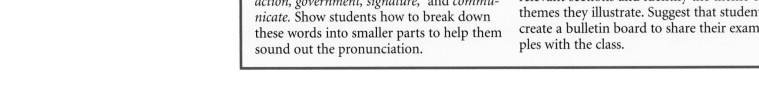

MapMaster Skills Handbook

Differentiated Instruction

For English Language Learners L1

Students may find it difficult to pronounce some of the multisyllable words in this section such as *relative, environment, interaction, government, signature,* and *communicate.* Show students how to break down these words into smaller parts to help them sound out the pronunciation.

For Advanced Readers L3

Have students find articles in newspapers or magazines that illustrate the themes of geography. Have students underline the relevant sections and identify the theme or themes they illustrate. Suggest that students create a bulletin board to share their examples with the class.

2 Regions are areas that share at least one common feature. Geographers divide the world into many types of regions. For example, countries, states, and cities are political regions. The people in any one of these places live under the same government. Other features, such as climate and culture, can be used to define regions. Therefore the same place can be found in more than one region. For example, the state of Hawaii is in the political region of the United States. Because it has a tropical climate, Hawaii is also part of a tropical climate region.

MOVEMENT

4 Movement answers the question, "How do people, goods, and ideas move from place to place?" Remember that what happens in one place often affects what happens in another. Use the theme of movement to help you trace the spread of goods, people, and ideas from one location to another.

PLACE

3 Place identifies the natural and human features that make one place different from every other place. You can identify a specific place by its landforms, climate, plants, animals, people, language, or culture. You might even think of place as a geographic signature. Use the signature to help you understand the natural and human features that make one place different from every other place.

INTERACTION

5 Human-environment interaction focuses on the relationship between people and the environment. As people live in an area, they often begin to make changes to it, usually to make their lives easier. For example, they might build a dam to control flooding during rainy seasons. Also, the environment can affect how people live, work, dress, travel, and communicate.

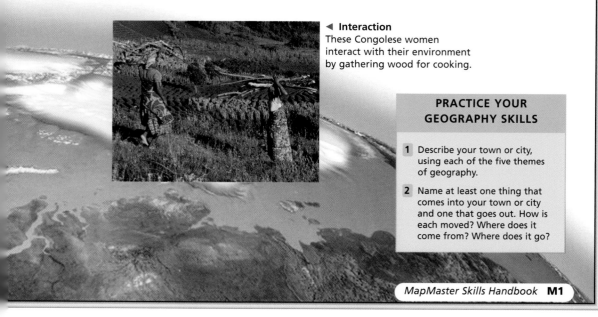

◀ **Interaction**
These Congolese women interact with their environment by gathering wood for cooking.

PRACTICE YOUR GEOGRAPHY SKILLS

1 Describe your town or city, using each of the five themes of geography.

2 Name at least one thing that comes into your town or city and one that goes out. How is each moved? Where does it come from? Where does it go?

MapMaster Skills Handbook **M1**

Independent Practice
Partner students and have them complete *The Five Themes of Geography.*

All in One Europe and Russia Teaching Resources, *The Five Themes of Geography,* p. 29

Monitor Progress
As students complete the worksheet, circulate to make sure that individuals comprehend the material. Provide assistance as needed.

Assess and Reteach

Assess Progress   L2
Have students complete the questions under Practice Your Geography Skills.

Reteach   L1
Help students create a concept web that identifies the five themes of geography. Start filling in blank *Transparency B17: Concept Web* to model how to identify information to clarify each theme. For example, under Regions students might write "share common features such as government, climate, and culture." Encourage students to refer to their webs to review the themes.

Europe and Russia Transparencies, *Transparency B17: Concept Web*

Extend   L3
To extend the lesson, ask students to find out about any plans for new buildings, highways, or other types of construction in your area. Ask students to predict how these changes will affect the community's environment.

Answers

PRACTICE YOUR GEOGRAPHY SKILLS

1. Answers should include an example of how each of the five themes relates to your community.

2. Students' answers should provide examples of goods, ideas, or things that move into and out of your community.

MapMaster Skills Handbook **M1**

Objective

- Explain how the movements of Earth cause night and day, as well as the seasons.

Prepare to Read

Build Background Knowledge   L2

Remind students that while Earth revolves around the sun, it also rotates on its own axis. Review the meanings of "revolve" and "rotate" in this context. Ask students to brainstorm ways that Earth's revolving and rotating might affect their lives. Conduct an Idea Wave (TE, p. T35) to generate a list of ideas.

Instruct

Understanding Movements of Earth   L2

Guided Instruction

- Read the text as a class using the Oral Cloze strategy (TE, p. T33). Explain the illustrations on pp. M2 and M3 show the information in the text visually. Clarify the meanings of any unfamiliar words.

- Ask students **How does Earth rotating on its axis cause day and night?** *(It is daytime on the side of Earth facing the sun, while the side facing away from the sun is dark.)*

- Ask **How does the tilt of Earth affect the seasons?** *(The farther away a part of Earth is from the sun's rays, the colder it is.)*

Independent Practice

Partner students and have them complete *Understanding the Movements of the Earth.*

All in One Europe and Russia Teaching Resources, *Understanding Movements of the Earth*, p. 30

Understanding Movements of Earth

The planet Earth is part of our solar system. Earth revolves around the sun in a nearly circular path called an orbit. A revolution, or one complete orbit around the sun, takes 365¼ days, or one year. As Earth orbits the sun, it also spins on its axis, an invisible line through the center of Earth from the North Pole to the South Pole. This movement is called a rotation.

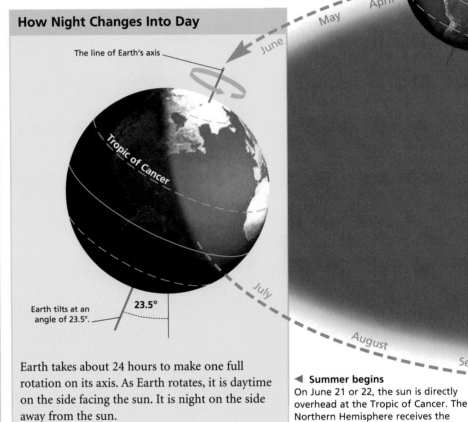

How Night Changes Into Day

The line of Earth's axis

Tropic of Cancer

Earth tilts at an angle of 23.5°.   **23.5°**

Earth takes about 24 hours to make one full rotation on its axis. As Earth rotates, it is daytime on the side facing the sun. It is night on the side away from the sun.

▼ **Spring begins**
On March 20 or 21, the sun is directly overhead at the Equator. The Northern and Southern Hemispheres receive almost equal hours of sunlight and darkness.

◄ **Summer begins**
On June 21 or 22, the sun is directly overhead at the Tropic of Cancer. The Northern Hemisphere receives the greatest number of sunlight hours.

M2 MapMaster Skills Handbook

Background: Links Across Place

Sunrise and Sunset Most people have heard the saying "The sun rises in the east and sets in the west." However, the sun does not ever actually change position. Every day, Earth rotates on its axis so that as each region faces the sun, it experiences day. The rotation continues so that as a region turns away from the sun, it experiences night. The sun stays in the same place. A person viewing sunrise or sunset is really seeing Earth's slow turn on its axis, not the sun rising or setting.

The Seasons

Earth's axis is tilted at an angle. Because of this tilt, sunlight strikes different parts of Earth at different times in the year, creating seasons. The illustration below shows how the seasons are created in the Northern Hemisphere. In the Southern Hemisphere, the seasons are reversed.

PRACTICE YOUR GEOGRAPHY SKILLS

1 What causes the seasons in the Northern Hemisphere to be the opposite of those in the Southern Hemisphere?

2 During which two days of the year do the Northern Hemisphere and Southern Hemisphere have equal hours of daylight and darkness?

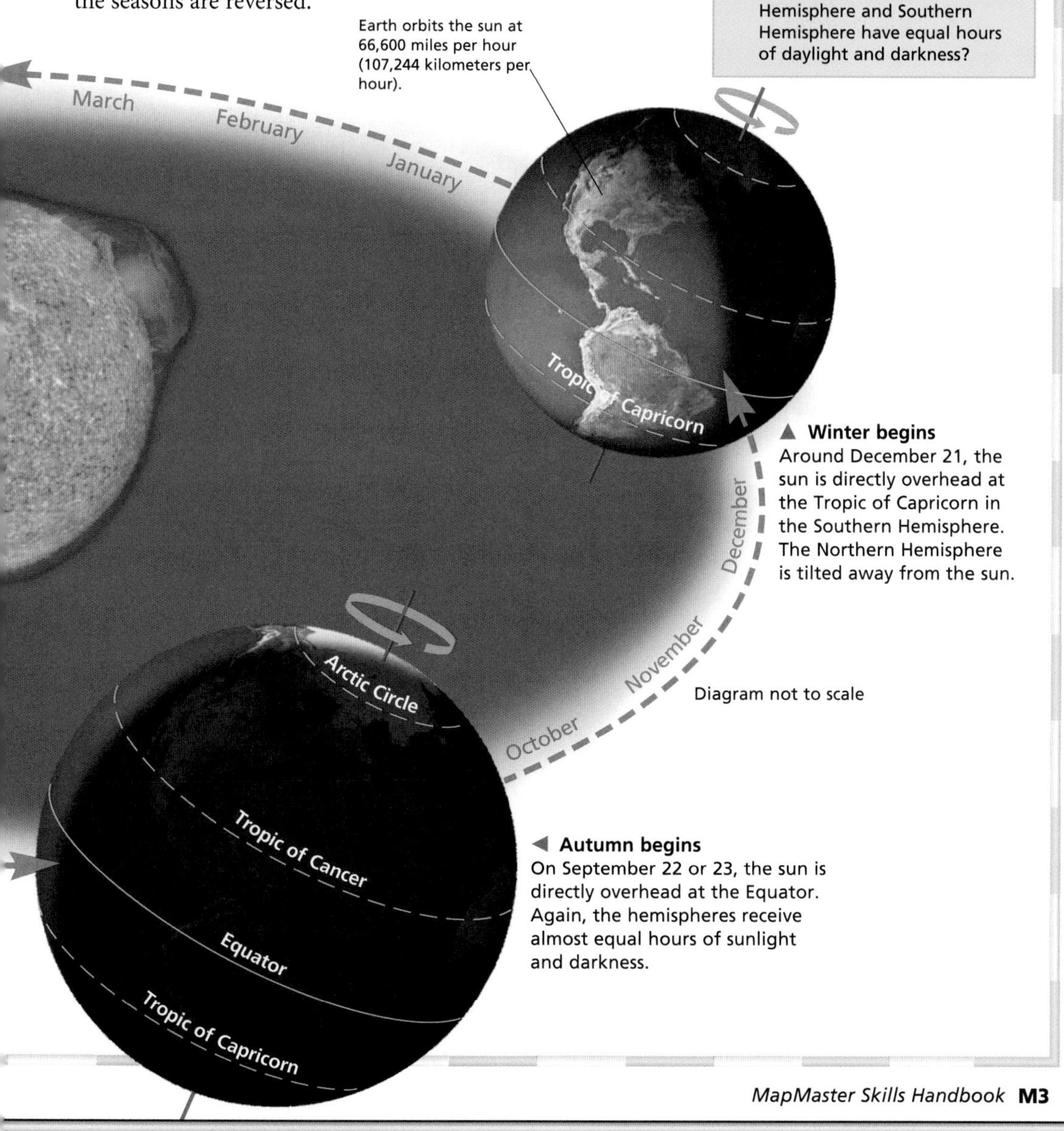

Earth orbits the sun at 66,600 miles per hour (107,244 kilometers per hour).

March
February
January

December
November
October

Tropic of Capricorn

Arctic Circle

Tropic of Cancer

Equator

Tropic of Capricorn

Diagram not to scale

▲ **Winter begins**
Around December 21, the sun is directly overhead at the Tropic of Capricorn in the Southern Hemisphere. The Northern Hemisphere is tilted away from the sun.

◄ **Autumn begins**
On September 22 or 23, the sun is directly overhead at the Equator. Again, the hemispheres receive almost equal hours of sunlight and darkness.

MapMaster Skills Handbook **M3**

Monitor Progress

As students do the worksheet, circulate to make sure individuals comprehend the key concepts. Provide assistance as needed.

Assess and Reteach

Assess Progress L2
Have students complete the Practice Your Geography Skills questions.

Reteach L1
If students are having trouble understanding these concepts, create a model to demonstrate Earth's revolution. Use a foam ball to represent Earth. Insert a pencil through the ball to represent Earth's axis, labeling the ends "North Pole" and "South Pole." Draw the Equator perpendicular to the axis. Place a light source in the center of a table to represent the sun. Then tilt the ball at a slight angle and move it around the light to mimic Earth's revolution. Have students notice the point at which each pole is nearest the sun and identify what season it would be in each hemisphere.

Extend L3
To extend the lesson, ask students to consider Earth's relationship to its satellite, the moon. Ask them to research on the Internet to answer these questions: "Does the moon rotate like Earth? Does the moon revolve around Earth as Earth revolves around the sun?" To help students start their research, give them *Doing Searches on the Internet*.

All in One **Europe and Russia Teaching Resources,** *Doing Searches on the Internet,* p. 31

Differentiated Instruction

For Special Needs Students L1

Have students act out the revolution of Earth around the sun. Assign one student the role of "the sun," and other students the roles of Earth at four different times of the year. Have them walk through a year's cycle. Show *Color Transparency ER 1: The Earth's Revolution and the*

Seasons to guide them. Ask them to simulate the tilt of Earth's axis as shown in the illustrations on pp. M2–M3.

Europe and Russia Transparencies, *Color Transparency ER 1: The Earth's Revolution and the Seasons*

Answers

PRACTICE YOUR GEOGRAPHY SKILLS

1. The seasons are reversed in the Northern Hemisphere and Southern Hemisphere because Earth is tilted. When one hemisphere is tilted towards the sun, the other hemisphere is tilted away from the sun.

2. September 22–23 and March 20–21

Objectives

- Understand how a globe is marked with a grid to measure features on Earth.
- Learn how to use longitude and latitude to locate a place.

Prepare to Read

Build Background Knowledge **L2**

Tell students that in this lesson, they will learn how to use globes. Ask students what it would be like to see Earth from a spacecraft. Discuss the shape that students would see. Then discuss why a globe is a more accurate rendering of Earth than a flat map. Point out that a globe is like a model car in that it is a small version of something larger. If a globe is available, have students examine it.

Instruct

Understanding Globes **L2**

Guided Instruction

- Read the text as a class using the Oral Cloze strategy (TE, p. T33). Have students study the illustrations carefully.

- Ask **What line of latitude divides the Northern and Southern Hemispheres?** *(the Equator)* **At what degrees latitude is this line?** *(0º)*

- Ask **Where do the lines of longitude come together?** *(at the North and South Poles)* **What is the name of the meridian at 0 degrees?** *(Prime Meridian)*

- Have students look at the global grid on *Color Transparency ER 3: The Global Grid.* Ask **What is the global grid?** *(a pattern of lines formed where the parallels of latitude and meridians of longitude cross)* **What continent in the Eastern Hemisphere does the 100E° meridian pass through?** *(Asia)*

    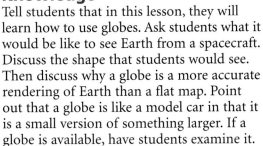 **Europe and Russia Transparencies,** *Color Transparency ER 3: The Global Grid*

Understanding Globes

A globe is a scale model of Earth. It shows the actual shapes, sizes, and locations of all Earth's landmasses and bodies of water. Features on the surface of Earth are drawn to scale on a globe. This means that a small unit of measure on the globe stands for a large unit of measure on Earth.

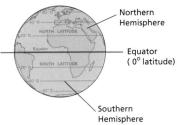

Northern Hemisphere

Equator (0° latitude)

Southern Hemisphere

Parallels of Latitude

Geographers divide the globe along imaginary horizontal lines called parallels of latitude. One of these latitude lines is the Equator, located halfway between the North and South poles. Parallels of latitude are measured in degrees (°). One degree of latitude represents a distance of about 69 miles (111 kilometers).

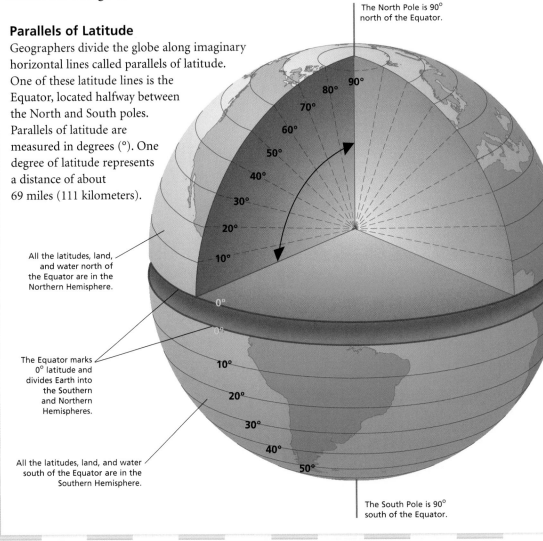

The North Pole is 90° north of the Equator.

90°
80°
70°
60°
50°
40°
30°
20°
10°
0°

All the latitudes, land, and water north of the Equator are in the Northern Hemisphere.

The Equator marks 0° latitude and divides Earth into the Southern and Northern Hemispheres.

0°
10°
20°
30°
40°
50°

All the latitudes, land, and water south of the Equator are in the Southern Hemisphere.

The South Pole is 90° south of the Equator.

Background: Links Across Time

The First Globes Historians believe that the first globe may have been made in the second century B.C. by a Greek geographer known as Crates of Mallus. The mathematician Ptolemy represented Earth as a globe in his written works in the second century A.D. In late 1492 Martin Behaim made a terrestrial globe that, although inaccurate by today's knowledge, reflected the best geographical knowledge of the time. This globe still exists and is on display in Behaim's hometown of Nuremberg, Germany.

Meridians of Longitude

Geographers also divide the globe along imaginary vertical lines called meridians of longitude, which are measured in degrees (°). The longitude line called the Prime Meridian runs from pole to pole through Greenwich, England. All meridians of longitude come together at the North and South Poles.

PRACTICE YOUR GEOGRAPHY MAP SKILLS

1 Which continents lie completely in the Northern Hemisphere? In the Western Hemisphere?

2 Is there land or water at 20° S latitude and the Prime Meridian? At the Equator and 60° W longitude?

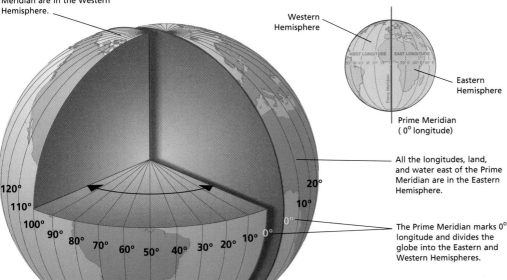

All the longitudes, land, and water west of the Prime Meridian are in the Western Hemisphere.

Western Hemisphere

Eastern Hemisphere

Prime Meridian (0° longitude)

All the longitudes, land, and water east of the Prime Meridian are in the Eastern Hemisphere.

The Prime Meridian marks 0° longitude and divides the globe into the Eastern and Western Hemispheres.

The Global Grid

Together, the pattern of parallels of latitude and meridians of longitude is called the global grid. Using the lines of latitude and longitude, you can locate any place on Earth. For example, the location of 30° north latitude and 90° west longitude is usually written as 30° N, 90° W. Only one place on Earth has these coordinates—the city of New Orleans, in the state of Louisiana.

▲ **Compass**
Wherever you are on Earth, a compass can be used to show direction.

MapMaster Skills Handbook **M5**

Independent Practice

Have students work in pairs to complete *Understanding Hemispheres* and *Understanding Latitude and Longitude.*

All in One Europe and Russia Teaching Resources, *Understanding Hemispheres,* p. 32; *Understanding Latitude and Longitude,* p. 33

Monitor Progress

As students do the worksheets, circulate to make sure pairs understand the key concepts. Show *Color Transparency ER 2: The Hemispheres* to help students.

Europe and Russia Transparencies, *Color Transparency ER 2: The Hemispheres*

Assess and Reteach

Assess Progress L2

Have students answer the questions under Practice Your Geography Map Skills.

Reteach L1

Use the DK Atlas activity *Understanding Latitude and Longitude* to review these skills with students. Have students complete the activity in pairs.

All in One Europe and Russia Teaching Resources, *DK Compact Atlas of the World Activity: Understanding Latitude and Longitude,* p. 34

Extend L3

To extend the lesson, have students complete *Using Latitude and Longitude.* Then have students use the map and with a partner, play a game of Can You Find ...? Each partner takes a turn giving the coordinates for a place on the map and the other partner must name the place.

All in One Europe and Russia Teaching Resources, *Using Latitude and Longitude,* p. 35

Differentiated Instruction

For Less Proficient Readers L1

For students having difficulty understanding the concept of a global grid, give them *Understanding Grids* and help them complete it. Then follow up with *Using a Grid.*

All in One Europe and Russia Teaching Resources, *Understanding Grids,* p. 36; *Using a Grid,* p. 37

For Advanced Readers L3

Have students complete *Comparing Globes and Maps.* Then ask them to make a chart showing the pros and cons of these two ways of representing Earth.

All in One Europe and Russia Teaching Resources, *Comparing Globes and Maps,* p. 38

Answers

PRACTICE YOUR GEOGRAPHY SKILLS

1. Northern Hemisphere: North America; Europe; Western Hemisphere: North America; South America

2. water; land

MapMaster Skills Handbook **M5**

Objectives

- Compare maps of different projections.
- Describe distortions in map projections.

Prepare to Read

Build Background Knowledge L1

In this lesson, students will learn how cartographers depict Earth on a two-dimensional map. Remind students that if they were traveling in a spaceship, Earth would look like a globe. Ask if they could ever see the entire Earth at one time from space. Help students recognize that a flat map is the only way to see all of Earth at one time.

Instruct

Map Projections L2

Guided Instruction

- Read the text as a class using the Choral Reading strategy (TE, p. T34). Direct students to look at the relevant maps after you read each section together. Follow up by having students do a second silent reading.

- Help students locate Greenland on the Mercator and Robinson maps. Ask **What difference do you notice in the way Greenland is shown?** *(It appears much larger on the Mercator Map.)* **How would you explain this?** *(The Mercator is a same-shape map and the shapes toward the poles are enlarged.)*

- Ask **Where does the distortion usually occur on an equal-shape map?** *(at the edges of the map)*

- Have students compare Antarctica on the three projections. *(It is largest and most distorted on the Mercator map; smallest on the equal-area map; covers the entire bottom edge of the Robinson map.)*

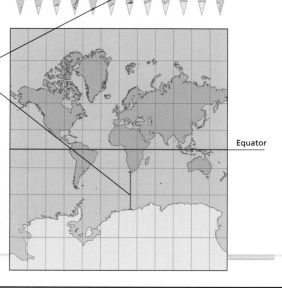

MAP MASTER™ | LOCATION | REGIONS | PLACE | MOVEMENT | INTERACTION

Map Projections

Maps are drawings that show regions on flat surfaces. Maps are easier to use and carry than globes, but they cannot show the correct size and shape of every feature on Earth's curved surface. They must shrink some places and stretch others. To make up for this distortion, mapmakers use different map projections. No one projection can accurately show the correct area, shape, distance, and direction for all of Earth's surface. Mapmakers use the projection that has the least distortion for the information they are presenting.

▲ **Global gores**
Flattening a globe creates a string of shapes called gores.

Same-Shape Maps

Map projections that accurately show the shapes of landmasses are called same-shape maps. However, these projections often greatly distort, or make less accurate, the size of landmasses as well as the distance between them. In the projection below, the northern and southern areas of the globe appear more stretched than the areas near the Equator.

To turn Earth into a same-shape map, mapmakers must stretch the gores into rectangles.

Equator

Stretching the gores makes parts of Earth larger. This enlargement becomes greater toward the North and South Poles.

Equator

Mercator projection ▶
One of the most common same-shape maps is the Mercator projection, named for the mapmaker who invented it. The Mercator projection accurately shows shape and direction, but it distorts distance and size. Because the projection shows true directions, ships' navigators use it to chart a straight-line course between two ports.

Differentiated Instruction

For Special Needs Students L1

If students have difficulty understanding why distortion occurs, draw a simple picture on an orange. Then have students try to peel the orange in one piece. Challenge students to place the peel flat on a piece of paper without any tears and spaces. Talk about what happens to the drawing. Explain that mapmakers face this same challenge when drawing Earth on a flat paper.

For Gifted and Talented L3

Have students complete *Great Circles and Straight Lines.* Then ask them to use their completed page and a globe to explain the concept of great circles to the class.

All in One Europe and Russia Teaching Resources, *Great Circles and Straight Lines,* p. 40

Equal-Area Maps

Map projections that show the correct size of landmasses are called equal-area maps. In order to show the correct size of landmasses, these maps usually distort shapes. The distortion is usually greater at the edges of the map and less at the center.

PRACTICE YOUR GEOGRAPHY SKILLS

1 What feature is distorted on an equal-area map?

2 Would you use a Mercator projection to find the exact distance between two locations? Tell why or why not.

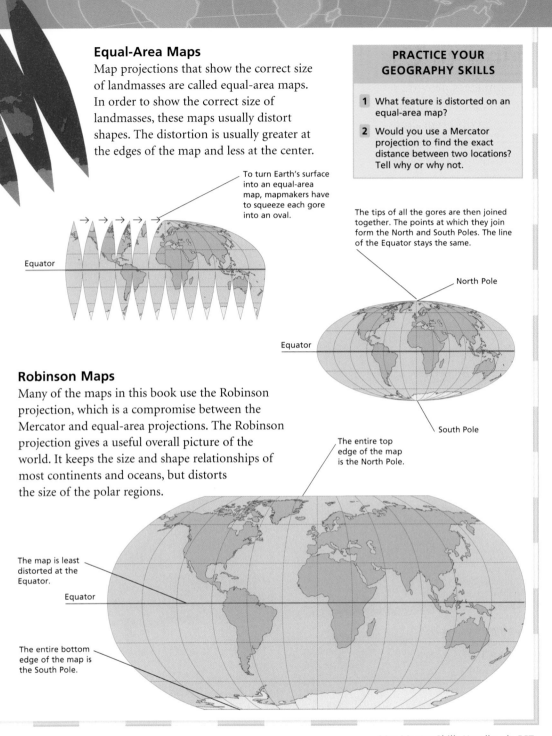

To turn Earth's surface into an equal-area map, mapmakers have to squeeze each gore into an oval.

Equator

The tips of all the gores are then joined together. The points at which they join form the North and South Poles. The line of the Equator stays the same.

North Pole

Equator

South Pole

Robinson Maps

Many of the maps in this book use the Robinson projection, which is a compromise between the Mercator and equal-area projections. The Robinson projection gives a useful overall picture of the world. It keeps the size and shape relationships of most continents and oceans, but distorts the size of the polar regions.

The entire top edge of the map is the North Pole.

The map is least distorted at the Equator.

Equator

The entire bottom edge of the map is the South Pole.

MapMaster Skills Handbook **M7**

Background: Biography

Gerardus Mercator (1512–1594) The Mercator projection takes its name from a Flemish geographer, Gerhard Kremer. Kremer, who used the Latin form of his name, Gerardus Mercator, wrote books on ancient geography and cartography. He made his first world map in 1538. In 1554 he made a map of Europe. In 1568, the first map using the Mercator projection bearing his name appeared. Mercator also began an atlas of his maps which was finished by his son and published in 1594.

Independent Practice

Have students work with partners to complete *Understanding Projection.*

All in One **Europe and Russia Teaching Resources,** *Understanding Projection,* p. 39

Monitor Progress

As students do the worksheet, circulate to make sure individuals comprehend the key concepts. Provide assistance as needed.

Assess and Reteach

Assess Progress L2

Have students complete the Practice Your Geography Skills questions.

Reteach L1

Use *Maps with Accurate Shapes: Conformal Maps* and *Maps with Accurate Areas: Equal-Area Maps* to help students go over the information in the lesson. Model thinking for each question and partner students to complete each page together. Circulate to provide explanations and help as students work.

All in One **Europe and Russia Teaching Resources,** *Maps with Accurate Shapes: Conformal Maps,* p. 41; *Maps with Accurate Areas: Equal-Area Maps,* p. 42

Extend L3

To extend the lesson, ask students to complete *Maps with Accurate Direction: Azimuthal Maps.* Then have students write a sentence or two describing the different projections they have learned about.

All in One **Europe and Russia Teaching Resources,** *Maps with Accurate Directions: Azimuthal Maps,* p. 43

Answers

PRACTICE YOUR GEOGRAPHY SKILLS

1. shapes
2. No; the Mercator projection distorts distances.

Objective

- Identify and use the parts of a map.

Prepare to Read

Build Background Knowledge L1

In this lesson, students will learn about the practical aspects of maps. Ask students to name reasons that they might use a map: for example, to find directions, boundaries, distances. Conduct an Idea Wave (TE, p. T35) to generate a list of ideas. List the ideas on the board.

Instruct

How to Use a Map L2

Guided Instruction

- Divide the text and captions in the lesson using the headings and ask students to read the pages using the Structured Silent Reading strategy (TE, p. T34). Remind students to use the illustrations to acquire additional understanding. Refer to the list on the board, then ask students which map part (key, compass rose, scale, symbol, title) would be helpful in using a map for a specific purpose.

- Ask **What is the purpose of a compass rose?** *(to show directions)*

- Talk about how the three maps show different amounts of Earth's surface. Ask **Which map shows the largest area?** *(Western Europe)* **Which map shows the smallest area?** *(Central London)*

- Ask **What are some symbols that you might find on a map key?** *(border, national capital, city, airport, park, point of interest)*

Independent Practice

Partner students and have them complete *Using the Map Key* and *Using the Compass Rose.*

> **All in One Europe and Russia Teaching Resources,** *Using the Map Key,* p. 44; *Using the Compass Rose,* p. 45

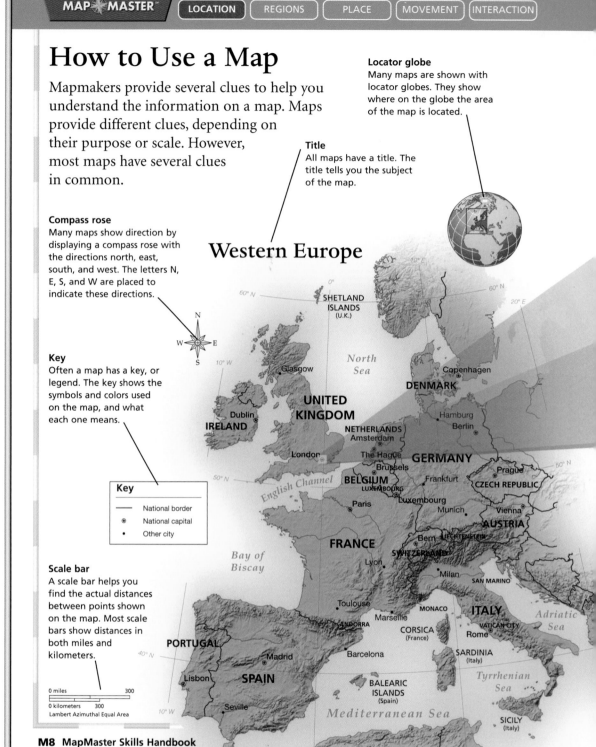

MAP MASTER | LOCATION | REGIONS | PLACE | MOVEMENT | INTERACTION

How to Use a Map

Mapmakers provide several clues to help you understand the information on a map. Maps provide different clues, depending on their purpose or scale. However, most maps have several clues in common.

Locator globe
Many maps are shown with locator globes. They show where on the globe the area of the map is located.

Title
All maps have a title. The title tells you the subject of the map.

Compass rose
Many maps show direction by displaying a compass rose with the directions north, east, south, and west. The letters N, E, S, and W are placed to indicate these directions.

Key
Often a map has a key, or legend. The key shows the symbols and colors used on the map, and what each one means.

Scale bar
A scale bar helps you find the actual distances between points shown on the map. Most scale bars show distances in both miles and kilometers.

Western Europe

Key
— National border
⊛ National capital
• Other city

M8 MapMaster Skills Handbook

Differentiated Instruction

For Less Proficient Readers L1

If students have difficulty recalling the purposes of different parts of a map, have them make a table using each map part as a heading. Under each heading, help students list the important function or functions of that map part. Students should refer to their table when they are working with maps.

For English Language Learners L1

Some of the words in the lesson, such as *symbol* and *scale,* may be unfamiliar to students acquiring English. Have students identify difficult words, look them up in the dictionary, and write sentences explaining what the terms mean.

Maps of Different Scales

Maps are drawn to different scales, depending on their purpose. Here are three maps drawn to very different scales. Keep in mind that maps showing large areas have smaller scales. Maps showing small areas have larger scales.

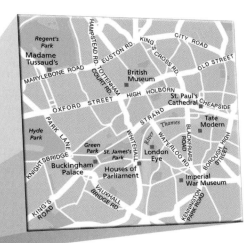

▲ **Greater London**
Find the gray square on the main map of Western Europe (left). This square represents the area shown on the map above. It shows London's boundaries, the general shape of the city, and the features around the city. This map can help you find your way from the airport to the center of town.

▲ **Central London**
Find the gray square on the map of Greater London. This square represents the area shown on the map above. This map moves you closer into the center of London. Like the zoom on a computer or a camera, this map shows a smaller area but in greater detail. It has the largest scale (1 inch represents about 0.9 mile). You can use this map to explore downtown London.

Key

■ Point of interest

▮ Park

```
0 miles       0.5        1
0 kilometers        1
```

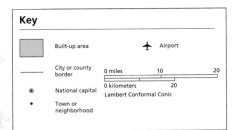

Key

▢ Built-up area   ✈ Airport

── City or county border

```
0 miles        10        20
0 kilometers        20
```
Lambert Conformal Conic

⦿ National capital

• Town or neighborhood

PRACTICE YOUR GEOGRAPHY SKILLS

1 What part of a map explains the colors used on the map?

2 How does the scale bar change depending on the scale of the map?

3 Which map would be best for finding the location of the British Museum? Explain why.

Monitor Progress
Circulate around the room as students complete the worksheets. Make sure that individuals comprehend the material. Provide assistance as needed.

Assess and Reteach

Assess Progress   L2
Have students complete the questions under Practice Your Geography Skills.

Reteach   L1
Some DK Atlas Activities will be helpful in reteaching the lesson. Give students more practice using these concepts by doing the activities for *Using the Map Key, Using the Compass Rose,* and *Using the Map Scale.*

 Europe and Russia Teaching Resources, *DK Compact Atlas of the World Activity: Using the Map Key,* p. 46; *DK Compact Atlas of the World Activity: Using the Compass Rose,* p. 47; *DK Compact Atlas of the World Activity: Using the Map Scale,* p. 48

Extend   L3
To extend the lesson, have students complete *Comparing Maps of Different Scale* and *Maps with Accurate Distances: Equidistant Maps.*

Europe and Russia Teaching Resources, *Comparing Maps of Different Scale,* p. 49; *Maps with Accurate Distances: Equidistant Maps,* p. 50

Answers

PRACTICE YOUR GEOGRAPHY SKILLS

1. key

2. Maps showing large areas have smaller scales. Maps showing small areas have larger scales.

3. the map of Central London; it shows the streets in more detail and includes the British Museum as a point of interest

Objectives

- Understand and use political maps.
- Understand and use physical maps.

Prepare to Read

Build Background Knowledge L1

Tell students that they will learn about political maps and physical maps in this lesson. Explain that a political map is one that shows the boundaries and cities of an area as established by its people. Physical maps show information about the physical features of the area. These physical features would exist whether people lived in a place or not.

Instruct

Political Maps L2
Physical Maps L2

Guided Instruction

- Read the text as a class using the Choral Reading strategy (TE, p. T34) and ask students to study the map.

- Ask students to identify what river forms the boundary between Zimbabwe and South Africa. (*Limpopo River*) Then ask them to name at least two capitals on the Mediterranean Sea. (*Tripoli, Algiers, Tunis*)

- Read the text with the class and draw students' attention to the map and its key.

- Explain that sea level is the average height of the ocean's surface; sea level is at zero elevation. Ask students what color represents sea level on the map key. (*dark green*)

- Have students find the Qattara Depression. Ask **What is its elevation?** (*from 0 to 650 feet*)

- Ask **What is the difference between elevation and relief?** (*Elevation is the height of land above sea level while relief shows how quickly the land rises or falls.*)

Answers

PRACTICE YOUR GEOGRAPHY SKILLS

1. solid line, star in a circle, dot
2. Luanda

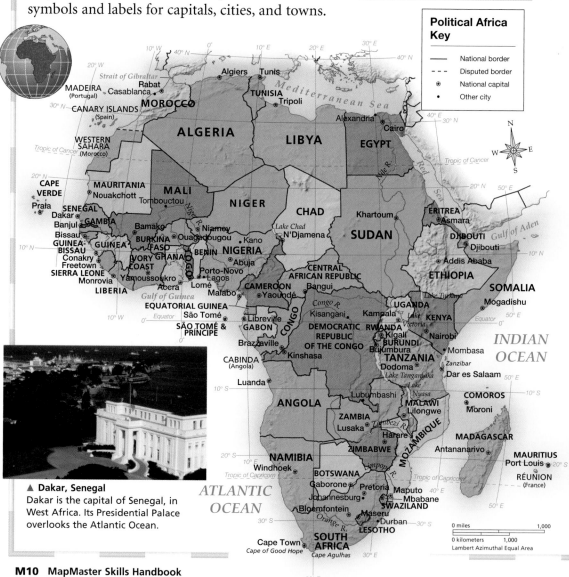

MAP MASTER™ LOCATION REGIONS PLACE MOVEMENT INTERACTION

Political Maps

Political maps show political borders: continents, countries, and divisions within countries, such as states or provinces. The colors on political maps do not have any special meaning, but they make the map easier to read. Political maps also include symbols and labels for capitals, cities, and towns.

PRACTICE YOUR GEOGRAPHY SKILLS

1 What symbols show a national border, a national capital, and a city?

2 What is Angola's capital city?

Political Africa Key

— National border
--- Disputed border
⊙ National capital
• Other city

▲ **Dakar, Senegal**
Dakar is the capital of Senegal, in West Africa. Its Presidential Palace overlooks the Atlantic Ocean.

M10 MapMaster Skills Handbook

Background: Global Perspectives

Africa's Highest Peaks Africa's two highest mountains are both extinct volcanoes that rise near the equator on the eastern part of the continent. The tallest mountain, Kilimanjaro in Tanzania, reaches 19,340 feet (5,895 meters) at its highest point. Although snow covers its peaks, farmers raise coffee and plantains on the lower southern slopes of Kilimanjaro. Africa's second highest mountain is Mt. Kenya at 17,058 feet (5,199 meters) located in central Kenya. Like Kilimanjaro, it is snowcapped in its highest regions. Both Kilimanjaro and Mt. Kenya are attractions for mountain climbers from all over the world.

Physical Maps

Physical maps represent what a region looks like by showing its major physical features, such as hills and plains. Physical maps also often show elevation and relief. Elevation, indicated by colors, is the height of the land above sea level. Relief, indicated by shading, shows how quickly the land rises or falls.

PRACTICE YOUR GEOGRAPHY SKILLS

1 Which areas of Africa have the highest elevation?

2 How can you use relief to plan a hiking trip?

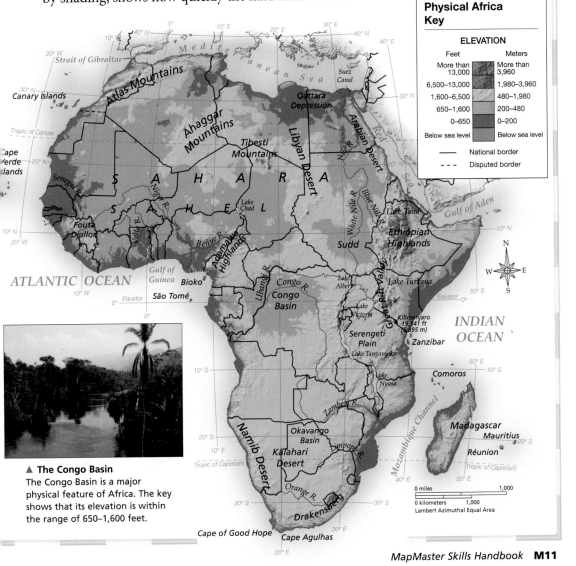

Physical Africa Key

ELEVATION

Feet	Meters
More than 13,000	More than 3,960
6,500–13,000	1,980–3,960
1,600–6,500	480–1,980
650–1,600	200–480
0–650	0–200
Below sea level	Below sea level

—— National border

- - - Disputed border

▲ The Congo Basin
The Congo Basin is a major physical feature of Africa. The key shows that its elevation is within the range of 650–1,600 feet.

MapMaster Skills Handbook **M11**

Independent Practice
Have students complete *Reading a Political Map*, *Reading a Physical Map*, and *Elevation on a Map* working with partners.

All in One Europe and Russia Teaching Resources, *Reading a Political Map*, p. 51; *Reading a Physical Map*, p. 56; *Elevation on a Map*, p. 57

Monitor Progress
As students complete the worksheets, circulate around the room to make sure individuals understand the key concepts. Provide assistance as needed.

Assess and Reteach

Assess Progress   L2
Have students answer the questions under Practice Your Geography Skills on pp. M10–M11.

Reteach   L1
Use the DK Atlas Activities *Reading a Political Map* and *Reading a Physical Map* to review the concepts in this lesson.

All in One Europe and Russia Teaching Resources, *DK Compact Atlas of the World Activity: Reading a Political Map*, p. 52; *DK Compact Atlas of the World Activity: Reading a Physical Map*, p. 58

Extend   L3
To extend the lesson, have students fill in the name of each country and its capital on the outline maps *North Africa*, *West and Central Africa*, and *East and Southern Africa*. Also, ask them to use colors and shading to indicate the Atlas Mountains, the Ethiopian Highlands, the Congo Basin, and the Namib Desert.

All in One Europe and Russia Teaching Resources, *Outline Map 22: North Africa*, p. 53; *Outline Map 23: West and Central Africa*, p. 54; *Outline Map 24: East and Southern Africa*, p. 55

Differentiated Instruction

For Special Needs Students   L1
Reuse *Reading a Political Map* to help students understand political maps. Point to the symbol for a national border in the key, then trace the borders of several countries. Invite students to trace others.

All in One Europe and Russia Teaching Resources, *Reading a Political Map*, p. 51

For Advanced Readers   L3
Challenge students to explore the concepts of relief and elevation further by completing *Relief on a Map* and *Maps of the Ocean Floor*.

All in One Europe and Russia Teaching Resources, *Relief on a Map*, p. 59; *Maps of the Ocean Floor*, p. 60

Answers

PRACTICE YOUR GEOGRAPHY SKILLS

1. Ethiopian Highlands and Great Rift Valley
2. It can help you find out where the land rises and falls.

Objectives

- Understand and use climate maps.
- Understand and use language maps.

Prepare to Read

Build Background Knowledge **L1**

Ask students to think of as many meanings for the word *special* as they can. Tell them that maps can be special too. Ask **What do you think a special-purpose map might show?** List suggestions on the board.

Instruct

Special-Purpose Maps: Climate **L1**

Guided Instruction

- Ask students to read the text using the Structured Silent Reading strategy (TE, p. T34). Point out that the map shows Bangladesh, Bhutan, Nepal, and parts of Myanmar and Pakistan as well as India.

- Point out the map and key. Ask **What areas have a tropical wet climate?** *(area along the southern western coast; eastern part of Bangladesh)*

- Ask **What color represents an arid climate?** *(brown)*

Independent Practice

Partner students and have them complete *Reading a Climate Map.*

All in One Europe and Russia Teaching Resources, *Reading a Climate Map,* p. 61

Monitor Progress

As students complete the worksheet, circulate around the room to make sure individuals comprehend the key concepts. Provide assistance as needed.

Answers

PRACTICE YOUR GEOGRAPHY SKILLS

1. the key

2. the northwestern part; No major cities are in the arid region.

Special-Purpose Maps: Climate

Unlike the boundary lines on a political map, the boundary lines on climate maps do not separate the land into exact divisions. For example, in this climate map of India, a tropical wet climate gradually changes to a tropical wet and dry climate.

<image-ref id="N" />

PRACTICE YOUR GEOGRAPHY SKILLS

1 What part of a special-purpose map tells you what the colors on the map mean?

2 Where are arid regions located in India? Are there major cities in those regions?

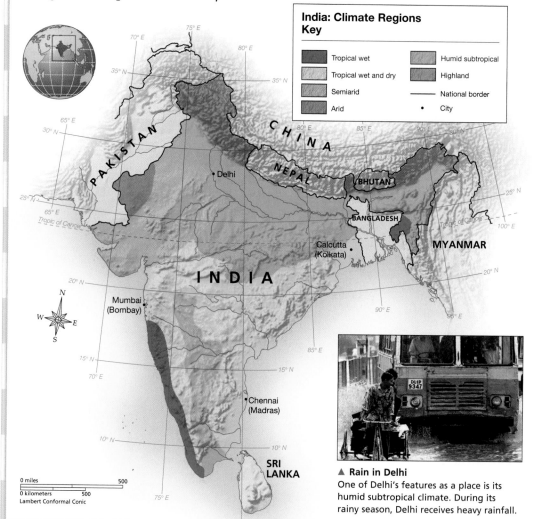

India: Climate Regions Key

- Tropical wet
- Tropical wet and dry
- Semiarid
- Arid
- Humid subtropical
- Highland
- —— National border
- • City

▲ **Rain in Delhi**
One of Delhi's features as a place is its humid subtropical climate. During its rainy season, Delhi receives heavy rainfall.

0 miles 500
0 kilometers 500
Lambert Conformal Conic

Differentiated Instruction

For English Language Learners **L1**

If students are unfamiliar with words in the lesson, help them identify and look up those words in the dictionary. For example: *arid*—adj. having little or no rainfall; dry *humid*—adj. having a lot of water; damp; *semi*—adj. part or partially

Follow up by having students determine the meaning of *semiarid.*

For Gifted and Talented **L3**

Give students *Reading a Climate Graph.* Ask students to compare the information in the graph with the information on the map above. Using the map and the graph, ask them to write a sentence about the climate of Mumbai.

All in One Europe and Russia Teaching Resources, *Reading A Climate Graph,* p. 62

Special-Purpose Maps: Language

This map shows the official languages of India. An official language is the language used by the government. Even though a region has an official language, the people there may speak other languages as well. As in other special-purpose maps, the key explains how the different languages appear on the map.

PRACTICE YOUR GEOGRAPHY SKILLS

1 What color represents the Malayalam language on this map?

2 Where in India is Tamil the official language?

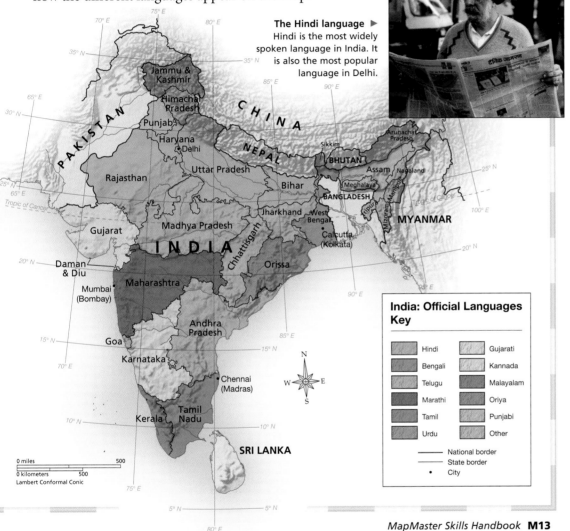

The Hindi language ▶ Hindi is the most widely spoken language in India. It is also the most popular language in Delhi.

India: Official Languages Key

Hindi	Gujarati
Bengali	Kannada
Telugu	Malayalam
Marathi	Oriya
Tamil	Punjabi
Urdu	Other

——— National border
——— State border
• City

MapMaster Skills Handbook **M13**

Background: Daily Life

The Hindi Language Hindi is the official language of India and is the primary language for about 300 million people. Hindi is the written form of Hindustani that is used by Hindus. English is also spoken by many Indians and is considered the language of politics and commerce. However, the diversity of the country is reflected in the enormous number of languages spoken there, more than 1,500 in all. Ten of India's major states are organized along linguistic lines, and the Indian constitution recognizes 15 regional languages.

Guided Instruction
- Read the text as a class. Draw students' attention to the map and its key.
- Have students consider the diversity of official languages. Ask **Why might it be important for a country to have a common language in addition to regional ones?** (*Communication is easier with a common language.*)

Independent Practice
Have students work with partners to read another special purpose map, *Reading a Natural Vegetation Map.*

> **All in One Europe and Russia Teaching Resources,** *Reading a Natural Vegetation Map,* p. 63

Monitor Progress
As students complete the worksheet, circulate around the room and make sure individuals understand key concepts. Provide assistance as needed.

Assess and Reteach

Assess Progress · L2
Have students answer the questions under Practice Your Geography Skills on pp. M12–M13.

Reteach · L1
To help students understand how to use a special purpose map, have them practice the skill using *Analyzing and Interpreting Special Purpose Maps.*

> ⊙ *Analyzing and Interpreting Special-Purpose Maps,* **Social Studies Skills Tutor CD-ROM**

Extend · L3
Have students learn about another type of special-purpose map by completing *Reading a Time Zone Map.* Then ask students to find out the time zones in India and create their own time zone map, using *Outline Map 26: South Asia: Political.*

> **All in One Europe and Russia Teaching Resources,** *Reading a Time Zone Map.* p. 65; *Outline Map 26: South Asia: Political,* p. 64

Answers

PRACTICE YOUR GEOGRAPHY SKILLS

1. dark purple
2. southeast India

Objectives

- Learn why people migrate.

- Understand how migration affects environments.

Prepare to Read

Build Background Knowledge **L1**

Remind students that they studied the theme of movement earlier in this unit. Brainstorm with students why people move from place to place, particularly those who move from one country to another. Use the Numbered Heads participation strategy (TE, p. T36) to generate ideas.

Instruct

Human Migration **L2**

Guided Instruction

- Divide the text using the headings and ask students to read the pages using the Paragraph Shrinking strategy (TE, p. T34). Clarify the meanings of any unfamiliar words.

- Have students look at the map. Ask **From what European countries did people migrate to the Americas in the years between 1500-1800?** *(Portugal, Spain, France, Netherlands, England)*

- Ask **Where did the French settle in Latin America?** *(French Guiana and Haiti)* **Which European country had the most possessions in the Americas?** *(Spain)*

- Ask **Why were some Africans forced to migrate?** *(They were imported as slaves from their homeland. Europeans wanted them to work on the land they claimed in the Americas.)*

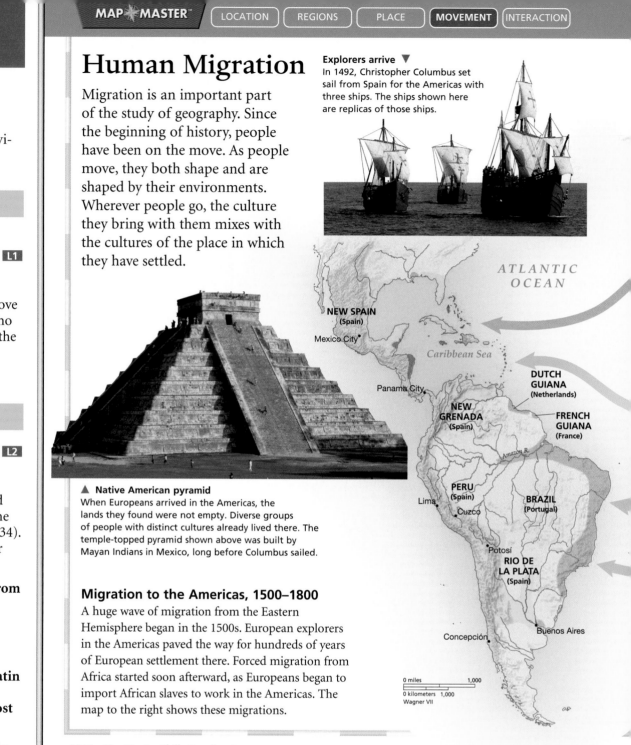

Human Migration

Migration is an important part of the study of geography. Since the beginning of history, people have been on the move. As people move, they both shape and are shaped by their environments. Wherever people go, the culture they bring with them mixes with the cultures of the place in which they have settled.

Explorers arrive ▼
In 1492, Christopher Columbus set sail from Spain for the Americas with three ships. The ships shown here are replicas of those ships.

ATLANTIC OCEAN

NEW SPAIN (Spain)
Mexico City

Caribbean Sea

Panama City

DUTCH GUIANA (Netherlands)

NEW GRENADA (Spain)

FRENCH GUIANA (France)

Amazon R.

PERU (Spain)
Lima
Cuzco

BRAZIL (Portugal)

Potosí

RIO DE LA PLATA (Spain)

Concepción

Buenos Aires

0 miles 1,000
0 kilometers 1,000
Wagner VII

▲ **Native American pyramid**
When Europeans arrived in the Americas, the lands they found were not empty. Diverse groups of people with distinct cultures already lived there. The temple-topped pyramid shown above was built by Mayan Indians in Mexico, long before Columbus sailed.

Migration to the Americas, 1500–1800

A huge wave of migration from the Eastern Hemisphere began in the 1500s. European explorers in the Americas paved the way for hundreds of years of European settlement there. Forced migration from Africa started soon afterward, as Europeans began to import African slaves to work in the Americas. The map to the right shows these migrations.

Differentiated Instruction

For Less Proficient Readers **L1**

Review with students the meaning of "push" and "pull" factors in terms of human migration. Model for students how to make a table with the headings Push and Pull. Then work with students to list as many factors as they can under each heading.

For Advanced Readers **L3**

Have students complete *Analyzing Statistics*. When they have finished, have them write a paragraph explaining how economic and social statistics are related to "push" and "pull" factors.

 Europe and Russia Teaching Resources, *Analyzing Statistics,* p. 67

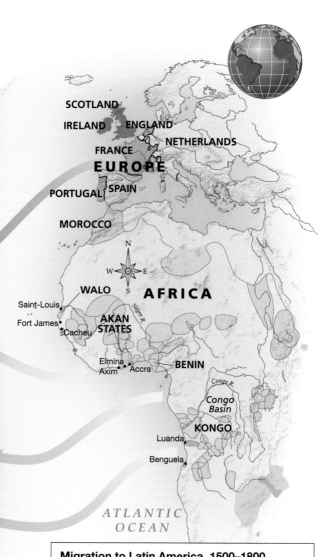

SCOTLAND
IRELAND ENGLAND
FRANCE NETHERLANDS
EUROPE
PORTUGAL SPAIN
MOROCCO

N
W   E
S

WALO AFRICA
Saint-Louis
Fort James
Cacheu AKAN
STATES
Niger R.
Elmina Accra
Axim BENIN
Congo R.
Congo
Basin
KONGO
Luanda
Benguela

ATLANTIC
OCEAN

Migration to Latin America, 1500–1800
Key

→ European migration		Spain and possessions	
→ African migration		Portugal and possessions	
— National or colonial border		Netherlands and possessions	
⋯ Traditional African border		France and possessions	
African State		England and possessions	

"Push" and "Pull" Factors

Geographers describe a people's choice to migrate in terms of "push" factors and "pull" factors. Push factors are things in people's lives that push them to leave, such as poverty and political unrest. Pull factors are things in another country that pull people to move there, including better living conditions and hopes of better jobs.

▲ **Elmina, Ghana**
Elmina, in Ghana, is one of the many ports from which slaves were transported from Africa. Because slaves and gold were traded here, stretches of the western African coast were known as the Slave Coast and the Gold Coast.

Independent Practice

Have students work with partners to complete *Reading a Historical Map.* Have students be ready to explain how the movement of European groups changed the map of Africa. (*Much of Africa was colonized by Europeans.*)

All in One Europe and Russia Teaching Resources, *Reading a Historical Map,* p. 66

Monitor Progress

As students complete the worksheet, circulate around the room to make sure individuals comprehend the key concepts. Provide assistance as needed.

Assess and Reteach

Assess Progress   L2
Have students complete the questions under Practice Your Geography Skills.

Reteach   L1
Help students make an outline of the lesson. Show *Transparency B15: Outline* as a model. Then work with students to identify the main points. Encourage students to refer to their outlines to review the material.

Europe and Russia Transparencies, *Transparency B15: Outline*

Extend   L3
To extend the lesson, have students complete *The Global Refugee Crisis.* Then ask them to choose a specific region on the graph and find out more about refugees from one country in that region.

Go Online
PHSchool.com **For:** Environmental and Global Issues: *The Global Refugee Crisis*
Visit: PHSchool.com
Web Code: ldd-7001

Answers

PRACTICE YOUR GEOGRAPHY SKILLS

1. Brazil

2. most likely push factors because people were forced to leave; the need for workers in the Americas was a pull factor although it was the Europeans who responded to it by importing Africans as slaves

Objectives

- Understand and use a land use map.
- Learn how land use and economic structures are linked.

Prepare to Read

Build Background Knowledge   **L1**

Discuss with the class the ways that people in your community are using land. For example, is all the land used for homes? How much is used for commercial purposes? What kinds? Are there farms or manufacturing facilities? Point out that communities in all parts of the world use land in different ways.

Instruct

World Land Use   **L2**

Guided Instruction

- Read the text as a class using the Oral Cloze strategy (TE, p. T33). Follow up by having students do a second silent reading. Encourage students to study the map and photographs.

- Talk about the difference between commercial and subsistence farming. Have them look closely at the photographs on pages M16 and M17. Ask **How do the tools and equipment people use differ in these types of farming?** (*Large power machines are used in commercial farming; hand tools are used in subsistence farming.*) **Why might people use more land in commercial farming?** (*Machines make it possible to cultivate more land. The more land cultivated, the more sales possible.*)

- Ask **What color represents nomadic herding on this map?** (*light purple*) **In what parts of the world is this an economic activity?** (*Africa, Asia, Europe*)

- Ask **Why might some parts of the world have little or no land use activity?** (*Land and/or climate might not be suitable for farming or other activity.*)

World Land Use

People around the world have many different economic structures, or ways of making a living. Land-use maps are one way to learn about these structures. The ways that people use the land in each region tell us about the main ways that people in that region make a living.

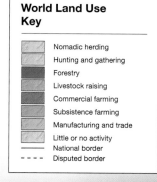

World Land Use Key

	Nomadic herding
	Hunting and gathering
	Forestry
	Livestock raising
	Commercial farming
	Subsistence farming
	Manufacturing and trade
	Little or no activity
——	National border
- - - -	Disputed border

▲ **Wheat farming in the United States**
Developed countries practice commercial farming rather than subsistence farming. Commercial farming is the production of food mainly for sale, either within the country or for export to other countries. Commercial farmers like these in Oregon often use heavy equipment to farm.

Levels of Development

Notice on the map key the term *subsistence farming*. This term means the production of food mainly for use by the farmer's own family. In less-developed countries, subsistence farming is often one of the main economic activities. In contrast, in developed countries there is little subsistence farming.

NORTH AMERICA

SOUTH AMERICA

▲ **Growing barley in Ecuador**
These farmers in Ecuador use hand tools to harvest barley. They will use most of the crop they grow to feed themselves or their farm animals.

0 miles 2,000
0 kilometers 2,000
Robinson

Background: Global Perspectives

Agriculture Almost 50 percent of the world's population is occupied in agriculture. A much higher proportion of this is in developing countries where dense populations, small land holdings, and traditional techniques predominate. In areas where there is intense cultivation using people and animals but few machines, the yield is low in relation to the output of energy. In leading food producing countries such as the United States, industrial farms make use of new technology and crop specialization to increase output.

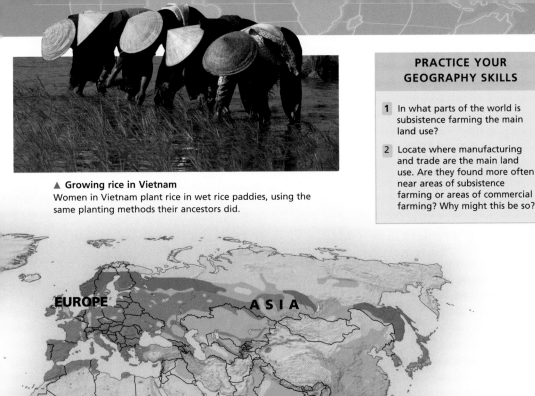

▲ **Growing rice in Vietnam**
Women in Vietnam plant rice in wet rice paddies, using the same planting methods their ancestors did.

PRACTICE YOUR GEOGRAPHY SKILLS

1 In what parts of the world is subsistence farming the main land use?

2 Locate where manufacturing and trade are the main land use. Are they found more often near areas of subsistence farming or areas of commercial farming? Why might this be so?

EUROPE

ASIA

AFRICA

AUSTRALIA

◀ **Herding cattle in Kenya**
Besides subsistence farming, nomadic herding is another economic activity in Africa. This man drives his cattle across the Kenyan grasslands.

MapMaster Skills Handbook **M17**

Independent Practice

Partner students and have them complete *Reading an Economic Activity Map.* Have students be ready to offer explanations for how the economic activity in Somalia might affect the lives of people there.

All in One **Europe and Russia Teaching Resources,** *Reading an Economic Activity Map,* p. 68

Monitor Progress

Circulate around the room as students complete the worksheet to make sure individuals comprehend the key concepts. Provide assistance as needed.

Assess and Reteach

Assess Progress L2

Have students complete the questions under Practice Your Geography Skills.

Reteach L1

Help students make a table to identify the main kinds of land use. Draw a model on the board for students to follow. Use these headings: Nomadic Herding, Forestry, Livestock Raising, Commercial Farming, Subsistence Farming, Manufacturing and Trade. Under each heading, help students write a short explanation. Then have students find one or two places on the map in their books where that activity takes place.

Extend L3

To extend the lesson, have students complete *Reading a Natural Resources Map.* Point out that this map shows mineral resources. Then ask students to write a paragraph relating mineral resources to land use.

All in One **Europe and Russia Teaching Resources,** *Reading a Natural Resources Map,* p. 69

Differentiated Instruction

For English Language Learners L1
Students may find it difficult to pronounce some of the multisyllable words in this section such as *nomadic, subsis-* *tence, commercial,* and *forestry.* Model how to break down these words into smaller parts to help students sound out the pronunciation.

Answers

PRACTICE YOUR GEOGRAPHY SKILLS

1. Africa, Asia, South America, North America

2. areas of commercial farming; both manufacturing and trade and commercial farming require technology which is found in developed countries

MapMaster Skills Handbook **M17**

Teaching the Target Reading Skills

The Prentice Hall *World Studies* program has interwoven essential reading skills instruction throughout the Student Edition, Teacher's Edition, and ancillary resources. In Europe and Russia, students will learn five reading skills.

Student Edition The *World Studies* Student Edition provides students with reading skills instruction, practice, and application opportunities in each chapter within the program.

Teacher's Edition The *World Studies* Teacher Edition supports your teaching of each skill by providing full modeling in each chapter's interleaf and modeling of the specific sub-skills in each section lesson.

All in One Teaching Resources The *World Studies* All-in-One Teaching Resources provides a worksheet explaining and supporting the elements of each Target Reading Skill. Use these to help struggling students master skills, or as more practice for every student.

How to Read Social Studies

Target Reading Skills

The Target Reading Skills introduced on this page will help you understand the words and ideas in this book and in other social studies reading you do. Each chapter focuses on one of these reading skills. Good readers develop a bank of reading strategies, or skills. Then they draw on the particular strategies that will help them understand the text they are reading.

Chapter 1 Target Reading Skill
Using the Reading Process Previewing can help you understand and remember what you read. In this chapter you will practice using these previewing skills: setting a purpose for reading, predicting what the text will be about, and asking questions before you read.

Chapter 2 Target Reading Skill
Clarifying Meaning If you do not understand something you are reading right away, you can use several skills to help clarify the meaning of the word or idea. In this chapter you will practice these strategies for clarifying meaning: rereading, reading ahead, and paraphrasing.

Chapter 3 Target Reading Skill
Identifying the Main Idea Since you cannot remember every detail of what you read, it is important that you identify the main ideas. The main idea of a section or paragraph is the most important point and the one you want to remember. In this chapter you will practice these skills: identifying stated and implied main ideas and identifying supporting details.

Chapter 4 Target Reading Skill
Using Context Using the context of an unfamiliar word can help you understand its meaning. Context includes the words, phrases, and sentences surrounding a word. In this chapter you will practice using these context clues: descriptions, definitions, comparisons, and examples.

Chapter 5 Target Reading Skill
Comparing and Contrasting You can use comparison and contrast to sort out and analyze information you are reading. Comparing means examining the similarities between things. Contrasting is looking at differences. In this chapter you will practice these skills: comparing and contrasting, identifying contrasts, making comparisons, and recognizing contrast signal words.

M18 Europe and Russia

Assessment Resources

Use the diagnosing readiness tests from **AYP Monitoring Assessments** to help you identify problems before students begin to study Europe and Russia.

Determine students' reading level and identify challenges:

📄 *Screening Tests,* pp. 1–11

Evaluate students' verbal skills:

📄 *Critical Thinking and Reading Tests,* pp. 25–34

📄 *Vocabulary Tests,* pp. 45–52

📄 *Writing Tests,* pp. 53–60

EUROPE and RUSSIA

Europe and Russia lie on a gigantic landmass that stretches from the Atlantic Ocean to the Pacific. The countries of this region are as diverse as their geography, with distinctive cultures and societies. Ancient civilizations that developed in Europe still influence people around the world. Today, the region contains countries with histories that stretch back hundreds of years as well as countries that were formed just a decade or two ago.

Guiding Questions

The text, photographs, maps, and charts in this book will help you discover answers to these Guiding Questions.

1. **Geography** What are the main physical features of Europe and Russia?

2. **History** How have Europe and Russia been affected by their history?

3. **Culture** How have the people of Europe and Russia been shaped by their cultures?

4. **Government** What types of government have existed in Europe and Russia?

5. **Economics** How have Russian and European economies developed into what they are today?

Project Preview

You can also discover answers to the Guiding Questions by working on projects. Several project possibilities are listed on page 208 of this book.

Europe and Russia **1**

Assess students' social studies skills:

- *Geographic Literacy Tests,* pp. 13–20
- *Visual Analysis Tests,* pp. 21–24
- *Communications Tests,* pp. 35–44

The *World Studies* program provides instruction and practice for all of these skills. Use students' test results to pinpoint the skills your students have mastered and the skills they need to practice. Then use *Correlation to Program Resources* to prescribe skills practice and reinforcement.

- *Diagnosing Readiness Test Correlations,* pp. 64–77

Guiding Questions

- This book was developed around five Guiding Questions about Europe and Russia. They appear on the reduced Student Edition page to the left. The Guiding Questions are intended as an organizational focus for the book. The Guiding Questions act as a kind of umbrella under which all of the material falls.

- You may wish to add your own Guiding Questions to the list in order to tailor them to your particular course.

- Draw students' attention to the Guiding Questions. Ask them to write the questions in their notebooks for future reference.

- In the Teacher's Edition, each section's themes are linked to a specific Guiding Question at the beginning of each chapter. Then, an activity at the end of the chapter returns to the Guiding Questions to review key concepts.

Project Preview

- The projects for this book are designed to provide students with hands-on involvement in the content area. Students are introduced to some projects on p. 208.

- *Book Projects* give students directions on how to complete these projects, and more.

  All in One **Europe and Russia Teaching Resources,** *Book Project: Changing Climates,* pp. 77–79; *Book Project: Tourism in Eastern Europe,* pp. 80–82; *Book Project: Olympic Cities,* pp. 83–85; *Book Project: Folklore Corner,* pp. 86–88

- Assign projects as small-group activities, whole-class projects, or individual projects. Consider assigning a project at the beginning of the course.

Objectives

- Describe the relative size and location of Europe and Russia.
- Locate the countries that make up Europe.
- Examine the physical features of Europe and Russia.
- Study the population density of Europe and Russia.

Prepare to Read

Build Background Knowledge   **L2**

Use the Give One, Get One strategy (TE, p. T37) to help students create a list of impressions related to Europe and Russia.

Instruct

Investigate Europe and Russia   **L2**

Guided Instruction

- Read the introductory, Location, and Regions paragraphs as a class.
- Hand out the *Regional Overview* work-sheet. Direct students to fill it in as they study the Regional Overview.

  All in One Europe and Russia Teaching Resources, *Regional Overview,* pp. 93–95

Independent Practice

Form students into pairs and have them write a statement comparing Europe and Russia's location and size to that of the United States.

Monitor Progress

Circulate and make sure the pairs are measuring correctly.

Answers

LOCATION Atlantic Ocean; west; both regions are about the same distance from the Equator; Alaska and the northern portions of Europe and Russia are located about the same distance from the Arctic Circle; Possible answer: their location.

REGIONS Europe and Russia are bigger than the United States. The United States is larger than Europe alone.

Investigate Europe and Russia

Europe and Russia extend across more than half the world's longitudes, from Iceland in the west at about 25° W to easternmost Siberia at 175° E. Europe is a continent made up of many countries, while Russia is one country that actually lies on two continents—Europe and Asia. Together, Europe and Russia form a rich pattern of different cultures, histories, and languages.

▲ **Amsterdam, the Netherlands**
Skating on one of the city's many frozen canals

LOCATION

1 Investigate Europe and Russia's Location

The location of an unfamiliar place can be described in relation to a familiar place. Use the map above to describe the location of Europe and Russia in relation to the United States. What ocean lies between Europe and the United States? If you were on the west coast of the United States, in what direction would you travel to get to the east coast of Russia? How close to the Equator are the two regions—Europe and Russia and the United States? How close are they to the Arctic Circle? Many people think the climates of Europe and the United States are similar. Look at the map, and explain why this might be so.

REGIONS

2 Estimate the Size of Europe and Russia

How big are Europe and Russia? To find out, compare the size of Europe and Russia together to that of the 48 states of the United States mainland. Now compare Europe alone to those states. Notice that Russia lies in two continents, Asia and Europe. The striped area shows the European part of Russia. The solid green area shows the Asian part of Russia.

Background: Global Perspectives

Europe-Asia Borders The Ural Mountains are not the only mountains that form a border between Europe and Asia. The Caucasus Mountains separate European Russia and the country of Georgia, which is part of Central Asia. The third land boundary between Europe and Asia is located where the country of Turkey borders the European countries of Greece and Bulgaria. Half of this border is formed by another natural feature—the Maritsa River, which serves as the boundary between Greece and Turkey.

Political Europe and Russia

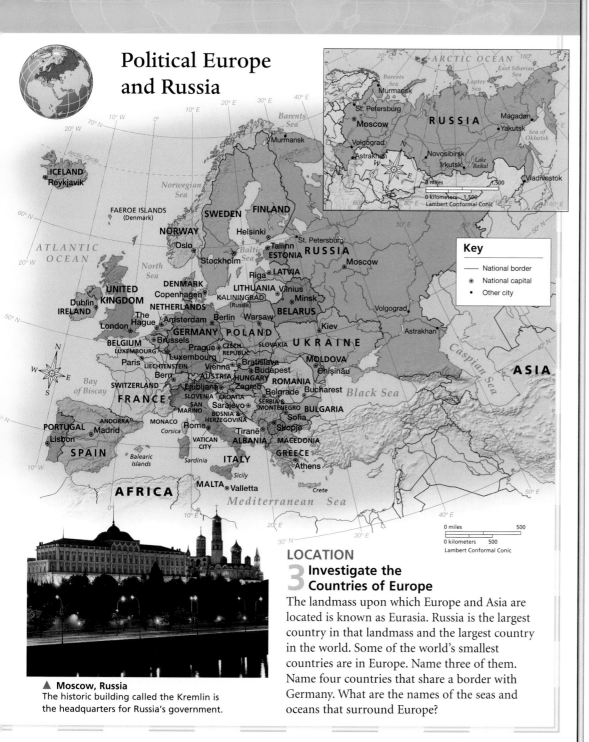

Regional Overview   3

Key
— National border
⊚ National capital
• Other city

LOCATION

3 Investigate the Countries of Europe

The landmass upon which Europe and Asia are located is known as Eurasia. Russia is the largest country in that landmass and the largest country in the world. Some of the world's smallest countries are in Europe. Name three of them. Name four countries that share a border with Germany. What are the names of the seas and oceans that surround Europe?

▲ **Moscow, Russia**
The historic building called the Kremlin is the headquarters for Russia's government.

Political Europe and Russia L2

Guided Instruction

- Read the Location paragraph. Direct students' attention to the political map of Europe and Russia. Ask students to try to locate the three biggest countries in Europe and write their answers on the board. Direct students to the Country Databanks on pp. 112–121 and 166–173 to check their answers. *(Ukraine, France, Spain)*

- Ask students to name the European countries that border Russia. *(Finland, Estonia, Latvia, Belarus, and Ukraine)* Then ask students to locate the small portion of Russia that is separate from the rest of the country. Ask **What countries border this part of Russia?** *(Lithuania and Poland)*

- Ask students to continue completing the *Regional Overview* worksheet.
  All in One **Europe and Russia Teaching Resources,** *Regional Overview,* pp. 93–95

Independent Practice

Distribute *Reading a Political Map.* Have students practice their map skills by answering the questions about the political map of Western Europe.
All in One **Europe and Russia Teaching Resources,** *Reading a Political Map,* p. 51

Monitor Progress

Circulate to make sure that individuals are filling in the correct answers on their worksheets. Provide assistance as needed.

Mental Mapping

Everything in Its Place Divide students into four groups. Assign each group one of the following European regions and distribute the appropriate outline map: Northern Europe, Southern Europe, Western Europe, and Eastern Europe and Russia. Write the names of some of the countries from each region on the board. Ask students to locate as many countries on the maps as they can without looking in their textbooks. They can fill in countries they could not locate as they study the region.

All in One **Europe and Russia Teaching Resources,** *Outline Map 14: Western Europe: Political,* p. 97; *Outline Map 15: Northern Europe,* p. 98; *Outline Map 16: Southern Europe,* p. 99; *Outline Map 18: Eastern Europe and Russia: Political,* p. 100

Answers

LOCATION Possible answers: Vatican City, Monaco, San Marino, Andorra, and Liechtenstein; Possible answers: Denmark, Poland, Czech Republic, Austria, Switzerland, France, Luxembourg, Belgium, Netherlands; Arctic and Atlantic oceans, North, Baltic, Mediterranean, Tyrrhenian, Ionian, Adriatic, Aegean, and Black seas

Physical Europe and Russia

Guided Instruction

- Read the Location paragraph. Point out that Europe is a peninsula, or a body of land nearly surrounded by water. Then ask students to name the four smaller peninsulas found on the continent. *(Iberian, Scandinavia, Italian, and Balkan peninsulas)*

- Ask students to continue completing the Regional Overview worksheet.

All in One Europe and Russia Teaching Resources, *Regional Overview,* pp. 93–95

Independent Practice

Have students do research to find the highest and lowest points in Europe, including European Russia. Ask them to write down the height of each in feet and meters. Then ask students to locate each point on the map on p. 4. Tell students to put their finger on each point and circulate to check their answers. *(Highest point: Elbrus located in the Caucasus Mountains—18,510 feet, or 5,642 meters; lowest point: Caspian Sea shore—92 feet, or 28 meters, below sea level)*

Monitor Progress

Circulate to be sure students have written down the correct heights of each point and that their fingers are on the correct locations.

Answers

LOCATION Pyrenees, Alps, Apennines, Carpathian Mountains, Dinaric Alps, Transylvanian Alps, Balkan Mountains, Pindus Mountains, Caucasus Mountains; Pyrenees

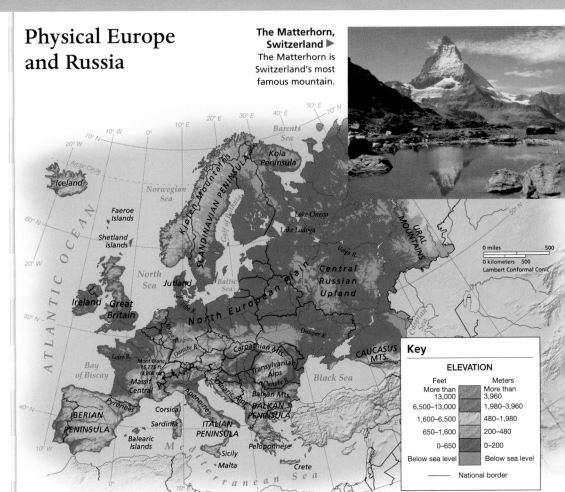

Physical Europe and Russia

The Matterhorn, Switzerland ▶
The Matterhorn is Switzerland's most famous mountain.

Key

ELEVATION

Feet	Meters
More than 13,000	More than 3,960
6,500–13,000	1,980–3,960
1,600–6,500	480–1,980
650–1,600	200–480
0–650	0–200
Below sea level	Below sea level

—— National border

LOCATION

4 Examine the Mountains of Europe and Russia

Several mountain ranges stretch through Central and Southern Europe, from the Bay of Biscay to the Caspian Sea. Find and name four of these mountain ranges. What mountain range separates France from Spain? Now locate Russia's Ural Mountains. Most of Russia lies in Asia, east of the Ural Mountains. Most Russians, however, live in the European part of Russia, west of the Ural Mountains.

4   Europe and Russia

Differentiated Instruction

For Less Proficient Readers L1

Show students the Europe and Russia flyover segment on the Passport to the World CD-ROM. Ask students to list several of the region's major landforms on the board after viewing the segment.

⊙ *Europe and Russia Flyover,* **Passport to the World CD-ROM**

Europe and Russia: Population Density

Population density describes how crowded a particular place is. Use the key below to determine what color on the map represents an area where many people live. What color represents an area where very few people live? Compare the parts of Europe where there are very few people with the parts of Europe where there are very many. How would you describe the population densities of the two regions?

KEY

Persons per sq. mile	Persons per sq. kilometer
More than 3,119	More than 1,204
520–3,119	200–1,204
260–519	100–199
130–259	50–99
25–129	10–49
1–24	1–9
Less than 1	Less than 1

Urban Areas
- ☐ 5,000,000–9,999,999
- ◉ 1,000,000–4,999,999
- ● Less than 1,000,000
- — National border

▼ Norway
Sami children on a snowmobile

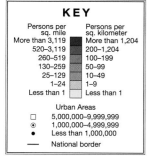

▲ Sergivev Posad, Russia
Trinity Monastery of St. Sergius

PRACTICE YOUR GEOGRAPHY SKILLS

1 You begin to explore Europe from its west coast. From Portugal you fly over the headwaters of the Danube and the Rhine rivers. In what direction are you flying?

2 You board a train in Moscow and travel east. When you get to the farthest point in Siberia, you have gone about one third of the way around the world. What mountain range did you cross?

3 You are going to drive from Warsaw to Moscow. In what direction will you travel?

Differentiated Instruction

For Advanced Readers L3
Have students do Internet or library research to identify the five most populated cities in Europe and Russia. Ask students to make a bar graph showing the populations of the cities in millions. Remind students to label both axes and give the graph a title.

Guided Instruction

- Read the Interaction paragraph and have students study the population density map.
- Ask students to list the areas with the highest population densities. (TK)
- Ask **Why do you think the population density of the Scandinavian Peninsula is less dense than that of Central and Southern Europe?** (*Possible answer: The climate of the Scandinavian Peninsula is colder because it is located closer to the Arctic Circle, so fewer people want to live there.*)
- Direct students to finish the *Regional Overview* worksheet.

  All in One **Europe and Russia Teaching Resources,** *Regional Overview,* pp. 93–95

Independent Practice

Have students complete *Reading a Population Density Map* to practice the skill.

All in One **Europe and Russia Teaching Resources,** *Reading a Population Density Map,* p. 101

Monitor Progress

Circulate to make sure that students are able to correctly answer the questions at the end of the activity. Provide assistance as needed.

Answers

Yellow represents an area where few people live. Answers will vary.

PRACTICE YOUR GEOGRAPHY SKILLS

1. east

2. Ural Mountains

3. east

Focus on Countries in Europe and Russia L2

Guided Instruction
- Assign a number from 1–4 to each caption. Have students pick a number (1–4) from a hat and divide the class according to the numbers they selected.
- Have each group read the text on the country relative to their group number and write down important details.

Independent Practice
Have each group use the Country Databanks on pp. 112–121 and 166–173, DK Compact Atlas of the World, and the DK World Desk Reference Online (see student pages for Web code) to research the country they have been assigned. Ask groups to focus on the geography, climate, government, and people of the countries. Then, have each group present the information they gathered to the class.

Monitor Progress
Use *Rubric for Assessing an Oral Presentation* to assess students' presentations.

All in One **Europe and Russia Teaching Resources,** *Rubric for Assessing an Oral Presentation, p. 103*

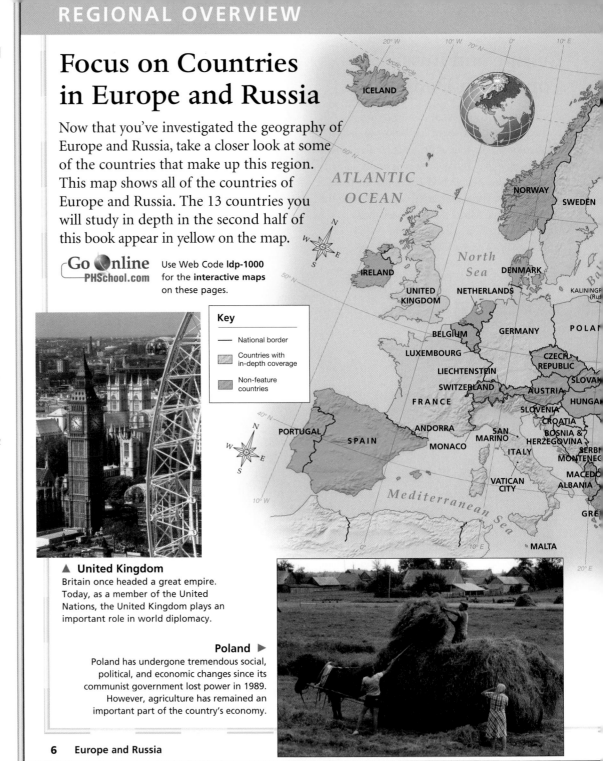

Focus on Countries in Europe and Russia

Now that you've investigated the geography of Europe and Russia, take a closer look at some of the countries that make up this region. This map shows all of the countries of Europe and Russia. The 13 countries you will study in depth in the second half of this book appear in yellow on the map.

Go Online PHSchool.com Use Web Code **ldp-1000** for the **interactive maps** on these pages.

Key
— National border
▨ Countries with in-depth coverage
▨ Non-feature countries

▲ **United Kingdom**
Britain once headed a great empire. Today, as a member of the United Nations, the United Kingdom plays an important role in world diplomacy.

Poland ▶
Poland has undergone tremendous social, political, and economic changes since its communist government lost power in 1989. However, agriculture has remained an important part of the country's economy.

6 Europe and Russia

Background: Links Across Time

Britain's Empire By 1820, Britain controlled so many colonies and territories around the world, that it governed more than 200 million people. This was 26 percent of the world's population at the time. Britain ruled territories on every continent.

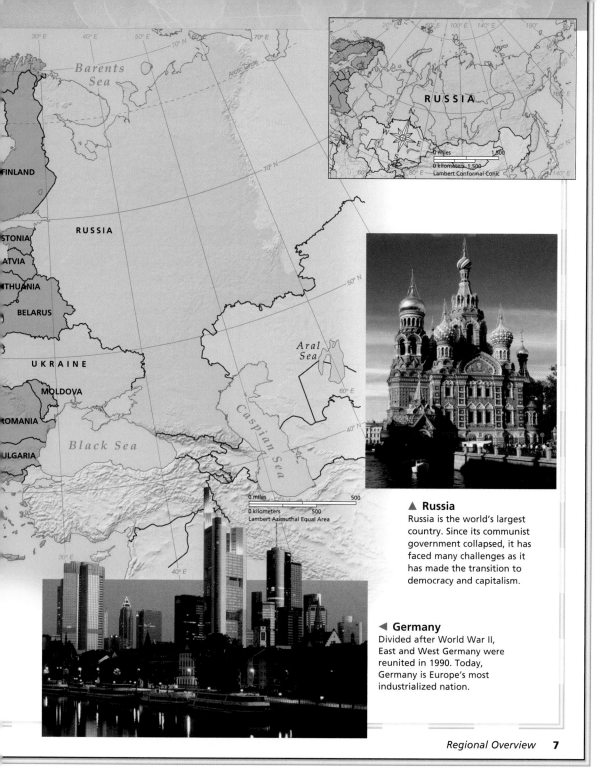

▲ Russia
Russia is the world's largest country. Since its communist government collapsed, it has faced many challenges as it has made the transition to democracy and capitalism.

◄ Germany
Divided after World War II, East and West Germany were reunited in 1990. Today, Germany is Europe's most industrialized nation.

Assess and Reteach

Assess Progress　L2

■ Have students revisit the impressions they brainstormed in Build Background Knowledge. Using the information they have learned so far, ask them to confirm or revise some of the impressions. If some aspects have yet to be touched on, tell students to write them in their notebooks and look for more information as they begin their study of Europe and Russia.

■ Ask students to complete the Practice Your Geography Skills questions on p. 5.

Reteach　L1

For more exploration of the region, have students view the Europe and Russia portion of the Passport to the World CD-ROM and complete the Customs Quiz.

◉ *Europe and Russia,* **Passport to the World CD-ROM**

Extend　L3

Portfolio Activity One way of assessing students' accomplishments is by having them build a portfolio of their best work. To begin their portfolios for Europe and Russia, have students choose a country in the region that they will not be exploring in depth in this textbook. Have students research their country to create a magazine advertisement that encourages people to visit the country. Tell students to use text, illustrations, and maps in their advertisements.

■ Give students *Doing Searches on the Internet* to teach them how they can gather information for their advertisements.

All in One Europe and Russia Teaching Resources, *Doing Searches on the Internet,* p. 31

Europe and Russia: Physical Geography

Overview

Section 1 — Land and Water
1. Learn about the size, location, and population of Europe and Russia.
2. Examine the major landforms of Europe and Russia.
3. Find out about the waterways of Europe and Russia.

Section 2 — Climate and Vegetation
1. Find out about the wide range of climates in Europe and Russia.
2. Learn about the major climate regions of Europe and Russia.
3. Examine the natural vegetation regions of Europe and Russia.

Section 3 — Resources and Land Use
1. Learn about the natural resources of Western Europe.
2. Find out about the natural resources of Eastern Europe.
3. Examine Russia's natural resources.

Discovery CHANNEL SCHOOL Video

The Geography of Europe and Russia
Length: 7 minutes, 2 seconds
Use with Section 1

This segment provides an overview of the geography of Europe and Russia, with a focus on population density. The climates, geographic features, and natural resources of the two regions are compared and contrasted.

Technology Resources

Students use embedded Web codes to access Internet activities, chapter self-tests, and additional map practice. They may also access Dorling Kindersley's Online Desk Reference to learn more about each country they study.

Use the Interactive Textbook to make content and concepts come alive through animations, videos, and activities that accompany the complete basal text—online and on CD-ROM.

PRENTICE HALL

Use this complete suite of powerful teaching tools to make planning lessons and administering tests quicker and easier.

Reading and Assessment

Reading and Vocabulary Instruction

⏱ Model the Target Reading Skill

Reading Process Previewing the text, setting a purpose for reading, predicting what the section will be about, and asking questions before reading all give students a task to complete while reading. This can sharpen students' focus and enhance their understanding of a selection. Model the reading process by thinking about this chapter aloud:

"This chapter's title is *Europe and Russia: Physical Geography*. I will read to learn about the physical features of Europe and Russia. The first section is called *Land and Water*. I predict that this section will explain whether the land in Europe and Russia is made up of deserts, forests, mountains, or something else. It will probably describe the rivers, lakes, oceans, and seas as well. The second section is called *Climate and Vegetation*. I wonder if I will learn about a connection between climate and plant life in Europe and Russia? If a place is rainy and not too cold, then I imagine it would be a good place for plants to grow. The third section is called *Resources and Land Use*. I know that *resources* are things that people use. I wonder if there is a connection between the resources people have and how they use the land. I predict that I will learn about the relationship between humans and the environment."

Use the following worksheets from All-in-One Europe and Russia Teaching Resources (pp. 118–120) to support the chapter's Target Reading Skill.

 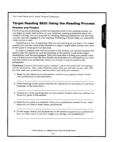

Vocabulary Builder
High-Use Academic Words

Use these steps to teach this chapter's high-use words:

1. Have students rate how well they know each word on their Word Knowledge worksheets (All-in-One Europe and Russia Teaching Resources, p. 121).

2. Pronounce each word and ask students to repeat it.

3. Give students a brief definition or sample sentence (provided on TE pp. 11, 18, and 27).

4. Work with students as they fill in the "Definition or Example" column of their Word Knowledge worksheets.

Assessment

Formal Assessment

Test students' understanding of core knowledge and skills.

Chapter Tests A and B, All-in-One Europe and Russia Teaching Resources, pp. 138–143

Customize the Chapter Tests to suit your needs.
ExamView® Test Bank CD-ROM

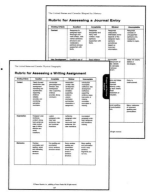

Skills Assessment

Assess geographic literacy.
MapMaster Skills, Student Edition, pp. 9, 12, 18, 21, 22, 27, 30, 34

Assess reading and comprehension.
Target Reading Skills, Student Edition, pp. 15, 19, 31, and in Section Assessments

Chapter 1 Assessment, Europe and Russia Reading and Vocabulary Study Guide, p. 15

Performance Assessment

Assess students' performance on this chapter's Writing Activities using the following rubrics from All-in-One Europe and Russia Teaching Resources.

Rubric for Assessing a Journal Entry, p. 136

Rubric for Assessing a Writing Assignment, p. 137

Assess students' work through performance tasks.

Small Group Activity: Europe and Russia Map and Climate Charts, All-in-One Europe and Russia Teaching Resources, pp. 124–127

Online Assessment

Have students check their own understanding.

Chapter Self-Test

Test Preparation

Assess students' skills and diagnose problems as students begin their study of this region.

Screening Tests and Diagnosing Readiness Tests, AYP Monitoring Assessments, pp. 1–11, 13–63

Section 1 Land and Water

 1.5 periods, .75 block

Social Studies Objectives

1. Learn about the size, location, and population of Europe and Russia.
2. Examine the major landforms of Europe and Russia.
3. Find out about the waterways of Europe and Russia.

Reading/Language Arts Objective

Set a purpose for reading in order to focus on important ideas.

Prepare to Read	Instructional Resources	Differentiated Instruction
Build Background Knowledge Ask students to preview the section and predict the geographic features they will learn about. **Set a Purpose for Reading** Have students evaluate statements on the *Reading Readiness Guide*. **Preview Key Terms** Teach the section's Key Terms. **Target Reading Skill** Introduce the section's Target Reading Skill of **setting a purpose for reading**.	**All in One Europe and Russia Teaching Resources** L2 Reading Readiness Guide, p. 107 L2 Preview and Set a Purpose, p. 118	**Spanish Reading and Vocabulary Study Guide** L1 Chapter 1, Section 1, pp. 7–8 ELL

Instruct	Instructional Resources	Differentiated Instruction
Size, Location, and Population Discuss how the size and location of Europe and Russia affect climate and population. **Major Landforms** Discuss the land regions of Europe and Russia. **Target Reading Skill** Review **setting a purpose for reading**. **Waterways of Europe and Russia** Discuss the Rhine and the Volga Rivers.	**All in One Europe and Russia Teaching Resources** L2 Guided Reading and Review, p. 108 L2 Reading Readiness Guide, p. 107 **Europe and Russia Transparencies** L2 Section Reading Support Transparency ER 32 **World Studies Video Program** L2 The Geography of Europe and Russia	**All in One Europe and Russia Teaching Resources** L3 Activity Shop Lab: Tracking the Midnight Sun, pp. 128–129 AR, GT **Teacher's Edition** L3 For Advanced Readers, TE p. 14 L1 For English Language Learners, TE p. 15 **Spanish Support** L2 Guided Reading and Review (Spanish), p. 4 ELL

Assess and Reteach	Instructional Resources	Differentiated Instruction
Assess Progress Evaluate student comprehension with the section assessment and section quiz. **Reteach** Assign the Reading and Vocabulary Study Guide to help struggling students. **Extend** Extend the lesson by assigning a Small Group Activity.	**All in One Europe and Russia Teaching Resources** L2 Section Quiz, p. 109 L3 Small Group Activity: Europe and Russia Map and Climate Charts, pp. 124–127 Rubric for Assessing a Journal Entry, p. 136 **Reading and Vocabulary Study Guide** L1 Chapter 1, Section 1, pp. 6–8	**Spanish Support** L2 Section Quiz (Spanish), p. 5 ELL

Key

L1 Basic to Average   L3 Average to Advanced   LPR Less Proficient Readers   GT Gifted and Talented
L2 For All Students   AR Advanced Readers   ELL English Language Learners
                                                 SN Special Needs Students

Section 2 Climate and Vegetation

 2 periods, 1 block (includes Skills for Life)

Social Studies Objectives
1. Find out about the wide range of climates in Europe and Russia.
2. Learn about the major climate regions of Europe and Russia.
3. Examine the natural vegetation regions of Europe and Russia.

Reading/Language Arts Objective
Make predictions about the text to help set a purpose for reading and remember what you read.

Prepare to Read	Instructional Resources	Differentiated Instruction
Build Background Knowledge Have students compare the climates of Barcelona and Irkutsk to that of their own region. **Set a Purpose for Reading** Have students evaluate statements on the *Reading Readiness Guide.* **Preview Key Terms** Teach the section's Key Terms. **Target Reading Skill** Introduce the section's Target Reading Skill of **predicting**.	**All in One Europe and Russia Teaching Resources** **L2** Reading Readiness Guide, p. 111 **L2** Preview and Predict, p. 119	**Spanish Reading and Vocabulary Study Guide** **L1** Chapter 1, Section 2, pp. 9–10 ELL

Instruct	Instructional Resources	Differentiated Instruction
A Wide Range of Climates Discuss how oceans and location affect the climates of Europe and Russia. **Target Reading Skill** Review **predicting**. **Major Climate Regions** Discuss the different climate regions in Europe and Russia. **Natural Vegetation Regions** Discuss different types of vegetation native to Europe and Russia.	**All in One Europe and Russia Teaching Resources** **L2** Guided Reading and Review, p. 112 **L2** Reading Readiness Guide, p. 111 **Europe and Russia Transparencies** **L2** Color Transparency ER 20: Western Europe: Physical-Political **L2** Transparency B2: Flow Chart **L2** Section Reading Support Transparency ER 33	**All in One Europe and Russia Teaching Resources** **L3** Doing Searches on the Internet, p. 133 AR, GT **L3** Preparing for Presentations, p. 134 AR, GT **L3** Book Project: Changing Climates, pp. 77–79 AR, GT **L1** Reading a Natural Vegetation Map, p. 130 ELL, LPR, SN **L2** Skills for Life, p. 123 AR, GT, LPR, SN **Teacher's Edition** **L3** For Advanced Readers, TE p. 19 **L1** For English Language Learners, TE p. 19 **L3** For Gifted and Talented, TE p. 22 **L1** For Less Proficient Readers, TE p. 22 **Reading and Vocabulary Study Guide** **L1** Chapter 1, Section 2, pp. 9–11 ELL, LPR, SN

Assess and Reteach	Instructional Resources	Differentiated Instruction
Assess Progress Evaluate student comprehension with the section assessment and section quiz. **Reteach** Assign the Reading and Vocabulary Study Guide to help struggling students. **Extend** Extend the lesson by assigning an Enrichment activity.	**All in One Europe and Russia Teaching Resources** **L2** Section Quiz, p. 113 **L3** Enrichment, p. 122 Rubric for Assessing a Writing Assignment, p. 137 **Reading and Vocabulary Study Guide** **L1** Chapter 1, Section 2, pp. 9–11	**Teacher's Edition** **L1** For Special Needs Students, TE p. 25 **Social Studies Skills Tutor CD-ROM** **L1** Analyzing and Interpreting Special Purpose Maps ELL, LPR, SN **Spanish Support** **L2** Section Quiz (Spanish), p. 6 ELL

Key
L1 Basic to Average   **L3** Average to Advanced
L2 For All Students

LPR Less Proficient Readers
AR Advanced Readers
SN Special Needs Students

GT Gifted and Talented
ELL English Language Learners

Section 3 Resources and Land Use

 3.5 periods, 1.75 blocks (includes Chapter Review and Assessment)

Social Studies Objectives

1. Learn about the natural resources of Western Europe.
2. Find out about the natural resources of Eastern Europe.
3. Examine Russia's natural resources.

Reading/Language Arts Objective

Preview and ask questions to help you remember important ideas in the section.

Prepare to Read

Build Background Knowledge
Discuss the importance of soil, water, and fuel.

Set a Purpose for Reading
Have students evaluate statements on the *Reading Readiness Guide*.

Preview Key Terms
Teach the section's Key Terms.

Target Reading Skill
Introduce the section's Target Reading Skill of **previewing and asking questions**.

Instructional Resources

All in One Europe and Russia Teaching Resources
- **L2** Reading Readiness Guide, p. 115
- **L2** Preview and Ask Questions, p. 120

Differentiated Instruction

Spanish Reading and Vocabulary Study Guide
- **L1** Chapter 1, Section 3, pp. 11–12 ELL

Instruct

Resources of Western Europe
Discuss natural resources and where they are found in Western Europe.

Resources of Eastern Europe
Discuss the benefits of having a variety of natural resources, and compare the resources of Eastern and Western Europe.

Resources of Russia
Discuss the challenge of collecting the natural resources of Russia.

Target Reading Skill
Review **previewing and asking questions**.

Instructional Resources

All in One Europe and Russia Teaching Resources
- **L2** Guided Reading and Review, p. 116
- **L2** Reading Readiness Guide, p. 115
- **L3** The Endless Steppe, pp. 131–132

Europe and Russia Transparencies
- **L2** Section Reading Support Transparency ER 34

Differentiated Instruction

Teacher's Edition
- **L3** For Gifted and Talented, TE p. 29
- **L1** For Less Proficient Readers, TE p. 30
- **L1** For Special Needs Students, TE p. 30
- **L3** For Advanced Readers, TE p. 31

Student Edition on Audio CD
- **L1** Chapter 1, Section 3 ELL, LPR, SN

PHSchool.com
- **L3** For: Environmental and Global Issues: World Oil Reserves
  Web Code: ldd-7104 AR, GT

Assess and Reteach

Assess Progress
Evaluate student comprehension with the section assessment and section quiz.

Reteach
Assign the Reading and Vocabulary Study Guide to help struggling students.

Extend
Extend the lesson by assigning an Internet activity.

Instructional Resources

All in One Europe and Russia Teaching Resources
- **L2** Section Quiz, p. 117
- **L2** Vocabulary Development, p. 135
- **L2** Word Knowledge, p. 121
- **L2** Chapter Tests A and B, pp. 138–143

Reading and Vocabulary Study Guide
- **L1** Chapter 1, Section 3, pp. 12–14

PHSchool.com
- **L3** For: Long-Term Integrated Projects: Reporting to an Environmental Conference
  Web Code: ldd-7105

Differentiated Instruction

Spanish Support
- **L2** Section Quiz (Spanish), p. 9 ELL
- **L2** Chapter Summary (Spanish), p. 10 ELL
- **L2** Vocabulary Development (Spanish), p. 11 ELL

Key

L1 Basic to Average	**L3** Average to Advanced	LPR Less Proficient Readers	GT Gifted and Talented
L2 For All Students		AR Advanced Readers	ELL English Language Learners
		SN Special Needs Students	

Reading Background

Previewing and Prereading

This chapter's Target Reading Skill asks students to preview each section and set a purpose for reading. Students who do a brief, preliminary reading of complex material are in a strategic position to take control of their learning and comprehension. Previewing helps students consider what they already know about a topic they will be studying and gives some idea of what a text selection is about before they read it. Previewing also helps students identify the text structure and develop a mental framework for ideas to be encountered in the text. This can help them formulate a more realistic reading and study plan. Follow the steps below to teach students how to preview and preread.

1. Tell students that previewing will help them identify the text structure and develop a mental outline of ideas they will encounter in the text.

2. List the various text features you will be previewing in the order in which you would like students to examine them: section title, text headings, introduction, list of Key Terms, questions or tasks in the reading selection, photographs, drawings, maps, charts, and other visuals in the text. Focus students' attention on some of these items, or ask them to look at all of them.

3. Prompt students to reflect after examining various text features. They may ask themselves questions such as: What is this reading selection about? What are some key words I will learn? How should I tackle this reading and divide up the task?

Mapping Word Definitions

Research shows that mapping word definitions can help students develop the ability to investigate word meanings independently and provide elaborated definitions.

Model mapping word definitions using the Key Term *fossil fuel.* Begin by asking students a series of questions: What are some examples of fossil fuels? *(oil, natural gas)* What are these used for? *(providing power for automobiles and other modes of transportation, heating homes)* Where are these found? *(deep inside Earth)*

Finally, develop a graphic organizer with information about the term *fossil fuel:*

the definition (in their own words)	*a source of energy that forms from ancient plant and animal remains*
a synonym	*petroleum*
a sentence using the word	*Fossil fuel is an important natural resource because it is used to provide energy throughout Earth.*

World Studies Background

Urban Development in Europe

Many European cities developed as Roman colonies and still reflect the typical Roman layout. Roman cities were often concentrated around a public gathering place. On the edge of this forum were the main commercial, governmental, and religious buildings. The streets usually emerged from this center in a grid design.

Siberia

The name of this vast region that lies mainly in Russia comes from a Tatar word meaning "sleeping land," in reference to the long, harsh winters during which much of the vegetation lies dormant.

Parts of Siberia have experienced temperatures as low as −90° Fahrenheit (−68° C). Because of its remoteness, Siberia has been used as a place of exile for criminals and political prisoners.

European Cheese

Many regions in Europe make local cheeses from the milk of sheep, goats, and cows. In the caves of Roquefort, France, cheese is left to gather the bacteria that give it a distinctive flavor and coloring. In Italy, provolone cheese is heated and kneaded. In Greece, feta cheese is cured in brine, giving it a salty flavor. In Holland, Gouda and Edam cheeses are preserved by a wax coating. True Gouda and Edam have the word "Holland" stamped on the rind.

Infoplease® provides a wealth of useful information for the classroom. You can use this resource to strengthen your background on the subjects covered in this chapter. Have students visit this advertising-free site as a starting point for projects requiring research.

Use Web code **ldd-7100** for **Infoplease®**.

Guiding Questions

Remind students about the Guiding Questions introduced at the beginning of the book.

Section 1 refers to **Guiding Question** ➊
What are the main physical features of Europe and Russia? *(Europe is a small continent made up of many small countries, while Russia is the largest country in the world. Both have mountains, plains, highlands, plateaus, and major waterways.)*

Section 2 refers to **Guiding Question** ➊
What are the main physical features of Europe and Russia? *(Europe and Russia have a wide range of climate regions; climates are affected by nearness to the ocean, the North Atlantic Current, and mountains. Europe and Russia also have diverse vegetation. Both are heavily forested, but plant life varies by climate.)*

Section 3 refers to **Guiding Question** ➊
What are the main physical features of Europe and Russia? *(Europe's natural resources include fertile soil used for farming, water used for drinking and creating hydroelectric power, and fuels used for producing energy. Russia has large fuel and forest reserves. Fish are an important resource, as is water, used for hydroelectric energy. However, it is difficult for Russia to transport and take advantage of its resources due to its size and climate.)*

➲ Target Reading Skill

In this chapter, students will learn and apply the reading process. Use the following worksheets to help students practice the skill.

    All in One **Europe and Russia Teaching Resources,** *Preview and Set a Purpose,* p. 118; *Preview and Predict,* p. 119; *Preview and Ask Questions,* p. 120

Differentiated Instruction

The following Teacher Edition strategies are suitable for students of varying abilities.

Advanced Readers, pp. 14, 19, 31
English Language Learners, pp. 15, 19
Gifted and Talented, pp. 22, 29
Less Proficient Readers, pp. 22, 30
Special Needs Students, pp. 25, 30

Europe and Russia: Physical Geography

Chapter Preview

This chapter will introduce you to the geography of Europe and Russia and show how geography affects the people who live there.

Section 1
Land and Water

Section 2
Climate and Vegetation

Section 3
Resources and Land Use

➲ **Target Reading Skill**

Reading Process In this chapter you will use previewing to help you understand and remember what you read.

▶ Waves splash against the rocky coast of Cornwall in southern England.

8 Europe and Russia

Bibliography

For the Teacher
Geography of the World. Dorling Kindersley Publishing, 2003.
Milner-Gulland, R.R., et al. *Cultural Atlas of Russia and the Former Soviet Union.* Checkmark Books, 1998.
Recht, Roland. *The Rhine.* Thames & Hudson, 2001.

For the Student
L1 Boraas, Tracey. *England (Countries and Cultures).* Bridgestone Books, 2002.
L2 Bramwell, Martyn. *Europe: The World in Maps.* Lerner Publications Company, 2000.
L3 Murrell, Kathleen Berton. *Eyewitness: Russia.* Dorling Kindersley Publishing, 2000.

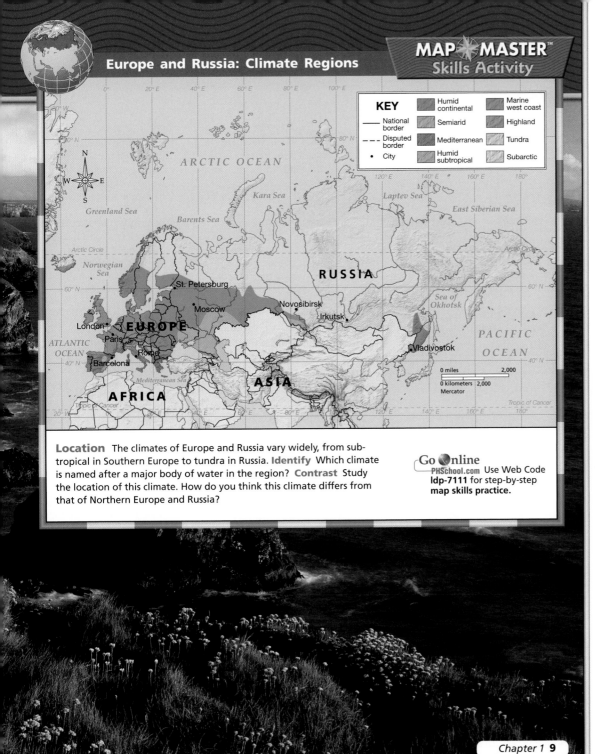

Europe and Russia: Climate Regions

MAP MASTER™ Skills Activity

KEY

— National border
- - - Disputed border
• City

Humid continental
Semiarid
Mediterranean
Humid subtropical
Marine west coast
Highland
Tundra
Subarctic

Location The climates of Europe and Russia vary widely, from subtropical in Southern Europe to tundra in Russia. **Identify** Which climate is named after a major body of water in the region? **Contrast** Study the location of this climate. How do you think this climate differs from that of Northern Europe and Russia?

Go Online PHSchool.com Use Web Code ldp-7111 for step-by-step **map skills practice.**

Chapter 1 **9**

- Direct students' attention to the map of Europe and Russia. Have students trace the borders of Europe and Russia with their fingers. Point out that Russia is much larger than Europe, and extends much farther north.

- Ask students to create a chart with two columns and label the columns "Climates of Europe" and "Climates of Russia." Have students use the map to list the climates of each region in the appropriate column.

Go Online PHSchool.com Students may practice their map skills using the interactive online version of this map.

Using the Visual   L2

Reach Into Your Background Draw students' attention to the caption accompanying the picture on pp. 8–9. Tell students that Cornwall is a county in southwestern England and is located on a peninsula. Point out that Cornwall's climate is greatly affected by its proximity to the sea; high winds, sea mists, and rainfall are common. Ask students to brainstorm ways that geography affects their own region. Conduct an Idea Wave (TE, p. T35) to elicit responses.

Answers

MAP MASTER™ Skills Activity **Identify** Mediterranean **Contrast** Because the Mediterranean climate is closer to the Equator, it is probably warmer than the climates of northern Europe and Russia.

Chapter Resources

Teaching Resources
Letter Home, p. 105
L2 Vocabulary Development, p. 135
L2 Skills for Life, p. 123
L2 Chapter Tests A and B, pp. 138–143

Spanish Support
Spanish Letter Home, p. 3
L2 Spanish Chapter Summary, p. 10
L2 Spanish Vocabulary Development, p. 11

Media and Technology
L1 Student Edition on Audio CD
L1 Guided Reading Audiotapes, English and Spanish
L2 Social Studies Skills Tutor CD-ROM
ExamView® Test Bank CD-ROM

Discovery CHANNEL SCHOOL World Studies Video Program

interactive Textbook

PRENTICE HALL

TeacherEXPRESS™ Plan • Teach • Assess

Objectives

Social Studies
1. Learn about the size, location, and population of Europe and Russia.
2. Examine the major landforms of Europe and Russia.
3. Find out about the waterways of Europe and Russia.

Reading/Language Arts
Set a purpose for reading in order to focus on important ideas.

Prepare to Read

Build Background Knowledge **L2**

Tell students that they will be reading about Europe and Russia's size, land, and bodies of water. Ask students to preview the section's headings and visuals. Have them predict the geographic features they expect to learn about, and conduct an Idea Wave (TE, p. T35) to generate a list. Then encourage students to share information they may already know about these features.

Set a Purpose for Reading **L2**
- Preview the Objectives.
- Read each statement in the *Reading Readiness Guide* aloud. Ask students to mark the statements true or false.

  All in One **Europe and Russia Teaching Resources,** *Reading Readiness Guide,* p. 107

- Have students discuss the statements in pairs or groups of four, then mark their worksheets again. Use the Numbered Heads participation strategy (TE, p. T36) to call on students to share their groups' perspectives.

Vocabulary Builder
Preview Key Terms **L2**
Pronounce each Key Term, then ask the students to say the word with you. Provide a simple explanation such as, "A navigable river is wide and deep enough for a ship to pass through."

Prepare to Read

Objectives
In this section you will
1. Learn about the size, location, and population of Europe and Russia.
2. Examine the major landforms of Europe and Russia.
3. Find out about the waterways of Europe and Russia.

Taking Notes
As you read this section, look for the main ideas about land and water. Copy the table below and record your findings in it.

Region	Landforms	Bodies of Water
Europe		
Russia		

Target Reading Skill

Set a Purpose for Reading When you set a purpose for reading, you give yourself a focus. Before you read this section, look at the headings, the maps, and the photographs to see what the section is about. Then set a purpose for reading the section. Your purpose might be to find out about the geography of Europe and Russia. As you read, use the Taking Notes table to help you achieve your purpose.

Key Terms
- **population density** (pahp yuh LAY shun DEN suh tee) *n.* the average number of people living in a square mile or a square kilometer
- **peninsula** (puh NIN suh luh) *n.* a land area nearly surrounded by water
- **plateau** (pla TOH) *n.* a large raised area of mostly level land bordered on one or more sides by steep slopes or cliffs
- **tributary** (TRIB yoo tehr ee) *n.* a river or stream that flows into a larger river
- **navigable** (NAV ih guh bul) *adj.* wide and deep enough for ships to travel through

A windmill in Friesland, the Netherlands

If you cross a field in the Netherlands (NETH ur lundz), you could be walking where sea waves once roared. Water formerly covered more than two fifths of the country. Centuries ago, the people of the Netherlands began an effort to create land where there was water. They built long walls called dikes to hold back the water. They pumped the water into canals that empty into the North Sea. In this way, they created polders (POHL durz), or patches of new land.

The polders that lie below sea level are always filling with water. Netherlanders must continually pump them out. Keeping the polders dry is important. Like much of Europe, the country's many people must find living space on a small amount of land. The richest farmlands and some cities in the Netherlands are located on polders.

10 Europe and Russia

Target Reading Skill **L2**

Set a Purpose for Reading Direct students' attention to the Target Reading Skill. Tell them that setting a purpose will give them a focus as they read.

Model setting a purpose for reading by thinking aloud as you preview the headings and photographs on p. 11: "The information on this page tells me that I will learn about land and people in Europe and Russia. My purpose for reading this page is to learn about the size, location, and population of that area."

Give students *Preview and Set a Purpose.* Have them complete the activity in groups.

All in One **Europe and Russia Teaching Resources,** *Preview and Set a Purpose,* p. 118

Size, Location, and Population

Europe and Russia are parts of Eurasia, the world's largest land-mass. This landmass is made up of two continents, Europe and Asia. The country of Russia stretches over both continents. About one fourth of Russia is in Europe; the rest is in Asia. The Ural (YOOR ul) Mountains divide Europe from Asia.

Stretching North Trace a latitude line from the United States to Eurasia in the world political map in the Atlas. You will see that much of Europe and nearly all of Russia are farther north than is the United States. Berlin, the German capital, lies at about the same latitude as the southern tip of Canada's Hudson Bay.

A Small Continent With Many People Europe is a small continent. Only Australia is smaller. While Europe lacks size, it has 47 different countries. As you might guess, most of the countries are small. Many are the size of an average state in the United States. Russia, on the other hand, is the largest country in the world. It is almost twice the size of the United States.

Most of the countries of Europe have a much higher population density than other countries in the world. **Population density** is the average number of people living in a square mile or a square kilometer. The Netherlands has more than 1,236 people per square mile (477 people per sq kilometer). By comparison, the world average is about 106 people per square mile (42 people per sq kilometer). Russia, on the other hand, has a much lower population density—only about 22 people per square mile (9 people per sq kilometer).

✓ **Reading Check** What is the largest landmass in the world?

Rural Regions of Europe and Russia
The Ural Mountains, shown at the bottom, mark the dividing line between Europe and Russia. The inset photo shows a church situated in the highlands of northern Scotland. **Analyze Images** Use clues from the photos to estimate the population densities of these two regions.

Vocabulary Builder

Use the information below to teach students this section's high-use words.

High-Use Word	Definition and Sample Sentence
landmass, p. 11	*n.* a large area of land Africa is the world's second largest **landmass**.
enable, p. 12	*v.* to allow; to make possible The loan **enabled** Cliff to attend college.
level, p. 13	*adj.* flat; horizontal We looked for a **level** spot to pitch our tent.
link, p. 15	*v.* to join together The two highways **link** and become one in the northern part of the state.

Size, Location, and Population   L2

Guided Instruction

■ **Vocabulary Builder** Clarify the high-use word **landmass** before reading.

■ Read Size, Location, and Population using the Choral Reading strategy (TE, p. T34).

■ Have students describe Europe and Russia's size and location. (*Eurasia is made up of the continents of Europe and Asia. Europe is a small continent with many small countries. Russia is the largest country in the world.*)

■ Ask students **Which natural feature divides Europe from Asia?** (*the Ural Mountains*) **Is Russia in Europe, Asia, or both?** (*Both—about one fourth of Russia is in Europe; the rest is in Asia.*)

■ Ask students to predict how the climate of Europe and Russia might compare to that of the United States. (*The climate of Europe and Russia is probably colder than that of the United States because Europe and Russia are mainly located farther north. Some of Europe probably has a similar climate to that of the United States.*) Tell students that they will learn more about the region's climate in the next section.

Independent Practice
Ask students to create the Taking Notes graphic organizer. Have them fill in the Landforms column with information about the Ural Mountains.

Monitor Progress
Circulate among students to make sure they are filling in the correct details. Provide assistance as needed.

Answers

Analyze Images Since the photo of the highlands of northern Scotland shows a church, and the photo of the Ural mountains does not show any buildings, the highlands probably have a higher population density.

✓ **Reading Check** Eurasia

Major Landforms

Guided Instruction

- **Vocabulary Builder** Clarify the high-use words **enable** and **level** before reading.

- Read Major Landforms with students. Circulate and make sure they can answer the Reading Check question.

- Ask students **Why is the continent of Europe described as a peninsula?** (*Europe is a peninsula because it is a body of land nearly surrounded by water.*)

- Ask students **What effect have Western Europe's harbors had on its economy?** (*Western Europe's harbors have helped it to become a world leader in the shipping industry.*)

- Have students look at the map on this page. Point out that although there are no physical barriers between Russia and other European countries, there are some barriers between other countries on the continent. Ask **Why might physical barriers impede travel today less than they may have in the past?** (*Today, people can travel by airplane. Roads have been built through some mountains, allowing cars to travel over them. In the past, people had to travel by foot or on animals, so physical barriers such as mountains were difficult to cross.*)

L2

Major Landforms

Study the shape of Europe on the map below. The continent of Europe forms a **peninsula** (puh NIN suh luh), or a body of land nearly surrounded by water. The European peninsula juts out into the Atlantic Ocean. Europe also has many smaller peninsulas with bays. These bays include harbors, or sheltered bodies of water where ships dock. Good harbors enabled Western European countries to become world leaders in the shipping industry.

Now find Russia on the political map of Asia in the Atlas. Notice how much of Russia lies on the Arctic Ocean. For most of the year, this body of water is frozen and cannot be used for shipping. Between Russia and the countries of Europe, however, there are no physical barriers. Movement between these two regions has always been easy.

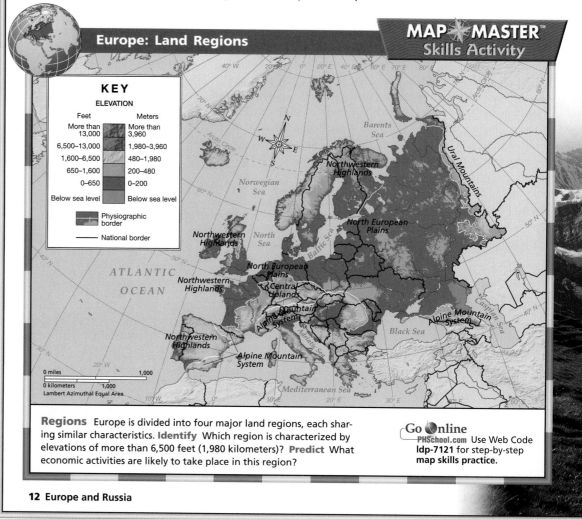

Europe: Land Regions

MAP MASTER Skills Activity

KEY
ELEVATION

Feet	Meters
More than 13,000	More than 3,960
6,500–13,000	1,980–3,960
1,600–6,500	480–1,980
650–1,600	200–480
0–650	0–200
Below sea level	Below sea level

— Physiographic border
— National border

0 miles 1,000
0 kilometers 1,000
Lambert Azimuthal Equal Area

Regions Europe is divided into four major land regions, each sharing similar characteristics. **Identify** Which region is characterized by elevations of more than 6,500 feet (1,980 kilometers)? **Predict** What economic activities are likely to take place in this region?

Go Online
PHSchool.com Use Web Code ldp-7121 for step-by-step map skills practice.

12 Europe and Russia

Answers

MAP MASTER Skills Activity **Identify** an area of the Alpine Mountain System east of the Black Sea **Predict** possible answers: animal raising; small scale farming

Go Online
PHSchool.com Students may practice their map skills using the interactive online version of this map.

Skills for Life Skills Mini Lesson

Using the Cartographer's Tools

1. Teach the skill by pointing out that there are certain elements common to most maps, such as a scale and compass rose.

2. Have students practice the skill by using the compass rose to determine where the North European Plain is located in relation to the Alpine Mountain System.

   (*It is northeast of the Alpine Mountain System.*)

3. Have students apply the skill by answering this question: Which land region extends the farthest east, the Central Uplands or the North European Plain? (*the North European Plain*)

Plains, Uplands, and Mountains of Europe Within the peninsula of Europe are four major land regions: the Northwestern Highlands, the North European Plain, the Central Uplands, and the Alpine Mountain System. Find these regions on the map on page 12.

The Northwestern Highlands stretch across the far north of Europe. It is a region of old mountains that have been worn down by wind and weather. Because they have steep slopes and thin soil, they are not good for farming, and few people live there. But the forests there support a successful timber industry. And people there raise goats and sheep, especially in Spain and Scotland.

Notice that the North European Plains cover more than half of Europe. These plains includes most of the European part of Russia and reach all the way to France. This region has the most productive farmland and the largest cities in Europe.

In the center of southern Europe are the Central Uplands. The Central Uplands are a region of highlands, made up of mountains and plateaus. **Plateaus** (pla TOHZ) are large raised areas of mostly level land bordered on one or more sides by steep slopes or cliffs. Most of the land there is rocky and not good for farming. But the uplands have other uses, including mining, industry, and tourism.

The mountains of the Alpine Mountain System stretch from France to the Balkan Peninsula. They include the Alps, the highest mountains in the system. Some families do small-scale farming in the mountain valleys and meadows of the Alps.

Learn about the geography of Europe and Russia.

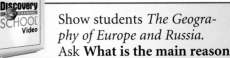

Show students *The Geography of Europe and Russia*. Ask **What is the main reason for Russia's low population density?** *(Large parts of the country have a harsh, cold climate.)*

Guided Instruction (continued)

- Ask students **What are Europe's four major land regions?** *(the Northwestern Highlands, the North European Plains, the Central Uplands, and the Alpine Mountain System)*

- Ask students **In which part of Europe are the Northwestern Highlands located?** *(They stretch across the far north of Europe.)* Have students discuss why this region is not good for farming. *(The Northwestern Highlands have steep slopes and thin soil.)*

- Ask students **Which land region has the most productive farmland and the largest cities in Europe?** *(the North European Plains)*

- Ask students **How do people use the land in the Alps?** *(Some land in the Alps is used for small-scale farming.)* Have students discuss why they think only small-scale farming takes place in the Alps. *(Students' responses may vary, but should reflect the understanding that large-scale farming is difficult in mountainous terrain.)*

Traveling in the Alps
A train carries people between alpine villages in southern Switzerland. The country has an extensive rail system. **Infer** *What geographical challenges does a nation like Switzerland face when building a rail system?*

Chapter 1 Section 1 **13**

Background: Links Across Place

The Alps When most people think of the mountains that form the Alps, they think of Switzerland and perhaps France, Italy, Germany, or Austria. In fact, the Alps stretch across a total of nine European countries, including Slovenia, Croatia, Bosnia and Herzegovina, and Serbia and Montenegro.

Major rivers that originate in the peaks of Alpine mountains include the Rhône, the Rhine, the Po, and a number of tributaries from the Danube River. As these rivers wind their way through Europe, they eventually drain into the Adriatic, Black, North, and Mediterranean seas.

Answer

Infer Possible answer: It is probably difficult to build a railroad over mountainous terrain.

Guided Instruction (continued)

- Ask students to name Russia's two largest cities. *(Moscow and St. Petersburg)*

- Ask students **Why do you think more people live in the North European Plain than in other regions of Russia?** *(Possible answer: The North European Plain has a milder climate than the rest of Russia.)*

Independent Practice

Have students continue filling in the table with details about Europe and Russia's landforms. Briefly model how to identify which details to record.

Monitor Progress

Provide assistance to individuals as needed as they add landforms to their tables.

Making a Living in Siberia
The nomadic Chukchi people make their living by herding reindeer in the uplands of northeastern Siberia. The name *Chukchi* means "rich in reindeer." **Infer** *Why does it make sense for the Chukchi to be nomadic—moving from place to place—rather than to live in fixed settlements?*

Plains, Uplands, and Mountains of Russia Europe and western Russia share the North European Plain. Russia's largest cities, Moscow (MAHS kow) and St. Petersburg, are in this region. Most of Russia's industries are there, too. More people live in this region than in any other part of Russia.

Where the plains end, the uplands begin. On the eastern border of the European Plain, you will find the Ural Mountains. To the east of the Urals is the Asian part of Russia—a region known as Siberia (sy BIHR ee uh). This region makes up about 75 percent of Russian territory, but the climate is so harsh that only about 20 percent of Russia's people live there.

If you continue east into Siberia from the Ural Mountains, you will cross the largest plain in the world—the West Siberian Plain. This low, marshy plain covers more than one million square miles (2.59 million sq kilometers). More than half of it rises only 328 feet (100 meters) above sea level. Farther east is the Central Siberian Plateau, which slopes upward from the West Siberian Plain. If you travel still farther east, you will need to watch your step. The East Siberian Uplands include more than 20 active volcanoes among the rugged mountains and plateaus.

✓ Reading Check **Where are most of Russia's industries located?**

14 Europe and Russia

Differentiated Instruction

For Advanced Readers   L3
Have students further explore life in the Arctic regions of Europe and Russia by completing *Activity Shop Lab: Tracking the Midnight Sun* in groups.

All in One **Europe and Russia Teaching Resources,** *Activity Shop Lab: Tracking the Midnight Sun,* pp. 128–129

Answers

Infer Possible answer: The Chukchi probably have to move often to find food for their reindeer herds.

✓ Reading Check Most of Russia's industries are located in the North European Plain.

Waterways of Europe and Russia

Rivers and lakes provide the people who live in Europe and Russia with water and transportation.

Major Rivers High in the Alps in Switzerland (SWIT sur lund), melting glaciers create two streams that combine to form the Rhine River. Winding through forests and plains, the Rhine makes a journey of 865 miles (1,392 kilometers), from Switzerland to the Netherlands and the North Sea. The Rhine River is connected to the farthest reaches of Western Europe by canals and **tributaries** (TRIB yoo tehr eez). A tributary is a river or stream that flows into a larger river.

Another major waterway is the Danube (DAN yoob) River. The Danube is Europe's second-longest river. It begins in the Black Forest region of western Germany. It travels 1,770 miles (2,850 kilometers) to the Black Sea of southeastern Europe. Along the way, the Danube passes through nine countries.

The longest river in Europe is Russia's Volga (VOHL guh) River. It flows 2,291 miles (3,687 kilometers) through western Russia and empties into the Caspian (KASP ee un) Sea. Canals link the Volga and its tributaries to the Baltic Sea and other seas. Unfortunately, the Volga freezes along much of its length for three months of each year. During the winter months, it is not **navigable** (NAV ih guh bul), or clear enough for ships to travel through.

Set a Purpose for Reading
If your purpose is to learn about the geography of Europe and Russia, how do these paragraphs help you meet your goal?

A Historical Waterway
The Rhine flows past old castles, mills, and factories along its course through Germany. Just as they did in ancient times, ships today use the river to transport goods. **Analyze Images** What advantages would this location have given the people who settled here?

Chapter 1 Section 1 **15**

Differentiated Instruction

For English Language Learners `L1`
Make the meanings of Key Terms and high-use words as concrete as possible by linking each to an object, photo, drawing, or movement. For instance, to demonstrate the word *navigable*, set up several desks and chairs so that there is enough space between them for students to walk through. Then move the desks closer together so that students cannot squeeze through to demonstrate a path that is not navigable.

Target Reading Skill `L2`

Set a Purpose for Reading As a follow up, ask students to answer the Target Reading Skill question in the Student Edition. (*The paragraphs describe Europe and Russia's major rivers, which are an important part of the geography of Europe and Russia.*)

Waterways of Europe and Russia `L2`

Guided Instruction

- **Vocabulary Builder** Clarify the high-use word **link** before reading.

- Read Waterways of Europe and Russia with students.

- Ask students **Where does the Rhine River begin and end?** (*It begins high in the Alps in Switzerland and flows to the Netherlands, where it empties into the North Sea.*)

- Have students compare and contrast the Rhine and Volga rivers. (*Both rivers have canals and tributaries and empty into the sea. Both rivers are long, although the Volga is longer. Both rivers serve as trade routes, although the Volga freezes for three months each year and during that time it is not navigable.*)

Independent Practice

Have students complete the graphic organizer by filling in details about the waterways of Europe and Russia.

Monitor Progress

- Show *Section Reading Support Transparency ER 32* and ask students to check their graphic organizers individually. Go over key concepts and clarify key vocabulary as needed.

  Europe and Russia Transparencies, *Section Reading Support Transparency ER 32*

- Tell students to fill in the last column of the *Reading Readiness Guide*. Probe for what they learned that confirms or invalidates each statement.

  All in One Europe and Russia Teaching Resources, *Reading Readiness Guide,* p. 107

Answer

Analyze Images They were located on a major trade route, so they would have had access to goods from many places and could have been able to prosper through trade.

Assess Progress L2

Have students complete the Section Assessment. Administer the *Section Quiz*.

All in One **Europe and Russia Teaching Resources,** *Section Quiz,* p. 109

Reteach L1

If students need more instruction, have them read this section in the Reading and Vocabulary Study Guide.

Chapter 1, Section 1, **Europe and Russia Reading and Vocabulary Study Guide,** pp. 6–8

Extend L3

Have students learn more about the physical geography of Europe and Russia by completing the *Small Group Activity: Europe and Russia Map and Climate Charts.* Have gifted and talented and special needs students work together in small groups to complete the activity.

All in One **Europe and Russia Teaching Resources,** *Small Group Activity: Europe and Russia Map and Climate Charts,* pp. 124–127

Answers

Analyze Images No, the river appears to be frozen.

✓ **Reading Check** the Volga River

Section 1 Assessment

Key Terms

Students' sentences should reflect knowledge of each Key Term.

Target Reading Skill

Answers will vary, but should reflect that having a purpose for reading helped students to focus on the main ideas of the section.

Comprehension and Critical Thinking

1. (a) Russia **(b)** Europe is a small continent with many small countries, while Russia is the largest country in the world.

2. (a) the Northwestern Highlands, the North European Plains, the Central Uplands, and the Alpine Mountain System **(b)** the North European Plain, the Ural Mountains, the West Siberian Plain, the Central Siberian Plateau, and the East Siberian Uplands **(c)** Possible responses: Much of the land in the Northwestern Highlands and the Central Uplands is not suitable for farming, so most

A Seasonal Harbor
Ships wait in the harbor of Nizhay Novgorod, Russia, on the Volga River. **Analyze Images** *Is it likely that the river was navigable at the time the photo was taken?*

Lakes Though Europe is criss-crossed by rivers, it contains few lakes compared to other regions. Russia, in contrast, has a huge number of lakes, both large and small. The world's largest freshwater lake is found in Russia. Called Lake Baikal (by KAHL), it is located in southern Russia. Lake Baikal is nearly 400 miles long and has an average width of 30 miles. It is also the world's deepest lake, with some parts reaching 5,315 feet (1,620 meters). Lake Baikal contains about one fifth of Earth's fresh water and is home to hundreds of animal and plant species. In fact, the Russian word *baikal* means "rich lake."

✓ **Reading Check** What is the longest river in Europe?

Section 1 Assessment

Key Terms

Review the key terms at the beginning of this section. Use each term in a sentence that explains its meaning.

Target Reading Skill

How did having a purpose for reading help you understand important ideas in this section?

Comprehension and Critical Thinking

1. (a) Locate Which country is located on both the continents of Europe and Asia?

(b) Compare and Contrast How does the land size of Europe differ from the land size of Russia?

2. (a) Name What are the four major land regions of Europe?
(b) Identify What are the major land regions of Russia?
(c) Draw Conclusions How have physical features affected life in Europe and Russia?

3. (a) Explain Why is the Volga River in Russia not navigable year-round?
(b) Identify Effects How might Russia's industries be affected by ships not being able to travel on the rivers all year long?

Writing Activity

Write an entry in your journal describing what you learned about the landforms and waterways of Europe or Russia.

Writing Tip Remember that writing in a journal is writing you do for yourself. In a journal, you can let your ideas flow without stopping to correct your writing.

farming is done in the North European Plains; frozen land and water in northern Russia limit settlement, industry, and movement; the rocky land in the Central Uplands favors grazing over farming.

3. (a) The Volga River is not navigable for three months of the year when much of it freezes over. **(b)** Possible response: Industries may not be able to make much money during the months in which they are unable to ship goods.

Writing Activity

Use the *Rubric for Assessing a Journal Entry* to evaluate students' journals.

All in One **Europe and Russia Teaching Resources,** *Rubric for Assessing a Journal Entry,* p. 136

Go Online
PHSchool.com Typing in the Web code when prompted will bring students to detailed instructions for this activity.

Prepare to Read

Objectives

In this section you will
1. Find out about the wide range of climates in Europe and Russia.
2. Learn about the major climate regions of Europe and Russia.
3. Examine the natural vegetation regions of Europe and Russia.

Taking Notes

As you read this section, look for details about factors that affect climate and vegetation. Copy the flowchart below, and write each detail under the correct heading.

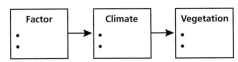

🎯 Target Reading Skill

Predict Making predictions about the text helps you set a purpose for reading and helps you remember what you read. Before you begin, preview the section by looking at the headings, photographs, charts, and maps. Then predict what the text might discuss about climate and vegetation. As you read this section, connect what you read to your prediction. If what you learn doesn't support your prediction, change your prediction.

Key Terms

• **rain shadow** (rayn SHAD oh) *n.* the area on the dry, sheltered side of a mountain, which receives little rainfall
• **steppes** (steps) *n.* the grasslands of fertile soil suitable for farming in Russia
• **tundra** (TUN druh) *n.* a cold, dry, treeless region covered with snow for most of the year
• **permafrost** (PUR muh frawst) *n.* a permanently frozen layer of ground below the top layer of soil

It is February in Barcelona (bahr suh LOH nuh), Spain. Twelve-year-old Pablo wakes up to the sun streaming through his bedroom window. It's another comfortable day, and the temperature is already 52°F (11°C). Pablo dresses quickly in jeans and a t-shirt and eats a breakfast of thick hot chocolate and *churros*, twisted loops of fried dough. He wants to go out and play soccer with his friends on this sunny Saturday morning.

At the very same moment, it is late afternoon in Irkutsk (ihr KOOTSK), a city in southern Siberia. Anya (AHN yuh) returns home from a day of cross-country skiing. She takes off her fur hat, gloves, boots, ski pants, and coat. The day has been sunny but cold, with an average temperature of −15°F (−26°C). Now Anya warms up with a dinner of *pelmeny* (PEL muh nee), chicken broth with meat-filled dumplings.

Boys in Siberia and in Spain

🎯 Target Reading Skill L2

Predict Point out the Target Reading Skill. Tell students that predicting will help them refine their purpose for reading and remember what they read.

Model predicting by previewing the headings and map on p. 18. Use the previewing process to make a prediction about what students will learn on this page: "I predict we will learn about various climates

and how the ocean affects them." Then tell students that they should connect and compare what they read to their predictions.

Give students *Preview and Predict*. Have them complete the activity in groups.

All in One Europe and Russia Teaching Resources, *Preview and Predict,* p. 119

Objectives
Social Studies
1. Find out about the wide range of climates in Europe and Russia.
2. Learn about the major climate regions of Europe and Russia.
3. Examine the natural vegetation regions of Europe and Russia.

Reading/Language Arts
Make predictions about the text to help set a purpose for reading and remember what you read.

Prepare to Read

Build Background Knowledge L2
Use the Think-Write-Pair-Share participation strategy (TE, p. T36) to structure the following activity. Ask students to describe the climate where they live. Then have students read the text on this page about the children in Barcelona and Irkutsk. Encourage students to summarize what this passage tells them about the variety of climates found in Europe and Russia. Ask students to compare the climates in Barcelona and Irkutsk in February to their own climate.

Set a Purpose for Reading L2
■ Preview the Objectives.

■ Read each statement in the *Reading Readiness Guide* aloud. Ask students to mark the statements true or false.

   All in One Europe and Russia Teaching Resources, *Reading Readiness Guide,* p. 111

■ Have students discuss the statements in pairs or groups of four, then mark their worksheets again. Use the Numbered Heads participation strategy (TE, p. T36) to call on students to share their group's perspectives.

Vocabulary Builder
Preview Key Terms L2
Pronounce each Key Term, then ask the students to say the term with you. Provide a simple explanation such as, "Some places are so cold that there is a layer of ground called permafrost that is frozen all the time."

A Wide Range of Climates L2

Guided Instruction

- **Vocabulary Builder** Clarify the high-use word **dramatic** before reading.

- Have students use the Paragraph Shrinking strategy (TE, p. T34) to read A Wide Range of Climates. Circulate throughout the classroom to ensure that individuals are able to answer the Reading Check question.

- Ask students **How do oceans affect climate?** *(Areas near an ocean or sea have mild weather, while areas farther from the ocean have more extreme weather.)*

- Have students describe the impact of the North Atlantic Current on climate in much of northwestern Europe. *(The North Atlantic Current carries warm water from the Gulf of Mexico to northwestern Europe and warms winds blowing across the Atlantic Ocean. The warm water and wind bring mild weather to much of northwestern Europe.)*

Achill Island, Ireland

A Wide Range of Climates

Barcelona, where Pablo lives, lies on the Mediterranean Sea. There, the summers are hot and dry, and the winters are mild. In Irkutsk, Anya's home, summers are short, and the winters are long and very cold. Temperatures in winter can drop to −50°F (−45°C). Snow covers the ground for about six months of the year.

How Oceans Affect Climate The two cities' distances from an ocean or a sea help explain their climate. Areas that are near an ocean or a sea have fairly mild weather year-round. Areas that are far from the ocean often have more extreme weather. Look at the map below and find the Gulf Stream. Notice that it becomes the North Atlantic Current as it crosses the Atlantic Ocean. This powerful ocean current carries warm water from the tropical waters of the Gulf of Mexico to northwestern Europe. It also warms winds blowing from the west across the Atlantic Ocean. The warm waters and winds bring mild weather to much of northwestern Europe.

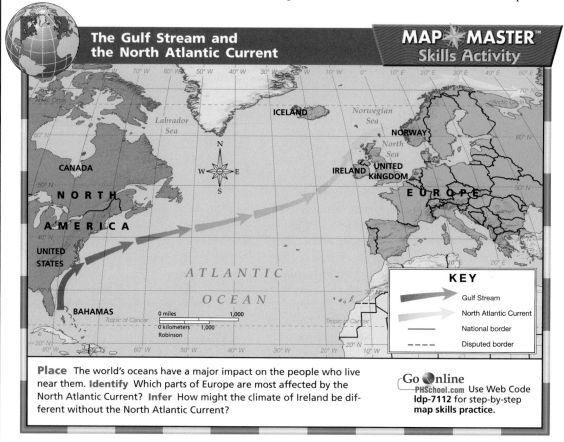

MAP MASTER Skills Activity

The Gulf Stream and the North Atlantic Current

KEY

→ Gulf Stream
→ North Atlantic Current
— National border
---- Disputed border

Place The world's oceans have a major impact on the people who live near them. **Identify** Which parts of Europe are most affected by the North Atlantic Current? **Infer** How might the climate of Ireland be different without the North Atlantic Current?

Go Online PHSchool.com Use Web Code ldp-7112 for step-by-step map skills practice.

Answers

MAP MASTER Skills Activity **Identify** Ireland, The United Kingdom, Norway **Infer** The climate of Ireland might be much colder without the North Atlantic Current.

Go Online PHSchool.com Students may practice their map skills using the interactive online version of this map.

Vocabulary Builder

Use the information below to teach students this section's high-use words.

High-Use Word	Definition and Sample Sentence
dramatic, p. 19	*adj.* striking in effect Marcus barely recognized his friend after her **dramatic** weight loss.
overlap, p. 21	*v.* to occupy the same area in part A Venn diagram is made up of two circles that **overlap.**
brief, p. 23	*adj.* short in time, duration, or length The **brief** quiz took up only five minutes of class time.

Two Cities, Two Climates

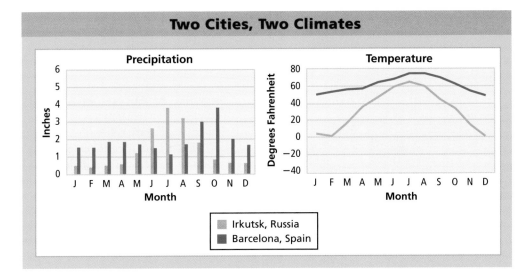

Precipitation

Inches (y-axis: 0–6)
Month (x-axis: J F M A M J J A S O N D)

Temperature

Degrees Fahrenheit (y-axis: −40 to 80)
Month (x-axis: J F M A M J J A S O N D)

■ Irkutsk, Russia
■ Barcelona, Spain

London, England, is farther north than any city in the continental United States, yet it has mild weather. How is this possible? The North Atlantic Current is the reason. But the most dramatic effect of the North Atlantic Current can be seen in northern Norway. Snow and ice cover most of this area in winter. Yet Norway's western coast is free of ice and snow all year. Snow melts almost as soon as it falls. Norway's ice-free ports have helped make its fishing industry one of the largest in Europe.

The ocean affects climate in other ways. Winds blowing across the ocean pick up a great deal of moisture. When these winds blow over land, they drop the moisture in the form of rain. Winds blowing from the west across the Atlantic bring a fairly wet climate to much of Western Europe.

How Mountains Affect Rainfall Mountains also affect the amount of rainfall in an area. In Europe, areas west of mountains receive heavy rainfall. These areas include parts of Great Britain, France, Germany, and Norway. Areas east of mountains have much lighter rainfall.

Why is this so? As winds rise up a mountain, they cool and drop their moisture. The air is dry by the time it reaches the other side of the mountain. Areas on the leeward side of a mountain, or the side away from the wind, are in a rain shadow. A **rain shadow** is an area on the dry, sheltered side of a mountain, which receives little rainfall.

✓ **Reading Check** How do mountains affect the climates of Western Europe?

■ **Graph Skills**

A city's climate is affected by its location and the geographical features that are located near it. **Identify** In how many months out of the year does Barcelona receive more precipitation than Irkutsk? **Draw Conclusions** What factors explain Irkutsk's low precipitation for most of the year?

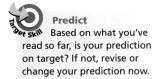

Predict Based on what you've read so far, is your prediction on target? If not, revise or change your prediction now.

Chapter 1 Section 2 **19**

Differentiated Instruction

For Advanced Readers　　　**L3**

Ask students to conduct research and prepare a presentation on the hydrologic cycle. Have them complete *Doing Searches on the Internet* and *Preparing for Presentations* to help them get started.

📖 **All in One** **Europe and Russia Teaching Resources,** *Doing Searches on the Internet,* p. 133; *Preparing for Presentations,* p. 134

For English Language Learners　　**L1**

Provide an oral synopsis of key content before asking students to read the text. Consider reading the section summary in the Reading and Vocabulary Study Guide aloud to preview section content.

📖 Chapter 1, Section 2, **Europe and Russia Reading and Vocabulary Study Guide,** pp. 9–11

Guided Instruction (continued)

■ Have students explain why London and Norway have mild climates despite being located far to the north. (*The North Atlantic Current keeps London and Norway mild, despite their distance from the Equator.*)

■ Ask students **Why is the climate in much of Western Europe wet?** (*Winds blowing east across the Atlantic Ocean pick up moisture. When the winds arrive over Western Europe, the moisture falls as rain.*)

■ Review the text of How Mountains Affect Rainfall with students. Then display *Color Transparency ER 20: Western Europe: Physical-Political.* Ask students to point to the areas described in the text as having heavy rainfall. (*the western portions of Great Britain, France, Germany, and Norway*) Then ask them to point to the areas they predict would have less rainfall. (*Students should point to areas east of mountain ranges, such as eastern Italy.*)

📖 **Europe and Russia Transparencies,** *Color Transparency ER 20: Western Europe: Physical-Political*

Independent Practice

Ask students to create the Taking Notes graphic organizer on a blank piece of paper. Then have them begin to fill in the flow chart by listing factors that affect climate. Display the blank *Flow Chart Transparency.* Briefly model how to identify which details to record.

📖 **Europe and Russia Transparencies,** *Transparency B2: Flow Chart*

Monitor Progress

As students begin to fill in the graphic organizer, circulate and help individuals understand which details to include in their charts. Provide assistance as needed.

↻ Target Reading Skill

Predict As a follow up, ask students to answer the Target Reading Skill question in the Student Edition. (*Students should either explain why their predictions are on target, or revise them if necessary.*)

Answers

Graph Skills Identify nine months **Draw Conclusions** possible answers: distance from the ocean, its low temperatures

✓ **Reading Check** In Europe, areas west of mountains receive heavy rainfall, while areas east of mountains are drier.

Major Climate Regions [L2]

Guided Instruction

- Have students read about the variety of climate regions found in Europe and Russia in Major Climate Regions.

- Ask students **What climate regions are found in Europe and Russia?** *(humid continental, subarctic, arctic, semiarid, marine west coast, Mediterranean, humid subtropical)*

- Have students compare the marine west coast climate to the subarctic climate region. *(The marine west coast climate is mild and rainy throughout the year, while the subarctic climate has short summers and long, cold winters.)*

- Ask students **In which climate regions would you expect most people to live?** *(Possible answer: More people probably live in the milder and wetter climates such as humid subcontinental, Mediterranean, and marine west coast.)*

Independent Practice

Have students continue to fill in their graphic organizers by adding details about the major climate regions of Europe and Russia in the climate box.

Monitor Progress

Circulate among students and provide assistance as needed.

Answers

Infer Possible answer: London probably has a much higher population density than Siberia.

✓ Reading Check marine west coast and Mediterranean

Two Very Different Climates
Much of Russia has a tundra climate, as shown in the top photo of Siberia. In contrast, London, England (at bottom), enjoys a mild climate year-round. **Infer** *How might the population densities of the places in these photos differ?*

Major Climate Regions

Considering the size of Europe and Russia, it is no surprise that this region contains many different climate regions.

Climate Regions of Europe and Russia
Look at the climate regions map on page 9. Notice that four climate regions are common to Europe and Russia. Find the humid continental climate region. This climate is characterized by long, cold winters and hot summers.

Now find Irkutsk, Russia, on the map. It is located in a huge subarctic climate region. There summers are short, and winters are long and cold. You can see how cold it is all year by looking at the temperature graph for Irkutsk on page 19. Notice that this climate also stretches across northern Europe.

Europe and Russia share two other climate regions. The northernmost areas of Europe and Russia have an arctic climate. It is very cold in these areas. On the warmest days of the short summer, temperatures sometimes barely reach 60°F (14°C). In contrast, southeastern Europe and southwestern Russia have a semiarid climate region, with hot temperatures and little rainfall.

Moderate Climate Regions of Europe As you can see on the climate regions map, Europe has moderate climate regions that Russia does not have. For example, the marine west coast climate affects much of northwestern Europe, stretching from northern Spain to northern Norway. As you have read, winds and currents from the Atlantic Ocean keep this climate mild and rainy all year.

Another climate region surrounds the Mediterranean Sea. It is easy to remember the name of this type of climate—Mediterranean, just like the sea. Remember that Barcelona, Spain, is on the Mediterranean Sea. In the Mediterranean climate, summers are hot and dry. Winters are mild and rainy.

Finally, a band of humid subtropical climate is located in southern Europe. Warm temperatures and year-round rainfall characterize this climate.

✓ Reading Check What two climate regions are found in Europe but not Russia?

Skills Mini Lesson

Comparing and Contrasting

1. Teach the skill by pointing out to students that to make comparisons and contrasts, they should look for ways things in a group are similar and different. Then, they should draw a conclusion based on their comparisons and contrasts.

2. Have students practice the skill by comparing and contrasting the climate of London with the climate in their own community.

3. Have students apply the skill by drawing a conclusion about the climates of the two cities.

Natural Vegetation Regions

The natural vegetation, or plant life, of Europe and Russia is as varied as the climate. Vegetation regions are related to climate regions. Vegetation in Europe and Russia varies from ice cap to desert. However, the main vegetation regions are forest, grassland, tundra, and Mediterranean. Compare the climate map on page 9 with the natural vegetation map below to see how the climate and vegetation regions overlap.

Forests of Europe and Russia The natural vegetation of much of Europe is forest. However, most of these forests have been cleared to make way for farms, factories, and cities. In northern Europe, you can still find large coniferous (koh NIF ur us) forests, which have evergreen trees with cones that carry and protect the seeds. Deciduous (dih SIJ oo us) forests, which contain trees that lose their leaves in fall, cover most of Western and Central Europe.

Russia is also heavily forested. One forest, called the taiga (TY guh), covers more than 4 million square miles (10 million square kilometers). Located in Siberia, it is the largest forest in the world.

Links Across The World

The Boreal Forest The boreal forest includes one third of all Earth's forests. The name comes from an ancient Greek god named Boreas, the god of the north wind. Russia's taiga makes up half of the boreal forest. The rest is located in the northern parts of Canada, Alaska, China, Mongolia, Scandinavia, and Scotland. Boreal forests play an important role in the environment, by filtering out carbon dioxide and other gases from the atmosphere.

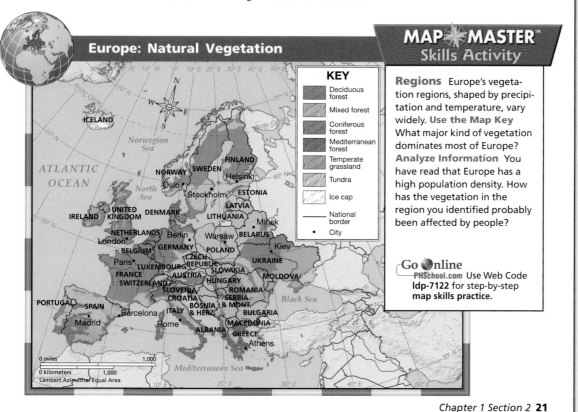

Europe: Natural Vegetation

MAP MASTER Skills Activity

KEY
- Deciduous forest
- Mixed forest
- Coniferous forest
- Mediterranean forest
- Temperate grassland
- Tundra
- Ice cap
- National border
- • City

Regions Europe's vegetation regions, shaped by precipitation and temperature, vary widely. **Use the Map Key** What major kind of vegetation dominates most of Europe? **Analyze Information** You have read that Europe has a high population density. How has the vegetation in the region you identified probably been affected by people?

Go Online PHSchool.com Use Web Code **ldp-7122** for step-by-step **map skills practice.**

Chapter 1 Section 2 **21**

Links

Read the **Links Across the World** on this page. Ask students **What role do boreal forests play in the environment?** (*They filter out carbon dioxide and other gases from the atmosphere.*)

Natural Vegetation Regions   L2

Guided Instruction

- **Vocabulary Builder** Clarify the high-use words **overlap** and **brief** before reading.

- Have students read Natural Vegetation Regions to learn about the many types of plant life found in Europe and Russia.

- Ask students **What natural vegetation covers much of Europe?** (*forests*)

- Have students discuss what has happened to most of the forests in Europe. (*The forests have been cleared to make way for farms, factories, and cities.*)

- Ask students **What is the land that was once covered by grasslands now used for?** (*farming*)

- Have students compare the vegetation map on this page with the climate map of Europe on p. 9. Ask them to draw a conclusion about how climate affects vegetation. (*Possible answer: Warmer, wetter climates such as the marine west coast climate promote the growth of more vegetation, while colder climates such as the subarctic climate region only allow for the growth of sparse vegetation.*)

Background: Daily Life

Country Homes On the weekends, many Russians travel to their *dacha* (DAH cha), or country home. Dachas are located in the countryside and provide Russians in urban areas with a retreat from busy city life. Traditionally, dachas are wooden shacks located on small areas of land, but today some people build dachas with many levels and swimming pools. Dacha owners usually have a small garden where they grow fruits and vegetables. Some people grow an entire year's supply of food for their families in these gardens.

Answers

MAP MASTER Skills Activity **Use The Map Key** deciduous forest **Analyze Information** Possible answer: Much of the forests has probably been cleared to make way for farms, factories, and cities.

Go Online PHSchool.com Students may practice their map skills using the interactive online version of this map.

Guided Instruction (continued)

- Ask students **What are the three main vegetation regions in Russia?** *(tundra, forest, and grassland)*

- Ask students **What are the grasslands called in Russia?** *(steppes)* **Why are the steppes good for farming?** *(The soil is fertile.)*

- Ask students **What is the tundra?** *(a cold, dry, treeless region that is covered with snow for most of the year)*

- Have students discuss their similarities and differences between the vegetation regions of Europe and Russia. *(Similarities—both have grasslands and forests; differences— much of Russia is covered by tundra and coniferous forest while Europe's vegetation is more varied.)*

Independent Practice

Have students complete their flowcharts by filling in details about the vegetation found in Europe and Russia.

Monitor Progress

- Show *Section Reading Support Transparency ER 33* and ask students to check their graphic organizers individually. Go over key concepts and clarify key vocabulary as needed.

    Europe and Russia Transparencies, *Section Reading Support Transparency ER 33*

- Tell students to fill in the last column of the *Reading Readiness Guide.* Probe for what they learned that confirms or invalidates each statement.

    Europe and Russia Teaching Resources, *Reading Readiness Guide,* p. 111

Answers

MAP★MASTER Skills Activity **Use a Scale** most of the region that borders the Arctic Ocean, an area of land approximately 4,000 miles long **Apply Information** The region is cold, treeless, and covered with snow most of the year.

Go Online
PHSchool.com Students may practice their map skills using the interactive online version of this map.

MAP★MASTER
Skills Activity

Russia: Natural Vegetation

KEY
- Deciduous forest
- Mixed forest
- Coniferous forest
- Temperate grassland
- Desert scrub
- Tundra
- Ice cap
- National border
- City

0 miles 1,500
0 kilometers 1,500
Lambert Azimuthal Equal Area

Location Russia is located far from the Equator and the warm ocean currents that bring mild climates to most of Europe. **Use a Scale** How much of Russia's land is tundra? **Apply Information** Why are few major cities located in this region?

Go Online
PHSchool.com Use Web Code ldp-7132 for step-by-step map skills practice.

Grasslands of Europe and Russia Grasslands, also called prairies, are a major vegetation region in Europe and Russia. In Europe, grasslands once covered the central and southern parts of the North European Plain. Like the forests, most of the prairies have also disappeared. Today, the land is used for farming.

In Russia, the grasslands are called **steppes.** Steppes are located mainly in the southwestern parts of the country. They contain a mix of grasses and low-growing vegetation such as mosses. Below that vegetation, the soil of the steppes is fertile and black and good for farming. The steppes are similar to the Great Plains of the United States.

Mediterranean Regions of Europe Just as the area of southern Europe near the Mediterranean Sea has its own climate, it also has its own vegetation region. Mediterranean vegetation is a mix of trees, scrub, and smaller plants, usually less than about 8 feet (2.5 meters) tall.

Differentiated Instruction

For Gifted and Talented [L3]
Form students into groups and have them begin working on the *Book Project: Changing Climates* to learn more about European climates.

Europe and Russia Teaching Resources, *Book Project: Changing Climates,* pp. 77–79

For Less Proficient Readers [L1]
Some students may have difficulty reading the vegetation map. Have them work in pairs to complete *Reading a Natural Vegetation Map.*

Europe and Russia Teaching Resources, *Reading a Natural Vegetation Map,* p. 130

Tundra of Europe and Russia Northern parts of Europe—including northern Scandinavia and Iceland—as well as northern Russia have a tundra vegetation region. **Tundra** is a cold, dry, treeless region that is covered with snow for most of the year. There winters last as long as nine months and the ground contains **permafrost,** a layer of permanently frozen ground below the top layer of soil. During the brief season when the top surface of the permafrost thaws, grasses, mosses, and other plant life grow quickly. Few people live in the tundra region.

✓ **Reading Check** Where is the world's largest forest located?

Flowers bloom during the short Siberian summer.

Section 2 Assessment

Key Terms
Review the key terms at the beginning of this section. Use each term in a sentence that explains its meaning.

Target Reading Skill
What did you predict about this section? How did your prediction guide your reading?

Comprehension and Critical Thinking
1. (a) Describe How do oceans affect climate?
(b) Identify Effects How does the North Atlantic Current affect northern Europe?

2. (a) Recall What are the major climate regions of Europe and Russia?
(b) Draw Conclusions Why are summers in Barcelona, Spain, hot and dry?
3. (a) List What are the natural vegetation regions of Europe and Russia?
(b) Summarize How are vegetation regions and climate regions related?
(c) Generalize What geographic features might lead someone to settle in Europe, rather than in Russia?

Writing Activity
Suppose you are planning a trip to one of the cities mentioned in this section. Decide what time of year you would want to go. Based on the climate of the city, make a list of the clothes that you would pack. Then write a brief paragraph explaining why you would pack the items on your list.

For: An activity about Ireland
Visit: PHSchool.com
Web Code: ldd-7101

Assess and Reteach

Assess Progress
Have students complete the Section Assessment. Administer the *Section Quiz.*

All in One **Europe and Russia Teaching Resources,** *Section Quiz,* p. 113

Reteach
If students need more instruction, have them read this section in the Reading and Vocabulary Study Guide.

Chapter 1, Section 2, **Europe and Russia Reading and Vocabulary Study Guide,** pp. 9–11

Extend
Extend students' knowledge by having them complete the *Enrichment* activity in which they will learn about a threat to some of Europe's forests.

All in One **Europe and Russia Teaching Resources,** *Enrichment,* p. 122

Answer
✓ **Reading Check** Siberia

Writing Activity
Use the *Rubric for Assessing a Writing Assignment* to evaluate students' paragraphs.

All in One **Europe and Russia Teaching Resources,** *Rubric for Assessing a Writing Assignment,* p. 137

Go Online
PHSchool.com Typing in the Web code when prompted will bring students to detailed instructions for this activity.

Section 2 Assessment

Key Terms
Students' sentences should reflect knowledge of each Key Term.

Target Reading Skill
Students should explain how their predictions helped them focus their reading on important ideas in the section.

Comprehension and Critical Thinking
1. (a) Areas near the ocean are fairly mild throughout the year. **(b)** The North Atlantic Current carries warm water from the Gulf of Mexico to northwestern Europe and warms the winds that blow from the west across the Atlantic Ocean. The warm waters and winds cause much of northwestern Europe to have a mild climate.

2. (a) humid continental, subarctic, arctic, semiarid, marine west coast, Mediterranean, and humid subtropical **(b)** Barcelona is located in a Mediterranean climate region, which is characterized by hot and dry summers.

3. (a) forest, grassland, tundra, and Mediterranean **(b)** Climate affects the type of vegetation that can grow in an area. **(c)** possible answer: the warmer climate of some areas

Objective

Learn how to use a precipitation map.

Prepare to Read

Build Background Knowledge L2

Tell students to look at the special purpose maps in the first two sections of the chapter. Have them identify what each map shows, and then think about why it is useful. Conduct an Idea Wave (TE, p. T35) to help students share their answers.

Instruct

Using a Precipitation Map L2

Guided Instruction

- Read the steps to using a precipitation map aloud and write them on the board.

- Practice the skill by following the steps on p. 25 as a class. Model each step in the activity by reading the map title and looking over the map to get a general idea of what it shows. *(The World: Precipitation shows how much precipitation different areas of the world receive.)* Students should continue by studying the key *(Different amounts of precipitation are shown using various colors.)*, looking at the precipitation amounts for different regions *(Most of North Africa, Central Asia, Australia, Greenland, and Antarctica receive less than ten inches of precipitation a year. Most of South America, Central Africa, and Southeast Asia receive more than 40 inches of precipitation a year.)*, and using the information to compare precipitation in the United States and Russia. *(Most of the U.S. and Russia receive between ten and 40 inches of precipitation each year, although the eastern and southern coasts of the U.S. receive an average of more than 40 inches a year. The U.S. has more variation in precipitation, and Russia is generally drier.)*

Using a Precipitation Map

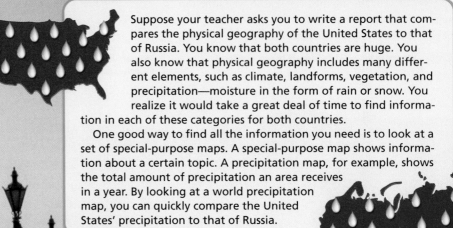

Suppose your teacher asks you to write a report that compares the physical geography of the United States to that of Russia. You know that both countries are huge. You also know that physical geography includes many different elements, such as climate, landforms, vegetation, and precipitation—moisture in the form of rain or snow. You realize it would take a great deal of time to find information in each of these categories for both countries.

One good way to find all the information you need is to look at a set of special-purpose maps. A special-purpose map shows information about a certain topic. A precipitation map, for example, shows the total amount of precipitation an area receives in a year. By looking at a world precipitation map, you can quickly compare the United States' precipitation to that of Russia.

A rainy day in St. Petersburg, Russia

24 Europe and Russia

Learn the Skill

Follow the steps below to learn how to use a precipitation map.

1 **Read the map title and look over the map to get a general idea of what it shows.** Notice that a precipitation map includes common map features, such as a title, key, scale, and labels.

2 **Read the key to understand how the map uses symbols, colors, and patterns.** A precipitation map often shows colors to represent different amounts of precipitation. Notice that the amounts are indicated in both inches and centimeters.

3 **Use the key to interpret the map.** Look on the map for the different colors shown in the key. Notice where areas with different amounts of precipitation are located on the map.

4 **Draw conclusions about what the map shows.** Information you discover when you analyze a precipitation map can help you draw conclusions about how precipitation affects people's lives.

Independent Practice

Assign *Skills for Life* and have students complete it individually.

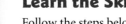 **Europe and Russia Teaching Resources,** *Skills for Life,* p. 123

Monitor Progress

As students are completing *Skills for Life,* circulate to make sure individuals are applying the skill steps effectively. Provide assistance as needed.

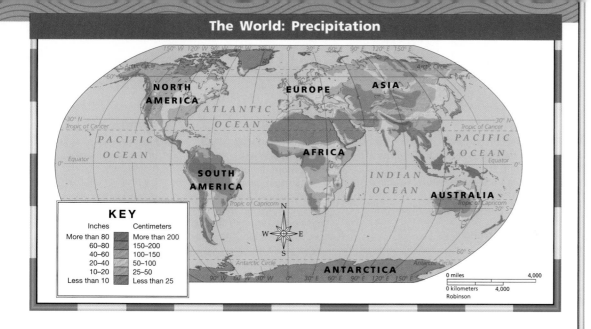

The World: Precipitation

KEY

Inches	Centimeters
More than 80	More than 200
60–80	150–200
40–60	100–150
20–40	50–100
10–20	25–50
Less than 10	Less than 25

0 miles 4,000
0 kilometers 4,000
Robinson

Practice the Skill

Use the precipitation map above to complete the following steps.

1 Become familiar with the map. What is the map's title? In general, what does it show?

2 Look at the key to see how different amounts of precipitation are shown. Familiarize yourself with the colors on the key.

3 Look for areas on the map with different amounts of precipitation. Because you want to compare the United States with Russia, find those two regions within the continents of North America, Asia, and Europe on the map. (If you need help finding the areas of the two countries, compare this map with the World: Political map in the Atlas).

4 Study the map. Use the information on it to compare precipitation in the United States and Russia. Which country has more variation in precipitation? Which country is generally drier? Write a conclusion that summarizes your comparison.

Apply the Skill

Turn to Section 2 of Chapter 1 and look at the Europe: Natural Vegetation map on page 21. Use the steps of this skill to analyze and draw conclusions about this special-purpose map.

Chapter 1 **25**

Differentiated Instruction

For Special Needs Students **L1**
Partner special needs students with more proficient students to do Level 1 of the *Analyzing and Interpreting Special Purpose Maps* lesson on the Social Studies Skill Tutor CD-ROM together. When students feel more confident, they can move on to Level 2 alone.

 Analyzing and Interpreting Special Purpose Maps, **Social Studies Skill Tutor CD-ROM**

Assess and Reteach

Assess Progress **L2**
Ask students to do the Apply the Skill activity.

Reteach **L1**
If students are having trouble applying the skill steps, have them review the skill using the interactive Social Studies Skills Tutor CD-ROM.

 Analyzing and Interpreting Special Purpose Maps, **Social Studies Skills Tutor CD-ROM**

Extend **L3**
Have students use the map on this page to create a chart with the amounts of precipitation for different areas of the world. Assign each student different cities, countries, and regions. Have them use an atlas, if necessary, to locate these places on the map in the Student Edition. Then display the finished charts on a class bulletin board.

Answer
Apply the Skill

Students should recognize that the Europe: Natural Vegetation map shows the vegetation regions of Europe. The key should help students identify the countries, major cities, and vegetation regions. Students may conclude that most of Europe is made up of deciduous forest, although it contains large areas of other types of vegetation as well.

Section 3
Step-by-Step Instruction

Objectives

Social Studies
1. Learn about the natural resources of Western Europe.
2. Find out about the natural resources of Eastern Europe.
3. Examine Russia's natural resources.

Reading/Language Arts
Preview and ask questions to help you remember important ideas in the section.

Prepare to Read

Build Background Knowledge `L2`

Write the following words on the board: *soil; water; fuel.* Tell students that in this section they will read about the distribution of these resources throughout Europe and Russia. Have students discuss and debate which of these resources they think are most important. Use the Give One, Get One participation strategy (TE, p. T37) to structure the discussion.

Set a Purpose for Reading `L2`

■ Preview the Objectives.

■ Read each statement in the *Reading Readiness Guide* aloud. Ask students to mark the statements true or false.

　All in One Europe and Russia Teaching Resources, *Reading Readiness Guide,* p. 115

■ Have students discuss the statements in pairs or groups of four, then mark their worksheets again. Use the Numbered Heads participation strategy (TE, p. T36) to call on students to share their group's perspectives.

Vocabulary Builder
Preview Key Terms `L2`

Pronounce each Key Term, then ask the students to say the word with you. Provide a simple explanation such as, "Hydroelectric power is electricity that is created by moving water."

Section 3
Resources and Land Use

Prepare to Read

Objectives
In this section you will
1. Learn about the natural resources of Western Europe.
2. Find out about the natural resources of Eastern Europe.
3. Examine Russia's natural resources.

Taking Notes
As you read this section, look for the natural resources located in Europe and Russia. Copy the Venn diagram below, and record your findings in it.

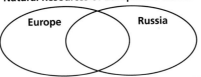

Natural Resources of Europe and Russia

Europe   Russia

🎯 Target Reading Skill

Preview and Ask Questions Before you read this section, preview the headings and illustrations to find out what the section is about. Write one or two questions that will help you understand or remember something important in the section. Then read this section to answer your questions.

Key Terms
• **loess** (LOH es) *n.* a type of rich, dustlike soil
• **hydroelectric power** (hy droh ee LEK trik POW ur) *n.* the power generated by water-driven turbines
• **fossil fuel** (FAHS ul FYOO ul) *n.* a source of energy that forms from the remains of ancient plants and animals

---

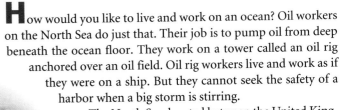

A North Sea oil rig

26 Europe and Russia

How would you like to live and work on an ocean? Oil workers on the North Sea do just that. Their job is to pump oil from deep beneath the ocean floor. They work on a tower called an oil rig anchored over an oil field. Oil rig workers live and work as if they were on a ship. But they cannot seek the safety of a harbor when a big storm is stirring.

The North Sea, located between the United Kingdom and mainland northwestern Europe, sometimes has violent weather. Severe storms with winds of as much as 100 miles (160 kilometers) an hour are common. Waves as high as 90 feet (27 meters) batter oil rig platforms. Despite the harsh conditions, crews work around the clock to operate, inspect, and repair the rigs.

Making sure a rig operates properly is a very important job. The United Kingdom and other nations around the North Sea depend on oil and natural gas from the rigs.

🎯 Target Reading Skill `L2`

Preview and Ask Questions Point out the Target Reading Skill. Tell students that previewing and asking questions can help them to focus on and remember important details about what they will read.

Model the skill by previewing the headings and the map on p. 27 and asking the following question: Why is fertile soil an important natural resource in Western Europe? Tell students to read the section and answer the question. (*It is needed to grow food.*)

Give students *Preview and Ask Questions.* Have them complete the activity in groups.

　All in One Europe and Russia Teaching Resources, *Preview and Ask Questions,* p. 120

Resources of Western Europe

Western Europe is a wealthy region and a world leader in economic development. Part of this wealth and success comes from Western Europe's rich and varied supply of natural resources. These natural resources include fertile soil, water, and fuels.

Fertile Soil Soil is one of Earth's most important natural resources because it is needed to grow food. Much of Western Europe is covered with rich, fertile soil, especially the region's broad river valleys.

Wind has helped create the fertile soil of the North European Plain. Over thousands of years, winds have deposited **loess** (LOH es), a type of rich, dustlike soil. This soil, combined with plentiful rain and moderate temperatures, provides for a long growing season. These conditions allow European farmers to produce abundant crops.

Tulips brighten the landscape at a flower farm in the Netherlands.

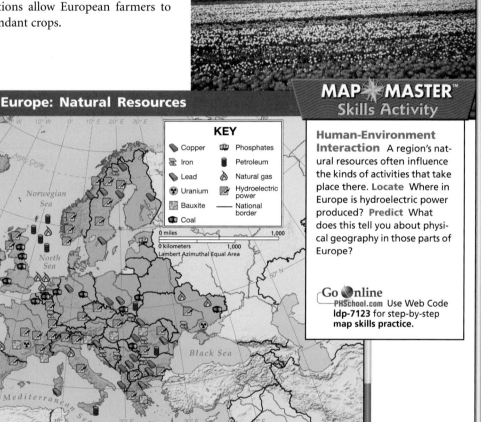

Europe: Natural Resources

KEY

- Copper
- Iron
- Lead
- Uranium
- Bauxite
- Coal
- Phosphates
- Petroleum
- Natural gas
- Hydroelectric power
- — National border

0 miles 1,000
0 kilometers 1,000
Lambert Azimuthal Equal Area

MAP★MASTER™ Skills Activity

Human-Environment Interaction A region's natural resources often influence the kinds of activities that take place there. **Locate** Where in Europe is hydroelectric power produced? **Predict** What does this tell you about physical geography in those parts of Europe?

Go Online
PHSchool.com Use Web Code **ldp-7123** for step-by-step map skills practice.

Vocabulary Builder

Use the information below to teach students this section's high-use words.

High-Use Word	Definition and Sample Sentence
deposit, p. 27	*v.* to set down or drop The storm **deposited** three feet of snow onto our roof.
nourish, p. 28	*v.* to promote growth For a garden to thrive, it must be **nourished** with water and sunlight.
element, p. 30	*n.* an essential part Exercise is an important **element** of a healthy lifestyle.
transport, p. 32	*v.* to carry from one place to another Overnight mail is a good way to **transport** small goods quickly.

Instruct

Resources of Western Europe L2

Guided Instruction

- **Vocabulary Builder** Clarify the high-use words **deposit** and **nourish** before reading.

- Read Resources of Western Europe, using the Paragraph Shrinking strategy (TE, p. T34).

- Have students scan the map of Europe's natural resources before they read the text. Ask students to choose a Western European country and describe its natural resources, using an atlas to locate the countries if necessary. *(Possible answer: Portugal has water for hydroelectric power.)*

- Ask students **What three factors contribute to the abundance of crops in Europe?** *(rich soil in the form of loess, plentiful rain, and moderate temperatures)*

Answers

MAP★MASTER Skills Activity **Locate** Most hydroelectric power in Europe is produced in the far north and in the south. **Predict** Possible answer: The regions where hydroelectric power is produced must have rivers. These areas may also have mountains, since many rivers that flow down mountains have been dammed to generate power.

Go Online
PHSchool.com Students may practice their map skills using the interactive online version of this map.

Guided Instruction (continued)

- Ask students **Why is water an important resource for Western Europe?** *(People need water for drinking; water is needed to grow crops; water can be used to generate hydroelectric power.)*

- Ask students **Where must hydroelectric power plants be located?** *(Hydroelectric plants must be located where there are sources of fast-flowing water, such as dammed rivers or waterfalls.)*

- Ask students **What are fossil fuels?** *(Fossil fuels are sources of energy such as natural gas, oil, and coal that are formed from the remains of ancient plants and animals.)*

- Ask students to name three countries in Western Europe that have large supplies of coal. *(the United Kingdom, Germany, and Norway)*

- Have students make generalizations about the natural resources of Western Europe. *(Possible generalizations: Western Europe has a rich variety of important natural resources; Western Europe is a leading world industrial power due to its rich natural resources; Western Europe's major natural resources include fertile soil, water, and fuel deposits.)*

Independent Practice

Have students create the Taking Notes graphic organizer on a blank piece of paper. Ask them to begin by listing the resources of Western Europe in the appropriate circle.

Monitor Progress

Circulate throughout the classroom to ensure that individuals are listing the appropriate resources. Help students as needed.

Answer

✓ Reading Check Hydroelectric power is generated by fast-flowing water from a river that has been dammed or a waterfall that is used to spin turbines. As the turbines spin, they create electric power.

Abundant Water Another important resource in Western Europe is water. People need water for drinking. Water nourishes crops. Water can also be used to produce electricity for industries and homes. To be used as a source of energy, water must flow very quickly. The force of water from a waterfall or a dam can be used to spin machines called turbines (TUR bynz). Spinning turbines generate, or create, electric power. Power generated by water-driven turbines is called **hydroelectric power** (hy droh ee LEK trik POW ur).

Many countries in Western Europe have favorable locations for the development of hydroelectric power. Some rivers that flow down through the mountains have been dammed to generate hydroelectric power. Norway gets almost all of its electric power from water. Hydroelectric power also keeps factories in Sweden, Switzerland, Austria, Spain, Scotland, and Portugal operating.

Fuel Deposits Like flowing water, fuel deposits are another source of energy for many industries. **Fossil fuels** are sources of energy that formed from the remains of ancient plants and animals. Fossil fuels include natural gas, oil, and coal.

Both the United Kingdom and Norway have large deposits of oil and natural gas. The United Kingdom also has large coal fields, as does Germany. The largest coal deposits in Germany are located in the Ruhr (ROOR), a region named for the Ruhr River. Because of its fuel resources, the Ruhr has long been one of Western Europe's most important industrial regions.

An abundance of coal and iron ore gave Western European industries a head start in the 1800s, when industries grew rapidly. Today, countries in Western Europe remain among the world's leading industrial powers.

✓ Reading Check How is hydroelectric power generated?

Producing hydroelectric power on the Tay River in Scotland

Background: Links Across Time

The Industrial Revolution Prior to the Industrial Revolution, the great majority of human labor was devoted to farming. However, technological innovations made farming more efficient and industries such as manufacturing, mining, and communications began to grow.

The Industrial Revolution began around 1760 in Great Britain. Initially, the British banned the export of their technology in an effort to keep their industrial advantages to themselves. However, this policy eventually failed as new inventions spread to nearby European countries, such as Belgium, as well as the United States.

Resources of Eastern Europe

Now, shift your view from Western to Eastern Europe. Turn back to the map on page 27 showing Europe's natural resources. Notice that Eastern Europe has resources similar to those of Western Europe. Place a finger on the area around 50° N and 15° E. This is where Poland, the Czech (chek) Republic, and Germany come together. This area is called Silesia (sy LEE zhuh). Large deposits of coal there have helped to make Silesia a major industrial center.

Ukraine (yoo KRAYN), a large country in Eastern Europe, has coal deposits, too. It also has other fuel resources—especially oil and natural gas. However, the most important resource is probably its soil. The region's black earth is very fertile. Not surprisingly, farming is an extremely important activity in Ukraine.

Eastern Europe has fewer water resources than does Western Europe. However, the nations of the Balkan Peninsula produce a large amount of hydroelectric power.

✓ **Reading Check** What is Silesia, and where is it?

Energy and Land Resources
The photo at the left shows miners on the job in a Silesian coal mine. Above, a Ukrainian woman harvests flowers to use in making perfume.
Compare and Contrast What do mining and farming have in common? How are they different?

Chapter 1 Section 3 **29**

Resources of Eastern Europe **L2**

Guided Instruction

■ Ask students to read Resources of Eastern Europe. As students read, circulate and make sure individuals can answer the Reading Check question.

■ Ask students **Why is fertile soil an important resource in Ukraine?** *(Farming is an important activity there.)*

■ Ask students **What natural resources do Eastern and Western Europe have in common?** *(They both have fertile soil and fuel resources, such as coal and oil.)*

■ Ask students **Why do you think it might be better for a country or region to have a variety of natural resources rather than just one type?** *(Possible answers: Varied resources help countries or regions to have diversified economies; possessing many natural resources provides a country or region with a certain amount of self-sufficiency.)*

Independent Practice

Have students continue to fill in the graphic organizer by listing all of Eastern Europe's natural resources.

Monitor Progress

Circulate among students to make sure individuals are using both the map and the text to compile their resource lists.

Answers

✓ **Reading Check** Silesia is a major industrial area with large coal deposits. It is located where Poland, the Czech Republic, and Germany meet.

Compare and Contrast They both require natural resources; farmers use the fertile soil to grow crops, and miners uncover resources like coal and oil. Mining generally occurs in deep pits of underground shafts; farming activities occur in open fields and barns.

Resources of Russia L2

Guided Instruction

- **Vocabulary Builder** Clarify the high-use words **element** and **transport** before reading.

- Have students read about the variety of Russia's natural resources in Resources of Russia.

- Ask students **What geographic factors make it difficult for Russia to take advantage of its resources?** (*Russia's harsh climate, huge size, and lack of navigable rivers; it also has few places suited for farming*)

- Ask students to name the four major energy resources that are found in Russia. (*oil, natural gas, coal, and hydroelectricity*)

- Ask students **Why do you think steel is useful for many industries in Russia?** (*Possible answer: Steel is a basic material used in industries such as automobile production, manufacturing, and construction.*)

A tugboat pushes a barge loaded with logs along a Russian river.

Resources of Russia

Russia has a much greater supply of natural resources than does the United States. The United States has used its resources to become the richest nation on Earth. You might wonder why Russia has not done the same.

One answer is that Russia's harsh climate, huge size, and few navigable rivers have made it difficult to turn the country's resources into wealth. In addition, Russia has relatively few places that are suited for farming. Much of Russia lacks one or more of the key elements for farming: favorable climate, good soil, and plentiful water.

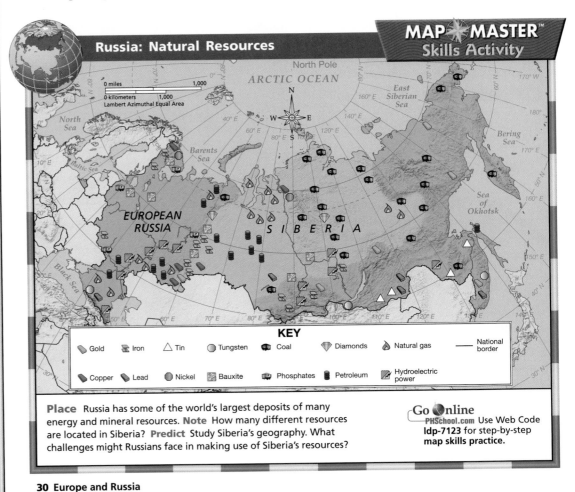

MAP MASTER™ Skills Activity

Russia: Natural Resources

KEY

- Gold
- Iron
- Tin
- Tungsten
- Coal
- Diamonds
- Natural gas
- Copper
- Lead
- Nickel
- Bauxite
- Phosphates
- Petroleum
- Hydroelectric power
- National border

Place Russia has some of the world's largest deposits of many energy and mineral resources. **Note** How many different resources are located in Siberia? **Predict** Study Siberia's geography. What challenges might Russians face in making use of Siberia's resources?

Go Online PHSchool.com Use Web Code **ldp-7123** for step-by-step map skills practice.

30 Europe and Russia

Answers

MAP MASTER™ Skills Activity **Note** fourteen **Predict** Possible answer: Siberia is so far north that its cold climate might make it difficult to access and transport its resources. Siberia's large size might restrict the transportation of resources.

Go Online PHSchool.com Students may practice their map skills using the interactive online version of this map.

Differentiated Instruction

For Less Proficient Readers L1

Have students read the section as they listen to the recorded version on the Student Edition on Audio CD. Check for comprehension by pausing the CD after each paragraph and asking students to summarize what they have just read.

⊙ Chapter 1, Section 3, **Europe and Russia Student Edition on Audio CD**

For Special Needs Students L1

Explain to students that they can use word roots to help find the meaning of unfamiliar words. Break down the word *hydroelectric* into its parts—*hydro* and *electric*. Explain that "hydro" is a prefix meaning "water." Ask students to explain what "electric" means. Then help students to understand the full meaning of the word.

From Fossils to Fuel

1. Peat is made of partially decayed plant material. ▶

2. Over millions of years, material ▶ built up over ancient peat deposits. The pressure of this material gradually changed the peat into brown coal.

◀ **3.** Continuing pressure gradually turned brown coal into soft coal. Soft coal is the most common coal found on Earth. It is often used in industry.

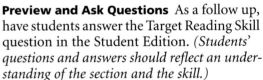

Fossil Fuels and Minerals Russia has the largest reserves, or available supply, of natural gas in the world. It is also one of the world's five leading oil producers. Scientists estimate that the country has about one third of the world's coal reserves. In addition, Russia has huge deposits of minerals, including cobalt, chromium, copper, and gold.

Russia also has the world's largest reserves of iron ore, which is used to make steel. Many of these iron ore deposits are in the part of Russia that is on the continent of Europe. That is one reason why most of Russia's industry is west of the Ural Mountains. Fueled by its natural resources, Russian factories produce automobiles, cloth, machinery, computers, and chemicals.

Forest, Fishing, and Energy Resources Russia has the world's largest forest reserves. Wood harvested from these forests is used to make paper and pulp, and it also supplies wood for houses and furniture.

Because of Russia's location on the Pacific Ocean, fish provide another abundant resource. Russians also fish the Black and Caspian seas, as well as the country's many inland lakes. The fishing industry is an important part of Russia's economy.

Finally, Russia has ample energy resources. It uses much of its fossil fuel resources to produce electricity. In addition, many Russian rivers are dammed to generate electricity in hydroelectric plants. Russia is one of the world's largest producers of electricity.

■ Diagram Skills

A man in Ireland cuts pieces of peat from the ground. **Explain** If this peat stayed in the ground, how long would it take to turn into brown coal? **Apply Information** Explain why coal is a nonrenewable resource, using information from the diagram.

 Preview and Ask Questions
Ask a question that will help you learn something important from this section. Then read the section, and answer your question.

Chapter 1 Section 3 **31**

Differentiated Instruction

For Advanced Readers ⬛L3
Have students read *The Endless Steppe* to learn more about the harsh lands of Siberia. Then ask them to answer the questions at the end of the selection.

All in One Europe and Russia Teaching Resources, *The Endless Steppe*, pp. 131–132

Guided Instruction (continued)

■ Ask students **What major natural resources are found in Siberia?** *(oil, natural gas, coal, and forests)*

■ Ask students **Why is it difficult for Russians to transport their natural resources from Siberia?** *(Siberia is far from the population and industrial centers of the country. Transport is difficult due to Russia's huge size. Transport via water is difficult because most of Siberia's rivers do not flow toward important cities.)*

■ Ask students **What generalization can you make about the natural resources of Russia?** *(Possible answer: Russia has an abundance of natural resources, yet they are often difficult to reach and transport.)*

Independent Practice
Have students complete the graphic organizer by moving the resources common to both Europe and Russia into the overlapping portion of the circles.

Monitor Progress
■ Show *Section Reading Support Transparency ER 34* and ask students to check their graphic organizers individually. Go over key concepts and clarify key vocabulary as needed.

Europe and Russia Transparencies, *Section Reading Support Transparency ER 34*

■ Tell students to fill in the last column of the *Reading Readiness Guide*. Probe for what they learned that confirms or invalidates each statement.

All in One Europe and Russia Teaching Resources, *Reading Readiness Guide*, p. 115

⟳ Target Reading Skill ⬛L2

Preview and Ask Questions As a follow up, have students answer the Target Reading Skill question in the Student Edition. *(Students' questions and answers should reflect an understanding of the section and the skill.)*

Answers
Diagram Skills **Explain** millions of years **Apply Information** Possible answers: Once all existing coal is used up, it will take millions of years for more to form.

Chapter 1 Section 3 **31**

Assess and Reteach

Assess Progress `L2`

Have students complete the Section Assessment. Administer the *Section Quiz*.

> **Europe and Russia Teaching Resources,** *Section Quiz,* p. 117

Reteach `L1`

If students need more instruction, have them read this section in the Reading and Vocabulary Study Guide.

> Chapter 1, Section 3, **Europe and Russia Reading and Vocabulary Study Guide,** pp. 12–14

Extend `L3`

Remind students that efforts to get and use resources in Siberia have led to some environmental problems. Have students begin to work on *Reporting to an Environmental Conference,* a long-term project that will help them learn more about environmental problems that affect regions in Europe and Russia and other parts of the world.

> **Go Online**
> PHSchool.com
>
> **For:** Long-Term Integrated Projects:
> *Reporting to an Environmental Conference*
> **Visit:** PHSchool.com
> **Web Code:** ldd-7105

Answers

Infer possible answer: pollution

✔ Reading Check Most of these resources are located in Siberia.

Section 3 Assessment

Key Terms

Students' sentences should reflect knowledge of each Key Term.

🔄 Target Reading Skill

Students' questions will vary. Students should explain how asking questions helped them as they read this section.

Comprehension and Critical Thinking

1. (a) fertile soil, water, and fuel **(b)** Water is used for drinking, growing crops, and producing hydroelectric power.

2. (a) coal, oil, natural gas, and fertile soil
(b) Many Ukrainians probably farm for a living and to feed their families.

3. (a) minerals, oil, natural gas, coal, iron ore, and forests **(b)** Western Europe has developed its resources to become an important industrial region while Russia has not been able to fully develop its resources.
(c) The size of the country, the cold climate, and a lack of river transportation routes have hindered Russia's ability to develop its resources fully and bring wealth to its people.

Writing Activity

Use the *Rubric for Assessing a Writing Assignment* to evaluate students' paragraphs.

> **Europe and Russia Teaching Resources,** *Rubric for Assessing a Writing Assignment,* p. 137

Breaking Up Old Ships
When ships are no longer seaworthy, they are broken apart like this oil tanker in the harbor of Murmansk, Russia. Breaking up ships often causes environmental and health problems. **Infer** *What specific problems might breaking up an oil tanker cause?*

Challenges to Using Russia's Resources Most of Russia's deposits of oil, natural gas, and coal are located in Siberia. Three fourths of Russia's forests are located there, too. These forests contain half of the world's reserves of softwood timber. However, Siberia is far from the population and industrial centers of the country.

Russia's huge size presents a major challenge to transporting Siberian resources to areas where they are needed. Except for the Volga, Russia's rivers are not very useful for transportation. Siberia's rivers do not flow toward Russia's most important cities. Instead, they flow north into the Arctic Ocean. In spite of these problems and the bitter-cold winter weather, Russia has found ways to move resources from Siberia. Pipelines carry oil and natural gas, and railroads transport coal to European Russia.

Extracting Russia's resources has created a new challenge—protecting the environment. Some of the world's worst cases of pollution are found in Russia, especially Siberia. Nuclear waste has been dumped into rivers for 40 years. Air pollution from factories is very severe. Besides finding ways to develop its valuable resources, Russia must also consider how to restore polluted areas.

✔ Reading Check Where are most of Russia's oil, natural gas, and coal deposits located?

 Section 3 Assessment

Key Terms

Review the key terms at the beginning of this section. Use each term in a sentence that explains its meaning.

🔄 Target Reading Skill

Look at the list of questions you asked. Which ones helped you learn and remember something from this section?

Comprehension and Critical Thinking

1. (a) List Name Western Europe's major natural resources.

(b) Summarize How is water used as a natural resource in Western Europe?
2. (a) Recall Which important natural resources are located in Ukraine?
(b) Draw Conclusions Why is farming important to Ukraine?
3. (a) List Name Russia's major natural resources.
(b) Compare and Contrast How do Western Europe and Russia differ in their use of natural resources?
(c) Draw Conclusions Why is Russia not as wealthy as Western Europe?

Writing Activity

What do you think is the most important natural resource in Europe and Russia? What makes that resource so important? Write a paragraph explaining your choice. Be sure to include a main idea statement in your paragraph.

> **Writing Tip** Before you begin writing, list all the natural resources discussed in the section. Then choose which you think is most important.

Chapter 1 Review and Assessment

◆ Chapter Summary

Section 1: Land and Water
- Europe and Russia are part of Eurasia, the world's largest landmass.
- Both Europe and Russia have plains, uplands, and mountains.
- Europe's major rivers are the Rhine and the Danube, and Russia's is the Volga.

Section 2: Climate and Vegetation
- Oceans and mountains both affect the climates of Europe and Russia.
- The climate regions of Europe and Russia range from Mediterranean to subarctic.
- The natural vegetation of Europe and Russia is as varied as its climate and includes forest, grassland, and tundra.

London

Section 3: Resources and Land Use
- The resources of Western Europe include fertile soil, water, and fossil fuels.
- Eastern Europe has resources similar to those of Western Europe, including coal, oil, and natural gas.
- Russia has abundant mineral, energy, and other resources, with the majority of these resources located in Siberia.

Ukraine

◆ Key Terms

Use each key term below in a sentence that shows the meaning of the term.

1. population density
2. navigable
3. peninsula
4. plateau
5. tributary
6. rain shadow
7. loess
8. tundra
9. permafrost
10. steppes
11. hydroelectric power
12. fossil fuel

Chapter 1 **33**

Vocabulary Builder

Revisit this chapter's high-use words:

landmass, enable, level, link, dramatic, overlap, brief, deposit, nourish, element, transport

Ask students to review the definitions they recorded on their *Word Knowledge* worksheets.

All in One Europe and Russia Teaching Resources, *Word Knowledge,* p. 121

Consider allowing students to earn extra credit if they use the words in their answers to the questions in the Chapter Review and Assessment. The words must be used correctly and in a natural context to win the extra points.

Chapter 1 Review and Assessment

Review Chapter Content
- Review and revisit the major themes of this chapter by asking students to classify what Guiding Question each bulleted statement in the Chapter Summary answers. Place students in groups to classify the statements. Use the Numbered Heads participation strategy (TE, p. T36) to have the groups share their answers in a group discussion. Refer to p. 1 in the Student Edition for the text of the Guiding Questions.
- Assign *Vocabulary Development* for students to review Key Terms.

  All in One Europe and Russia Teaching Resources, *Vocabulary Development,* p. 135

Answers
Key Terms
1–12. Students' sentences should reflect knowledge of each Key Term.

Chapter 1 **33**

13. (a) The countries of Europe are more densely populated than Russia. More people live in the North European Plains than in any other part of Russia. **(b)** The North European Plains are less mountainous than other areas and has a relatively mild climate. The most productive farmland is found there.

14. (a) The Central Uplands are a region of Europe made up of mountains and plateaus. **(b)** The uplands are used for raising sheep and goats, as well as mineral mining. **(c)** The Central Uplands are characterized by mountains and plateaus, while the North European Plain consists of a broad plain that is more favorable for human settlement.

15. (a) two of the following: oceans, the North Atlantic Current, and mountains **(b)** Warm ocean currents bring warm air and winds to northwestern Europe, making the region's climate mild. The fact that much of Russia is far from oceans is one reason for the climate's harshness.

16. (a) A Mediterranean climate has hot, dry summers and mild, rainy winters. **(b)** A Mediterranean climate is much milder and enjoys longer summers than a subarctic climate.

17. (a) Western and Eastern Europe both share fertile soil, water, fuel deposits, and iron ore; Russia has fuel deposits, iron ore, and forests. **(b)** If a river flows toward major cities and is navigable year-round, ships can easily travel along it to transport goods at any time of the year. **(c)** Western Europe's resources are more fully developed than Russia's because they are accessible, and it is easier to transport them along Europe's many rivers. Russia's resources are often located far from industrial centers, and transportation of resources along rivers is hampered by the fact that many rivers either flow away from industrial centers or freeze during winter.

18. (a) oil, coal, natural gas **(b)** The development of natural resources affects how people in an area make a living. For example, in areas with rich oil deposits, many people might work at oil refineries.

Skills Practice
Students' conclusions should use accurate information from the map and show that they are able to apply the skill steps.

◆ Comprehension and Critical Thinking

13. (a) Identify Which areas of Europe and Russia are the most densely populated?
(b) Summarize What physical features encouraged people to settle in those areas?

14. (a) Define What are the European Central Uplands?
(b) List Name two uses of these uplands.
(c) Contrast How do the Central Uplands differ from the North European Plain?

15. (a) Name List two factors that affect the climates of Europe and Russia.
(b) Summarize What effect do large bodies of water have on climate in Europe and Russia?

16. (a) Describe Explain what a Mediterranean climate is.
(b) Compare and Contrast How is a Mediterranean climate similar to or different from a subarctic climate?

17. (a) Identify What are the major natural resources of Western Europe, of Eastern Europe, and of Russia?
(b) Predict What factors might influence how well a river can be used to transport resources?
(c) Identify Cause and Effect Why are Western Europe's natural resources more fully developed than Russia's natural resources?

18. (a) List Name three kinds of fossil fuels.
(b) Draw Conclusions How does the development of natural resources affect the way that people live?

◆ Skills Practice

Using a Precipitation Map In the Skills for Life activity in this chapter, you learned how to use a precipitation map. The steps you followed to learn this skill can be applied to other kinds of special purpose maps.

Review the steps you used to learn the skill. Then turn to the map titled Europe: Natural Resources on page 27. Use the map title and key to read and interpret the map. Then write a conclusion about the information the map contains.

◆ Writing Activity: Geography

Suppose you are visiting a fourth-grade classroom. You have been asked to report to the students on Europe and Russia's geography. Write a brief report on this subject. To get started, write down the various kinds of landforms and bodies of water that are discussed in the chapter. Do the same for the human and natural resources of Europe and Russia. Then explain in your report how life is similar and difficult for the people who live in different regions of Europe and Russia.

Skills Activity
Europe and Russia

Place Location For each place listed below, write the letter from the map that shows its location.
1. France
2. Ural Mountains
3. Alps
4. Siberia
5. Rhine River
6. Volga River
7. North Sea

Go Online
PHSchool.com Use Web Code ldp-7183 for an interactive map.

Writing Activity
Students' reports will vary, but should compare and contrast the ways in which landforms, waterways, climate, vegetation, and natural resources affect the lives of people in Europe and Russia.

Use the *Rubric for Assessing a Writing Assignment* to evaluate students' reports.

All in One Europe and Russia Teaching Resources, *Rubric for Assessing a Writing Assignment,* p. 137

Standardized Test Prep

Test-Taking Tips

Some questions on standardized tests ask you to make mental maps. Read the passage below. Then follow the tips to answer the sample question.

Ben is playing a trivia game. One of the geography questions asks, "Which mountain range divides Russia between two continents, Europe and Asia?" What is the correct answer?

Choose the letter that best answers the question.

A Kjolen Mountains

B Ural Mountains

~~C Pyrenees~~

~~D Alps~~

TIP Rule out choices that do not make sense. Then choose the best answer from the remaining choices.

Think It Through You can rule out the Alps and Pyrenees because both are inside Europe. Which sounds more familiar to you, the Ural Mountains or the Kjolen Mountains? The correct answer is an important range and is likely to be a name you have heard. As it turns out, the Kjolen Mountains are in Scandinavia—in northern Europe. The correct answer is B.

TIP Try to picture a physical map of Europe and Russia. Then try to place each of these mountain ranges on your mental map.

Practice Questions

Use the tips above and other tips in this book to help you answer the following questions.

1. Which Russian feature covers more than 4 million square miles (10 million square kilometers)?

A grasslands   B taiga

C polders   D tundra

2. Because of its location near the Mediterranean Sea, Barcelona's summers are

A mild and wet.

B cold and snowy.

C hot and dry.

D short and wet.

3. The climate of the northernmost areas of Europe and Russia is called

A marine west coast.

B Mediterranean.

C humid continental.

D arctic.

4. What is the location of Siberia relative to that of Spain?

A northeast

B southeast

C northwest

D west

5. The major vegetation region of Europe and Russia that is now mainly used for farming is

A grasslands.

B tundra.

C taiga.

D Mediterranean.

Go Online PHSchool.com

Use Web Code lda-7101 for a **Chapter 1 self-test.**

Chapter 1 **35**

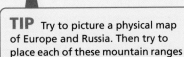
Standardized Test Prep

Answers

1. B

2. C

3. D

4. A

5. A

Chapter Overview

Overview

 Section 1

From Ancient Greece to the Middle Ages
1. Learn how the heritage of ancient Greece influences life today.
2. Discover the glory of the ancient Roman Empire.
3. Learn about Europe in the Middle Ages.

 Section 2

Renaissance and the Age of Revolution
1. Discover what the Renaissance was like at its peak.
2. Examine the effects of increased trade and stronger rulers in the Renaissance.
3. Learn about revolutions in government and science in the 1600s and 1700s.

 Section 3

Industrial Revolution and Nationalism
1. Learn how the Industrial Revolution changed people's lives.
2. Examine how nationalism and war can be related.

 Section 4

Imperial Russia to the Soviet Union
1. Discover how Russia built its empire.
2. Understand the fall of the Russian tsars.
3. Examine the rise and fall of the Soviet Union.
4. Learn the causes and effects of the Cold War.
5. Learn about the Russian Federation today.

 **Section 5**

The European Union
1. Learn about the history of the European Union.
2. Understand the purpose of the European Union.
3. Examine the structure of the European Union.
4. Find out what the future holds for the European Union.

Discovery CHANNEL SCHOOL Video

St. Petersburg and Peter the Great
Length: 3 minutes, 30 seconds
Use with Section 4
This segment describes how Peter the Great built the city of Saint Petersburg. It concentrates on how the city was important to Russia, and how it brought Eastern and Western Europe together.

Technology Resources

Go Online
PHSchool.com

Students use embedded Web codes to access Internet activities, chapter self-tests, and additional map practice. They may also access Dorling Kindersley's Online Desk Reference to learn more about each country they study.

Interactive Textbook

Use the Interactive Textbook to make content and concepts come alive through animations, videos, and activities that accompany the complete basal text—online and on CD-ROM.

PRENTICE HALL
TeacherEXPRESS
Plan · Teach · Assess

Use this complete suite of powerful teaching tools to make planning lessons and administering tests quicker and easier.

Reading and Assessment

Reading and Vocabulary Instruction

↩ Model the Target Reading Skill

Clarifying Meaning Explain to students that they can use several strategies to clarify the meanings of new words and ideas. They can reread a passage and try to link familiar and unfamiliar words and ideas. They can also read ahead to see if the author provides definitions or examples later in the passage. After reading, students can paraphrase or summarize the information to better understand and remember it.

Write the following selection from page 46 of the Student Edition on the board. Model techniques for clarifying meaning by thinking aloud as you read it to the class.

Michelangelo was an accomplished painter, poet, architect, and sculptor. Think aloud: "I'll reread to make sure I understand. I'm not sure what *accomplished* means. I'll read ahead to find out." *His lifelike statues were remarkably realistic and detailed. In some, you can see veins bulging in the hands. Or the drape of a cloak across the sculpted person looks so real that it appears to be made of cloth rather than of marble.* Think aloud: "I'll paraphrase this segment: Michelangelo was so skilled at carving that he could make marble appear to be flesh or cloth. Therefore, *accomplished* must mean very skillful. To summarize, Michelangelo was remarkably skilled in many art forms."

Use the following worksheets from All-in-One Europe and Russia Teaching Resources (pp. 169–171) to support the chapter's Target Reading Skill.

Vocabulary Builder
High-Use Academic Words
Use these steps to teach this chapter's high-use words:

1. Have students rate how well they know each word on their Word Knowledge worksheets (All-in-One Europe and Russia Teaching Resources, p. 172).

2. Pronounce each word and ask students to repeat it.

3. Give students a brief definition or sample sentence (provided on TE pp. 39, 46, 54, 63, and 71).

4. Work with students as they fill in the "Definition or Example" column of their Word Knowledge worksheets.

Assessment

Formal Assessment
Test students' understanding of core knowledge and skills.

Chapter Tests A and B, All-in-One Europe and Russia Teaching Resources, pp. 203–208

Customize the Chapter Tests to suit your needs.
ExamView Test Bank CD-ROM

Skills Assessment
Assess geographic literacy.

MapMaster Skills, Student Edition, pp. 37, 40, 57, 63, 71, 76

Assess reading and comprehension.

Target Reading Skills, Student Edition, pp. 42, 48, 57, 65, 73, and in Section Assessments

Chapter 2 Assessment, Europe and Russia Reading and Vocabulary Study Guide, p. 31

Performance Assessment

Assess students' performance on this chapter's Writing Activities using the following rubrics from All-in-One Europe and Russia Teaching Resources.

Rubric for Assessing a Journal Entry, p. 200

Rubric for Assessing a Writing Assignment, p. 201

Rubric for Assessing a Letter to the Editor, p. 202

Assess students' work through performance tasks.

Small Group Activity: Castle Mural, All-in-One Europe and Russia Teaching Resources, pp. 175–178

Online Assessment

Have students check their own understanding.

Chapter Self-Test

Section 1 From Ancient Greece to the Middle Ages

 *1.5 periods, .75 block*

Section Lesson Planner

Social Studies Objectives
1. Learn how the heritage of ancient Greece influences life today.
2. Discover the glory of the ancient Roman Empire.
3. Learn about Europe in the Middle Ages.

Reading/Language Arts Objective
Reread to look for connections among words and sentences.

Prepare to Read	**Instructional Resources**	**Differentiated Instruction**
Build Background Knowledge Discuss how Greek and Roman cultures have influenced modern culture. **Set a Purpose for Reading** Have students evaluate statements on the *Reading Readiness Guide*. **Preview Key Terms** Teach the section's Key Terms. **Target Reading Skill** Introduce the section's Target Reading Skill of **rereading**.	**All in One Europe and Russia Teaching Resources** **L2** Reading Readiness Guide, p. 150 **L2** Reread or Read Ahead, p. 169	**Spanish Reading and Vocabulary Study Guide** **L1** Chapter 2, Section 1, pp. 14–15 ELL

Instruct	**Instructional Resources**	**Differentiated Instruction**
The Greek Heritage Discuss ancient Greek influence on modern culture. **The Glory of Ancient Rome** Discuss the Roman Empire and its demise. **Target Reading Skill** Review **rereading**. **Europe in the Middle Ages** Discuss the changes that occurred during the Middle Ages.	**All in One Europe and Russia Teaching Resources** **L2** Guided Reading and Review, p. 151 **L2** Reading Readiness Guide, p. 150 **Europe and Russia Transparencies** **L2** Section Reading Support Transparency ER 35	**All in One Europe and Russia Teaching Resources** **L3** A Spartan Reply, p. 182 AR, GT **L3** Storm in the State, p. 183 AR, GT **Teacher's Edition** **L3** For Advanced Readers, TE p. 40 **L3** For Gifted and Talented, TE p. 40 **L1** For English Language Learners, TE p. 42 **Spanish Support** **L2** Guided Reading and Review (Spanish), p. 12 ELL

Assess and Reteach	**Instructional Resources**	**Differentiated Instruction**
Assess Progress Evaluate student comprehension with the section assessment and section quiz. **Reteach** Assign the Reading and Vocabulary Study Guide to help struggling students. **Extend** Extend the lesson by assigning a Small Group Activity.	**All in One Europe and Russia Teaching Resources** **L2** Section Quiz, p. 152 **L3** Small Group Activity: Castle Mural, pp. 175–178 Rubric for Assessing a Journal Entry, p. 200 **Reading and Vocabulary Study Guide** **L1** Chapter 2, Section 1, pp. 16–18	**Spanish Support** **L2** Section Quiz (Spanish), p. 13 ELL

Key

L1 Basic to Average	**L3** Average to Advanced	LPR Less Proficient Readers	GT Gifted and Talented
L2 For All Students		AR Advanced Readers	ELL English Language Learners
		SN Special Needs Students	

Section 2 Renaissance and the Age of Revolution

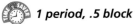 *1 period, .5 block*

Social Studies Objectives
1. Discover what the Renaissance was like at its peak.
2. Examine the effects of increased trade and stronger rulers in the Renaissance.
3. Learn about revolutions in government and science in the 1600s and 1700s.

Reading/Language Arts Objective
Paraphrase to restate what you have read in your own words.

Prepare to Read	**Instructional Resources**	**Differentiated Instruction**
Build Background Knowledge Discuss how the invention of the printing press has influenced people's lives. **Set a Purpose for Reading** Have students begin to fill out the *Reading Readiness Guide*. **Preview Key Terms** Teach the section's Key Terms. **Target Reading Skill** Introduce the section's Target Reading Skill of **paraphrasing.**	**All in One Europe and Russia Teaching Resources** L2 Reading Readiness Guide, p. 154 L2 Paraphrase, p. 170	**Spanish Reading and Vocabulary Study Guide** L1 Chapter 2, Section 2, pp. 16–17 ELL

Instruct	**Instructional Resources**	**Differentiated Instruction**
Glories of the Renaissance Discuss cultural and ideological changes that occurred during the Renaissance. **More Trade, Stronger Rulers** Discuss how overseas trade affected Europe. **Target Reading Skill** Review **paraphrasing.** **Revolutions in Government** Discuss the American and French Revolutions. **Revolutions in Science** Discuss the Scientific Revolution.	**All in One Europe and Russia Teaching Resources** L2 Guided Reading and Review, p. 155 L2 Reading Readiness Guide, p. 154 **Europe and Russia Transparencies** L2 Section Reading Support Transparency ER 36	**All in One Europe and Russia Teaching Resources** L3 Enrichment, p. 173 AR, GT **Teacher's Edition** L1 For Less Proficient Readers, TE p. 47 L3 For Gifted and Talented, TE p. 47 **Spanish Support** L2 Guided Reading and Review (Spanish), p. 14 ELL

Assess and Reteach	**Instructional Resources**	**Differentiated Instruction**
Assess Progress Evaluate student comprehension with the section assessment and section quiz. **Reteach** Assign the Reading and Vocabulary Study Guide to help struggling students. **Extend** Extend the lesson by assigning a primary source reading.	**All in One Europe and Russia Teaching Resources** L2 Section Quiz, p. 156 L3 Testing a Theory, p. 184 Rubric for Assessing a Writing Assignment, p. 201 **Reading and Vocabulary Study Guide** L1 Chapter 2, Section 2, pp. 19–21	**Spanish Support** L2 Section Quiz (Spanish), p. 15 ELL

Key
L1 Basic to Average	L3 Average to Advanced	LPR Less Proficient Readers	GT Gifted and Talented
L2 For All Students		AR Advanced Readers	ELL English Language Learners
		SN Special Needs Students	

Section 3 Industrial Revolution and Nationalism

2 periods, 1 block (includes Skills for Life)

Social Studies Objectives

1. Learn how the Industrial Revolution changed people's lives.
2. Examine how nationalism and war can be related.

Reading/Language Arts Objective

Summarize to better understand the text.

Prepare to Read	Instructional Resources	Differentiated Instruction
Build Background Knowledge Discuss ways that countries show nationalism. **Set a Purpose for Reading** Have students evaluate statements on the *Reading Readiness Guide*. **Preview Key Terms** Teach the section's Key Terms. **Target Reading Skill** Introduce the section's Target Reading Skill of **summarizing**.	**All in One Europe and Russia Teaching Resources** **L2** Reading Readiness Guide, p. 158 **L2** Summarize, p. 171	**Spanish Reading and Vocabulary Study Guide** **L1** Chapter 2, Section 3, pp. 18–19 ELL

Instruct	Instructional Resources	Differentiated Instruction
The Industrial Revolution Discuss changes in Europe during and after the Industrial Revolution. **Eyewitness Technology** Discuss a textile mill. **Target Reading Skill** Review **summarizing**. **A Century of War and Nationalism** Discuss nationalism and World Wars I and II.	**All in One Europe and Russia Teaching Resources** **L2** Guided Reading and Review, p. 159 **L2** Reading Readiness Guide, p. 158 **Europe and Russia Transparencies** **L2** Transparency B6: Flow Chart **L2** Section Reading Support Transparency ER 37	**All in One Europe and Russia Teaching Resources** **L3** A Child in Prison Camp, pp. 185–187 AR, GT **L2** Skills for Life, p. 174 AR, GT, LPR, SN **Teacher's Edition** **L1** For English Language Learners, TE p. 55 **L3** For Advanced Readers, TE p. 58 **L1** For Special Needs Students, TE p. 58 **Student Edition on Audio CD** **L1** Chapter 2, Section 3 ELL, LPR, SN

Assess and Reteach	Instructional Resources	Differentiated Instruction
Assess Progress Evaluate student comprehension with the section assessment and section quiz. **Reteach** Assign the Reading and Vocabulary Study Guide to help struggling students. **Extend** Extend the lesson by assigning an online activity.	**All in One Europe and Russia Teaching Resources** **L2** Section Quiz, p. 160 Rubric for Assessing a Writing Assignment, p. 201 **Reading and Vocabulary Study Guide** **L1** Chapter 2, Section 3, pp. 22–24 **PHSchool.com** **L3** For: Long-term Integrated Projects: Making a Book About World Technologies Web Code: ldd-7206	**Spanish Support** **L2** Section Quiz (Spanish), p. 17 ELL **Teacher's Edition** **L1** For Special Needs Students, TE p. 61 **Social Studies Skills Tutor CD-ROM** **L1** Problem Solving ELL, LPR, SN

Key

L1 Basic to Average   **L3** Average to Advanced

L2 For All Students

LPR Less Proficient Readers
AR Advanced Readers
SN Special Needs Students

GT Gifted and Talented
ELL English Language Learners

Section 4 Imperial Russia to the Soviet Union

 1 period, .5 block

Social Studies Objectives
1. Discover how Russia built its empire.
2. Understand the fall of the Russian tsars.
3. Examine the rise and fall of the Soviet Union.
4. Learn the causes and effects of the Cold War.
5. Learn about the Russian Federation today.

Reading/Language Arts Objective
Read ahead to help clarify an unfamiliar word or passage.

Prepare to Read	Instructional Resources	Differentiated Instruction
Build Background Knowledge Ask students to generate a list of words that describe Catherine the Great. **Set a Purpose for Reading** Have students evaluate statements on the *Reading Readiness Guide* worksheet. **Preview Key Terms** Teach the section's Key Terms. **Target Reading Skill** Introduce the section's Target Reading Skill of **reading ahead.**	**All in One Europe and Russia Teaching Resources** L2 Reading Readiness Guide, p. 162 L2 Reread or Read Ahead, p. 169	**Spanish Reading and Vocabulary Study Guide** L1 Chapter 2, Section 4, pp. 20–21 ELL

Instruct	Instructional Resources	Differentiated Instruction
Building a Vast Empire Discuss the Russian Empire. **The Fall of the Tsars** Discuss some of the challenges Russia faced in the early 1900s. **Target Reading Skill** Review **reading ahead.** **The Rise and Fall of the Soviet Union** Ask about Lenin, Stalin, and World War II. **The Cold War** Discuss the Cold War and the collapse of the Soviet Union. **The Russian Federation** Discuss some of the challenges the Russian Federation has faced.	**All in One Europe and Russia Teaching Resources** L2 Guided Reading and Review, p. 163 L2 Reading Readiness Guide, p. 162 **Europe and Russia Transparencies** L2 Section Reading Support Transparency ER 38 **World Studies Video Program** L2 St. Petersburg and Peter the Great	**All in One Europe and Russia Teaching Resources** L3 A Letter from Napoleon's Army, pp. 188–189 AR, GT L3 Lenin's Deathbed Words, p. 190 AR, GT L3 Kampf, p. 191 AR, GT **Teacher's Edition** L3 For Advanced Readers, TE p. 65 L2 For English Language Learners, TE p. 65 L3 For Gifted and Talented, TE p. 67 L1 For Less Proficient Readers, TE pp. 67, 68 **Reading and Vocabulary Study Guide** L1 Chapter 2, Section 4, pp. 25–27 ELL, LPR, SN

Assess and Reteach	Instructional Resources	Differentiated Instruction
Assess Progress Evaluate student comprehension with the section assessment and section quiz. **Reteach** Assign the Reading and Vocabulary Study Guide to help struggling students. **Extend** Extend the lesson by assigning The Endless Steppe.	**All in One Europe and Russia Teaching Resources** L2 Section Quiz, p. 164 L3 The Endless Steppe, pp. 192–193 Rubric for Assessing a Writing Assignment, p. 201 **Reading and Vocabulary Study Guide** L1 Chapter 2, Section 4, pp. 25–27	**Spanish Support** L2 Section Quiz (Spanish), p. 19 ELL

Key
L1 Basic to Average   L3 Average to Advanced
L2 For All Students

LPR Less Proficient Readers
AR Advanced Readers
SN Special Needs Students

GT Gifted and Talented
ELL English Language Learners

Section 5 The European Union

 4 periods, 2 blocks (includes Chapter Review and Assessment and Literature)

Social Studies Objectives

1. Learn about the history of the European Union.
2. Understand the purpose of the European Union.
3. Examine the structure of the European Union.
4. Find out what the future holds for the European Union.

Reading/Language Arts Objective

Reread or read ahead to help understand words and ideas in the text.

Prepare to Read	Instructional Resources	Differentiated Instruction
Build Background Knowledge Discuss the word *union*. **Set a Purpose for Reading** Have students evaluate statements on the *Reading Readiness Guide* worksheet. **Preview Key Terms** Teach the section's Key Terms. **Target Reading Skill** Introduce the section's Target Reading Skill of **rereading or reading ahead.**	**All in One Europe and Russia Teaching Resources** **L2** Reading Readiness Guide, p. 166 **L2** Reread or Read Ahead, p. 169	**Spanish Reading and Vocabulary Study Guide** **L1** Chapter 2, Section 5, p. 22–23 ELL

Instruct	Instructional Resources	Differentiated Instruction
History of the European Union Discuss the history of the European Union. **What does the European Union Do?** Discuss goals and policies of the EU. **Structure of the European Union** Discuss the institutions responsible for making policy. **Future of the European Union** Ask questions about nations joining the European Union in the future. **Target Reading Skill** Review **rereading or reading ahead.**	**All in One Europe and Russia Teaching Resources** **L2** Guided Reading and Review, p. 167 **L2** Reading Readiness Guide, p. 166 **Europe and Russia Transparencies** **L2** Section Reading Support Transparency ER 39	**All in One Europe and Russia Teaching Resources** **L3** Whose Falkland Islands Are They? pp. 194–196 AR, GT **Teacher's Edition** **L1** For Special Needs Students, TE p. 72 **L3** For Advanced Readers, TE p. 72 **L3** For Gifted and Talented, TE p. 80 **Reading and Vocabulary Study Guide** **L1** Chapter 2, Section 5, pp. 28–30 ELL, LPR, SN **Spanish Support** **L2** Guided Reading and Review (Spanish), p. 20 ELL

Assess and Reteach	Instructional Resources	Differentiated Instruction
Assess Progress Evaluate student comprehension with the section assessment and section quiz. **Reteach** Assign the Reading and Vocabulary Study Guide to help struggling students. **Extend** Extend the lesson by assigning a map activity.	**All in One Europe and Russia Teaching Resources** **L2** Section Quiz, p. 168 **L3** Outline Maps 14, 17, and 18, pp. 179–181 Rubric for Assessing a Letter to the Editor, p. 202 **L2** Vocabulary Development, p. 199 **L2** Word Knowledge, p. 172 **L2** Rubric for Assessing a Writing Assignment, p. 201 **L2** Chapter Tests A and B, pp. 203–208 **Reading and Vocabulary Study Guide** **L1** Chapter 2, Section 5, pp. 28–30	**All in One Europe and Russia Teaching Resources** **L3** Lords and Vassals, p. 197 AR, GT Rubric for Assessing a Writing Assignment, p. 201 **Spanish Support** **L2** Section Quiz (Spanish), p. 21 ELL **L2** Chapter Summary (Spanish), p. 22 ELL **L2** Vocabulary Development (Spanish), p. 23 ELL

Key

L1 Basic to Average	**L3** Average to Advanced	LPR Less Proficient Readers	GT Gifted and Talented
L2 For All Students		AR Advanced Readers	ELL English Language Learners
		SN Special Needs Students	

Reading Background

Pre-Teaching Vocabulary

Research literature on academic vocabulary instruction indicates that effective strategies require students to go beyond simply looking up dictionary definitions or examining the context. Vocabulary learning needs to be based on the learner's dynamic engagement in constructing understanding.

If students are not retaining the meaning of the Key Terms or high-use words, use this extended vocabulary sequence to engage them in learning new words.

1. Present the word in writing and point out the part of speech.
2. Pronounce the word and then have students pronounce the word.
3. Provide a range of familiar synonyms (or "it's like" words) before offering definitions.
4. Provide an accessible definition and concrete examples, or "showing sentences."
5. Rephrase the simple definition or example sentence, asking students to complete the statement by substituting the word aloud.
6. Check for understanding by providing an application task/question requiring critical thinking.

Sample instructional sequence:

1. Our first word is *monarch*. It is a noun, a word that names a person, place, or thing.
2. Say the word *monarch* after me. (Students repeat.)
3. A *monarch* is like a *king* or *queen*.
4. The word *monarch* means *a ruler of a kingdom or empire*; A *monarch* has power over his or her people.
5. A _____ usually inherits his or her title, whereas a president is an elected official. (Students substitute the word.)
6. What are some of the differences between a monarch and a president? (Students answer the question.)

Encourage Active Participation

In this chapter, students may use an Idea Wave to share their ideas. Remind students that if their idea is closely related to another person's idea, they should acknowledge the other person's ideas when they share theirs. Below are some language strategies for active classroom participation:

> *My idea is similar to _____'s idea.*
> *As _____ already pointed out, it seems like….*
> *I don't agree with _____ because….*

World Studies Background

Michelangelo

Like Leonardo da Vinci, Michelangelo Buonarroti (1475–1564) was an important figure during the Renaissance. He worked in his native Italy as a sculptor, painter, architect, and poet. Some of his most famous works include the sculpture *David* and the paintings on the ceiling of the Sistine Chapel at the Vatican in Rome. At the rear of the chapel is *The Last Judgment*, thought by many to be Michelangelo's greatest masterpiece.

Luddites

Bands of handicraft workers known as Luddites led uprisings in the industrial areas of England during the early 1800s. These textile workers took their name from a mythical figure, King Ludd. Their riots, in which they destroyed power looms and other machines, were carried out in anger over low wages and employment issues.

A Great Debate

A famous debate about the differences in Soviet and American lifestyles took place during the Cold War. While touring a U.S. exhibit of a model home in Moscow in 1959, then Vice President Richard Nixon and Russian Premier Nikita Khrushchev began an argument over which nation had the better economic system. This informal debate over capitalism and communism became known as the "kitchen debate."

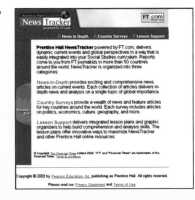

Get in-depth information on topics of global importance with **Prentice Hall Newstracker,** powered by FT.com.

 Use Web code **ldd-7200** for **Prentice Hall Newstracker.**

Guiding Questions

Remind students about the Guiding Questions at the beginning of the book.

Section 1 relates to **Guiding Question ②**
How have Europe and Russia been affected by their history? (*Ancient Greek and Roman ideas influenced many European legal systems.*)

Section 2 relates to **Guiding Question ③**
How have the people of Europe and Russia been shaped by their culture? (*Europeans were influenced by Renaissance ideas in the 1500s.*)

Section 3 relates to **Guiding Question ②**
How have Europe and Russia been affected by their history? (*The Industrial Revolution changed industry and society. During the 1900s, destructive nationalism contributed to two world wars and the deaths of millions.*)

Section 4 relates to **Guiding Question ④**
What types of government have existed in Europe and Russia? (*Tsars ruled Russia until 1917. The Communists established the Soviet Union, which broke apart in 1991. Russia became more democratic.*)

Section 5 relates to **Guiding Question ⑤**
How have Russian and European economies developed into what they are today? (*The European Union was formed to promote a strong economy among European nations.*)

⟳ Target Reading Skill

In this chapter, students will learn and apply the reading skill of clarifying meaning. Use the following worksheets to help students practice this skill:

All in One Europe and Russia Teaching Resources, *Reread or Read Ahead,* p. 169; *Paraphrase,* p. 170; *Summarize,* p. 171

Differentiated Instruction

The following Teacher's Edition strategies are suitable for students of varying abilities.

Advanced Readers, pp. 40, 58, 65, 72
English Language Learners, pp. 42, 55, 65
Gifted and Talented, pp. 40, 47, 67, 80
Less Proficient Readers, pp. 47, 67, 68
Special Needs Students, pp. 58, 61, 72

Chapter Preview

This chapter presents the history of Europe and Russia and shows how that history affects the region to this day.

Section 1
From Ancient Greece to the Middle Ages

Section 2
Renaissance and the Age of Revolution

Section 3
Industrial Revolution and Nationalism

Section 4
Imperial Russia to the Soviet Union

Section 5
The European Union

⟳ Target Reading Skill

Clarifying Meaning In this chapter you will focus on clarifying, or better understanding, the meaning of what you read.

▶ A bridge built in the 1100s still spans the Rhone River in Avignon, France.

Bibliography

For the Teacher
Carlson, Laurie. *Classical Kids: An Activity Guide to Life in Ancient Greece and Rome.* Chicago Review Press, 1998.
Cole, Alison, *The Renaissance.* Dorling Kindersley, 2000.
Fitzpatrick, Sheila. *Everyday Stalinism: Ordinary Life in Extraordinary Times: Soviet Russia in the 1930s.* Oxford University Press, 2000.

For the Student
L1 Collins, Mary. *The Industrial Revolution* (Cornerstones of Freedom Series). Children's Book Press, 2001.
L2 Herbert, Janis. *Marco Polo for Kids.* Chicago Review Press, 2001.
L3 Rogers, Stillman D. *Russia* (Enchantment of the World Series). Children's Book Press, 2002.

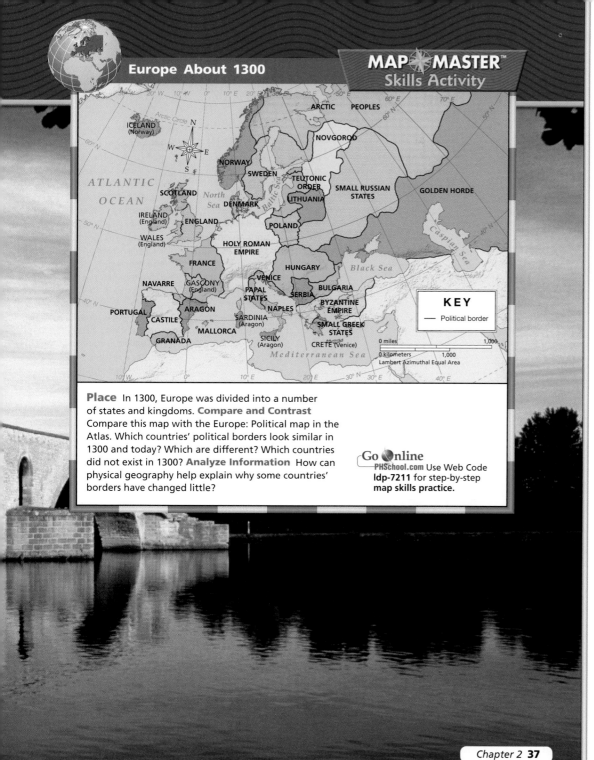

MAP MASTER™
Skills Activity

ARCTIC PEOPLES

ICELAND
(Norway)

NOVGOROD

NORWAY

SWEDEN

TEUTONIC
ORDER

SMALL RUSSIAN
STATES

GOLDEN HORDE

ATLANTIC
OCEAN

SCOTLAND

North
Sea DENMARK

LITHUANIA

IRELAND
(England) ENGLAND

POLAND

WALES
(England)

HOLY ROMAN
EMPIRE

FRANCE

HUNGARY

Black Sea

NAVARRE

GASCONY
(England)
PAPAL
STATES

VENICE

SERBIA

BULGARIA

PORTUGAL

ARAGON

NAPLES

BYZANTINE
EMPIRE

Caspian Sea

CASTILE

SARDINIA
(Aragon)

SMALL GREEK
STATES

GRANADA

MALLORCA

SICILY
(Aragon)

CRETE (Venice)

Mediterranean Sea

KEY
— Political border

0 miles   1,000
0 kilometers   1,000
Lambert Azimuthal Equal Area

Place In 1300, Europe was divided into a number of states and kingdoms. **Compare and Contrast** Compare this map with the Europe: Political map in the Atlas. Which countries' political borders look similar in 1300 and today? Which are different? Which countries did not exist in 1300? **Analyze Information** How can physical geography help explain why some countries' borders have changed little?

Go Online
PHSchool.com Use Web Code
ldp-7211 for step-by-step
map skills practice.

MAP MASTER™
Skills Activity

Have students carefully study the map on this page. Then have them create a two-column chart on a piece of paper. In the first column, students should make a list of all of the countries on the map. Then, have students study the political map of Europe in the Atlas, and identify which present-day countries correspond to the countries of Europe around 1300. Have them write these countries in the second column of their charts.

Go Online
PHSchool.com Students may practice their map skills using the interactive online version of this map.

Using the Visual L2

Reach Into Your Background Point out the photograph on pp. 36–37 and its caption. Ask students to think about how the bridge in the photograph is similar to and different from modern bridges. Use an Idea Wave (TE, p. T35) to create a list of responses.

Answers

MAP MASTER™
Skills Activity **Compare and Contrast**
Similar: Iceland, Norway, Denmark, Ireland, Portugal, Serbia, Bulgaria; Different: Sweden, Hungary, Lithuania, Poland, France; Did not exist: Finland, Belarus, Ukraine, Romania, Moldova, Macedonia, Albania, Bosnia and Herzegovina, Croatia, Slovakia, Austria, Czech Republic, Switzerland, Belgium, the Netherlands, Latvia, Estonia, Russia, United Kingdom, Germany, Turkey, Spain, Italy, Greece **Analyze Information** Physical barriers that form a border may prevent a country from changing in size.

Chapter Resources

Teaching Resources
L2 Vocabulary Development, p. 199
L2 Skills for Life, p. 174
L2 Chapter Tests A and B, pp. 203–208

Spanish Support
L2 Spanish Chapter Summary, p. 22
L2 Spanish Vocabulary Development, p. 23

Media and Technology
L1 Student Edition on Audio CD
L1 Guided Reading Audiotapes, English and Spanish
L2 Social Studies Skills Tutor CD-ROM
ExamView Test Bank CD-ROM

DISCOVERY World Studies
CHANNEL Video Program
SCHOOL

Interactive Textbook

PRENTICE HALL
TeacherEXPRESS™
Plan · Teach · Assess

Objectives

Social Studies

1. Learn how the heritage of ancient Greece influences life today.
2. Discover the glory of the ancient Roman Empire.
3. Learn about Europe in the Middle Ages.

Reading/Language Arts

Reread to look for connections among words and sentences.

Prepare to Read

Build Background Knowledge [L2]

Tell students that in this section they will learn about Europe's history, beginning with ancient Greece. Have students briefly preview the headings and visuals in this section, paying careful attention to the examples of architecture. Explain that aspects of modern architecture can be traced to ancient Greek and Roman cultures. If possible, show students a photo of the White House, and explain that its columns were inspired by Greek and Roman architecture. Ask students to think of other ancient architectural features (*arches, aqueducts*) that are still in use today. Conduct an Idea Wave (TE, p. T35) to generate ideas.

Set a Purpose for Reading [L2]

■ Preview the Objectives.

■ Read each statement in the *Reading Readiness Guide* aloud. Ask students to mark the statements true or false.

■ Have students discuss the statements in pairs or groups of four, then mark their worksheets again. Use the Numbered Heads participation strategy (TE, p. T36) to call on students to share their group's perspectives.

All in One Europe and Russia Teaching Resources, *Reading Readiness Guide*, p. 150

Vocabulary Builder

Preview Key Terms [L2]

Pronounce each Key Term, then ask students to say the word with you. Provide a simple explanation such as, "In a democracy such as the United States, citizens elect officials to represent them in the government."

From Ancient Greece to the Middle Ages

Prepare to Read

Objectives

In this section you will
1. Learn how the heritage of ancient Greece influences life today.
2. Discover the glory of the ancient Roman Empire.
3. Learn about Europe in the Middle Ages.

Taking Notes

As you read this section, look for information about ancient times and the Middle Ages. Copy the outline below and record your findings in it.

> **I. The Greek heritage**
>   **A. Democracy**
>   **B.**
> **II.**

Target Reading Skill

Reread Rereading is a strategy that can help you to understand words and ideas in the text. If you do not understand a certain passage, reread it to look for connections among the words and sentences. For example, rereading the first paragraph below can make it clear that marathons today are modeled after an event from ancient times.

Key Terms

- **Middle Ages** (MID ul AY juz) *n.* the time between the ancient and modern times, about A.D. 500–1500
- **democracy** (dih MAHK ruh see) *n.* a kind of government in which citizens govern themselves
- **city-state** (SIH tee stayt) *n.* a city with its own government that was both a city and an independent state
- **feudalism** (FYOOD ul iz um) *n.* a system in which people had obligations based on their position in society

Runners beginning the Boston Marathon

38 Europe and Russia

Every April thousands of people from around the world gather in a small Massachusetts town. At noon, they begin a marathon race that requires great strength and willpower. The race ends in the city of Boston, some 26 miles (42 kilometers) away.

The Boston Marathon was inspired by an event that is said to have happened 2,500 years ago in the ancient Greek city of Athens. In 490 B.C., the people of Athens were at war with the Persians. The Athenians defeated the Persians at the Battle of Marathon. To announce their victory, an Athenian soldier named Pheidippides (fuh DIP ih deez) ran all the way to Athens, about 25 miles (40 kilometers) away. Pheidippides shouted, "Rejoice, we conquer!" as he entered the city. Then he died of exhaustion.

The Greeks loved the story, and people all over the world still run marathons. When they do, they show how history lives on. This chapter discusses three periods in the history of Europe and Russia—ancient times, modern times, and the Middle Ages, or the time between the ancient and modern times. We will see how the past affects the present in Europe and Russia.

Target Reading Skill [L2]

Reread Point out the Target Reading Skill. Tell students that rereading can help them understand words and ideas in the text.

Model the skill by reading and rereading the second paragraph on p. 41. Tell students that rereading can help them better understand the Roman system of roads.

Give students *Reread or Read Ahead.* Have them complete the activity in groups.

All in One Europe and Russia Teaching Resources, *Reread or Read Ahead*, p. 169

The Greek Heritage

The Athenians and other ancient Greeks were Europe's first great philosophers, historians, poets, and writers. They invented new ideas about how the world worked and how people should live.

The Growth of Democracy One such idea was **democracy,** or a kind of government in which citizens, not a king or other ruler, govern themselves. In ancient times, Greece had more than a hundred **city-states,** or cities with their own governments that were both cities and independent states. The Greek city-states had several different kinds of government. Many of them were democracies.

One of the most famous democratic Greek city-states was Athens. Every citizen there voted on laws and government policies, or the methods and plans a government uses to do its work. Citizens were either elected or chosen at random for government positions.

Democracy was a fresh idea for the Greeks. However, it was not the same as the democracy we practice today. Most Greeks were not citizens. Only freeborn males whose fathers held Athenian citizenship were citizens of Athens. Women, slaves, freed slaves, non-Greeks, and people whose families came from other parts of Greece were not citizens. They could not vote. Still, the Greek idea that citizens should have a voice in their own government had a strong influence on people in later times.

The Golden Age of Athens Democracy reached its highest point in Athens from about 479 to 431 B.C., during Athens' "Golden Age." During that period, the arts, literature, and philosophy also flourished. The Greeks studied the nature of plants, animals, and the human body. In the process, they developed ways of thinking that still influence life today.

Chart Skills

Greek ideas that developed over two thousand years ago still influence societies around the world today. **Note** When were democratic ideals of government formed in Athens? **Apply Information** Which of these ideals can be seen in today's United States government?

The Legacy of the Greeks

Topic	Influence on Modern Society
Drama	Aristotle created the rules for drama in his work *The Poetics.* Today, playwrights and movie scriptwriters still use his ideas.
Architecture	Many modern building designs reflect the common Greek styles known as Ionic, Doric, and Corinthian.
Science	The ancient Greeks introduced many principles of modern medicine, physics, biology, and mathematics.
Politics	The democratic ideals of government by the people, trial by jury, and equality under the law were formed in Athens around 500 B.C.
History	Herodotus collected information from people who remembered the events of the Persian wars. This method of research set the standard for the way history is recorded today.

Vocabulary Builder

Use the information below to teach students this section's high-use words.

High-Use Word	Definition and Sample Sentence
process, p. 39	*n.* a series of actions We had to be careful to follow the steps for the chemical **process** carefully.
rely, p. 41	*v.* to depend on I **relied** on my brother to give me a ride to school.
collapse, p. 43	*n.* a breakdown The **collapse** of the economy led to the government's defeat.

Instruct

The Greek Heritage L2

Guided Instruction

- **Vocabulary Builder** Clarify the high-use word **process** before reading.

- Read The Greek Heritage with students using the Choral Reading strategy (TE, p. T34).

- Ask students **Why are the ancient Greeks considered Europe's first great philosophers, poets, and writers?** *(They did not accept old ways of thinking; they had new ideas about how people should live.)*

- Have students discuss how ancient Greek democracy differed from democracy in the United States today. *(In ancient Greece, only male citizens were allowed to vote. In the United States, all citizens 18 and older have the right to vote.)*

- Draw students' attention to the chart of Greek achievements. Ask **What are the fields in which Greece made important contributions?** *(drama, architecture, science, politics, history)*

Answers

Chart Skills Note around 500 B.C.
Apply Information government by the people, trial by jury, and equality under the law

Guided Instruction (continued)

■ Ask students **How did Alexander the Great spread Greek ideas?** *(He established Greek cities, the Greek language, and Greek ideas throughout the empire he built.)*

Independent Practice

Ask students to create the Taking Notes outline on a blank piece of paper. Then have students begin to fill it in using information from the text they have read so far. Briefly model how to organize information on an outline.

Monitor Progress

As students work on their outlines, circulate around the room and make sure individuals are choosing the correct information. Provide assistance as needed.

Answers

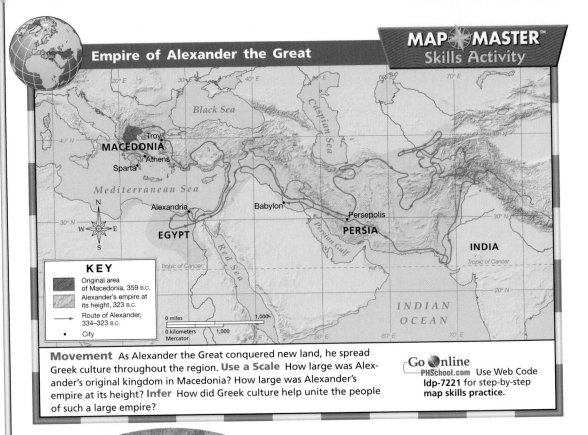

Empire of Alexander the Great

MAP MASTER™ Skills Activity

KEY

- Original area of Macedonia, 359 B.C.
- Alexander's empire at its height, 323 B.C.
- → Route of Alexander, 334–323 B.C.
- • City

0 miles 1,000
0 kilometers 1,000
Mercator

Movement As Alexander the Great conquered new land, he spread Greek culture throughout the region. **Use a Scale** How large was Alexander's original kingdom in Macedonia? How large was Alexander's empire at its height? **Infer** How did Greek culture help unite the people of such a large empire?

Go Online PHSchool.com Use Web Code ldp-7221 for step-by-step map skills practice.

MAP MASTER Skills Activity **Use a Scale** His original kingdom was about 200 miles (520 kilometers) wide and 200 miles (520 kilometers) long. His empire at its height stretched over about 3,000 miles (7,800 kilometers) from east to west and was almost 1,000 miles (2,600 kilometers) long from north to south in some places. **Infer** It provided a common way of life for all of the people in the empire.

Go Online PHSchool.com Students may practice their map skills using the interactive online version of this map.

✓ **Reading Check** a collection of lands ruled by a single government

The Spread of Greek Ideas A young man named Alexander, later called Alexander the Great, helped spread the ideas of the Greeks. At age 20, he became king of Macedonia (mas uh DOH nee uh) in northern Greece. But he was not satisfied with his small kingdom. In 334 B.C., Alexander set out to conquer the world. Within only ten years, he had conquered an empire almost as great in size as the United States is today. An empire is a collection of lands ruled by a single government. The map above shows Alexander's travels and the lands he conquered.

In all his new lands, Alexander established Greek cities, the Greek language, and Greek ideas. At the time of his death in 323 B.C., Greek culture linked the entire Mediterranean world. The people who next ruled the region, the Romans, also borrowed much from the Greeks.

This ancient Italian mosaic shows Alexander the Great in battle.

✓ **Reading Check** What is an empire?

40 Europe and Russia

Differentiated Instruction

For Advanced Readers [L3]

Have students read about Alexander the Great's father, King Philip, in the primary source *A Spartan Reply*. Have students follow up by writing sentences using the words "laconic" and "Spartan." Ask students to explain the origins of these words to the class.

All in One **Europe and Russia Teaching Resources,** *A Spartan Reply*, p. 182

For Gifted and Talented [L3]

Ask students to read the poem *Storm in the State* by Alcaéus of Mytiléne. After reading the poem and answering the questions, suggest that students do research to learn about the kinds of political struggles with which an ancient Greek nobleman might be involved.

All in One **Europe and Russia Teaching Resources,** *Storm in the State*, p. 183

The Glory of Ancient Rome

Have you ever heard someone say, "All roads lead to Rome" or "Rome was not built in a day"? These expressions refer to the Roman Empire. At its peak, the Roman Empire covered a huge area, and Romans built magnificent cities and structures.

About 50,000 miles (80,500 kilometers) of hard-surfaced roads linked the cities of the Roman Empire. The Roman system of roads was one of the most outstanding transportation networks ever built. Constructed more than 2,000 years ago, many of these roads are still in use today.

The Romans also built aqueducts, or canals that carried water to the cities from distant sources. Like Roman roads, some of these aqueducts are still in use.

The Pax Romana The Romans began building their empire soon after the death of Alexander the Great. The first emperor of Rome, Augustus, took control in 27 B.C. This began the *Pax Romana* (paks roh MAH nah), which means "Roman peace." It lasted for about 200 years. During the Pax Romana, Rome was the most powerful state in Europe and in the Mediterranean. With Rome in control, these regions remained stable.

Roman Law One of Rome's greatest gifts to the world was a system of written laws. Roman lawmakers were careful and organized. They did not rely on word of mouth to pass their laws from one generation to the next. Instead, they wrote the laws down. When a judge made a decision, he based it on written law. His decision was also put in writing to guide other judges. After a while, the law became so complex that it was difficult to learn. Various groups were appointed to gather the laws together into an organized system. Today, the legal system of almost every European country reflects the organization of ancient Roman law.

Roman laws protected all citizens. At first, citizens included only free people who lived in Rome. In time, the term came to include people all over the empire. Roman laws thus protected the rights of all citizens, not just the powerful and wealthy. Modern laws and government are based on this idea.

Roman Art and Architecture
The Colosseum (above) held as many as 50,000 people for public events. The sculpture below is of Rome's first emperor, Augustus. **Conclude** *What does the art a society produces tell you about its culture and wealth?*

Guided Instruction

- **Vocabulary Builder** Clarify the high-use word **rely** before reading.

- Have students read The Glory of Ancient Rome to learn more about the Roman Empire. As students read, circulate and make sure individuals can answer the Reading Check question.

- Ask **Why would a good network of roads be important in building an empire?** *(Possible answer: it would enable people to travel, ideas and information to be communicated, and allow the government in Rome to control a large territory.)*

- Point out the photo of the Colosseum in the Student Edition and tell students that like many ancient Roman roads and aqueducts, the Colosseum is still standing today. Ask **What does this tell you about the Roman Empire?** *(Possible answer: Their civilization was technically advanced enough to create buildings that have lasted thousands of years.)*

- Have students discuss why the Roman system of written laws was so important. *(Roman laws were organized and documented, and almost every modern European country is influenced by them.)*

Answer

Conclude Art can show what is important to a society. For example, the Colosseum reflects the fact that the Romans enjoyed attending public events. Generally, a wealthy society has more elaborate and expensive art than a less wealthy society.

Skills Mini Lesson

Analyze Images

1. Tell students that by analyzing an image, they can learn more about a topic. They should look for clues to help them by asking themselves: Who or what is this image? When and where did the scene take place? What feeling does the image suggest? Who created the image and why?

2. Have students analyze the statue of Augustus on this page. Suggest that they make a chart listing the type of details they notice (clothing, posture, etc.) and the conclusions they suggest.

3. Have students apply the skill by analyzing the image of Jesus on p. 42.

Guided Instruction (continued)

■ Ask students **How did Emperor Constantine help spread Christianity?** *(He encourage the spread of Christianity and it became the official religion of the Roman Empire.)*

■ Ask students to list some reasons for the fall of the Roman Empire. *(centuries of warfare; higher taxes to pay for warfare weakened the economy; the empire grew too large and was divided, after which the western Roman Empire was attacked and collapsed in A.D. 476)*

Independent Practice

Have students add information about the Roman Empire to their outlines. Suggest that students use the different headings in the text to help them organize information.

Monitor Progress

As students continue to fill in the graphic organizer, circulate and make sure individuals are choosing the correct details. Provide assistance as needed.

⟳ Target Reading Skill ▨

Reread As a follow up, have students perform the Target Reading Skill activity in the Student Edition. *(Students should reread the paragraphs to understand that a spiritual leader is a person who serves as a leader for people who observe a certain religion.)*

Answer

Analyze Information They might have wanted to keep their faith secret from groups that might persecute them, and using symbols that only early Christians understood was one way to do this.

Christian Art
This mosaic of Jesus, at the right, decorates the dome of a monastery in Daphni, Greece. Symbols of Christianity—a cross and a fish—are shown below. Early Christians used the symbol of the fish because each letter in the Greek word for fish, *ichthys*, stood for a Christian phrase. **Analyze Information** *Why might early Christians have depended on symbols to express their faith, rather than doing so openly?*

⟳ **Reread**
Target Skill Reread the paragraphs under Beginnings of Christianity to understand the phrase "spiritual leader."

Beginnings of Christianity Roman emperors allowed a certain amount of religious freedom within the empire. Jews were allowed to practice their religion as long as they obeyed Roman law. For centuries, the Jewish people had believed that God would send them a messiah, or a savior, who would free them from outside rule. Many Jews were content to cooperate with the Romans, but others began resisting Roman rule. In present-day Israel, the Romans crushed their attempts to revolt.

In about A.D. 30 a spiritual leader, named Jesus of Nazareth, traveled and preached throughout the region. His followers believed that God was acting through him. They called him Jesus Christ. *Christ* meant "someone anointed, or a savior sent by God." After the Romans put Jesus to death for troublemaking, his followers began spreading his teachings. They eventually became known as Christians. At first, they were treated poorly by Roman emperors.

After three centuries, Christianity had become so strong that a Roman emperor, Constantine, became a Christian. He encouraged the spread of Christianity. It became the official religion of the Roman Empire. Many people who had suffered under Roman rule turned to the church for comfort at this time.

The Decline of Rome Over time, it grew more difficult to govern the huge Roman empire. Germanic invaders outside the empire grew strong and broke through Roman lines of defense. Sometimes they terrorized and looted Rome itself.

42 Europe and Russia

Differentiated Instruction

For English Language Learners ▨
Suggest that students use sticky notes to mark words with which they are unfamiliar. Students can go back to these words and use a dictionary to find the meaning. For a concrete noun such as *canal,* have students draw pictures based on their definition.

To fight the invaders, the empire needed more and more soldiers. The government raised taxes to pay for the warfare. This hurt the empire's economy. The empire had grown too large for one person to govern, so it was divided into two empires, one in the eastern Mediterranean and one in the west. The eastern empire remained strong. But the western one continued to weaken. In the 450s A.D., invaders attacked Rome itself. Finally in 476 A.D., invaders overthrew the Roman emperor, and the western Roman Empire collapsed.

✓ **Reading Check** What was the Pax Romana?

Europe in the Middle Ages

The collapse of the Roman Empire in western Europe led to a time of uncertainty and confusion. The legal system of the Roman Empire no longer protected people. The invading peoples did gradually settle down and establish kingdoms. But no kingdom was able to provide the unity and security that the Roman Empire had provided. Europe entered a long period of turmoil and warfare. Government, law, and trade broke down.

In such a time of chaos, people needed order and security. Eventually, a new structure of European society arose. It was based on a new political system and the Roman Catholic Church. The Roman Catholic Church was the name for the Christian church in the former western Roman Empire.

Feudalism To bring about order, people in western Europe needed a way to organize their society. The political system that developed is called **feudalism,** or a system in which land was owned by kinds of lords, but held by vassals in return for their loyalty. In each country, the king held the highest position. His greatest obligation was to provide security for his kingdom, which meant that he needed soldiers to build an army. Nobles provided the king with knights and foot soldiers. In exchange for knights and soldiers—as well as for the nobles' loyalty—the king, also called a lord, gave land to the nobles, also called vassals.

The noble landholders needed people to work their estates, or manors. They gave peasants the right to farm their land in exchange for the larger portion of the crops and any other income from the land. In exchange, they maintained order, enforced laws, and protected the peasants. This economic system is called manorialism. It provided a basis for the feudal political system.

Details from books and calendars dating from the 1400s show farming scenes at medieval manors.

Background: Biography

Julius Caesar Before the days of the Roman Empire, one of Rome's leaders was Julius Caesar. Born in about 100 B.C., Julius Caesar was a natural leader. He was known for his military strategies and led Roman armies to victory over Gaul (parts of today's France, Belgium, and Italy). Many in Rome thought Caesar had too much power. When he refused to give up that power, a civil war began. Caesar's army won, and he became dictator in 49 B.C. He was assassinated five years later, in 44 B.C. The continuing civil strife after his death finally led to new leadership and to the beginnings of the Roman Empire.

Guided Instruction

- **Vocabulary Builder** Clarify the high-use word **collapse** before reading.

- Have students read Europe in the Middle Ages.

- Discuss how the fall of the Roman Empire affected life in western Europe. Ask students **What were some of the problems that the collapse of Rome created?** *(Roman laws no longer protected people, and kingdoms established by invading peoples could not provide unity and security. Government and trade broke down. It was a time of turmoil and warfare.)*

- Have students explain the role of kings, nobles, and peasants in the feudal political system. *(The king held the highest position and kept the kingdom secure. Nobles provided the king with knights and soldiers and in return were provided with land. Noble landholders gave peasants the right to farm their land in exchange for a portion of the crop.)*

- Ask **What role did Christianity play in the Middle Ages?** *(It offered people a sense of community and security in a time of hardship.)*

- Ask **How had Europe changed by the 1400s?** *(Trade increased, and towns grew into cities.)*

Independent Practice

Have students complete their graphic organizers with information about Europe in the Middle Ages.

Monitor Progress

Show *Section Reading Support Transparency ER 35* and ask students to check their graphic organizers individually. Go over key concepts and clarify key vocabulary as needed.

  Europe and Russia Transparencies, *Section Reading Support Transparency ER 35*

Tell students to fill in the last column of their *Reading Readiness Guides*. Probe for what they learned that confirms or invalidates each statement.

  Europe and Russia Teaching Resources, *Reading Readiness Guide,* p. 150

Answer

✓ **Reading Check** the Roman peace that lasted for 200 years

Assess and Reteach

Assess Progress `L2`

Have students complete the Section Assessment. Administer the *Section Quiz*.

📄 **One** **Europe and Russia Teaching Resources,** *Section Quiz*, p. 152

Reteach `L1`

If students need more instruction, have them read this section in the Reading and Vocabulary Study Guide.

📖 Chapter 2, Section 1, **Europe and Russia Reading and Vocabulary Study Guide,** pp. 16–18

Extend `L3`

Have students work in pairs to complete the *Small Group Activity: Castle Mural*. Ask students to discuss their research before they begin work on their murals. Follow up with a discussion about the functions of castles during the Middle Ages.

📄 **One** **Europe and Russia Teaching Resources,** *Small Group Activity: Castle Mural,* pp. 175–178

Answers

Analyze Images large, elaborate stained glass windows and carved statues

✓ **Reading Check** Unlike slaves, serfs could not be sold, although they were bound to the land and could not leave without their lord's permission.

Section 1 Assessment

Key Terms
Students' sentences should reflect knowledge of each Key Term.

🔁 Target Reading Skill
Answers will vary, but students should identify a word or idea they were able to clarify by rereading.

Comprehension and Critical Thinking
1. (a) democracy **(b)** In ancient Athens, only freeborn males whose fathers were citizens could participate in the government. In the United States, all citizens can participate in government.

2. (a) Many modern legal systems are based on the Romans' system of written laws and their idea that laws should protect the rights of all citizens. **(b)** Invaders grew strong and broke through Roman defenses; the govern-

Cathedral of Notre Dame
The Notre Dame cathedral in Paris, France, dates from the 1100s. It is one of the largest and most spectacular in the world. A carved figure from the roof of the cathedral is shown at the right. **Analyze Images** *What features from the cathedral do you think were meant to inspire awe in the people who worshipped there?*

The peasants who worked the land were called serfs. Serfs were not free people. They were bound to the land and could not leave without their lord's permission. But serfs were not slaves. They could not be sold away from the land.

Christianity Religious faith helped give people a sense of security and community during the Middle Ages. Most people's lives centered on the Roman Catholic Church. Religious ceremonies marked the major events in the calendar, as well as important events in the lives of individual members.

Wealthy nobles and kings donated large amounts of money for the construction of grand cathedrals, churches, and monasteries. In a world where most people's lives were marked by hardship and uncertainty, these grand buildings were awe-inspiring. They soared higher than any other buildings nearby. Their brilliant stained-glass windows taught religious stories to peasants who were unable to read.

Europe Begins to Change As the centuries passed, life in Europe changed. Trade increased. Towns offered excitement and opportunity to the merchants and other tradespeople who lived there. Towns grew into cities. By the A.D. 1400s, a new way of life centered around cities had begun to develop in Europe.

✓ **Reading Check** **How did serfs differ from slaves?**

 Section 1 Assessment

Key Terms
Review the key terms at the beginning of this section. Use each term in a sentence that explains its meaning.

 Target Reading Skill
What word or idea did you clarify by rereading certain passages?

Comprehension and Critical Thinking
1. (a) Recall What kind of government did ancient Athens have?

(b) Contrast How was the government of ancient Athens different from today's United States government?
2. (a) List What were the most important lasting ideas of the ancient Romans?
(b) Sequence Explain how the Roman Empire declined.
3. (a) Name Which institutions brought order and security to people in the Middle Ages?
(b) Summarize How did the feudal system work?
(c) Draw Conclusions Who benefited the most from feudalism? Explain.

Writing Activity
Suppose you are a Roman governor in Britain, far from your home and family in Rome. Write a journal entry describing the things you miss about Rome.

> **Writing Tip** Remember to write your description in the first person, using the pronouns *I* or *we*. Use vivid words to describe Rome. You might write about things such as Rome's weather, art, and architecture.

---

ment raised taxes to pay for the warfare, which hurt the economy; the empire was divided, and eventually the western Roman empire collapsed and was overrun by invaders.

3. (a) feudalism and the Roman Catholic Church **(b)** The king held the highest position and provided security for his kingdom. The nobles provided the king with knights and soldiers in exchange for land. The noble landholders allowed peasants to farm land in exchange for some of the crops.

(c) Possible answer: The king and nobles benefited from feudalism more than peasants because they held more power and were free.

Writing Activity
Use the *Rubric for Assessing a Journal Entry* to evaluate students' journal entries.

📄 **One** **Europe and Russia Teaching Resources,** *Rubric for Assessing a Journal Entry,* p. 200

Renaissance and the Age of Revolution

Prepare to Read

Objectives
In this section you will
1. Discover what the Renaissance was like at its peak.
2. Examine the effects of increased trade and stronger rulers in the Renaissance.
3. Learn about revolutions in government and science in the 1600s and 1700s.

Taking Notes
As you read this section, look for details about the Renaissance and the Age of Revolution. Copy the chart below and record your findings in it.

Target Reading Skill
Paraphrase When you pharaphrase, you restate what you have read in your own words. You could paraphrase the first two paragraphs of this section this way: "Marco Polo recorded his world travels in a book that influenced Christopher Columbus." As you read, paraphrase the information following each red or blue heading.

Key Terms
- **Renaissance** (REN uh sahns) *n.* a period of European history that included the rebirth of interest in learning and art
- **monarch** (MAHN urk) *n.* the ruler of a kingdom or empire, such as a king or a queen
- **revolution** (rev uh LOO shun) *n.* a far-reaching change
- **colony** (KAHL uh nee) *n.* a territory ruled by another nation

In about A.D. 1324 an elderly explorer named Marco Polo said before he died, "I have only told the half of what I saw!" Marco Polo indeed had an interesting life. For a time, he was a messenger of the great Mongol (MAHN gul) emperor Kublai Khan (KOO bly kahn), ruler of China. Polo also traveled across burning deserts and sailed south of the Equator. He visited the Spice Islands, which were the sources of the spices cinnamon, nutmeg, and cloves that Europeans valued. He earned great riches, only to be robbed on his way home to Italy.

These stories were published in a book we know today as *The Travels of Marco Polo.* Two hundred years later, Marco Polo's book inspired Christopher Columbus, another explorer. When Columbus sailed west from Europe, he was searching for a new route to the rich lands Marco Polo had described: China, Japan, and India.

Marco Polo and Kublai Khan

Chapter 2 Section 2 **45**

Target Reading Skill L2

Paraphrase Point out the Target Reading Skill. Tell students that paraphrasing, or restating what they have read in their own words, will help them better understand what they have read.

Model paraphrasing by restating the information in the first paragraph under the heading Printing Spreads the Renaissance on p. 47. (*The printing press, invented in Germany around 1450, encouraged the spread of the ideas during the Renaissance. Instead of being copied by hand, books could now be made quickly on a printing press.*)

Give students *Paraphrase.* Have them complete the activity in groups.

All in One Europe and Russia Teaching Resources, *Paraphrase,* p. 170

Objectives
Social Studies
1. Discover what the Renaissance was like at its peak.
2. Examine the effects of increased trade and stronger rulers in the Renaissance.
3. Learn about revolutions in government and science in the 1600s and 1700s.

Reading/Language Arts
Paraphrase to restate what you have read in your own words.

Prepare to Read

Build Background Knowledge L2
Tell students that in this section they will read about the Renaissance and important inventions of the Renaissance, such as the printing press. Ask students to suppose that the printing press had never been invented, and books were very difficult to obtain. How would this affect their lives? For example, would this affect their knowledge about places far away from where they live? Use the Think-Write-Pair-Share participation strategy (TE, p. T36) to encourage class discussion.

Set a Purpose for Reading L2
- Preview the Objectives.

- Form students into pairs or groups of four. Distribute the *Reading Readiness Guide.* Ask students to fill in the first two columns of the chart. Use the Numbered Heads participation strategy (TE, p. T36) to call on students to share one piece of information they already know and one piece of information they want to know.

All in One Europe and Russia Teaching Resources, *Reading Readiness Guide,* p. 154

Vocabulary Builder
Preview Key Terms L2
Pronounce each Key Term, then ask students to say the word with you. Provide a simple explanation such as, "Queen Elizabeth II is the monarch of the United Kingdom today."

Glories of the Renaissance

L2

Guided Instruction

- **Vocabulary Builder** Clarify the high-use word **focus** before reading.

- Have students read Glories of the Renaissance, using the Paragraph Shrinking strategy (TE, p. T34).

- Ask **How did cultural life change during the Renaissance?** (*There was a renewed interest in learning and the arts, especially poetry, plays, architecture, sculpture, and painting.*)

- Explain to students that humanism is both the revival of the study of Greek and Roman ideas, and a theory that focuses on human dignity and values. Then ask **How did humanism affect the way people thought about life and death?** (*They began thinking about improving the world they lived in rather than hoping for a better life after death.*)

- Ask students **Who was Michelangelo?** (*an Italian painter, poet, architect, and sculptor*) **How did his statues reflect the ideas of humanism?** (*His statues were lifelike and incredibly realistic, rather than being stiff symbols.*)

Answer

Compare and Contrast Alike—both have pointed spires extending upward; Different—Notre Dame has stained glass windows and a pointed roof, whereas St. Peter's has no stained glass and a domed roof.

Works of Michelangelo
Michelangelo used themes from the Bible in many of his art works. Above is his sculpture of Moses. As an architect, Michelangelo worked on the dome of St. Peter's, the church of the Pope, in Rome. **Compare and Contrast** *Compare the photo of St. Peter's with that of Notre Dame on page 44. How are they alike? How are they different?*

46 Europe and Russia

Glories of the Renaissance

Columbus's search for a new route to the riches of the East was only one example of the movement sweeping Europe. The changes began in Italy in the 1300s and spread over the continent. Traders bought and sold goods across the region. The rich grew even richer. They had the time to enjoy art and learning—and the money to support artists and scholars. This period is called the **Renaissance** (REN uh sahns), or the rebirth of interest in learning and art. The Renaissance reached its peak in the 1500s.

Looking to the Past In trying to understand the world around them, Renaissance thinkers re-examined, or looked at once again, the ideas of Greek and Roman thinkers. People learned again about the ancient world's great poetry, plays, ideas, buildings, and sculpture. What they learned changed them. Writers began writing fresh, powerful poetry. The wealthy built glorious new buildings and filled them with breathtaking paintings.

Humanism: A New View Recall that during the Middle Ages much of Europe was in chaos, and religion was a way to bring order to people's lives. Renaissance thinkers began to focus on improving this world rather than hoping for a better life after death. This new approach to knowledge was called humanism (HYOO muh niz um). Humanistic thinkers emphasized the importance of human nature and the abilities of human beings to change the world.

Humanism affected every part of Renaissance life. For example, in the early Middle Ages, statues had been carved as stiff symbols. In contrast, during the Renaissance period artists carved lifelike statues.

An Important Renaissance Artist The Italian Michelangelo (my kul AN juh loh) was one such artist. Michelangelo was an accomplished painter, poet, architect, and sculptor. His lifelike statues were remarkably realistic and detailed. In some, you can see veins bulging in the hands. Or the drape of a cloak across the sculpted person looks so real that it appears to be made of cloth rather than of marble. Like other Renaissance artists, Michelangelo's work gave art a new importance. During the Renaissance, the role of art changed.

Vocabulary Builder

Use the information below to teach students this section's high-use words.

High-Use Word	Definition and Sample Sentence
focus, p. 46	*v.* to concentrate Nick made sure to **focus** on the teacher during science class.
radical, p. 50	*adj.* extreme or sweeping The new chef made **radical** changes to the restaurant's menu.

Art came to be seen as an important way to understand man, God, and nature. You can read about another important Renaissance figure, Leonardo da Vinci (lee uh NAHR doh duh VIN chee) in the box below.

Printing Spreads the Renaissance An important invention encouraged the spread of the Renaissance. Around 1450, the printing press was invented in Germany. Before printed books, books were made by carefully copying them by hand—a process that took a very long time. With the printing press, books could be made quickly.

Printed books made in large quantities could reach far more people than could books copied by hand. For that reason, the spread of printing had two important effects. First, it increased literacy, or the ability of people to read and write. Second, it allowed ideas of the Renaissance, written in books, to spread to large numbers of people. To understand the difference that the printing press made, consider this example. Before the printing press, there were a few thousand hand-copied books in Europe. Within 50 years after the printing press was invented, there were about 9 million books in Europe.

✓ **Reading Check** What is literacy?

- Ask students **Where and when was the printing press invented?** *(around 1450; Germany)*

- Ask students **What two important effects did the spread of printing have on the people of Europe?** *(It increased literacy and allowed the ideas of the Renaissance to spread to large numbers of people.)*

- Draw students' attention to the graphic Leonardo da Vinci: Renaissance Man. Ask students **What makes da Vinci a Renaissance man?** *(his talents in many different fields, including art and science)*

Independent Practice
Have students create the Taking Notes graphic organizer on a blank piece of paper. Ask them to begin filling in causes and effects of the Renaissance. Briefly model how to choose details.

Monitor Progress
Circulate as students work on their charts and make sure individuals are choosing the correct information. Provide assistance as needed.

Leonardo da Vinci: Renaissance Man

◄ Painting
Leonardo's *Mona Lisa* (1503–1506) is one of the most famous paintings in the world. The lady is believed to have been a merchant's wife. The style of her portrait and the misty background behind her continue to influence artists today.

Inventions ►
Leonardo built machines of all kinds, but was especially interested in the possibility of human flight. He studied birds and drew imaginary flying machines. This helicopter-like machine, designed in 1487, was inspired by a child's toy.

Science ►
Leonardo studied the anatomy of the living and the dead to learn how the human body works. He often referred to his studies, like this one done in 1510, to make his paintings more realistic.

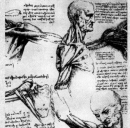

Mirror Writing ►
Leonardo used "mirror writing"—writing from right to left—in his journals. No one is sure why, but some believe that because he was left-handed, he found it easier to write from right to left. This signature says "Io, Lionardo" or "I, Leonardo."

Chapter 2 Section 2 **47**

Differentiated Instruction

For Less Proficient Readers **L1**
Remind students that it is useful to read the captions that appear with photographs or other visual material. Have students choose two captions in this section. Within each caption, have them find one noun that names the topic of the illustration and one verb that provides more information. Then ask students to describe each object without referring to the caption.

For Gifted and Talented **L3**
Have students learn more about Leonardo da Vinci by reading and completing the *Enrichment* activity. Students may work in pairs to complete the activity.

All in One Europe and Russia Teaching Resources, *Enrichment,* p. 173

More Trade, Stronger Rulers L2

Guided Instruction

- Read More Trade, Stronger Rulers with students. As students read, circulate and make sure individuals can answer the Reading Check question.

- Ask **Why did traders begin to travel outside of Europe?** (*exploration, trade of gold, silver, ivory, slaves, and spices*)

- Ask **Which European countries were active in overseas trade and settlement?** (*Portugal, Spain, France, England, and the Netherlands*)

- Ask **How did the wealth from trade affect feudalism?** (*Traders and merchants formed a middle class between the nobles and the peasants. The taxes they paid made monarchs even richer and less dependent on feudal lords. Feudalism declined and kings gained power.*)

⟳ Target Reading Skill L2

Paraphrase As a follow up, ask students to complete the Target Reading Skill activity in the Student Edition. (*Europeans searched for wealth in the Americas, and brought back precious metals and trade goods to Europe. Most of the wealth went to European monarchs, while some went to traders and merchants who formed a new middle class. Taxes on these goods paid by merchants and traders made monarchs wealthier and ultimately led to the decline of feudalism.*)

Answers

Diagram Skills Identify dishes of various metals **Analyze Information** Possible answer: monarchs, traders, and other merchants probably bought items from merchants such as this one; they had the most wealth to purchase such goods.

■ **Diagram Skills**

By the mid-1400s, European merchants like the one shown here sold a wide variety of goods, some from as far away as China. **Identify** What items in the diagram were made in Germany? **Analyze Information** What kinds of people most likely bought things from merchants such as this one? Why do you think so?

Woolen cloth came from the British Isles, while other kinds of cloth were made in France.

Dishes of various metals were made in present-day Germany.

Leather goods, such as shoes, came from towns in Spain.

More Trade, Stronger Rulers

During the Renaissance, traders began to travel more often outside of Europe. In the 1400s, Portuguese explorers traveled along the western coast of Africa. There they traded in gold, ivory, and slaves. This trade was very profitable. Some Portuguese traders traveled as far east as the Indian Ocean.

Then in 1492, a discovery brought even more possibilities for wealth. While searching for a shortcut to the Indian Ocean spice trade, Christopher Columbus landed in the Americas. He claimed the lands for Spain. Other Spanish explorers soon followed.

While Portugal grew rich from spices, Spain grew wealthy from American gold and silver. Other European countries grew envious. By the 1600s, France, England, and the Netherlands took a growing share of the riches to be gained from overseas trade and settlement.

 Paraphrase Paraphrase the paragraph under the blue heading The Effects of Trade.

The Effects of Trade Europeans raced to the Americas in search of wealth. Precious metals, such as gold and silver, and trade goods, such as fur and tobacco, poured into Europe. Much of the wealth went to European **monarchs** (MAHN urks), or rulers such as kings and queens. Some of it went to traders and merchants. These people formed a new social class. They became the middle class, the class between the privileged nobles and the lowly peasants or farmers. The taxes paid by prosperous merchants and traders made monarchs even wealthier. Soon, kings no longer needed the support of feudal lords. Feudalism declined, local lords grew weaker, and kings gained power.

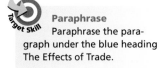 **Skills Mini Lesson**

Identifying Cause and Effect

1. Explain that a cause is an event or condition that makes something else, an effect, happen. Students should identify an event or condition as a starting point, look at earlier events for causes, look at later events for effects, and summarize the relationships they find.

2. Have students work in groups to identify cause and effect using The Effects of Trade on p. 48 of the Student Edition.

3. Have students identify causes and effects independently using Revolutions in Government on p. 50 of the Student Edition.

The Age of Monarchs The period in European history from the 1600s to the 1700s can be called the Age of Monarchs. During this time, many European monarchs became absolute monarchs, meaning that they exercised great power over their subjects.

One such monarch was France's King Louis (LOO ee) XIV, who ruled from 1643 to 1715. One of Europe's most powerful kings, Louis XIV ruled at a time when France was a leading world power. Like other kings of his time, Louis was an absolute monarch; that is, he exercised complete power over his subjects. As he said, "I am the state." His wishes were law, and no one dared to disagree with him. Like other European monarchs, Louis believed that his power to rule came from God. To oppose him was the same as opposing God.

Louis used his power to make people pay heavy taxes. These taxes, in part, paid for his very expensive lifestyle. But Louis also wanted to make France strong. Other rulers wanted their countries to be strong as well. Over time, these monarchs made their countries stronger and more unified. As these changes took place, people began thinking again about government. Should the monarchs have such great power? What should the role of the government be?

✓ Reading Check **What is an absolute monarch?**

A Wealthy Monarch
Louis XIV, king of France, rides a horse in this painting from the mid-1600s. He built the palace of Versailles, shown below, to be his personal residence as well as the center of France's government. **Analyze Images** *How does Versailles reflect Louis XIV's lifestyle? What does it say about his vision of government?*

Background: Daily Life

Versailles Louis XIV spent his days at Versailles, the palace where he also had his official court. This magnificent palace includes formal gardens and could accomodate up to 5,000 people. The famous Hall of Mirrors, which stretches across the west façade of the palace, was designed by French architect Jules Hardouin-Mansart. After the French Revolution, Versailles was never again used as a royal residence. However, several important treaties were signed there, including the 1919 Treaty of Versailles at the conclusion of World War I.

Read the **Citizen Heroes** on this page. Ask students **Why is Lavoisier considered one of the founders of modern chemistry?** *(Because, among many other achievements, he was the first scientist to recognize oxygen as an element and give it a name.)*

Revolutions in Government L2

Guided Instruction

- **Vocabulary Builder** Clarify the high-use word **radical** before reading.

- Read Revolutions in Government aloud.

- Ask students **Why are the 1600s and 1700s often called the Age of Revolution?** *(Because many significant revolutions, or far-reaching changes, occurred during this time.)*

- Discuss how revolutions can change governments. Ask **How did revolutionary ideas about government in Great Britain affect the American colonists?** *(The idea that people should have a say in government spread to the colonists, who rebelled against the British king because they felt the laws were unfair. This led to the independence of the United States.)*

- Ask **What was the immediate result of the French Revolution?** *(It created chaos in France.)* **What was a long-term result?** *(Ideas born in the French Revolution influenced Europe long afterwards.)*

Independent Practice

Instruct students to continue filling in their graphic organizers.

Monitor Progress

Circulate to make sure individuals are choosing appropriate information for their charts.

Answer

✓ Reading Check The English removed King Charles from the throne for claiming too much power, causing a revolutionary change in England's government; the American Revolution and the French Revolution brought political change to those nations.

Chemistry and Revolution
Antoine Laurent Lavoisier (1743–1794) is considered one of the founders of modern chemistry. He was the first scientist to recognize oxygen as an element, and he gave it its name. He was also an important public servant. He built workhouses, savings banks, and canals to improve the lives of people in his district.

During the French Revolution, people turned against Lavoisier and other people who were wealthy or had been part of the government. In 1793, Lavoisier was arrested and given an unfair trial. On May 8, 1794, he and 28 others were executed. Lavoisier is shown in this 1788 painting by Jacques-Louis David with his wife Marie-Anne, who helped her husband in his lab.

Revolutions in Government

The 1600s and 1700s are often called the Age of Revolution. A **revolution** is a far-reaching change. European thought, beliefs, and ways of life all changed. This period was the beginning of the modern age of science and democracy that we know today.

New Ideas in Government One sign of revolutionary change in Europe was that people began questioning their governments. People began to believe that kings should not have all the power. For example, in England, King Charles I refused to share power with Parliament (PAHR luh munt), the elected legislature. Following a civil war, he was put on trial and put to death. After this period in England's history, no ruler could again claim absolute power or ignore the law.

The American Revolution The idea that people should have a say in government spread to North America, where Great Britain had several colonies. A **colony** is a territory ruled by another nation, usually one far away. In 1776, 13 of the colonies rebelled against the British king because they felt that the laws applied to them were not fair. The colonists defeated the British and formed the independent nation of the United States.

In 1789, 13 years after the Americans declared their independence, a revolution occurred in France. In order to create a democracy, the French people used extreme violence to overthrow their government. They did this in the name of freedom, equality, and brotherhood. The French Revolution created chaos in France. It also inspired new, radical theories about political and economic change. Ideas born in the French Revolution continued to influence Europeans long after the revolution ended.

✓ Reading Check **What revolutions took place during the 1600s and 1700s?**

This painting captures the scene of angry colonists pulling down a statue of British King George III after declaring independence in 1776.

Background: Links Across Place

In Defense of Revolutions In 1776, a Virginia colonist named Thomas Paine wrote a pamphlet called *Common Sense.* Paine argued that it was time the American colonies separated from Britain, and he urged the colonies to fight for independence. Paine's writings greatly influenced the American Revolution. Paine later wrote a two-part document called *The Rights of Man,* published in 1791 and 1792, that defended the French Revolution of 1789. In these documents Paine asserted that there are natural rights common to all people and only democratic governments can guarantee these rights.

Revolutions in Science

For centuries, Europeans had based their view of the world on their religious faith. Scientists had studied nature to explain how the world fit with their religious beliefs. Slowly, scientists began to change their approach. Influenced by humanism and the Renaissance, scientists began to observe nature carefully and record only what they observed. Then they based their theories on facts instead of making the facts fit their religious beliefs. This change in outlook is called the Scientific Revolution.

The Scientific Method It is difficult to pinpoint the exact beginning of the Scientific Revolution. Yet many sources agree that it started at least in part with the work of a scientist named Copernicus (koh PUR nih kus), who lived during the Middle Ages. Before Copernicus, people believed that Earth was the center of the universe. Copernicus shocked the world by suggesting that the sun was the center of the universe, and that Earth moved around the sun. Over time, he was proved to be right. His theories sparked other scientists to look at the world in different ways.

Copernicus and other scientists needed new procedures to test their ideas. These procedures make up what is called the scientific method, in which ideas are tested with experiments and observations. Scientists will accept an idea only if it has been tested repeatedly. The chart on the right shows the steps of the scientific method. Using the scientific method, scientists made dramatic advances.

Other Scientific Developments Some of the greatest advances were in the fields of chemistry and medicine. Before the 1600s, chemistry as we know it today did not exist. Instead, the main idea of chemistry was that any metal could be turned into gold. A scientist named Robert Boyle changed that. Boyle's ideas about temperatures and the behavior of gases set the stage for modern chemistry.

New ideas in medicine came about at that same time. People made efforts to learn about the human body, both inside and out. An English doctor named William Harvey discovered how blood circulates inside the body. The Dutch inventor Antonie van Leeuwenhoek (ahn TOH ne van LAY vun hook) developed techniques for making lenses for microscopes. He used his microscopes to study small lifeforms, such as insects and bacteria.

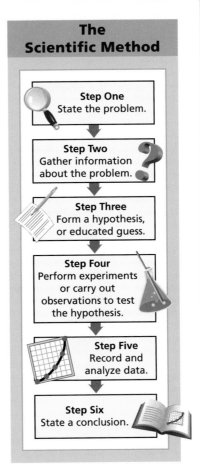

The Scientific Method

Step One
State the problem.

Step Two
Gather information about the problem.

Step Three
Form a hypothesis, or educated guess.

Step Four
Perform experiments or carry out observations to test the hypothesis.

Step Five
Record and analyze data.

Step Six
State a conclusion.

■ Diagram Skills

Though the scientific method is simple, it greatly changed the way science is done. **Explain** What is a hypothesis? How is it tested? **Apply Information** What was Copernicus's hypothesis about the universe?

Revolutions in Science L2

Guided Instruction

- Ask **What was the Scientific Revolution?** *(It was a change in thinking in which scientists formed theories based on facts observed from nature. Previously, scientists had tried to make facts fit religious beliefs.)*

- Ask students **What is the scientific method?** *(a series of procedures in which ideas are tested with experiments and observations)* **How did the use of the scientific method reflect changes in European attitudes?** *(It showed that Europeans had been influenced by humanism and the Renaissance, since they began basing their theories on facts rather than making them fit with their religious beliefs.)*

Independent Practice

Have students complete their graphic organizers with additional information from their reading.

Monitor Progress

- Show *Section Reading Support Transparency ER 36* and ask students to check their graphic organizers individually. Go over key concepts and clarify key vocabulary as needed.

   📖 **Europe and Russia Transparencies,** *Section Reading Support Transparency ER 36*

- Tell students to fill in the last column of the *Reading Readiness Guide.* Ask them to evaluate if what they learned was what they had expected to learn.

   All in One Europe and Russia Teaching Resources, *Reading Readiness Guide,* p. 154

Answers

Diagram Skills **Explain** an educated guess; by performing experiments or making observations **Apply Information** that the sun was the center of the universe, and that Earth moved around the sun

Assess and Reteach

Assess Progress `L2`

Have students complete the Section Assessment. Administer the *Section Quiz*.

All in One Europe and Russia Teaching Resources, *Section Quiz*, p. 156

Reteach `L1`

If students need more instruction, have them read this section in the Reading and Vocabulary Study Guide.

Chapter 2, Section 2, **Europe and Russia Reading and Vocabulary Study Guide**, pp. 19–21

Extend `L3`

Partner students and have them read the primary source *Testing a Theory* to learn how scientists in the seventeenth century tested their ideas. Have pairs work together to answer the questions.

All in One Europe and Russia Teaching Resources, *Testing a Theory*, p. 184

Answer

✓ Reading Check a new branch of mathematics called calculus

Section 2 Assessment

Key Terms

Students' sentences should reflect knowledge of each Key Term.

Target Reading Skill

Isaac Newton was one of the greatest scientists of the Scientific Revolution. He invented calculus to test his ideas, because existing mathematics could not explain them. With calculus and other simple laws, he was able to explain the movement of the moon and planets. His laws are still used today.

Comprehension and Critical Thinking

1. (a) a rebirth of interest in learning and art that reached its peak in the 1500s **(b)** the printing press

2. (a) a shortcut to the Indian Ocean spice trade **(b)** Their desire for wealth led them to travel outside Europe for goods that they could bring back and sell.

Isaac Newton and the title page of his book about gravity and the solar system

These and other developments led to a new way of thinking among scientists. With each new discovery, scientists began to see the universe as a giant machine. They believed this machine worked in a regular way, with set rules. They also believed that they could eventually learn everything about it.

Isaac Newton One of the greatest scientists of the Scientific Revolution was Isaac Newton. You may have heard a story about Newton, in which he saw an apple fall from a tree. He wondered if the force that pulled the apple to the ground was the same force that kept the moon in orbit around Earth.

To test this idea, Newton invented a new branch of mathematics called calculus (KAL kyoo lus). He had to invent calculus because the mathematics that existed at the time could not be used to explain his ideas. Using calculus and a few simple laws, Newton was able to demonstrate how the moon and planets move. Newton's laws and his mathematics are still used in science today.

By the end of the Age of Revolution, the nations of Europe were bustling with trade and bursting with new scientific ideas. Europe was about to begin a new kind of revolution. This time it would be an economic one.

✓ **Reading Check** What did Isaac Newton invent?

✦ Section 2 Assessment

Key Terms

Review the key terms at the beginning of this section. Use each term in a sentence that explains its meaning.

Target Reading Skill

Paraphrase the text under the blue heading Isaac Newton above.

Comprehension and Critical Thinking

1. (a) Define What was the Renaissance?
(b) Identify Causes What invention helped spread the ideas of the Renaissance?

2. (a) Recall What was Christopher Columbus searching for when he landed in the Americas?
(b) Identify Effects How did Europeans' desire for wealth lead to voyages of exploration?

3. (a) Explain Why are the 1600s and 1700s called the Age of Revolution?
(b) Summarize How did the thinking of European scientists change during this period?
(c) Make Inferences How did humanism and advances in art help bring about changes in science?

Writing Activity

Marco Polo's writings excited readers and made them want to explore the places he had visited. Think about a place that you have visited. What makes it special? Describe in detail the features that you especially liked. Write about the place in a way that would make a reader want to go there.

Go Online
PHSchool.com

For: An activity about Leonardo da Vinci
Visit: PHSchool.com
Web Code: ldd-7202

---

3. (a) European thought, beliefs, and ways of life changed dramatically during this time. **(b)** Scientists began using new methods of experimentation and observation. **(c)** Scientists changed their approaches based on the ideas of humanism and the Renaissance, observing nature carefully and recording what they observed.

Writing Activity

Use the *Rubric for Assessing a Writing Assignment* to evaluate students' work.

All in One Europe and Russia Teaching Resources, *Rubric for Assessing a Writing Assignment*, p. 201

 Typing in the Web code when prompted will bring students directly to detailed instructions for this activity.

Industrial Revolution and Nationalism

Prepare to Read

Objectives
In this section you will
1. Learn how the Industrial Revolution changed peoples' lives.
2. Examine how nationalism and war can be related.

Taking Notes
As you read this section, look for details about how life changed as a result of the Industrial Revolution. Copy the chart below and record your findings in it.

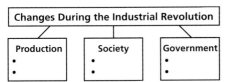

Changes During the Industrial Revolution
- Production
  - •
  - •
- Society
  - •
  - •
- Government
  - •
  - •

Target Reading Skill
Summarize You can better understand a text if you pause to restate the key points briefly in your own words. A good summary includes important events and details, notes the order in which the events occurred, and makes connections between the events or details. Because a summary leaves out less important details, it is shorter than the original text.

Key Terms
- **Industrial Revolution** (in DUS tree ul rev uh LOO shun) *n.* the life-changing period in the 1800s when products began to be made by machines in factories
- **textile** (TEKS tyl) *n.* a cloth product
- **imperialism** (im PIHR ee ul iz um) *n.* the political and economic control of one country by another
- **nationalism** (NASH uh nul iz um) *n.* pride in one's country
- **alliance** (uh LY uns) *n.* an agreement between countries to protect and defend each other

It was dawn. Thick, black smoke rose from the tall smokestack of the factory. The smoke and the roar of machines signaled that the factory workday had begun. Inside, women and children worked at rows of machines that wove cotton thread into cloth. Their work was dirty, noisy, and dangerous. The day before, a worker had severely injured his hand in a machine. Today, another worker stood in his place. Both were only 13 years old. But the machines kept going. Workers fed them thread for 12 hours every day—six days a week. Vacations did not exist, and there were few breaks.

Factories like this one could be found all across Europe in the early 1800s. They were a result of the **Industrial Revolution,** a life-changing period when goods changed from being made by hand to being made by machines in factories. Industrialization caused great suffering at first, but in time brought an easier way of life to people all over the world.

Workers grind razors at a factory in Sheffield, England, in 1866.

Target Reading Skill [L2]
Point out the Target Reading Skill. Tell students that when summarizing text, they should include only the key points in the correct order, and omit the less important details.

Model the skill by summarizing the second paragraph on this page aloud. "The Industrial Revolution occurred in Europe during the 1800s. Goods changed from being made by hand to being made by machines. Although it first caused great suffering for many, it eventually made life easier for people worldwide."

Give students *Summarize*. Have them complete the activity in their groups.

All in One Europe and Russia Teaching Resources, *Summarize,* p. 171

Objectives

Social Studies
1. Learn how the Industrial Revolution changed peoples' lives.
2. Examine how nationalism and war can be related.

Reading/Language Arts
Summarize to better understand the text.

Prepare to Read

Build Background Knowledge [L2]
Tell students that in this section they will learn about nationalism, or pride in one's country. Ask them to think of the ways that Americans show pride in their country. Have them discuss how events, such as Memorial Day or Veterans Day, and symbols, such as the American flag or the Statue of Liberty, reflect American nationalism. If you have students from different countries in your classroom, have them explain ways in which their home countries use events or symbols to reflect their citizens' nationalism, and how they are different than or similar to those in the United States. Use the Give One, Get One participation strategy (TE, p. T37) for this activity.

Set a Purpose for Reading [L2]
- Preview the Objectives.
- Read each statement in the *Reading Readiness Guide* aloud. Ask students to mark the statements true or false.
- Have students discuss the statements in pairs or groups of four, then mark their worksheets again. Use the Numbered Heads participation strategy (TE, p. T36) to call on students to share their group's perspectives.

All in One Europe and Russia Teaching Resources, *Reading Readiness Guide,* p. 158

Vocabulary Builder
Preview Key Terms
Pronounce each Key Term, then ask students to say the word with you. Provide a simple explanation such as, "Cotton is an important material in the textile industry."

Instruct

The Industrial Revolution **L2**

Guided Instruction

- **Vocabulary Builder** Clarify the high-use word **policy** before reading.

- Have students read The Industrial Revolution, using the Structured Silent Reading strategy (TE, p. T34).

- Ask **Where did the Industrial Revolution begin?** *(Great Britain)* **What did the first machines make?** *(textiles)*

- Ask **What do you think were the advantages of making goods by machine rather than by hand?** *(Possible answer: goods could be made more quickly and cheaply and in greater numbers. This enabled business owners to earn greater profits.)*

- Ask **What other improvements did the new factory system bring about?** *(new inventions in machinery, transportation, and communication, and improvements in agriculture)*

Improvements in Making Cloth
For generations, people used spinning wheels like the one above to spin cloth. After the Industrial Revolution, huge machines called "spinning mules" in factories like the one at the right produced cloth cheaper and more quickly. **Evaluate Information** *How do you think the shift from using simple tools to complex machinery affected the average worker?*

The Industrial Revolution

Until the late 1700s, nearly all goods were made by hand. People made what they needed, or bought it from a craftsperson or at a store for a high price. The Industrial Revolution—a revolution in the way goods were made and in the ways people lived and worked—changed all that.

Changes in Production The first machines of the Industrial Revolution were invented in Great Britain to speed up the weaving of **textiles,** or cloth products. Large factories housed the machines. Factory work was very different from work done by hand. For example, a person weaving cloth would first spin the thread, then dye it, and then weave it. He or she might work on every step of the finished product. In contrast, in a factory each worker tended a specific machine, which performed a specific job over and over again. The machine worked much faster than a person could. This meant that goods could be made quickly and much more cheaply than they had been by hand.

This new factory system was improved by new inventions in machinery, transportation, and communication. Other new inventions also brought about improvements in agriculture. Food could be grown in larger quantities by fewer people, and transported quickly to supply factory workers in the cities.

54 Europe and Russia

Answer

Evaluate Information Possible answer: It allowed the average worker to produce more goods in less time.

Vocabulary Builder

Use the information below to teach students this section's high-use words.

High-Use Word	Definition and Sample Sentence
policy, p. 57	*n.* a plan adopted by a government, organization, or individual The school's **policy** was to reward students who had perfect attendance.
invade, p. 58	*v.* to enter by force The war started after the country **invaded** its neighboring country.
generation, p. 58	*n.* a group of individuals born and living at the same time My parents belong to a different **generation** than my sister and I.

Changes in Society Because Great Britain's factories were so successful, business people in other countries began to build factories. By 1900, factories produced many of the goods made in the United States and Western Europe.

The Industrial Revolution changed life in almost every way. Inventions created to fuel the Industrial Revolution were soon used in everyday life. Improved transportation meant that people could travel more quickly and often more cheaply. Better communications meant that people separated by long distances could talk to one another almost instantly.

Yet not all of the effects of the Industrial Revolution were positive. For hundreds of years, families had farmed the land. Now they moved to industrial centers to work in factories. Cities grew rapidly. People lived in cramped, dirty housing. Because of unclean and crowded conditions, diseases spread rapidly.

Factory work was also difficult. Factory owners took advantage of workers. Wages were low. Factory conditions were not safe. However, workers slowly began to form labor unions and to demand better working conditions. In the early 1900s, governments began passing laws to protect workers. Over time, conditions improved and wages rose. The Industrial Revolution helped give working people a greater voice in government. Many European nations became more democratic as a result.

■ **Timeline Skills**

Important inventions of the late 1700s and early 1800s had a major impact on industry and society. **Note** When was the spinning jenny invented? **Apply Information** Which inventions helped improve the process of making textiles?

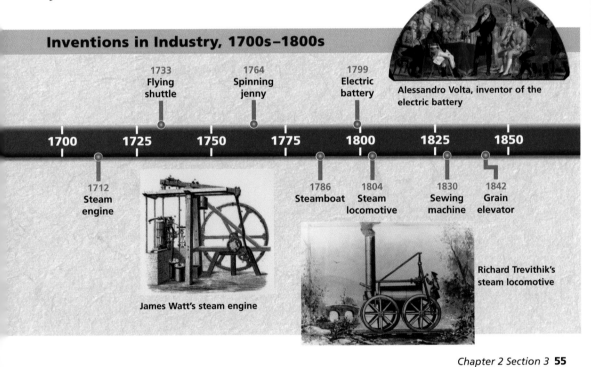

Inventions in Industry, 1700s–1800s

1733 Flying shuttle

1764 Spinning jenny

1799 Electric battery

Alessandro Volta, inventor of the electric battery

1700   1725   1750   1775   1800   1825   1850

1712 Steam engine

1786 Steamboat

1804 Steam locomotive

1830 Sewing machine

1842 Grain elevator

James Watt's steam engine

Richard Trevithik's steam locomotive

Chapter 2 Section 3 **55**

Guided Instruction (continued)

■ Have students discuss how the Industrial Revolution affected the growth of cities. *(Cities grew quickly as people moved from farms to work in new factories in the cities.)*

■ Ask **Why did factory workers form unions?** *(Wages were low; factory owners took advantage of workers; working conditions were unsafe. Unions had more influence than individuals in fighting management.)*

■ Have students discuss how the Industrial Revolution caused European nations to become more democratic. *(Making and selling goods was a big part of a country's economy, so governments had to listen to workers. As a result, working people got a greater voice in government.)*

■ Ask **How did the Industrial Revolution lead to imperialism?** *(Colonies served useful purposes for European nations. They supplied raw material for industry and buyers for European products.)*

Differentiated Instruction

For English Language Learners L1
Students may find it difficult to pronounce some of the words on these pages, such as *industrial, economy, imperialism,* and *aggressive.* Show students how to break these words down into smaller parts to help them sound out the pronunciations.

Answers
Timeline Skills Note in 1764 **Apply Information** the spinning jenny; the sewing machine

Textile Mill

Guided Instruction

Have students read the main paragraph on this page. As a class, look at the diagram and read the numbered captions. Direct students' attention to the photo and its caption. Then have students discuss their answers to the Analyzing Images question.

Independent Practice

Display *Transparency B6: Flow Chart,* and have students work in pairs to create a flow chart showing the activities in a mill. Using the diagram and numbered captions, have students identify the features of the mill and the jobs each feature performs. Remind students to put the descriptions in the correct order, to show how the features of the mill are linked.

Europe and Russia Transparencies, *Transparency B6: Flow Chart*

Textile Mill

Weaving, or making cloth from threads or yarns, is one of the oldest crafts in the world. It was also the first to take advantage of the inventions that fed the Industrial Revolution. Water, and then steam, powered the first textile factories and their machines. In England, this new form of manufacturing produced goods for trade and export, and wealth and power for the nation.

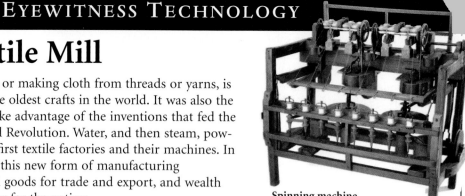

Spinning machine
A water-powered spinning machine (called a water frame) was invented by Sir Richard Arkwright.

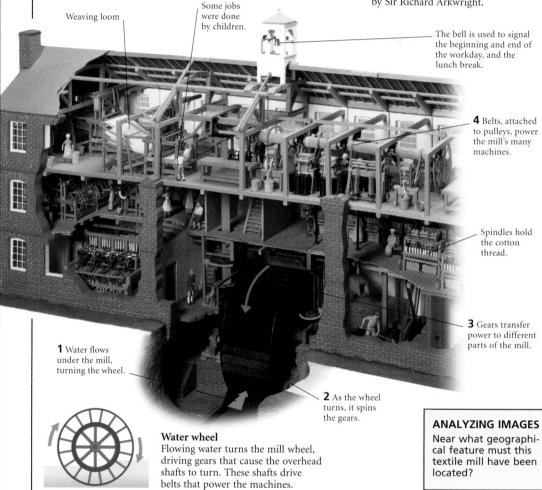

Weaving loom

Some jobs were done by children.

The bell is used to signal the beginning and end of the workday, and the lunch break.

4 Belts, attached to pulleys, power the mill's many machines.

Spindles hold the cotton thread.

3 Gears transfer power to different parts of the mill.

1 Water flows under the mill, turning the wheel.

2 As the wheel turns, it spins the gears.

Water wheel
Flowing water turns the mill wheel, driving gears that cause the overhead shafts to turn. These shafts drive belts that power the machines.

ANALYZING IMAGES
Near what geographical feature must this textile mill have been located?

56 Europe and Russia

Answer
ANALYZING IMAGES flowing water

Changes in Government At the same time, though, European governments were becoming more aggressive abroad. Beginning in the 1600s, many European nations had followed the policy of **imperialism**, or taking over other countries and turning them into colonies. Colonies provided the raw materials, such as cotton, wood, and metals, that industry needed. Colonies also supplied markets for European goods. Finally, European countries hoped to spread their influence over people in those colonies by converting them to their own religions.

The late 1800s are called the Age of Imperialism. During this time, the nations of Belgium, France, Italy, Spain, Portugal, Germany, and Great Britain colonized most of Africa. Some of these countries also took over much of Southeast Asia and many South Pacific islands. In time, struggles among the colonial powers would bring disaster to Europe.

✓ **Reading Check** Why are the late 1800s called the Age of Imperialism?

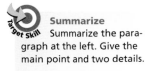
Summarize Summarize the paragraph at the left. Give the main point and two details.

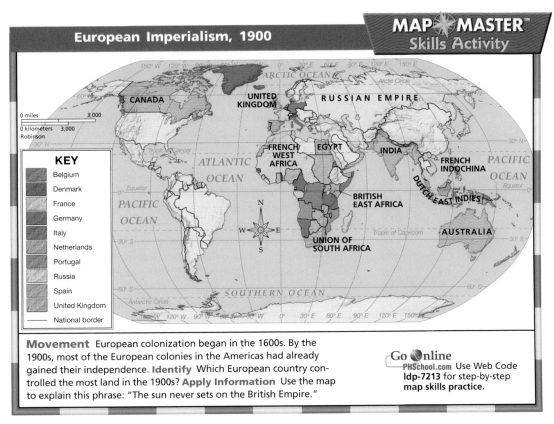

European Imperialism, 1900

MAP MASTER™ Skills Activity

KEY
- Belgium
- Denmark
- France
- Germany
- Italy
- Netherlands
- Portugal
- Russia
- Spain
- United Kingdom
- — National border

Movement European colonization began in the 1600s. By the 1900s, most of the European colonies in the Americas had already gained their independence. **Identify** Which European country controlled the most land in the 1900s? **Apply Information** Use the map to explain this phrase: "The sun never sets on the British Empire."

Go Online PHSchool.com Use Web Code **ldp-7213** for step-by-step map skills practice.

 Skills Mini Lesson

Sequencing

1. Tell students that sequencing—showing events in chronological order—helps them to keep track of historical events. To make a timeline, students should determine the topic and time span, identify the events, and place them in order.

2. Have students study the timeline on p. 55 of the Student Edition. Ask them to find one or two events to add to the timeline and indicate where on the timeline they would place these events.

3. Have students make a timeline of events leading up to World War II. Students may do library or Internet research to add to their timelines.

Summarize As a follow up, have students perform the Target Reading Skill activity in the Student Edition. *(Main Idea: European nations used the policy of imperialism to colonize other countries. Students' examples of details will vary, but should be drawn from the paragraph.)*

Independent Practice

Have students create the Taking Notes graphic organizer on a blank piece of paper and begin filling it in with details about the Industrial Revolution.

Monitor Progress

As students work on their graphic organizers, circulate and make sure individuals are choosing appropriate information. Provide assistance as needed.

Answers

✓ **Reading Check** During these years, many European nations took over much of Africa, parts of Southeast Asia, and many South Pacific Islands and turned them into colonies.

MAP MASTER Skills Activity **Identify** the United Kingdom **Apply Information** Because the United Kingdom colonized countries all over the world, there was always daylight in at least one British colony.

Go Online PHSchool.com Students may practice their map skills using the interactive online version of this map.

A Century of War and Nationalism

L2

Guided Instruction

- **Vocabulary Builder** Clarify the high-use words **invade** and **generation** before reading.

- Read A Century of War and Nationalism with students. As students read, circulate and make sure individuals can answer the Reading Check question.

- Ask **How was nationalism a destructive force in Europe in the early 1900s?** *(European nations feared one another and were afraid of invasion. As a result, they made alliances to protect themselves. Soon, Europe was divided into two major alliances. Eventually, fighting broke out between them.)*

- Ask **Who were the two opposing alliances in World War II?** *(Axis Powers: Germany, Italy, and Japan; Allies: Great Britain, the Soviet Union, France, China, and the United States.)*

- Ask **How did nationalism in Western Europe change after World War II?** *(Nations began to work together as trading partners and in building a common European community.)*

Independent Practice

Have students complete their graphic organizers by filling in details about World War II.

Monitor Progress

- Show *Section Reading Support Transparency ER 37* and have students check their graphic organizers individually. Go over key concepts and clarify key vocabulary as needed.

   Europe and Russia Transparencies, *Section Reading Support Transparency ER 37*

- Ask students to fill in the last column of the *Reading Readiness Guide*. Probe for what they learned that confirms and invalidates each statement.

   All in One Europe and Russia Teaching Resources, *Reading Readiness Guide,* p. 158

A Century of War and Nationalism

At the start of the 1900s, the people of Europe were filled with **nationalism,** or pride in their countries. Nationalism can be either a destructive or a constructive force, depending on what it leads people to do. It can make one nation harm another in an effort to get ahead. It can also prevent nations from working with one another. Then, hatred and warfare can erupt between countries. Between 1900 and 1950, destructive nationalism played a part in causing two world wars and the deaths of millions of people.

World War I During the early 1900s, European nations feared one another. Each nation was afraid another would invade, or try to take over, its territory. To protect themselves, nations made **alliances** (uh LY un sez), or agreements with one another. In such alliances, a nation promises to protect its friends if someone attacks them. Soon, Europe was divided into two major alliances. On one side were Germany, Austria-Hungary, and Turkey. On the other side were Great Britain, France, and Russia.

In 1914, fighting between the alliances broke out into what is now called World War I. Over the course of the war, most of the nations of Europe became involved. The United States—on the side of Great Britain, France, and Russia—also joined the war in 1917. The alliance of Germany, Austria-Hungary, and Turkey was defeated, but at an enormous cost. By the end of the war in 1918, more than 9 million soldiers had been killed. About 13 million civilians, or non-soldiers, had also died. Europe had lost almost an entire generation of young men.

World War II But the flame of nationalism still burned. In 1939, another war broke out. This war was called World War II. As in World War I, there were two alliances. On one side were the Axis Powers—Germany, Italy, and Japan. These countries sought to increase their national wealth and power by means of military conquest. They quickly captured most of Europe and parts of China and the South Pacific. Germany also attacked the Soviet Union.

The Allies—Great Britain, the Soviet Union, France, and China—opposed the Axis Powers. In 1941, the United States joined the Allies. More than 50 nations took part in this war, which was the most destructive ever fought. More people died, more property was damaged, and more money was spent than in any other war in history. The fighting finally ended in August of 1945. The Allies had won.

During World War I, countries on both sides of the fight used posters to promote their causes.

Differentiated Instruction

For Advanced Readers L3
Ask students to read the primary source *A Child in Prison Camp.* Students should work with a partner to answer and discuss the questions. Ask students to summarize this account for the class.

   All in One Europe and Russia Teaching Resources, *A Child in Prison Camp,* pp. 185–187

For Special Needs Students L1
Have students reread the section as they listen to the recorded version on the Student Edition on Audio CD. Check for comprehension by pausing the CD and asking students to share their answers to the Reading Check questions.

    Chapter 2, Section 3, **Student Edition on Audio CD**

Two Paths Emerge in Europe After World War II, the Soviet Union and the United States emerged as the world's two superpowers. These nations had very different ideas about government and its role in society. Both nations used their ideas to influence people around the world.

After the war, much of Europe was in ruins. It was time to rebuild. The nations of Western Europe allied themselves with the United States. They also grew together as a region. With the shared values of peace and prosperity, they worked together to restore the economies and standards of living that had been shattered by war.

The nations of Eastern Europe, in contrast, took a different path. Many of the nations of Eastern Europe followed the example of the Soviet Union. Their economies failed to recover after the war, and their governments suspended many of their people's freedoms. You will read more about the Soviet Union and its influence on Eastern Europe in the next section.

Eastern and Western Europe remained divided, with very different governments and standards of living, until the 1990s. You will read about their recent history in Chapters 4 and 5.

 Reading Check Which countries made up the Axis Powers? Which made up the Allies?

The United States led an effort called the Marshall Plan to rebuild the economies of Europe. In this photo, a parade in Greece celebrates the delivery of Marshall Plan food supplies.

Section 3 Assessment

Key Terms
Review the key terms at the beginning of this section. Use each term in a sentence that explains its meaning.

Target Reading Skill
Summarize the information in the paragraphs on this page.

Comprehension and Critical Thinking
1. (a) Recall Where did the Industrial Revolution begin?

(b) Find the Main Idea How did the Industrial Revolution change the way that goods were made?
(c) Identify Effects How did this change affect the lives of Europeans?
2. (a) Describe Give an example of destructive nationalism.
(b) Identify Cause and Effect How did nationalism help to cause World War I and World War II?
(c) Predict How might nationalism be used in the future as a creative force for peace?

Writing Activity
After World War II, colonies in Africa and Asia demanded their freedom. Suppose you were a citizen of a colony of one of the European nations. Write a paragraph explaining why you would want your country to be independent.

> **Writing Tip** Use the following topic sentence to help you organize your thoughts: It is important for people to control their own destiny.

Chapter 2 Section 3 **59**

Objective

Learn how to solve problems.

Prepare to Read

Build Background Knowledge ⬛L2

Tell students that problem solving is a skill that they can use every day to solve small or large problems. Introduce students to the skill by asking them to think of a problem they had recently, either at school or in some other aspect of their lives. If students are uncomfortable talking about their personal experiences, they may make up a fictional problem. Ask students to think about how they solved or did not solve the problem. If they were able to solve it, what strategies did they use? If the problem was not solved, why do they think that was so? Could they have done anything differently? Use the Numbered Heads participation strategy (TE, p. T36) to elicit responses.

Instruct

Problem Solving ⬛L2

Guided Instruction

■ Read the steps to problem solving as a class and write them on the board.

■ Practice the skill by following the steps on p. 61 as a class. Model each step in the activity by identifying the problem *(invaders were attacking the Roman empire)*, listing possible solutions *(have a better organized army of only trained military officers; invest more time in training peasants and slaves; station all soldiers in one place; repair roads so travel would be easier)*, reviewing the possible solutions *(having only trained officers would mean fewer people to fight in the army; spending more time training peasants and slaves would require more work and time and would mean that peasants and slaves would not be performing their other jobs; stationing all soldiers in one place would require soldiers to travel to the location and might make it difficult for them to return home; repairing roads would require money and workers, but traveling from place to place would be easier)*, and iden-

In 1275, Marco Polo arrived at the court of Kublai Khan in China. The Mongol leader appointed Marco Polo governor of Yangchow, a busy Chinese city. After three years had passed, Marco Polo wanted to return to Venice. He had enemies within the court. The khan was getting older. Marco Polo worried that when the khan died, those enemies would have him killed. But the khan refused to let him return to Venice.

One year, a Mongol princess was promised as a bride to the Persian khan. Marco Polo proposed that he accompany the princess on the journey, to keep her safe. He knew that at the end of the trip he could escape to Venice. The khan agreed, and Marco Polo set out by sea with the princess and hundreds of men. The trip was dangerous, and most of the men died. But it might have been even more dangerous to go by land, because of robbers.

Marco Polo dressed in clothes worn by the Tatars, a nomadic tribe of eastern Asia

Solving a problem requires a range of skills. You must first state the problem clearly and identify the possible solutions. Then you must think about the likely outcome of each solution and choose the best option. In the passage above, Marco Polo identified and solved two problems.

Learn the Skill

Follow the steps below to learn how to solve problems.

1 **Identify the problem.** State the problem in a direct, complete, and accurate way. Your statement should contain facts, not opinions. The facts should be directly related to the problem.

2 **List possible solutions.** There may be more than one way to solve the problem. Identify all possible solutions.

3 **Review the possible solutions.** Identify the resources that would be needed to carry out each solution. Also identify consequences of each solution.

4 **Choose the best solution.** Decide which solution is the most effective, or the easiest to carry out. What will the likely outcome be?

60 Europe and Russia

tifying the solution they think is best *(Students' answers will vary, but they should identify the solution they think is the best, why it is best, and what they think its outcome would be)*.

Independent Practice

Assign *Skills for Life* and have students complete it individually.

All in One **Europe and Russia Teaching Resources,** *Skills for Life,* p. 174

Monitor Progress

As students are completing *Skills for Life,* circulate to make sure individuals are applying the skill steps effectively. Provide assistance as needed.

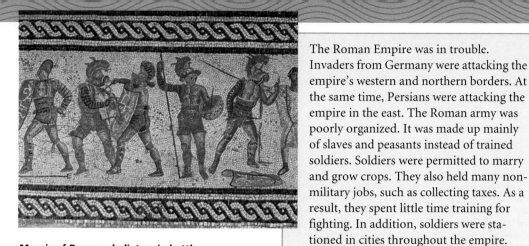
Mosaic of Roman gladiators in battle

The Roman Empire was in trouble. Invaders from Germany were attacking the empire's western and northern borders. At the same time, Persians were attacking the empire in the east. The Roman army was poorly organized. It was made up mainly of slaves and peasants instead of trained soldiers. Soldiers were permitted to marry and grow crops. They also held many non-military jobs, such as collecting taxes. As a result, they spent little time training for fighting. In addition, soldiers were stationed in cities throughout the empire. When attacks on the empire occurred, it was difficult to gather the soldiers together in one place for defense. Finally, the government had not kept the roads in repair, so travel was very difficult.

Practice the Skill

Read the passage above. Use the steps from Learn the Skill to identify the Roman Empire's problem and possible solutions.

1 Identify the Roman Empire's problem. State the problem in a clear sentence or two.

2 Identify possible solutions. Does the passage bring to mind any obvious solutions? Does it suggest any solutions that aren't as obvious?

3 Review the possible solutions. What kind of resources would each solution require? Think of what the possible outcome would be for each solution.

4 Identify the solution you think is best. Explain why you think it is the best one, and what its outcome would be.

Apply the Skill

Reread the passage titled Revolutions in Government on page 50. Then use the steps in this skill to identify the problem described in the passage, note its possible effects, and explain the solutions used.

**Bronze statue of a
Roman soldier**

Assess Progress L2
Ask students to do the Apply the Skill activity.

Reteach L1
If students are having trouble applying the skill steps, have them review the skill using the interactive Social Studies Skills Tutor CD-ROM.

⊙ *Problem Solving,* **Social Studies Tutor CD-ROM**

Extend L3
To extend the lesson, have students turn to p. 55 and reread the passage under Changes in Society. Have them identify the problem in the passage, and think of possible solutions that are not in the text. Have students make a list of their solutions to the problem, reminding them to use the skill steps they learned. Then have them share their ideas with the class.

Answers
Apply the Skill
Problem: In England, North America, and France, the people wanted more say in their governments. Solutions: In England, a civil war was fought and the king was put on trial and condemned to death, after which no ruler could claim absolute power or ignore the law; in North America, the colonies rebelled against the British king, defeated the British soldiers, and formed an independent nation; in France, the French people used extreme violence to overthrow the government.

Differentiated Instruction

For Special Needs Students L1
Partner special needs students with more proficient readers to do Level 1 of the Problem Solving lesson on the Social Studies Skills Tutor CD-ROM together. When students feel more confident, they can move onto Level 2 alone.

⊙ *Problem Solving,* **Social Studies Skills Tutor CD-ROM**

Objectives

Social Studies

1. Discover how Russia built its empire.
2. Understand the fall of the Russian tsars.
3. Examine the rise and fall of the Soviet Union.
4. Learn the causes and effects of the Cold War.
5. Learn about the Russian Federation today.

Reading/Language Arts

Read ahead to help clarify an unfamiliar word or passage.

Prepare to Read

Build Background Knowledge   L2

Draw students' attention to the photo of Catherine the Great on this page. Help students get a sense of the Russian court by conducting an Idea Wave (TE, p. T35) to generate a list of words and phrases that might describe Catherine. Provide an example to get students started. *(regal, wealthy, powerful)*

Set a Purpose for Reading   L2

■ Preview the Objectives.

■ Read each statement in the *Reading Readiness Guide* aloud. Ask students to mark the statements true or false.

■ Have students discuss the statements in pairs or groups of four, then mark their worksheets again. Use the Numbered Heads participation strategy (TE, p. T36) to call on students to share their group's perspectives.

All in One **Europe and Russia Teaching Resources,** *Reading Readiness Guide,* p. 162

Vocabulary Builder
Preview Key Terms   L2

Pronounce each Key Term, then ask students to say the word with you. Provide a simple explanation such as, "Ivan IV was the first tsar, or emperor, of Russia."

Prepare to Read

Objectives

In this section you will

1. Discover how Russia built its empire.
2. Understand the fall of the Russian tsars.
3. Examine the rise and fall of the Soviet Union.
4. Learn the causes and effects of the Cold War.
5. Learn about the Russian Federation today.

Taking Notes

As you read this section, look for important dates in Russia's development as an empire. Copy the timeline below and record your findings on it.

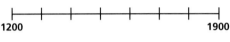

1200   1900

Target Reading Skill

Read Ahead Reading ahead can help you understand something you are not sure of in the text. If you do not understand a certain word or passage, keep reading. The word or idea may be clarified further on. For example, in the last paragraph below you may not be sure what is meant by the word *expansion.* As you read the section, that word will be clarified by the text.

Key Terms

• **westernization** (wes tur nuh ZAY shun) *n.* the adoption of western European culture

• **tsar** (zahr) *n.* a Russian emperor

• **revolutionary** (rev uh LOO shuh neh ree) *adj.* ideas that relate to or cause the overthrow of a government, or other great change

• **communism** (KAHM yoo niz um) *n.* a political system in which the central government owns farms, factories, and offices

Catherine the Great

62 Europe and Russia

The Russian court under Catherine the Great was dazzling. Catherine loved the arts, literature, philosophy, and French culture. She dreamed of creating a great nation, as glorious as France had been under Louis XIV.

Early in her rule, she made many efforts to improve the lives of the Russian people. She built schools and hospitals and gave people more religious freedom. She also became interested in ideas about liberty. Catherine did not bring freedom to all of her people, but she did make Russia a great empire. By the time of her death in 1796, she had expanded Russia southward to the Black Sea and westward into parts of Poland.

The history of Russia is a story with four themes: invasion and expansion, harsh treatment of the common people, slow **westernization,** or the process of becoming more like Western Europe, and autocratic (aw toh KRAT ik) government. An autocratic government is one in which one person has absolute power. As you read Russia's story, notice how these four themes appear again and again.

Target Reading Skill   L2

Read Ahead Point out the Target Reading Skill. Tell students to keep reading if they come across a word or passage they do not understand, because it may be clarified later on in the text.

Model reading ahead by reading aloud the third sentence in the second paragraph on this page. "She also became interested in ideas about liberty." Tell students to read the next sentence in the paragraph to clarify the meaning of the word "liberty". *(freedom)*

Give students *Reread or Read Ahead.* Have them complete the activity in groups.

All in One **Europe and Russia Teaching Resources,** *Reread or Read Ahead,* p. 169

MAP MASTER™
Skills Activity

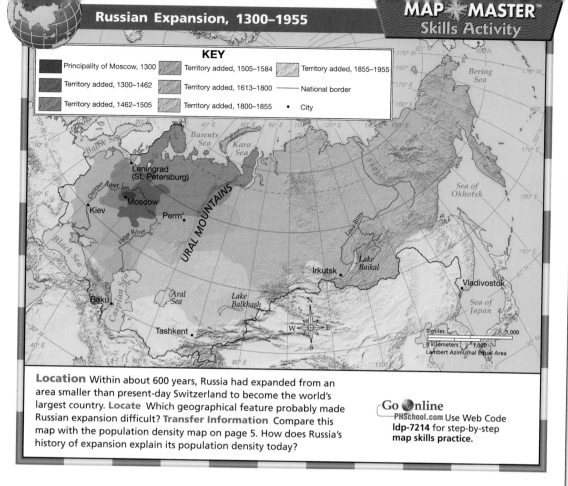

KEY

Principality of Moscow, 1300	Territory added, 1505–1584	Territory added, 1855–1955
Territory added, 1300–1462	Territory added, 1613–1800	National border
Territory added, 1462–1505	Territory added, 1800–1855	• City

Lambert Azimuthal Equal Area

Location Within about 600 years, Russia had expanded from an area smaller than present-day Switzerland to become the world's largest country. **Locate** Which geographical feature probably made Russian expansion difficult? **Transfer Information** Compare this map with the population density map on page 5. How does Russia's history of expansion explain its population density today?

Go Online
PHSchool.com Use Web Code
ldp-7214 for step-by-step
map skills practice.

Building a Vast Empire

Russia's story begins long before Catherine the Great. Many centuries before, various groups of people known as Slavs (slahvz) lived in small settlements. The Slavs lived in the region that eventually became the Russian Empire. In the 1200s, Mongol invaders from Asia swept in and conquered them.

The Rise of Moscow The prince of Moscow made clever agreements with the Mongols that helped him grow rich and powerful. By the 1330s, he had become the strongest ruler in the region. Slowly Moscow conquered surrounding territory. By the end of the 1400s, Moscow had freed itself entirely from Mongol rule. The map above shows how the small principality, or territory ruled by a prince, of Moscow grew into a huge country.

Chapter 2 Section 4 **63**

Instruct

Building a Vast Empire
L2

Guided Instruction

- **Vocabulary Builder** Clarify the high-use word **reign** before reading.

- Have students use the Oral Cloze reading strategy (TE, p. T33) to read Building a Vast Empire. They should also study the map showing Russian expansion.

- Ask **Which groups of people lived in the region that became the Russian Empire?** *(Slavs lived in the region in small settlements; Mongol invaders from Asia conquered the Slavs in the 1200s.*

- Have students study the map of Russian Expansion. Ask **In what time period was Kiev added to Russian territory?** *(1613–1800)*

— Vocabulary Builder —

Use the information below to teach students this section's high-use words.

High-Use Word	Definition and Sample Sentence
reign, p. 64	*n.* period of time during which a monarch rules During the queen's **reign**, there was peace in the country.
reform, p. 65	*n.* a change for the better The principal made **reforms** to the school schedule, giving us more time to use the computer room.
withdraw, p. 66	*v.* to move back or out We **withdrew** from the room so we would not disturb the sleeping baby.

Answers

MAP MASTER Skills Activity **Locate** the Ural Mountains **Transfer Information** Russia has a low population density, partly because it is such a large country.

Go Online
PHSchool.com Students may practice their map skills using the interactive online version of this map.

Show students *St. Petersburg and Peter the Great.* Ask **Who was Peter the Great?** *(He was the tsar of Russia from 1682–1725.)* **How did he make St. Petersburg into a great city?** *(He brought artists and architects from around the world to make a beautiful city; he made it the capital of the Russian Empire.)*

Guided Instruction (continued)

- Ask **Who was the first tsar of Russia?** *(Ivan IV, known as Ivan the Terrible)* **What happened in Russia after his death?** *(Russia entered the Time of Troubles, during which there were 20 years of civil wars and invasions by the Poles.)*

- Ask **What changes did Peter the Great bring to Russia?** *(He encouraged the westernization of the country, founded new schools, reorganized the government and army, conquered land on the Baltic and Black Seas, and moved the capital to St.Petersburg.)*

- Ask **How was Napoleon's army in Russia defeated in 1812?** *(The early Russian winter surprised the troops and about 90,000 soldiers died.)*

Independent Practice

Have students create the Taking Notes graphic organizer on a blank piece of paper and begin to fill in dates and events from Building a Vast Empire.

Monitor Progress

As students begin work on their timelines, circulate and make sure individuals are choosing correct information. Provide assistance as needed.

Answers

Analyze Images the man on the horse; he appears to be leading the army

✓ **Reading Check** He wanted seaports to help Russia become a world power.

The Rise of the Tsars In the 1540s, Ivan IV became the leader of Moscow. He called himself **tsar** (zahr), or emperor. Ivan IV expanded Moscow's control of the territories to its south and east. He earned the name Ivan the Terrible for his cruelty both to those he conquered and to his own people.

After the death of Ivan the Terrible, Russia entered the Time of Troubles. During that period, the Russians endured about 20 years of civil wars and invasions by the Poles.

Finally, in 1613, Michael Romanov (ROH muh nawf) became tsar. During his reign, order was restored to Russia. The Romanovs continued expanding Russian territory throughout the 1600s and continued to rule Russia for more than 300 years.

Peter the Great Peter the Great came to power in 1689. Peter began bringing Western European ideas and culture to Russia. He hired foreign professors, scientists, and advisors, and encouraged Russians to adopt European customs. He also established new schools and reorganized his government and the army.

Peter believed that Russia needed good seaports to become a world power. He conquered land on the Baltic (BAWL tik) and Black seas, and moved the capital to St. Petersburg. Later tsars continued to expand Russian territory. Russia gained control over territories in present-day Poland, Turkey, China, and Sweden. With so many lands under its rule, Russia became an empire.

Invasion Being an empire did not mean that Russia was safe from invasion. A French army under Napoleon Bonaparte invaded Russia in 1812. Fierce fighting erupted as Napoleon's army approached Moscow. Napoleon's invasion plan, which did not take into account Russia's early winter, resulted in disastrous losses for the French. Of the 100,000 soldiers that reached Moscow, only about 10,000 survived.

✓ **Reading Check** Why did Peter the Great want to control land on the Baltic Sea?

Napoleon's First View of Moscow Napoleon and his troops approach Moscow in 1812 in this historical painting. **Analyze Images** *Which figure in the painting is Napoleon? How can you tell?*

Skills Mini Lesson

Using Reliable Information

1. Tell students that they should answer these questions when checking if a source is reliable: Is the information recent enough for your purposes? Is it accurate? What are the author's qualifications and methods? Does the author have a bias or one-sided view?

2. Ask students if a speech by Peter the Great about the value of his policy of westernization would be a reliable source of information about Russian history during the late 1600s.

3. Ask students to apply the skill using an article about Russia from a current source, such as a newspaper article.

The Fall of the Tsars

Russia had become a powerful empire, but the lives of most of its people had not improved. For hundreds of years, the tsar made all the important decisions. Below the tsar, Russian society was divided into two main groups. The first was a small number of landowners. The second group was a large number of very poor serfs. Tensions between the two groups began to rise.

Freeing of the Serfs In 1855, Alexander II became tsar. He soon freed the serfs and gave them their own land. He also gave towns more control over their own affairs. However, Alexander's son, Alexander III, reversed many of his father's reforms. Once again, the tsar ruled with absolute power.

Rumblings of Revolution In 1894, Nicholas II became tsar. He would be the last Russian tsar. Russia was badly beaten in a war with Japan in 1904 and 1905, and unrest grew among peasants, workers, and a small middle class. In 1905, thousands of workers in St. Petersburg marched to the tsar's Winter Palace. They wanted to appeal directly to the tsar for reforms. Troops stopped them and fired into the crowd, killing hundreds. This mass killing was known as Bloody Sunday.

Tsar Nicholas II was forced to agree to establish the Duma (DOO mah), a kind of congress. The people elected its members. In theory, the Duma shared power with the tsar. In fact, the Duma had very little power. Some progress toward reform was made, but many people wanted more.

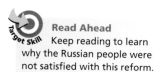

Read Ahead Keep reading to learn why the Russian people were not satisfied with this reform.

✓ **Reading Check** What event is known as Bloody Sunday?

The Fall of the Tsars L2

Guided Instruction

- **Vocabulary Builder** Clarify the high-use word **reform** before reading.

- Read The Fall of the Tsars with the class.

- Have students discuss why there were tensions between serfs and landowners. (*A small number of people owned all the land, but there was a large number of very poor serfs.*)

- Ask students to explain what happened when workers sought reforms in 1905. (*Troops killed hundreds of workers marching to the Winter Palace to ask the tsar for reforms. Tsar Nicholas II was forced to establish the Duma and share power with its elected members.*)

Independent Practice

Have students add information about the freeing of the serfs and the beginnings of revolution in Russia to their graphic organizers.

Monitor Progress

As students work on their graphic organizers, circulate to make sure individuals are choosing the correct events and placing them in order. Provide assistance as needed.

⟳ Target Reading Skill L2

Read Ahead As a follow up, ask students to perform the Target Reading Skill activity in the Student Edition. (*Students should read ahead to find out why the Russian people were not satisfied with this reform.*)

Differentiated Instruction

For Advanced Readers L3
Have students read about Napoleon's campaign on the Russian battlefield in *A Letter from Napoleon's Army*. Have students share their responses to the questions in a discussion with a partner.

All in One **Europe and Russia Teaching Resources,** *A Letter from Napoleon's Army,* pp. 188–189

For English Language Learners L2
You may wish to have Spanish-speaking students complete the *Guided Reading and Review (Spanish)* for Section 4 of this chapter.

📄 **Europe and Russia Spanish Support,** *Guided Reading and Review (Spanish),* p. 18

Answers

Compare and Contrast The tsar and his family were wealthy and probably lived much more comfortably than poor Russians.

✓ **Reading Check** the mass killing of protesting workers at the Winter Palace in 1905

The Rise and Fall of the Soviet Union ⬛ L2

Guided Instruction

- **Vocabulary Builder** Clarify the high-use word **withdraw** before reading.

- Read The Rise and Fall of the Soviet Union with students.

- Ask **Why did communism appeal to the Russian people?** *(The nation was made up of mostly poor people who suffered terribly while a few rich people lived in luxury. Communism seemed to offer the poor the hope of making everyone equal and improving life for many Russians.)*

- Ask **What country did Lenin create when the Communists won the Russian civil war?** *(the Soviet Union)* **What did it include?** *(Russia and several smaller republics under Russian control—most of the territory of the old Russian Empire)*

- Ask **How did Stalin achieve his goals for the Soviet Union?** *(He developed industry by forcing peasants to give their crops to the government to feed factory workers and sending millions who opposed this policy to their death in Siberian prison camps.)*

- Have students discuss how the Soviet Union became involved in World War II. *(Despite an agreement between the Soviet Union and Germany, the Germans invaded the Soviet Union in 1941.)*

Independent Practice

Have students continue to work on their timelines, adding new dates and events.

Monitor Progress

Circulate to make sure individuals are choosing appropriate events.

Answer

Synthesize the idea that everyone would be equal and would enjoy a better standard of living

Promoting Communism
At the top, Lenin gives a speech to a crowd in Moscow in 1918. The poster above promotes communism, reading, "You are still not a member of the cooperative? Sign up immediately!" **Synthesize** *What about communism might have appealed to poverty-stricken Russians?*

The Rise and Fall of the Soviet Union

On an afternoon in April 1917, a small group of Russians gathered at a German railroad station. Among them was a man named Vladimir Ulyanov, who was also called Lenin. Earlier, the Russian government had imprisoned Lenin for spreading ideas that they believed were **revolutionary,** or ideas that could cause the overthrow of a government. Later, the government gave him permission to leave Russia.

Now the Germans were taking Lenin back to Russia. The Germans made two rules. First, no member of Lenin's group could leave the train, and second, none of them could talk to any Germans during their journey. The Germans, like the Russians, knew that ideas could be more powerful than any army. At the time, Germany was at war with Russia and hoped that Lenin would cause changes in Russia. And he did.

The Russian Revolution To understand why the Germans helped Lenin, you need to go back to 1914. That year, Russia entered World War I against Germany. Millions of Russian soldiers were killed or wounded. At home, people suffered severe food and fuel shortages. By March 1917, the Russian people began rioting. Troops were sent to put down the uprising. They joined the rioters instead. Tsar Nicholas II was forced to give up his throne. The tsar and his family were held as prisoners, and were later killed by Lenin's followers. A weak government took over.

In November 1917, after his return to Russia, Lenin and his supporters pushed the weak government aside. Lenin knew that Russians wanted peace more than anything else. In March 1918, Russia signed an agreement with Germany and withdrew from World War I. Under Lenin's leadership, Russia also agreed to give up the Baltic republics, a large area of its territory that had been occupied by the Germans. This was just what the Germans had hoped for.

As the new leader of Russia, Lenin wanted to establish a communist government. **Communism** (KAHM yoo niz um) is a political system in which the central government owns farms, factories, and offices. No one person can own factories or land. Each person is supposed to work and share equally in the rewards of this work.

The idea of communism appealed greatly to many Russians. For hundreds of years, Russia's poor had suffered terrible hardships while the rich lived in luxury. Lenin promised that everyone would be equal and enjoy a better standard of living, but he broke that promise. Instead, the government took all power and most of the wealth for itself.

66 Europe and Russia

Background: Biography

Joseph Stalin Joseph Stalin, the leader of the USSR from 1925–1953, was one of the most brutal dictators of modern times. In 1928, he launched programs that dramatically changed Soviet economic and social structures. Stalin crushed any opposition to his policies. In 1932–33, he created a famine in the Ukraine that killed 3 million farmers who had protested giving their lands to the state. In 1936, he conducted purges that resulted in the execution of many military officers and Communist party members that he believed were plotting against him. Stalin accomplished many of his goals, such as industrialization and involving the Soviet Union in international affairs, but after his death his methods were denounced by the Soviet government.

Building a Communist State The treaty with Germany ended the war, but peace still did not come to Russia. After the Communists came to power, there was a terrible civil war. On one side were Lenin's followers. On the other side were many groups who opposed them.

The Russian civil war lasted three years and cost millions of lives. Eventually, the Communists won. In 1922, Lenin created the Union of Soviet Socialist Republics (USSR), also called the Soviet Union. The Soviet Union was made up of Russia and several smaller republics under Russian control. It included most of the territory of the old Russian Empire. And as in the old empire, most of the people in the smaller republics were not Russian.

Lenin began turning the Soviet Union into a communist country. He jailed and even killed people who opposed him, calling them enemies of the revolution. Lenin died in 1924. Josef Stalin became the next leader. Under Stalin's form of Soviet communism, the government tried to control all aspects of citizens' lives.

Stalin's Dictatorship Josef Stalin was a dictator (DIK tayt ur), a leader who has absolute power. Stalin did not care about the suffering his decisions caused the Russian people. For example, he wanted to develop more industry in the Soviet Union. He knew that the increased number of factory workers would require great amounts of food. Therefore, Stalin forced the peasants to give their farm products to the government. Many peasants opposed the plan. As punishment, Stalin sent millions of peasants to prison camps in Siberia. Most died there. Stalin eventually succeeded in industrializing Russia. But all of the Soviet Union lived in terror of Stalin.

World War II Stalin signed an agreement with the Germans in 1939. It stated that the two countries would not go to war against each other. Despite the agreement, the Germans invaded the Soviet Union two years later. Three million German soldiers, with tanks and airplanes, advanced deep into the Soviet Union.

For a time, a German victory appeared likely. Many Soviet cities were destroyed. Millions of soldiers died or were captured. But the Soviet people fought bravely. By 1943, the Soviets had begun pushing the Germans out of Russia. Two years later, Soviet troops had captured Berlin, the capital of Germany.

✓ **Reading Check** Why was Stalin called a dictator?

Ending World War II
In the photo at the top, a Russian soldier celebrates the Soviet victory in Berlin by raising the Soviet flag. Above, the leaders of the Soviet Union, the United States, and the United Kingdom meet to discuss their countries' roles in the post-war world. **Recognize Causes** How did the Soviet Union's role in World War II help it become a world power?

Guided Instruction

- Have students read about growing tension between the United States and the Soviet Union in The Cold War.

- Ask students **What were the world's two superpowers after World War II?** *(the United States and the Soviet Union)* **Why were they called "superpowers"?** *(They were extremely powerful countries.)*

- Ask **What were the main causes of the Cold War?** *(The Soviet Union forced Eastern European nations to become Communist and cut off their contact with the West. The Soviets attempted to expand their power in the world by encouraging rebels in other countries to turn to communism. The United States was determined to stop the spread of communism.)*

- Have students discuss some of the causes of the collapse of the Soviet Union. *(Its economy did not grow fast enough; basic consumer goods were in scarce supply; people did not want to be controlled by the government in every part of their lives.)*

Independent Practice
Have students add events from The Cold War to their graphic organizers.

Monitor Progress
As students continue to work on their timelines, circulate to make sure individuals are choosing the correct events. Provide assistance as needed.

Differentiated Instruction

For Gifted and Talented   L3
Have students read *Lenin's Deathbed Words* and *Kampf*, by Joseph Stalin. Ask students to write a brief paragraph explaining if they think Lenin's concerns about Joseph Stalin were valid.

All in One **Europe and Russia Teaching Resources,** *Lenin's Deathbed Words*, p. 190; *Kampf*, p. 191

For Less Proficient Readers   L1
Students who are less proficient readers may have difficulty absorbing the information in this section. Pair students with more proficient readers and have them create an outline of the material. Tell students to use the headings in the section as guidelines for their outline.

Answers

Recognize Causes It had a major role in the victory against Germany, which ultimately gave it more power after World War II.

✓ **Reading Check** because he ruled with absolute power

The Russian Federation

L2

Guided Instruction

- Have students read about the Russian Federation. Circulate to make sure individuals can answer the Reading Check question.

- Ask **What is the Russian Federation?** (*the name that Russia took after the breakup of the Soviet Union; it includes Russians and many different ethnic groups.*)

- Ask **What are some of the challenges the Russian Federation has faced?** (*The transition from a Communist system to a western-style economy has caused economic chaos; ethnic conflict has arisen.*)

- Have students discuss the ways in which some groups have decided to break away from Russian rule. (*The republic of Tatarstan negotiated with the Russians to have more rights, while the republic of Chechnya has fought for its independence.*)

Independent Practice

Have students complete their timelines by adding events from The Russian Federation.

Monitor Progress

- Show *Section Reading Support Transparency ER 38* and ask students to check their graphic organizers individually. Go over key concepts and clarify key vocabulary as needed.

    📖 **Europe and Russia Transparencies,** *Section Reading Support Transparency ER 38*

- Tell students to fill in the last column of the *Reading Readiness Guide*. Probe for what they learned that confirms or invalidates each statement.

    All in One Europe and Russia Teaching Resources, *Reading Readiness Guide,* p. 162

A Nuclear Threat
By the 1980s, the superpowers had built enough powerful nuclear weapons to destroy the entire world. The top photo shows the explosion of a nuclear bomb. The bottom photo shows the universal yellow and black symbol of fallout shelters—underground rooms meant to protect people from fallout, or dangerous particles, after a nuclear explosion.
Sequence *What events led to the buildup of nuclear weapons by the Soviet Union and the United States?*

The Cold War

As you have read, after World War II the United States and the Soviet Union were so powerful that people called them superpowers. Relations between the superpowers became extremely tense. However, the two sides never fought each other. This time of tension without actual war is called the Cold War. It lasted roughly from 1945 until 1991, and shaped events within the two nations, and around the world.

Causes of the Cold War The first cause of the Cold War was the situation in Eastern Europe. During World War II the Soviet army moved westward to Berlin, freeing the Eastern European countries that the Germans had conquered. But after the war, the Soviet troops did not leave. They forced those countries to become communist. Trade and most contact with the West were cut off. British leader Winston Churchill said that it was as if an "iron curtain" had fallen across Eastern Europe, dividing the East from the West.

Second, the Soviets tried to expand their power beyond Eastern Europe. They encouraged rebels in other nations to turn to communism. The United States was determined to stop this. The superpowers often backed opposing sides in conflicts in Latin America, Asia, and Africa. They also built powerful nuclear (NOO klee ur) weapons to use against each other.

Collapse of an Empire The Soviet Union's economy grew weak during the Cold War. The government had invested most of its money in heavy industries and weapons. It did not produce enough basic consumer goods, such as food and clothing. Also, the government's central control of the economy was not working.

Almost all of the Soviet people had lost faith in the communist system by the early 1980s. They were still poor and no longer believed the government's promises. One Soviet leader responded. Mikhail Gorbachev (mee kah EEL GAWR buh chawf), who took power in 1985, made many changes in the Soviet system. He allowed more personal freedom. He also reduced the government's control of the economy.

When people who have lived under harsh rule are given a taste of freedom, they often want more. This happened across Eastern Europe and the Soviet Union by the late 1980s. Eastern European countries abandoned communism. The Soviet republics demanded their independence. Finally, at the end of 1991, the Soviet Union broke apart.

✓ **Reading Check** What was the "Iron Curtain"?

Answers

Sequence the United States and the Soviet Union became superpowers after World War II; the Soviet Union took over Eastern Europe; the Soviet Union tried to spread communism in other parts of the world; the United States tried to stop the spread of communism; both countries built powerful nuclear weapons to use against each other.

✓ **Reading Check** a term used to describe the division between Eastern and Western Europe after World War II

Differentiated Instruction

For Less Proficient Readers **L1**
Have students read the section in the Reading and Vocabulary Study Guide. This version provides basic-level instruction in an interactive format with questions and write-on lines.

📖 Chapter 2, Section 4, **Europe and Russia Reading and Vocabulary Study Guide,** pp. 25–27

The Russian Federation

After the breakup of the Soviet Union, all of its republics became independent nations. The republic of Russia changed its name to the Russian Federation. A federation is a union of states or republics. In a federation, each member agrees to give certain powers to a central government. The Russian Federation includes Russians and peoples of many different ethnic groups. However, the Russian Federation is smaller in size than the old Soviet Union.

The Russian Federation has made efforts to build a free-market economy, or an economy in which producers compete freely for consumers' business. It sold its state-owned factories and businesses to private individuals. It has also tried to become more democratic. The transition away from a communist system has been difficult, however. Russia experienced economic chaos.

Russia also experienced conflicts among its ethnic groups. Many of these other peoples were tired of being ruled by Russians, who are the majority in Russia. The republic of Tatarstan, for example, negotiated with the Russians to have more rights. The republic of Chechnya (CHECH nee uh), however, has fought for its independence. Russia today faces many challenges to building a new way of life.

Russian president Vladimir Putin in 2000

✔ **Reading Check** Why did the Russian Federation sell businesses to private individuals?

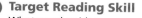

Section 4 Assessment

Key Terms
Review the key terms at the beginning of this section. Use each term in a sentence that explains its meaning.

🎯 Target Reading Skill
What word or idea were you able to clarify by reading ahead?

Comprehension and Critical Thinking
1. (a) Name Who was the first Russian leader to begin westernization?
(b) Draw Conclusions Why did he encourage Russians to adopt western customs?

2. (a) Define What was the Russian Duma?
(b) Identify Causes Why did Tsar Nicholas II create the Duma?
3. (a) Explain Why had Lenin been imprisoned by the Russian government?
(b) Sequence How did Lenin become Russia's leader?
4. (a) Define What is a federation?
(b) Summarize How did the Russian Federation try to westernize its economy?

Writing Activity
Today, some people in Russia want to return to their lives under communist rule. Write a paragraph arguing either for or against returning to communism.

Go Online
PHSchool.com

For: An activity about Leo Tolstoy
Visit: PHSchool.com
Web Code: ldd-7204

Chapter 2 Section 4 **69**

Assess and Reteach

Assess Progress   L2
Have students complete the Section Assessment. Administer the *Section Quiz*.

All in One Europe and Russia Teaching Resources, *Section Quiz,* p. 164

Reteach   L1
If students need more instruction, have them read this section in the Reading and Vocabulary Study Guide.

📖 Chapter 2, Section 4, **Europe and Russia Reading and Vocabulary Study Guide,** pp. 25–27

Extend   L3
To extend students' understanding of the hardships people who were sent to Siberia suffered, have them read the primary source *The Endless Steppe* by Esther Hautzig. Have students work with partners to answer the questions.

All in One Europe and Russia Teaching Resources, *The Endless Steppe,* pp. 192–193

Answer

✔ **Reading Check** to begin building a free-market economy

Writing Activity
Use the *Rubric for Assessing a Writing Assignment* to evaluate students' paragraphs.

All in One Europe and Russia Teaching Resources, *Rubric for Assessing a Writing Assignment,* p. 201

Go Online
PHSchool.com Typing in the Web code when prompted will bring students directly to detailed instructions for this activity.

Section 4 Assessment

Key Terms
Students' sentences should reflect knowledge of each Key Term.

🎯 Target Reading Skill
Answers will vary, but students should identify a word or idea in the section that they were able to clarify by reading ahead.

Comprehension and Critical Thinking
1. (a) Peter the Great **(b)** To make Russia a world power, Peter the Great probably felt that Russians needed to be familiar with western culture and ideas.

2. (a) a kind of congress with elected members that was set up in Russia **(b)** He needed to meet the people's demand for reforms after the events of Bloody Sunday.

3. (a) The government felt he had been spreading dangerous revolutionary ideas. **(b)** After the tsar was forced to give up his throne, a weak government was formed. Lenin and his supporters pushed that government aside.

4. (a) a union of states or republics **(b)** It sold state-owned businesses to individuals and tried to become more democratic.

Objectives

Social Studies

1. Learn about the history of the European Union.
2. Understand the purpose of the European Union.
3. Examine the structure of the European Union.
4. Find out what the future holds for the European Union.

Reading/Language Arts

Reread or read ahead to help understand words and ideas in the text.

Prepare to Read

Build Background Knowledge L2

Tell students that in this section they will learn about the European Union. Write the word *union* on the board and invite students to suggest how this applies to governments and international affairs. Use an Idea Wave (TE, p. T35) to generate ideas. To get students started, ask them to think about how *union* applies to the United States. *(The word expresses how the individual states are united to make one country.)*

Set a Purpose for Reading L2

■ Preview the Objectives.

■ Read each statement in the *Reading Readiness Guide* aloud. Ask students to mark the statements true or false.

■ Have students discuss the statements in pairs or groups of four, then mark their worksheets again. Use the Numbered Heads participation strategy (TE, p. T36) to call on students to share their group's perspectives.

All in One Europe and Russia Teaching Resources, *Reading Readiness Guide,* p. 166

Vocabulary Builder

Preview Key Terms L2

Pronounce each Key Term, then ask students to say the word with you. Provide a simple explanation such as, "Many countries in Europe use the same currency, the euro."

Prepare to Read

Objectives

In this section you will

1. Learn about the history of the European Union.
2. Understand the purpose of the European Union.
3. Examine the structure of the European Union.
4. Find out what the future holds for the European Union.

Taking Notes

As you read this section, look for details about the European Union. Copy the concept web below and record your findings in it.

Target Reading Skill

Reread or Read Ahead
Both rereading and reading ahead can help you understand words and ideas in the text. If you do not understand a word or passage, use one or both of these techniques. In some cases, you may wish to read ahead first to see if the idea is clarified later on. If it is not, try going back and rereading the original passage.

Key Terms

- **euro** (YUR oh) *n.* the official currency of the European Union
- **single market** (SING ul MAHR ket) *n.* a system in which goods, services, and capital move freely, with no barriers
- **foreign minister** (FAWR MIN is tur) *n.* a government official who is in charge of a nation's foreign affairs

Robert Schuman worked to repair war-torn Europe.

70 Europe and Russia

At the end of World War II, Europe lay in ruins. Many of the nations of Europe had been at war with one another for years. Europeans needed to work together to bring about peace, rebuild their nations, and strengthen their shattered economies.

A French government official named Robert Schuman had a plan. He wanted European nations to work together to control their coal and steel industries. He proposed a new organization called the European Coal and Steel Community (ECSC). Six nations—Belgium, France, Italy, Luxembourg, the Netherlands, and West Germany—joined the group in 1951.

Over time, this small group grew into a much larger group, with many more roles and responsibilities. Today, it is called the European Union (EU), and has 25 member states. Many additional countries are waiting to become members.

Target Reading Skill L2

Reread or Read Ahead Point out the Target Reading Skill. Tell students to reread or read ahead to help them understand unfamiliar words or clarify ideas.

Model rereading and reading ahead using the two paragraphs on this page. Tell students that rereading the first paragraph can help clarify why European nations needed to rebuild and strengthen their economies.

Then tell students that reading ahead to the second paragraph will help them understand one of the ways in which Europeans wanted to rebuild their nations after World War II.

Give students *Reread or Read Ahead.* Have them complete the activity in their groups.

All in One Europe and Russia Teaching Resources, *Reread or Read Ahead,* p. 169

European Union, 1957–2005

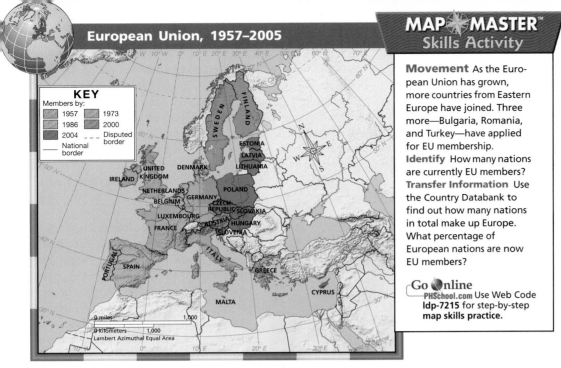

MAP MASTER™
Skills Activity

KEY
Members by:
1957	1973
1986	2000
2004	- - - Disputed border
— National border	

Movement As the European Union has grown, more countries from Eastern Europe have joined. Three more—Bulgaria, Romania, and Turkey—have applied for EU membership. **Identify** How many nations are currently EU members? **Transfer Information** Use the Country Databank to find out how many nations in total make up Europe. What percentage of European nations are now EU members?

Go Online
PHSchool.com Use Web Code ldp-7215 for step-by-step **map skills practice.**

History of the European Union

The ECSC created the European Economic Community (EEC) in 1957. The EEC expanded the ECSC, giving it greater economic powers. It also added the power to make social policies.

Expanding Membership Throughout the 1970s and 1980s, more and more nations wanted to join the EEC. The United Kingdom, Ireland, and Denmark joined in 1973. Greece followed in 1981. Portugal and Spain joined in 1986. Soon, the member nations began working on a new plan for an even stronger union.

The EEC Becomes the EU In 1992 the member nations of the EEC signed the Maastricht (MAH strikt) Treaty. This treaty established the European Union. It also laid out the plan for EU nations to adopt a single currency, or money. The currency is called the **euro,** (YUR oh). By 2001, twelve countries had adopted the euro. Denmark, Sweden, and the United Kingdom chose not to adopt the euro.

At first, only businesses and financial markets used the euro. In 2002, most EU nations withdrew their own coins and paper bills from circulation and began using euros instead.

✓ **Reading Check** What is the currency of the European Union?

Instruct

History of the European Union [L2]

Guided Instruction

- Have students read History of the European Union using the Paragraph Shrinking reading strategy (TE, p. T34).

- Ask **What was the origin of the EU?** (*Six European nations formed the European Coal and Steel Community, which eventually became the EU.*)

- Ask **Which countries joined the EEC in 1973?** (*the United Kingdom, Ireland, and Denmark*) **Which joined in 1986?** (*Portugal and Spain*)

- Ask **What did the Treaty of Maastricht accomplish?** (*It established the European Union and laid out the plan for its members to adopt a single currency.*)

Independent Practice

Have students create the Taking Notes graphic organizer on a blank piece of paper. Briefly model how to begin filling in the concept web.

Monitor Progress

As students work on their graphic organizers, circulate to make sure individuals are choosing correct information. Provide assistance as needed.

Vocabulary Builder

Use the information below to teach students this section's high-use words.

High-Use Word	Definition and Sample Sentence
legal, p. 73	*adj.* relating to the law
	The presidents signed the bill, making the new law **legal.**
debate, p. 73	*v.* to discuss both sides of an issue
	We spent a long time **debating** whether to go away or stay at home during the vacation.

Answers

MAP MASTER™ *Skills Activity* **Identify** twenty-five
Transfer Information about 60 percent

Go Online
PHSchool.com Students may practice their map skills using the interactive online version of this map.

✓ **Reading Check** the euro

What does the European Union Do? L2

Guided Instruction

- **Vocabulary Builder** Clarify the high-use word **legal** before reading.

- Read What does the European Union Do? with students. As they read, circulate and make sure individuals can answer the Reading Check question.

- Ask **What is the main goal of the European Union?** *(to make future wars impossible by binding together the people and governments of Europe)* **How does the EU work to achieve this goal?** *(by promoting economic and social progress)*

- Ask **How does the EU make it easy for the citizens of its member nations to move freely through the EU?** *(Citizens can travel to any member nation without a passport and can move permanently to another member nation without receiving official permission.)*

- Ask **How do EU member nations still retain control over many of their own policies?** *(Each nation makes its own decisions about health care, national defense, education, and housing policies.)* **Why might this be important?** *(Answers will vary, but students should recognize that each country has its own culture, heritage, language, and sense of pride.)*

Independent Practice

Have students add information about the origins of the European Union to their graphic organizers.

Monitor Progress

As students work on their graphic organizers, circulate to make sure individuals are choosing correct information. Provide assistance as needed.

Answer

Generalize Possible answer: People traveling between countries do not have to carry many different currencies to buy goods.

A Market With Two Currencies
A Spanish market lists prices in both euros (top) and pesetas, the old Spanish currency. Many European markets used both currencies before changing over completely to euros. **Generalize** *What are some advantages of having just one currency throughout several countries?*

What Does the European Union Do?

The EU was created at a time when the memory of a terrible war was fresh in the minds of all Europeans. For that reason, the goal of the EU was to make future wars impossible by binding together the people and governments of Europe. The EU works to achieve that goal by cooperating to promote economic and social progress. Unlike the United States or Russia, the EU is not a federation of states. It is a group of individual countries that have agreed to give certain powers to the EU. Each EU nation remains an independent nation. But by working together, the EU has strength and influence that no individual nation could have alone.

Common Social Policies The citizens of all EU member nations are considered equal. Throughout the EU, people can move around freely without needing special visas or permits. For example, citizens of the EU can travel to any EU member nation without a passport. They can even move permanently to another EU nation without receiving official permission.

EU member nations also establish common policies in areas such as education, the environment, and fighting crime. For example, EU nations have similar policies for combating poverty. EU nations also follow over 200 environmental guidelines set up by the EU.

Finally, the EU strives to protect European heritage and culture. European students are encouraged to learn foreign languages and study in other EU countries. The EU also sponsors cultural projects—such as theater, dance, and film—that are produced by EU member nations working together.

Common Economic Policies EU member nations can trade freely with one another without having to pay tariffs, or taxes, on international trade. In effect, the EU has a **single market**, or a system in which goods, services, and capital move freely, with no barriers. EU nations also cooperate to create jobs for citizens in all countries throughout the EU.

All EU member nations help plan and contribute to the EU's central budget. A special bank manages this budget, which pays for all of the EU's expenses.

Differentiated Instruction

For Special Needs Students L1

To help students access the material, have students read the section in the Reading and Vocabulary Study Guide before they begin reading.

📖 Chapter 2, Section 5, **Europe and Russia Reading and Vocabulary Study Guide,** pp. 28–30

For Advanced Readers L3

Have students read and analyze the primary source *Whose Falkland Islands Are They?* and think about why Great Britain operated on its own instead of involving the European Communities.

All in One Europe and Russia Teaching Resources, *Whose Falkland Islands Are They?,* pp. 194–196

Common Government and Foreign Policies

The EU has many different roles relating to government and foreign policy. It creates laws that govern its member nations. It also signs treaties with non-EU countries and organizations. Most of these treaties have to do with trade or industry. Finally, the EU oversees policies that have to do with crime and the national security of the region.

A court called the Court of Justice ensures that the EU's policies are applied fairly in every EU member nation. It settles any legal disputes between member nations, EU organizations, or EU citizens. The Court is made up of one judge from each EU member state.

Things the EU Does Not Handle Recall that all EU member nations still remain independent countries. Although EU member nations work together, they keep control over many of their countries' own policies. For example, each nation decides how best to handle its own healthcare, national defense, education, and housing policies. Still, member nations try to make policies that agree with the policies made by other member nations.

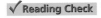 **Reading Check** What is the court that ensures EU policies are applied fairly?

Structure of the European Union

The EU has three main policy-making institutions. These institutions are the European Parliament, the Council of the European Union, and the European Commission.

European Parliament The European Parliament passes the majority of the EU's laws. It is the only EU institution that meets and debates in public. It is elected by all the citizens of the EU and represents their interests.

The number of representatives to Parliament differs according to the size of each country. When the Parliament meets, the representatives are assembled by political party, not by nation.

Council of the European Union The Council of the European Union is made up of the foreign ministers from individual EU nations. A **foreign minister** is a government official who is in charge of a nation's foreign affairs, or relations with other nations. The Council represents the separate national interests of the member nations.

A Seat of Government
The European Parliament is located in Strasbourg, France. **Infer** What challenges might EU nations have faced in deciding on where to locate its parliament?

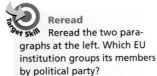 **Reread** Reread the two paragraphs at the left. Which EU institution groups its members by political party?

Chapter 2 Section 5 **73**

Assess and Reteach

Assess Progress L2

Have students complete the Section Assessment. Administer the *Section Quiz.*

All in One **Europe and Russia Teaching Resources,** *Section Quiz,* p. 168

Reteach L1

If students need more instruction, have them read this section in the Reading and Vocabulary Study Guide.

📖 Chapter 2, Section 5, **Europe and Russia Reading and Vocabulary Study Guide,** pp. 28–30

Extend L3

To help students extend their understanding, have them use *Outline Maps 14, 17,* and *18* to label the nations currently in the European Union and those expecting to join in the near future. They may do library or Internet research to help them find countries being considered for membership.

All in One **Europe and Russia Teaching Resources,** *Outline Map 14: Western Europe: Political,* p. 179, *Outline Map 17: Eastern Europe: Physical,* p. 180, *Outline Map 18: Eastern Europe and Russia: Political,* p. 181

Answers

✓ **Reading Check** the Council of the European Union

✓ **Reading Check** It must accept existing EU laws, values, and policies.

Section 5 Assessment

Key Terms
Students' sentences should reflect knowledge of each Key Term.

🎯 Target Reading Skill
Answers will vary, but students should identify how rereading or reading ahead helped their understanding of an idea in the text.

Comprehension and Critical Thinking
1. (a) Denmark, Sweden, and the United Kingdom **(b)** Possible answer: They might have taken pride in their own currency as part of their national identity.

2. (a) People can move freely between member countries; common policies have been established for the countries; European heritage and culture are protected. **(b)** It wants

to improve the quality of life for its citizens and protect their national identities.

3. (a) European Commission, Council of the European Union, European Parliament **(b)** Members of the same political groups probably have more goals in common than representatives of the same country.

4. (a) EU laws, values, and policies **(b)** Possible answer: They do not agree with EU laws and policies; they may feel as though joining

the EU will compromise their sense of nationalism.

Writing Activity
Use the *Rubric for Assessing a Letter to the Editor* to evaluate students' letters.

All in One **Europe and Russia Teaching Resources,** *Rubric for Assessing a Letter to the Editor,* p. 202

Members of the EU discuss energy resources with non-EU members.

Other EU Institutions The European Commission represents the interests of the whole EU community. It is made up of several different offices, each overseeing a certain area of policy. Each EU member nation sends representatives to the Commission. Other EU institutions perform services such as monitoring the EU's income and spending, advising on economic policy, and overseeing long-term investment.

✓ **Reading Check** **Which institution in the European Union represents each nation's national interests?**

Future of the European Union

In just over 50 years, the EU has enjoyed great success. It has brought peace and prosperity to almost 500 million Europeans.

The EU continues to expand. In 2004, ten nations from Eastern and Southern Europe joined. Three more countries have applied to join and are working to meet EU requirements. To join, new members must accept existing EU laws, values, and policies. The EU will continue to draw its strength from following its own rules and honoring its traditions. Its long-term goal is to bring all the democracies of Europe together. This process will be a careful and gradual one.

✓ **Reading Check** **What must a nation do to join the EU?**

 ## Section 5 Assessment

Key Terms
Review the key terms at the beginning of this section. Use each term in a sentence that explains its meaning.

🎯 Target Reading Skill
How did rereading or reading ahead help your understanding?

Comprehension and Critical Thinking
1. (a) Name Which three nations in the EU did not adopt the euro? **(b) Infer** Why might these countries not have wanted to adopt a single currency?

2. (a) List What are some examples of the EU's social policies? **(b) Analyze Information** What do these policies tell you about how the EU views its citizens?

3. (a) Recall What are the EU's main policy institutions? **(b) Draw Conclusions** Why do you think the representatives in Parliament are assembled by political group and not by nation?

4. (a) Recall What must new members of the EU accept before they can join the EU? **(b) Infer** Why might some European countries not want to join the EU?

Writing Activity
Suppose that you are a citizen of a nation that is interested in joining the European Union. Write a letter to your local newspaper describing both the benefits and the disadvantages of joining.

Writing Tip A letter should begin with an overview sentence or two. After describing the benefits and disadvantages, end the letter with a closing statement.

Review and Assessment

◆ Chapter Summary

Section 1: From Ancient Greece to the Middle Ages

- The first great philosophers, historians, and writers were the ancient Greeks.
- Ancient Romans created a system of written laws that are still in use today.
- In the Middle Ages, many people found order and security in feudalism and Christianity.

Section 2: Renaissance and the Age of Revolution

- The ideas, writing, and art of the ancient world later inspired Renaissance scholars and artists.
- Explorers began to travel beyond Europe in search of wealth.
- Revolutions in government and science changed European ways of life.

Section 3: Industrial Revolution and Nationalism

- The Industrial Revolution changed the way that goods were made and how people lived and worked.
- Workers began to demand better working conditions and a voice in government.
- Europe experienced a century of war and nationalism in the 1900s.

Section 4: Imperial Russia to the Soviet Union

- By the 1900s, Russia was a huge empire.
- Following the Russian Revolution, Vladimir Lenin came to power and a communist state was established.
- The Cold War was a time of great tension between the United States and Russia that lasted for nearly 50 years.
- After the collapse of the Soviet Union, the Russian Federation was formed.

Section 5: The European Union

- The European Union was officially created in 1992.
- The European Union works to achieve common security and economic goals.
- Three main institutions create European Union policy.
- The European Union continues to expand.

Euro bills and coins

◆ Key Terms

Match the vocabulary words with their correct definitions.

1. Industrial Revolution
2. euro
3. foreign minister
4. alliance
5. Renaissance
6. tsar

A a Russian emperor

B a government official who is in charge of relations with other nations

C the currency of the European Union

D the period of history when products began to be made by machines in factories

E a period of history that included the rebirth of interest in learning and art

F an agreement between countries to protect and defend each other

Chapter 2 **75**

┌ Vocabulary Builder

Revisit this chapter's high-use words:

process	policy	withdraw
rely	invade	legal
collapse	generation	debate
focus	reign	
radical	reform	

Ask students to review the definitions they recorded on their *Word Knowledge* worksheets.

All in One Europe and Russia Teaching Resources, *Word Knowledge,* p. 172

Consider allowing students to earn extra credit if they use the words in their answers to the questions in the Chapter Review and Assessment. The words must be used correctly and in a natural context to win the extra points.

- Review and revisit the major themes of this chapter by asking students to classify what Guiding Question each bulleted statement in the Chapter Summary answers. Have students work in groups to classify the statements. Use the Numbered Heads participation strategy (TE, p. T36) to have the groups share their answers in a class discussion. Refer to p. 1 in the Student Edition for the text of the Guiding Questions.

- Assign *Vocabulary Development* for students to review Key Terms.
  All in One Europe and Russia Teaching Resources, *Vocabulary Development,* p. 199

Answers

Key Terms

1. D
2. C
3. B
4. F
5. E
6. A

Review and Assessment

Comprehension and Critical Thinking

7. (a) democracy and the idea of learning through observation **(b)** He acquired a huge empire in which he established Greek cities, the Greek language, and Greek ideas.

8. (a) in the 1500s **(b)** the ancient world of Greek and Roman thinkers **(c)** The art of the Renaissance was more lifelike than the stiff art of the Middle Ages.

9. (a) People worked long hours in unsafe factories for low wages. The rapid growth of cities caused people to live in cramped, dirty housing where diseases spread rapidly. **(b)** to fight for better working conditions **(c)** As governments responded to workers' demands, people gained a greater voice in government and many European nations became more democratic.

10. (a) Millions of soldiers had been killed or wounded in World War I, and people at home were suffering shortages of food and fuel. **(b)** He promised poor Russians that everyone would be equal and enjoy a better standard of living to convince them to support communism.

11. (a) In the 1300s, the prince of Moscow conquered the territory surrounding Moscow. Ivan IV expanded Moscow's control; Peter the Great and Catherine the Great later added to the empire. **(b)** Under the tsars most people were poor and lived lives of hardship. **(c)** Under the tsars, only a few people owned the land and the rest were poor peasants. Under communism, the state owned everything. People were supposed to work and share the rewards equally, but the government took all the power.

12. (a) to promote security and a strong economy **(b)** to preserve national independence and identity

Skills Practice
Possible Answer: Problem—Wages were low and factory conditions were not safe. Solution—Workers formed labor unions and demanded better working conditions.

◆ Comprehension and Critical Thinking

7. (a) List Name two important ideas given to us by the ancient Greeks.
(b) Synthesize How did Alexander the Great spread Greek ideas?

8. (a) Recall When did the Renaissance reach its peak?
(b) Explain To what culture did Renaissance scholars and artists look for inspiration?
(c) Contrast How did the art of the Renaissance differ from the art of the Middle Ages?

9. (a) Name In what ways did people suffer as a result of industrialization?
(b) Draw Conclusions Why did labor unions begin to form during the Industrial Revolution?
(c) Identify Effects How did changes in society during the Industrial Revolution lead to changes in government?

10. (a) Explain Why was there rioting in Russia in 1917?
(b) Identify Effects How did Lenin use the power of ideas to persuade Russians to follow him?

11. (a) Explain How did Russia gain more territory and become an empire?
(b) Summarize Why did the Russian people come to oppose the tsars?
(c) Contrast How was Russia under the tsars different from the Soviet Union under communism?

12. (a) Recall What are the main goals of the European Union?
(b) Analyze Why might EU member nations prefer to handle some issues, such as healthcare, education, and housing policies, on their own?

◆ Skills Practice

Problem Solving In the Skills for Life activity in this chapter, you learned how to solve problems. Review the steps you followed to learn this skill. Then turn to the section titled Changes in Society on page 55 of this chapter. Identify the problem that factory workers faced. Then explain how the problem was solved.

◆ Writing Activity: Math

Rome's emperor Hadrian had a wall built from coast to coast across northern England, in order to defend his empire's land. The wall extends 73 miles (118 kilometers) from Wallsend in the east to Bowness in the west. There are many towers and gates along the wall. About every seven miles there is a fort. Calculate how long it would have taken an army to march the entire length of the wall, if their marching speed was three miles per hour. Write a paragraph explaining your opinion on whether a wall would work as a type of defense.

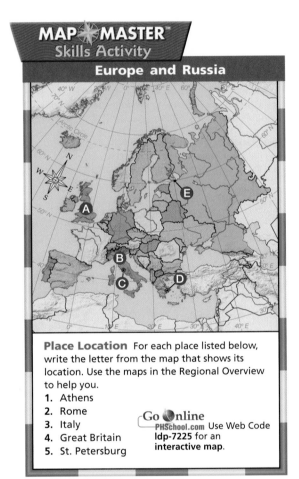

MAP MASTER™ Skills Activity

Europe and Russia

Place Location For each place listed below, write the letter from the map that shows its location. Use the maps in the Regional Overview to help you.
1. Athens
2. Rome
3. Italy
4. Great Britain
5. St. Petersburg

Go Online PHSchool.com Use Web Code ldp-7225 for an interactive map.

Writing Activity: Math

Students should note that it would take a soldier about 24 hours and 20 minutes to walk the length of the entire wall. Students might point out that this figure does not take into account resting or eating. Most students will conclude that this is not the best defense, although they should note the period in which it was used. They might also mention other walls erected for defense, such as the Great Wall of China. Use the *Rubric for Assessing a Writing Assignment* to evaluate students' paragraphs.

All in One Europe and Russia Teaching Resources, *Rubric for Assessing a Writing Assignment,* p. 201

Standardized Test Prep

Test-Taking Tips

Some questions on standardized tests ask you to find main ideas or topic sentences. Read the paragraph below. Then follow the tips to answer the sample question.

> In 334 B.C., Alexander the Great set out from Greece to conquer the world. Within ten years, his empire extended from Egypt to northern India. He founded many new cities across these lands. Greek culture linked the whole Mediterranean world by the time of his death in 323 B.C.

Pick the letter that best answers the question.

Which topic sentence is missing from this paragraph?

- **A** Alexander the Great was a great soldier, thinker, and artist.
- **B** Alexander the Great was one of the world's greatest military minds.
- **C** The accomplishments of Alexander the Great were enormous.
- **D** Alexander's conquest spread Greek language, culture, and ideas.

TIP Some paragraphs have a topic sentence that states the main idea. All the other sentences in the paragraph support this point.

Think It Through What is the main point of the paragraph? You can eliminate C because it is too general. Answer A may or may not be true, but even if it is true, it doesn't completely describe every sentence in the paragraph. That leaves B and D. Alexander was a great military mind, but the paragraph includes other accomplishments as well. The correct answer is D.

TIP Make sure that you read each answer choice carefully. Carelessness can easily cost points on a multiple-choice test.

Practice Questions

Use the tips above and other tips in this book to help you answer the following questions.

1. In a feudal system, there is a special relationship between
   - **A** knights and foot soldiers.
   - **B** lords and vassals.
   - **C** peasants and knights.
   - **D** peasants and kings.

2. Which of the following would not be discussed under the topic sentence, Renaissance sculptors made powerful lifelike statues?
   - **A** the work of Michelangelo
   - **B** the importance of human beings to Renaissance artists
   - **C** the role of printing in the Renaissance
   - **D** the 1500 sculpture named *David*

3. After World War II, Eastern Europe was under the influence of which country?
   - **A** the Soviet Union
   - **B** France
   - **C** Germany
   - **D** the United States

4. What type of leader was Joseph Stalin?
   - **A** president
   - **B** tsar
   - **C** prime minister
   - **D** dictator

Use Web Code lda-7201 for a **Chapter 2 self-test**.

MAP MASTER
Skills Activity

1. D   2. C
3. B   4. A
5. E

Go Online PHSchool.com Students may practice their map skills using the interactive online version of this map.

Standardized Test Prep

Answers

1. B
2. C
3. A
4. D

Go Online PHSchool.com Students may use the Chapter 2 self-test on PHSchool.com to prepare for the Chapter Test.

Assessment Resources

Use *Chapter Tests A and B* to assess students' mastery of chapter content.

All in One **Europe and Russia Teaching Resources,** *Chapter Tests A and B,* pp. 203–208

Tests are also available on the *ExamView Test Bank CD-ROM.*

⊙ *ExamView Test Bank CD-ROM*

Objectives

1. Learn about the everyday life of a young serf in the Middle Ages.
2. Understand the importance of work on a feudal manor.
3. Determine the author's purpose and point of view.

Prepare to Read

Build Background Knowledge L2

Ask students to recall what they have read about feudalism. Discuss what it would have been like to be a serf in the Middle Ages. Use the Think-Write-Pair-Share participation strategy (TE, p. T36) to have students identify what responsibilities someone their own age might have had as a serf.

Instruct

Pearl in the Egg L2

Guided Instruction

- Point out that some potentially unfamiliar words are defined for students in the margin. Clarify the meaning of the words before reading.

- Pair students and have them use the Paragraph Shrinking strategy (TE, p. T34) to read the selection.

- Ask students **What is Pearl's home like?** (*It is a hut made of mud and timber that has a dirt floor, a bed of straw, and is lit by a rushlight.*)

- Ask students **Why is it important for Pearl to work in the fields?** (*It is harvest time and her family needs the food for the coming winter. Her father is ill and cannot help, so her brother has to take their father's place working in the manor fields.*)

From Pearl in the Egg
By Dorothy Van Woerkom

Prepare to Read

Background Information
In Europe in the Middle Ages, a typical day for a person your age was quite different than it is for you. For one thing, a child at that time was considered much closer to being an adult than is a child today. This is because people had shorter life expectancies. More people in those days died of diseases that today can be cured.

Pearl in the Egg was the name of a real girl who lived in the 1200s. Historians know little about her. Dorothy Van Woerkom has written a book of historical fiction about Pearl. Her descriptions of Pearl's life are based on what historians know about life in England in the 1200s. At that time, people in Europe were just beginning to use family names. Usually they gave themselves names that described their work or their families in some way.

In this part of Pearl's story, you will read about a typical day in her life.

Objectives
In this selection you will
1. Learn about the everyday life of a young serf in the Middle Ages.
2. Understand the importance of work on a feudal manor.

---

rushlight (RUSH lyt) *n.* a lamp made with grease and part of a rush, or swamp plant

dripping (DRIP ing) *n.* fat and juices drawn from cooking meat

serfs (surfs) *n.* peasant farmers who worked the land as the slaves of a wealthy landowner

earl set the bowl of cabbage soup down on the floor near the rushlight. She knelt beside the box of straw that was her father's bed. She wiped his forehead, listening to his heavy breathing.

"Please, Fa," she coaxed. She broke off a piece from a loaf of black bread and dipped it into the soup. She placed it on his lips, letting the soup trickle into his mouth. She ate the chunk of bread, and dipped another.

"I will be in the fields until the nooning," she said, "so you must try to eat a little now. See, I have put a bit of dripping in the soup."

She forced the warm, mild liquid down his throat until the bowl was half empty. She drank the rest herself, chewing hungrily on the lump of fat that the sick man had not been able to swallow.

Again she wiped his face, and then she blew out the light. She crossed the smooth dirt floor, and pulled a sack from a peg on the wall near the door as she left the hut. Outside, the sky was gray with the dawn. Ground fog swirled around her feet. The air smelled of ripening grain and moist earth.

From other huts of mud and timber, serfs hurried out into the early morning mist. Some, like Pearl, would spend the day in their own small holdings in the fields. It was the time for har-

78 Europe and Russia

Read Fluently

Partner students and have them choose a paragraph from the selection. Have students take turns reading the paragraph aloud. Ask them to underline words that give them trouble as they read. Then, have them decode the problem words with their partner. Provide assistance as needed. Have students reread the paragraph two more times to improve their reading speed. Remind them to stop at the commas and periods and to read with expression.

vesting their crops, which would feed their families through the winter. Others, like Pearl's older brother, Gavin, had already left for work in the manor fields to bring in Sir Geoffrey's crops.

Sir Geoffrey was lord of the manor, which included his great stone house and all the land surrounding it. He owned this tiny village. He even owned most of the people in it. A few, like the baker, the miller, and the soapmaker, were freemen and free women. They worked for themselves and paid the lord taxes. For tax, Sir Geoffrey collected a portion of everything they produced. No one in the village had money.

But the serfs were not free. They could never leave the manor, or marry without the lord's permission. They could not fish in the streams or hunt in the forest. They owned only their mud huts and small gardens, called holdings, and an ox or cow, or a few geese or sheep. The serfs also paid taxes. Each year they gave Sir Geoffrey a portion of their crops. He took a share of their eggs; if a flock of sheep or geese increased, he took a share; and if a cow had a calf, he took that also. On certain days of the week each family had to send a man—and an ox if they had one—to help plow the lord's fields, harvest his crops, and do their work. Each woman had to weave one garment a year for the lord and his family.

The sun was up when Pearl reached the long <u>furrows</u> of her field, where the flat green bean pods weighed down their low bushes. She bent to see if the leaves were dry. Wet leaves would wither when she touched them.

The sun had dried them. Pearl began filling her sack, wondering how she could finish the harvest all by herself before the first frost. She had other plots to work as well.

Now that their father was ill, twelve-year-old Gavin was taking his place for three days each week in the manor fields. Sir Geoffrey would get his crops safely in! But if the frost came early, or if the only one left at home to work was an eleven-year-old like Pearl, that was of small matter to Sir Geoffrey.

Pearl stood up to rub her back. A serf's life was a hard life. Her father's was, and his father's before him. She sighed. Who could hope to change it?

Old <u>Clotilde</u> came swaying up the narrow path between her field and Pearl's. She waved her empty sack by way of greeting and squatted down among her plants.

"How be your Fa this morning?" she asked Pearl.

A page from a French book dating from around 1460 shows people planting seeds.

furrows (FUR ohz) *n.* grooves in the earth made by a plow

Clotilde (kluh TILD)

✓ Reading Check

Why does Pearl work alone in her family's holdings?

Literature **79**

Guided Instruction (continued)

- Ask students **What responsibilities do the freemen and free women in the village have to the lord?** (*Though they work for themselves, they are required to pay the lord taxes.*)

- Ask students **How does Sir Geoffrey control the lives of the serfs?** (*They cannot leave the manor or marry without the lord's permission; they cannot fish in the streams or hunt in the forest; they own only their mud huts, their small gardens, and some livestock; Sir Geoffrey takes a portion of any gains in their livestock each year. Each family must send a man to work in the lord's fields on certain days, and each woman must weave one garment per year for the lord and his family.*)

- Ask students **Why do you think the author includes the flashback to Pearl's meeting with Jack in the woods?** (*Possible answer: The author wanted to show how unfairly and cruelly the serfs were treated.*)

- Ask students **What will be the result of the hunters' damage to the crops?** (*Many villagers won't have enough to eat.*)

- Have students discuss what the author's purpose might have been in writing this story. (*Possible answers: to share the story of a real girl's life in the 1200s; to let readers know what feudalism was like*)

- Ask students **Based on the selection, how do you think the author feels about feudalism?** (*Possible answer: It was a hard and unfair life for serfs.*)

Answer

✓ **Reading Check** Her mother is dead, her father is ill, and her brother must take the place of their father in the manor fields, so Pearl is the only one left at home to work in her family's holdings.

Independent Practice

If students are having trouble following the selection, have them reread it with a partner, taking turns reading every few paragraphs aloud to each other. Ask them to write down the answers to the Reading Check questions as they read.

Monitor Progress

Circulate to make sure students are communicating effectively and are able to answer the Reading Check questions. Provide assistance as needed.

A painting of nobles hunting illustrates this manuscript, created in 1515.

bowmen (BOH mun) *n.* men with bows and arrows; archers

defiant (dee FY unt) *adj.* bold or resistant

"He took some soup. But he wanders in his head. He thinks I am my mother, though she's been dead three summers now."

"Ah, and he'll join her soon, Big Rollin will." Clotilde's wrinkled face was nearly the same dirty gray as her cap. "They all do, soon as they take a mite of sickness. For the likes of us to stay alive, we must stay well! Get the priest for him! He won't plow these fields again."

Before Pearl could reply, the shrill blare of a hunting horn sounded across the meadow, followed by the baying of hounds on the trail of a wild boar. Startled to their feet, the serfs watched the terrified boar running in and out among the rows of crops.

"Run, lest you get trampled!" Clotilde screamed, dashing down the path toward the forest. The others followed her. Someone pulled Pearl along as she stumbled forward, blinded by angry tears, her fingers tightly gripping her sack.

The hounds came running in pursuit of the boar. Behind the hounds rode the hunting party of twenty horsemen, led by Sir Geoffrey. At the rear was another man Pearl recognized. Jack, one of Sir Geoffrey's <u>bowmen</u>, had come upon her one day as she scrounged for dead branches near the edge of the forest. He had baited her with cruel words, rudely ruffling her hair with the shaft end of an arrow.

"Jack's my name. What's yours?" he had demanded, taking pleasure in her discomfort. For answer she had spat at him, and he had pressed the arrow's metal tip against her wrist until she'd dropped her bundle. Laughing, he had scattered the branches with his foot and grabbed her hair.

"Spit at me again, girl, and that will be the end of you!" Though his mouth had turned up in a grin, his eyes had been bright with anger. His fingers had tightened on the nape of her neck, bending her head back. She stared up at him, frightened, but <u>defiant</u>.

"Perhaps you need a lesson in manners right now," he'd said, raising his other hand. He probably would have struck her, but for the rattle of a wagon and the tuneless whistle signaling someone's approach. He had let her go with a suddenness that had left her off balance, and had stalked away.

Shaken, Pearl had turned to see Sir Geoffrey's woodcutter driving out of the forest with a wagonload of wood for the manor house.

80 Europe and Russia

Differentiated Instruction

For Gifted and Talented L3

Ask students to create a schedule for a day in Pearl's life. Remind them that her day depended on the hours of light available. Then have each student make another schedule showing a day in his or her own life. Ask students to write a paragraph comparing their lives with Pearl's. Students should include hours spent at work or other responsibilities, hours spent learning, hours spent at recreation, sleeping, and any other categories they can think of.

Now Pearl shuddered at the memory; but Jack was taking no notice of her. His eyes were on the boar and on his master. If the boar became maddened during the chase and turned on one of the hunters, Jack was ready with his arrows to put an end to the beast.

Over the meadow they galloped, and onto the fields. They churned up the soft earth, trampled down the precious bean plants, crushed the near-ripe ears of the barley and oats, tore up the tender pea vines. They chased the boar across the fields and back again, laughing at the sport.

When they had gone, Pearl ran back to her field. She crawled in the turned-up earth, searching for unbroken bean pods. The other serfs were doing the same.

"What is the matter with us?" she demanded of Clotilde, "Why do we stay silent, with spoiled crops all around us, just so Sir Geoffrey will have his sport?"

"Shish!" Clotilde warned, looking quickly around to see who might have heard. "Do you want a flogging for such bold words? Hold your tongue, as you see your elders do."

For the rest of the morning they worked in silence. At midday, Pearl picked up her half-filled sack. It should have been full by now. She glared fiercely across the meadow at the manor house, but she held her tongue.

Pearl returned home to find that her father had worsened. When she could not rouse him, she went for the priest.

About the Selection

Pearl in the Egg: A Tale of the Thirteenth Century, with illustrations by Joe Lasker, was published in 1980. Pearl in the Egg and Matil Makejoye, another character who appears in the book, were listed in the king's account books as minstrels in the court of King Edward I. The story of Pearl's life is fiction, but it is based on the life of real people in the 1200s.

flogging (FLAHG ing) *n.* a beating or whipping

✓ **Reading Check**

What stopped Jack from hitting Pearl?

Review and Assessment

Thinking About the Selection

1. (a) Recall What did the serfs use to pay their taxes?
(b) Explain Why did the serfs give Sir Geoffrey a portion of their crops every year?
(c) Infer The feudal system existed for more than 400 years. Why do you think it lasted for such a long time?
2. (a) Explain What did Clotilde mean when she said, "Do you want a flogging for such bold words?"

(b) Predict Based on what you know about Pearl, how do you think she might act the next time she sees the lord or one of his men?

Writing Activity
Write a Short Story
Write a preface to Pearl's story telling how she received the name Pearl in the Egg. Or write a short story in which Pearl awakens in 2005. She is still 11 years old, and her father is still ill. Describe her reaction to today's world.

About the Author

Dorothy Van Woerkom (b. 1924) was born in Buffalo, New York. She was an elementary school teacher before becoming a writer. She is most noted for her folktale translations and her religious stories. She often rewrites folktales, sometimes changing the characters' names and the settings, but keeping the plot.

Literature **81**

Assess and Reteach

Assess Progress L2
Have students answer the assessment questions.

Reteach L1
To help students understand and analyze the characters, have them make a chart listing each of these characters—Pearl, Clotilde, Jack—as a heading. Under each name, have students write words that describe the character in terms of feelings and actions. (*Pearl: worried about her father and the harvest; hard worker at home and in the fields: angry and defiant toward Jack; angry at the hunters. Clotilde: concerned and resigned about Pearl's father; fearful about the hunters; fearful about speaking out about the ruined crops. Jack: cruel and bold toward Pearl; angry at her resistance; dutiful during the hunt.*)

Extend L3
To broaden students' understanding of how feudalism worked, have them read *Lords and Vassals.* Partner students to discuss this selection and to compare it with *Pearl in the Egg.*

 Europe and Russia Teaching Resources, *Lords and Vassals,* p. 197

Review and Assessment

Thinking About the Selection
1. (a) They gave the lord part of their crops, livestock, and labor. **(b)** He owned the village and the land they farmed. **(c)** Possible answer: The lords benefited from it, and probably did not want the system to end; many of the serfs were probably too afraid to speak up for their rights.

2. (a) She meant that Pearl could be punished for criticizing Sir Geoffrey and his men.
(b) Answers will vary but students might suggest that Pearl will have angry words for the lord and his men.

Writing Activity
Use *Rubric for Assessing a Writing Assignment* to evaluate students' work.

 Europe and Russia Teaching Resources, *Rubric for Assessing a Writing Assignment,* p. 201

Answer
✓ **Reading Check** The woodcutter drove his wagon past them.

Chapter Overview

Overview

Section 1

The Cultures of Western Europe
1. Find out how industry has led to the growth of cities and increased wealth.
2. Learn about the cultural centers of Western Europe.
3. Understand how open borders affect life in Western Europe.

Section 2

The Cultures of Eastern Europe
1. Learn about the different ethnic groups in Eastern Europe.
2. Understand the impact of foreign domination on the region.
3. Find out about ethnic conflict in Eastern Europe.
4. Learn about Eastern Europe's cultural centers.

Section 3

The Cultures of the Russian Federation
1. Learn about Russia's ethnic groups.
2. Find out about the Russian culture and its educational system.

Discovery CHANNEL SCHOOL Video

Uniting Europe: Football
Length: 4 minutes, 43 seconds
Use with Section 1
Explores the origins of the game of soccer, or "football," as it is known in Europe. Explains how the game has brought Europeans together.

Technology Resources

Go Online
PHSchool.com

Students use embedded Web codes to access Internet activities, chapter self-tests, and additional map practice. They may also access Dorling Kindersley's Online Desk Reference to learn more about each country they study.

Interactive Textbook

Use the Interactive Textbook to make content and concepts come alive through animations, videos, and activities that accompany the complete basal text—online and on CD-ROM.

PRENTICE HALL
TeacherEXPRESS
Plan • Teach • Assess

Use this complete suite of powerful teaching tools to make planning lessons and administering tests quicker and easier.

Reading and Assessment

Reading and Vocabulary Instruction

↻ Model the Target Reading Skill

Main Idea The main idea is the most important point in a written passage. All of the details in a well-written paragraph or section should add up to the main idea. Write the paragraph below, from page 86 of the Student Edition, on the board. Explain that the main idea is often stated in the first or last sentence.

Model identifying the main idea by thinking aloud: "I will read the first and last sentences to see if either may be the main idea. I think the first sentence is the main idea because it is more general. Now I will read the entire paragraph to see if I can find details that support the first sentence."

Point out the supporting details by underlining each one:

Most Western European cities are a mix of the old and the new. Both public buildings and houses from the Middle Ages are a common sight. They stand next to modern apartments and office buildings. Cars and buses drive along cobblestone streets once used by horse-drawn carriages. Monuments honor leaders who lived hundreds of years ago.

Think aloud: "What do these details have in common? They all describe features of Western European cities. They support the main idea, that *Most Western European cities are a mix of the old and the new.*"

Use the following worksheets from All-in-One Europe and Russia Teaching Resources (pp. 227–229) to support the chapter's Target Reading Skill.

Vocabulary Builder
High-Use Academic Words

Use these steps to teach this chapter's high-use words:

1. Have students rate how well they know each word on their Word Knowledge worksheets (All-in-One Europe and Russia Teaching Resources, p. 230).
2. Pronounce each word and ask students to repeat it.
3. Give students a brief definition or sample sentence (provided on TE pp. 85, 92, and 101).
4. Work with students as they fill in the "Definition or Example" column of their Word Knowledge worksheets.

Assessment

Formal Assessment

Test students' understanding of core knowledge and skills.

Chapter Tests A and B, All-in-One Europe and Russia Teaching Resources, pp. 247–252

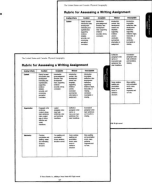

Customize the Chapter Tests to suit your needs.

ExamView Test Bank CD-ROM

Skills Assessment

Assess geographic literacy.

MapMaster Skills, Student Edition, pp. 83, 86, 92, 94, 101, 108

Assess reading and comprehension.

Target Reading Skills, Student Edition, pp. 87, 93, 102, and in Section Assessments

Chapter 3 Assessment, Europe and Russia Reading and Vocabulary Study Guide, p. 41

Performance Assessment

Assess students' performance on this chapter's Writing Activities using the following rubrics from All-in-One Europe and Russia Teaching Resources.

Rubric for Assessing a Writing Assignment, p. 244

Rubric for Assessing a Student Poster, p. 245

Rubric for Assessing an Oral Presentation, p. 246

Assess students' work through performance tasks.

Small Group Activity: European and Russian Music, All-in-One Europe and Russia Teaching Resources, pp. 233–236

Online Assessment

Have students check their own understanding.

Chapter Self-Test

Test Preparation

Europe and Russia Benchmark Test 1, AYP Monitoring Assessments, pp. 105–108

Section 1 The Cultures of Western Europe

 *1 period, .5 block*

Social Studies Objectives

1. Find out how industry has led to the growth of cities and increased wealth.
2. Learn about the cultural centers of Western Europe.
3. Understand how open borders affect life in Western Europe.

Reading/Language Arts Objective

Learn how to identify main ideas.

Prepare to Read

Build Background Knowledge
Discuss countries in Western Europe and their capital cities.

Set a Purpose for Reading
Have students begin to fill out the *Reading Readiness Guide.*

Preview Key Terms
Teach the section's Key Terms.

Target Reading Skill
Introduce the section's Target Reading Skill of **identifying main ideas.**

Instructional Resources

All in One Europe and Russia Teaching Resources
- L2 Reading Readiness Guide, p. 216
- L2 Identify Main Ideas, p. 227

Europe and Russia Transparencies
- L2 Color Transparency ER 16: Western Europe: Political

Differentiated Instruction

Spanish Reading and Vocabulary Study Guide
- L1 Chapter 3, Section 1, pp. 25–26 ELL

Instruct

Growth of Industry
Discuss changes in industry after World War II.

Centers of Culture
Discuss cultural attractions and popular recreational activities.

Target Reading Skill
Review **identifying main ideas.**

Open Borders
Discuss travel in Europe.

Instructional Resources

All in One Europe and Russia Teaching Resources
- L2 Guided Reading and Review, p. 217
- L2 Reading Readiness Guide, p. 216

Europe and Russia Transparencies
- L2 Section Reading Support Transparency ER 40

World Studies Video Program
- L2 Uniting Europe: Football

Differentiated Instruction

All in One Europe and Russia Teaching Resources
- L3 Small Group Activity: European and Russian Music, pp. 233–236 AR, GT

Teacher's Edition
- L3 For Advanced Readers, TE p. 86
- L1 For Special Needs Students, TE p. 86

Spanish Support
- L2 Guided Reading and Review (Spanish), p. 24 ELL

Assess and Reteach

Assess Progress
Evaluate student comprehension with the section assessment and section quiz.

Reteach
Assign the Reading and Vocabulary Study Guide to help struggling students.

Extend
Extend the lesson by assigning an Enrichment activity.

Instructional Resources

All in One Europe and Russia Teaching Resources
- L2 Section Quiz, p. 218
- L3 Enrichment, p. 231
  Rubric for Assessing a Writing Assignment, p. 244

Reading and Vocabulary Study Guide
- L1 Chapter 3, Section 1, pp. 32–34

Differentiated Instruction

Spanish Support
- L2 Section Quiz (Spanish), p. 25 ELL

Key

- L1 Basic to Average   L3 Average to Advanced
- L2 For All Students

- LPR Less Proficient Readers
- AR Advanced Readers
- SN Special Needs Students

- GT Gifted and Talented
- ELL English Language Learners

Section Lesson Planner

Section 2 The Cultures of Eastern Europe

 2 periods, 1 block (includes Skills for Life)

Social Studies Objectives
1. Learn about the different ethnic groups in Eastern Europe.
2. Understand the impact of foreign domination on the region.
3. Find out about ethnic conflict in Eastern Europe.
4. Learn about Eastern Europe's cultural centers.

Reading/Language Arts Objective
Learn how to identify supporting details in a text to help understand the main idea.

Prepare to Read	Instructional Resources	Differentiated Instruction
Build Background Knowledge Discuss the origins of different ethnic groups. **Set a Purpose for Reading** Have students evaluate statements on the *Reading Readiness Guide*. **Preview Key Terms** Teach the section's Key Terms. **Target Reading Skill** Introduce the section's Target Reading Skill of **identifying supporting details**.	**All in One Europe and Russia Teaching Resources** L2 Reading Readiness Guide, p. 220 L2 Identify Supporting Details, p. 228	**Spanish Reading and Vocabulary Study Guide** L1 Chapter 3, Section 2, pp. 27–28 ELL

Instruct	Instructional Resources	Differentiated Instruction
Eastern Europe's Ethnic Groups Discuss the Slavs. **Target Reading Skill** Review **identifying supporting details.** **Foreign Domination Ethnic Conflict** Discuss conflicts in Czechoslovakia and Yugoslavia. **European Centers of Culture** Discuss the major cities of Prague and Budapest.	**All in One Europe and Russia Teaching Resources** L2 Guided Reading and Review, p. 221 L2 Reading Readiness Guide, p. 220 L2 Your Government Has Returned to You! pp. 237–238 **Europe and Russia Transparencies** L2 Section Reading Support Transparency ER 41	**All in One Europe and Russia Teaching Resources** Rubric for Assessing a Student Poster, p. 245 AR, GT L2 Skills for Life, p. 232 AR, GT, LPR, SN **Teacher's Edition** L3 For Gifted and Talented, TE p. 95 L3 For Advanced Readers, TE p. 96 **PHSchool.com** L3 For: Long Term Integrated Project: Genocide in the Balkans AR, GT **Web Code:** ldd-7304

Assess and Reteach	Instructional Resources	Differentiated Instruction
Assess Progress Evaluate student comprehension with the section assessment and section quiz. **Reteach** Assign the Reading and Vocabulary Study Guide to help struggling students. **Extend** Extend the lesson by assigning a Book Project.	**All in One Europe and Russia Teaching Resources** L2 Section Quiz, p. 222 L3 Book Project: Tourism in Eastern Europe, pp. 80–82 Rubric for Assessing a Writing Assignment, p. 244 **Reading and Vocabulary Study Guide** L1 Chapter 3, Section 2, pp. 35–37	**Spanish Support** L2 Section Quiz (Spanish), p. 27 ELL **Teacher's Edition** L1 For Special Needs Students, TE p. 99 **Social Studies Skills Tutor CD-ROM** L1 Supporting a Position ELL, LPR, SN

Key
L1 Basic to Average	L3 Average to Advanced	LPR Less Proficient Readers	GT Gifted and Talented
L2 For All Students		AR Advanced Readers	ELL English Language Learners
		SN Special Needs Students	

Section Lesson Planner

Section 3 The Cultures of the Russian Federation

⏱ *3 periods, 1.5 blocks (includes Chapter Review and Assessment)*

Social Studies Objectives
1. Learn about Russia's ethnic groups.
2. Find out about the Russian culture and its educational system.

Reading/Language Arts Objective
Learn how to identify implied main ideas to help remember the most important information.

Prepare to Read	Instructional Resources	Differentiated Instruction
Build Background Knowledge Ask students to discuss works of art that they like or dislike. **Set a Purpose for Reading** Have students evaluate statements on the *Reading Readiness Guide*. **Preview Key Terms** Teach the section's Key Terms. **Target Reading Skill** Introduce the section's Target Reading Skill of **identifying main ideas**.	**All in One Europe and Russia Teaching Resources** L2 Reading Readiness Guide, p. 224 L2 Identify Implied Main Ideas, p. 229	**Spanish Reading and Vocabulary Study Guide** L1 Chapter 3, Section 3, pp. 29–30 ELL

Instruct	Instructional Resources	Differentiated Instruction
Russia's Ethnic Groups Discuss ethnic groups in Russia. **Target Reading Skill** Review **identifying main ideas**. **Eyewitness Technology** Discuss the beginning of the space age. **Russian Culture and Education** Discuss art and education in Russia.	**All in One Europe and Russia Teaching Resources** L2 Guided Reading and Review, p. 225 L2 Reading Readiness Guide, p. 224 **Europe and Russia Transparencies** L2 Section Reading Support Transparency ER 42	**All in One Europe and Russia Teaching Resources** Rubric for Assessing an Oral Presentation, p. 246 AR, GT L3 Writing Plays, p. 242 AR, GT **Teacher's Edition** L1 For Less Proficient Readers, TE p. 102 L3 For Gifted and Talented, TE p. 102 L2 For English Language Learners, TE p. 103 L3 For Advanced Readers, TE p. 105 L1 For Special Needs Students, TE p. 105 **Student Edition on Audio CD** L1 Chapter 3, Section 3 ELL, LPR, SN **Passport to the World CD-ROM** L1 Russia ELL, LPR, SN

Assess and Reteach	Instructional Resources	Differentiated Instruction
Assess Progress Evaluate student comprehension with the section assessment and section quiz. **Reteach** Assign the Reading and Vocabulary Study Guide to help struggling students. **Extend** Extend the lesson by assigning a literature reading.	**All in One Europe and Russia Teaching Resources** L2 Section Quiz, p. 226 L3 Lenin's Deathbed Words, p. 239 L2 Vocabulary Development, p. 243 L2 Word Knowledge, p. 230 L2 Chapter Tests A and B, pp. 247–252 **Reading and Vocabulary Study Guide** L1 Chapter 3, Section 3, pp. 38–40	**Spanish Support** L2 Section Quiz (Spanish), p. 29 ELL L2 Chapter Summary (Spanish), p. 30 ELL L2 Vocabulary Development (Spanish), p. 31 ELL

Key
L1 Basic to Average   L3 Average to Advanced   LPR Less Proficient Readers   GT Gifted and Talented
L2 For All Students   AR Advanced Readers   ELL English Language Learners
SN Special Needs Students

82e

Reading Background

Applying New Words Outside the Classroom

Expand students' understanding of this chapter's vocabulary by assigning an activity which applies the chapter's Key Terms and high-use words to students' lives. Choose five or six vocabulary words from the chapter, such as *urbanization, immigrant, ethnic group, conflict,* and *campaign,* and ask students to list them in their notebooks.

Next, ask students where they might *see* these words outside of their textbook. List the responses on the board. Suggestions might include signs, newspapers, magazines, history books, fiction books, and biographies. Then ask students where they might *hear* these words. Answers might include television or radio news broadcasts, conversations with parents or other adults, and political speeches. Finally, ask students how they might *use* these words. Students can suggest sample sentences or topics of conversation.

Have students keep a log for one week in which they record where and how they see their selected words printed or spoken. Have students share their logs at the end of the week.

Encourage Active Participation

In this chapter, students may use the Choral Reading strategy to engage them in actively reading the chapter. Remember that the following tips can help improve the effectiveness of the Choral Reading strategy:

1. Make sure that students say the words with you, without lagging behind or racing ahead in their speech.
2. Use only short passages of less than 500 words. Follow the choral reading with a silent reading of the same passage to allow students to review the materials silently now that they have heard the content.

World Studies Background

Languages of Western Europe

The two major language divisions in Western Europe are Romance and Germanic languages. Both divisions stem from the language of the ancient peoples who migrated to Europe from Asia. The Romance languages, such as French, Spanish, and Italian, are prevalent in western and Mediterranean regions. The Germanic languages, such as German, Netherlandic (Dutch or Flemish), and Swedish, are found in central, northern, and northwestern regions of Europe.

Roma of Eastern Europe

One of the least-understood groups in Eastern Europe is the Roma, sometimes mistakenly called Gypsies. They are descended from a group of people who originated in India. The Roma reside throughout the world, although most live in Europe. Many still speak the Romany language and live a nomadic lifestyle, traveling from place to place to find work. Few non-Roma know or understand much about this culture. In some countries of Europe, Roma have often been a persecuted minority.

Infoplease® provides a wealth of useful information for the classroom. You can use this resource to strengthen your background on the subjects covered in this chapter. Have students visit this advertising-free site as a starting point for projects requiring research.

 Use Web Code **ldd-7300** for **Infoplease®**.

Guiding Questions

Remind students about the Guiding Questions introduced at the beginning of the book.

Section 1 relates to **Guiding Question** ③ **How have the people of Europe and Russia been shaped by their culture?** *(Many European cities are centers of culture, and have museums, concert halls, restaurants, nightclubs, theaters, and stores.)*

Section 2 relates to **Guiding Question** ② **How have Europe and Russia been affected by their history?** *(Most ethnic groups in Eastern Europe are descended from Slavs. Throughout European history, as the Slavs separated and migrated across Eastern Europe, they developed different languages and dialects, and adopted different religions.)*

Section 3 relates to **Guiding Question** ② **How have Europe and Russia been affected by their history?** *(Under communism, artistic creativity nearly ended because the government only approved art that supported its propaganda campaign. The collapse of communism in 1991 led to a revival of artistic traditions in Russia.)*

⊙ Target Reading Skill

In this chapter, students will learn and apply the reading skill of identifying main ideas. Use the following worksheets to help students practice this skill:

All in One Europe and Russia Teaching Resources, *Identify Main Ideas,* p. 227; *Identify Supporting Details,* p. 228; *Identify Implied Main Ideas,* p. 229

Differentiated Instruction

The following Teacher Edition strategies are suitable for students of varying abilities.

Advanced Readers, pp. 86, 96, 105
English Language Learners, p. 103
Gifted and Talented, pp. 95, 102
Less Proficient Readers, p. 102
Special Needs Students, pp. 86, 99, 105

Chapter
3 Cultures of Europe and Russia

Chapter Preview

This chapter will introduce you to the cultures of Europe and Russia.

Section 1
The Cultures of Western Europe

Section 2
The Cultures of Eastern Europe

Section 3
The Cultures of the Russian Federation

⊙ Target Reading Skill

Identify Main Ideas In this chapter you will focus on finding and remembering the main idea, or the most important point, of sections and paragraphs.

▶ The golden domes of the Annunciation Cathedral brighten up the sky above Moscow, Russia.

Bibliography

For the Teacher
Egert-Romanowska, Joanna, and Magorzata Omilanowska. *Eyewitness Travel Guide to Germany.* Dorling-Kindersley Publishing, 2001.
Hancock, Ian. *We Are the Romani People.* University of Hertfordshire Press, 2003.
Richmond, Yale. *From Nyet to Da: Understanding the Russians.* Intercultural Press, 2003.

For the Student
L1 Flux, Paul. *Wassily Kandinsky.* Heinemann Library, 2002.
L2 Lane, Kathryn. *Germany: The Culture.* Bt Bound, 2002.
L3 Marcovitz, Hal. *The Balkans: People in Conflict (People at Odds).* Chelsea House Publications, 2002.

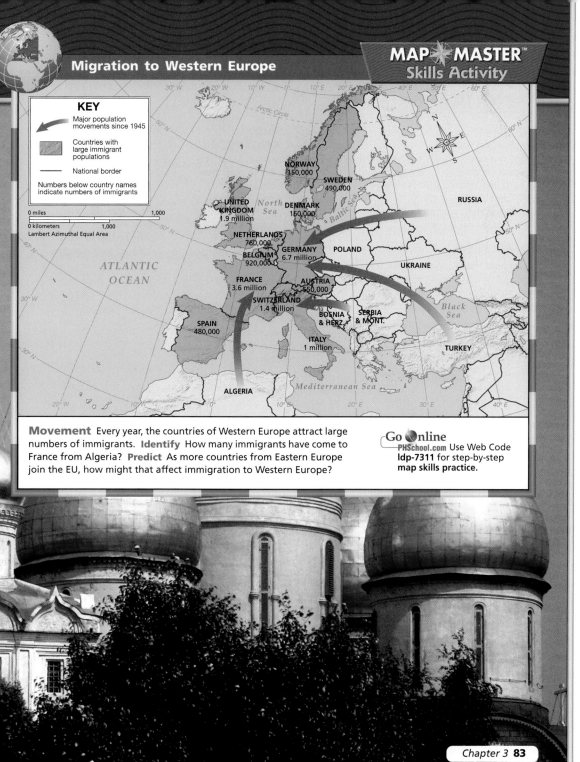

Migration to Western Europe

KEY

Major population movements since 1945

Countries with large immigrant populations

National border

Numbers below country names indicate numbers of immigrants

0 miles 1,000
0 kilometers 1,000
Lambert Azimuthal Equal Area

NORWAY 150,000
SWEDEN 490,000
RUSSIA
UNITED KINGDOM 1.9 million
DENMARK 150,000
NETHERLANDS 760,000
GERMANY 6.7 million
BELGIUM 920,000
POLAND
UKRAINE
FRANCE 3.6 million
AUSTRIA 550,000
ATLANTIC OCEAN
SWITZERLAND 1.4 million
BOSNIA & HERZ.
SERBIA & MONT.
Black Sea
SPAIN 480,000
ITALY 1 million
TURKEY
ALGERIA
Mediterranean Sea
North Sea
Baltic Sea
Arctic Circle

Movement Every year, the countries of Western Europe attract large numbers of immigrants. **Identify** How many immigrants have come to France from Algeria? **Predict** As more countries from Eastern Europe join the EU, how might that affect immigration to Western Europe?

Go Online PHSchool.com Use Web Code ldp-7311 for step-by-step map skills practice.

Chapter 3 **83**

MAP MASTER™
Skills Activity

Make a chart on the board with three columns labeled "Migration To," "Migration From," and "Number of People." Have student volunteers come to the board and fill in the information based on the map. Then lead a discussion as to why Western Europe might attract so many immigrants.

Go Online PHSchool.com Students may practice their map skills using the interactive online version of this map.

Using the Visual L2

Reach Into Your Background Draw students' attention to the caption accompanying the photograph on pp. 82–83. Ask students to compare and contrast the cathedral in the photograph to houses of worship that they have seen in their own community. Conduct an Idea Wave (TE, p. T35) with students to create a list of similarities and differences on the board.

Answers

MAP MASTER Skills Activity **Identify** 3.6 million
Predict It might increase migration to Western Europe.

Chapter Resources

Teaching Resources
L2 Vocabulary Development, p. 243
L2 Skills for Life, p. 232
L2 Chapter Tests A and B, pp. 247–252

Spanish Support
L2 Spanish Chapter Summary, p. 30
L2 Spanish Vocabulary Development, p. 31

Media and Technology
L1 Student Edition on Audio CD
L1 Guided Reading Audiotapes, English and Spanish
L2 Social Studies Skill Tutor CD-ROM
ExamView Test Bank CD-ROM

DISCOVERY CHANNEL **SCHOOL** World Studies Video Program

interactive Textbook
PRENTICE HALL
TeacherEXPRESS™
Plan · Teach · Assess

Objectives

Social Studies

1. Find out how industry has led to the growth of cities and increased wealth.
2. Learn about the cultural centers of Western Europe.
3. Understand how open borders affect life in Western Europe.

Reading/Language Arts

Learn how to identify main ideas.

Prepare to Read

Build Background Knowledge `L2`

Tell students that they will learn about the cultures of Western Europe in this section. Show students *Color Transparency ER 16: Western Europe: Political*, and identify the locations of several countries' capital cities. Point out to students the close proximity of the countries and their capitals, and have students list the ways they think that this might affect the people living in Western Europe. Use the Think-Write-Pair-Share strategy (TE, p. T36) to elicit student responses, and then list them on the board.

📖 **Europe and Russia Transparencies,** *Color Transparency ER 16: Western Europe: Political*

Set a Purpose for Reading `L2`

■ Preview the Objectives.

■ Form students into pairs or groups. Distribute the *Reading Readiness Guide*. Ask the students to fill in the first two columns of the chart. Use the Numbered Heads participation strategy (TE, p. T36) to call on students to share one piece of information they already know and one piece of information they want to know.

All in One Europe and Russia Teaching Resources, *Reading Readiness Guide,* p. 216

Vocabulary Builder
Preview Key Terms

Pronounce each Key Term, then ask the students to say the word with you. Provide a simple explanation such as, "Urbanization occurs when large numbers of people move from the countryside into cities."

Prepare to Read

Objectives

In this section you will

1. Find out how industry has led to the growth of cities and increased wealth.
2. Learn about the cultural centers of Western Europe.
3. Understand how open borders affect life in Western Europe.

Taking Notes

As you read this section, look for the main ideas and details about the cultures of Western Europe. Copy the web diagram below and record your findings in it.

Western European Cultures

🔁 Target Reading Skill

Identify Main Ideas It is impossible to remember every detail that you read. Good readers identify the main idea in every section. The main idea is the most important or the biggest point—the one that includes all the other points in the section. Sometimes this idea is stated directly. As you read, record the main ideas of this section in the Taking Notes chart.

Key Terms

• **urbanization** (ur bun ih ZAY shun) *n.* the movement of populations toward cities

• **immigrant** (IM uh grunt) *n.* a person who moves to one country from another

A high-speed train travels across Europe.

84 Europe and Russia

As the train speeds down the track, the passengers hear hardly a whisper. As the passengers sit in their comfortable seats, they can look out the window at the highway next to the railroad. They know that the cars are traveling at least 60 miles (96 kilometers) per hour, but the cars seem to be moving backward. That's because the train is traveling three times faster than the cars—about 180 miles (289 kilometers) per hour.

Would you like to take a trip like that? You can if you go to France, which has some of the world's fastest trains. Great Britain also has speedy rail travel. Some British trains reach speeds of 140 miles (225 kilometers) per hour. In Western Europe, high-speed trains have made travel between countries easy and fast. Someone in a European country can be in another country in hours. Such easy movement through Western Europe affects the entire culture of the region.

🔁 Target Reading Skill `L2`

Identify Main Ideas Point out the Target Reading Skill. Tell students that identifying main ideas will help them remember the most important information in their reading.

Model identifying main ideas by reading the second paragraph on p. 86. Point out that the main idea of the paragraph is that European cities have a mixture of old and new

structures. Note that this idea is stated in the first sentence of the paragraph.

Give students *Identify Main Ideas*. Have them complete the activity in their groups.

All in One Europe and Russia Teaching Resources, *Identify Main Ideas,* p. 227

Growth of Industry

Most Western European countries are prosperous, or wealthy. This prosperity is based on strong economies. The economies of Western Europe have grown because of productive industries and high-quality services.

Agricultural Revolution

The Industrial Revolution of the late 1700s sped up the development of industry in Western Europe. Before the Industrial Revolution, most people worked on farms. They could grow little beyond their basic food needs. There were few machines to help them do their work. Over time, new and better farm machines were able to do tasks that once required many workers. Farmers also learned ways to improve soil quality and fight insects. With these advances, farms could produce more and better crops with fewer laborers.

This revolution in farming, called the Agricultural Revolution, took place around the same time as the Industrial Revolution. Thus, as the need for farm workers declined, the need for industrial workers grew. Many people began moving to cities, where factories were located.

The Growth of Cities

Urbanization (ur bun ih ZAY shun), or the movement of populations toward cities, was a trend throughout the 1800s and 1900s. Following World War II, it increased rapidly. The United States provided billions of dollars to help Western Europe recover from the war. With this help, the region's industries came back stronger than ever. And even more people left rural areas to work in cities.

Today, the majority of Western Europeans have a comfortable life. They earn good wages working in factories or in service industries such as banking and food service.

✓ **Reading Check** What was the Agricultural Revolution?

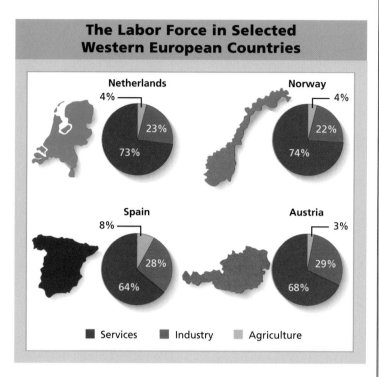

The Labor Force in Selected Western European Countries

Netherlands: 4%, 23%, 73%
Norway: 4%, 22%, 74%
Spain: 8%, 28%, 64%
Austria: 3%, 29%, 68%

■ Services ■ Industry ■ Agriculture

■ Diagram Skills

The economies of most Western European countries today are based on service industries. **Identify** Which country has the second-highest percentage of its labor force in services? **Apply Information** Recall the description of this country's geography in Chapter 1. Use this information to explain why its economy depends on services.

Vocabulary Builder

Use the information below to teach students this section's high-use words.

High-Use Word	Definition and Sample Sentence
revolution, p. 85	*n.* a complete or drastic change Modern sewing machines brought about a **revolution** in the fashion industry.
scholar, p. 87	*n.* a person with great knowledge in a particular area The history professor was a **scholar** in his field.
recreational, p. 87	*adj.* for the purpose of play or amusement Soccer is Sarah's favorite **recreational** activity.
exchange, p. 90	*v.* to give and receive The friends **exchanged** phone numbers and agreed to talk that evening.

Instruct

Growth of Industry L2

Guided Instruction

- **Vocabulary Builder** Clarify the high-use word **revolution** before reading.

- Read Growth of Industry, using the Choral Reading strategy (TE, p. T34).

- Ask students **What kinds of improvements led to the Agricultural Revolution?** *(New and better farm machines could do tasks that had once required many workers, and farmers learned ways to improve soil quality and fight insects.)*

- Explain the factors that increased urbanization in Europe after World War II. *(Billions of dollars from the United States helped European industries rebuild, causing more people to move to cities in search of jobs.)*

Independent Practice

Ask students to create the Taking Notes graphic organizer on a blank piece of paper. Then have them fill in one of the circles with the information they have just learned. Briefly model how to identify which details to record.

Monitor Progress

As students fill in the graphic organizer, circulate to make sure individuals are recording the correct details.

Answers

Diagram Skills Identify the Netherlands **Apply Information** Much of the land is covered by water and must be constantly maintained, so the Netherlands relies on the service sector.

✓ **Reading Check** the time during which new and better farm machines improved farm production while reducing the number of laborers needed

Centers of Culture L2

Guided Instruction

- **Vocabulary Builder** Clarify the high-use words **scholar** and **recreational** before reading.

- With students, read Centers of Culture. As students read, circulate and make sure individuals can answer the Reading Check question.

- Ask **What kinds of cultural attractions can be found in European cities?** *(museums, concert halls, restaurants, nightclubs, theaters, and stores)*

- Have students carefully examine the map on this page. List the names of the countries found on the map on the board. Divide students into pairs, and have each pair identify what language group or groups are found in each country.

MAP★MASTER™ Skills Activity   **Western Europe: Languages**

Place Though more than 50 languages are spoken in Western Europe, many of these languages are related. **Locate** Where are languages other than Indo-European languages spoken? **Infer** For what geographical feature was the Uralic language group named?

Go Online
PHSchool.com Use Web Code ldp-7321 for step-by-step map skills practice.

KEY

Indo-European Languages
- Celtic
- Germanic
- Romance
- Greek

Other Language Groups
- Uralic
- Basque
- — National border
- ⊛ National capital

Centers of Culture

It is difficult to travel far in Europe without coming across a city. People travel from small towns and villages to cities to find jobs. Some people go to cities to attend school. People also travel to cities to enjoy cultural attractions. These include museums, concerts, restaurants, nightclubs, theaters, and stores.

A modern entrance was added to the over-400-year-old Louvre Museum in Paris, France.

The Old and the New Most Western European cities are a mix of the old and the new. Both public buildings and houses from the Middle Ages are a common sight. They stand next to modern apartments and office buildings. Cars and buses drive along cobblestone streets once used by horse-drawn carriages. Monuments honor leaders who lived hundreds of years ago. Market plazas dating back to medieval times still thrive today.

86 Europe and Russia

Answers

MAP★MASTER Skills Activity **Locate** Spain, France, Finland **Infer** Ural Mountains

Go Online
PHSchool.com Students may practice their map skills using the interactive online version of this map.

Differentiated Instruction

For Advanced Readers L2
To learn more about aspects of different cultures in Europe and Russia, assign students the *Small Group Activity: European and Russian Music*. Students may work in pairs or groups to complete the activity.

All in One **Europe and Russia Teaching Resources**, *Small Group Activity: European and Russian Music*, pp. 233–236

For Special Needs Students L1
Ask students to pick out a paragraph or sentence under Centers of Culture that describes life in a European area or city. Have them draw a picture that illustrates what the text describes. *(To illustrate the description of Madrid in the text, students might draw images of people eating.)*

Vibrant Cities Each city in Western Europe is different from every other city. However, they all share certain characteristics. The majority of Western Europeans live and work in cities. Cities are also the centers of Western European culture.

Let's take a look at some Western European capital cities. Paris, the capital of France, attracts scholars, writers, and artists from all over the world. England's capital, London, is known for its important financial center as well as for its grand historic buildings and lovely parks. The Spanish capital city of Madrid (muh DRID) is known as a place with a vibrant street life, a place where people meet on cafe terraces to relax outdoors after work. As publishing capital of the Spanish-speaking world, it is also an important literary city. The German capital, Berlin, is always full of activity and attracts many visitors to its theaters and museums.

Work and Leisure Let's focus on life in Germany for a moment. Most visitors to Germany think that the Germans are efficient. In other words, Germans do their work without waste or extra effort. Visitors get this idea from what they see. German cities, streets, and buses are kept clean. Hotels are well run. German cars are well designed. Travel is swift on an excellent system of highways. Travel is equally fast on high-speed trains.

But life in Germany is not all hard work and fast-paced activity. Many workers enjoy as much as six weeks of vacation each year. Skiing, hiking, and camping are popular recreational activities throughout the country's mountains and highlands. The country's many rivers, as well as the North and Baltic seas, are good for swimming and boating. Those who prefer city life enjoy the museums, concerts, and plays. Life is similar in countries throughout Western Europe.

The European Union and the Arts One of the goals of the European Union is to support Europe's cultural community. Although different from one another geographically and politically, European nations often share a common history and cultural heritage. They all belong to the European community. The EU organizes concerts, cultural events, exhibits, and conferences to bring Europeans together. The EU's goal is to respect individual cultures, while encouraging cooperation among them.

European City Scenes
A trolley passes by historical buildings in Amsterdam, the Netherlands, in the top photo. The photo above shows Germany's Parliament building, called the Reichstag, in Berlin. It was built in 1995 after the country was reunified. **Infer** *Why do you think the German government chose a modern style of architecture for its new Parliament building?*

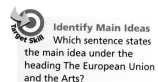

Identify Main Ideas Which sentence states the main idea under the heading The European Union and the Arts?

Chapter 3 Section 1 **87**

Guided Instruction (continued)

■ Discuss with students the examples of recreational activities that Germans participate in. Ask **How are these similar to or different from the recreational activities where you live?** (*Answers will vary, but students should identify which of their recreational activities are similar and which are different.*)

■ Ask students **What kinds of events does the EU organize to bring Europeans together?** (*concerts, cultural events, exhibits, and conferences*)

■ Ask students **What is the DEBORA project?** (*a project that gives Internet users access to documents from the Renaissance*) **How did EU support help this project?** (*Access to the collections of books and materials stored in libraries throughout Europe was often limited, but with support from the EU, people are now able to view the collections on the Internet.*)

Target Reading Skill

Identify Main Ideas As a follow up, ask students to answer the Target Reading Skill question in the Student Edition. (*One of the goals of the European Union is to support Europe's cultural community.*)

Skills for Life ## Skills Mini Lesson

Making Valid Generalizations

1. Teach the skill by telling students that valid generalizations can be made about a group if the statement is supported by facts that relate to the vast majority of the group.

2. Help students practice the skill by identifying a generalization in the first paragraph on this page.

3. Have students apply the skill by identifying a generalization in the section Growth of Industry on p. 85. Then have them explain what details support the generalization.

Answer

Infer Possible answer: Germany had just reunified, so it may have wanted to break away from the past by using a new style of architecture unlike the style used when the country was divided.

Chapter 3 Section 1 **87**

Have students read the **Links Across Time** on this page. Ask **How are the UK's immigration patterns expected to change?** *(As more countries from Eastern and Central Europe join the EU, large numbers of people from those regions are expected to immigrate to the UK.)*

Guided Instruction (continued)

- Ask students **Why did millions of Western Europeans leave Europe in the 1800s and early 1900s?** *(They left in search of more opportunities and better lives.)* **Where did they go?** *(Most went to the United States, Canada, and South America.)*

- Ask students **Where do most of the current immigrants to Western Europe come from?** *(Eastern Europe, North Africa, South Asia, and the Middle East)*

- Ask students **How have many Western European countries become multicultural?** *(Immigrants to these countries have brought their own languages, religious beliefs, values, and customs, causing the cultures of these countries to blend and change.)*

Independent Practice

Have students continue filling in the graphic organizer with details about Western European cultures. Encourage them to add extra circles as necessary.

Monitor Progress

As students continue to fill in the graphic organizer, circulate and make sure individuals are including as many details as possible.

Links Across
Time

Immigrants in the United Kingdom The United Kingdom's immigrant population today reflects its history as a world power. In 2001, nine of the ten countries from which the most immigrants came—including Ireland, Pakistan, Somalia, India, and Nigeria—were once under British rule. In the future, the UK's immigration patterns are expected to change. As more countries from Eastern and Central Europe join the EU, large numbers of people from those regions are expected to immigrate to the UK and other Western European countries.

To achieve that goal, the EU finances programs that help cultural development and encourage cultural exchange. One of the programs that the EU funds is the DEBORA (Digital Access to Books of the Renaissance) project. It gives Internet users access to documents from the Renaissance. The books and materials dating from the 1500s are stored in libraries throughout Europe. However, access to these collections is often limited. With the EU's support, Internet technology now makes viewing the collections possible. The EU helps museums, libraries, and other cultural institutions make these collections accessible to more people. By doing so, it helps connect people to their cultural heritage.

Changing Immigration Patterns Although life in Western Europe is good now, it was not always so. In the 1800s and early 1900s, millions of Western Europeans left Europe. Most went to the United States, Canada, and South America. They left in search of more opportunities and better lives.

Since World War II, patterns of human movement have been reversed. Large numbers of people stopped leaving Western Europe. Industry continued to expand in the postwar years and more workers were needed. As a result, people from other countries began moving to Western Europe.

Today's Immigrants Today, about 6 percent of workers in Western Europe are **immigrants** (IM uh grunts), or people who move to one country from another. Most of the immigrants in Western Europe are from Eastern Europe, North Africa, South Asia, and the Middle East. The four largest countries in the European Union—France, Germany, Italy, and the United Kingdom—all have large immigrant populations.

88 Europe and Russia

Background: Links Across Place

German Expressionism and Hollywood Germany has a long history of artistic achievements, ranging from opera to great works of literature. One German art form that had a strong influence on popular culture in the United States was early German filmmaking, especially during the period from 1919 to 1933. During this time a group of German artists created a style of filmmak-ing called German Expressionism. Their films, which were mostly thrillers, experimented with uses of light, settings, and make-up to create feelings of fear in audiences. This style greatly influenced most early American horror films. After the Nazi Party came to power in 1933, many German filmmakers moved to the United States and became leaders in the Hollywood movie industry.

More than 4 million immigrants live in France, making up 6 percent of the total population. Algerians make up the largest group of immigrants in the country. In 2000, the number of immigrants in Germany accounted for nearly 9 percent of its total population, or more than 7 million people. The majority of Germany's immigrants are citizens from Turkey and the former Yugoslavia, with smaller numbers of other Europeans and Asians.

About 2 percent of Italy's population is foreign-born, with Moroccans and Albanians being the largest groups. Increasing numbers of immigrants are also arriving in Italy from South America and China. Most of the United Kingdom's 2 million immigrants come from Ireland, India, and Central and Eastern Europe. They make up about 3 percent of the country's population.

Blending Cultures Immigrants do not leave their cultures behind when they leave their homelands. They bring their languages, religious beliefs, values, and customs to their new homes. But most immigrants make changes in their ways of life. They may change the way they dress. They may try new foods and discover new ways of cooking. Most immigrants learn the language of their new country.

In many ways, immigration has changed the cultures of Western Europe. In countries like the United Kingdom and France, people from many different backgrounds live and work together. They learn about one another's ways of life. In the process, the cultures blend and change. In this way, many Western European countries have become multicultural.

√ Reading Check **What does the European Union hope to gain by supporting the arts?**

Learn how soccer brings Europeans together.

Faces of Western European Immigration
The photos from left to right show Africans in France, Caribbean Islanders in the UK, a Turkish woman in Germany, and a South American in Italy. All are immigrants.
Analyze Images *Identify some cultural traditions that these people have brought with them.*

Background: Daily Life

Religious Diversity One change that has occurred as Western European countries have become more multicultural is a greater diversity of religions. In some countries, there is still primarily one religion—for example, nearly 90 percent of the French population is Roman Catholic. In the United Kingdom, however, where the Anglican Church has been the official religion for centuries, there has been a growth in the number of Catholics, Hindus, Jews, and Muslims. In Germany, a little over one third of the country is Protestant and one third is Catholic, with other religions practiced by the remaining population.

Show students *Uniting Europe: Football.* Ask **How does European football bring people together?** (*Many Europeans share a common love of the game, which brings them together, regardless of nationality.*)

Open Borders

Guided Instruction

■ **Vocabulary Builder** Clarify the high-use word **exchange** before reading.

■ As students read Open Borders, ask them to think back to the examples they listed in the Build Background Knowledge activity at the beginning of the lesson.

■ Ask students **How does geography influence travel in Europe?** (*Since most of the countries are small and close together, travel between them is quick and easy.*)

■ Ask students to look at the map on p. 86. Then ask **What language skills would be helpful to a person traveling across Western Europe?** (*Knowledge of several languages would probably be helpful, since there are many different language groups in Western Europe.*)

Independent Practice
Have students complete the graphic organizer with information from the section.

Monitor Progress

■ Show *Section Reading Support Transparency ER 40* and ask students to check their graphic organizers individually. Go over key concepts and clarify key vocabulary as needed.

📖 **Europe and Russia Transparencies,** *Section Reading Support Transparency ER 40*

■ Tell students to fill in the last column of the *Reading Readiness Guide.* Probe for what they learned that confirms or invalidates each statement.

All in One **Europe and Russia Teaching Resources,** *Reading Readiness Guide,* p. 216

Answers

Analyze Images Possible answer: their traditional style of dress

√ Reading Check It hopes to respect individual cultures, while encouraging cooperation among them.

Assess and Reteach

Assess Progress L2
Have students complete the Section Assessment. Administer the *Section Quiz*.

All in One Europe and Russia Teaching Resources, *Section Quiz,* p. 218

Reteach L1
If students need more instruction, have them read this section in the Reading and Vocabulary Study Guide.

📖 Chapter 3, Section 1, **Europe and Russia Reading and Vocabulary Study Guide,** pp. 32–34

Extend L3
Remind students that elements of a country's culture also include literature, such as plays. Have them learn more about one of England's most famous playwrights, William Shakespeare, by completing the *Enrichment* activity.

All in One Europe and Russia Teaching Resources, *Enrichment,* p. 231

Answer

✔ **Reading Check** the transportation of goods and people flowing freely across borders, and the use of the euro

Section 1 Assessment

Key Terms
Students' sentences should reflect knowledge of each Key Term.

↩ **Target Reading Skill**
Possible answers: Western European cultures are a combination of old and new. The growth of industry has led to urbanization and prosperity. Western Europeans of different countries easily share goods and ideas.

Comprehension and Critical Thinking
1. (a) industry **(b)** Cities grew, along with the immigrant population.

2. (a) France, Germany, Italy and the United Kingdom **(b)** They bring their languages, religious beliefs, values, and customs to their new homes.

3. (a) The countries are small and close together. **(b)** Possible answer: It would be difficult for people to travel across borders, and there might not be such a large exchange of cultural ideas.

Goods are transferred from a train to a truck in Munich-Reim, Germany.

Open Borders

You read that on a high-speed train, travelers can go from one country to another in a matter of hours. Ideas, goods, and raw materials can travel quickly as well. In addition to the closeness of the countries and the good train service, Western Europe is becoming more prosperous because goods and people can now flow freely across its borders.

Adding to the ease of movement across the borders is the use of a single European currency, the euro, which you read about in Chapter 2. Think about how different it was when a traveler had to stop at every country's border to show a passport and to change money to the local currency. Since 2002, the euro has replaced old currencies such as the French franc, the German mark, and the Italian lira.

Adopting the euro is one step in a series of efforts to move Europe toward both economic and political unity. Even the colorful design of the euro coins and bills reflects this effort. They do not have any famous people on them. Instead, they symbolize European unity by featuring a map of Europe, flags of the EU member nations, and bridges, gateways, and windows. The open exchange of ideas, goods, and money is an outcome of the European Union and has helped Western Europe thrive.

✔ **Reading Check** **Which factors have created a prosperous Western Europe?**

 ## Section 1 Assessment

Key Terms
Review the key terms at the beginning of this section. Use each term in a sentence that explains its meaning.

 **Target Reading Skill**
State the main ideas in Section 1.

Comprehension and Critical Thinking
1. (a) Recall What is Western Europe's prosperity based on?

(b) Identify Effects How has the growth of industry affected cities in Western Europe?
2. (a) List Which four Western European countries have large immigrant populations?
(b) Summarize How have immigrants changed the cultures of Western Europe?
3. (a) Explain Why is it easy to travel among Western European countries?
(b) Make Generalizations How would life be different for travelers in Western Europe if borders were not open?

Writing Activity
Write down two facts about Western Europe that you were surprised to learn. How has this new information changed the way you think about Western Europe or its people?

Go Online
PHSchool.com
For: An activity on the European Union
Visit: PHSchool.com
Web Code: ldd-7301

Writing Activity
Use the *Rubric for Assessing a Writing Assignment* to evaluate students' answers.

All in One Europe and Russia Teaching Resources, *Rubric for Assessing a Writing Assignment,* p. 244

 **Go Online**
PHSchool.com Typing in the Web code when prompted will bring students to detailed instructions for this activity.

Prepare to Read

Objectives

In this section you will
1. Learn about the different ethnic groups in Eastern Europe.
2. Understand the impact of foreign domination on the region.
3. Find out about ethnic conflict in Eastern Europe.
4. Learn about Eastern Europe's cultural centers.

Taking Notes

As you read, create an outline of this section. The outline below has been started for you.

```
I. Eastern Europe's ethnic groups
   A. Slavic heritage
      1.
      2.
   B. Non-Slavic groups
II.
```

 Target Reading Skill

Identify Supporting Details The main idea of a section is supported by details that explain or develop the main idea with reasons or examples. The main idea of the section titled Eastern Europe's Ethnic Groups is stated in the first sentence of the first paragraph under the heading Slavic Cultures. As you read, note the details following each of the blue headings that tell more about the cultures of Eastern Europe.

Key Terms

- **migration** (my GRAY shun) *n.* movement from place to place
- **ethnic group** (ETH nik groop) *n.* a group of people who share the same ancestors, culture, language, or religion
- **dialect** (DY uh lekt) *n.* a version of a language found only in a certain region

If you look at a map of Europe as it was one hundred years ago, you may notice something odd. Many of today's Eastern European countries are missing. Until 1918, three large empires ruled most of this region.

Eastern Europe formed a crossroads between east and west. To the east lay the Russian and Ottoman empires. To the west lay Germany and Austria. There were few mountains or other natural barriers to keep invaders out of Eastern Europe. For example, Russia, Prussia, and Austria moved into Poland and divided it among themselves in 1795. Poland did not become independent again until the end of World War I in 1918.

Movement throughout much of Eastern Europe has always been easy. For thousands of years, various groups have entered or crossed this region. This movement from place to place, called **migration** (my GRAY shun), is still happening today.

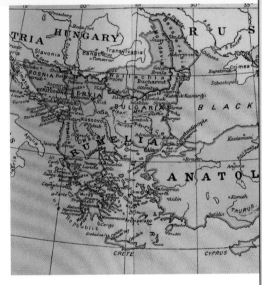

An Ottoman Empire map from the 1800s

 Target Reading Skill L2

Identify Supporting Details Point out the Target Reading Skill. Tell students that identifying supporting details in the text will help them remember the most important ideas in their reading.

Model identifying supporting details by reading the first paragraph on p. 93. Note that the main idea is that most of Eastern Europe's ethnic groups are descendants of Slavs. Identify supporting details that can help students remember this idea. *(One main Slavic group existed two thousand years ago. It separated, developing into about ten different Slavic language groups.)*

Give students *Identify Supporting Details*. Have them complete the activity in their groups.

All in One **Europe and Russia Program Resources,** *Identify Supporting Details,* p. 228

Objectives

Social Studies
1. Learn about the different ethnic groups in Eastern Europe.
2. Understand the impact of foreign domination on the region.
3. Find out about ethnic conflict in Eastern Europe.
4. Learn about Eastern Europe's cultural centers.

Reading/Language Arts
Learn how to identify supporting details in a text to help understand the main idea.

Prepare to Read

Build Background Knowledge L2

Tell students that in this section they will learn about the different ethnic groups in Eastern Europe. Ask students to list some of the different ethnic groups in their community. Then have them identify where these groups originally came from. Are any of them from Eastern Europe? Conduct an Idea Wave (TE, p. T35) to generate a list. Point out that ethnic groups move for different reasons, such as finding better jobs or escaping religious or political persecution.

Set a Purpose for Reading L2

- Preview the Objectives.

- Read each statement in the *Reading Readiness Guide* aloud. Ask students to mark each statement true or false. Have students discuss the statements in pairs or groups of four, then mark their worksheets again. Use the Numbered Heads participation strategy (TE, p. T36) to call on students to share their group's perspective.

  All in One Europe and Russia Teaching Resources, *Reading Readiness Guide,* p. 220

Vocabulary Builder
Preview Key Terms

Pronounce each Key Term, then ask the students to say the word with you. Provide a simple explanation such as, "The movement of people from one place to another is called migration."

Instruct

Eastern Europe's Ethnic Groups L2

Guided Instruction

- **Vocabulary Builder** Clarify the high-use word **descendant** before reading.

- Read Eastern Europe's Ethnic Groups, using the Paragraph Shrinking strategy (TE, p. T34).

- Ask **What ethnic groups are most Eastern Europeans descended from?** *(Slavs)*

- Ask **How did differences develop among the descendants of the Slavs?** *(As the Slavs separated, they developed different languages and dialects, and adopted different religions.)*

- Ask students **What might have happened if the Slavs had not migrated across Eastern Europe?** *(Possible answer: They probably would not have divided into so many groups, and another ethnic group might have populated Eastern Europe.)*

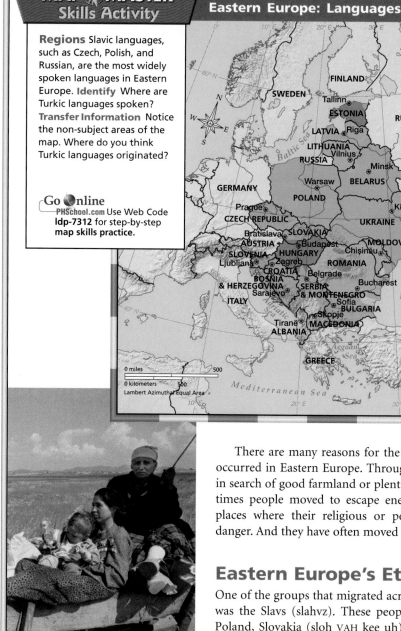

MAP★MASTER™ Skills Activity
Eastern Europe: Languages

Regions Slavic languages, such as Czech, Polish, and Russian, are the most widely spoken languages in Eastern Europe. **Identify** Where are Turkic languages spoken?
Transfer Information Notice the non-subject areas of the map. Where do you think Turkic languages originated?

Go Online
PHSchool.com Use Web Code **ldp-7312** for step-by-step map skills practice.

KEY
Indo-European Languages
- Baltic
- Slavic
- Romance
- Albanian

Other Language Groups
- Uralic
- Turkic

— National border
⊛ National capital

0 miles 500
0 kilometers 500
Lambert Azimuthal Equal Area

There are many reasons for the frequent migration that has occurred in Eastern Europe. Throughout history, people moved in search of good farmland or plentiful natural resources. Sometimes people moved to escape enemies. People have also fled places where their religious or political beliefs put them in danger. And they have often moved in search of a better life.

Eastern Europe's Ethnic Groups

One of the groups that migrated across Eastern Europe long ago was the Slavs (slahvz). These people first lived in present-day Poland, Slovakia (sloh VAH kee uh), and Ukraine. By the 700s, the Slavs had spread south to Greece, west to the Alps, north to the Baltic Sea, and east into Russia.

A Roma family

92 Europe and Russia

Answers

MAP★MASTER Skills Activity **Identify** Bulgaria, Ukraine
Transfer Information Turkey

Go Online
PHSchool.com Students may practice their map skills using the interactive online version of this map.

Vocabulary Builder

Use the information below to teach students this section's high-use words.

High-Use Word	Definition and Sample Sentence
descendant, p. 93	*n.* a person related to an earlier ancestor or family Paul is a **descendant** of his grandfather.
conflict, p. 95	*n.* a disagreement My sister and I were in a **conflict** over who would have the bigger bedroom.
thrive, p. 96	*v.* to grow vigorously; flourish Mia's boat rental business **thrives** in the summer.

Slavic Cultures Today, descendants of Slavs make up most of Eastern Europe's ethnic groups. An **ethnic group** is a group of people with a shared culture, language, or religion that sets them apart from their neighbors. Two thousand years ago, there was a single Slavic language. As the Slavs separated and moved to different areas, different Slavic languages developed. Today, about ten Slavic languages are spoken in Eastern Europe. These include Czech, Polish, and Russian.

Some countries in Eastern Europe are almost entirely Slavic-speaking. These countries include Poland, Croatia (kroh AY shuh), Slovenia (sloh VEE nee uh), and the Czech Republic.

However, even two people who speak the same Slavic language may not speak the same dialect. A **dialect** (DY uh lekt) is a version of a language that can be found only in a certain region.

There are also major religious differences among descendants of Slavs. Most follow the Eastern Orthodox faith or Roman Catholicism. Others may be Protestant or Muslim.

Other Ethnic Groups Many other ethnic groups live in Eastern Europe as well. About 90 percent of the people of Hungary belong to an ethnic group called the Magyars (MAG yahrz). In Romania, most people are Romanians. Similarly, in Albania, most people are Albanian. Roma, sometimes called Gypsies, and Germans live in several of the countries of Eastern Europe.

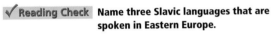 **Reading Check** Name three Slavic languages that are spoken in Eastern Europe.

 **Identify Supporting Details**
What details in these paragraphs give examples of Slavic languages?

Worshiping in Different Ways
Below, hundreds of Muslims pray at a mosque in Bosnia. At the left, women participate in a religious ceremony in an Eastern Orthodox church in Macedonia.
Synthesize *Though these Eastern Europeans practice different religions, what other cultural traditions might they share?*

Chapter 3 Section 2 **93**

Target Reading Skill L2

Identify Supporting Details As a follow up, ask students to answer the Target Reading Skill question in the Student Edition. (*Two thousand years ago there was one Slavic language; as Slavs separated, different Slavic languages developed; today there are about ten Slavic languages in Eastern Europe.*)

Independent Practice
Ask students to create the Taking Notes graphic organizer on a blank piece of paper. Then have them fill in the outline with headings and details from the section. Briefly model how to identify which details to record.

Monitor Progress
Circulate to make sure students are filling in their outlines correctly. Provide assistance as needed.

Answers

Synthesize They might share similar ways of dressing, similar languages, and other ways of life.

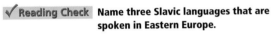 **Reading Check** Czech, Polish, and Russian

Foreign Domination [L2]

Ethnic Conflict [L2]

Guided Instruction

- **Vocabulary Builder** Clarify the high-use word **conflict** before reading.

- Read Foreign Domination and Ethnic Conflict as a class. As students read, circulate to make sure individuals can answer the Reading Check questions.

- Ask **How did the Soviets try to control people's lives in Eastern Europe?** *(They took private land, punished people for criticizing the government, and discouraged cultural traditions such as religion.)*

- Discuss the role cultural traditions played in Eastern Europe. *(Cultural traditions brought people together. For example, in Poland, Roman Catholics united in their opposition to the Soviets.)*

- Ask **Who controlled Czechoslovakia after World War II?** *(Communists heavily influenced by the Soviet Union)*

- Discuss how many Czechoslovakians reacted to the Communist government. *(Many were unhappy, and students and writers formed groups protesting communism and calling for a return to democracy.)*

MAP MASTER™ Skills Activity

Eastern Europe: Political

Regions This book uses the term *Eastern Europe* to describe the region including the former Yugoslavia and the nations dominated by the Soviet Union after World War II. **Identify** Which nation is physically in the eastern half of Europe, but is not part of what we call Eastern Europe? **Apply Information** Why is this country not considered part of Eastern Europe?

Go Online
PHSchool.com Use Web Code **ldp-7322** for step-by-step **map skills practice.**

KEY
— National border
⊛ National capital
• Other city

0 miles 400
0 kilometers 400
Lambert Azimuthal Equal Area

Foreign Domination

As you read at the beginning of this section, Eastern Europe is a region with a history of foreign domination. As you read in Chapter 2, most of Eastern Europe came under Soviet control following World War II. Communist leaders, influenced by the Soviet Union, led the governments of most Eastern European countries.

As in the Soviet Union, the Communists tried to control almost every aspect of people's lives. They took private land, and punished people for criticizing the government. They discouraged traditional expressions of culture such as religion. However, they did not succeed in destroying Eastern European culture. Instead, the cultural traditions you have read about brought people together. In Poland, for example, the Roman Catholic faith unified people in opposition to the Soviets. In Ukraine, people continued to speak Ukrainian even though Russian was the official language.

✓ **Reading Check** What country influenced Eastern Europe's leaders?

Answers

MAP MASTER Skills Activity **Identify** Russia **Apply Information** because much of Russia is located in Asia

✓ **Reading Check** the Soviet Union

 Skills for Life Skills Mini Lesson

Analyzing Primary Sources

1. Teach the skill by telling students that when they read a primary source, they should identify who wrote or spoke the information, and when and why they did so. They should then identify the main idea, identify facts and opinions, and determine whether the source is reliable.

2. Help students practice the skill by analyzing the primary source on p. 95 using the steps above.

3. Have students apply the skill by analyzing another of Havel's speeches, *Your Government Has Returned to You!*

All in One Europe and Russia Teaching Resources, *Your Government Has Returned to You!*, pp. 237–238

Ethnic Conflict

Eastern Europe's long history of migration and foreign domination have made it an ethnically diverse region. At times, that diversity has brought ethnic conflict. Ethnic conflict in the region has been resolved both peacefully and violently.

Czechs and Slovaks: A Peaceful Division Czechoslovakia (chek uh sloh VAH kee uh) had two main ethnic groups. The Czechs lived mostly in the western regions of Bohemia and Moravia. The Slovaks lived mostly in the eastern region of Slovakia. Hungarians, Ukrainians, Germans, and Poles lived in both areas.

Czechoslovakia was taken over by Communists, heavily influenced by the Soviet Union, after World War II. From the 1960s to the 1980s, students and writers formed groups protesting communism and calling for a return to democracy. Vaclav Havel, a playwright, explained his reasons for staying in Czechoslovakia.

> **❝I am Czech. . . . This is my language, this is my home. I don't feel myself to be patriotic, because I don't feel that to be Czech is to be something more than French, English, or European, or anybody else. . . . I try to do something for my country because I live here. ❞**
>
> —Vaclav Havel

Such protests helped end communism in Czechoslovakia. However, Czechs and the Slovaks disagreed about how to run the newly democratic country. In 1993, they agreed to peacefully separate into two countries—the Czech Republic and Slovakia.

Yugoslavia: A Violent Division Unlike in Czechoslovakia, ethnic differences in the former country of Yugoslavia (yoo goh SLAH vee uh) led to violence and the breakup of the country. You will read more about this conflict in Chapter 5.

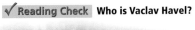 **Reading Check** Who is Vaclav Havel?

The Velvet Revolution
Crowds celebrate Czechoslovakia's transition to a democratic government, which took place in a peaceful movement called the Velvet Revolution. Playwright Vaclav Havel, shown below, became the country's first president. **Infer** *Why was Czechoslovakia's change in government called the "Velvet Revolution"?*

Chapter 3 Section 2 **95**

Differentiated Instruction

For Gifted and Talented `L3`
To learn more about the conflicts that occurred during the breakup of Yugoslavia, have students read *Genocide in the Balkans*, and answer the questions.

Go Online
PHSchool.com

For: Long Term Integrated Project: *Genocide in the Balkans*
Visit: PHSchool.com
Web Code: ldd-7304

Guided Instruction (continued)

■ Ask **Why did Czechoslovakia divide in 1993?** *(The Czechs and Slovaks disagreed about the future of the country.)* **What countries emerged as a result of this split?** *(the Czech Republic and Slovakia)*

■ Ask **How did the division of Yugoslavia differ from that of Czechoslovakia?** *(Conflicts and violence broke out within Yugoslavia, leading to its breakup.)*

Independent Practice
Have students continue to fill in their outlines as they read the section.

Monitor Progress
As students fill in details from the section, circulate to check students' outlines and provide assistance as needed.

Answers

Infer Possible answer: Velvet is a smooth fabric, and the transition went smoothly and peacefully.

✔ **Reading Check** the playwright who became the first president of Czechoslovakia

Chapter 3 Section 2 **95**

European Centers of Culture

L2

Guided Instruction

- **Vocabulary Builder** Clarify the high-use word **thrive** before reading.

- Read European Centers of Culture as a class.

- Discuss the ways in which Prague has been an important center of culture through history. *(In the past, several famous composers lived there. Today, the music of these composers is still performed there. The city is well-known for its theaters, and is an important center for art.)*

- Ask **How did geography play a part in the development of Prague and Budapest into major cities?** *(Possible answer: Both are located on major rivers which may have provided transportation, ports for trade, and water for drinking, making these locations good for the development of cities.)*

- Ask **How was Budapest different from many other European cities during Communist rule?** *(It was able to remain a thriving cultural center because Hungary's ties to Western Europe were stronger than those of other Eastern European countries.)*

Independent Practice

Have students complete their outlines with the information they have just read.

Monitor Progress

- Show *Section Reading Support Transparency ER 41* and ask students to check their graphic organizers individually. Go over key concepts and clarify key vocabulary as needed.

  📖 **Europe and Russia Transparencies,** *Section Reading Support Transparency ER 41*

- Tell students to fill in the last column of their *Reading Readiness Guides*. Probe for what they learned that confirms or invalidates each statement.

  All in One Europe and Russia Teaching Resources, *Reading Readiness Guide,* p. 220

Answer

Apply Information Because of the Czech Republic's architecture and cultural attractions, tourism is probably an important part of the economy.

Prague: A Historic City
Prague's buildings are a rich mix of architectural styles, including Renaissance, Gothic, and modern. Many of Prague's historic buildings house art collections. **Apply Information** *What role do you think tourism plays in the economy of the Czech Republic?*

European Centers of Culture

As in Western Europe, Eastern Europe's cities are important centers of life and culture throughout the region. These cities have thrived particularly since the fall of communist governments in the region in the 1980s.

Prague: A City Rich in Culture Prague (prahg) is the capital of the Czech Republic. Though people settled in the region thousands of years ago, the city first developed in the A.D. 800s. The Vltava (VUL tuh vuh) River winds its way through the city. Prague Castle, built in the late 800s, sits high on a hill overlooking the city. Houses dating back hundreds of years line the narrow streets of the historic city center.

Prague has always been an important center of culture. Antonín Dvořák (AHN toh nin DVAWR zhahk) and several other famous Czech composers lived in Prague. Today, their music is performed every year at a spring music festival in the city. The composer Wolfgang Mozart, an Austrian, also lived and wrote some of his famous pieces in Prague.

Prague is well known for its many theaters. It is also an important center for art, with its many museums and galleries.

96 Europe and Russia

Differentiated Instruction

For Advanced Readers L3
Have students work in pairs to research other famous Czech artists, such as Franz Kafka, Rainer Maria Rilke, or Antonín Dvořák. Then have them create a poster with biographical information about the artist, as well as his or her artistic achieve- ments. Use *Rubric for Assessing a Student Poster* to evaluate students' work.

All in One Europe and Russia Teaching Resources, *Rubric for Assessing a Student Poster,* p. 245

Budapest: Queen of the Danube

Budapest (BOO duh pest) is Hungary's capital and its largest city. The Danube River runs through the city and separates it into two regions, Buda and Pest. These two regions, once separate cities, were joined together in 1873. Budapest got the nickname "Queen of the Danube" because of the beauty of the Danube and the hills surrounding the city.

The history of Budapest stretches back to pre-Roman times. Ruins of Roman houses and baths can still be seen in Budapest. Today, it is a bustling capital city where more than one fifth of all Hungarians live. Unlike many Eastern European cities, Budapest remained a thriving cultural center even during communist times. This was because Hungary had stronger ties to Western Europe than other Eastern European countries had.

Like Prague, Budapest has produced famous composers such as Béla Bartók (BAY lah BAHR tawk) and Franz Liszt (frahntsz list). It is also an important center of art, theater, and scientific research.

Hungarian composers Béla Bartók (seated at left) and Zoltán Kodály (seated at right), with other Hungarian musicians, in the early 1900s

√ **Reading Check** What is the capital of the Czech Republic?

Section 2 Assessment

Key Terms
Review the key terms at the beginning of this section. Use each term in a sentence that explains its meaning.

Target Reading Skill
State the details that support the main idea on page 95.

Comprehension and Critical Thinking
1. (a) Locate Where did Slavs first live in Europe?
(b) Generalize What are some differences among Slavic groups?

(c) Summarize How did Poles use their culture to oppose the Soviet Union?
2. (a) Note Give an example of an Eastern European ethnic conflict that was solved peacefully.
(b) Conclude Why were the groups in this conflict able to come to an agreement without violence?
3. (a) Identify Name two important Eastern European cities that are centers of culture.
(b) Predict How might EU membership affect life in these two cities?

Writing Activity
Write a paragraph about ethnic diversity in Eastern Europe. In your paragraph, explain how ethnic diversity can enrich a country's culture and how it can create challenges as well.

> **Writing Tip** Begin your paragraph with a topic sentence that states your main idea. Be sure to include examples that support your main idea.

Chapter 3 Section 2 **97**

Objective

Learn how to support a position.

Prepare to Read

Build Background Knowledge L2

On the board, write the following statements: "I think students should be assigned homework over the weekend. I think students should not be assigned homework over the weekend." Ask students to choose which statement they agree with. Discuss with students which position they agree with, using the Idea Wave participation strategy (TE, p. T35). Then ask them how they chose which position to support.

Instruct

Supporting a Position L2

Guided Instruction

- Read the steps to supporting a position as a class and write them on the board.

- Practice the skill by following the steps on p. 99 as a class. Model each step in the activity by writing a statement that supports your position (*answers will vary, but should be in favor of or against immigration*), identifying three reasons that support the position (*answers will vary, but should identify three reasons that support the chosen position*), supporting each reason with accurate evidence (*answers will vary, but should include accurate evidence for the three reasons*), organizing the reasons and supporting evidence and identifying connections (*answers will vary, but should show connections between pieces of information for the chosen position*), and adding a reasoned conclusion (*conclusions will vary, but should restate and summarize the chosen position*).

Independent Practice

Assign *Skills for Life* and have students complete it individually.

All in One Europe and Russia Teaching Resources, *Skills for Life*, p. 232

Skills for Life Supporting a Position

A French police officer checks an immigrant's passport.

Mr. St. Jean's debate class was discussing immigration. Mr. St. Jean had chosen that topic because he knew people had strong—and often opposing—opinions about the subject. For example, he pointed out that some people believe that when a country's economy is not doing well, immigration should be limited. They reason that immigrants might take jobs from people who have lived in the country for many years. Mr. St. Jean asked his class to think about this issue. Should countries limit immigration? And if so, what should the limits be?

Asiya thought about her own family. They had emigrated from Algeria to France. Her mother worked in a restaurant, and her father worked in a library. She did not think her parents had taken jobs from any French people. And if they had stayed in Algeria, they would not have had as good a life as they had in France. She decided to argue in favor of immigration.

When you support a position, you present the reasoning and the evidence that back up your opinion or statement.

Learn the Skill

To learn how to support a position, follow the steps below:

1. **Write a statement that summarizes the position you want to support.** In general, a position is a broadly stated opinion that can be supported with facts. For her position statement, Asiya wrote, *Countries should not limit immigration.*

2. **Identify at least three reasons that support your position.** You may want to make notes or create a chart. Add as many details as you can to strengthen your argument. Use examples.

3. **Support each reason with accurate evidence.** Use reliable sources to strengthen your argument.

4. **Organize your reasons and supporting evidence.** Explain the connections between pieces of information, such as cause and effect.

5. **Add a reasoned conclusion.** Your conclusion should restate your position and summarize your reasons for it.

98 Europe and Russia

Monitor Progress

As students are completing *Skills for Life*, circulate to make sure individuals are applying the skill steps effectively. Provide assistance as needed.

Practice the Skill

Reread the passages about immigration and culture on pages 88–89. Then decide what *your* position is about immigration. Use the steps in Learn the Skill to support your position.

1 Prepare to write a statement summarizing your position by first jotting down your ideas about immigration. Think about these questions as you decide on your position: Why do people emigrate? Why do some countries welcome immigrants? Why do other countries sharply limit immigration? How do immigrants affect the countries they move to? Now choose a position, and write a statement that summarizes it.

2 Add at least three reasons to explain why you hold your position. Clarify your reasons with examples or other details.

3 Research your position using reliable sources. Add additional reasons, details, and examples.

4 Review the information you have gathered and organize it in order to strengthen your argument. Does one reason lead to another?

5 Summarize your position about immigration in a one-sentence conclusion.

I support immigration because....

I do not support immigration because....

Apply the Skill

Reread the passage titled Growth of Industry on page 85. Use the steps you have learned in this lesson to identify and support a position on whether the trend toward urbanization in Europe is a positive or a negative thing.

Assess Progress   L2

Ask students to do the Apply the Skill activity.

Reteach   L1

If students are having trouble applying the skill steps, have them review the skill using the interactive Social Studies Skills Tutor CD-ROM.

 Supporting a Position, **Social Studies Skills Tutor CD-ROM**

Extend   L3

Write the following on the board: "Immigrants should try and blend into their new country's culture as much as possible." Then write, "Immigrants should learn about their new country's culture, but should also retain some of their own customs and traditions." Have students reread the text under the subheading Blending Cultures on p. 89. Working together in pairs, have students write a paragraph that supports one of the positions.

Differentiated Instruction

For Special Needs Students   L1
Partner special needs students with more proficient students to do Level 1 of the Supporting a Position lesson on the Social Studies Skill Tutor CD-ROM together.

When students feel more confident, they can move onto Level 2 alone.

Supporting a Position, **Social Studies Skill Tutor CD-ROM**

Answer
Apply the Skill

Answers will vary, but students should identify and support a position on whether or not they think urbanization in Europe is a positive or negative trend.

Objectives

Social Studies
1. Learn about Russia's ethnic groups.
2. Find out about Russia's culture and its educational system.

Reading/Language Arts
Learn how to identify implied main ideas to help remember the most important information.

Prepare to Read

Build Background Knowledge L2

Tell students that in this section they will learn about the cultural achievements of Russia. Ask students to preview the headings, photographs, art, and captions in the section, keeping the following questions in mind: **What artwork did they like? Did they dislike any artwork? Do they think that artists should be able to create whatever they like without outside interference, such as government involvement?** Use the Give One, Get One participation strategy (TE, p. T37) to elicit student responses, and then record them on the board.

Set a Purpose for Reading L2

■ Preview the Objectives.

■ Form students into pairs or groups. Distribute the *Reading Readiness Guide*. Ask the students to fill in the first two columns of the chart. Use the Numbered Heads participation strategy (TE, p. T36) to call on students to share one piece of information they already know and one piece of information they want to know.

All in One Europe and Russia Teaching Resources, *Reading Readiness Guide*, p. 224

Vocabulary Builder
Preview Key Terms

Pronounce each Key Term, then ask the students to say the word with you. Provide a simple explanation such as, "A government represses a group of people when it does not allow them to practice their religion freely."

Prepare to Read

Objectives
In this section you will
1. Learn about Russia's ethnic groups.
2. Find out about Russia's culture and its educational system.

Taking Notes
As you read this section, look for information about how cultural expression differed in the Soviet Union and Russia. Copy the table below and record your findings in it.

Cultural Expression	
Soviet Union	**Russia**
•	•
•	•
•	•
•	•

Moscow's St. Basil's Cathedral was built in the 1500s.

100 Europe and Russia

Target Reading Skill

Identify Main Ideas
Identifying main ideas can help you remember what you read. Sometimes the main idea is not stated directly. To find the main idea, add up all the details in the paragraphs and then state the main idea in your own words. Carefully read the details in the two paragraphs below. Then state the main idea of that section.

Key Terms
• **heritage** (HEHR uh tij) *n.* the customs and practices passed from one generation to the next
• **propaganda** (prahp uh GAN duh) *n.* the spread of ideas designed to support a cause or hurt an opposing cause

For many years, Russians passing the Church of Saints Cosmas and Damian in Moscow never heard a choir. They never saw a bride and groom leave the church. They never heard religious services. The only sound they heard was the hum of machines printing government documents. The government of the Soviet Union owned the church and used it as a printing shop. In the Soviet Union, the government tried to prevent people from practicing religion.

In 1991, the Soviet Union collapsed. Two years later, Russians who had never given up their faith took back their church. Now the Church of Saints Cosmas and Damian is filled with people singing songs of worship. In recent years, hundreds of other churches in Moscow have reopened their doors. The same return to religion can be seen in places of worship across all of Russia.

Target Reading Skill L2

Identify Main Ideas Point out the Target Reading Skill. Tell students that when the main idea of a text is not stated directly, they must read the text carefully to figure out the implied idea, and then state it in their own words.

Model identifying implied main ideas by reading the second paragraph on p. 106. Note that the first sentence of the passage states important information, but not the main idea. State the main idea in your own words. (*After the fall of the Soviet Union, free education continued, but students had greater freedom to study what they wanted.*)

Give students *Identify Implied Main Ideas*. Have them complete the activity in their groups.

All in One Europe and Russia Teaching Resources, *Identify Implied Main Ideas*, p. 229

Russia's Ethnic Groups

The Russian Orthodox religion is a branch of Christianity closely related to the Eastern Orthodox Church. It has been a powerful bond among many Russians for hundreds of years. It is part of the Russian **heritage** (HEHR uh tij), or the customs and practices that are passed from one generation to the next.

Russia's ethnic culture is another part of the Russian heritage. More than 80 percent of Russian citizens belong to the ethnic group of Russian Slavs. These people generally speak the Russian language. Most of them live in the western parts of the Russian Federation. However, Russia is also home to many non-Russian ethnic groups.

Both of the families at the right live in Siberia.

Russia: Languages

MAP MASTER™
Skills Activity

KEY

Indo–European
- Slavic
- Iranian

Altaic
- Turkic
- Mongolic
- Tungusic

Other language groups
- Uralic
- Caucasian
- Other
- Uninhabited
- National border
- ⊛ National capital
- • Other city

Place Altaic languages, originating in Asia, are spoken in Russia today along with Indo-European and other languages. **Locate** In what parts of Russia are Asian languages spoken? **Analyze Information** How has Russia's location on two continents shaped its culture?

Go Online
PHSchool.com Use Web Code **ldp-7313** for step-by-step **map skills practice.**

Vocabulary Builder

Use the information below to teach students this section's high-use words.

High-Use Word	Definition and Sample Sentence
unify, p. 102	*v.* to combine into one A common language and culture **unified** the community.
intricate, p. 104	*adj.* full of detail, complex The beading on the fancy dress was very **intricate.**
campaign, p. 104	*n.* series of activities to achieve a goal The goal of the election **campaign** was to get as many votes as possible for the candidate.

Instruct

Russia's Ethnic Groups L2

Guided Instruction

- **Vocabulary Builder** Clarify the high-use word **unify** before reading.

- Read Russia's Ethnic Groups, using the Oral Cloze reading strategy (TE, p. T33).

- Discuss what ethnic group has had the greatest influence on Russia's heritage. *(Russian Slavs, who make up over 80 percent of the population and speak the Russian language)*

Answers

MAP MASTER™ Skills Activity **Locate** Asian languages are spoken mainly in northern and eastern Russia, as well as a few areas in southern and western Russia. **Analyze Information** Russia's culture is influenced by both European and Asian cultures.

Go Online
PHSchool.com Students may practice their map skills using the interactive online version of this map.

Guided Instruction (continued)

■ Discuss how other ethnic groups have shaped Russia. (*More than 60 other ethnic groups live within Russia, mostly far from the western Russian areas. They speak languages other than Russian and practice Islam, Buddhism, and other religions. Some groups, like the Chechens, have tried to break away from Russia politically.*)

■ Ask students **Why do you think some non-Russian ethnic groups have not tried to break away from Russia?** (*Answers will vary, but students might argue that some groups might be afraid of Russia's military power, while others might say that many groups do not feel the need to break away since they are allowed to rule themselves.*)

Independent Practice

Assign *Guided Reading and Review*.

All in One **Europe and Russia Teaching Resources**, *Guided Reading and Review*, p. 225

Monitor Progress

As students complete the worksheet, circulate to answer questions and provide assistance as needed.

🎯 Target Reading Skill   L2

Identify Main Ideas As a follow up, ask students to perform the activity of the Target Reading Skill in the Student Edition. (*The Russian government wants to keep the country united.*)

Answers

Compare and Contrast The people in the three photographs live in different areas, and are probably from different ethnic groups. They also may of different socio-economic backgrounds.

✓ Reading Check Russian Orthodox

Buddhism in Russia
A Buddhist monastery in southern Siberia reflects the Tibetan heritage of the people who live there.
Compare and Contrast *Compare this photo with the ones on page 93. Besides religion, what other cultural differences might there be among the three groups?*

🎯 **Identify Main Ideas**
In one sentence, summarize all the details in the paragraph at the right.

Other Ethnic Groups More than 60 non-Russian ethnic groups live in Russia. Most of them live far from the heavily populated western areas. People speaking languages related to Finnish and Turkish live near the Ural and Caucasus (KAW kuh sus) mountains. Armenians and Mongolians live along Russia's southern edges. The Yakuts (yah KOOTS) live in small areas of Siberia. These groups speak languages other than Russian.

They also follow different religions. Muslims make up Russia's second-largest religious group, after Russian Orthodox. Many followers of Buddhism (BOOD iz um) live near Russia's border with China.

Ethnic Majorities Recall that the Soviet Union was made up of many republics. Each Soviet republic was the homeland of a large ethnic group. When the Soviet Union came apart, the non-Russian republics broke away and formed their own countries. For example, Armenia is a former Soviet republic with a majority of ethnic Armenians. It gained its independence in 1991.

Other ethnic groups remained part of Russia, sometimes unwillingly. Many of them have called for more rights to rule themselves. Some have even called for independence. These efforts have brought much ethnic tension. Yet despite this great tension, fighting has broken out only between Russia and one other ethnic group—the Chechens. You will read about their independence movement, and the Russian government's repression of it, in Chapter 5.

The government of the Russian Federation has tried to keep the country unified. It has given many ethnic groups the right to rule themselves. However, it must work hard to turn the nation's ethnic diversity into an asset, rather than a source of conflict.

✓ Reading Check **What is Russia's largest religious group?**

Differentiated Instruction

For Less Proficient Readers   L1
To learn more about Russia, have students view the maps, photo tour, and timeline about Russia on the Passport to the World CD-ROM.

🔘 *Russia,* **Passport to the World CD-ROM**

For Gifted and Talented   L3
Have students research and give an oral presentation on one of the non-Russian ethnic groups that live in Russia. Use the *Rubric for Assessing an Oral Presentation* to assess students' work.

All in One **Europe and Russia Teaching Resources**, *Rubric for Assessing an Oral Presentation*, p. 246

The Space Age Begins

When the Soviet Union launched the first artificial satellite on October 4, 1957, it took the world by surprise. Less than four years later, the Soviet Union shocked the world again by sending the first human being into space. On April 12, 1961, twenty-seven-year-old Cosmonaut Yuri Gagarin spent one hour and 48 minutes in space. Gagarin completed a single orbit in the spacecraft *Vostok I*, before returning to Earth.

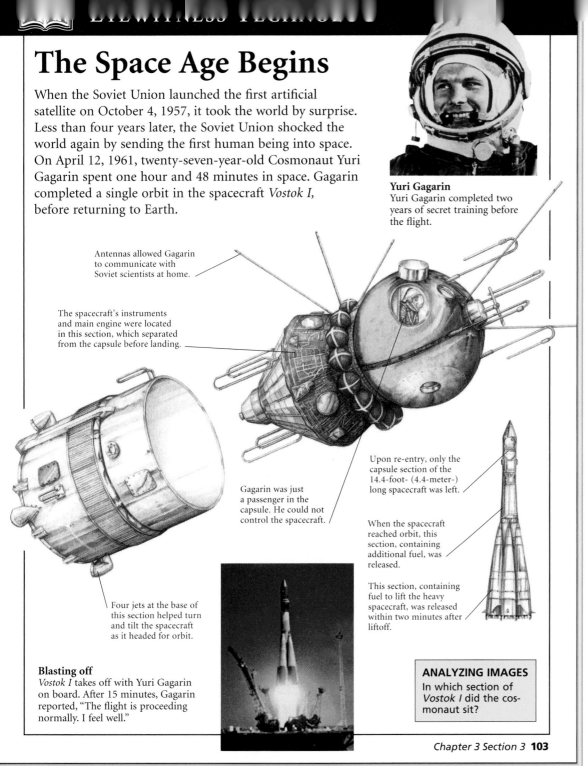

Yuri Gagarin
Yuri Gagarin completed two years of secret training before the flight.

Antennas allowed Gagarin to communicate with Soviet scientists at home.

The spacecraft's instruments and main engine were located in this section, which separated from the capsule before landing.

Gagarin was just a passenger in the capsule. He could not control the spacecraft.

Four jets at the base of this section helped turn and tilt the spacecraft as it headed for orbit.

Upon re-entry, only the capsule section of the 14.4-foot- (4.4-meter-) long spacecraft was left.

When the spacecraft reached orbit, this section, containing additional fuel, was released.

This section, containing fuel to lift the heavy spacecraft, was released within two minutes after liftoff.

Blasting off
Vostok I takes off with Yuri Gagarin on board. After 15 minutes, Gagarin reported, "The flight is proceeding normally. I feel well."

> **ANALYZING IMAGES**
> In which section of *Vostok I* did the cosmonaut sit?

Chapter 3 Section 3 **103**

The Space Age Begins L2

Guided Instruction
Have students read the text on this page of the Student Edition. As a class, study the art and photographs and read the captions. Then have students answer the Analyzing Images question.

Independent Practice
Ask students to suppose it is April 1961, and Yuri Gagarin has just become the first person to orbit Earth. Using the information in the captions and text, ask them to write a short paragraph from the point of view of Yuri Gagarin describing what happened as he traveled in the spacecraft.

Differentiated Instruction

For English Language Learners L2
Students may have trouble understanding some of the more difficult words on this page, such as *antennas, capsule, proceeding,* and *tilt.* Have students use a dictionary to find the meaning of the words, their parts of speech, and their pronunciations.

Answer
ANALYZING IMAGES He sat in the capsule.

Russian Culture and Education

Guided Instruction

- **Vocabulary Builder** Clarify the high-use words **intricate** and **campaign** before reading.

- Read about Russian Culture and Education. Draw students attention to the graphic Artistic Traditions in Russia at the bottom of pp. 104–105 and read the captions together.

- Identify some of the kinds of art produced by Russian artists, musicians, and writers. *(Fabergé eggs, works by Leo Tolstoy, music by Peter Tchaikovsky, paintings by Wassily Kandinski)*

- Discuss how communism affected Russian art. *(Artistic creativity nearly ended because the government only approved art that supported its propaganda campaign.)*

- Ask **What event in 1991 led to the return of artistic traditions in Russia?** *(the collapse of Soviet communism)*

Elaborately decorated Fabergé eggs like this one were made in St. Petersburg in the late 1800s.

Russian Culture and Education

Russia has produced many great artists. Russia's artistic heritage includes outstanding architecture, fine paintings, great plays, and intricate art objects like Fabergé (FAB ur zhay) eggs.

Russian Artists The novelist Leo Tolstoy (TOHL stoy) wrote powerful stories of life in Russia in the 1800s. Peter Tchaikovsky (chy KAWF skee) composed moving classical music. Russian painters, such as Wassily Kandinsky (VAS uh lee kan DIN skee), were leaders in the modern art movement in the early 1900s. Creating works of art has been a tradition among Russians.

Under Soviet communism, the creation of new works of art nearly came to a halt. The Soviet government believed that the purpose of art was to serve political goals. The government only approved art that supported its propaganda campaigns. **Propaganda** is the spread of ideas designed to support some cause or to hurt an opposing cause.

The Soviet Union broke apart in 1991. With the collapse of Soviet communism, the Russian people eagerly returned to their artistic traditions. Creating new works was once again possible.

Artistic Traditions in Russia

Cinema ▶
Motion pictures came to Russia in 1896. The cinema was extremely popular there before the 1917 revolution and during World War I. After the revolution, Soviet leaders used the cinema to spread communist ideas. The golden age of Russian cinema was the 1920s, although filmmaking techniques continued to develop under Stalin.

A 1929 Russian movie poster

Painting ▲
Russian painter Wassily Kandinsky (1866–1944), above, was an influential abstract artist. Abstract artists do not try to depict things the way that they appear to the eye. His style ranged from pure bursts of color to exact geometric shapes.

Tolstoy and Chekhov in 1901

◀ Literature
Russian literature is rich and varied, from the short stories of Nikolay Gogol to the novels of Leo Tolstoy and the plays of Anton Chekhov. Often writing in a harsh political environment, Russian authors have influenced writers all over the world with their wit, expressiveness, and insight into the human mind.

104 Europe and Russia

 Skills Mini Lesson

Distinguishing Fact and Opinion

1. Teach the skill by explaining that facts are statements that can be proved or disproved, while opinions are statements that cannot be proved or disproved.

2. Help students practice the skill by writing the following sentences on the board, and then having them determine if the statements are fact or opinion and

why. "Leo Tolstoy was born in 1828." *(Fact: it can be proven true or false.)* "I think *War and Peace* is the greatest book ever written. *(Opinion: it cannot be proven true or false.)*

3. Have students apply the skill by finding other examples of facts and opinions in the text as they read.

St. Petersburg: A Cultural Symbol The second-largest city and the largest seaport in Russia, the city of St. Petersburg lies on the Gulf of Finland and is an important center of Russian culture. Visitors to the city can clearly see the mixture of Russian and other European cultures. St. Petersburg was founded by Peter the Great in 1703. His goal was to create a Russian city as beautiful as any Western European city. He employed Western architects to design the city. St. Petersburg was the capital of Russia for more than 200 years before it was renamed Leningrad in 1924. In September 1991, its name was changed back to St. Petersburg.

Because of its grand architecture and many canals, St. Petersburg was once called Venice of the North. The Neva (NEE vuh) River winds gracefully through the city. Along the river's banks are palaces and public buildings hundreds of years old. St. Petersburg's grandest sight, the Winter Palace, is on the Neva. The palace has more than 1,000 rooms and was the winter home of Russia's tsars. Part of the palace is now the Hermitage (HUR muh tij) Museum. Built in 1764, it houses one of the world's finest art collections of Russian, Asian, and European art.

Guided Instruction (continued)

- Ask students to describe the Winter Palace. *(It is a palace on the Neva River, with more than 1,000 rooms, and was the winter home of Russia's tsars. Part of the palace is now the Hermitage Museum.)*

- Ask students **How did old Soviet Union policies lead to a more educated population?** *(Education was free, increasing the percentage of the population that could read and write from 40 percent to almost 100 percent.)*

- Ask students **What other new courses do you think Russia's young people might be interested in?** *(Possible answers: art, religion, music, politics)*

Independent Practice
Have students create the Taking Notes graphic organizer on a piece of paper. Then have them complete it using the information from this section.

Monitor Progress
- Show *Section Reading Support Transparency ER 42* and ask students to check their graphic organizers individually. Go over key concepts and clarify key vocabulary as needed.

  📖 **Europe and Russia Transparencies,** *Section Reading Support Transparency ER 42*

- Tell students to fill in the last column of their *Reading Readiness Guides*. Probe for what they learned that confirms or invalidates each statement.

  All in One Europe and Russia Teaching Resources, *Reading Readiness Guide,* p. 224

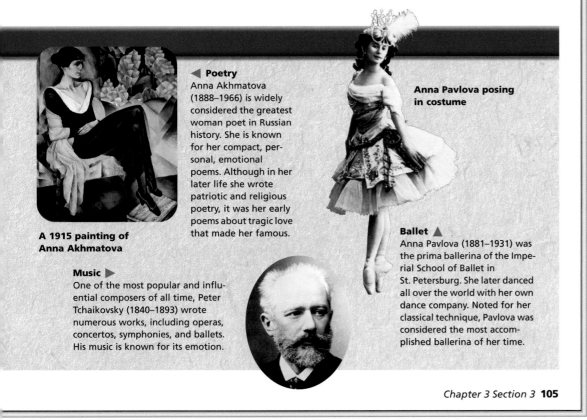

Poetry
Anna Akhmatova (1888–1966) is widely considered the greatest woman poet in Russian history. She is known for her compact, personal, emotional poems. Although in her later life she wrote patriotic and religious poetry, it was her early poems about tragic love that made her famous.

A 1915 painting of Anna Akhmatova

Anna Pavlova posing in costume

Ballet
Anna Pavlova (1881–1931) was the prima ballerina of the Imperial School of Ballet in St. Petersburg. She later danced all over the world with her own dance company. Noted for her classical technique, Pavlova was considered the most accomplished ballerina of her time.

Music
One of the most popular and influential composers of all time, Peter Tchaikovsky (1840–1893) wrote numerous works, including operas, concertos, symphonies, and ballets. His music is known for its emotion.

Differentiated Instruction

For Advanced Readers L2
Divide students into groups and have them do research about Leo Tolstoy. Then have each group write and present a short play, highlighting two or three episodes from Tolstoy's life. Give students *Writing Plays* to help them get started.

All in One Europe and Russia Teaching Resources, *Writing Plays,* p. 242

For Special Needs Students L1
Have students read the section as they listen to the recorded version on the Student Edition on Audio CD. Check for comprehension by pausing the CD and asking students to share their answers to the Reading Checks.

⊙ Chapter 3, Section 3, **Student Edition on Audio CD**

Assess and Reteach

Assess Progress   L2

Have students complete the Section Assessment. Administer the *Section Quiz*.

AlI in One **Europe and Russia Teaching Resources,** *Section Quiz,* p. 226

Reteach   L1

If students need more instruction, have them read this section in the Reading and Vocabulary Study Guide.

Chapter 3, Section 3, **Europe and Russia Reading and Vocabulary Study Guide,** pp. 38–40

Extend   L3

Have students learn more about Russia's political history and how it affected the people of Russia by reading *Lenin's Deathbed Words, Kampf,* and *Housekeeping in Russia Soon After the Revolution.*

AlI in One **Europe and Russia Teaching Resources,** *Lenin's Deathbed Words,* p. 239; *Kampf,* p. 240; *Housekeeping in Russia Soon After the Revolution,* p. 241

Section 3 Assessment

Key Terms

Students' sentences should reflect knowledge of each Key Term.

Target Reading Skill

Possible answers: While most Russians share a common ethnic background, many different groups live there. Russia has a rich artistic heritage that includes great artists, thinkers, and writers. St. Petersburg is an important center of Russian culture. Education is also an important part of Russia's culture, and has been since it came under Communist rule.

Comprehension and Critical Thinking

1. (a) Russian Slavs **(b)** Some ethnic groups want to rule themselves. **(c)** Some groups have tried to break ties with the Russians, leading the Russians to use force against them.

2. (a) There has been a return to religion since the fall of the Soviet Union. Artistic traditions that were not allowed under the Soviets are being practiced once more. **(b)** The Soviet Union introduced free education. After the end of Soviet rule, education

---

Children learning computer skills in a Russian school

Russia's Educational System One of the strengths of the Soviet Union was its free public education system. Under that system, the number of Russians who could read and write rose from about 40 percent to nearly 100 percent. Higher education was also free for Soviet citizens.

The Russian Federation continued free public schooling for children between ages 6 and 17. When students finish ninth grade, they can choose to continue their education in a secondary school or a vocational school. Secondary schools emphasize academic subjects such as mathematics and science, while the vocational schools prepare students for careers in industry and agriculture. Schools are updating their old courses of study, which used to emphasize only one official point of view.

These changes show that Russia is trying to recover the riches of its past even as it prepares for a new future. Religion and art, two important parts of Russia's cultural heritage, can now be freely expressed. And Russia's young people, unlike their parents, can grow up deciding their future for themselves.

✓ **Reading Check** Who founded the city of St. Petersburg?

Section 3 Assessment

Key Terms

Review the key terms at the beginning of this section. Use each term in a sentence that explains its meaning.

Target Reading Skill

State the main ideas in Section 3.

Comprehension and Critical Thinking

1. (a) Recall What is Russia's major ethnic group?
(b) Identify Point of View Why do some ethnic groups in Russia seek independence?

(c) Draw Conclusions How has Russia's ethnic mix created challenges for the new Russian government?

2. (a) List Give some examples of the ways in which Russians are reconnecting with their past.
(b) Identify Effects How have political changes in Russia led to changes in education?
(c) Predict How might the lives of young people in Russia today be different from those of their parents' generation?

Writing Activity

Suppose that you are visiting St. Petersburg. Write a postcard to your family describing the works of art, architecture, and other expressions of Russian culture that you have seen.

For: An activity on Russian cities
Visit: PHSchool.com
Web Code: ldd-7303

---

continued to be free, and schools have updated their courses. **(c)** Answers will vary, but students might say that they probably have more freedom and more choices than their parents did.

Writing Activity

Use the *Rubric for Assessing a Writing Assignment* to evaluate students' postcards.

AlI in One **Europe and Russia Teaching Resources,** *Rubric for Assessing a Writing Assignment* p. 244

Go Online PHSchool.com Typing in the Web code when prompted will bring students to detailed instructions for this activity.

Review and Assessment

Celebrating Carnival in London

◆ Chapter Summary

Section 1: The Cultures of Western Europe

- Industry has made many Western European countries wealthy.
- Western European cities are the cultural centers of their countries.
- Goods, materials, and ideas can travel easily and quickly across Western Europe.

Section 2: The Cultures of Eastern Europe

- Long ago, many ethnic groups migrated across Eastern Europe.
- Under foreign domination, some expressions of Eastern European culture were discouraged.
- Ethnic conflict has influenced the modern history of Eastern Europe.
- Prague and Budapest are important cultural centers of Eastern Europe.

Section 3: The Cultures of the Russian Federation

- Russia has more than 60 different ethnic groups.
- Russia has a rich cultural heritage.

A Fabergé egg from Russia

◆ Key Terms

Each of the statements below contains a key term from the chapter. If the statement is true, write *true*. If it is false, change the term to make it true.

1. A tariff is a different version of a language.
2. Propaganda is the spread of ideas designed to support a cause.
3. Someone who moves to one country from another is an immigrant.
4. People in the same ethnic group share the same ancestors, culture, or religion.
5. Heritage is the customs and practices passed from one generation to the next.
6. Diversification is the movement of populations toward cities and the resulting city growth.
7. Migration is a movement from place to place.

┌ Vocabulary Builder ──────

Revisit this chapter's high-use words:

revolution	descendant	intricate
scholar	conflict	campaign
recreation	thrive	
exchange	unify	

Ask students to review the definitions they recorded on their *Word Knowledge* worksheets.

All in One Europe and Russia Teaching Resources, *Word Knowledge*, p. 230

Consider allowing students to earn extra credit if they use the words in their answers to the questions in the Chapter Review and Assessment. The words must be used correctly and in a natural context to win the extra points.

Review Chapter Content

- Divide the class into pairs, and have them review the major themes of this chapter by reading each bulleted statement of the Chapter Summary. Then have each group identify which Guiding Question each bulleted statement in the Chapter Summary answers. Discuss the answers as a class using the Idea Wave participation strategy (TE, p. T35). Refer to p. 1 in the Student Edition for the Guiding Questions.

- Assign *Vocabulary Development* for students to review Key Terms.

  All in One Europe and Russia Teaching Resources, *Vocabulary Development*, p. 243

Answers

Key Terms

1. False. A dialect is a different version of a language.
2. True.
3. True.
4. True.
5. True.
6. False. Urbanization is the movement of populations toward cities and the result of city growth.
7. True.

Review and Assessment

Comprehension and Critical Thinking

8. (a) Answers may vary; possible answers include: Paris, London, Madrid, Berlin **(b)** museums, parks, theaters, nightclubs, shops, restaurants, monuments, historical sites

9. (a) People, goods, and ideas can travel easily between countries. **(b)** The Industrial Revolution, urbanization, and continued economic development before and after World War II has made them prosperous.

10. (a) An ethnic group found in many parts of Eastern Europe. **(b)** Today, descendants of Slavs make up most of Eastern Europe's ethnic groups. The different groups of Slavs speak 10 different, but related, languages and practice many different languages.

11. (a) Czechs and Slovaks **(b)** The breakup of Czechoslovakia was peaceful, while the breakup of Yugoslavia led to many conflicts. **(c)** The Czechs and Slovaks already lived in separate parts of the country, which made it easier to divide the land.

12. (a) more than 60 **(b)** Some groups have tried to form their own countries.

13. (a) 1991 **(b)** There is greater political, religious, and cultural freedom. **(c)** Students' answers will vary, but might predict greater artistic, financial, and political achievements.

Skills Practice

Answers will vary, but students should show that they used the skill steps to support their positions.

Writing Activity: Language and Arts

Students' travel guides will vary, but should reflect accurate information about the places they have chosen.

Use the *Rubric for Assessing a Writing Assignment* to evaluate students' answers.

All in One **Europe and Russia Teaching Resources,** *Rubric for Assessing a Writing Assignment,* p. 244

Review and Assessment (continued)

◆ Comprehension and Critical Thinking

8. (a) List Name three cities in Western Europe.
(b) Summarize What features make cities in Western Europe centers of culture?

9. (a) Explain What does the concept of open borders mean?
(b) Infer Why do Western Europeans generally have a higher standard of living than do Eastern Europeans?

10. (a) Identify Who were the Slavs?
(b) Synthesize How does Slavic culture live on in Eastern Europe today?

11. (a) Recall Name two of Czechoslovakia's ethnic groups.
(b) Compare and Contrast How was the breakup of Czechoslovakia different from the breakup of Yugoslavia?
(c) Draw Conclusions Why was Czechoslovakia able to break up peacefully?

12. (a) Note About how many ethnic groups live in Russia?
(b) Analyze How have non-Russian ethnic groups reacted to recent changes in Russia?

13. (a) Recall When did the Soviet Union break apart?
(b) Find Main Ideas How has life changed for the Russian people since the collapse of the Soviet Union?
(c) Predict What might the future hold for the Russian people?

◆ Skills Practice

Supporting a Position In the Skills for Life activity in this chapter, you learned how to support a position. Review the steps you followed to learn this skill. Then turn to the section titled Ethnic Majorities on page 102. Read about Russia's republics. Decide whether you support or oppose independence for Russia's republics and then support your position.

◆ Writing Activity: Language Arts

Suppose you had friends who were visiting Europe and Russia for the first time. What information would you want to share with them? Create a brief travel guide that your friends could use to plan their trip. Mention interesting places and activities, and provide background information on the cultures of the people they will meet.

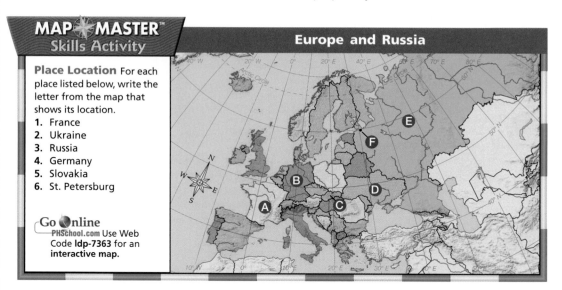

MAP MASTER™
Skills Activity

Europe and Russia

Place Location For each place listed below, write the letter from the map that shows its location.
1. France
2. Ukraine
3. Russia
4. Germany
5. Slovakia
6. St. Petersburg

Go Online
PHSchool.com Use Web Code **ldp-7363** for an **interactive map.**

108 Europe and Russia

Standardized Test Prep

Test-Taking Tips

Some questions on standardized tests ask you to analyze graphic organizers. Study the concept web below. Then follow the tips to answer the sample question at the right.

> **TIP** Preview the question. Keep it in mind as you study the information in the web.

Pick the letter that best answers the question. Another name that belongs on this web is

A Peter the Great.

B Tsar Nicholas II.

C Pablo Picasso.

D Peter Tchaikovsky.

> **TIP** Be sure that you read all four options. If you don't read each one, you can't be certain that you've found the best choice.

Think It Through What other name belongs in the web? The center of the web says Russian Artists—meaning painters, writers, musicians, dancers, and so on. You can rule out A and B, because both are political figures in Russian history. That leaves C and D. You may know that Picasso is Spanish. That leaves Tchaikovsky, answer D.

Go Online
PHSchool.com Students may practice their map skills using the interactive online version of this map.

Standardized Test Prep

Answers

1. C

2. D

3. A

4. B

Go Online
PHSchool.com Students may use the Chapter 3 self-test on PHSchool.com to prepare for the Chapter Test.

Practice Questions

Use the tips above and other tips in this book to help you answer the following questions.

1. Advances in farming about 200 years ago led to

 A the Velvet Revolution.

 B increased immigration.

 C the growth of cities.

 D open borders in Western Europe.

2. Which group's descendants make up most of Eastern Europe's ethnic groups?

 A the Romanians

 B the Albanians

 C the Russians

 D the Slavs

3. More than 80 percent of Russian citizens belong to this ethnic group.

 A Russian Slavs   **B** Mongolians

 C Yakuts   **D** Buddhists

Study the concept web and answer the question that follows.

4. What other country belongs on the web?

 A Russia

 B Bosnia and Herzegovina

 C Austria

 D Romania

Go Online
PHSchool.com

Use Web Code lda-7303 for a **Chapter 3 self-test.**

Assessment Resources

Use *Chapter Tests A and B* to assess students' mastery of the chapter content.

All in One **Europe and Russia Teaching Resources,** *Chapter Tests A and B,* pp. 247–252

Tests are also available on the *ExamView Test Bank CD-ROM.*

⊚ *ExamView Test Bank CD-ROM*

Use a benchmark test to evaluate students' cumulative understanding of what they have learned in Chapters 1 through 3.

▤ *Europe and Russia Benchmark Test 1,* **AYP Monitoring Assessments,** pp. 105–108

Overview

Introducing Western Europe
1. Analyze the data to compare the countries.
2. Identify the characteristics that the countries of Western Europe share.
3. Find out some of the key differences among the countries.

The Geography of Western Europe
Length: 5 minutes, 9 seconds
Gives overview of the different regions and landforms of Western Europe.

 Section 1

The United Kingdom: Democracy and Monarchy
1. Examine the regions that make up the United Kingdom.
2. Learn about the United Kingdom's democratic heritage.
3. Find out how the United Kingdom combines democracy and monarchy.
4. Understand why trade is important to the United Kingdom.

Great Britain: London Fog and Suburbia
Length: 4 minutes, 17 seconds
Explains how the suburbs in Britain reflect British history.

 Section 2

France: Cultural Heritage and Diversity
1. Find out why the French take pride in their traditional culture.
2. Learn about growing cultural diversity in France.

France: The Rise of Napoleon Bonaparte
Length: 5 minutes, 53 seconds
Explores Napoleon's power.

 Section 3

Sweden: A Welfare State
1. Learn about Sweden's welfare state.
2. Find out how Sweden became a welfare state.
3. Examine possible solutions to Sweden's economic problems.

Sweden: Land of Forests
Length: 4 minutes, 15 seconds
Discusses the importance of forestry in Sweden.

 Section 4

Italy: Northern and Southern Divisions
1. Discover that there is another country within Italy called Vatican City.
2. Understand why there are divisions between northern and southern Italy.

Ancient Rome
Length: 4 minutes, 37 seconds
Describes the daily lives and achievements of the Romans.

 Section 5

Germany: A Unified Nation
1. Learn about Germany's past.
2. Find out how Germany became reunited.

Germany: The Berlin Wall
Length: 4 minutes, 22 seconds
Discusses the history of the Berlin Wall.

Technology Resources

Students use embedded Web codes to access Internet activities, chapter self-tests, and additional map practice. They may also access Dorling Kindersley's Online Desk Reference to learn more about each country they study.

Use the Interactive Textbook to make content and concepts come alive through animations, videos, and activities that accompany the complete basal text—online and on CD-ROM.

PRENTICE HALL
TeacherEXPRESS™
Plan · Teach · Assess

Use this complete suite of powerful teaching tools to make planning lessons and administering tests quicker and easier.

Reading and Assessment

Reading and Vocabulary Instruction

🔁 Model the Target Reading Skill

Context Understanding how to derive meaning from context clues can help students become more confident and better readers. Learning the importance of context allows students to see patterns between terms and understand larger concepts.

Model using context clues by thinking aloud about the following selection from p. 129. Begin by writing the selection on the board.

The United Kingdom has many strong industries, or businesses. For example, it has good supplies of fossil fuels—especially oil from deposits beneath the North Sea. It also continues to export many manufactured goods, such as clothing and electronic products.

Think aloud: "The first sentence uses the word *industries*. I think this is an important word, but I'm not completely sure of its meaning. The word *or* comes after the word *industries*. This is a clue that a definition might follow. Reading ahead, I see that *industries* means *businesses*. Why are the United Kingdom's industries strong? I will underline the items in the next two sentences that give me clues. (*underline* good supplies of fossil fuels *and* export many manufactured goods) By looking at the context, I was able to determine that the United Kingdom has strong businesses because a great deal of goods are manufactured for export, and a large amount of fossil fuel is found there."

Use the following worksheets from All-in-One Europe and Russia Teaching Resources (pp. 277–279) to support the chapter's Target Reading Skill.

Vocabulary Builder
High-Use Academic Words

Use these steps to teach this chapter's high-use words:

1. Have students rate how well they know each word on their Word Knowledge worksheets (All-in-One Europe and Russia Teaching Resources, p. 280).

2. Pronounce each word and ask students to repeat it.

3. Give students a brief definition or sample sentence (provided on TE pp. 123, 131, 139, 146, and 155).

4. Work with students as they fill in the "Definition or Example" column of their Word Knowledge worksheets.

Assessment

Formal Assessment

Test students' understanding of core knowledge and skills.

Chapter Tests A and B, All-in-One Europe and Russia Teaching Resources, pp. 300–305

Customize the Chapter Tests to suit your needs.

ExamView Test Bank CD-ROM

Skills Assessment

Assess geographic literacy.

MapMaster Skills, Student Edition, pp. 111, 123, 155, 162

Country Profile Map and Chart Skills, Student Edition, pp. 124, 134, 140, 147, 156

Assess reading and comprehension.

Target Reading Skills, Student Edition, pp. 125, 136, 142, 146, 158, and in Section Assessments

Chapter 4 Assessment, Europe and Russia Reading and Vocabulary Study Guide, p. 57

Performance Assessment

Assess students' performance on this chapter's Writing Activities using the following rubrics from All-in-One Europe and Russia Teaching Resources.

Rubric for Assessing a Writing Assignment, p. 298

Rubric for Assessing a Journal Entry, p. 299

Assess students' work through performance tasks.

Small Group Activity: Comparing Types of Government, All-in-One Europe and Russia Teaching Resources, pp. 283–286

Portfolio Activity, Teacher Edition, p. 121

Online Assessment

Have students check their own understanding.

Chapter Self-Test

Section 1 The United Kingdom: Democracy and Monarchy

 2 periods, 1 block (includes Country Databank)

Social Studies Objectives
1. Examine the regions that make up the United Kingdom.
2. Learn about the United Kingdom's democratic heritage.
3. Find out how the United Kingdom combines democracy and monarchy.
4. Understand why trade is important to the United Kingdom.

Reading/Language Arts Objective
Use context clues to clarify unfamiliar words and ideas.

Prepare to Read	Instructional Resources	Differentiated Instruction
Build Background Knowledge Ask students to discuss words having to do with the United Kingdom's government. **Set a Purpose for Reading** Have students begin to fill out the *Reading Readiness Guide*. **Preview Key Terms** Teach the section's Key Terms. **Target Reading Skill** Introduce the section's Target Reading Skill of **using context clues**.	**All in One Europe and Russia Teaching Resources** L2 Reading Readiness Guide, p. 258 L2 Use Context Clues: Definition and Description, p. 277	**Spanish Reading and Vocabulary Study Guide** L1 Chapter 4, Section 1, pp. 32–33 ELL **World Studies Video Program** L2 The Geography of Western Europe AR, GT, LPR, SN

Instruct	Instructional Resources	Differentiated Instruction
Regions of the United Kingdom Discuss the formation of Great Britain. **Country Profile** Ask students to derive information from maps, charts, and graphs. **Target Reading Skill** Review **using context clues**. **A Democratic Heritage** Discuss democracy in the United Kingdom. **A Changing Monarchy** Discuss aspects of the British constitution. **The Importance of Trade** Discuss trade and colonies.	**All in One Europe and Russia Teaching Resources** L2 Guided Reading and Review, p. 259 L2 Reading Readiness Guide, p. 258 L2 Reading a Circle Graph, p. 287 **Europe and Russia Transparencies** L2 Section Reading Support Transparency ER 43 **World Studies Video Program** L2 Great Britain: London Fog and Suburbia	**All in One Europe and Russia Teaching Resources** Rubric for Assessing a Writing Assignment, p. 298 AR, GT, LPR, SN L3 Enrichment, p. 281 AR, GT **Teacher's Edition** L3 Gifted and Talented, p. 118 L3 For Advanced Readers, TE pp. 118, 126 L1 For Less Proficient Readers, TE p. 126 L1 For English Language Learners, TE p. 127 **Student Edition on Audio CD** L1 Chapter 4, Section 1 ELL, LPR, SN **Spanish Support** L2 Guided Reading and Review (Spanish), p. 32 ELL

Assess and Reteach	Instructional Resources	Differentiated Instruction
Assess Progress Evaluate student comprehension with the section assessment and section quiz. **Reteach** Assign the Reading and Vocabulary Study Guide to help struggling students. **Extend** Extend the lesson by assigning a Small Group Activity.	**All in One Europe and Russia Teaching Resources** L2 Section Quiz, p. 260 L3 Small Group Activity: Comparing Types of Government, pp. 283–286 **Reading and Vocabulary Study Guide** L1 Chapter 4, Section 1, pp. 42–44	**Spanish Support** L2 Section Quiz (Spanish), p. 33 ELL

Key
L1 Basic to Average   L3 Average to Advanced
L2 For All Students

LPR Less Proficient Readers
AR Advanced Readers
SN Special Needs Students

GT Gifted and Talented
ELL English Language Learners

Section 2 France: Cultural Heritage and Diversity

 *1.5 periods, .75 block*

Social Studies Objectives
1. Find out why the French take pride in their traditional culture.
2. Learn about growing cultural diversity in France.

Reading/Language Arts Objective
Use context clues to understand new words.

Prepare to Read

Build Background Knowledge
Have students learn about France using the Passport to the World CD-ROM.

Set a Purpose for Reading
Have students begin to fill out the *Reading Readiness Guide*.

Preview Key Terms
Teach the section's Key Terms.

Target Reading Skill
Introduce the section's Target Reading Skill of **using context clues**.

Instructional Resources

All in One Europe and Russia Teaching Resources
- L2 Reading Readiness Guide, p. 262
- L2 Use Context Clues: Compare and Contrast p. 278

Passport to the World CD-ROM
- L2 France

Differentiated Instruction

Spanish Reading and Vocabulary Study Guide
- L1 Chapter 4, Section 2, pp. 34–35 ELL

Instruct

Pride in French Culture
Discuss various aspects of French culture.

Country Profile
Ask students to derive information from maps, charts, and graphs.

Diversity in France
Discuss how other cultures have influenced that of France.

Target Reading Skill
Review **using context clues**.

Instructional Resources

All in One Europe and Russia Teaching Resources
- L2 Guided Reading and Review, p. 263
- L2 Reading Readiness Guide, p. 262
- L2 Reading a Table, p. 288

Europe and Russia Transparencies
- L2 Section Reading Support Transparency ER 44

World Studies Video Program
- L2 France: The Rise of Napoleon Bonaparte

Differentiated Instruction

Teacher's Edition
- L3 For Gifted and Talented, TE p. 132
- L3 For Advanced Readers, TE p. 136

Spanish Support
- L2 Guided Reading and Review (Spanish), p. 34 ELL

Assess and Reteach

Assess Progress
Evaluate student comprehension with the section assessment and section quiz.

Reteach
Assign the Reading and Vocabulary Study Guide to help struggling students.

Extend
Extend the lesson by assigning a research project.

Instructional Resources

All in One Europe and Russia Teaching Resources
- L2 Section Quiz, p. 264
  Rubric for Assessing a Writing Assignment, p. 298

Europe and Russia Transparencies
- L3 Color Transparency 24: The Cathedral at Reims
- L3 Color Transparency 25: The Cathedral at Reims: Interior

Reading and Vocabulary Study Guide
- L1 Chapter 4, Section 2, pp. 45–47

Differentiated Instruction

Spanish Support
- L2 Section Quiz (Spanish), p. 35 ELL

Key
L1 Basic to Average	L3 Average to Advanced
L2 For All Students	

LPR Less Proficient Readers
AR Advanced Readers
SN Special Needs Students

GT Gifted and Talented
ELL English Language Learners

Section Lesson Planner

Section 3 Sweden: A Welfare State

1.5 periods, .75 block

Social Studies Objectives
1. Learn about Sweden's welfare state.
2. Find out how Sweden became a welfare state.
3. Examine possible solutions to Sweden's economic problems.

Reading/Language Arts Objective
Learn to use context clues to determine how familiar words are being used in the text.

Prepare to Read	Instructional Resources	Differentiated Instruction
Build Background Knowledge Ask students to discuss benefits the government provides. **Set a Purpose for Reading** Have students evaluate statements on the *Reading Readiness Guide*. **Preview Key Terms** Teach the section's Key Terms. **Target Reading Skill** Introduce the section's Target Reading Skill of **using context clues**.	**All in One Europe and Russia Teaching Resources** **L2** Reading Readiness Guide, p. 266 **L2** Use Context Clues: General Knowledge, p. 279	**Spanish Reading and Vocabulary Study Guide** **L1** Chapter 4, Section 3, pp. 36–37 ELL

Instruct	Instructional Resources	Differentiated Instruction
A Welfare State Discuss the welfare system in Sweden. **Country Profile** Ask students to derive information from maps, charts, and graphs. **Building a Welfare State** Discuss change in Sweden during the 1800s and 1900s and the way the country became a welfare state. **Target Reading Skill** Review **using context clues**. **Problems and Solutions** Discuss challenges that Sweden's government and businesses faced in the late 1900s.	**All in One Europe and Russia Teaching Resources** **L2** Guided Reading and Review, p. 267 **L2** Reading Readiness Guide, p. 266 **L2** Reading a Line Graph, p. 289 **Europe and Russia Transparencies** **L2** Section Reading Support Transparency ER 45 **World Studies Video Program** **L2** Sweden: Land of Forests	**Teacher's Edition** **L1** For Special Needs Students, TE p. 142 **L3** For Gifted and Talented, TE p. 142 **Europe and Russia Transparencies** **L3** Transparency B5: Flow Chart AR, GT **Student Edition on Audio CD** **L1** Chapter 4, Section 3 ELL, LPR, SN **Spanish Support** **L2** Guided Reading and Review (Spanish), p. 36 ELL

Assess and Reteach	Instructional Resources	Differentiated Instruction
Assess Progress Evaluate student comprehension with the section assessment and section quiz. **Reteach** Assign the Reading and Vocabulary Study Guide to help struggling students. **Extend** Extend the lesson by assigning a literature excerpt.	**All in One Europe and Russia Teaching Resources** **L2** Section Quiz, p. 268 **L3** The Boy, pp. 292–295 Rubric for Assessing a Writing Assignment, p. 298 **Reading and Vocabulary Study Guide** **L1** Chapter 4, Section 3, pp. 48–50	**Spanish Support** **L2** Section Quiz (Spanish), p. 37 ELL

Key
L1 Basic to Average	**L3** Average to Advanced
L2 For All Students	

LPR Less Proficient Readers
AR Advanced Readers
SN Special Needs Students

GT Gifted and Talented
ELL English Language Learners

Section 4 Italy: Northern and Southern Divisions

 2.5 periods, 1.25 blocks (includes Skills for Life)

Social Studies Objectives

1. Discover that there is another country within Italy called Vatican City.
2. Understand why there are divisions between northern and southern Italy.

Reading/Language Arts Objective

Use what you already know about an unfamiliar word to confirm information given in context clues.

Section Lesson Planner

Prepare to Read	Instructional Resources	Differentiated Instruction
Build Background Knowledge Show a video and discuss the Roman influence in Italy today. **Set a Purpose for Reading** Have students evaluate statements on the *Reading Readiness Guide*. **Preview Key Terms** Teach the section's Key Terms. **Target Reading Skill** Introduce the section's Target Reading Skill of **using context clues**.	**All in One Europe and Russia Teaching Resources** **L2** Reading Readiness Guide, p. 270 **L2** Use Context Clues: General Knowledge, p. 279 **World Studies Video Program** **L2** Ancient Rome	**Spanish Reading and Vocabulary Study Guide** **L1** Chapter 4, Section 4, pp. 38–39 ELL

Instruct	Instructional Resources	Differentiated Instruction
Target Reading Skill Review **using context clues**. **A Unifying Force** Discuss Vatican City. **Country Profile** Ask students to derive information from maps, charts, and graphs. **Divisions Between North and South** Discuss the differences between northern and southern Italy and the challenges they face.	**All in One Europe and Russia Teaching Resources** **L2** Guided Reading and Review, p. 271 **L2** Reading Readiness Guide, p. 270 **L2** Reading a Bar Graph, p. 290 **Europe and Russia Transparencies** **L2** Transparency B16: Venn Diagram **L2** Section Reading Support Transparency ER 46	**All in One Europe and Russia Teaching Resources** **L2** Skills for Life, p. 282 AR, GT, LPR, SN **Teacher's Edition** **L1** For Special Needs Students, TE p. 147 **L3** For Advanced Readers, TE p. 148 **L1** For English Language Learners, TE p. 150 **Europe and Russia Transparencies** **L1** Transparency B17: Concept Web ELL **PHSchool.com** **L3** **For:** Long-Term Integrated Projects: Keeping a Scrapbook of Daily Life Around the World AR, GT **Web Code:** ldd-7406

Assess and Reteach	Instructional Resources	Differentiated Instruction
Assess Progress Evaluate student comprehension with the section assessment and section quiz. **Reteach** Assign the Reading and Vocabulary Study Guide to help struggling students. **Extend** Extend the lesson by assigning an online activity.	**All in One Europe and Russia Teaching Resources** **L2** Section Quiz, p. 272 Rubric for Assessing a Writing Assignment, p. 298 **Reading and Vocabulary Study Guide** **L1** Chapter 4, Section 4, pp. 51–53 **PHSchool.com** **L3** **For:** Environmental and Global Issues: Urban Population, Past and Projected **Web Code:** ldd-7407	**Spanish Support** **L2** Section Quiz (Spanish), p. 39 ELL **Teacher's Edition** **L1** For Less Proficient Readers, TE p. 153 **Social Studies Skills Tutor CD-ROM** **L1** Transferring Information from One Medium to Another ELL, LPR, SN

Key

L1 Basic to Average   **L3** Average to Advanced   LPR Less Proficient Readers   GT Gifted and Talented
L2 For All Students   AR Advanced Readers   ELL English Language Learners
                                                      SN Special Needs Students

Section 5 Germany: A Unified Nation

 3.5 periods, 1.75 blocks (includes Chapter Review and Assessment)

Social Studies Objectives
1. Learn about Germany's past.
2. Find out how Germany became reunited.

Reading/Language Arts Objective
Learn to use context clues in several paragraphs to determine the meaning of an unfamiliar word.

Prepare to Read	Instructional Resources	Differentiated Instruction
Build Background Knowledge Discuss the concept of the Berlin Wall with students. **Set a Purpose for Reading** Have students begin to fill out the *Reading Readiness Guide*. **Preview Key Terms** Teach the section's Key Terms. **Target Reading Skill** Introduce the section's Target Reading Skill of **using context clues.**	**All in One Europe and Russia Teaching Resources** **L2** Reading Readiness Guide, p. 274 **L2** Use Context Clues: Definition and Description, p. 277	**Spanish Reading and Vocabulary Study Guide** **L1** Chapter 4, Section 5, pp. 40–41 ELL

Instruct	Instructional Resources	Differentiated Instruction
Germany's Past Discuss World War I, World War II, the Cold War, and the fall of the Berlin Wall in Germany. **Country Profile** Ask students to derive information from maps, charts, and graphs. **Target Reading Skill** Review **using context clues.** **Germany Reunited** Discuss the effects of the fall of the Berlin Wall on Germany.	**All in One Europe and Russia Teaching Resources** **L2** Guided Reading and Review, p. 275 **L2** Reading Readiness Guide, p. 274 **L2** Reading a Timeline, p. 291 **Europe and Russia Transparencies** **L2** Section Reading Support ER Transparency 47 **World Studies Video Program** **L2** Germany: The Berlin Wall	**Teacher's Edition** **L3** For Gifted and Talented, TE p. 156 **L1** For English Language Learners, TE p. 158 **L1** For Less Proficient Readers, TE p. 159 **Europe and Russia Transparencies** **L1** Color Transparency ER Set 1: Europe Today With Eastern Europe Updated ELL, LPR, SN **PHSchool.com** **L3** For: Environmental and Global Issues: The Universal Declaration of Human Rights AR, GT Web Code: ldd-7408

Assess and Reteach	Instructional Resources	Differentiated Instruction
Assess Progress Evaluate student comprehension with the section assessment and section quiz. **Reteach** Assign the Reading and Vocabulary Study Guide to help struggling students. **Extend** Extend the lesson by assigning a research project.	**All in One Europe and Russia Teaching Resources** **L2** Section Quiz, p. 276 **L3** Writing to Inform and Explain, p. 296 Rubric for Assessing a Journal Entry, p. 299 **L2** Vocabulary Development, p. 297 **L2** Word Knowledge, p. 280 **L2** Chapter Tests A and B, pp. 300–305 **Reading and Vocabulary Study Guide** **L1** Chapter 4, Section 5, pp. 54–56	**Spanish Support** **L2** Section Quiz (Spanish), p. 41 ELL **L2** Chapter Summary (Spanish), p. 42 ELL **L2** Vocabulary Development (Spanish), p. 43 ELL

Key

L1 Basic to Average	**L3** Average to Advanced	LPR Less Proficient Readers	GT Gifted and Talented
L2 For All Students		AR Advanced Readers	ELL English Language Learners
		SN Special Needs Students	

Professional Development

Reading Background

Summarizing

Research shows that summarizing can help students comprehend and recall text. Use the following steps to model how to write a one-sentence summary using the following paragraph from p. 141 of the Student Edition:

1. Write the selection on the board, and read it aloud to students.
2. Underline the important ideas:
   Swedish people believe that welfare benefits are very important. They are willing to pay the highest taxes in Europe in order to have these benefits. Swedes pay as much as 60 percent of their income in taxes. Food is taxed at 12 percent. Clothing and other goods are taxed at 25 percent. But in exchange for these high taxes, all Swedes have financial security.
3. Show how to combine these ideas into one sentence.

(Swedish people are willing to pay taxes for welfare benefits in exchange for financial security.)

Seed Discussions

Give students the opportunity to lead their own discussions about what they are reading in the chapter. Tell students that in order to lead a discussion with their classmates, they will need a strong "seed" to start with. Have the class list ideas for strong seeds, such as questions or opinions about what they have learned, or things in the chapter that surprised them.

Model a strong seed versus a weak seed. A strong seed might be an opinion, such as: "I believe the fall of the Berlin Wall was good for Germany." A weak seed might be a restatement of fact, such as: "Hitler was the dictator of Germany."

Once students are comfortable with the concept of a strong seed, have each student write a seed on a sheet of paper. Then have students form small groups. In the groups, each person should take a turn leading a discussion from the seed he or she has written. Divide time equally so every person gets an equal opportunity to lead the discussion.

Professional Development

World Studies Background

The Chunnel

Although France and England are separated by the English Channel, they are now connected by the Channel Tunnel (often called "the Chunnel"). This tunnel consists of three passages: two are for trains and their passengers, and one is for maintenance and ventilation. Train service began in 1994. The train ride between Folkestone, England and Calais, France takes about 35 minutes.

Brittany

Before the Chunnel, history connected England and France. The Bretons, a Celtic people who lived in England, were driven out of England by the Anglo-Saxon invasion in the A.D. 400s and 500s. They settled in the northwest part of France, called Brittany. Brittany fought for independence, but was integrated into France in 1532. The Breton language is still spoken in some areas.

Swedish Holidays

Many people in Sweden celebrate St. Lucia day on December 13, in honor of the saint also known as St. Lucy. Traditionally on this day, the oldest daughter in the family wears a white robe and a candle-lit wreath on her head and serves pastries to her family. People also celebrate with parades and bonfires. On Midsummer Day, the longest day of the year, many Swedes celebrate by singing and dancing around a May pole.

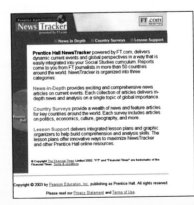

Get in-depth information on topics of global importance with **Prentice Hall Newstracker,** powered by FT.com.

 Use Web code **ldd-7400** for **Prentice Hall Newstracker.**

Chapter 4

Guiding Questions

Remind students about the Guiding Questions at the beginning of the book.

Section 1 relates to **Guiding Question 4**
What types of government have existed in Europe and Russia? (*The United Kingdom is a constitutional monarchy.*)

Section 2 relates to **Guiding Question 3**
How have the people of Europe and Russia been shaped by their culture? (*The French have made important contributions to the arts, architecture, food, philosophy, and fashion.*)

Section 3 relates to **Guiding Question 5**
How have Russian and European economies developed into what they are today? (*Economic problems led to the establishment of Sweden's modern welfare programs.*)

Section 4 relates to **Guiding Question 2**
How have Europe and Russia been affected by their history? (*Roman Catholicism has been a strong influence on Italy.*)

Section 5 relates to **Guiding Question 2**
How have Europe and Russia been shaped by their history? (*Germany was divided into two countries after World War II; they were reunited in 1990.*)

🎯 Target Reading Skill

In this chapter, students will learn to use context clues. Use the following worksheets to help students practice this skill:

All in One Europe and Russia Teaching Resources, *Use Context Clues: Definition and Description,* p. 277; *Use Context Clues: Compare or Contrast,* p. 278; *Use Context Clues: General Knowledge,* p. 279

Differentiated Instruction

The following Teacher Edition strategies are suitable for students of varying abilities.

Advanced Readers, pp. 118, 126, 136, 148
English Language Learners, pp. 127, 150, 158
Gifted and Talented, pp. 118, 132, 142, 156
Less Proficient Readers, pp. 126, 153, 159
Special Needs Students, pp. 142, 147

Chapter 4 Western Europe

Chapter Preview

This chapter focuses on key countries in Western Europe: the United Kingdom, France, Sweden, Italy, and Germany.

Country Databank
The Country Databank provides data and descriptions of each of the countries in Western Europe.

Section 1
The United Kingdom
Democracy and Monarchy

Section 2
France
Cultural Heritage and Diversity

Section 3
Sweden
A Welfare State

Section 4
Italy
Northern and Southern Divisions

Section 5
Germany
A Unified Nation

🎯 Target Reading Skill

Using Context In this chapter you will focus on using context to help you understand unfamiliar words. Context includes the words, phrases, and sentences surrounding the word.

▶ Boats on one of the many canals in Venice, Italy

110 Europe and Russia

Bibliography

For the Teacher
Cannon, John Ashton, ed. *The Oxford Companion to British History.* Oxford Press, 2003.
Hilton, Christopher. *The Wall: The People's Story.* Sutton Publishing, Limited, 2003.
Subervie, Maurice. *Paris in 500 Photos.* Flammarion, 2003.

For the Student
[L1] Thomas, Keltie. *Sweden: The People.* Crabtree, 2003.
[L2] Stanley, Diane. *Michelangelo.* HarperTrophy, 2003.
[L3] Rochman, Hazel, ed. *Bearing Witness: Stories of the Holocaust.* Orchard Books, 1999.

Western Europe: Political

MAP MASTER Skills Activity

KEY
- —— National border
- ⊛ National capital
- • Other city

0 miles 500
0 kilometers 500
Lambert Azimuthal Equal Area

Place Western Europe stretches from just north of Africa to the Arctic Circle, and from the Atlantic Ocean to the Mediterranean Sea. **Identify** Which countries lie partly within the Arctic Circle? **Apply Information** How do the climates of these countries differ from those countries that border the Mediterranean Sea?

Go Online
PHSchool.com Use Web Code **ldp-7411** for step-by-step map skills practice.

MAP MASTER Skills Activity

Tell students to trace the outline of Western Europe with their fingertips. Point out that much of the region is bordered by either seas or oceans. Ask them to brainstorm how this fact may have affected the region. Use the Think-Write-Pair-Share strategy (TE, p. T36) to elicit responses.

Go Online
PHSchool.com Students may practice their maps skills using the interactive online version of this map.

Using the Visual   L2

Reach Into Your Background Direct students' attention to the caption accompanying the photo on pp. 110–111. Tell students that people in Venice use canals and bridges to travel within the city. Then ask **How does Venice differ from where you live? Are there any similarities?**

Answers

MAP MASTER Skills Activity **Identify** Russia, Norway, Sweden, and Finland lie partly within the Arctic Circle. Iceland lies very close to the circle's edge. **Apply Information** The climate is much colder within the Arctic Circle.

Chapter Resources

Teaching Resources
- L2 Vocabulary Development, p. 297
- L2 Skills for Life, p. 282
- L2 Chapter Tests A and B, pp. 300–305

Spanish Support
- L2 Spanish Chapter Summary, p. 42
- L2 Spanish Vocabulary Development, p. 43

Media and Technology
- L1 Student Edition on Audio CD
- L1 Guided Reading Audiotapes, English and Spanish
- L2 Social Studies Skills Tutor CD-ROM
- *ExamView Test Bank CD-ROM*

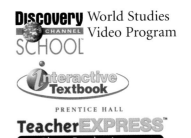

Discovery CHANNEL SCHOOL World Studies Video Program

interactive Textbook

PRENTICE HALL
TeacherEXPRESS
Plan • Teach • Assess

Objectives

- Look at the map on the previous page and then read the paragraphs to learn more about each nation.

- Analyze the data to compare the countries.

- Identify the characteristics that the countries of Western Europe share.

- Find out some of the key differences among the countries.

Show *The Geography of Western Europe.* Then ask **What are the four major geographic regions of Western Europe?** *(Northwestern Highlands, the Alpine Mountain system, the Central Uplands, and the European Plain)* **What are the major bodies of water?** *(Students may mention the Rhine River and the Mediterranean Sea.)*

Prepare to Read

Build Background Knowledge
L2

Write a list of the countries that students will be learning about across the top of the board. Then ask students what they already know about the countries listed. *(For example, students may say that France's capital is Paris, or that the United Kingdom is also sometimes referred to as Britain.)* Conduct an Idea Wave (TE, p. T35) to share students' answers, and add their responses under the name of the country on the board. Tell students that they will be learning more about these countries as they read the Country Databank.

Guide for Reading

This section provides an introduction to the 24 countries of Western Europe.

- Look at the map on the previous page and then read the paragraphs to learn about each nation.

- Analyze the data to compare the countries.

- What characteristics do most of these countries share?

- What are some key differences among the countries?

Viewing the Video Overview

View the World Studies Video Overview to learn more about each of the countries. As you watch, answer these questions:

- What are the four major geographic regions of Western Europe?

- What are the major bodies of water and why are they important?

Explore the geography of Western Europe.

Andorra

Capital	Andorra la Vella
Land Area	181 sq mi; 468 sq km
Population	68,403
Ethnic Group(s)	Spanish, Andorran, French, Portuguese
Religion(s)	Roman Catholic
Government	parliamentary democracy
Currency	euro
Leading Exports	tobacco products, furniture
Language(s)	Catalan (official), Spanish, French, Portuguese

The small country of Andorra (an DAWR uh) lies high in the eastern Pyrenees mountain range between France and Spain. France and Spain together ruled Andorra from the 1200s until the first full elections were held in 1993. Today, a 28-member legislature governs the country. Andorra's main source of income is its tourist industry. Most tourists come from France, Italy, or Spain to shop in the tax-free stores or to ski. Andorra's wealthiest citizens are its hotel owners.

The town of Andorra la Vella, Andorra

112 Europe and Russia

Austria

Capital	Vienna
Land Area	31,945 sq mi; 82,738 sq km
Population	8.2 million
Ethnic Group(s)	German, Croatian, Slovene, Hungarian, Czech, Slovak, Roma
Religion(s)	Roman Catholic, Protestant, Muslim, Jewish
Government	federal republic
Currency	euro
Leading Exports	machinery and equipment, motor vehicles and parts, paper and paperboard, metal goods, chemicals, iron and steel, textiles, foodstuffs
Language(s)	German (official), Croatian, Slovenian

Austria (AWS tree uh) borders several countries including the Czech Republic, Germany, Hungary, Italy, and Slovenia. In 1273, Austria came under the control of the Hapsburg Empire. Present-day Austria was established in 1918 after the fall of the Austro-Hungarian Empire during World War I. In 1938, Germany took control of Austria. Austria regained full independence 17 years later, in 1955. Having few natural resources, Austria imports large amounts of fossil fuels and energy from Russia.

A poster for the 1924 Commercial Fair in Brussels, Belgium

Belgium

Capital	Brussels
Land Area	11,672 sq mi; 30,230 sq km
Population	10.3 million
Ethnic Group(s)	Fleming, Walloon
Religion(s)	Roman Catholic, Protestant
Government	federal parliamentary democracy under a constitutional monarch
Currency	euro
Leading Exports	machinery and equipment, chemicals, diamonds, metals and metal products
Language(s)	Dutch (official), French (official), German (official)

Belgium (BEL jum) is a small country bordered by Germany, France, Luxembourg, and the Netherlands. It only takes about four hours to cross Belgium by car or by train. Belgium is one of the most densely populated countries in Europe. More than 95 percent of its citizens live in cities. The city of Antwerp is Belgium's main commercial center and Europe's second-largest port. Antwerp is important because Belgium has few natural resources and depends on the export of goods and services from other countries.

Denmark

Capital	Copenhagen
Land Area	16,368 sq mi; 42,394 sq km
Population	5.4 million
Ethnic Group(s)	Scandinavian, Inuit, Faeroe, Southwest Asian, Central Asian
Religion(s)	Protestant, Roman Catholic, Muslim
Government	constitutional monarchy
Currency	Danish krone
Leading Exports	machinery and instruments, meat and meat products, dairy products, fish, chemicals, furniture, ships, windmills
Language(s)	Danish (official)

Denmark (DEN mahrk) is the southernmost country in the region of northern Europe known as Scandinavia (skan duh NAY vee uh). Denmark contains many hundreds of islands, including self-governing Greenland. Greenland, located in the North Atlantic Ocean, is the world's largest island. Denmark itself is one of the flattest countries in the world. More than 65 percent of its land is used to raise crops. The North Atlantic current creates a damp but usually mild climate. These conditions help to make the region's farming profitable.

- Point out the Religions data on pp. 114–115. Ask students **Which religions do almost all the countries on these pages share?** *(Roman Catholicism and Protestantism)*

- Ask students to compare the ethnic groups of France and Germany. Ask **Which ethnic group do they have in common?** *(German)* **Which ethnic groups are unique to France?** *(French, Breton, North African, Basque)* **Which are found only in Germany?** *(Turkish, Southeast Asian)*

- Ask students why they think Swedish is one of the official languages of Finland. *(Sweden borders Finland, so perhaps this is why many people speak Swedish there.)*

COUNTRY DATABANK

Introducing Western Europe

A brown bear in Lappi, Finland

Finland

Capital	Helsinki
Land Area	11,610 sq mi; 305,470 sq km
Population	5.2 million
Ethnic Group(s)	Finnish, Swedish, Sami, Roma, Tartar
Religion(s)	Protestant, Russian Orthodox
Government	republic
Currency	euro
Leading Exports	machinery and equipment, chemicals, metals, timber, paper, pulp
Language(s)	Finnish (official), Swedish (official), Sami

Bordered by Norway, Sweden, and Russia, Finland (FIN lund) is a low-lying country that can be divided into three geographic zones. There is a low-lying coastal strip in the south and west, where most of the cities are located. The interior of Finland is made up of vast forests and woodlands. This area also contains more than 60,000 lakes. Finland's third region is thinly wooded or barren and lies north of the Arctic Circle. The climate is extreme there. Temperatures fall well below zero degrees Fahrenheit during the six-month winter.

France

Capital	Paris
Land Area	210,668 sq mi; 545,630 sq km
Population	59.8 million
Ethnic Group(s)	French, North African, German, Breton, Basque
Religion(s)	Roman Catholic, Protestant, Jewish, Muslim
Government	republic
Currency	euro
Leading Exports	machinery and transportation equipment, aircraft, plastics, chemicals, pharmaceutical products, iron and steel, beverages
Language(s)	French (official), Provençal, German, Breton, Catalan, Basque

Located between the English Channel and the Mediterranean Sea, France (frans) is bordered by Italy, Switzerland, Germany, Belgium, and Spain. France has a long history of wars, invasions, and foreign occupations. Though it suffered great damage during both world wars, France is currently an economic leader among the nations of Europe. France helped to establish the European Union. It is the fourth-largest exporter in the world. Paris, the capital, is considered to be one of the world's great cultural centers.

114 Europe and Russia

Background: Global Perspectives

France and the New World French culture has had a significant influence on North America. The Canadian province of Quebec was originally founded by the French. Although later conquered by the British, Quebec was allowed to retain its French language and institutions. Today, many French-speaking Canadians feel that they might be better represented and their French traditions better preserved if Quebec broke away from Canada and formed its own country.

Germany

Capital	Berlin
Land Area	134,835 sq mi; 349,223 sq km
Population	83 million
Ethnic Group(s)	German, Turkish, Southeast Asian
Religion(s)	Protestant, Roman Catholic, Muslim
Government	federal republic
Currency	euro
Leading Exports	machinery, vehicles, chemicals, metals and manufactured goods, foodstuffs, textiles
Language(s)	German (official), Turkish

Germany (JUR muh nee) is located in Central Europe, with coastlines on the Baltic and North seas. It is bordered by nine countries, including France, Poland, and Austria. Germany was divided into two countries from 1949 to 1990. Today the country faces problems such as unemployment and an aging population. Germans are also still working to rebuild the former East Germany. However, Germany, an EU member, is now an economic leader. It is the second-largest exporter in the world. Germany's economy—based mainly on services and industry—is Europe's largest.

Greece

Capital	Athens
Land Area	50,502 sq mi; 130,800 sq km
Population	10.6 million
Ethnic Group(s)	Greek
Religion(s)	Eastern Orthodox, Muslim
Government	parliamentary republic
Currency	euro
Leading Exports	food and beverages, manufactured goods, petroleum products, chemicals, textiles
Language(s)	Greek (official), Turkish, Macedonian, Albanian

Greece (grees) is located in southern Europe. It is made up of the southern tip of the Balkan Peninsula and more than 2,000 islands. It is surrounded by the Aegean, Ionian, and Mediterranean seas. Greece's landscape is dominated by mountains and coastlines. Greece is famous for its ancient culture, which influenced the development of the modern world. Today, Greece is a member of the EU. However, it has one of the weakest economies in that organization. Efforts to strengthen the Greek economy have been slowed by government policies and conflicts with Greece's neighbors.

Iceland

Capital	Reykjavík
Land Area	38,707 sq mi; 100,250 sq km
Population	279,384
Ethnic Group(s)	Norse, Celtic
Religion(s)	Protestant, Roman Catholic
Government	constitutional republic
Currency	Icelandic króna
Leading Exports	fish and fish products, animal products, aluminum, diatomite, ferrosilicon
Language(s)	Icelandic (official)

Iceland (EYES lund) is an island in northern Europe, between the Greenland Sea and the North Atlantic Ocean. Located just south of the Arctic Circle, Iceland's climate is generally cold. However, the warm waters of the Gulf Stream keep its ports ice-free in the winter. Iceland's varied landscape includes volcanoes, glaciers, fjords, and hot springs. More than half the population of Iceland lives in or near Reykjavík, the capital city. Fishing is the country's largest industry. The people of Iceland enjoy a high standard of living and a strong economy.

- Ask **What is the capital of Germany?** *(Berlin)* **What is the capital of Greece?** *(Athens)*

- Have students compare and contrast the geography and economies of Greece and Iceland. *(Geography—Much of both countries border the ocean; Greece is made up of the southern tip of the Balkan Peninsula and over 2,000 islands, while Iceland is a large island off the coast of northern Europe. Greece is closer to the Equator than Iceland. Economies—Greece's economy is relatively weak, while Iceland's is strong.)*

Guided Instruction (continued)

- Tell students that the countries on pp. 116–117 vary greatly in size. Have students read through the data tables to find the land area for each country. Then ask them to list the countries from largest to smallest. *(Italy, Ireland, Luxemburg, Malta, Liechtenstein, Monaco)*

- Ask students **Which country on these two pages has a land area less than one square mile?** *(Monaco)* Then ask **Are any countries in the Country Databank smaller than Monaco?** *(Vatican City is smaller than Monaco.)*

- Have students compare and contrast the religions and governments of Ireland and Italy. *(They are both republics, and both have Roman Catholics, but Ireland also has Protestants.)*

- Ask students to study Italy's leading exports. Then ask **What do these exports tell you about land use in Italy?** *(Possible answer: Much of the land is probably used for agriculture.)*

Introducing Western Europe

Ireland

Capital	Dublin
Land Area	26,598 sq mi; 68,890 sq km
Population	3.9 million
Ethnic Group(s)	Celtic, English
Religion(s)	Roman Catholic, Protestant
Government	republic
Currency	euro
Leading Exports	machinery and equipment, computers, chemicals, pharmaceuticals live animals, animal products
Language(s)	Irish Gaelic (official), English (official)

Ireland (EYER lund) is located in the North Atlantic Ocean off the west coast of Britain. It is an independent republic that occupies most of the island of Ireland. About one sixth of the island is Northern Ireland, which is part of the United Kingdom. Despite decades of violent conflict with Northern Ireland, Ireland's economy has grown at a remarkable rate in recent years. Its low taxes have brought in businesses from around the world. It is a member of the European Union and helped launch the euro currency. Often called the Emerald Isle, Ireland is known for its rolling green hills and mild, damp climate.

Italy

Capital	Rome
Land Area	113,521 sq mi; 294,020 sq km
Population	57.7 million
Ethnic Group(s)	Italian, Sardinian
Religion(s)	Roman Catholic
Government	republic
Currency	euro
Leading Exports	fruits, vegetables, grapes, potatoes, sugar beets, soybeans, grain, olives, beef, dairy products, fish
Language(s)	Italian (official), German, French, Rhaeto-Romanic, Sardinian

Italy (IT ul ee) is a peninsula in southern Europe. It lies in the Mediterranean Sea northeast of Tunisia. Italy also includes Sicily, Sardinia, and several other islands. Italy has a long and influential history. As the center of the Roman Empire, it was once a world leader. A system of law developed in Rome more than 2,000 years ago still influences law and citizenship in many countries today. Modern Italy became a democratic republic in 1946. Italy, a founding member of the European Union, has a strong economy based largely on manufacturing and industry.

Liechtenstein

Capital	Vaduz
Land Area	62 sq mi; 160 sq km
Population	32,842
Ethnic Group(s)	Alemannic, Italian, Southwest Asian
Religion(s)	Roman Catholic, Protestant
Government	hereditary constitutional monarchy
Currency	Swiss franc
Leading Exports	small specialty machinery, dental products, stamps, hardware, pottery
Language(s)	German (official), Alemannic dialect, Italian

Liechtenstein (LIK tun styn) is a small country in the Alps of central Europe, between Austria and Switzerland. Despite its small size, Liechtenstein has a strong free-enterprise economy and a high standard of living. It has a low tax rate, which attracts businesses from other countries. It also has many banks, with laws that protect international investors. Liechtenstein is closely tied to Switzerland, which provides the smaller country's defense. Liechtenstein uses Switzerland's franc as its national currency. Tourists visit Liechtenstein to ski, climb, and hike in the mountains.

116 Europe and Russia

Background: Links Across Time

The Cradle of Civilization The Mediterranean Sea is located between three continents — Africa, Asia, and Europe. The early civilizations of Egypt, Greece, and Phoenicia developed in the area surrounding the Mediterranean, which is often called the "cradle of civilization." By the first century A.D., the region was controlled by the Romans. The sea has a long history of trade; it was used by many early civilizations to transport goods between Asia and Europe. The Mediterranean declined as a trade route in the late fifteenth century with the establishment of an ocean route around Africa. However, much of the oil transported today from Southwest Asia to Europe crosses the Mediterranean Sea.

Luxembourg

Capital	Luxembourg-Ville
Land Area	998 sq mi; 2,586 sq km
Population	448,569
Ethnic Group(s)	Celtic, French, German, Portuguese, Italian, Slavic
Religion(s)	Roman Catholic, Protestant, Jewish, Muslim
Government	constitutional monarchy
Currency	euro
Leading Exports	machinery and equipment, steel products, chemicals, rubber products, glass
Language(s)	French (official), German (official), Luxembourgish (official)

Luxembourg (LUK sum burg) is bordered by France, Germany, and Belgium. Luxembourg became wealthy from steel production before World War II and today is a financial center. Its capital city has more banks than any other city in the world. Luxembourg is also the home of important EU organizations. The people of Luxembourg enjoy high income, low unemployment, and few social problems. More than 90 percent of the population lives in cities. Tourists visit Luxembourg to see its forests, mountains, and historic castles.

Malta

Capital	Valletta
Land Area	122 sq mi; 316 sq km
Population	397,499
Ethnic Group(s)	Maltese
Religion(s)	Roman Catholic
Government	republic
Currency	Maltese lira
Leading Exports	machinery and transport equipment, manufactured goods
Language(s)	Maltese (official), English (official)

Malta (MAWL tuh) is a group of islands south of Italy in the Mediterranean Sea. Only three islands of this rocky archipelago are inhabited. Malta fell under British rule in 1814, and the United Kingdom defended Malta through World War I and World War II. In 1964, Malta gained its independence and ten years later became a republic. Since that time, Malta has become an important transportation port, financial center, and tourist destination. Economically, it depends on trade with other countries, manufacturing, and tourism. Malta has recently joined the European Union.

Monaco

Capital	Monaco
Land Area	0.75 sq mi; 1.95 sq km
Population	31,987
Ethnic Group(s)	French, Monégasque, Italian
Religion(s)	Roman Catholic
Government	constitutional monarchy
Currency	euro
Leading Exports	no information available
Language(s)	French (official), Italian, Monégasque, English

Monaco (MAHN uh koh) is located on the southeastern coast of France, bordering the Mediterranean Sea. In the late 1800s, Monaco was linked to France with a railroad. This event brought tourists and money to the small country. Since that time, Monaco has grown into a popular vacation destination for tourists seeking beautiful scenery, a pleasant climate, and shopping. The government is focused on developing other services and industries as well. Monaco has no income tax and low business taxes. However, the cost of living is high.

Chapter 4 **117**

Guided Instruction (continued)

- Ask students **Why is Monaco such a popular tourist spot?** (*It offers beautiful scenery, a pleasant climate, and shopping.*)

- Ask **What do Luxembourg and Lichtenstein have in common?** (*Their ethnic groups both include Italians; the Roman Catholic and Protestant religions are practiced in both; their governments are both constitutional monarchies; they both produce machinery; German is an official language in both.*)

Guided Instruction (continued)

■ Have students read the data tables on pp. 118–121.

■ Ask **What ethnic groups live in the Netherlands?** (*Dutch, Southwest Asian, North African, Southeast Asian, South American, West Indian*)

■ Ask **Which of Norway's exports might be related to its long coastline?** (*ships, fish*)

■ Ask students **What religion is practiced in all the countries on pp. 118–119?** (*Roman Catholicism*)

Introducing Western Europe

The Netherlands

Capitals	Amsterdam and The Hague
Land Area	13,082 sq mi; 33,883 sq km
Population	16.1 million
Ethnic Group(s)	Dutch, Southwest Asian, North African, Southeast Asian, South American, West Indian
Religion(s)	Roman Catholic, Protestant, Muslim
Government	constitutional monarchy
Currency	euro
Leading Exports	machinery and equipment, chemicals, fuels, foodstuffs
Language(s)	Dutch (official), Frisian

The Netherlands (NETH ur lundz) is located in northwest Europe between Belgium and Germany, bordering the North Sea. The country is also known by the name *Holland*. The Netherlands suffered through German invasion and occupation during World War II. Very active in international politics, the nation helped to form both NATO and the European Union. Stable relationships with other industrial countries help to keep its economy strong and growing. The Netherlands also serves as an important transportation center in Europe— particularly Rotterdam, on the Mans River.

Norway

Capital	Oslo
Land Area	118,865 sq mi; 307,860 sq km
Population	4.5 million
Ethnic Group(s)	Norwegian, Sami
Religion(s)	Protestant, Roman Catholic
Government	constitutional monarchy
Currency	Norwegian krone
Leading Exports	petroleum and petroleum products, machinery and equipment, metals, chemicals, ships, fish
Language(s)	Norwegian (official), Sami

Norway (NAWR way) is located in northern Europe west of Sweden. In 995, Norway's king converted to Christianity. He also ended two hundred years of Viking raids. In 1397, the nation became part of Denmark, and it remained so for more than four hundred years. The following two hundred years saw Norway gain independence, fall under Swedish rule, gain its independence again, fall under German rule, and regain its independence a third time, in 1945. In the 1960s, the discovery of oil and gas strengthened the Norwegian economy. Like Sweden, Norway has a mix of modern capitalism with many social welfare benefits, and has a very high standard of living. Norway has decided not to join the European Union.

A Sami man trains a reindeer to pull a sleigh.

Differentiated Instruction

For Advanced Readers   L3

Have students scan the Country Databank for languages or ethnic groups they may not be familiar with, such as the Monégasque of Monaco, or the Sami language, spoken in Norway. Have students choose one of these languages or ethnic groups to research in the library or on the Internet. Ask students to write a one-page summary of their research, to be read aloud for the class.

For Gifted and Talented   L3

Using a calculator, ask students to find the population density of each country in the Databank by dividing each country's population by its land area. Students should record the population density for each nation, then organize the information in a poster-sized chart, table, or bar graph. Allow students to explain to the class how they chose to organize their information.

Portugal

Capital	Lisbon
Land Area	35,502 sq mi; 91,951 sq km
Population	10.1 million
Ethnic Group(s)	Portuguese, African
Religion(s)	Roman Catholic, Protestant
Government	parliamentary democracy
Currency	euro
Leading Exports	clothing and footwear, machinery, chemicals, cork and paper products, hides
Language(s)	Portuguese (official)

Portugal (PAWR chuh gul) is located in southwestern Europe. It is west of Spain, bordered by the North Atlantic Ocean. Though Portugal is a fairly small country, it has played a major role in world history. From the 1400s to the 1600s, Portugal dominated the world sea trade. Portuguese explorers sailed the world, seeking wealth and colonies. They established colonies throughout the Americas and in Africa, some of which they ruled into the 1900s. Portugal became part of the European Union in 1986. Since then, the Portuguese economy has grown stronger, but a poor educational system is hindering greater growth.

San Marino

Capital	San Marino
Land Area	23.6 sq mi; 61.2 sq km
Population	27,730
Ethnic Group(s)	Sammarinese, Italian
Religion(s)	Roman Catholic
Government	independent republic
Currency	euro
Leading Exports	building stone, lime, wood, chestnuts, wheat, baked goods, hides, ceramics
Language(s)	Italian (official)

San Marino (sahn mah REE noh) is located in southern Europe, in the Italian Apennine Mountains. It is completely surrounded by the nation of Italy. San Marino is the third-smallest country in Europe and claims to be the world's oldest republic. It has remained independent since around A.D. 300. San Marino's political and social trends are similar to those of Italy. The tourist industry is extremely important to San Marino. Other industries include banking, clothing, electronics, ceramics, and cheese-making. San Marino enjoys a standard of living similar to the wealthiest areas of Italy.

Spain

Capital	Madrid
Land Area	192,873 sq mi; 499,542 sq km
Population	40.1 million
Ethnic Group(s)	Castilian Spanish, Catalan, Galician, Basque, Roma
Religion(s)	Roman Catholic
Government	parliamentary monarchy
Currency	euro
Leading Exports	machinery, motor vehicles, foodstuffs, other consumer goods
Language(s)	Spanish (official), Galician (official), Catalan (official), Basque (official)

Spain (spayn) is located in southwestern Europe between Portugal and France. It has coasts on the North Atlantic Ocean, the Mediterranean Sea, and the Bay of Biscay. Spain was a powerful world empire in the 1500s and 1600s. However, Spain's economy did not industrialize as quickly in later centuries as did other Western European countries such as Britain, Germany, and France. Spain was neutral during World War I and World War II but suffered through its own civil war in the 1930s. Spain joined the EU in 1986, and was among the first countries to begin using the euro currency. The country's economy is generally strong, though high unemployment continues to be a problem.

Chapter 4 **119**

- Ask students **Why do you think the official language of San Marino is Italian?** *(Possible answer: San Marino is completely surrounded by Italy, so Italy has probably had a strong influence on its culture.)*

- Have students compare the information given about San Marino and Italy. Ask **What other characteristics do they have in common?** *(Their ethnic groups both include Italian, their religions both include Roman Catholicism, they are both republics, and they both use the euro.)*

- Have students compare and contrast the populations, languages, and governments of Portugal and Spain. *(Portugal has 10.1 million people, while Spain has roughly four times as many; Portugal's official language is Portuguese, while Spain's four official languages are Spanish, Galician, Catalan, and Basque; Portugal is a parliamentary democracy, while Spain is a parliamentary monarchy.)*

- Have students compare and contrast the governments and political histories of Sweden and Switzerland. (*Sweden is a constitutional monarchy, while Switzerland is a federal republic. Both countries have maintained peace over time by not taking sides in wars.*)

- Ask students **What is the currency of Sweden?** (*the Swedish krona*) **What is the currency of the United Kingdom?** (*the pound sterling*)

- Have students describe how the United Kingdom has changed since the 1800s. (*In the 1800s, the United Kingdom was a growing empire with industrial and military strength. The nation was weakened by World War I and World War II, gradually withdrew from its colonies, and rebuilt itself to become a modern world power.*)

- Ask students **What characteristics make Vatican City different from the rest of the places you have learned about?** (*Vatican City is the smallest independent state in the world; it is an enclave of the city of Rome; its government is ecclesiastical and is headed by the pope; it has no exports; its economy is supported by a yearly tax on Catholics around the world.*)

Independent Practice

Explain to students that the euro is the monetary unit and currency of many of the nations of the European Union, and notes and coins began being used by participating countries in 2002. Have students make a list of the countries in Western Europe that use the euro, and another list of those that do not. Then ask students to write a paragraph explaining what they think the benefits of many countries having the same currency are, and think about why some countries have not adopted the euro. Use the *Rubric for Assessing a Writing Assignment* to review students' paragraphs.

All in One **Europe and Russia Teaching Resources,** *Rubric for Assessing a Writing Assignment,* p. 298

Monitor Progress

Circulate to make sure students are organizing their ideas appropriately.

Introducing Western Europe

Sweden

Capital	Stockholm
Land Area	158,662 sq mi; 410,934 sq km
Population	8.9 million
Ethnic Group(s)	Swedish, Finnish, Sami
Religion(s)	Protestant, Roman Catholic, Muslim, Jewish, Buddhist
Government	constitutional monarchy
Currency	Swedish krona
Leading Exports	machinery, motor vehicles, paper products, pulp and wood, iron and steel products, chemicals
Language(s)	Swedish (official), Finnish, Sami

Sweden (SWEED un) is located in northern Europe between Norway and Finland, bordering the Baltic Sea and the Gulf of Bothnia. Sweden has a high standard of living, with a mixture of modern capitalism and broad social welfare benefits. The nation joined the EU in 1995 but has not accepted the euro as its own currency. Beginning in the 1990s, Sweden faced high unemployment and other economic problems. However, with a population of skilled workers, rich resources, and a modern transportation system, Sweden's economy is still relatively strong. Sweden is one of the world's leaders in equal rights for women.

Swedish soccer player Malin Moestroem in 2003

Switzerland

Capital	Bern
Land Area	15,355 sq mi; 39,770 sq km
Population	7.3 million
Ethnic Group(s)	German, French, Italian, Romansch
Religion(s)	Roman Catholic, Protestant
Government	federal republic
Currency	Swiss franc
Leading Exports	machinery, chemicals, metals, watches, agricultural products
Language(s)	French (official), German (official), Italian (official), Swiss German, Romansch

Switzerland (SWIT sur lund) is located between France and Italy. It is the source of all four of the region's major river systems: the Po, the Rhine, the Rhône, and the Inn-Danube. Politically, Switzerland is famous for its neutrality. Switzerland is also economically neutral and has so far remained outside the European Union. Switzerland does, however, participate in international organizations, including the UN. This small, landlocked Alpine country has one of the strongest market economies in Europe. It is a center of international finance.

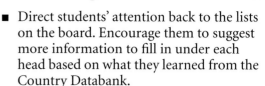

United Kingdom

Capital	London
Land Area	93,278 sq mi; 241,590 sq km
Population	59.8 million
Ethnic Group(s)	English, Scottish, Irish, Welsh, Ulster, West Indian, South Asian
Religion(s)	Protestant, Roman Catholic, Muslim
Government	constitutional monarchy
Currency	pound sterling
Leading Exports	manufactured goods, fuels, chemicals, food, beverages, tobacco
Language(s)	English (official), Welsh (official), Scottish Gaelic, Irish Gaelic

The United Kingdom (yoo NYT id KING dum) is made up of several islands lying northwest of France, between the North Atlantic Ocean and the North Sea. In the 1800s, the United Kingdom was an expanding empire with great industrial and military strength. However, World War I and World War II seriously weakened the nation. In the following decades, the United Kingdom withdrew from its colonies around the world. It then rebuilt itself into a modern world power. The United Kingdom is a founding member of NATO and one of the five permanent members of the UN Security Council. It is also a member of the European Union, although the British have not accepted the euro.

Vatican City

Capital	Vatican City
Land Area	0.17 sq mi; 0.44 sq km
Population	900
Ethnic Group(s)	Italian, Swiss, Polish
Religion(s)	Roman Catholic
Government	ecclesiastical
Currency	euro
Leading Exports	none
Language(s)	Latin (official), Italian (official)

Vatican City (VAT ih kun SIH tee), also known as the Holy See, is an enclave of Rome. This means it is entirely surrounded by Italy's capital city. The Vatican is the world's smallest independent state. It is the home of the pope, who is the leader of the Roman Catholic Church. The pope is also the head of the Vatican City government. The Vatican's unique economy is supported by donations from Roman Catholics around the world. It also earns income from investments and tourism.

SOURCES: DK World Desk Reference Online; CIA World Factbook Online, 2002; *The World Almanac*, 2003

Assessment

Comprehension and Critical Thinking

1. Compare and Contrast Which countries in the region are the largest and the smallest?

2. Make Generalizations What are some characteristics that many of the region's countries share?

3. Infer Which countries do not have any exports? Why might this be so?

4. Categorize What kinds of exports do many of the countries of Western Europe rely on?

5. Make a Circle Graph The total population of Western Europe is about 392 million. Find the Western European country with the largest population. Make a circle graph that shows this country's population as a percent of the population of Western Europe as a whole.

Keeping Current

Access the **DK World Desk Reference Online** at **PHSchool.com** for up-to-date information about the 24 countries in this region.

Go Online
PHSchool.com

Web Code: lde-7400

Assess Progress L2

- Direct students' attention back to the lists on the board. Encourage them to suggest more information to fill in under each head based on what they learned from the Country Databank.

- Ask students to answer the Assessment questions.

Reteach L1

Ask students to create a bar graph showing the populations of the countries of Western Europe. Have them display the countries in order, from the smallest population to the largest population. Remind them to label their information and give the graph a title.

Extend L3

Portfolio Activity

Have students choose one country in the Country Databank. Ask students to learn more about one or two aspects of the country's culture, using the Internet or other reference sources. Have students create a poster explaining their topic and what they learned through their research to the class.

Answers

Assessment

1. France is the largest; Vatican City is the smallest.

2. Many countries in Western Europe use the euro; many share the Roman Catholic and Protestant religions; many are members of the European Union; many countries export machinery and equipment.

3. Monaco and Vatican City; probably because they are so small

4. machinery and equipment, motor vehicles and parts, paper, metals, chemicals, textiles, foodstuffs, ships, wood products, manufactured goods

5. Germany has the largest population in Western Europe, with 83 million. Students' graphs should show that Germany's population is about 21 percent of the total population of Western Europe.

Section 1
Step-by-Step Instruction

Objectives

Social Studies
1. Examine the regions that make up the United Kingdom.
2. Learn about the United Kingdom's democratic heritage.
3. Find out how the United Kingdom combines democracy and monarchy.
4. Understand why trade is important to the United Kingdom.

Reading/Language Arts
Use context clues to clarify unfamiliar words and ideas.

Prepare to Read

Build Background Knowledge L2
Tell students that in this section, they will learn about the United Kingdom and its democratic heritage. Then write the following words on the board: *King, President, Parliament, Congress, Representative, Constitution,* and *Democracy*. Give students several minutes to write down what they think about when they see or hear these words. Then conduct an Idea Wave (TE, p. T35) to allow students to share their responses.

Set a Purpose for Reading L2
■ Preview the Objectives

■ Form students into pairs or groups of four. Distribute the *Reading Readiness Guide.* Ask students to fill in the first two columns of the chart. Use the Numbered Heads participation strategy (TE, p. T36) to call on students to share one piece of information they already know and one piece of information they want to know.

All in One Europe and Russia Teaching Resources, *Reading Readiness Guide,* p. 258

Vocabulary Builder
Preview Key Terms L2
Pronounce each Key Term, then ask students to say the word with you. Provide a simple explanation such as, "A country's constitution is its plan of government."

Section 1 The United Kingdom
Democracy and Monarchy

Prepare to Read

Objectives
In this section you will
1. Examine the regions that make up the United Kingdom.
2. Learn about the United Kingdom's democratic heritage.
3. Find out how the United Kingdom combines democracy and monarchy.
4. Understand why trade is important to the United Kingdom.

Taking Notes
As you read this section, look for important events that have taken place in British history. Copy the table below, and write each event in the correct time period.

Events in British History			
1500s	1700s	1800s	1900s

Target Reading Skill

Use Context Clues When reading, you may come across a word that is used in an unfamiliar way. Look for clues in the context—the surrounding words, sentences, and paragraphs—to help you understand the meaning. Sometimes the context will define the word. In the first paragraph below, for example, you know the words *crown* and *jewels,* but may not know what the term *crown jewels* means. The context of the second paragraph helps explain this term.

Key Terms
- **Parliament** (PAHR luh munt) *n.* the lawmaking body of the United Kingdom
- **representative** (rep ruh ZEN tuh tiv) *n.* a person who represents, or speaks for, a group of people
- **constitution** (kahn stuh TOO shun) *n.* a set of laws that describes how a government works
- **constitutional monarchy** (kahn stuh TOO shuh nul MAHN ur kee) *n.* a government in which a monarch is the head of state but has limited powers

A Beefeater in front of the Tower of London

122 Europe and Russia

The line of tourists seems to go on forever. People in the line are speaking English, French, Arabic, and Japanese. In all of these languages, the tourists are talking about the same thing: the British crown jewels.

The jewels are kept under guard in the Tower of London. The priceless collection includes crowns worn by the kings and queens of England. After a long wait, the tourists finally reach the amazing jewels. Their eyes widen at the sight of huge diamonds, bright-red rubies, and cool-blue sapphires.

British history can be felt everywhere in and around the Tower of London. Near the Tower, rebellious nobles met their deaths on the executioner's block. Young King Edward V and his brother were most likely murdered in the Tower of London. The Tower is watched over by guards called Beefeaters. No one knows for sure where this name came from. But Beefeaters in their colorful red uniforms have guarded the Tower for hundreds of years.

Target Reading Skill L2

Use Context Clues Point out the Target Reading Skill. Tell students that using context clues will help them determine the meaning of unfamiliar words or ideas in a text.

Model using context clues with the word *specific* from the first paragraph on p. 123. *(Since the paragraphs following the sentence explain that each name for the United King-* *dom has a slightly different meaning, students should be able to determine that* specific *means "exact" or "particular.")*

Give students *Use Context Clues: Definition and Description.* Have them complete the activity in groups.

All in One Europe and Russia Teaching Resources, *Use Context Clues: Definition and Description,* p. 277

Regions of the United Kingdom

You may have heard people use different names for the nation located on the British Isles: England, Great Britain, and the United Kingdom. Each name has a specific meaning.

England England is a region within the United Kingdom. Find England on the map below. About two thousand years ago, Romans ruled over present-day England. After the Roman Empire fell, many small kingdoms arose. Over time, one of these kingdoms, Wessex, grew stronger than the others. By conquering other kingdoms, Wessex unified England into a single nation by the 800s.

Great Britain England grew in power and strength. Soon, it began to exert power over its neighbors, including Wales and Scotland. Wales officially became part of the English nation in the 1500s. By the early 1700s, England and Scotland had joined together. Now all of the nations on the island of Great Britain were united. The name of the nation changed to Great Britain.

Hadrian's Wall, built in about A.D.122 by the Roman emperor Hadrian, marked the northern boundary of the Roman Empire. It still stands today in northern England.

Regions of the United Kingdom

KEY

- England
- Great Britain
- United Kingdom
- ——— National border

0 miles 200
0 kilometers 200
Lambert Azimuthal Equal Area

Shetland Islands
Orkney Islands
Outer Hebrides
SCOTLAND
NORTHERN IRELAND
UNITED KINGDOM
IRELAND
Isle of Man
GREAT BRITAIN
WALES
ENGLAND
Isle of Wight
ATLANTIC OCEAN
North Sea
Irish Sea
Celtic Sea
English Channel
N

MAP MASTER™ Skills Activity

Regions The United Kingdom is a single nation made up of several smaller regions. **Identify** Which three regions do the islands called the Outer Hebrides belong to? **Compare and Contrast** How does the political structure of the United Kingdom compare to that of the United States?

Go Online
PHSchool.com Use Web Code ldp-7421 for step-by-step map skills practice.

Chapter 4 Section 1 **123**

Vocabulary Builder

Use the information below to teach students this section's high-use words.

High-Use Word	Definition and Sample Sentence
exert, p. 123	*v.* to apply Hiking requires one to **exert** great energy.
symbol, p. 126	*n.* something that represents or suggests another thing An olive branch is a **symbol** of peace.
finance, p. 129	*n.* the management of money matters The treasurer of our book club is in charge of **finance**.

Instruct

Regions of the United Kingdom ▢L2

Guided Instruction

- **Vocabulary Builder** Clarify the high-use word **exert** before reading.

- Read Regions of the United Kingdom, using the Structured Silent Reading strategy (TE, p. T34).

- Have students discuss the formation of Great Britain. *(England became a united nation by the 800s and began to exert power over its neighbors. Wales became a part of England in the 1500s, and Scotland joined later, in the 1700s, forming Great Britain.)*

- Discuss the Act of Union with students. Ask **Do you think Ireland was in favor of joining with Great Britain? Why or why not?** *(Answers will vary, but students should point out that the southern part of Ireland became an independent nation in the 1920s, and some Northern Irish groups seek to break away from Great Britain and join Ireland, which might indicate that the Irish did not want to join with Great Britain.)*

Independent Practice

Ask students to create the Taking Notes graphic organizer on a blank piece of paper. Then have them enter the details of important events in British history. Briefly model how to identify which details to include.

Monitor Progress

As students fill in the graphic organizer, circulate to make sure individuals are placing the events in the correct boxes. Provide assistance as needed.

Answers

MAP MASTER™ Skills Activity **Identify** Scotland **Compare and Contrast** Possible answer: Just as the United States is made up of fifty separate states, the United Kingdom is comprised of separate regions.

Go Online PHSchool.com Students may practice their map skills using the interactive online version of this map.

COUNTRY PROFILE
Focus on Economics

Guided Instruction [L2]

Ask students to study the Country Profile on this page. As a class, answer the Map and Chart Skills questions. Allow students to briefly discuss their responses with a partner before sharing answers.

Independent Practice

Distribute *Reading a Circle Graph*. Have students work in pairs to complete the worksheet. Then direct their attention to the two circle graphs on this page. Ask **What is the United Kingdom's leading export?** *(manufactured goods)* **What is the United Kingdom's leading import?** *(manufactured goods)*

All in One Europe and Russia Teaching Resources, *Reading a Circle Graph,* p. 287

COUNTRY PROFILE
Focus on Economics

United Kingdom

The United Kingdom has few mineral resources. Yet it has more energy resources—including coal, natural gas, and petroleum—than any other EU member. In the early 2000s, it was among the world's top ten oil producers. From about the mid-1970s on, the United Kingdom has produced enough fuel to export it to other countries. The United Kingdom also uses its energy resources to run the factories that produce manufactured goods, the country's most important export. Study the map and graphs to learn more about the United Kingdom's economy.

United Kingdom: Natural Resources
KEY
- Iron
- Tin
- Coal
- Peat
- Kaolin
- Salt
- Petroleum
- Natural gas
- Hydroelectric power
- National border
- National capital
- Other city

0 miles 200
0 kilometers 200
Lambert Azimuthal Equal Area

Leading Exports

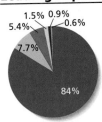

1.5% 0.9%
0.6%
5.4%
7.7%
84%

Leading Imports

2.6% 0.6%
0.4%
3.7%
8.3%
84.4%

- Manufactured goods
- Oil
- Food, beverages, and tobacco
- Raw materials
- Non-oil fuels
- Other

Note: Numbers may not equal 100% due to rounding.
SOURCE: U.K. Office for National Statistics, 2002

Fossil Fuel Production, 1972–2001

Millions of Tons of Oil or Oil Equivalent
1,500
1,200
900
600
300
0
1972–1976 1977–1981 1982–1986 1987–1991 1992–1996 1997–2001
Years

SOURCE: U.K. Office for National Statistics, 2002

Map and Chart Skills

1. **Identify** Where is the United Kingdom's petroleum located?
2. **Locate** Compare the United Kingdom's exports and imports. Which products are the only ones that the country exports more of than it imports?
3. **Synthesize Information** How does the information in the bar graph explain the answer to the question above?

Go Online PHSchool.com Use Web Code ldp-7431 for step-by-step **map skills practice.**

124 Europe and Russia

Answers

Map and Chart Skills

1. in the North Sea
2. oil
3. Fossil fuel production in the United Kingdom has increased steadily since 1972.

Go Online PHSchool.com Students can find more information about this topic on the DK World Desk Reference Online.

Skills Mini Lesson

Transferring Information from One Medium to Another

1. Tell students that to transfer information from one medium to another, they should state the main idea they wish to communicate, identify key information, choose a format to express the information, and transfer the information into the new format.

2. Practice the skill by having students write a paragraph expressing the information on the Leading Imports circle graph on this page in pairs.

3. Apply the skill by having students write a paragraph expressing the information on the bar graph on this page independently.

United Kingdom In 1801, Great Britain officially brought Ireland under its control with a law called the Act of Union. The name of the nation changed to the United Kingdom of Great Britain and Ireland. In the 1920s, the southern part of Ireland became an independent nation. The rest of the island, Northern Ireland, has remained part of the United Kingdom. However, some Northern Irish groups seek to break away from Great Britain and join Ireland.

Today, the full name of this nation is the United Kingdom of Great Britain and Northern Ireland. Most people use the shortened form of the name, United Kingdom, or UK. Within the United Kingdom are four regions: England, Scotland, Wales, and Northern Ireland. Each region continues to have its own culture, traditions, and customs. The British government unifies them all.

Use Context Clues
How do the sentences in this paragraph explain what an *Act of Union* is?

✓ **Reading Check** Which regions make up Great Britain?

A Democratic Heritage

Today, the United Kingdom is headed by Queen Elizabeth II. As the country's monarch, she is a symbol of Britain's past and its customs. The United Kingdom also has a strong democratic government. The roots of British democracy go back many centuries.

The Magna Carta During the Middle Ages, kings needed large sums of money for major undertakings, such as going to war. If they did not have the money themselves, they asked the nobles to provide the funds. In the 1200s, the nobles used the influence their money gave them to limit the power of the king. In 1215, a group of nobles required King John to sign a document called the Magna Carta, or "Great Charter." The Magna Carta required the king to obey the laws of the land.

Links Across
Time

The Magna Carta King John signed the Magna Carta in 1215 in a meadow called Runnymede, beside the River Thames in southeastern England. The Magna Carta holds an important place in history because it was the first written document that limited the power of a monarch. Hundreds of years later, British colonists in the Americas used the Magna Carta to support their fight for more rights. The document itself was written in Latin, which was the language of formal documents at that time. Four copies of the original charter still exist today in England, including the one shown at the right. Two are held in the British Library, while the other two are stored in the archives of the cathedrals at Lincoln and Salisbury.

Chapter 4 Section 1 **125**

Background: Biography

Another Elizabeth Queen Elizabeth I (1533–1603) reigned as queen of England from 1558 to 1603. The period of her reign is called the "Elizabethan Age," and it marked one of England's greatest eras. During her rule, England became a major power in Europe, building a navy formidable enough to defeat the great Spanish Armada. England also experienced a cultural golden age during her reign, as exemplified by writers such as William Shakespeare.

A Changing Monarchy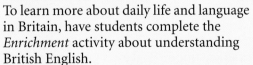

L2

Guided Instruction

- **Vocabulary Builder** Clarify the high-use word **symbol** before reading.

- Have students read about the current basis of British government in A Changing Monarchy. As students read, circulate to make sure individuals can answer the Reading Check question.

- Ask students **What is a constitutional monarchy?** *(a government in which the power of kings and queens is limited)* **What role does Britain's monarchy play today?** *(It is a symbol of Britain's past and helps to unify the British people.)*

- Discuss the components of the British constitution. *(laws passed by Parliament, significant court decisions, and certain legal practices)* Ask **How is this different from the United States Constitution?** *(The Constitution of the United States is a single written document.)*

- Ask students **What do you think are some of the benefits and challenges of devolution?** *(Answers will vary, but may include: benefits—regional assemblies have a better idea of what their citizens need and can adopt specific laws for their citizens; challenges—regional assemblies may pass laws that conflict with one another; the national Parliament might lose some of its power over certain areas)*

Answers

Compare Possible answer: The seating arrangements and clothing of the monarch and members of Parliament are very similar in both images.

✓ **Reading Check** Its purpose was to force the king to obey the law of the land.

Parliament, Past and Present
Below, an illustration shows King Edward I before the Parliament in the late 1200s. At the bottom, Queen Elizabeth II attends a session of Parliament in 1995. **Compare** *Compare the two images. What traditions has Parliament kept throughout its history?*

126 Europe and Russia

Parliament In time, the group of nobles became known as the Parliament. **Parliament** is the legislature, or lawmaking body, of the United Kingdom. This word comes from the French word *parler* (PAHR lay), which means "to talk." Parliament is the place where officials discuss laws and other government business. Parliament changed over time. It later came to include common people as well as nobles. As it became more responsive to the needs of the people, it also gained more power. It helped decide the kinds of taxes paid by citizens. People elected from each region of the country served as representatives in the Parliament. A **representative** represents, or speaks for, a group of people.

The modern Parliament is made up of the House of Lords and the House of Commons. Members of the House of Lords are not elected. They are high-ranking clergy and judges or people who have distinguished themselves in public life. Their power has become limited over the years. In contrast, members of the House of Commons are elected. They govern the nation.

✓ **Reading Check** What was the purpose of the Magna Carta?

A Changing Monarchy

Today, the monarchy serves as an important symbol of Britain's past. It also helps to unify the British people. The British honor the monarchy in many ways. When the queen is in London, a royal flag is flown over her home at Buckingham (BUK ing um) Palace. A ceremony called the changing of the guard takes place there every day. Trumpets blare and guardsmen march back and forth at the palace gate.

A Constitutional Monarchy While Parliament gained power, the power of British monarchs lessened. They no longer make laws or collect taxes. The United Kingdom is now governed by a constitution. A **constitution** is a set of laws that describes how a government works. Some nations have one written document that serves as a constitution, such as the Constitution of the United States. The British constitution is different. It is not one written document. Instead, the British constitution is made up of laws passed by Parliament, important court decisions, and certain legal practices. Parliament can change it as necessary. One of the greatest strengths of the United Kingdom's government is its ability to adopt modern ideas while keeping old ideas that still work.

Differentiated Instruction

For Less Proficient Readers　　L1
Have students read the section as they listen to the recorded version on the Student Edition on Audio CD. Check for comprehension by pausing the CD after a paragraph or two and asking students to paraphrase what they have read.

🔘 Chapter 4, Section 1, **Student Edition on Audio CD**

For Advanced Readers　　L3
To learn more about daily life and language in Britain, have students complete the *Enrichment* activity about understanding British English.

All in One **Europe and Russia Teaching Resources,** *Enrichment,* p. 281

The British government is a **constitutional monarchy,** or a government in which the power of kings and queens is limited. In a constitutional monarchy, kings and queens must obey the laws. And in the United Kingdom, the laws are made by Parliament, not by the monarch. This is very different from an absolute monarchy. An absolute monarch makes all the laws and has the power to ignore them as he or she chooses.

Devolution Until the late 1990s, Parliament made the laws for the entire nation. It even made specific laws for each of the country's regions—laws that affected only England, Scotland, Wales, or Northern Ireland. By the end of the 1990s, the national Parliament turned over some of its lawmaking powers to regional assemblies. Now, the Scottish Parliament makes certain laws that apply only to Scotland. The Welsh Assembly makes laws for Wales, and the Northern Ireland Assembly makes laws for Northern Ireland. Only England does not have a regional assembly. Its laws are still made by the national Parliament. The process of moving lawmaking power from the national level to the regional level is called devolution.

✓ Reading Check **What is devolution?**

Regional Seats of Government
At the left, Queen Elizabeth II opens the Scottish Parliament in 1999—Scotland's first parliament in nearly 300 years. Northern Ireland's Assembly building is shown below. **Apply Information** *In what ways does allowing more power to regional lawmakers strengthen the United Kingdom's government?*

Links Across
The World

The Brightest Jewel Rare spices, silks, and other riches attracted the British East India Company to India in the 1600s. The company established trading outposts in India, with the goal of making huge profits. Over time, the company's goals changed. It gained great political power, and called for social change such as ending India's system of discrimination against people of lower class. In 1858, the British government took over the company, and officially turned India into a colony. Many people called India the "brightest jewel" in the British "crown" of colonies. The coat of arms shown here was a symbol of the British East India Company.

Chapter 4 Section 1 **127**

The Importance of Trade

Guided Instruction

- **Vocabulary Builder** Clarify the high-use word **finance** before reading.

- Have students read The Importance of Trade.

- Discuss how the United Kingdom acquired the natural resources it needed during the period of the British Empire. *(It traded with other nations and established colonies in other areas of the world.)*

- Ask students **How has the United Kingdom become successful in today's world economy?** *(It has become a leading member of the European Union, with expertise in shipping and finance; its membership also allows easy access to European markets for trade.)*

Independent Practice

Have students complete the graphic organizer with events from this section.

Monitor Progress

- Show *Section Reading Support Transparency ER 43* and ask students to check their graphic organizers individually.

  📖 **Europe and Russia Transparencies,** *Section Reading Support Transparency ER 43*

- Tell students to fill in the last column of the *Reading Readiness Guide.*

  All in One Europe and Russia Teaching Resources, *Reading Readiness Guide,* p. 258

Show students *Great Britain: London Fog and Suburbia.* Ask **What was the main cause of the "London Fog" of the 1800s?** *(The smoke from burning coal mixed with natural fog and created a thick smog.)*

Answer

Analyze Images the feeling of unity among the different regions of the British Empire

A Far-Flung Empire
The postcard below shows several of the British Empire's colonies in 1919. At the right, Lord Curzon, the British monarch's deputy in India, poses with an Indian prince in 1907. **Analyze Images** *Read the words and phrases on the postcard. What kind of image of the British Empire is the postcard trying to convey?*

Learn about the suburbs of Great Britain.

The Importance of Trade

As an island nation, the United Kingdom has limited natural resources. It must trade with other nations for resources. For that reason, trade has been important throughout the United Kingdom's history.

The British Empire In the 1500s, trade enabled the British to begin building a large empire. The British Empire grew to include colonies in British-ruled areas on six continents. Its empire was so vast that one could say in the 1800s, "The sun never sets on the British Empire." Recall that 13 of today's United States used to be British colonies. The American and other colonies provided British factories with raw materials. They also provided markets to sell the goods made in British factories. Its many colonies helped the United Kingdom become a world economic power.

But that changed in the 1900s. Fighting World War I and World War II weakened the United Kingdom. In the years after World War II, most of the colonies within the British Empire began seeking independence. The British Empire rapidly came to an end. It had turned over most of its colonies by the mid-1960s. The last colony, Hong Kong, was returned to China in 1997. However, the United Kingdom continues to trade with its former colonies.

Background: Links Across Time

The American Colonies Great Britain suffered a major setback when it lost the 13 colonies in North America that became the United States. This setback occurred in the late 1700s, when Britain was nearing the height of its power. Some believe that the British government failed to take the colonists' complaints regarding trade and taxation seriously. Also, not only had the colonists inherited strong democratic values from England, but much of the motivation for migrating to the colonies had been centered on individual freedom and independence. Ultimately, Britain's attempts to control commerce in the colonies for its own benefit led first to widespread protest and then the American Revolution.

A European Union Member The United Kingdom has many strong industries, or businesses. For example, it has good supplies of fossil fuels—especially oil from deposits beneath the North Sea. It also continues to export many manufactured goods, such as clothing and electronic products. However, the United Kingdom is not as strong a world power as it once was.

The United Kingdom no longer relies on its colonies to boost its economy. In 1973, the United Kingdom joined the European Union. As you have read, the EU is a group of nations that promotes trade and other forms of cooperation among its members.

The United Kingdom today is a leading member of the EU. Its experience in such areas as shipping and finance has strengthened the EU in global trade. In turn, easier access to European markets has helped replace the trade the United Kingdom lost when its empire broke apart. With new links to the resources and markets of other European countries, the British look forward to a bright economic future.

A woman paints figures by hand at a British company that exports tableware and gifts.

✓ **Reading Check** In what ways did the United Kingdom rely on its colonies?

Section 1 Assessment

Key Terms
Review the key terms at the beginning of this section. Use each term in a sentence that explains its meaning.

Target Reading Skill
Find the phrase *common people* on page 126. How do the other words in the same sentence explain its meaning?

Comprehension and Critical Thinking
1. (a) Explain What is the difference between the terms *Great Britain* and *United Kingdom*?

(b) Sequence List four events, in order, that led to the formation of the United Kingdom.
2. (a) Name What are the two houses of the British Parliament?
(b) Contrast How do the two houses of Parliament differ?
3. (a) Recall What kind of government does the United Kingdom have?
(b) Contrast How does the British constitution differ from that of the United States?
4. (a) Note What factor led the British to build a large empire?
(b) Draw Conclusions How did the United Kingdom remain strong after losing its colonies?

Writing Activity
Suppose that you are a British tour guide operator. You tell an American tourist that you are from three places: England, Great Britain, and the United Kingdom. Write a paragraph that explains to the tourist how this can be so.

For: An activity on the British Empire
Visit: PHSchool.com
Web Code: ldd-7401

Chapter 4 Section 1 **129**

Section 1 Assessment

Key Terms
Students' sentences should reflect knowledge of each Key Term.

Target Reading Skill
The phrase *as well as of nobles* tells students that *common people* are people who are not nobles or royalty, but ordinary citizens.

Comprehension and Critical Thinking
1. (a) *Great Britain* refers to England, Scotland, and Wales. *United Kingdom* refers to those three regions plus Northern Ireland.
(b) The Roman Empire fell; the kingdom of Wessex conquered other kingdoms to unify England; England incorporated Scotland and Wales; Great Britain brought Ireland under its control.

2. (a) the House of Lords and the House of Commons **(b)** In the House of Lords, the members are not elected, and they have limited power; in the House of Commons, the members are elected, and they govern the nation.

3. (a) a constitutional monarchy **(b)** The British constitution is not a single written document, but is made up of laws passed by Parliament, significant court decisions, and certain legal practices.

4. (a) trade **(b)** The United Kingdom's participation in the European Union has replaced some of the trade it lost with its colonies.

Assess and Reteach

Assess Progress [L2]
Have students complete the Section Assessment. Administer the *Section Quiz*.

All in One Europe and Russia Teaching Resources, *Section Quiz,* p. 260

Reteach [L1]
If students need more instruction, have them read this section in the Reading and Vocabulary Study Guide.

Chapter 4, Section 1, **Europe and Russia Reading and Vocabulary Study Guide,** pp. 42–44

Extend [L3]
Have students complete the *Small Group Activity: Comparing Types of Government* to learn more about the governments of Great Britain and the United States.

All in One Europe and Russia Teaching Resources, *Small Group Activity: Comparing Types of Government,* pp. 283–286

Answer

✓ **Reading Check** It relied on the colonies for raw materials and as markets for goods made in British factories.

Writing Activity
Use the *Rubric for Assessing a Writing Assignment* to assess students' paragraphs.

All in One Europe and Russia Teaching Resources, *Rubric for Assessing a Writing Assignment,* p. 298

Go Online PHSchool.com Typing in the Web code when prompted will bring students directly to detailed instructions for this activity.

Section 2
Step-by-Step Instruction

Objectives

Social Studies
1. Find out why the French take pride in their traditional culture.
2. Learn about growing cultural diversity in France.

Reading/Language Arts
Use context clues to understand new words.

Prepare to Read

Build Background Knowledge **L2**

In this section, students will learn about France and French culture. Have students begin their exploration of France by viewing the Passport to the World CD-ROM section about France. As they use the CD-ROM, ask students to note several facts about France to share with the class using the Give One, Get One strategy (TE, p. T37).

 France, **Passport to the World CD-ROM**

Set a Purpose for Reading **L2**

■ Preview the Objectives

■ Form students into pairs or groups of four. Distribute the *Reading Readiness Guide.* Ask students to fill in the first two columns of the chart. Use the Numbered Heads participation strategy (TE, p. T36) to call on students to share one piece of information they already know and one piece of information they want to know.

All in One **Europe and Russia Teaching Resources,** *Reading Readiness Guide,* p. 262

Preview Key Terms **L2**

Pronounce the Key Term, then ask students to say the word with you. Provide a simple explanation such as, "A person's philosophy often influences his or her lifestyle."

Section 2 France
Cultural Heritage and Diversity

Prepare to Read

Objectives
In this section you will
1. Find out why the French take pride in their traditional culture.
2. Learn about growing cultural diversity in France.

Taking Notes
As you read this section, look for details about French culture, including recent influences on it. Copy the chart below, and record your findings in it.

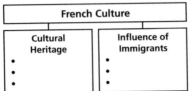

Target Reading Skill

Use Context Clues
Context, the words and phrases surrounding a word, can help you understand a new word. In this example, the phrase in italics helps explain what Impressionism is: French Impressionist artists such as Claude Monet developed *new techniques to paint light and shadow.*

Key Term
• **philosophy** (fil LAHS uh fee) *n.* a system of ideas and beliefs

In 1998, the words "world champions" were projected onto France's Arc de Triomphe.

130 Europe and Russia

It's July of 1998 in Paris, France. Hundreds of thousands of people crowd onto the Champs Elysées (shawnz eh lee ZAY), one of the most fashionable streets in the world. The sidewalks are packed. Some people have even climbed to the tops of lampposts or newspaper stands for a better view. They're all here for a huge celebration. The French soccer team has just won the World Cup championship for the first time ever.

Fans are waving French flags. Others have their faces painted in the colors of the French flag—red, white, and blue. But in the crowd, many fans are waving the Algerian flag and chanting, "Zizou! Zizou!" They are calling for Zinedine Zidane, the midfielder who scored two of the goals in the winning game. Like many of the team's players, Zidane, of Algerian descent, is the son of immigrants.

This victory celebration is symbolic of a new France—a France that is fiercely proud of its culture and is increasingly diverse.

Target Reading Skill **L2**

Use Context Clues Point out the Target Reading Skill. Tell students that sometimes, the context will contain a contrast word that tells the reader that the next idea will be different than the idea it follows.

Model using contrast in the context using the word *permanent* from the second paragraph on p. 136. *(Students should recognize that the word "instead" signals a contrast*

between "temporarily" and "permanent." Therefore, "permanent" means the opposite of "temporarily.")

Have students complete *Use Context Clues: Compare and Contrast* in their groups.

All in One **Europe and Russia Teaching Resources,** *Use Context Clues: Compare and Contrast,* p. 278

Pride in French Culture

French people generally take great pride in their culture—for good reason. Over centuries, the French have made many important contributions to art, religion, music, literature, and philosophy. A **philosophy** is a system of ideas and beliefs. Many French people are committed to preserving their traditional French culture.

The French Language Some people want to prevent the French language from changing too much. An organization called the French Academy determines which words are officially accepted as part of the French language. Since 1635, it has published dictionaries explaining the usage of these words. The Academy is one example of how the French strive to preserve their culture.

Enduring Philosophies Many important philosophies originated in France. Some of these philosophies had to do with government, and they had a great influence on many other nations. For example, the idea that government should be divided into three branches comes from a French philosopher named Baron de Montesquieu (MAHN tus kyoo). A Swiss philosopher living in France named Jean-Jacques Rousseau (zhahn zhahk roo SOH) developed the idea that no laws are binding unless the people have agreed to them. These ideas helped shape the United States Constitution.

Achievements in the Arts French painters are world-famous for their achievements. For example, Eugène Delacroix (ooh ZHEHN deh la KWAH) painted works full of intense emotion and rich color in the early 1800s. Impressionist artists such as Claude Monet (moh NAY) developed new techniques for painting light and shadow.

French composers have written beautiful works of classical music. Claude Debussy (deh boo SEE), for example, composed music in the late 1800s and early 1900s. His work was influenced by artists such as Monet. In turn, Debussy influenced other composers.

French literature is world-famous. For example, Alexandre Dumas (doo MAH) wrote novels in the 1800s. Even today, many of his novels are read by people around the world and have been made into movies.

French Cultural Milestones

1637 René Descartes publishes *Discourse on Method*, one of the world's most important works in philosophy.

1664 Molière, considered to be France's greatest comic playwright, writes his masterpiece, *Tartuffe*.

1751 Denis Diderot publishes an important encyclopedia of science and philosophy that reflects the ideals of the Scientific Revolution.

1790 Marie Louise Élisabeth Vigée-Lebrun, one of France's most successful woman painters, paints her self-portrait.

1830s A French artist and a French inventor together develop the first methods for making photographs.

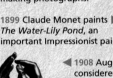

1899 Claude Monet paints *The Water-Lily Pond*, an important Impressionist painting.

1908 Auguste Rodin, considered to be France's finest sculptor, creates *The Cathedral*.

1939 Film director Jean Renoir produces his masterpiece *The Rules of the Game*, which influences cinema around the world.

1957 Writer Albert Camus, who wrote about human emotion in the post–World War II world, wins the Nobel Prize in Literature.

■ Diagram Skills

The French have made major contributions to the world's art, literature, cinema, and philosophy. **Identify** Which event had an influence on cinema around the world? **Identify Causes** What earlier event in this diagram paved the way for this event?

Vocabulary Builder

Use the information below to teach students this section's high-use words.

High-Use Word	Definition and Sample Sentence
contribution, p. 131	*n.* the act of giving something We made a **contribution** to the library with the money we raised at the bake sale.
standard, p. 133	*n.* anything taken as a basis for comparison The taste of my meal did not live up to my high **standards.**

Instruct

Pride in French Culture L2

Guided Instruction

- **Vocabulary Builder** Clarify the high-use words **contribution** and **standard** before reading.

- Read Pride in French Culture, using the Oral Cloze strategy (TE, p. T33).

- Ask students **What is the role of the French Academy?** (*It determines which words are officially accepted as part of the French language, and publishes dictionaries that explain the usage of these words.*)

- Discuss two major ideas of French philosophy that influenced the creation of the United States. (*The ideas that the government should be divided into three branches and that no laws are binding unless agreed to by the people.*)

- Have students compare the art of Eugéne Delacroix and Claude Monet. (*Eugéne Delacroix created works full of emotion and color; Claude Monet was part of a movement that developed new techniques to paint light and shadow.*)

- Ask students **In what other artistic areas have the French made significant contributions?** (*French composers have written classical music; French architects have created medieval cathedrals and modern buildings; French writers have written enduring works of literature.*)

Answers

Diagram Skills Identify Director Jean Renoir produced *The Rules of the Game*. **Identify Causes** the invention of the first photographic methods in the 1830s

- Ask students to describe Gothic architecture. *(Gothic architecture developed in and around Paris in the 1100s. It is characterized by high ceilings, thin walls, and the use of columns and arches.)*

- Ask students **How did French style influence other parts of the world in the 1700s and 1800s?** *(In the 1700s, Russian aristocrats followed French fashion, used French manners, and spoke French. In the 1800s, wealthy British and American women had their clothes made in France, and less wealthy women copied French styles.)*

The Eiffel Tower
Paris's Eiffel Tower was built in 1889 to celebrate the French Revolution. The 984-foot- (300-meter-) tall tower was the tallest structure in the world until 1930. **Infer** *What feelings about the French Revolution might this tower bring about in French people?*

Innovative Architecture French architects have created magnificent buildings. In the 1100s, a style of art and architecture called Gothic developed in and around Paris. Gothic architecture is characterized by high ceilings, thin walls, and the use of columns and arches. French architects built stunning Gothic-style medieval cathedrals, like the Cathedral of Notre Dame (noh truh DAHM). Built in the 1200s in Paris, Notre Dame is one of Europe's most famous cathedrals. It has a number of huge stained-glass windows, one of which is 42 feet (13 meters) in diameter.

In later years, French architects designed other important buildings. For example, work on the Louvre (LOO vruh) Museum was begun during the Renaissance. At first, the Louvre was a royal palace. Over time, many of France's monarchs added to the original building. As they collected great works of art, they housed them in different parts of the Louvre. By the late 1700s, monarchs no longer used the Louvre as a palace, and it became a national museum.

French architects today continue to design great buildings, such as the national library that opened in 1998. This library is made up of four glass skyscrapers surrounding an open square. Though the building is new and modern, the collection it holds is one of the oldest in the world.

Differentiated Instruction

For Gifted and Talented   [L3]
Have students do research to find examples of artwork created by any of the French artists named in the section. Using the artwork, have them create a poster that identifies the artist, the name of the artwork, a brief description of what materials the artwork is composed of, what the art represents, and, if possible, why the artist chose to create it.

Answer

Infer Possible answer: They may view it as symbol of their national pride and as a celebration of their history.

The Department Store In 1852, a French merchant named Aristide Boucicaut (BOO sih koh) took over the Bon Marché, a fabric shop in Paris. By 1914, he had transformed it into the world's first single department store. The department store allowed people, mainly women, to choose from a variety of ready-made clothing and household items in one attractive store. Before this, people went to individuals who specialized in making or selling one type of product. The department store also introduced innovations such as advertising, fixed prices on goods, and a system of returns or exchanges. Department stores were also introduced in the late 1800s in the United States and England.

The Bon Marché, in an engraving made around 1880

New Styles in Fashion For centuries, many people looked to France for the latest styles. Russian aristocrats of the 1700s followed French fashion and used French manners. They even spoke French. Wealthy British and American women traveled to Paris in the 1800s to have their clothes made. Less wealthy women admired French fashions in magazines. They often had their local seamstresses make copies of French originals.

French fashion continued to set trends in the 1900s. For example, a French fashion designer named Christian Dior (dee AWR) created a "New Look" in 1947. His designs featured narrow shoulders and long, full skirts. His fashions became popular all over the world.

Paris continues to be one of the most important centers of the fashion industry. Each year, people come from countries around the world to see the latest fashions from French designers.

Fine Food French cooking has long been one of the most respected styles of cooking in the world. In about 1805, a French pastry chef named Marie-Antoine Carême (muh REE ahn TWAHN kuh REM) delighted the rich and powerful people of France with his desserts. Some of his cakes looked like buildings or monuments. His puddings looked like birds or flowers.

In 1833, Carême wrote a book on the art of French cooking. His book was similar to the dictionaries of the French Academy. It set strict standards of excellence for cooking. Today, many of the world's best chefs are trained in France.

✓ **Reading Check** Name two examples of the influence of French culture on the rest of the world.

Learn about Napoleon Bonaparte.

"Coco" Chanel (1883–1971) Gabrielle "Coco" Chanel created fashion designs that dominated Parisian and international *haute couture* (oht koo TOOR) for much of the 1900s. Orphaned at age six, Chanel was raised by her aunts, who taught her how to sew and gave her the nickname "Coco." Chanel's styles attracted the attention of wealthy women seeking style and comfort. Her classic innovations included jersey dresses, bell-bottom pants, trench coats, turtleneck sweaters, and the "little black dress." She also created a line of perfumes, including the famous Chanel No. 5, which brought her company great financial success.

Guided Instruction (continued)

■ Ask students **How did French clothing styles change after World War II?** (*Designers set new trends that became popular around the world.*)

■ Ask students **How was Marie-Antoine Carême's book similar to the dictionary of the French Academy?** (*It set strict standards of excellence in French cooking.*)

Independent Practice

Ask students to create the Taking Notes graphic organizer on a blank piece of paper. Then have them begin filling in the box titled Cultural Heritage. Briefly model how to identify which details to record.

Monitor Progress

As students fill in the graphic organizer, circulate and make sure they are choosing the correct details.

Show students *France: The Rise of Napoleon Bonaparte.* Then ask **Why did the French people overthrow the monarchy?** (*The people demanded equal rights and more power to govern themselves, but the king refused to grant them these things.*)

Answer

✓ **Reading Check** Some examples include philosophy, art, fashion, and cooking.

Guided Instruction L2

Ask students to study the Country Profile on this page. As a class, answer the Map and Chart Skills questions. Allow students to briefly discuss their responses with a partner before sharing answers.

Independent Practice

Distribute *Reading a Table*. Have students work in partners to complete the worksheet. Then have students transform the information in the two circle graphs on this page into tables similar to the Export Partners table.

All in One **Europe and Russia Teaching Resources,** *Reading a Table*, p. 288

Answers

Map and Chart Skills

1. 35 percent; Large areas of arable land are located in southern and northwestern France. Commercial agriculture also takes place near the English Channel, along the Mediterranean coast, and in parts of the interior.

2. Using modern agricultural techniques, a small number of laborers can farm a large amount of land.

3. 50 percent; the EU is very important to the economy of France

Go **Online** Students can find more
PHSchool.com information about this topic on the DK World Desk Reference Online.

France

Like most developed countries, France's economy is increasingly based on services. Agriculture, however, is still very important to the nation's economy. France is the leading agricultural exporter among EU nations. Agricultural products, mainly cereals such as wheat and corn, make up about 16 percent of France's total exports. Use the data on this page to learn more about France's land use and economy.

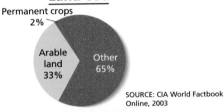

France: Farming and Land Use
KEY

- Livestock raising
- Commercial agriculture
- Forestry
- Mountain region
- Wetland
- National border
- ⊛ National capital
- • Other city
- Cereals   Vineyards
- Root crops   Cattle
- Market gardening

Export Partners

Export Destination	Percent of France's Exports
European Union	
Germany	15
United Kingdom	10
Spain	9
Italy	9
Belgium	7
United States	8
Other	42

SOURCE: CIA World Factbook Online, 2003

Labor Force by Occupation

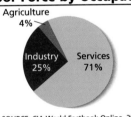

Agriculture 4%
Industry 25%
Services 71%

SOURCE: CIA World Factbook Online, 2003

Land Use

Permanent crops 2%
Arable land 33%
Other 65%

SOURCE: CIA World Factbook Online, 2003

Map and Chart Skills

1. **Note** How much of France's land can be used to grow crops? Where is this land located?

2. **Infer** Compare the percentage of France's arable land and cropland with the percentage of France's labor force in agriculture. From this information, what can you infer about how many laborers are needed to carry out modern agriculture?

3. **Transfer Information** What is the total percentage of France's exports to EU countries? What does this tell you about the importance of the EU to France's economy?

 Use Web Code **lde-7412** for **DK World Desk Reference Online.**

Diversity in France

Many French citizens believe French culture is both unique and valuable. Yet life in France is changing. The cultures of other nations are influencing French culture more and more.

The French language, for example, has picked up words from other languages. French has borrowed words from English, such as *weekend, barbecue, laser,* and *cross-country*. It has borrowed German words, such as *Bretzel* (pretzel) and *Knödel* (dumpling). French also includes words from languages such as Italian, Malaysian, Turkish, and Hindi. These words are a sign of France's ties with many other nations.

Cultural influences from other nations come from many different sources, such as film, television, and radio. Another source is immigration.

A History of Immigration From the mid-1800s on, France was especially welcoming to immigrants. In fact, between 1850 and about 1940, over 7 million immigrants entered France. In the late 1800s and early 1900s, these immigrants were from European countries such as Poland, Italy, Spain, Belgium, and Switzerland. Because these immigrants came from cultures similar to that of France, they quickly and easily adopted French culture.

Influences on French Culture
At the top, Indian immigrants celebrate a Hindu festival. Above, a cable advertisement on a bus uses both French and English words.
Identify Effects *How might increasing immigration continue to affect the French language?*

Guided Instruction

- Read Diversity in France to learn how outside influences have affected French culture. As students read, circulate to make sure individuals can answer the Reading Check question.

- Ask students **How has the French language changed?** (*It has picked up words from other languages.*) Ask students to name some other outside influences not listed in the text. (*Possible answers: books, magazines, the Internet, plays*)

- Discuss the ways in which immigration after World War II affected France. (*Algerians and other immigrants helped France rebuild its economy; many North African immigrants remained in France. As larger numbers of immigrants moved to France in the 1970s, the economy became weak and tensions began building between native-born French citizens and some immigrants. In the 1970s, the French government began to limit immigration.*)

Answer

Identify Effects It might increase the influence of other languages on the French language.

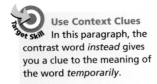

Guided Instruction (continued)

- Discuss the ways in which North African immigrants have contributed to French culture. (*They have brought their Arab culture with them, including different kinds of food, clothing, and music.*)

- Ask students **Why do you think there are more restaurants and grocery stores in France selling foreign foods?** (*Possible answer: There are more immigrants from other countries, and they wish to preserve their traditional customs, including special foods.*)

Independent Practice

Have students complete their graphic organizers with information from this section.

Monitor Progress

- Show *Section Reading Support Transparency ER 44* and ask students to check their graphic organizers individually. Go over key concepts and clarify key vocabulary as needed.

    Europe and Russia Transparencies, *Section Reading Support Transparency ER 44*

- Tell students to fill in the last column of the *Reading Readiness Guide.* Ask them to evaluate if what they learned was what they had expected to learn.

    All in One Europe and Russia Teaching Resources, *Reading Readiness Guide, p. 262*

Target Reading Skill   L2

Use Context Clues As a follow up, have students answer the Target Reading Skill question on this page. (*The text says that the French government thought that Algerian immigrants would be in France only temporarily. The next sentence says that many stayed permanently* instead, *so students should conclude that* temporarily *means "not permanently" or "for a short while."*)

A Political Protest

Muslim women protest a French law proposed in 2004 to ban students from wearing headscarves, Jewish caps, or other religious symbols in school. The women are holding a French flag. **Evaluate Information** *What point are the women making by displaying a French flag?*

Use Context Clues In this paragraph, the contrast word *instead* gives you a clue to the meaning of the word *temporarily.*

After World War II France had a shortage of workers, because repeated wars had resulted in many deaths and a lowered birth rate. The French government began to encourage people from other countries to immigrate to France. By the 1950s, the largest group of immigrants came from Algeria, a French colony in North Africa. In the past few decades, many immigrants have arrived from northern and southern Africa, as well as Southeast Asia.

Rising Tensions After World War II, Algerians and other immigrants helped rebuild France's economy. They took jobs that French employers found hard to fill. The French government assumed that these immigrants would work in France temporarily and then return home. Instead, many North African immigrants decided to make France their permanent home. Large numbers of immigrants along with their families moved to France in the 1970s, a time when the French economy was weak. Tension began to build between native-born French citizens and recent immigrants.

Some native French people had questions about the immigrants. Would they take jobs away from people already in France? Would the immigrants adopt French culture, or would they try to change it? Unlike earlier European immigrants, these recent immigrants often came from very different cultures. As they thought about these questions, some French people felt threatened by the immigrants. In the 1970s, the French government began to limit immigration.

136 Europe and Russia

Differentiated Instruction

For Advanced Readers   L3

Working in pairs, have students do research in the library or on the Internet to find the numbers and origins of immigrants to France for the last five years. Then have them create a table that shows this information.

Answer

Evaluate Information Possible answer: that French citizens should unite and protect each other's freedoms

Immigrants' Influences Today the debate over immigration continues. Immigrants from Algeria, Morocco, and Tunisia bring African and Arab cultures with them. Their food, dress, and music are quite different from those of traditional French culture. The same is true of immigrants from Asia and other regions. The influence of all these groups can be seen especially in the big cities. In Paris and in many other large cities in France, it is common to hear people speaking languages other than French. Every year, there are more and more restaurants and stores that sell foreign food.

France has always been a diverse society. But unlike in the past, recent immigrants have arrived from countries with very different cultures from that of France. France and its people are making adjustments. Many French people were shocked when a politician who promoted an anti-immigrant message won significant popular support in the 2002 presidential election. But most people have come to value the benefits of a diverse population.

An African immigrant selling fresh fish

✓ Reading Check **How are France's immigrants different from those of the past?**

Section 2 Assessment

Key Terms
Review the key terms at the beginning of this section. Use each term in a sentence that explains its meaning.

Target Reading Skill
Find the word *aristocrat* on page 133. What clues in that paragraph helped you figure out its meaning?

Comprehension and Critical Thinking
1. (a) List Name two French cultural contributions to the arts.
(b) Explain What were Montesquieu's and Rousseau's philosophies about government?
(c) Synthesize How did these philosophies influence the United States?
2. (a) Recall Why did the French government encourage immigration following World War II?
(b) Summarize Why did tensions arise between native-born French citizens and immigrants to France in the 1970s?
(c) Identify Effects When immigrants move to a new country, how do they change a country for better or worse?

Writing Activity
Suppose that you are a television reporter covering a story on French culture. You interview an elderly woman for your report. What questions might you ask her to determine how French culture has changed and how it has stayed the same over the past few decades?

Writing Tip Use the blue headings in this section to help you decide on topics. Reread the text under the headings to get ideas for your questions.

Assess and Reteach

Assess Progress L2
Have students complete the Section Assessment. Administer the *Section Quiz.*

All in One **Europe and Russia Teaching Resources,** *Section Quiz,* p. 264

Reteach L1
If students need more instruction, have them read this section in Reading and Vocabulary Study Guide.

Chapter 4, Section 2, **Europe and Russia Reading and Vocabulary Study Guide,** pp. 45–47

Extend L3
To learn more about France's historical architecture, show students *Color Transparency 24* and *Color Transparency 25* of the Cathedral at Reims. Then have students research the history of the Cathedral, and write a short paragraph about one historical event that occurred there.

Europe and Russia Transparencies, *Color Transparency 24: The Cathedral at Reims; Color Transparency 25: The Cathedral at Reims: Interior*

Answer
✓ Reading Check Most of France's immigrants today come from North Africa, and unlike those in the past, bring cultures that are very different from that of France.

Writing Activity
Use the *Rubric for Assessing a Writing Assignment* to assess students' interviews.

All in One **Europe and Russia Teaching Resources,** *Rubric for Assessing a Writing Assignment,* p. 298

Section 2 Assessment

Key Terms
Students' sentences should reflect knowledge of each Key Term.

Target Reading Skill
Because the paragraph states that Russian aristocrats followed French manners, fashion, even spoke French, and that French clothing was very expensive, students can deduce that an aristocrat is a wealthy, educated person.

Comprehension and Critical Thinking
1. (a) Answers should include two of the following: painting, music, architecture, literature. **(b)** The government should be divided into three branches; no law is binding unless agreed to by the people. **(c)** The United States government has three branches and is a republic, which means that laws are voted on by representatives of the people.

2. (a) because there was a shortage of workers in France **(b)** As the French economy became weak, native French people worried that immigrants would take jobs from them and would change French culture and traditions. **(c)** Better—They bring their own culture and traditions to the country, including foods, religions, and languages. Worse—Some might think that immigrants take jobs away from people who already live in the country, or cause the traditional culture of the country to change.

Objectives

Social Studies

1. Learn about Sweden's welfare state.
2. Find out how Sweden became a welfare state.
3. Examine possible solutions to Sweden's economic problems.

Reading/Language Arts

Learn to use context clues to determine how familiar words are being used in the text.

Prepare to Read

Build Background Knowledge   L2

Tell students that they will learn about government benefits in Sweden. Ask them if they know of any benefits that their local, state, or federal government provides for citizens in the United States. Model the thought process by encouraging them to think about transportation, education, and protection. Provide simple examples to get students started. Conduct an Idea Wave (TE, p. T35) to generate a class list.

Set a Purpose for Reading   L2

■ Preview the Objectives.

■ Read each statement in the *Reading Readiness Guide* aloud. Ask students to mark the statements true or false.

   All in One Europe and Russia Teaching Resources, *Reading Readiness Guide,* p. 266

■ Have students discuss the statements in pairs or groups of four, then mark their worksheets again. Use the Numbered Heads participation strategy (TE, p. T36) to call on students to share their group's perspectives.

Vocabulary Builder
Preview Key Terms   L2

Pronounce each Key Term, then ask students to say the word with you. Provide a simple explanation such as, "In a welfare state, the government provides services and benefits to citizens."

Prepare to Read

Objectives
In this section you will
1. Learn about Sweden's welfare state.
2. Find out how Sweden became a welfare state.
3. Examine possible solutions to Sweden's economic problems.

Taking Notes

As you read this section, look for details about Sweden's welfare state. Copy the table below and record your findings in it.

Sweden's Welfare State	
Benefits	**Economic Challenges**
•	•
•	•
•	•

Target Reading Skill

Use Context Clues
Remember that a word that looks familiar to you may have a different meaning in the context of the text you are reading. For example, you have probably heard of the word *welfare*. As you read the text under the red heading A Welfare State, you will learn that the word has a different meaning than the one you have thought of. The last sentence of the first paragraph under A Welfare State makes that difference clear.

Key Terms
• **welfare state** (WEL fayr stayt) *n.* a country in which many services and benefits are paid for by the government
• **national debt** (NASH uh nul det) *n.* the amount of money a government owes

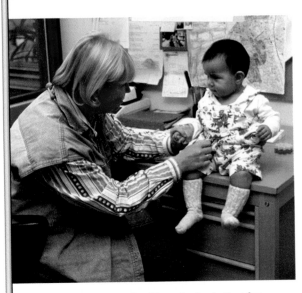

A baby being examined by a doctor in Sweden

138 Europe and Russia

A young Swedish couple is expecting a new baby any day now. Excited, they decorate the baby's room and talk about how they will raise her. They even joke about where she will go to college and what career she might choose when she grows up.

   Like all new parents, they have many hopes and plans for their baby. They have concerns, too—concerns about her health and well-being. But they feel confident about certain things. For example, both parents will have paid time off from work to care for the baby. The baby will also receive excellent health care, child care, and schooling—all for free or at a very low cost. To understand why the government provides these services, you need to understand the nature of Sweden's society.

Target Reading Skill   L2

Use Context Clues Point out the Target Reading Skill. Tell students that a word that looks familiar to them may have a different meaning in the context of the text they are reading. Students can use their own knowledge and context clues to determine how the word is being used.

   Model the skill using the term *cradle-to-grave* on p. 139. *(Students will be familiar with the words "cradle" and "grave," and from* the context should be able to discern that the term cradle-to-grave means "lifelong" or "at every stage of life.")

   Give students *Use Context Clues: General Knowledge.* Have them complete the activity in their groups.

   All in One Europe and Russia Teaching Resources, *Use Context Clues: General Knowledge,* p. 279

A Welfare State

Sweden is a welfare state. In a **welfare state,** the government provides many services and benefits either for free or for a very low cost. These services and benefits include medical care, paid time off from work, and child care. A welfare system means something very different in Sweden than it does in the United States. The American welfare system helps people who are in great need—people who cannot afford medical care or food. The Swedish system helps everyone.

A Cradle-to-Grave System Sweden has a "cradle-to-grave" welfare system. That means that the system provides basic services for all people at every stage of life. When a child is born, the government pays for parents to stay home from work for as long as 15 months. The state then provides child care at a reduced cost, so that parents can work or continue their education. The government pays the costs of schooling, including books and lunches for all students. College education is also paid for everyone. And every Swedish citizen—child or adult—has access to free or inexpensive health care.

As part of the government benefits program, all workers receive five weeks paid vacation. Most workers generally take their vacation at the same time during the summer. That is because in the summer, the nights in this far-northern country are very short. It is daylight for most of the day.

Swedish people are allowed more paid sick days than the workers of any other European nation. Some of the money to pay for this leave comes from the government. And when Swedish workers retire, they receive a monthly payment from the government. This payment nearly equals the pay they received when they were working.

Daily Life in Sweden
Sweden's government funds this day care center (below) and senior citizen community center (bottom left). Both are located in Stockholm, Sweden's capital. **Summarize** *What other benefits do Swedes receive from the government?*

Vocabulary Builder

Use the information below to teach students this section's high-use words.

High-Use Word	Definition and Sample Sentence
benefit, p. 139	*n.* money or service provided by a government to its citizens Her **benefits** allowed her to get job training.
productive, p. 142	*adj.* having the ability to make goods and services in large amounts. Last year's **productive** corn crop provided enough food for the village.

Instruct

A Welfare State   L2

Guided Instruction

- **Vocabulary Builder** Clarify the high-use word **benefit** before reading.

- Read A Welfare State, using the Choral Reading strategy (TE, p. T34).

- Discuss the difference between the meaning of a welfare system in the United States and in Sweden. (*The American welfare system helps people who are in great need. The Swedish system helps everyone.*)

- Ask students **Explain why Sweden is said to have a "cradle-to-grave" welfare system?** (*The government pays for benefits at every stage of life, including day care, education, health care, vacation, sick days, and retirement payments.*)

- Discuss with students how the Swedish government pays for benefits. (*Swedish people pay very high taxes on take-home pay, food, and clothing to pay for the benefits.*)

Independent Practice

Ask students to create the Taking Notes graphic organizer on a blank piece of paper. Have them fill in details in the Benefits column. Briefly model how to identify which details to record.

Monitor Progress

As students fill in the graphic organizer, circulate to make sure individuals are choosing the correct details. Provide assistance as needed.

Answer

Summarize The government pays for the costs of schooling, including higher education, and provides access to inexpensive or free health care. Workers receive five weeks of paid vacation, and Swedish people are allowed more paid sick days than the workers of any other European nation. The government pays for parents to stay home from work with their newborn children. When workers retire, they receive a monthly payment from the government.

Guided Instruction L2

Ask students to study the Country Profile on this page. As a class, answer the Map and Chart Skills questions. Allow students to briefly discuss their responses with a partner before sharing answers.

Independent Practice

Distribute *Reading a Line Graph*. Have students work in partners to complete the worksheet. Then draw their attention to the line graph on this page. Ask **How does the rainfall in Sweden fluctuate over a year?** *(Slightly more rain falls in the summer months of June, July, and August, but overall rainfall does not fluctuate very much.)*

All in One Europe and Russia Teaching Resources, *Reading a Line Graph,* p. 289

Answers

Map and Chart Skills

1. in the southern half of Sweden

2. The northern interior is cold and receives heavy snowfall, while in the south temperatures are more moderate and coastal waters do not freeze.

3. Sweden's large cities are located there in the south, where temperatures are more moderate and coastal waters do not freeze.

Go Online PHSchool.com Students can find more information about this topic on the DK World Desk Reference Online.

Sweden

Sweden is located far to the north, with about a fifth of its land within the Arctic Circle. Because of its great length from north to south, its climate varies greatly. The northern interior receives heavy snowfall and is cold for months, while in the southern regions temperatures are moderate, and the coastal waters do not freeze. The country is heavily forested, especially in the northern part of the country. Study the map and the charts to learn how Sweden's geography shapes the lives of its people.

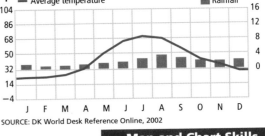

Sweden: Natural Vegetation
KEY
- Deciduous forest
- Mixed forest
- Coniferous forest
- Highland (vegetation varying with elevation)
- Tundra
- National border
- ⊛ National capital
- • Other city

Lambert Azimuthal Equal Area

Largest Cities

City	Population (2002)
Stockholm	👤👤👤👤👤👤👤
Göteborg	👤👤👤👤👤
Malmö	👤👤👤
Uppsala	👤👤
Linköping	👤

SOURCE: Statistics Sweden

👤 This figure represents 100,000 people.

Sweden's Weather

— Average temperature   ■ Rainfall

SOURCE: DK World Desk Reference Online, 2002

Urban and Rural Population

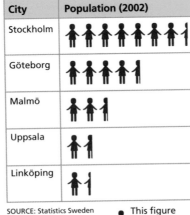

83% Urban   17% Rural

Map and Chart Skills

1. **Locate** Where are Sweden's five largest cities located?
2. **Contrast** How is the vegetation of that area different from that of the regions with no large cities?
3. **Synthesize Information** What factors might explain the location of the majority of Sweden's population?

 Use Web Code Ide-7413 for **DK World Desk Reference Online.**

140 Europe and Russia

Background: Global Perspectives

Health Insurance National health insurance has been adopted throughout Europe and in parts of Asia. For example, Great Britain has provided comprehensive health coverage since 1948, while Canada has had similar coverage since 1971. The United States, by contrast, is the only Western industrialized nation without a form of national comprehensive health insurance. However, the U.S. government does provide health coverage to older retired persons and low-income citizens. Many people in the United States have no health care coverage. This issue has been an important one in recent elections.

High Taxes Swedish people believe that welfare benefits are very important. They are willing to pay the highest taxes in Europe in order to have these benefits. Swedes pay as much as 60 percent of their income in taxes. Food is taxed at 12 percent. Clothing and other goods are taxed at 25 percent. But in exchange for these high taxes, all Swedes have financial security. Whether they are rich or poor, they know that their children will get a good education. Medical costs are low. Rents are affordable.

✓ Reading Check **What is a "cradle-to-grave" system?**

Building a Welfare State

As it has been for hundreds of years, Sweden is a monarchy. Yet the government has changed greatly throughout Sweden's history.

Sweden's History The history of Sweden begins with the Vikings—an early sailing people from Scandinavia who colonized many parts of Europe. Beginning in about the 900s, Sweden was ruled by a series of kingdoms. In the 1600s, Sweden emerged as a great power in northern Europe. From its capital city, Stockholm, Sweden ruled a thriving empire. However, the country's strength declined in the 1700s after Sweden lost a war with Russia. Sweden remained neutral in both world wars.

Like the monarchy in the United Kingdom, Sweden's monarchy changed over time. The monarch slowly gave more and more power to the people, represented in a parliament. And political parties arose to represent the people and bring about change in government. Today Sweden is a constitutional monarchy. The monarch is the ceremonial leader, but parliament makes the laws.

Learn the importance of Swedish forests.

Show students *Sweden: Land of Forests*. Then ask **Why are forests important to Sweden?** (*Forests cover much of Sweden, and the forestry industry pays taxes that help to provide the many benefits Swedes enjoy.*)

Building a Welfare State L2

Guided Instruction

- Read about Sweden's past in Building a Welfare State. As students read, circulate and make sure individuals can answer the Reading Check question.

- Discuss why life in Sweden was not always so secure. (*By the late 1800s, industry had not grown, farming methods had not changed, and many people were poor.*)

- Ask students **How did the country change in the early 1900s?** (*Sweden became an industrial country and the economy grew stronger.*)

- Discuss how Sweden became a welfare state. (*A political party called the Social Democrats came to power in the mid-1900s, promised Swedes a better life, and changed Sweden into a welfare state.*)

Independent Practice

Have students continue to fill in the graphic organizer with details about Sweden's welfare state. Ask them to include details under the Economic Challenges column.

Monitor Progress

As students fill in the graphic organizer, make sure individuals are entering the correct details. Provide assistance as necessary.

A 2002 photo shows the current Swedish monarch, King Carl Gustaf XVI, with other members of the royal family.

Chapter 4 Section 3 **141**

Background: Biography

Alfred Nobel (1833-1896) Industry came to Sweden slowly, but Swedish inventor and businessman Alfred Nobel became a successful industrialist in the 1800s. Nobel developed a safer form of the explosive nitroglycerin, which he called dynamite. He opened factories throughout Europe to manufacture dynamite and soon became rich. He also opened laboratories to develop new products. He registered more than 350 patents for his inventions, which included artificial leather and silk. In his will, he left money for the establishment of the Nobel Prizes. These prizes honor people who have made advances in science, literature, economics, and peace.

Answer

✓ Reading Check a system that provides basic services for all people at every stage of life

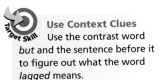

Target Reading Skill L2

As a follow up, have students answer the Target Reading Skill question on this page. (*Using the previous sentence and the contrast word* but, *students should answer that* lagged *means "delayed" or "fail to keep up."*)

Problems and Solutions L2

Guided Instruction

■ **Vocabulary Builder** Clarify the high-use word **productive** before reading.

■ Read how Sweden is trying to meet its challenges in Problems and Solutions.

■ Discuss Sweden's tax problem in the late 1980s. (*Because taxes were high, people bought fewer products, and Swedish companies became less productive.*)

■ Ask **What measures did the government take to continue to pay for benefits?** (*The government borrowed money, which raised the national debt. It then increased taxes and cut some spending to try to control the debt.*)

Use Context Clues Use the contrast word *but* and the sentence before it to figure out what the word *lagged* means.

■ Chart Skills

Sales tax is a tax on goods and services. This chart shows the rate, or percent, of sales tax in various Western European countries and two American states. **Compare** How does Sweden's sales tax compare to those of the other European countries shown? To the states shown? **Generalize** Do you think governments with very low taxes generally provide many or few social services? Why do you think so?

Sales Tax Rates in Western Europe and the United States

Country or State	Standard Rate (%)
France	19.6
Germany	16.0
Sweden	25.0
United Kingdom	17.5
United States: Florida	6.0
United States: New York	4.25

142 Europe and Russia

Meeting Economic Challenges Economic problems led to the rise of Sweden's modern welfare state. By the late 1800s, industry had grown in the United States and most of Europe. But Sweden lagged far behind. There were few factories or railroad lines or even good roads. Farming methods had not changed much since the Middle Ages. Many people were very poor. By the end of the 1800s, about 1.5 million Swedes had left the country in search of a better life. Most of them settled in the midwestern states of the United States, such as Minnesota and Wisconsin.

In 1932, a political party called the Social Democrats came to power. The Social Democrats promised a better life for Swedes. Over the next few decades, the party made Sweden into a welfare state. At the same time, Sweden became an industrial country, and its economy grew stronger. Today the Social Democrats are still the country's largest political party.

✔ **Reading Check** Which political party created Sweden's welfare state?

Problems and Solutions

Sweden's welfare state has served as a model for government throughout Europe. Still, the system has its problems. Everyone in Sweden receives benefits, but the government has faced challenges in providing those benefits.

Sweden's Troubles For decades, Sweden was able to offer its citizens very generous benefits, no matter how poorly the economy performed. But that changed in the late 1980s. People bought fewer items because of the high taxes on groceries, clothing, and other goods. Thus, there was less spending to boost the economy. Sweden's companies were less productive than companies in other nations. Long vacations meant that workers spent less time on the job. Sweden's economic growth stalled.

The benefits of the welfare system continued to be very important to Swedish citizens. To continue paying these benefits, the government had to borrow money. Soon, the **national debt**, or the amount of money their government owed, began to grow. The government increased taxes and cut some spending to try controlling the debt. But paying down the national debt remains a challenge.

Differentiated Instruction

For Special Needs Students L1

Have students read the section as they listen to the recorded version on the Student Edition on Audio CD. Check for comprehension by pausing the CD after each paragraph and asking students to summarize what they have just read.

 Chapter 4, Section 3, **Student Edition on Audio CD**

For Gifted and Talented L3

Have students create a flow chart using the information in the first paragraph under "Sweden's Troubles," using arrows to connect causes and effects. Show the *Transparency B5: Flow Chart* to aid students.

📖 **Europe and Russia Transparencies,** *Transparency B5: Flow Chart*

Answers

✔ **Reading Check** the Social Democrats

Chart Skills Compare Sweden's sales tax is about 5–9 percent higher than the other European countries shown, and about twenty percent higher than those of Florida and New York. **Generalize** Possible answer: probably fewer, because they have less money to spend on social services than governments with higher taxes

A Graying Population Sweden has 1.5 million retired people out of a population of about 9 million. This means that about one out of six people is retired. That is the highest proportion of retired people in the world. Sweden's aging population presents many challenges for the nation. Elderly people often need increased health care and medicines. Many elderly people who cannot take care of themselves must be cared for by other people.

Yet an aging population presents an even greater problem. As you have read, Swedes receive many benefits, such as low medical costs and low rents. The money for these benefits comes from the paychecks of Swedish workers, who pay high taxes on their salaries. In an aging population, there are fewer workers, because so many people are retired. As a result, there is less tax money to pay for benefits.

Over time, the money received from taxes is not enough to pay for the extra care needed by an elderly population. Some studies say that unless Sweden's government reforms its welfare benefits, there will not be any money left by 2015. Raising taxes even higher to cover the high costs of benefits has been proposed, but it is not a popular idea.

Government Solutions Sweden's government is looking for ways to solve these problems. One solution would be for the government to reduce benefits and spend less money. The government made many attempts to reduce benefits in the 1990s. It reduced the payments for sickness benefits. It also required workers to save more of their own money for retirement. But these reforms angered Swedish voters, who voted against their leaders in two major elections.

Links to
Science

Sun at Midnight It is midnight in northern Sweden, and some friends are playing volleyball outside. How is this so? From about March 20 to September 23 in the most northern arctic regions, the sun can be seen on the horizon 24 hours a day. This is because the northern hemisphere is tilted directly toward the sun at this time. In northern Sweden, the sun never sets for a few days around June 21. The Swedes celebrate this time as Midsummer's Eve, with dancing (below), food, and music.

12:05 AM

Chapter 4 Section 3 **143**

Links

Read the **Links to Science** on this page. Then ask **When do Swedes celebrate Midsummer's Eve?** *(for a few days around June 21, when the sun never sets)*

Guided Instruction (continued)

■ Discuss how Sweden has tried to solve its problems and whether its efforts were successful. *(It tried to reduce benefits and required workers to save more of their own money for retirement, but angry Swedish voters voted against their leaders.)*

■ Ask **Why have Swedish companies had problems competing with firms in other countries?** *(Companies became less productive because they could not make products as quickly and cheaply as other countries.)*

■ Ask **How might businesses help solve Sweden's problems?** *(Sweden's businesses might take advantage of natural resources.)*

Independent Practice

Have students complete the graphic organizer by filling in additional details in the Economic Challenges column.

Monitor Progress

■ Show *Section Reading Support Transparency ER 45* and ask students to check their graphic organizers individually. Go over key concepts and clarify key vocabulary as needed.

Europe and Russia Transparencies, *Section Reading Support Transparency ER 45*

■ Tell students to fill in the last column of the *Reading Readiness Guide*. Probe for what they learned that confirms or invalidates each statement.

All in One Europe and Russia Teaching Resources, *Reading Readiness Guide*, p. 266

 Skills Mini Lesson

Decision Making

1. Teach the skill by explaining the steps used in decision making: identify a problem, gather information, list and evaluate the options, and choose the best option.

2. Help students practice the skill by identifying the problems Sweden has faced

in continuing to provide benefits to all its citizens.

3. Have students apply the skill by answering these questions: What are some options the government and businesses have to solve this problem? What might be possible negative effects of these options? What would you decide?

Assess and Reteach

Assess Progress
L2

Have students complete the Section Assessment. Administer the *Section Quiz.*

 Europe and Russia Teaching Resources, *Section Quiz,* p. 268

Reteach
L1

If students need more instruction, have them read this section in the Reading and Vocabulary Study Guide.

📖 Chapter 4, Section 3, **Europe and Russia Reading and Vocabulary Study Guide,** pp. 48–50

Extend
L3

Have students learn more about comparing daily life today to life in the past by reading the literature excerpt *The Boy* by Erik Christian Haugaard in pairs or groups. Discuss the Think It Over questions at the end. Ask students how Dag's government might have been able to help him if it offered benefits like Sweden's today.

 Europe and Russia Teaching Resources, *The Boy,* pp. 292–295

Answer

✓ Reading Check Natural resources such as iron ore, steel, rivers, waterfalls, and timber could help the Swedish economy.

Section 3 Assessment

Key Terms
Students' sentences should reflect knowledge of each Key Term.

🎯 Target Reading Skill
Because the forests are large enough to supply Sweden's timber needs as well as those of other countries, *vast* must mean "large" or "extensive."

Comprehension and Critical Thinking
1. (a) Swedish citizens receive medical care, family leave, child care, education, five weeks paid vacation, sick leave, and retirement payments. **(b)** Many Swedes are willing to pay high taxes for the security the benefits give them.

2. (a) There were few factories or railroad lines or good roads, farming methods had changed little, many people were poor. Many left the country in search of a better life. **(b)** With industrialization, Sweden's economy grew stronger.

A woman assembles parts at a car factory in Göteborg, Sweden.

Business Solutions Another solution would be for businesses to earn more, giving more money to the government in the form of taxes. One way for businesses to grow is to take better advantage of Sweden's natural resources. Sweden has high-grade iron ore and produces enough steel for itself and for export. Hydroelectric turbines run by Sweden's fast rivers and many waterfalls produce half of Sweden's electricity. Sweden's vast forests support the timber industry, which supplies Sweden's needs as well as those of other countries.

Even with these ample resources, Swedish companies have had trouble competing with firms in other countries. Most Swedish products are of high quality. But the Swedes have not been able to make them as quickly and cheaply as other countries. Some companies have found a solution to this problem. Swedish automakers, for example, have followed the example of American companies. Using the methods of American auto factories, the Swedes can now make a car in about 40 hours. It used to take them about 100 hours.

Improving the economy means changing the ways that things are done in Sweden. The welfare system is very important to Swedes. However, they need to find better ways of paying for it. That is the greatest challenge facing Sweden today.

✓ Reading Check **What natural resources could help the Swedish economy?**

Section 3 Assessment

Key Terms
Review the key terms at the beginning of this section. Use each term in a sentence that explains its meaning.

🎯 Target Reading Skill
Find the word *vast* in the first paragraph on this page. How does its context explain its meaning?

Comprehension and Critical Thinking
1. (a) Describe What benefits do Swedish citizens receive?

(b) Identify Frame of Reference Why are some Swedes willing to pay such high taxes?

2. (a) Explain Why did many Swedes leave their country in the late 1800s?

(b) Identify Effects What effect did industrialization have on Sweden's economy?

3. (a) Explain Why did the Swedish economy stall in the late 1980s?

(b) Apply Information How could the government and businesses work together to solve Sweden's financial problems?

Writing Activity
Consider that in the United States, most people pay 20 to 30 percent of their income in taxes, compared to about 60 percent in Sweden. What lessons do you think the two countries might learn from each other? Write a paragraph summarizing your thoughts.

For: An activity on the Vikings
Visit: PHSchool.com
Web Code: ldd-7403

---

3. (a) People were buying fewer items because of high taxes, and companies were less productive. **(b)** The government could reduce benefits and allow businesses to take advantage of Sweden's natural resources, so they can earn more money to pay more in taxes.

Writing Activity
Use the *Rubric for Assessing a Writing Assignment* to evaluate students' paragraphs.

 Europe and Russia Teaching Resources, *Rubric for Assessing a Writing Assignment,* p. 298

Go Online PHSchool.com Typing in the Web code when prompted will bring students directly to detailed instructions for this activity.

Section 4 · Italy
Northern and Southern Divisions

Prepare to Read

Objectives
In this section you will
1. Discover that there is another country within Italy called Vatican City.
2. Understand why there are divisions between northern and southern Italy.

Taking Notes
As you read this section, look for ways that life is similar and different in northern and southern Italy. Copy the Venn diagram below and record your findings in it.

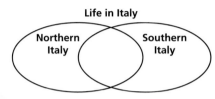

Life in Italy

Northern Italy · Southern Italy

🎯 Target Reading Skill
Use Context Clues To make sure you have correctly determined the meaning of an unfamiliar word by looking at its context, look at the word itself for clues. For example, examine the word *guidance* in the first paragraph below. The sentence in which the word appears tells you that it has something to do with the leader. To double check, look at the word itself. What verb sounds like *guidance*?

Key Terms
- **basilica** (buh SIL ih kuh) *n.* a Roman Catholic church that has special, high status because of its age or history
- **manufacturing** (man yoo FAK chur ing) *n.* the process of turning raw materials into finished products
- **land reform** (land ree FAWRM) *n.* the process of dividing large properties into smaller ones

Can you solve this riddle? A magazine photographer spent about a year exploring a certain country, yet the country is so tiny that he was able to walk around it in 40 minutes. Its population is only about 1,000. But about one billion people look to its leader for guidance. What is the country?

The tiny country is called Vatican City (VAT ih kun SIH tee). It is the world headquarters of the Roman Catholic Church. The pope is its leader. Every day, Roman Catholics all over the world look to him for leadership. Politically, Vatican City is not part of Italy. Yet it holds an important place in the culture of all Italians.

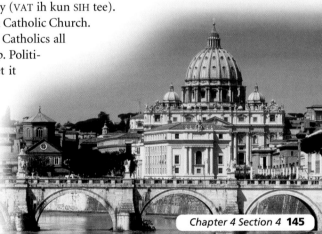

St. Peter's Basilica rises above Vatican City.

Chapter 4 Section 4 **145**

🎯 Target Reading Skill L2
Point out the Target Reading Skill. Tell students that when they use context clues to determine the meaning of a word, they can double check the meaning by studying the word itself for clues.

Model the skill using the word *modernize* in the fourth paragraph on p. 150. *(Students should use what they know about the word "modern" to determine that mod-* ernize *means to "renovate" or "bring up to date.")*

Give students *Use Context Clues: General Knowledge.* Have them complete the activity in groups.

All in One Europe and Russia Teaching Resources, *Use Context Clues: General Knowledge,* p. 279

Section 4
Step-by-Step Instruction

Objectives
Social Studies
1. Discover that there is another country within Italy called Vatican City.
2. Understand why there are divisions between northern and southern Italy.

Reading/Language Arts
Use what you already know about an unfamiliar word to confirm information given in context clues.

Prepare to Read

Build Background Knowledge
Tell students that they will learn about similarities and differences between the northern and southern regions of Italy. Show the video *Ancient Rome.* Ask students how the Roman Empire's legacy is evident in Italy today, and if they think it contributes to the unity or division of the Italian people. Use the Give One, Get One strategy (TE, p.T37) to encourage class discussion.

Ancient Rome, **World Studies Video Program**

Set a Purpose for Reading L2
- Preview the Objectives.
- Read each statement in the *Reading Readiness Guide* aloud. Ask students to mark the statements true or false.

    All in One Europe and Russia Teaching Resources, *Reading Readiness Guide,* p. 270

- Have students discuss the statements in pairs or groups of four, then mark their guides again. Use the Numbered Heads participation strategy (TE, p. T36) to call on students to share their group's perspectives.

Vocabulary Builder
Preview Key Terms
Pronounce each Key Term, then ask students to say the word with you. Provide a simple explanation such as, "A basilica is a Roman Catholic church that has special importance."

Use Context Clues As a follow up, have students answer the Target Reading Skill question on this page of the Student Edition. (*Students should conclude that* priceless *means "too valuable to be assigned a price" or "irreplaceable".*)

Instruct

A Unifying Force L2

Guided Instruction

- Read A Unifying Force, using the Oral Cloze reading strategy (TE, p. T33).

- Ask students **How is the Vatican both a city and a country?** (*The Vatican is located within the city of Rome. It has its own police force, radio station, newspaper, and fire department. Like other countries, it is a member of the United Nations and has its own banks and money.*)

- Discuss why tourists come to the Vatican. (*Tourists come to see St. Peter's Basilica, the Vatican's palace, the Sistine Chapel, and art museums.*)

Independent Practice

Assign *Guided Reading and Review*.

All in One **Europe and Russia Teaching Resources**, *Guided Reading and Review*, p. 271

Monitor Progress

As students complete *Guided Reading and Review*, circulate and make sure that individuals are completing the worksheet correctly.

Answers

✓ Reading Check The Vatican is an independent city-state and country within Rome. It symbolizes the Roman Catholic Church and unites most Italians.

Apply Information Many famous Renaissance artists and architects contributed to St. Peter's Basilica.

A Unifying Force

Vatican City is also known as the Vatican. It is a country within a country. Located within Rome, the capital of Italy, the Vatican is an independent city-state. The Vatican has its own banks and its own money, although you can also use euros there. It is a member of the United Nations. It also has its own police force, radio station, newspaper, and fire department.

Vatican City symbolizes the Roman Catholic Church that unites most Italians. Every day, Catholics and non-Catholics stream into this little country. Most visitors come to see St. Peter's Basilica. A **basilica** is a Roman Catholic church that has a special, high status because of its age or history. The Vatican's palace and art museums are also popular attractions. These museums have priceless collections of religious art, as well as artwork from ancient Greece and Rome.

The Sistine (SIS teen) Chapel, located inside the Vatican, contains many famous paintings, sculptures, and other works of art. Tourists crowd into this chapel, but there is nearly perfect silence inside. No one is allowed to speak above a whisper. Everyone leans back to see the religious scenes painted on the ceiling. The artist Michelangelo painted the ceiling in the 1500s. It is the most famous ceiling in the world.

✓ Reading Check **What is the Vatican?**

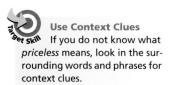

Use Context Clues If you do not know what *priceless* means, look in the surrounding words and phrases for context clues.

A View Inside St. Peter's Tourists gaze in awe at the art decorating St. Peter's Basilica, including these sculptures by the Italian Renaissance artist Bernini. **Apply Information** *How was the Vatican influenced by the Renaissance?*

Vocabulary Builder

Use the information below to teach students this section's high-use words.

High-Use Word	Definition and Sample Sentence
influence, p. 148	*n.* power to affect others With his mother's **influence**, he became a great writer.
abundant, p. 149	*adj.* plentiful The **abundant** rain allowed the flowers to bloom.

Italy

Historically, Italy's location on the Mediterranean Sea made it an important agricultural center and a crossroads of world trade. Today, Italy's economy is shifting toward services, and its main trade partners are other EU members. The "two Italies"—northern and southern—continue to have unequal economies. Use the data on this page to learn more about the economy of Italy.

Italy: Land Use KEY
- Wheat, rice, and dairy
- Livestock raising
- Fruit and mixed farming
- Grapes
- Forestry
- Industrial areas
- Little or no activity
- National border
- ⊛ National capital
- • Other city

SWITZERLAND · AUSTRIA · SLOVENIA · CROATIA · FRANCE · BOSNIA & HERZEGOVINA · SAN MARINO · ITALY · VATICAN CITY · Milan · Brescia · Venice · Turin · Florence · Pisa · Rome · Naples · CORSICA (France) · SARDINIA · Sicily · Ligurian Sea · Adriatic Sea · Tyrrhenian Sea · Ionian Sea · Mediterranean Sea

0 miles 200 / 0 kilometers 200 / Albers Equal Area

Economic Output per Person, 2001

$66,538 (North); $25,337 (South)
U.S. Dollars / Region

SOURCES: The European Commission; The World Bank Group

Structure of Italy's Economy

Percent of Annual Economic Output — Years 1983–2001
Legend: Agriculture, Industry, Services

SOURCE: The World Bank Group

Trade, 2001

Exports: 54% / 46%
Imports: 56% / 44%
Percentage of Total Trade
Legend: EU Countries, Non-EU Countries

SOURCE: Italy in Figures

Map and Chart Skills

1. **Identify** Where is most of Italy's industry?
2. **Compare and Contrast** How does northern Italy's economic output per person compare to that of southern Italy?
3. **Predict** What changes might southern Italy need to make to its economy in order to catch up with the economy of northern Italy?

Use Web Code lde-7414 for DK World Desk Reference Online.

COUNTRY PROFILE · Focus on **Economics**

Guided Instruction
Ask students to study the Country Profile on this page. As a class, answer the Map and Chart Skills questions. Allow students to briefly discuss their responses with a partner before sharing answers.

Independent Practice
Distribute *Reading a Bar Graph*. Have students work in pairs to complete the worksheet. Then ask them to study the bar graphs on this page. Ask them to describe what information the bar graph Trade, 2001 tells them. (*EU countries traded more than non-EU countries in 2001.*)

All in One **Europe and Russia Teaching Resources,** *Reading a Bar Graph,* p. 290

Answers
Map and Chart Skills
1. in northern Italy, especially near Milan
2. The north's economic output per person is much higher than the south's.
3. Possible answer: building factories to increase manufacturing

Go Online PHSchool.com Students can find more information about this topic on the DK World Desk Reference Online.

Differentiated Instruction

For Special Needs Students
Tell students that to paint the ceiling of the Sistine Chapel, Michelangelo had to paint lying on his back on top of a platform raised 60 feet above the ground. Help students appreciate the difficulties the artist faced by having each student first draw a picture sitting at a table. Then have them try to duplicate their efforts by drawing the same picture while lying on their backs. Students might tape their papers to the bottoms of chairs or desks. Have students compare their two drawings.

Show students *Ancient Rome.* Ask **What empire was once centered in what is now Italy?** *(the Roman Empire)*

Divisions Between North and South ⬛²

Guided Instruction

- **Vocabulary Builder** Clarify the high-use words **influence** and **abundant** before reading.

- Read about Italy's past and present in Divisions between North and South.

- Ask students **How does the Roman Catholic Church unite the people of Italy?** *(Though not every Italian is Catholic, Italy's history is closely tied to the history of Catholicism.)*

- Ask students **What are some differences among Italians?** *(Italians in the north live, work, and practice Roman Catholicism differently from those in the south.)*

- Have students discuss how northern and southern Italy developed differently after the fall of the Roman Empire. *(Italy was divided into many separate city-states, territories, and small kingdoms. Northern Italy was influenced by invaders from Western Europe. Southern Italy was colonized by invaders from the south. Their different cultures influenced northern and southern Italy—northern Italy is more industrial, while the south is more agricultural.)*

Links

Read the **Links Across Time** on this page. Ask students **How is the Risorgimento remembered in Italy today?** *(Italian schoolchildren learn about and celebrate the movement, and streets and squares are named after its heroes.)*

Learn about life in ancient Rome.

Links Across Time

The Risorgimento: "Rising Again" The Risorgimento was a movement in the 1800s that inspired the Italian people to unite as one nation. Poets and philosophers used words and ideas to create a sense of nationalism. Today, Italian school children learn about and celebrate the movement. Cities have streets and squares that bear the names of many of the Risorgimento's heroes. Giuseppe Garibaldi (right) was one of the Risorgimento's leaders and is today considered an Italian patriot.

Divisions Between North and South

Roman Catholicism, with its base in the Vatican, unites about one billion people around the world. It also unites most Italians. Not every Italian is a Catholic, but Italy's history is closely tied to the history of Catholicism. Other things also bring Italians together. Most people living in Italy are ethnic Italians. There are few ethnic minorities. Strong family ties are common among Italians. Even a love of soccer unites many Italians.

Despite these things that many Italians have in common, there are many differences among Italians. Some of the major differences are regional. Italians in the north and Italians in the south live, work, and even practice Roman Catholicism in different ways.

A Divided History For hundreds of years, there was no single, unified Italy. What we now call Italy was once the center of the Roman Empire. Around 2,000 years ago, the Roman Empire stretched across Europe and into northern Africa. When the Roman Empire broke up, Italy itself was divided into many separate city-states, territories, and small kingdoms. The people in these areas had different governments and spoke different languages.

Over time, a regional pattern emerged. Northern Italy was influenced by invaders from Western Europe, who came by land after the breakup of the Roman Empire. Over time, their culture shaped the peoples who lived there. In contrast, southern Italy was colonized by invaders from the south and east, who arrived by way of the Mediterranean Sea. Their culture influenced the region of southern Italy.

The two regions also developed differently in terms of government and economy. In northern Italy, city-states became bustling cities. In modern times, this region became a center of industry. In contrast, in southern Italy, feudal kingdoms dominated, with large numbers of peasants working the land. As a result, southern Italy has always been heavily agricultural.

Italy Unites In the late 1800s, the regions of Italy were united into one nation. A standard form of the Italian language was introduced to help unify the people. After hundreds of years of a divided history, it was not always easy for Italians to identify themselves with this new nation. Even today, there are strong differences between life in the north and in the south.

Differentiated Instruction

For Advanced Readers ⬛³
Have students learn more about daily life in Italy and the rest of the world by working on *Keeping a Scrapbook of Daily Life Around the World.*

Go Online PHSchool.com

For: Long-Term Integrated Projects: *Keeping a Scrapbook of Daily Life Around the World*
Visit: PHSchool.com
Web Code: ldd-7406

Life in the North Milan (mih LAN) is typical of northern Italy. Abundant minerals, fast rivers, and a well-developed economy have brought wealth to the region. Many international businesses are located there. Northern Italy is much more prosperous than southern Italy.

The cities of Milan, Turin, and Genoa are home to most of Italy's manufacturing industries. **Manufacturing** is the process of turning raw materials into finished products. Milan's factories produce cars, planes, leather goods, and plastics.

Milan has a more stylish side, too. Every season, people interested in fashion crowd into Milan to see the new collections from clothing designers. Milan is now second only to Paris as a fashion capital.

Like many European cities, Milan is a mix of the old and the new. In a 400-year-old palace, you can see one of the oldest public libraries in Europe. Millions of dollars have been spent to keep it in good condition. Less than a mile away, you can drive past modern steel and glass office buildings.

Cars being assembled at the Ferrari factory in Maranello, Italy

Life in the South Southern Italy is very different from Milan. Southern Italy is mostly agricultural. Fertile areas near the coast receive enough rainfall to grow abundant crops. Olives, tomatoes, fruits, and other crops grow there. Inland, farmers have difficulty making a living because of the thin soil and dry climate.

Locorotondo (loh koh roh TOHN doh) is a small town located in the southernmost part of Italy. It is on the "heel" of the Italian "boot." Most people in Locorotondo make a living by farming. They grow wheat, olives, and fruits there. Fishing is also an important business for people there.

Most people in southern Italy follow a more traditional way of life. Many people in southern Italy talk about northern Italy as if it were another country. There are fewer large cities in southern Italy. The high fashions of Milan and the busy city of Turin seem very far away.

Making Cheese
These men use traditional methods to make cheese. **Contrast** *How does this work differ from that performed by the men in the photo at the top of this page?*

- Ask students to explain how Milan is typical of northern Italy. (*Milan has abundant minerals, fast rivers, a developed economy, international businesses, manufacturing industries, and fashion designers, and is more prosperous than areas of southern Italy.*)

- Have students discuss how Locorotondo is typical of southern Italy. (*Locorotondo is a small town where most people make a living in agriculture and live a more traditional way of life than northern Italians.*)

Background: Links Across Time

A Papal Division The establishment of the Holy Roman Empire in the early 800s is linked to the division of north and south evidenced in Italy today. The pope was given political power over central Italy, and the Papal States effectively separated northern and southern Italy. The separation was heightened by the influence that France, Spain, and Austria exerted on northern Italy. These associations led northern city-states to create commercial and financial empires. Italy was unified in 1861.

Answer

Contrast The men in the photo at the top of the page are assembling machinery and seem to be working in an urban environment. The man in the photo at the bottom of the page seems to be using tools that are less modern. He probably works in a more rural area.

Guided Instruction (continued)

- Discuss with students how life is organized in small towns in Italy's countryside. (*Life is organized around the Roman Catholic Church and family.*)

- Ask **How did Italy's government work to improve life in southern Italy after World War II?** (*The government introduced land reform and modernized the region by building new roads and irrigation systems.*)

- Ask **Why do you think that the Northern League want to turn northern Italy into a separate country?** (*Possible answer: because the two regions are so different; perhaps so northern Italy would not have to support the poorer southern part of Italy*)

- Ask **Do you think northern and southern Italy will become separate countries?** (*Possible answer: Probably not, because Italians have a strong identity and are linked by religion and their focus on family.*)

Independent Practice

Ask students to create and complete the Taking Notes graphic organizer on a blank piece of paper. Have them fill in the graphic organizer with details about similarities and differences between the northern and southern regions of Italy. Briefly model how to identify which details to record. As an additional aid, show the blank *Venn Diagram Graphic Organizer Transparency*.

> 📖 **Europe and Russia Transparencies,** *Transparency B16: Venn Diagram*

Monitor Progress

- Show *Section Reading Support Transparency ER 46* and ask students to check their graphic organizers individually. Go over key concepts and clarify key vocabulary as needed.

> 📖 **Europe and Russia Transparencies,** *Section Reading Support Transparency ER 46*

- Tell students to fill in the last column of the *Reading Readiness Guide*. Probe for what they learned that confirms or invalidates each statement.

> 📖 **Europe and Russia Teaching Resources,** *Reading Readiness Guide,* p. 270

Answer

Analyze Images There is a large church in the lower righthand corner of the photgraph.

Religion in the Two Italies The Roman Catholic Church provides a focus particularly for southern Italians. Today, in the small towns of the south, life is organized around the larger family of the Church and the smaller family in the home. In the north, these ties may not be as strong.

Many religious events are celebrated in the streets of southern towns. Every year, the Feast of Corpus Christi, a Catholic religious festival, takes place several weeks after Easter. In this festival, women hang their wedding clothes over their balconies and place flowers on them. Additional displays are set up on the streets around town. People walk together around the town, from church to church and from display to display.

Economics and the Two Italies After World War II, Italy's economy boomed. Because most of its large cities and industrial centers are located in the north, northern Italy boomed, too. Meanwhile, the agriculture-based economy of southern Italy failed to thrive. Southern Italians moved to the north in large numbers to find jobs.

Italy's government took measures to help the south catch up with the north. First, it introduced land reform. **Land reform** is a process of dividing large properties into smaller ones. Governments sponsor land reform so that more people can own land. Italy's government hoped that land reform would increase agricultural production. The government also modernized the southern region by building roads and new irrigation systems.

A Coastal Scene
The town of Positano clings to a steep cliff on the edge of the ocean in southern Italy. **Analyze Images** *What evidence do you see in the photo of the importance of religion to southern Italians?*

Differentiated Instruction

For English Language Learners `L1`
As a vocabulary-building activity, create a word web using the blank *Concept Web Graphic Organizer Transparency* as an aid. Write "agriculture" in the center circle and invite students to suggest words on p. 150 that are related to that topic. Students may include related words not found in the text.

> 📖 **Europe and Russia Transparencies,** *Transparency B17: Concept Web*

These measures increased agricultural output in the south. Still, southern Italy today lags behind northern Italy. Unemployment in southern Italy is higher than elsewhere in the country. And many southern Italians still move north, particularly to the cities of Rome and Milan. There, they seek jobs and a better standard of living.

Politics and the Two Italies Northern and southern Italy are so different that some Italians have urged northern Italy to become a separate country. Throughout the 1990s, a party called the Northern League called for northern Italy to secede, or leave the rest of Italy to form its own country. In 1996, the party won 10 percent of the vote in a national election.

However, in recent elections, the Northern League has not done so well. For most Italians, no matter how much they differ, they will never lose their strong Italian identity. Religion and family will probably keep the people of Italy unified for many years to come.

 ✓ Reading Check Why do some Northern Italians support the Northern League?

Links to Art

Futurism Italian Futurism was an art movement in the early 1900s inspired by the speed and energy of modern life. As their name suggests, Futurists believed that art should look to the future rather than remain tied to traditions from the past. Beauty, they said, lies in modern machinery—factories, cars, planes, or even machine guns. Boccioni's 1913 sculpture *Unique Forms of Continuity in Space* shows a human figure in motion. More than just a person walking, the piece gives an idea of energy and movement. It even suggests how currents of air might rush around a body moving quickly through space.

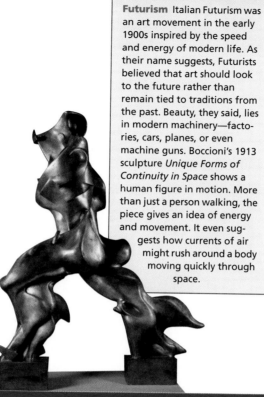

Section 4 Assessment

Key Terms
Review the key terms listed at the beginning of this section. Use each term in a sentence that explains its meaning.

Target Reading Skill
Use context clues to explain the meaning of the word *secede* in the second paragraph on this page.

Comprehension and Critical Thinking
1. **(a) Locate** Where is Vatican City?
(b) Summarize How does the Vatican operate as a city-state?

(c) Synthesize Information How does the Roman Catholic religion unite Italians?
2. **(a) List** Name three differences between life in northern Italy and life in southern Italy.
(b) Sequence How did regional differences emerge in Italy over time?
(c) Make Generalizations Do you think Italy's government should continue to introduce reforms to make northern Italy and southern Italy equal? Explain why or why not.

Writing Activity
Write a letter as if you are an Italian writing to a relative about life in either northern or southern Italy. Write details about your life, including what you do for fun, what kinds of work your parents do, and so on.

Writing Tip Be sure to include a greeting, a closing, and a signature in your letter. Also decide on the age, gender, and personality of the person writing the letter.

Assess and Reteach

Assess Progress L2
Have students complete the Section Assessment. Administer the *Section Quiz.*

 Europe and Russia Teaching Resources, *Section Quiz,* p. 272

Reteach L1
If students need more instruction, have them read this section in the Reading and Vocabulary Study Guide.

📖 Chapter 4, Section 4, **Europe and Russia Reading and Vocabulary Study Guide,** pp. 51–53

Extend L3
Have students complete the *Urban Population, Past and Projected* online activity.

Go Online
PHSchool.com

For: Environmental and Global Issues: *Urban Population, Past and Projected*
Visit: PHSchool.com
Web Code: ldd-7407

Answer

 ✓ Reading Check Possible answer: Some northern Italians may feel that northern and southern Italy are too different to remain one country.

Writing Activity
Use the *Rubric for Assessing a Writing Assignment* to evaluate students' letters.

 Europe and Russia Teaching Resources, *Rubric for Assessing a Writing Assignment,* p. 298

Section 4 Assessment

Key Terms
Students' sentences should reflect knowledge of each Key Term.

Target Reading Skill
The phrase following *secede* explains that it means that a part of the country breaks away to form its own country.

Comprehension and Critical Thinking
1. **(a)** The Vatican is in Rome, the capital of Italy. **(b)** It has its own money, police force, radio station, newspaper, and fire department, and is located entirely within the city of Rome. **(c)** Though not all Italians are Roman Catholic, Roman Catholicism is an important part of the history of Italy.

2. **(a)** Northern Italy has international businesses, manufacturing industries, and is more prosperous. Southern Italy is mostly agricultural and more traditional. **(b)** After the fall of the Roman Empire, different groups settled in northern and southern Italy. Their cultures shaped the people who lived in the regions. **(c)** Answers and explanations will vary, but should be supported with evidence from the text.

Objective

Learn how to transfer information from one medium to another by using visual information to write a paragraph.

Prepare to Read

Build Background Knowledge **L2**

Tell students that there are many ways to present information, such as photographs, numbers, charts, tables, and text. Ask students to look through the sections they have covered so far in this chapter. Have them choose a visual from the chapter, such as a chart or a photograph, and make a list of the information that the image communicates. Then have each student share what they found with the class.

Instruct

Using Visual Information to Write a Paragraph **L2**

Guided Instruction

- Read the steps to using visual information to write a paragraph as a class and write them on the board.

- Practice the skill by following the steps on p. 153 as a class. Model each step in the activity by identifying the title and what it reveals about the subject of the table (*The title, "Italy: Population Statistics," tells you that the table will focus on the population of Italy.*), studying the headings of the table and what they indicate (*The table is comparing and contrasting population, birth rate, death rate, fertility rate, and life expectancy in Italy in 1990 with an estimate of what they would be in 2003.*), analyzing the meaning of the facts and drawing conclusions, and writing a paragraph with the major pieces of information from the table, including conclusions that can be drawn from the information. (*Possible conclusions: The population of Italy has not changed very much in 13 years. The birth rate has gone down slightly, while the death rate has gone up slightly. This means that the population of Italy is not growing significantly through births.*)

Skills for Life
Using Visual Information to Write a Paragraph

> Jerry had to write a report on Rome's Vatican City. He was surprised to discover that Vatican City is a country. He had thought that it was only a religious center in Italy. To write his report, Jerry looked at different charts, graphs, maps, and diagrams. He found that the Vatican has been a country since 1929. From a chart, Jerry learned that the Vatican is about 109 acres (44 hectares) in area. Looking at a diagram, he saw that it is surrounded by a wall with gates that can be locked at night. Its population is fewer than a thousand people. The number of tourists who visit the Vatican each day is far greater than the number of its residents.

St. Peter's Basilica

Information can be presented as pictures, as numbers, or as text. When you translate the meaning of visual information into words, you are transferring information from one medium into another. Jerry transferred visual information from charts, graphs, and diagrams into a written report.

Learn the Skill

Use these steps to transfer visual information into a paragraph.

1 **Identify the topic of the chart, diagram, or graph by reading the title.** Then look at it to get a general idea of its purpose.

2 **Identify the key pieces of information.** Read headings and other key pieces of information carefully. The headings are usually set off in some way. If you are using a chart or a table, look for similarities and differences among the types of information in the columns.

3 **Analyze the meaning of the information.** Write down several conclusions that can be drawn from the information you have put together.

4 **Rewrite the key pieces of information and your conclusions in a clear paragraph.**

Independent Practice

Assign *Skills for Life* and have students complete it individually.

All in One **Europe and Russia Teaching Resources,** *Skills for Life,* p. 282

Monitor Progress

As students are analyzing the table, circulate and make sure individuals are applying the skill steps effectively.

Practice the Skill

Use the steps in Learn the Skill to translate the information in the table into a paragraph.

1 What is the title of the table? What does it tell you about the subject of the table?

2 What are the important headings in the table? Do they indicate key pieces of information? Note the information that is compared and contrasted in the table. How are all the statistics shown on this table related? In what ways are the two sets of numbers similar and different? Which categories have changed over time? Why do you think they have changed?

3 Analyze the meaning of the facts you have learned. What conclusions can you draw? For example, how might the change in the birth rate have affected Italy's population? How might the change in the death rate have affected Italy's population? Is the population getting older or younger? In what ways might the changes in Italy's population affect life in Italy in the future? Consider jobs, school, family life, health care, and so on.

4 Write a paragraph that contains the major pieces of information you have learned. Include the conclusions you have drawn.

ITALY: POPULATION STATISTICS		
	1990	2003 (Estimated)
Population	57,664,405	57,998,353
Birth Rate	10 births per 1,000 population	9 births per 1,000 population
Death Rate	9 deaths per 1,000 population	10 deaths per 1,000 population
Fertility Rate	1.4 children born per woman	1.3 children born per woman
Life Expectancy	74, male; 81, female	76, male; 83, female

Italian Workforce by Occupation

1990: 5%, 37%, 58%
2003: 5%, 32%, 63%

■ Services ■ Industry ■ Agriculture

Apply the Skill

Compare the circle graphs. Then use the steps above to write a short paragraph. Include key facts from the graphs, explaining what has changed from 1990 to 2003. Note that agriculture has remained the same. Why do you think that is so? Look at the two graphs and draw some conclusions about how these changes might have affected the country.

Chapter 4 **153**

Section 5
Step-by-Step Instruction

Objectives

Social Studies
1. Learn about Germany's past.
2. Find out how Germany became reunited.

Reading/Language Arts
Learn to use context clues over several paragraphs to determine the meaning of an unfamiliar word.

Prepare to Read

Build Background Knowledge `L2`

Ask students to suppose that there is a wall around their city or town. They are not allowed to cross the wall, and people on the other side of the wall are not allowed to cross either. Ask students how they would feel in this situation. Conduct an Idea Wave (TE, p. T35) to generate a list of student responses. Then tell them that until 1989 Germany was divided by a wall into two separate countries—East Germany and West Germany.

Set a Purpose for Reading `L2`
- Preview the Objectives.

- Form students into pairs or groups of four. Distribute the *Reading Readiness Guide.* Ask students to fill in the first two columns of the chart. Use the Numbered Heads participation strategy (TE, p. T36) to call on students to share one piece of information they already know and one piece of information they want to know.

  All in One Europe and Russia Teaching Resources, *Reading Readiness Guide,* p. 274

Vocabulary Builder
Preview Key Terms `L2`
Pronounce each Key Term, then ask students to say the word with you. Provide a simple explanation such as, "The reunification of Germany brought people from East and West Germany together for the first time since the end of World War II."

Section 5 Germany
A Unified Nation

Prepare to Read

Objectives
In this section you will
1. Learn about Germany's past.
2. Find out how Germany became reunited.

Taking Notes
As you read this section, look for the events that caused Germany to be divided and later reunited. Copy the flowchart below and record your findings in it.

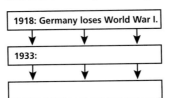

Target Reading Skill

Use Context Clues When you first encounter an unfamiliar word, jot down some ideas about its meaning. As you read and reread the paragraphs that provide its context, adjust the word's definition until you are certain of it. For example, find the word *desperate* in the first paragraph on the next page. You may need to read several paragraphs before you can be certain of its meaning.

Key Terms
- **Holocaust** (HAHL uh kawst) *n.* the mass murder of six million Jews
- **reunification** (ree yoo nih fih KAY shun) *n.* the process of becoming unified again
- **standard of living** (STAN durd uv LIV ing) *n.* the level of comfort in terms of the goods and services that people have

A guard stands watch while East Berlin workmen add blocks to the Berlin Wall in October, 1961.

154 Europe and Russia

In 1961, Conrad Schumann, a 19-year-old policeman, stood guard at a barbed-wire fence in East Berlin. His job was to shoot anyone who tried to get across the fence. East Berlin was part of communist East Germany. The fence was built to prevent East Berliners from escaping to West Berlin, where they could reach democratic West Germany.

To Schumann, the fence was a terrible thing. He could see the buildings of West Berlin on the other side. They seemed very beautiful. On television, he had seen a program from West Berlin that showed people dancing to Western music and speaking their views freely. In East Germany, the government did not approve of Western music and free speech. The stores had few interesting things to buy.

Schumann thought about all these things. Then he made a decision and jumped over the barbed wire. A moment later, he was on the other side—in the freedom of the West. Just a few days after Schumann jumped to freedom, a concrete wall replaced the barbed-wire fence. The Berlin Wall separated families and friends. On one side of it, communism ruled. On the other side, the people did. What were the effects of a divided Germany?

Target Reading Skill `L2`
Point out the Target Reading Skill. Tell students that clues to the meaning of an unfamiliar word may appear near the word, or later on in the text.

Model using context clues using the word *communism* from the last paragraph on this page. Point out to students that more information about life under communism can be found throughout the section. *(Students should be able to determine that communism is a system under which people have few individual rights, and the government controls most of the economy.)*

Give students *Use Context Clues: Definition and Description.* Have them complete the activity in their groups.

All in One Europe and Russia Teaching Resources, *Use Context Clues: Definition and Description,* p. 277

For the flowchart:
1918: Germany loses World War I.

1933:

Germany's Past

To understand the importance of the Berlin Wall, you need to understand part of Germany's past. Germany lost World War I in 1918. The German government had to pay billions of dollars as punishment for attacking other countries. In the early 1920s, the German economy collapsed. Prices soared. Germans became desperate.

Hitler and World War II When World War I began, Adolf Hitler (AD awlf HIT lur) was a 25-year-old Austrian soldier in the German army. When Germany lost the war, he promised himself that Germany would never suffer such a defeat again. Hitler became deeply involved in politics. In speech after speech, he promised to make Germany great again. By 1933, this former soldier had become dictator of Germany.

Hitler blamed Germany's economic problems on Jews. He spread hateful theories about Jews, Roma, and other ethnic groups in Germany. He claimed that they were inferior to other Germans. He claimed that Germans were a superior ethnic group—and that they should rule Europe.

Adolf Hitler salutes a crowd of people in 1934.

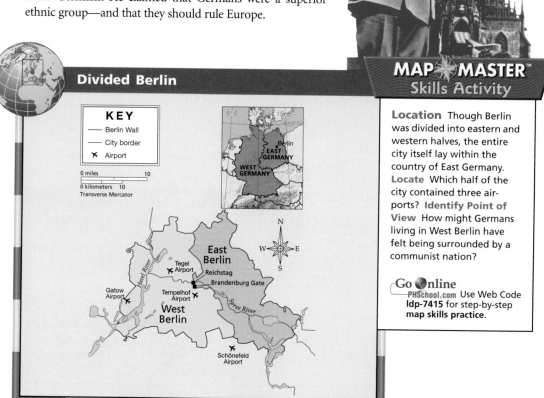

Divided Berlin

KEY
- Berlin Wall
- City border
- ✈ Airport

0 miles 10
0 kilometers 10
Transverse Mercator

EAST GERMANY
WEST GERMANY
Berlin

East Berlin
Tegel Airport
Reichstag
Brandenburg Gate
Gatow Airport
Tempelhof Airport
West Berlin
Havel River
Spree River
Schönefeld Airport

MAP MASTER Skills Activity

Location Though Berlin was divided into eastern and western halves, the entire city itself lay within the country of East Germany. **Locate** Which half of the city contained three airports? **Identify Point of View** How might Germans living in West Berlin have felt being surrounded by a communist nation?

Go Online
PHSchool.com Use Web Code ldp-7415 for step-by-step map skills practice.

Vocabulary Builder

Use the information below to teach students this section's high-use words.

High-Use Word	Definition and Sample Sentence
theory, p. 155	*n.* an idea or a plan about what something is or how it should be done It was Steve's **theory** that if the team practiced harder, they would win more games.
superior, p. 155	*adj.* greater in quality My new bicycle is **superior** to the old one.
elimination, p. 160	*n.* removal The **elimination** of sugar from the recipe made the cake less sweet.
aid, p. 160	*v.* to help Many charities **aid** people in need.

Germany's Past L2

Guided Instruction

- **Vocabulary Builder** Clarify the high-use words **theory** and **superior** before reading.

- Together with students, read Germany's Past, using the Oral Cloze reading strategy (TE, p. T33). As students read, circulate to make sure individuals can answer the Reading Check question.

- Have students discuss the effects of Germany's loss of World War I. (*The German government had to pay billions of dollars as punishment for attacking other countries, and the German economy collapsed while prices soared.*)

- Ask students **Who was Adolf Hitler?** (*an Austrian who became dictator of Germany in 1933*) **How did his actions lead to the start of World War II?** (*Hitler ordered attacks on neighboring countries and forced them under German rule. Great Britain, the Soviet Union, and the United States joined other nations to stop the Germans.*)

Answers

MAP MASTER Skills Activity **Locate** West Berlin **Identify Point of View** they might have felt isolated and vulnerable

Go Online
PHSchool.com Students may practice their map skills using the interactive online version of this map.

Guided Instruction

Ask students to study the Country Profile on this page. As a class, answer the Map and Chart Skills questions. Allow students to briefly discuss their responses with a partner before sharing answers.

Independent Practice

Distribute *Reading a Timeline*. Have students work in partners to complete the worksheet. After they have finished, direct their attention to the timeline on this page and ask the following questions: **How many years after Germany was divided was the Berlin Wall built?** *(12 years)* **How many years after that did the Berlin Wall fall?** *(28 years)*

All in One Europe and Russia Teaching Resources, *Reading a Timeline,* p. 291

Germany

Germany has a long, complex history. At the time of the Roman Empire, various Germanic tribes lived all across Central Europe and into Scandinavia. Present-day Germany developed in the late 1800s out of a patchwork of kingdoms and small states. Just a few decades later, the country dramatically altered its history by fighting a global war. Use the data on this page to learn about modern Germany's history.

Germany: Population Density

KEY

Persons per sq. mile	Persons per sq. kilometer
More than 519	More than 199
260–519	100–199
130–259	50–99
25–129	10–49

Urban Areas

☐ More than 4,999,999
⊙ 1,000,000–4,999,999
● 500,000–999,999
· Less than 500,000

— National border

0 miles 300
0 kilometers 300
Lambert Azimuthal Equal Area

Germany Since 1914

1914–1918 Germany is defeated in World War I; loses land, colonies, and wealth.

1933 Adolf Hitler and Nazi Party take political control.

1939–1945 Germany fights in World War II; is defeated by Allies.

1961 Berlin Wall is built.

1990 East Germany and West Germany reunite; Helmut Kohl is elected chancellor.

1900	1920	1940	1960	1980	2000

1920s Germany faces severe economic challenges.

1935 Nuremberg Laws legalize the persecution of Jews.

1949 Germany divides into communist East Germany and democratic West Germany.

1989 Berlin Wall falls.

1998 Gerhard Schröder becomes chancellor.

2002 Schröder is re-elected; Germany adopts euro as its currency.

A World War I gas mask

SOURCE: DK World Desk Reference Online, 2002

German Capital Cities

Years	German Region	Region's Capital
1871–1918	German Empire	Berlin
1919–1949	Germany	Berlin
1949–1990	East Germany	East Berlin
1949–1990	West Germany	Bonn
1990–1999	Germany	Bonn
1999–present	Germany	Berlin

SOURCE: Encyclopedia Britannica Online

Map and Chart Skills

1. **Note** What was the capital of West Germany from 1949 to 1990?

2. **Explain** Why did Germany have two different capitals during the years 1949–1990?

3. **Predict** How might the population density of eastern Germany change as long as Berlin remains the capital?

Go Online PHSchool.com
Use Web Code **Ide-7415** for **DK World Desk Reference Online.**

Answers

Map and Chart Skills

1. Bonn

2. because the country was divided into East Germany and West Germany

3. It might increase as more businesses and people move to Berlin.

Go Online PHSchool.com Students can find more information about this topic on the DK World Desk Reference Online.

Differentiated Instruction

For Gifted and Talented **L3**

Tell students that since the end of World War II, countries and organizations around the world have taken steps to try to prevent another Holocaust. Have students read *The Universal Declaration of Human Rights* to see one example of this.

Go Online PHSchool.com

For: Environmental and Global Issues: *The Universal Declaration of Human Rights*
Visit: PHSchool.com
Web Code: ldd-7408

Freedom From Concentration Camps
Soviet soldiers free Holocaust survivors from an Austrian concentration camp in 1945. **Synthesize** *How might images like this one have helped Europeans' resolve to avoid another world war?*

Many people did not believe Hitler's ideas. But Hitler was deadly serious. He ordered attacks on neighboring countries and forced them to submit to German rule. His actions led to the start of World War II in 1939. Great Britain, the Soviet Union, and finally the United States joined other nations to stop the Germans.

By the end of the war, Europe was in ruins. People around the world learned that the Germans had forced countless Jews, Roma, Slavs, and others into brutal concentration camps. Millions of people were murdered in these camps. The majority of them were Jews. This horrible mass murder of six million Jews is called the **Holocaust** (HAH luh kawst).

A Divided Capital At the end of the war, the victors divided up Germany. The Americans, British, and French joined their sections together to create the Federal Republic of Germany. This democratic country was also known as West Germany. The Soviet Union created a communist system in the German Democratic Republic, or East Germany.

The city of Berlin was in East Germany. But the western half of the city, called West Berlin, became part of democratic West Germany. The western half of Berlin was turned into an island of democracy in the middle of communism. The Berlin Wall separated the two halves of Berlin. It also stood as a symbol of a divided world.

Berlin had once been the capital of all of Germany. But now Germany was divided. The city of Bonn became the new capital of West Germany. East Berlin was the capital of East Germany.

Citizen Heroes

Raoul Wallenberg

Raoul Wallenberg (rah OOL WAHL un burg) came from a wealthy Swedish family of bankers and diplomats. Wallenberg studied architecture in the United States. But in 1944, with World War II raging, he persuaded the Swedish government to send him to Hungary as a diplomat. In Hungary, Wallenberg used Sweden's status as a neutral nation to create "safe houses" for Hungarian Jews. Wallenberg's safe houses sheltered several thousand Hungarian Jews and ultimately saved their lives. Wallenberg's efforts put his own life at great risk. In 1945, he was mistakenly arrested as a spy by Soviet troops in Hungary. Wallenberg died in a Soviet prison.

Guided Instruction (continued)

■ Ask students **How did Hitler's theories lead to the Holocaust?** *(He blamed Germany's problems on Jews and claimed Jews and other ethnic groups were inferior to other Germans. The Germans forced millions of Jews, Gypsies, Slavs, and others into concentration camps, where millions were murdered.)*

■ Discuss how Germany was divided at the end of World War II. *(The victors of the war divided Germany: the American, British, and French joined their sections to create a democratic country called the Federal Republic of Germany, also known as West Germany. The Soviet Union created a communist system called the German Democratic Republic, also known as East Germany. In addition, Berlin was divided by the Berlin Wall, creating West Berlin and East Berlin. East Berlin became the capital of East Germany and Bonn became the capital of West Germany.)*

Citizen Heroes

Read the **Citizen Heroes** on this page. Ask students **How did Raoul Wallenburg work to help Hungarian Jews during World War II?** *(He created "safe houses" to hide them during the Holocaust.)*

Drawing Inferences and Conclusions

1. Tell students that to draw inferences and conclusions, they should identify what they know to be true, make an educated guess based on what they assume to be true, and use inferences to draw a conclusion.

2. Help students practice the skill using this situation: On Friday, students always have a spelling test. Today is Friday, and the teacher tells them to take out a piece of paper. *(Conclusion: The teacher is giving a spelling test.)*

3. Have students draw a conclusion about what life was like in Germany after the end of World War II.

Answer

Synthesize Pictures like these probably strengthened European's resolve to work for peace by reminding them how victims of the Holocaust suffered during World War II.

Use Context Clues As a follow up, have students perform the Target Reading Skill activity on this page. *(By reading ahead, students learn that* installed *means "established" or "set up.")*

Guided Instruction (continued)

- Have students compare the United States and its partners with the Soviet Union and its partners during the Cold War. *(The United States and its Western European partners had democratic governments and opposed communism. The Soviet Union and its Eastern European partners had communist governments.)*

- Ask students **What were some of the effects of the Cold War on European countries?** *(Cold War borders separated families, friends, and relatives.)*

- Ask students **What was life like for people living in East Germany?** *(The government of East Germany required people to obey without asking questions and encouraged people to spy on family members and neighbors. Children were taught to respect only communist ideals. Western ideas and products were banned.)*

- Ask students **What happened on November 9, 1989?** *(Crowds of East Germans were allowed to cross into West Berlin; people climbed on top of the Berlin Wall, dancing and celebrating, and began to take the wall apart.)*

- Ask students **Why do you think Germans wanted to be united again?** *(Possible answer: East Germans wanted more democracy and a better economy, and did not want to be separated from friends and family any longer.)*

Independent Practice

Have students create the Taking Notes graphic organizer on a blank piece of paper. Then have them fill it with dates and events from the section.

Monitor Progress

As students fill in their graphic organizers, check to make sure they are listing events in chronological order. Provide assistance as needed.

⟲ **Use Context Clues** If you are unsure of the meaning of *installed,* read on. The next sentence clarifies its meaning.

While Eastern German border guards look on, a protestor hammers against the Berlin Wall in November, 1989.

158 Europe and Russia

The Cold War During the Cold War, the United States and Western Europe became partners. These countries had democratic governments and were opposed to communism. Eastern European countries had communist governments that had been installed by the Soviet Union. Soviet troops stayed in Eastern Europe to make sure that these countries remained communist.

Think about the effects of the Cold War on European countries. Recall that these countries are small and close together. Cold War borders separated families and friends. Even some who had managed to escape to the West suffered. They could no longer see the relatives they had left behind.

East Germans led far different lives from West Germans. The communist government required people to obey without asking questions. It even encouraged people to spy on family members and neighbors. Children were taught to respect only those things that promoted communism. Western movies, music, and magazines were seen as harmful influences.

The Communists Weaken In time, communist rule started to change. The East German economy fell far behind the West German economy. The average West German had a much more comfortable life than the average East German had. Many East Germans wanted to go to the West, but the East German government did not let them.

In the late 1980s, changes in the Soviet Union weakened the East German government. It became clear that the Soviets would no longer use force to protect communism in Eastern Europe. Fear of the Soviets had helped keep the East German government in power. Now this fear was gone, and the people were ready for change.

Some East Germans began to escape to West Germany by way of Hungary, Czechoslovakia, and Poland. Others began protesting in the streets. To stop the protests, the East German government softened its rules. It announced that under certain conditions, East Germans could visit West Germany.

The East German Government Falls Many people misunderstood the announcement. They thought that the government was opening the Berlin Wall permanently. On November 9, 1989, huge crowds of people demanded to cross into West Berlin. The border guards let them.

Differentiated Instruction

For English Language Learners L1
To help students visualize the countries that were formed after the end of the Cold War, show them *Color Transparency ER Set 1: Europe Today With Eastern Europe Updated.* Using the Think-Write-Pair-Share strategy (TE, p. T36), have students examine each map and note the differences and similarities between the maps.

📖 **Europe and Russia Transparencies,** *Color Transparency ER Set 1: Europe Today With Eastern Europe Updated*

Thousands of East Berliners crossed into West Berlin that night. People climbed on top of the wall. They danced and celebrated their new freedom. They also began to destroy the wall, taking it apart piece by piece. The hated wall that had separated them for so long was now gone.

The destruction of the Berlin Wall was the beginning of the end for the East German government. People continued protesting against the government. They wanted more democracy. They wanted Germany to be united again. Less than a year later, the governments of East Germany and West Germany united. Germany had become a single country again.

✓ **Reading Check** How was Germany divided after World War II?

Germany Reunited

Most Germans were thrilled about the fall of the Berlin Wall. Despite having been separate countries for about 50 years, the cultures of East Germany and West Germany had remained similar in many ways. People in both East Germany and West Germany spoke the same language and ate the same foods. They knew the same German composers, writers, and painters. Still, **reunification** (ree yoo nih fih KAY shun), or the process of becoming unified again, would not be easy.

Changing East Germany The East German economy was very weak. Germans in the west had to spend huge amounts of money to improve the economy in the east. The government sold the state-owned factories of East Germany to private companies. They modernized factories and businesses. They cleaned up toxic waste sites. They began producing more consumer goods, such as televisions and cars. This process was very expensive.

East Germans had some concerns about life after communism. For example, in communist East Germany, people had had guaranteed jobs. There were no such guarantees under the democratic system of West Germany. Even today, there are many more people in the east without jobs than there are in the west. Even so, Germans in the east now enjoy a much better standard of living than they did under communism. **A standard of living** is the level of comfort in terms of the goods and services that people have.

Links to Science

Albert Einstein German-born scientist Albert Einstein (below) was teaching physics at the University of Berlin when World War I broke out. He was also developing the important scientific theories that would make him world famous. Einstein was strongly opposed to the war. When Hitler rose to power, Einstein gave up his German citizenship and emigrated to the United States. When scientists began to investigate ways to create the atomic bomb in the 1930s, Einstein urged U.S. President Roosevelt to develop the bomb first, before Germany could. Yet Einstein was still opposed to war and spent the last years of his life promoting peace.

Learn about the history of the Berlin Wall.

Links

Read the **Links to Science** on this page. Ask students **Why do you think Einstein urged President Roosevelt to develop the atomic bomb?** (*Possible answer: Einstein believed Hitler was dangerous and had to be defeated.*)

Germany Reunited   L2

Guided Instruction

- **Vocabulary Builder** Clarify the high-use words **elimination** and **aid** before reading.

- Read Germany Reunited with students.

- Discuss the steps Germans took to improve the economy in East Germany. (*Germans spent money to improve the economy; the government sold state-owned factories to private companies; factories were modernized and toxic waste sites were cleaned; more consumer goods were produced.*)

Independent Practice

Have students complete their graphic organizers.

Monitor Progress

- Show *Section Reading Support Transparency ER 47* and ask students to check their graphic organizers individually.

   📖 **Europe and Russia Transparencies,** *Section Reading Support Transparency ER 47*

- Tell students to fill in the last column of the *Reading Readiness Guide.*

   All in One Europe and Russia Teaching Resources, *Reading Readiness Guide,* p. 274

Show students *Germany: The Berlin Wall.* Ask **Why was the Berlin Wall built?** (*to prevent East Germans from defecting to West Germany*)

Differentiated Instruction

For Less Proficient Readers   L1
To help students who are having trouble absorbing all of the information in the section, have them work in pairs to create an outline of the material. Tell them to use the headings in the section as a framework for their outlines.

Answer

✓ **Reading Check** It was divided into two parts—East Germany and West Germany.

Assess and Reteach

Assess Progress L2
Have students complete the Section Assessment. Administer the *Section Quiz*.

All in One Europe and Russia Teaching Resources, *Section Quiz, p. 276*

Reteach L1
If students need more instruction, have them read this section in the Reading and Vocabulary Study Guide.

Chapter 4, Section 5, **Europe and Russia Reading and Vocabulary Study Guide,** pp. 54–56

Extend L3
Have students choose one aspect of one topic discussed in this section, such as the Holocaust or the Cold War, for further study. Have them research and then write a short essay about their topic that presents new information not found in the lesson. Give students *Writing to Inform and Explain* to help get them started.

All in One Europe and Russia Teaching Resources, *Writing to Inform and Explain, p. 296*

Answer

✓**Reading Check** It was chosen because of its central location and because it had previously been the capital of a united Germany.

Section 5 Assessment

Key Terms
Students' sentences should reflect knowledge of each Key Term.

Target Reading Skill
Using the surrounding text, students should be able to determine that *elimination* means "removal" or "taking something away."

Comprehension and Critical Thinking
1. (a) It had to pay billions of dollars. **(b)** It led to soaring prices and the collapse of the economy. Hitler promised that he would make Germany great again. **(c)** After the defeat of Germany, the victorious countries divided the country among themselves. The Americans, British, and French joined their sections to create the Federal Republic of Germany, also known as West Germany. The Soviet Union created a communist system in the German Democratic Republic, or East Germany.

Moving Forward When Germany reunited, the German legislature decided Berlin would be the nation's capital once more. By 1999, most government offices had been moved back to Berlin from Bonn.

The cost of moving the capital was enormous. It led to budget cuts and the elimination of many public-service jobs. Still, Germans believed that the move benefited the "new Germany." Berlin's central location, they said, would aid reunification by linking Germans in the east with Germans in the west.

Reunification has been a huge undertaking. It has been difficult and expensive to merge two countries into one unified nation. Even so, Germany remains strong. Despite the high cost of reunification, Germany still has one of the world's strongest economies. It is also a powerful member of the European Union. As the European Union adds new members from Eastern Europe, Germany's central location will be to its advantage. Finally, because Germany was divided for only about 50 years, its people remember their shared history and culture. They will build on this common heritage as they move forward.

The German flag flies in front of the Reichstag, Germany's parliament building.

✓**Reading Check** Why was Berlin chosen as the reunified nation's capital?

Section 5 Assessment

Key Terms
Review the key terms listed at the beginning of this section. Use each term in a sentence that explains its meaning.

Target Reading Skill
Find the word *elimination* at the top of this page. How do the surrounding phrases help explain it?

Comprehension and Critical Thinking
1. (a) Explain What was Germany's punishment for its role in World War I?

(b) Identify Effects How did that punishment lead to the rise of Adolf Hitler and the beginning of World War II?

(c) Sequence Describe the events that led to the division of Germany.

2. (a) Recall How did most Germans feel about the fall of the Berlin Wall?

(b) Sequence Describe the events that led to the reunification of Germany.

(c) Identify Effects How has the reunification of Germany affected life in the former East Germany?

Writing Activity
Write a journal entry from the point of view of an East Berliner. Describe the night the Berlin Wall was torn down. How did you feel? Whom and what did you want to see?

> **Writing Tip** Before you write, decide what your age will be. If you are a young East Berliner, write as if you have never lived without the wall. If you are older, write as if you have experienced life both with and without the wall.

160 Europe and Russia

---

2. (a) They were happy. **(b)** After the destruction of the Berlin Wall, people continued to protest against the government, demanding democracy. A year later, the country became united again. **(c)** The government privatized state-owned factories, modernized factories and businesses, cleaned up toxic waste sites, and began producing more consumer goods. However, many more people are unemployed because there are no guaranteed jobs.

Writing Activity
Use the *Rubric for Assessing a Journal Entry* to evaluate students' journal entries.

All in One Europe and Russia Teaching Resources, *Rubric for Assessing a Journal Entry, p. 299*

Review and Assessment

◆ Chapter Summary

Section 1: The United Kingdom
- There are four regions within the United Kingdom: England, Scotland, Wales, and Northern Ireland.
- The Magna Carta and Parliament played important roles in the development of British democracy.
- The United Kingdom is a constitutional monarchy.
- Trade is important to the United Kingdom because it is an island with limited natural resources.

Section 2: France
- France has made important contributions to art, philosophy, architecture, fashion, and cooking.
- France is becoming more culturally diverse.

Boccioni's *Unique Forms of Continuity in Space* (1913)

Section 3: Sweden
- Sweden is a welfare state that provides many services to its citizens.
- Sweden became an industrialized country in the early 1900s.
- In order to continue providing benefits to everyone, the Swedish government needs to find better ways of paying for them.

Section 4: Italy
- Vatican City is an important city-state within Rome, Italy.
- Many Italians have close ties to the Roman Catholic Church.
- Life in northern Italy differs in many ways from life in southern Italy.

Section 5: Germany
- The Berlin Wall divided communist East Germany from democratic West Germany.
- After the fall of the Berlin Wall, the governments of East and West Germany reunited.

◆ Key Terms

Complete each sentence with a key term from the list.

Parliament

standard of living

land reform

philosophy

national debt

reunification

welfare state

constitutional monarchy

1. A _____ is a system of ideas or beliefs.
2. _____ is the lawmaking body of the United Kingdom.
3. A _____ is the level of comfort in terms of the goods and services that people have.
4. A _____ is a government in which a monarch is the head of state but has limited powers.
5. The process of dividing large properties into smaller ones is called _____.
6. In a _____, the government provides many services and benefits free or at a low cost.
7. _____ is the amount of money a government owes.
8. The process of becoming unified again is called _____.

Chapter 4 **161**

┌ **Vocabulary Builder** ─────────

Revisit this chapter's high-use words:

exert	standard	theory
symbol	benefit	superior
productive	elimination	aid
finance	influence	abundant
contribution		

Ask students to review the definitions they recorded on their *Word Knowledge* worksheets.

All in One **Europe and Russia Teaching Resources,** *Word Knowledge*, p. 280

Consider allowing students to earn extra credit if they use the words in their answers to the questions in the Chapter Review and Assessment. The words must be used correctly and in a natural context to win the extra points.

Chapter 4

Review and Assessment

Review Chapter Content

- Review and revisit the major themes of this chapter by asking students to classify what Guiding Question each bulleted statement in the Chapter Summary answers. Form students into groups and ask them to complete the activity together. Refer to p. 1 in the Student Edition for text of the Guiding Questions.

- Assign *Vocabulary Development* for students to review Key Terms.

 All in One **Europe and Russia Teaching Resources,** *Vocabulary Development*, p. 297

Answers

Key Terms
1. philosophy
2. Parliament
3. standard of living
4. constitutional monarchy
5. land reform
6. welfare state
7. national debt
8. reunification

Chapter 4 **161**

Review and Assessment

Comprehension and Critical Thinking

9. (a) The British monarch is a symbol of Britain's past and customs. **(b)** to unify the British people **(c)** Answers will vary, but should show clear reasoning and examples from the text.

10. (a) It is an organization that determines which words are officially accepted as part of the French language. **(b)** Possible answer: Because of the variety of cultures in Western Europe, different languages probably influence each other regularly.

11. (a) The Swedish government provides child care at a reduced cost, access to free or inexpensive health care, generous vacation and sick days for all workers, and money for retirement. The government also pays for parents to stay at home from work with their newborn children for up to 15 months, and pays for the costs of schooling through college. **(b)** Sweden does not have enough money to pay for all the benefits to its citizens. **(c)** The government may provide fewer benefits and businesses may pay more in taxes by taking advantage of Sweden's natural resources.

12. (a) Italians are united by a common ethnicity, the Roman Catholic faith, the legacy of the Roman Empire, and strong family ties. **(b)** It is both a city and an independent country that is led by the pope. **(c)** Northern Italy has international businesses and manufacturing industries, and is more prosperous. Southern Italy is mostly agricultural and more traditional, and religion plays a major part in daily life.

13. (a) The victors of World War II divided the country into democratic and communistic nations. **(b)** After the destruction of the Berlin Wall, East Germans continued to protest against the East German government and demand reunification. **(c)** West Germans had to spend much money to modernize factories, clean up toxic waste, and to improve the economy of East Germany.

14. (a) The East German government disapproved of Western movies and free speech. **(b)** East Germans could not travel where they wanted, question the government, or enjoy things produced by a noncommunist country. West Germans enjoyed the movies, music, and magazines they wanted, and freedom of speech.

Review and Assessment (continued)

◆ Comprehension and Critical Thinking

9. (a) Explain What is the role of the British monarch?
(b) Draw Conclusions Why does Britain remain a monarchy even though the monarch now has little power?
(c) Predict Do you think the United Kingdom will continue to have a monarch in the future? Explain why or why not.

10. (a) Explain What is the French Academy?
(b) Infer Why do foreign words enter the French language even though the French Academy tries to limit them?

11. (a) Explain What benefits does Sweden's welfare system provide?
(b) Summarize What problems does Sweden face today?
(c) Predict How might Sweden solve some of its economic problems?

12. (a) Identify What is the political status of Vatican City?
(b) List Which things do most Italians have in common?
(c) Compare and Contrast How is life in northern Italy different from life in southern Italy?

13. (a) Recall How was Germany divided?
(b) Explain Why was Germany reunified?
(c) Summarize What challenges has reunification brought to Germany?

14. (a) List Name two things that the East German government did not allow.
(b) Compare and Contrast Compare personal freedom in East Germany and West Germany during the Cold War.

◆ Skills Practice

In the Skills for Life activity in this chapter, you learned how to use visual information to write a paragraph. Review the steps you followed to learn this skill. Then turn to the Country Profile on page 156. Use the data on this page to write a paragraph titled *A History of Germany Since World War I*.

◆ Writing Activity: Government

You read about Germany's division after World War II. Recall that some Italians today are in favor of dividing Italy. Write a paragraph comparing Germany's situation after World War II with Italy's situation today.

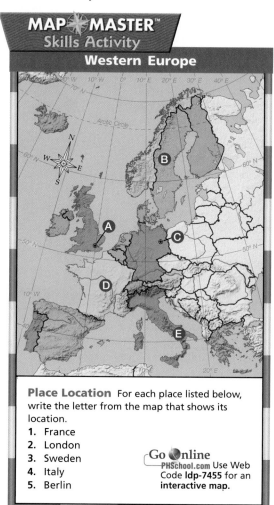

MAP MASTER™ Skills Activity
Western Europe

Place Location For each place listed below, write the letter from the map that shows its location.
1. France
2. London
3. Sweden
4. Italy
5. Berlin

Go Online
PHSchool.com Use Web Code ldp-7455 for an interactive map.

Skills Practice
Students' paragraphs should accurately reflect the information from the Country Profile.

Writing Activity: Government
Students' essays should use at least five key terms to explain the role of government in Western Europe.

Use the *Rubric for Assessing a Writing Assignment* to evaluate students' essays.

All in One **Europe and Russia Teaching Resources,** *Rubric for Assessing a Writing Assignment,* p. 298

Standardized Test Prep

Test-Taking Tips

Some questions on standardized tests ask you to analyze a point of view. Read the passage below. Then follow the tips to answer the sample question.

> On November 9, 1989, crowds began to tear down the Berlin Wall, block by block. People helped each other over the wall to the other side. Someone watching from a window nearby said, "Today they are happy. But will they still be cheering when they realize that they no longer have the promise of either a job or food to eat?"

Choose the letter that best answers the question.

Who might have made this statement?

- **A** an old East German who wants to have his son visit from West Germany
- **B** a young East German who dreams of finding a job in West Germany
- **C** an East German communist with a job running a state business
- **D** a West German whose parents live in East Germany

Think It Through
The person who made this statement is not happy that the wall is coming down. He or she wonders whether the people tearing it down will still be cheering about it in the future. Who would not be happy about the wall coming down? You can eliminate A and D because both people have families that will be reunited with the wall torn down. You can also rule out B because that person will now be able to go to West Germany to look for work. The correct answer is C.

TIP Use good reasoning to help you choose an answer that makes sense.

TIP Be sure that you understand the question: Who might have said the words that begin, *Today they are happy. But will they still be cheering . . .?*

Go Online PHSchool.com Students may practice their map skills using the interactive online version of this map.

Standardized Test Prep
Answers

1. A
2. C
3. B
4. D

Go Online PHSchool.com Students may use the Chapter 4 self-test on PHSchool.com to prepare for the Chapter Test.

Practice Questions

Use the tips above and other tips in this book to help you answer the following questions.

1. What historical document first limited the power of the British king?
   - **A** the Magna Carta
   - **B** Parliament
   - **C** the British constitution
   - **D** the Northern League

2. Which style of architecture began in the region of Paris hundreds of years ago?
   - **A** Renaissance
   - **B** French Academic
   - **C** Gothic
   - **D** classical

3. What happened when the Roman Empire broke up?
   - **A** The nation of Italy was formed.
   - **B** It broke into a number of kingdoms, city-states, and territories.
   - **C** Italy became part of the United Kingdom.
   - **D** The Italian language became standardized.

4. When was Germany divided into two countries?
   - **A** at the end of the Cold War
   - **B** at the end of World War I
   - **C** during the Cold War
   - **D** at the end of World War II

Go Online
PHSchool.com
Use Web Code lda-7405 for a **Chapter 4 self-test.**

Assessment Resources

Use *Chapter Tests A and B* to assess students' mastery of chapter content.

All in One **Europe and Russia Teaching Resources,** *Chapter Tests A and B,* pp. 300–305

Tests are also available on the *ExamView Test Bank CD-ROM.*

◉ *ExamView Test Bank CD-ROM*

Overview

DISCOVERY CHANNEL SCHOOL Video

Introducing Eastern Europe and Russia
1. Look at the map and study the data to learn about Russia and the countries of Eastern Europe.
2. Analyze data to compare the countries.
3. Identify characteristics that most of these countries share.
4. Find some of the key differences among the countries.

The Geography of Eastern Europe and Russia
Length: 5 minutes, 52 seconds
Provides overview of the countries, geography and resources of Eastern Europe and Russia.

Section 1 Poland: Preserving Tradition Amidst Change
1. Find out about Polish traditions.
2. Learn about economic changes that have taken place in Poland since the collapse of communism.
3. Understand the future challenges that Poland faces.

Jewish Life in Poland
Length: 3 minutes, 32 seconds
Explores the experience of Polish Jews before, during, and after World War II.

Section 2 Five Balkan Nations: A Region Tries to Rebuild
1. Identify the groups of people who live in the Balkans.
2. Understand how Yugoslavia was created and how it broke up.
3. Identify issues that these Balkan nations face in the future.

Rebuilding Kosovo
Length: 3 minutes, 48 seconds
Describes the rebuilding of Kosovo after years of struggle with the Serbian government.

Section 3 Ukraine: Independence and Beyond
1. Understand how Ukraine's history has been shaped by foreign rule.
2. Explain the major issues that Ukrainians have faced since independence.
3. Describe life in Ukraine today.

The After-Effects of Chernobyl
Length: 3 minutes, 27 seconds
Explains how Ukrainians have coped with the accident at Chernobyl.

Section 4 Russia: A Huge Country Takes a New Path
1. Investigate the changes that capitalism has brought to Russia.
2. Understand the cultural traditions that have endured throughout Russia.
3. Identify the issues that create challenges for Russians.

Life in the "New" Russia
Length: 4 minutes, 6 seconds
Discusses how the collapse of the Soviet Union improved the lives of Russians. Shows how old traditions and modern ways mix in the "new" Russia.

Technology Resources

Students use embedded Web codes to access Internet activities, chapter self-tests, and additional map practice. They may also access Dorling Kindersley's Online Desk Reference to learn more about each country they study.

Use the Interactive Textbook to make content and concepts come alive through animations, videos, and activities that accompany the complete basal text—online and on CD-ROM.

PRENTICE HALL
TeacherEXPRESS™
Plan • Teach • Assess

Use this complete suite of powerful teaching tools to make planning lessons and administering tests quicker and easier.

Reading and Assessment

Reading and Vocabulary Instruction

⟳ Model the Target Reading Skill

Comparison and Contrast Tell students that comparing and contrasting can be a helpful tool both for clarifying what they read and for remembering information. Comparing allows students to see patterns of similarities, and contrasting elucidates patterns of difference. Help students learn this skill by comparing and contrasting the Serbs and the Croats after reading the selection Land of Many Peoples from pp. 183–184 of the Student Edition.

Ask students **What are some similarities between the Serbs and the Croats?** *(Both are ethnic groups of the Balkan Peninsula; both groups speak Serbo-Croatian.)* Then ask **What are some differences between the two groups?** *(They use different alphabets; most Serbs belong to the Christian Orthodox Church, while most Croats are Roman Catholic.)* Finally, have students summarize what they learned to help them remember the information. *(Serbs and Croats, two ethnic groups of the Balkan Peninsula, both speak the same language. However, they use different alphabets and have different religions.)*

Use the following worksheets from All-in-One Europe and Russia Teaching Resources (pp. 329–331) to support the chapter's Target Reading Skill.

Vocabulary Builder
High-Use Academic Words

Use these steps to teach this chapter's high-use words:

1. Have students rate how well they know each word on their Word Knowledge worksheets (All-in-One Europe and Russia Teaching Resources, p. 332).

2. Pronounce each word and ask students to repeat it.

3. Give students a brief definition or sample sentence (provided on TE pp. 175, 182, 190, and 199).

4. Work with students as they fill in the "Definition or Example" column of their Word Knowledge worksheets.

Assessment

Formal Assessment

Test students' understanding of core knowledge and skills.

Chapter Tests A and B, and **Final Exams A and B,** All-in-One Europe and Russia Teaching Resources, pp. 351–356, pp. 363–368

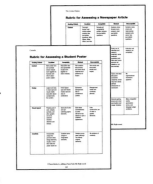

Customize the Chapter Tests to suit your needs.
ExamView Test Bank CD-ROM

Skills Assessment

Assess geographic literacy.

MapMaster Skills, Student Edition, pp. 165, 184, 187, 206

Country Profile Map and Chart Skills, Student Edition, pp. 176, 182, 190, 201

Assess reading and comprehension.

Target Reading Skills, Student Edition, pp. 178, 184, 192, 202, and in Section Assessments

Chapter 5 Assessment, Europe and Russia Reading and Vocabulary Study Guide, p. 70

Performance Assessment

Assess students' performance on this chapter's Writing Activities using the following rubrics from All-in-One Europe and Russia Teaching Resources.

Rubric for Assessing a Bar Graph, p. 347

Rubric for Assessing a Newspaper Article, p. 348

Rubric for Assessing a Timeline, p. 349

Assess students' work through performance tasks.

Small Group Activity, All-in-One Europe and Russia Teaching Resources, pp. 335–338

Portfolio Activity, Teacher Edition, p. 173

Online Assessment

Have students check their own understanding.

Chapter Self-Test

Test Preparation

Europe and Russia Practice Tests A, B and C, Test Prep Workbook, pp. 37–48

Europe and Russia Benchmark Test 2 and Outcome Test, AYP Monitoring Assessments, pp. 109–112, 188–193

Section 1 Poland: Preserving Tradition Amidst Change

 2 periods, 1 block (includes Country Databank)

Social Studies Objectives

1. Find out about Polish traditions.
2. Learn about economic changes that have taken place in Poland since the collapse of communism.
3. Understand the future challenges that Poland faces.

Reading/Language Arts Objective

Compare and contrast to help you sort out and analyze information.

Prepare to Read	Instructional Resources	Differentiated Instruction
Build Background Knowledge Discuss traditions in students' communities. **Set a Purpose for Reading** Have students evaluate statements on the *Reading Readiness Guide*. **Preview Key Terms** Teach the section's Key Terms. **Target Reading Skill** Introduce the section's Target Reading Skill of **comparing and contrasting**.	**All in One Europe and Russia Teaching Resources** **L2** Reading Readiness Guide, p. 314 **L2** Compare and Contrast, p. 329	**Spanish Reading and Vocabulary Study Guide** **L1** Chapter 5, Section 1, pp. 43–44 ELL **World Studies Video Program** **L2** The Geography of Eastern Europe and Russia AR, GT, LPR, SN

Instruct	Instructional Resources	Differentiated Instruction
Tradition in Poland Discuss the major religions in Poland and how language links the Polish people. **Country Profile** Ask students to derive and use information from maps, charts, and graphs. **Great Economic Changes** Ask about how the transition from communism to capitalism improved Poland's economy. **Target Reading Skill** Review **comparing and contrasting**. **Future Challenges** Discuss how Poland is repairing its damaged environment and working to reduce the level of unemployment.	**All in One Europe and Russia Teaching Resources** **L2** Guided Reading and Review, p. 315 **L2** Reading Readiness Guide, p. 314 **L2** Reading a Table, p. 342 **Europe and Russia Transparencies** **L2** Transparency B15: Outline **L2** Section Reading Support Transparency ER 48 **World Studies Video Program** **L2** Jewish Life in Poland	**All in One Europe and Russia Teaching Resources** **L2** Outline Map 18: Eastern Europe and Russia: Political, p. 344 AR, ELL, GT, LPR, SN **L2** Using a Map Key, p. 341 AR, GT, LPR, SN Rubric for Assessing a Newspaper Article, p. 348 AR, GT **Teacher's Edition** **L1** For Special Needs Students, TE pp. 167, 177 **L3** For Gifted and Talented, TE pp. 168, 177 **L1** For Less Proficient Readers, TE pp. 169, 176, 179 **L3** For Advanced Readers, TE p. 170 **Europe and Russia Transparencies** **L1** Transparency B16: Venn Diagram ELL, LPR, SN

Assess and Reteach	Instructional Resources	Differentiated Instruction
Assess Progress Evaluate student comprehension with the section assessment and section quiz. **Reteach** Assign the Reading and Vocabulary Study Guide to help struggling students. **Extend** Ask students to research the collapse of Poland's communist government and create a timeline based on their findings.	**All in One Europe and Russia Teaching Resources** **L2** Section Quiz, p. 316 Rubric for Assessing a Timeline, p. 349 Rubric for Assessing a Writing Assignment, p. 350 **Reading and Vocabulary Study Guide** **L1** Chapter 5, Section 1, pp. 58–60	**All in One Europe and Russia Teaching Resources** Rubric for Assessing a Bar Graph, p. 347 AR, GT, LPR, SN **Spanish Support** **L2** Section Quiz (Spanish), p. 45 ELL

Key

L1 Basic to Average	**L3** Average to Advanced	
L2 For All Students		
	LPR Less Proficient Readers	GT Gifted and Talented
	AR Advanced Readers	ELL English Language Learners
	SN Special Needs Students	

Section 2 Five Balkan Nations: A Region Tries to Rebuild

 *1.5 periods, .75 block*

Social Studies Objectives
1. Identify the groups of people who live in the Balkans.
2. Understand how Yugoslavia was created and how it broke up.
3. Identify issues that these Balkan nations face in the future.

Reading/Language Arts Objective
Make comparisons to find out how two or more situations are alike.

Prepare to Read	**Instructional Resources**	**Differentiated Instruction**
Build Background Knowledge Show students the video for this section and discuss the lasting effects of land mines. **Set a Purpose for Reading** Have students evaluate statements on the *Reading Readiness Guide*. **Preview Key Terms** Teach the section's Key Terms. **Target Reading Skill** Introduce the section's Target Reading Skill of **making comparisons**.	**All in One Europe and Russia Teaching Resources** L2 Reading Readiness Guide, p. 318 L2 Make Comparisons, p. 330 **World Studies Video Program** L2 Rebuilding Kosovo	**Spanish Reading and Vocabulary Study Guide** L1 Chapter 5, Section 2, pp. 45–46 ELL

Instruct	**Instructional Resources**	**Differentiated Instruction**
Country Profile Ask students to derive and use information from maps, charts, and graphs. **Land of Many Peoples** Discuss the Slavic groups in the Balkans. **Target Reading Skill** Review **making comparisons**. **The Creation of Yugoslavia** Discuss Yugoslavia's government before and after World War II. **Yugoslavia Breaks Up** Discuss war and conflict in Yugoslavia. **The Region's Future** Discuss Slobodan Milosevic and the future of the Balkan nations.	**All in One Europe and Russia Teaching Resources** L2 Guided Reading and Review, p. 319 L2 Reading Readiness Guide, p. 318 L2 Using a Map Key, p. 341 **Europe and Russia Transparencies** L2 Section Reading Support Transparency ER 49	**All in One Europe and Russia Teaching Resources** L1 DK Compact Atlas of the World Activity: Reading a Political Map, p. 343 ELL, LPR, SN **Teacher's Edition** L1 For Special Needs Students, TE p. 184 L1 For English Language Learners, TE p. 185 L3 For Gifted and Talented, TE p. 187 **PHschool.com** L3 **For:** Environmental and Global Issues: Genocide in the Balkans **Web Code:** ldd-7506 AR, GT **Spanish Support** L2 Guided Reading and Review (Spanish), p. 46 ELL

Assess and Reteach	**Instructional Resources**	**Differentiated Instruction**
Assess Progress Evaluate student comprehension with the section assessment and section quiz. **Reteach** Assign the Reading and Vocabulary Study Guide to help struggling students. **Extend** Extend the lesson by assigning an Enrichment activity.	**All in One Europe and Russia Teaching Resources** L2 Section Quiz, p. 320 L3 Enrichment, p. 333 Rubric for Assessing a Writing Assignment, p. 350 **Reading and Vocabulary Study Guide** L1 Chapter 5, Section 2, pp. 61–63	**Spanish Support** L2 Section Quiz (Spanish), p. 47 ELL

Key
L1 Basic to Average   L3 Average to Advanced   LPR Less Proficient Readers   GT Gifted and Talented
L2 For All Students   AR Advanced Readers   ELL English Language Learners
                                                 SN Special Needs Students

Section 3 Ukraine: Independence and Beyond

 2.5 periods, 1.25 blocks (includes Skills for Life)

Social Studies Objectives
1. Understand how Ukraine's history has been shaped by foreign rule.
2. Explain the major issues that Ukrainians have faced since independence.
3. Describe life in Ukraine today.

Reading/Language Arts Objective
Compare and contrast different points in history to understand how a nation has changed over time.

Prepare to Read	**Instructional Resources**	**Differentiated Instruction**
Build Background Knowledge Discuss how independence affected Ukraine. **Set a Purpose for Reading** Have students evaluate statements on the *Reading Readiness Guide*. **Preview Key Terms** Teach the section's Key Terms. **Target Reading Skill** Introduce the section's Target Reading Skill of **comparing and contrasting**.	**All in One Europe and Russia Teaching Resources** L2 Reading Readiness Guide, p. 322 L2 Compare and Contrast, p. 329	**Spanish Reading and Vocabulary Study Guide** L1 Chapter 5, Section 3, pp. 47–48 ELL

Instruct	**Instructional Resources**	**Differentiated Instruction**
Country Profile Ask students to derive and use information from maps, charts, and graphs. **A History of Occupation** Discuss Ukraine's relationship with the Soviet Union. **Target Reading Skill** Review **comparing and contrasting**. **Independence Brings Challenges** Ask about changes after independence. **Life in Ukraine** Discuss life in Ukraine before and after independence and ask about the future of the nation.	**All in One Europe and Russia Teaching Resources** L2 Guided Reading and Review, p. 323 L2 Reading Readiness Guide, p. 322 **Europe and Russia Transparencies** L2 Section Reading Support Transparency ER 50 **World Studies Video Program** L2 The After-Effects of Chernobyl	**All in One Europe and Russia Teaching Resources** L2 Guided Reading and Review, p. 323 ELL L3 Small Group Activity: Chernobyl: Report on a Disaster, pp. 335–338 AR, GT L2 Skills for Life, p. 334 AR, GT, LPR, SN **Teacher's Edition** L2 For English Language Learners, TE p. 191 L1 For Special Needs Students, TE p. 191 L3 For Gifted and Talented, TE p. 192 L3 For Advanced Readers, TE p. 193 **Student Edition on Audio CD** L1 Chapter 5, Section 3 ELL, LPR, SN

Assess and Reteach	**Instructional Resources**	**Differentiated Instruction**
Assess Progress Evaluate student comprehension with the section assessment and section quiz. **Reteach** Assign the Reading and Vocabulary Study Guide to help struggling students. **Extend** Extend the lesson by assigning an online activity.	**All in One Europe and Russia Teaching Resources** L2 Section Quiz, p. 324 Rubric for Assessing a Newspaper Article, p. 348 **Reading and Vocabulary Study Guide** L1 Chapter 5, Section 3, pp. 64–66 **PHSchool.com** L3 **For:** Environmental and Global Issues: Using Nuclear Power **Web Code:** ldd-7507	**Spanish Support** L2 Section Quiz (Spanish), p. 49 ELL **Teacher's Edition** L1 For Special Needs Students, TE p. 197 **Social Studies Skills Tutor CD-ROM** L1 Identifying Frame of Reference and Point of View ELL, LPR, SN

Key
L1 Basic to Average   L3 Average to Advanced   LPR Less Proficient Readers   GT Gifted and Talented

L2 For All Students   AR Advanced Readers   ELL English Language Learners

SN Special Needs Students

Section 4 Russia: A Huge Country Takes a New Path

 3.5 periods, 1.75 blocks (includes Chapter Review and Assessment)

Social Studies Objectives
1. Investigate the changes that capitalism has brought to Russia.
2. Understand the cultural traditions that have endured throughout Russia.
3. Identify the issues that create challenges for Russians.

Reading/Language Arts Objective
Identify contrasts to find out how two things are different.

Prepare to Read	**Instructional Resources**	**Differentiated Instruction**
Build Background Knowledge Discuss the effects of capitalism on Moscow. **Set a Purpose for Reading** Have students evaluate statements on the *Reading Readiness Guide*. **Preview Key Terms** Teach the section's Key Terms. **Target Reading Skill** Introduce the section's Target Reading Skill of **identifying contrasts**.	**All in One Europe and Russia Teaching Resources** L2 Reading Readiness Guide, p. 326 L2 Identify Contrasts, p. 331 **World Studies Video Program** L2 Life in the "New" Russia	**Spanish Reading and Vocabulary Study Guide** L1 Chapter 5, Section 4, pp. 49–50 ELL

Instruct	**Instructional Resources**	**Differentiated Instruction**
Emerging Capitalism Discuss the dissolution of the Soviet Union. **Country Profile** Ask students to analyze maps, charts, and graphs. **Target Reading Skill** Review **identifying contrasts**. **Cultural Traditions Continue** Discuss how old and new cultural traditions are mixing in Russia. **Uniting a Vast Nation** Discuss changes in Russia after the dissolution of the Soviet Union.	**All in One Europe and Russia Teaching Resources** L2 Guided Reading and Review, p. 327 L2 Reading Readiness Guide, p. 326 **Europe and Russia Transparencies** L2 Transparency B2: Flow Chart L2 Section Reading Support Transparency ER 51	**All in One Europe and Russia Teaching Resources** L3 Activity Shop Interdisciplinary: Plan a New Railroad Line, pp. 339–340 **Teacher's Edition** L1 For Less Proficient Readers, TE p. 201 L3 For Advanced Readers, TE pp. 201, 203 **Europe and Russia Transparencies** L1 Color Transparency ER 13 ELL, LPR, SN L1 Color Transparency ER 15 ELL, LPR, SN **PHSchool.com** L3 **For:** Environmental and Global Issues: Why Do Wars Begin? **Web Code:** ldd-7508 AR, GT

Assess and Reteach	**Instructional Resources**	**Differentiated Instruction**
Assess Progress Evaluate student comprehension with the section assessment and section quiz. **Reteach** Assign the Reading and Vocabulary Study Guide to help struggling students. **Extend** Extend the lesson by assigning a primary source reading.	**All in One Europe and Russia** L2 Section Quiz, p. 328 L3 Housekeeping in Russia Soon After the Revolution, p. 345 L2 Vocabulary Development, p. 346 L2 Word Knowledge, p. 332 L2 Chapter Tests A and B, pp. 351–356 **Reading and Vocabulary Study Guide** L1 Chapter 5, Section 4, pp. 67–69	**Spanish Support** L2 Section Quiz (Spanish), p. 51 ELL L2 Chapter Summary (Spanish), p. 52 ELL L2 Vocabulary Development (Spanish), p. 53 ELL

Key
L1 Basic to Average   L3 Average to Advanced   LPR Less Proficient Readers   GT Gifted and Talented
L2 For All Students   AR Advanced Readers   ELL English Language Learners
                                         SN Special Needs Students

Reading Background

Learning Vocabulary by Making Choices

Help students build their understanding of Key Terms and high-use words from the chapter by asking them to make choices between correct and incorrect examples of the words. For each word below, read the two examples and ask students to say which example best shows the true meaning of the word.

Word: *entrepreneur*
Description 1: Seth started a business to buy and sell baseball cards, and opened offices around the world. *(correct)*
Description 2: The employee followed her boss' orders to get the job done.

Word: *secede*
Description 1: The organization withdrew its membership. *(correct)*
Description 2: The student joined the study group.

Word: *inflation*
Description 1: The price of food has increased over the years. *(correct)*
Description 2: The price of food has decreased over the years.

Using the Choral Reading Strategy Effectively

For many less proficient readers, it is often a lack of confidence that is key to their reading difficulties. You can use a combination of reading strategies, such as Choral Reading followed by silent reading, to teach students the skills they need to read confidently.

Keep the following points in mind as you practice the Choral Reading strategy:

1. Encourage students to stay with your voice as you read rather than racing ahead or lagging behind.
2. Use shorter passages of about 300 to 500 words.
3. For students to have a better understanding of the text, follow with a silent reading of the same passage. Then begin to ask questions about the content of the passage.

World Studies Background

Lech Walesa (1943–)

Poland was still under communist control in 1980 when Lech Walesa, a shipyard electrician, led a strike against a government-owned shipyard in Gdansk. Walesa soon became the leader of Solidarity, an independent labor federation that challenged the communist government. The government outlawed Solidarity in 1981. Walesa was arrested and detained by the government for a year. He and other union activists were harassed by the government throughout the 1980s, until a new wave of labor unrest swept Poland in 1988. The government was forced to negotiate with Walesa and restore Solidarity. Walesa won the Nobel Peace Prize in 1983. In 1990, he became the first democratically elected president of a free Poland.

The Original Yugoslavia

The Kingdom of Serbs, Croats, and Slovenes was created in 1918 as a result of World War I. It was formed from regions that had been part of the Ottoman Empire and the Austro-Hungarian Empire and ruled by a Serb dynasty. In 1929, King Alexander, a Serb, attempted to unite the different ethnic groups and officially changed the country's name to Yugoslavia. After World War II, Yugoslavia was controlled by Joseph Broz Tito's Communist Party.

Infoplease® provides a wealth of useful information for the classroom. You can use this resource to strengthen your background on the subjects covered in this chapter. Have students visit this advertising-free site as a starting point for projects requiring research.

 Use Web code **ldd-7500** for **Infoplease**®.

Build Vocabulary by Developing Expanded Definitions

Give students a tool to create rich definitions, discover word relationships, and learn vocabulary independently by teaching them to develop expanded definitions. Students can build their understanding of a word by answering the three questions below. Students can then combine the answers into a definition to which they can relate. Model the skill by walking students through the steps with a high-use word from the chapter, such as *consume.*

1. What does it mean?
    to purchase goods and services
2. What is a synonym for *consume*?
    buy
3. Provide a sentence using the word.
    It becomes a problem when a society consumes goods faster than they can be produced.

As a class, create an expanded definition of *consume: To consume means to purchase goods or services. People who buy food are consumers.*

Ask students to use this skill to create definitions for other Key Terms and high-use words from the chapter.

Tips for Writing Paragraphs

Knowing the components that make up a paragraph is essential for writing successful paragraphs. Model the following steps using a paragraph from p. 175 of the Student Edition before students write paragraphs related to this chapter:

1. Begin with a topic sentence. *(Poland has experienced great change in its long history.)*
2. Provide examples that support the topic sentence. *(Borders have shifted. Rulers have come and gone. Economic systems have changed.)*
3. End with a summary sentence. *(But throughout all these changes, some parts of Polish life have remained the same.)*

Have students write their own paragraphs that relate to the chapter. Remind students to use transition words and vary the length and structure of their sentences.

Siberian Chronicles

The Siberian Chronicles are a series of stories and historical accounts about Siberia dating from the 1500s through the 1700s. Historians hold conflicting theories about the origins of the chronicles. One widely held hypothesis is that survivors of a Siberian expedition in the 1500s wrote a work which was copied and reinterpreted, then eventually modified into the Siberian Chronicles. The chronicles describe the travels of Yermak Timofeyevich, who led an expedition to explore Siberia and defeat local tribes. The chronicles also include aspects of Russian folklore.

Black Earth

Chernozem, the black soil abundant in Ukraine, occurs in other parts of the world as well. Present in the middle latitudes of both hemispheres, chernozem forms in regions with cold winters and hot summers. In the United States, the Black Belt is a fertile area that spans Alabama and northeastern Mississippi. Beef cattle and soybeans are raised in this region of dark, rich soil. Similar soils are also found in India and in the Pampas region of Argentina.

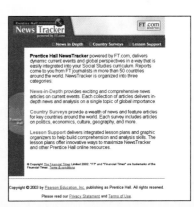

Get in-depth information on topics of global importance with **Prentice Hall Newstracker,** powered by FT.com.

 Use Web code **ldd-7501** for **Prentice Hall Newstracker.**

Guiding Questions

Remind students about the Guiding Questions introduced at the beginning of the book.

Section 1 relates to **Guiding Question 5**
How have Russian and European economies developed into what they are today? *(Poland transitioned from communism to capitalism, which has strengthened the economy.)*

Section 2 relates to **Guiding Question 2**
How have Europe and Russia been affected by their history? *(The formation of Yugoslavia brought together many ethnic groups. Tensions between the groups have led many to break away.)*

Section 3 relates to **Guiding Question 5**
How have Russian and European economies developed into what they are today? *(After Ukraine gained independence from the Soviet Union, Ukrainians had to learn how to build their economy.)*

Section 4 relates to **Guiding Question 3**
How have the people of Europe and Russia been shaped by their cultures? *(Today, traditional ways exist alongside new ways in Russia.)*

⟳ Target Reading Skill

In this chapter, students will learn and apply the reading skill of compare and contrast. Use the following worksheets to help students practice this skill:

All in One Europe and Russia Teaching Resources, *Compare and Contrast,* p. 329; *Make Comparisons,* p. 330; *Identify Contrasts,* p. 331

Differentiated Instruction

The following Teacher's Edition strategies are suitable for students of varying abilities.

Advanced Readers, pp. 170, 193, 201, 203
English Language Learners, pp. 185, 191
Gifted and Talented, pp. 168, 177, 187, 192
Less Proficient Readers, pp. 169, 176, 179, 201
Special Needs Students, pp. 167, 177, 184, 191, 197

Chapter Preview

This chapter focuses on Poland, five Balkan nations, Ukraine, and Russia.

Country Databank
The Country Databank provides data and descriptions of Russia and each of the countries in Eastern Europe.

Section 1
Poland
Preserving Tradition Amidst Change

Section 2
Five Balkan Nations
A Region Tries to Rebuild

Section 3
Ukraine
Independence and Beyond

Section 4
Russia
A Huge Country Takes a New Path

 Target Reading Skill

Comparing and Contrasting In this chapter you will focus on comparison and contrast to help you sort out and analyze information.

▶ Harvesting lavender on a hillside in Croatia

Bibliography

For the Teacher
Hudgins, Sharon. *The Other Side of Russia: A Slice of Life in Siberia and the Russian Far East.* Texas A&M University Press, 2003.
Prazmowska, Anita J. *A History of Poland.* Palgrave, Macmillan, 2004.
Rogel, Carole. *The Breakup of Yugoslavia and Its Aftermath: Revised Edition.* Greenwood Publishing Group, 2004.

For the Student
L1 Steele, Philip. *Moscow.* Gareth Stevens, 2003.
L2 Bryan, Nichol. *Chernobyl: Nuclear Disaster.* Gareth Stevens, 2003.
L3 Taylor, David. *The Wars of Former Yugoslavia (Troubled World).* Raintree/Steck Vaughn, 2003.

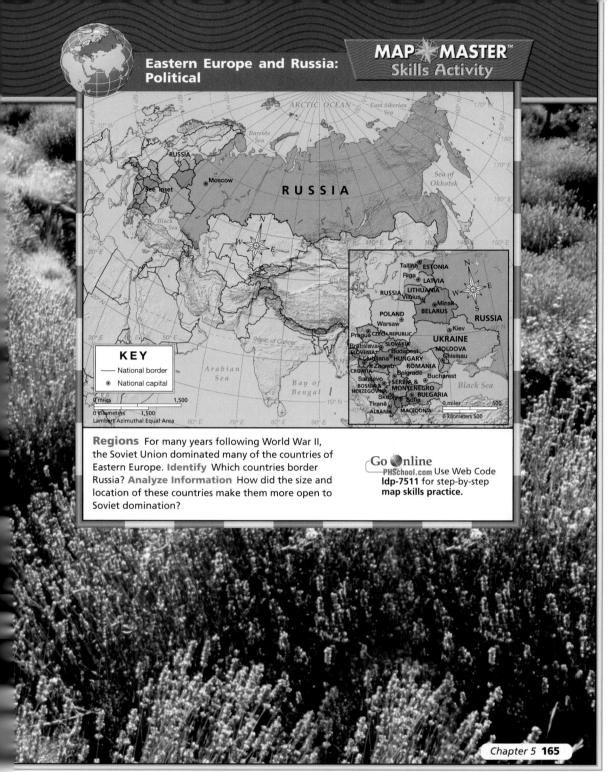

Eastern Europe and Russia: Political

MAP MASTER™
Skills Activity

KEY
— National border
⊛ National capital

0 miles 1,500
0 kilometers 1,500
Lambert Azimuthal Equal Area

0 miles 500
0 kilometers 500

Regions For many years following World War II, the Soviet Union dominated many of the countries of Eastern Europe. **Identify** Which countries border Russia? **Analyze Information** How did the size and location of these countries make them more open to Soviet domination?

Go Online
PHSchool.com Use Web Code **ldp-7511** for step-by-step **map skills practice.**

Chapter 5 **165**

MAP MASTER™
Skills Activity

Create a blank chart with two columns on the board. Label the columns "Countries of Eastern Europe and Russia" and "Capitals." Call on students to list the countries from the map on this page, and write them in the first column of the chart. Then, have students name the capital of each country, and fill them in the second column.

Go Online
PHSchool.com Students may practice their map skills using the intermediate online version of this map.

Using the Visual   L2

Reach Into Your Background Draw students' attention to the photograph on pages 164–165. Discuss the photograph with students. Have them discuss what details stand out to them. Can they relate this scene to something in their own lives? Encourage students to share their ideas with the class.

Answers

MAP MASTER Skills Activity **Identify** The map shows that Estonia, Latvia, Belarus, and Ukraine border Russia. **Analyze Information** They are relatively small and close to Russia, making it easier for Soviets to enter and gain control over them.

Chapter Resources

Teaching Resources
L2 Vocabulary Development, p. 346
L2 Skills for Life, p. 334
L2 Chapter Tests A and B, pp. 351–356

Spanish Support
L2 Spanish Chapter Summary, p. 52
L2 Spanish Vocabulary Development, p. 53

Media and Technology
L1 Student Edition on Audio CD
L1 Guided Reading Audiotapes, English and Spanish
L2 Social Studies Skills Tutor CD-ROM
ExamView Test Bank CD-ROM

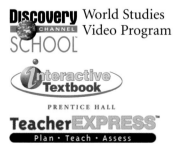

Discovery CHANNEL SCHOOL World Studies Video Program

interactive Textbook
PRENTICE HALL
TeacherEXPRESS™
Plan • Teach • Assess

Objectives

- Look at the map and study the data to learn about Russia and the countries of Eastern Europe.

- Analyze data to compare the countries.

- Identify characteristics that most of these countries share.

- Find some of the key differences among the countries.

Show *The Geography of Eastern Europe and Russia.* Ask **What are the major land regions in Eastern Europe?** *(East European Plains, Alpine Mountain System, and the plains and plateaus of Siberia)* **How is the terrain both different from and similar to that in Western Europe?** *(Both have plains that contain valuable resources, and the Alpine Mountain System runs through both. Western Europe, however, does not contain a region as large and barren as Siberia.)*

Prepare to Read

Build Background Knowledge

L2

Tell students that Russia and the Eastern European countries they saw in the video have many similarities and differences. Have students brainstorm any similarities or differences among these countries that they can recall from the video. Conduct an Idea Wave (TE, p. T35) to elicit student responses and write them on the board in two columns labeled "Similarities" and "Differences."

The Geography of Eastern Europe and Russia, **World Studies Video Program**

Introducing
Eastern Europe and Russia

Guide for Reading

This section provides an introduction to Russia and the 18 countries of Eastern Europe.

- Look at the map on the previous page and then read the paragraphs to learn about each nation.
- Analyze the data to compare the countries.
- What characteristics do most of these countries share?
- What are some key differences among the countries?

Viewing the Video Overview

View the World Studies Video Overview to learn more about each of the countries. As you watch, answer these questions:

- What are the major land regions in Eastern Europe?
- How is the terrain both different from and similar to that in Western Europe?

Explore the geography of Eastern Europe and Russia.

Albania

Capital	Tirana
Land Area	10,578 sq mi; 27,398 sq km
Population	3.5 million
Ethnic Group(s)	Albanian, Greek
Religion(s)	Muslim, Eastern Orthodox, Roman Catholic
Government	emerging democracy
Currency	lek
Leading Exports	textiles and footwear, asphalt, metals and metallic ores, crude oil, vegetables, fruits, tobacco
Language(s)	Albanian (official), Greek

Albania (al BAY nee uh) is located in southeastern Europe on the Adriatic and Ionian Seas. It is bordered by Serbia and Montenegro, Macedonia, and Greece. Albania became a communist state during World War II. In the early 1990s, the country tried to establish democracy. But government instability, high unemployment rates, and violence have prevented Albania from achieving that goal. Economically, the country is poor and struggling. Today, the country depends on aid from other countries to survive. However, the Albanians are slowly creating an open-market economy.

Belarus

Capital	Minsk
Land Area	80,154 sq mi; 207,600 sq km
Population	10.3 million
Ethnic Group(s)	Belarusian, Russian, Polish, Ukrainian
Religion(s)	Eastern Orthodox, Roman Catholic, Protestant, Muslim, Jewish
Government	republic
Currency	Belarusian ruble
Leading Exports	machinery and equipment, mineral products, chemicals, textiles, foodstuffs, metals
Language(s)	Belarusian (official), Russian (official)

Belarus (bay luh ROOS) is located between Poland and Russia. It was a Soviet republic for seven decades until its independence in 1991. Unlike many other former Soviet republics, Belarus has remained politically close to Russia. Russia also supplies Belarus with resources, as the country has few natural resources of its own. Belarus does have the potential, however, to develop its agriculture and forestry industries. Belarus faces major health and environmental problems caused by the 1986 Chernobyl explosion in neighboring Ukraine.

Bosnia and Herzegovina

Capital	Sarajevo
Land Area	19,741 sq mi; 51,129 sq km
Population	4.0 million
Ethnic Group(s)	Serb, Bosniak, Croat
Religion(s)	Muslim, Eastern Orthodox, Roman Catholic, Protestant
Government	emerging federal democratic republic
Currency	marka
Leading Exports	miscellaneous manufactured goods, raw materials
Language(s)	Serbo-Croat (official)

Bosnia and Herzegovina (BAHZ nee uh and hurt suh goh VEE nuh) is located on the Adriatic Sea in southeastern Europe, between Croatia and Serbia and Montenegro. Bosnia and Herzegovina declared independence from Yugoslavia in 1992. However, conflict among Serbs, Bosniaks, and Croats drew the country immediately into civil war. Peace was reached in 1995 with the help of NATO. Today, Bosnia and Herzegovina is struggling to recover from the years of war. Because of its natural resources, it has the potential to develop a thriving economy.

Bulgaria

Capital	Sofia
Land Area	42,683 sq mi; 110,550 sq km
Population	7.6 million
Ethnic Group(s)	Bulgarian, Southwest Asian, Roma, Macedonian, Armenian, Tartar, Circassian
Religion(s)	Eastern Orthodox, Muslim, Roman Catholic, Jewish
Government	parliamentary democracy
Currency	lev
Leading Exports	clothing, footwear, iron and steel, machinery and equipment, fuels
Language(s)	Bulgarian (official), Turkish, Macedonian, Romany

Bulgaria (bul GEHR ee uh) is located in southeastern Europe between Romania and Greece, bordering the Black Sea. The first Bulgarian state was created in the 600s when a central Asian Turkic tribe merged with the Slavic people of the region. Bulgaria was ruled by the Ottoman Empire for hundreds of years. The country regained its independence in 1878 but fell under communist rule after World War II. In 1990 the first open elections were held. Since then, the country has continued to develop a democratic political system with a free-market economy. Bulgaria is a member of NATO and has taken the first steps to becoming part of the EU.

Croatia

Capital	Zagreb
Land Area	21,781 sq mi; 56,414 sq km
Population	4.4 million
Ethnic Group(s)	Croat, Serb, Bosniak, Hungarian, Slovene, Czech, Albanian, Montenegrin, Roma
Religion(s)	Roman Catholic, Eastern Orthodox, Muslim
Government	presidential-parliamentary democracy
Currency	kuna
Leading Exports	transport equipment, textiles, chemicals, foodstuffs, fuels
Language(s)	Croation (official)

Croatia (kroh AY shuh) is located in southeastern Europe between Slovenia and Bosnia and Herzegovina. It borders the Adriatic Sea. Croatia was formerly part of the nation called Yugoslavia. Croatia declared its independence in 1991, but Serbian armies remained and fought on Croatian land for several years afterward. Economically, the country is struggling to recover from costly war damage and a high unemployment rate. The EU has spent over $1 billion in aid to help Croatia rebuild. The nation has rich fishing resources in the Adriatic Sea.

Chapter 5 **167**

Instruct

Introducing Eastern Europe and Russia L2

Guided Instruction

■ Read each country paragraph as a class using the Choral Reading strategy (TE, p. T34). Then, ask students to read through each data table.

■ Ask **What religions are common to all of the countries on pp. 166–167?** (*Muslim, Eastern Orthodox, and Roman Catholic*)

■ Have students study the Belarus data. Ask **In what ways are Belarus' ties to Russia visible?** (*Russian is one of Belarus' official languages, and Russian is one of the country's major ethnic groups.*)

■ Discuss the changes that have taken place in Bulgaria since 1990. (*The country now holds free elections, it is moving toward democracy and a free-market economy, it is a member of NATO, and it has taken the first steps to joining the EU.*)

Guided Instruction (continued)

- Have students study the paragraphs and data for the countries on pp. 168–169. Tell them to think about what the countries have in common and what the major differences are as they read. Encourage them to make a table to keep track of the similarities and differences.

- Ask students to find the similarities between the Czech Republic and Hungary. *(population size; Slovak is a major ethnic group; parliamentary democracy as government; machinery and equipment, manufactured goods, and raw materials are major exports; Hungarian language; once under communist rule; both have strengthening economies)*

Introducing Eastern Europe and Russia

Czech Republic

Capital	Prague
Land Area	29,836 sq mi; 78,276 sq km
Population	10.3 million
Ethnic Group(s)	Czech, Moravian, Slovak, Polish, German, Silesian
Religion(s)	Roman Catholic, Protestant, Eastern Orthodox
Government	parliamentary democracy
Currency	Czech koruna
Leading Exports	machinery and transportation equipment, intermediate manufactured goods, chemicals, raw materials, fuel
Language(s)	Czech (official), Slovak, Hungarian

The Czech Republic (chek rih PUB lik) is a landlocked nation surrounded by Germany, Slovakia, Austria, and Poland. In 1918, the Slovaks joined with the Czechs to form Czechoslovakia. Czechoslovakia fell under Soviet rule after World War II but gained back its freedom in 1989. In 1993, the Czechs and the Slovaks peacefully separated into two nations, the Czech Republic and Slovakia. The Czech Republic has become one of the most stable and successful countries of those dominated by the Soviet Union during the Cold War. It has strong industries, mineral resources, and a thriving tourist industry. The Czech Republic has become a member of NATO and the EU.

Estonia

Capital	Tallinn
Land Area	16,684 sq mi; 43,211 sq km
Population	1.4 million
Ethnic Group(s)	Estonian, Russian, Ukrainian, Belarusian, Finnish
Religion(s)	Protestant, Eastern Orthodox, Jewish
Government	parliamentary republic
Currency	kroon
Leading Exports	machinery and equipment, wood products, textiles, food products, metals, chemical products
Language(s)	Estonian (official), Russian

Estonia (es TOH nee uh) borders the Baltic Sea, Latvia, and Russia. It is actually a small peninsula, and includes more than 1500 small islands. For centuries, foreign powers controlled the region. But in 1918, Estonia gained its independence. Like several other eastern European states, it was taken over by the Soviet Union in 1940 and regained its independence in 1991. Since then, Estonia has adopted political and economic ideas from Western Europe. Its three major trading partners are Finland, Sweden, and Germany. The country has joined the EU and NATO.

A hawk moth in Viidumae Nature Reserve, Estonia

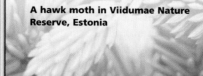

Differentiated Instruction

For Gifted and Talented L3

Have students choose two of the five countries found on pp. 168–169. Tell them to use the DK World Desk Reference Online to make information cards similar to the ones in the Country Databank using different statistics, such as the percentage of people living in rural and urban areas and literacy rates. Ask them to use the same types of statistics for both countries. Then have them write a short paragraph explaining the similarities and differences between the countries based on what they found.

Hungary

Capital	Budapest
Land Area	35,652 sq mi; 92,340 sq km
Population	10.1 million
Ethnic Group(s)	Hungarian, Roma, German, Serb, Slovak, Romanian
Religion(s)	Roman Catholic, Protestant
Government	parliamentary democracy
Currency	forint
Leading Exports	machinery and equipment, other manufactured goods, food products, raw materials, fuels and electricity
Language(s)	Hungarian (official)

Hungary (HUNG guh ree) is landlocked among Austria, Romania, and five other countries in central Europe. For hundreds of years the nation was part of the Austro-Hungarian Empire. After World War II, the country came under communist rule. In the late 1960s, Hungary took some steps away from a government-controlled economy. But real reforms came in 1990 with the first open elections and a free-market economy. Since then, Hungary has had strong economic growth, and has become a member of both NATO and the EU. Hungary's capital, Budapest, has long been a cultural center of the region.

Latvia

Capital	Riga
Land Area	24,552 sq mi; 63,589 sq km
Population	2.4 million
Ethnic Group(s)	Latvian, Russian, Belarusian, Ukrainian, Polish, Lithuanian
Religion(s)	Protestant, Roman Catholic, Eastern Orthodox
Government	parliamentary democracy
Currency	lat
Leading Exports	wood and wood products, machinery and equipment, metals, textiles, foodstuffs
Language(s)	Latvian (official), Russian

Located between Estonia and Lithuania, Latvia (LAT vee uh) sits on the eastern coast of the Baltic Sea. The entire country lies on a flat, low plain. Its climate is temperate, with cool summers and cold winters. Between World War I and World War II, Latvia enjoyed a period of independence, but in 1940 it was taken over by the Soviet Union. Along with many other Soviet republics, it declared its independence in 1991. Since then it has adopted many of the political and economic ideas of Western Europe. After a Russian economic crisis in 1998, Latvia further decreased is dependence on Russia. It has joined the EU and NATO.

Lithuania

Capital	Vilnius
Land Area	25,174 sq mi; 65,200 sq km
Population	3.6 million
Ethnic Group(s)	Lithuanian, Russian, Polish, Belarusian
Religion(s)	Roman Catholic, Protestant, Russian Orthodox, Muslim, Jewish
Government	parliamentary democracy
Currency	litas
Leading Exports	mineral products, textiles and clothing, machinery and equipment, chemicals, wood and wood products, foodstuffs
Language(s)	Lithuanian (official), Russian

Lithuania (lith oo AY nee uh) is located between Latvia and Poland and borders the Baltic Sea. It was an independent state before World War II, but the Soviet Union claimed it in 1940. Lithuania was the first Soviet republic to declare independence in 1990. Since independence, the Lithuanians have taken steps toward establishing a free-market economy and privatizing businesses. Most of Lithuania's income is from services and agriculture. However, it has few natural resources and is one of the poorer nations in the region. Lithuania has joined the EU and NATO.

Chapter 5 **169**

Guided Instruction (continued)

- Ask **Which countries on pp. 168–169 were once under Soviet rule?** *(Czech Republic, Estonia, Latvia, and Lithuania)* **What types of government do these countries have now?** *(Czech Republic, Latvia, and Lithuania are parliamentary democracies; Estonia is a parliamentary republic.)*

- Ask students **Do you think migration is common within Eastern Europe? Why or why not?** *(Students should see that many Eastern European countries contain major ethnic groups from other Eastern European countries. For example, Latvia's major ethnic groups include Russian, Belarusian, Ukrainian, Polish, and Lithuanian. Therefore, migration among Eastern European countries is probably fairly common.)*

Differentiated Instruction

For Less Proficient Readers   **L1**

Have students create a Venn diagram to show the similarities and differences between Estonia and Latvia. Display the *Venn Diagram Transparency* to show students how to sketch the organizer. Circulate to make sure students are filling in the organizers correctly.

Europe and Russia Transparencies, *Transparency B16: Venn Diagram*

Guided Instruction (continued)

■ Have students place the countries on pp. 170–171 in order from largest population to smallest population. *(Russian Federation, Poland, Romania, Moldova, Macedonia)* Remind students how to find population density. *(Divide the population by the land area.)* Ask them to find out which country on these pages has the highest population density. *(Moldova)* Ask **Which has the lowest?** *(Russian Federation)* **Why does the Russian Federation have the lowest when it is the largest country in the world and has a large population?** *(Its large population is spread out over a very large land area.)*

■ Ask **Why is Moldova's economy based mostly on farming?** *(It has a good climate for farming, and it has few minerals and energy resources to fuel the economy.)* **Why do you think Moldova's economy has not improved as much as Poland's economy?** *(Moldova had few free market reforms and in 2001 elected a communist president who would most likely not implement any more. Poland changed rapidly to an open economy.)*

Introducing Eastern Europe and Russia

Macedonia

Capital	Skopje
Land Area	9,597 sq mi; 24,856 sq km
Population	2.1 million
Ethnic Group(s)	Macedonian, Albanian, Southwest Asian, Serb, Roma
Religion(s)	Eastern Orthodox, Muslim
Government	emerging democracy
Currency	Macedonian denar
Leading Exports	food, beverages, tobacco, miscellaneous manufactured goods, iron and steel
Language(s)	Macedonian (official), Albanian (official), Serbo-Croat

Macedonia (mas uh DOH nee uh) is located in southeastern Europe north of Greece. It gained its independence from Yugoslavia in 1991. Macedonia is the poorest of the countries that used to make up Yugoslavia. The nation has a weak economy, and one third of its labor force is unemployed. Macedonia faces ethnic conflict and government instability. It has also faced political conflict with its neighbor, Greece. Because Macedonia is the name of a region in northern Greece, Greece opposed the country's choice of name. However, a treaty signed in 1995 settled the dispute.

A woman spins wool into yarn in her home in Moldova, 1995.

Moldova

Capital	Chisinau
Land Area	12,885 sq mi; 33,371 sq km
Population	4.4 million
Ethnic Group(s)	Moldovan, Ukrainian, Russian, Bulgarian, Gagauz
Religion(s)	Eastern Orthodox, Jewish
Government	republic
Currency	Moldovan leu
Leading Exports	foodstuffs, textiles and footwear, machinery
Language(s)	Moldovan (official), Romanian, Russian

Moldova (mohl DOH vuh) is located between Romania and Ukraine. Before World War II, Moldova was ruled by Romania. It became part of the Soviet Union after World War II and gained its independence in 1991. With few minerals and energy sources, Moldova's economy is based mostly on farming. One of the poorest nations in Europe, it recently saw an improvement in its economy due to some free-market reforms. However, in 2001 Moldova became the first former Soviet state to elect a communist president. Consequently, fewer free-market reforms are expected in the future.

170 Europe and Russia

Differentiated Instruction

For Advanced Readers   L3

Help students learn the capitals of each of the countries in the Country Databank by dividing the class into pairs, and having each pair create a set of flashcards. One side of the flashcard should have the country name, and the other side should have the country capital. Have students take turns quizzing each other. Once students have learned the country capitals, you may choose to have students repeat the exercise using different information, such as currency or government.

Poland

Capital	Warsaw
Land Area	117,554 sq mi; 304,465 sq km
Population	38.6 million
Ethnic Group(s)	Polish, German, Ukrainian, Belarusian
Religion(s)	Roman Catholic, Eastern Orthodox
Government	republic
Currency	zloty
Leading Exports	machinery and transport equipment, intermediate manufactured goods, miscellaneous manufactured goods, food and live animals
Language(s)	Polish (official)

Polish postage stamps

Poland (POH lund) is located in central Europe between Germany and Ukraine. Poland was taken over by Germany and the Soviet Union during World War II. Following the war, Poland was dominated by the Soviet Union. Since the fall of the Soviet Union, Poland has changed successfully from a government-controlled economy to an open economy, and has entered the EU and NATO. Poland has an almost homogeneous population, and the vast majority of Poles are Roman Catholic.

Romania

Capital	Bucharest
Land Area	88,934 sq mi; 230,340 sq km
Population	22.3 million
Ethnic Group(s)	Romanian, Hungarian, Roma, Ukrainian, German, Russian
Religion(s)	Eastern Orthodox, Protestant, Roman Catholic
Government	republic
Currency	Romanian leu
Leading Exports	textiles and footwear, metals and metal products, machinery and equipment, minerals and fuels
Language(s)	Romanian (official), Hungarian, German, Romany

Romania (roh MAY nee uh) is located in southeastern Europe between Ukraine and Bulgaria, bordering the Black Sea. Following World War II, Romania was occupied by the Soviet Union. It became a communist republic in 1947. A single harsh dictator ruled Romania from 1965 to 1989. In the late 1990s, the country became a limited democracy. Today, the country still struggles with widespread poverty and government instability. Romania would like to become part of the EU, but must achieve more political and economic reforms before it can apply.

Russian Federation

Capital	Moscow
Land Area	6,592,100 sq mi; 16,995,800 sq km
Population	145 million
Ethnic Group(s)	Russian, Tatar, Ukrainian, Chuvash, Bashkir, Belarusian, Moldavian
Religion(s)	Russian Orthodox, Muslim, Jewish
Government	federation
Currency	Russian ruble
Leading Exports	petroleum and petroleum products, natural gas, wood and wood products, metals, chemicals
Language(s)	Russian (official), Tatar, Ukrainian, Chuvash, and others

Russia (RUSH uh), the world's largest country, is located in northern Asia between Ukraine and China, bordering the Arctic and North Pacific Oceans. The region west of the Ural Mountains is considered part of Europe. Throughout most of its history, Russia was ruled by royal families. The last royal dynasty was overthrown in 1917. The world's first communist government, the Soviet Union, was formed after World War I and ruled for decades. In 1991, the USSR split into 15 independent nations. Today, Russians are moving toward a more democratic political system and a free-market economy.

Chapter 5 **171**

Guided Instruction (continued)

- Ask students to describe Romania's population. (*Romania has a population of about 22.3 million people. It has a diverse population, with seven major ethnic groups including Romanian, Hungarian, and Southwest Asian. Most people are Christian or Muslim.*) Ask **How does it differ from Poland's population?** (*Poland has a more homogenous population, and Islam is not a major religion practiced there.*)

- Ask **What challenges do you think Russia's large land area presents to its people and government?** (*Possible answer: Extensive transportation and communication systems are needed so that people and goods can be transported throughout the country and the government can rule the large territory effectively.*)

- Ask **How do Russia's leading exports reflect the country's standing as one of the world's leaders in natural resources?** (*Russia's leading exports include natural resources such as petroleum, natural gas, and wood.*)

Background: Links Across Time

St. Petersburg The name of the second largest city in Russia, now called St. Petersburg, has changed several times during the country's history. Peter the Great, who founded the city in the early 1700s, used the German word *burg*, meaning "city," as part of his city's name. In 1914, however, when Russia and Germany went to war, the city's name was changed to the more Russian-sounding Petrograd. After the communists came to power, the city's name was changed again, this time to Leningrad, in honor of one of Russian Communism's founders, Vladimir Lenin. Finally when the Soviet Union collapsed in the early 1990s, the city's name was changed back to its original, St. Petersburg.

Guided Instruction (continued)

- Ask students to compare and contrast Serbia and Montenegro and Slovenia. *(Similarities: Both have Serb and Hungarian ethnic groups, Christians and Muslims, manufactured goods and food as leading exports, and Serbo-Croat as a language; both were once part of Yugoslavia. Differences: Slovenia has a better economy and is more stable. There are also differences in land area, population size, some ethnic groups, government, currency, some exports, and some languages.)*

- Have students create a short timeline showing important events in Slovakia's history. *(1918: Slovaks join with Czechs to form Czechoslovakia; 1989: gains independence from Soviet rule; 1993: Slovaks and Czechs peacefully separate into Slovakia and the Czech Republic)*

- Have students review the map on p. 165, and ask them to draw conclusions about Ukraine's geographic location and its different ethnic groups. *(Ukraine is bordered by several countries, including Russia, Belarus, Poland, Hungary, and Moldova. A number of its ethnic groups come from these places.)*

Independent Practice

Have students complete *Using a Map Key,* and then divide the class into pairs and distribute *Outline Map 18: Eastern Europe and Russia: Political.* Then ask students to use the Country Databank to help them create a map that shows the official language for each country in the region. Tell students to use different colors for each official language, and shade the countries with the color that corresponds to the official language. If a country has more than one official language, have them alternate bands of two or three colors to show that information. They should explain what each color represents in their map keys.

All in One **Europe and Russia Teaching Resources,** *Using a Map Key,* p. 341; *Outline Map 18: Eastern Europe and Russia: Political,* p. 344

Monitor Progress

Circulate to make sure students are filling in their maps correctly. Provide assistance as needed.

Introducing Eastern Europe and Russia

Serbia and Montenegro

Capital	Belgrade
Land Area	39,435 sq mi; 102,136 sq km
Population	10.7 million
Ethnic Group(s)	Serb, Albanian, Montenegrin, Hungarian
Religion(s)	Eastern Orthodox, Muslim, Roman Catholic
Government	republic
Currency	dinar and euro
Leading Exports	manufactured goods, food and live animals, raw materials
Language(s)	Serbo-Croat (official), Albanian, Hungarian

Serbia and Montenegro (SUR bee uh and mahnt uh NEE groh) are located in southeastern Europe between Croatia and Romania, bordering the Adriatic Sea. These two republics were once part of Yugoslavia. They experienced years of ethnic conflict and civil war after Yugoslavia broke up. Serbia's violence against ethnic Albanians in Kosovo caused NATO troops to invade the region in 1999 to restore peace. In 2003, Serbia and Montenegro agreed to become a loose partnership of two states. Both republics are currently focused on rebuilding their troubled economies and recovering from years of war.

Slovakia

Capital	Bratislava
Land Area	18,842 sq mi; 48,800 sq km
Population	5.4 million
Ethnic Group(s)	Slovak, Hungarian, Roma, Czech, Moravian, Silesian, Ruthenian, Ukrainian, German, Polish
Religion(s)	Roman Catholic, Protestant, Eastern Orthodox
Government	parliamentary democracy
Currency	Slovak koruna
Leading Exports	machinery and transport equipment, manufactured goods, chemicals
Language(s)	Slovak (official), Hungarian, Czech

Slovakia (sloh VAH kee uh) is located in Central Europe between the Czech Republic and Ukraine. In 1918, the Slovaks joined with the Czechs to form Czechoslovakia. Czechoslovakia fell under Soviet domination after World War II but gained back its freedom in 1989. In 1993, the Slovaks and the Czechs peacefully separated into two democratic nations, Slovakia and the Czech Republic. Slovakia has a stable economy and has joined the EU and NATO.

An Eastern Orthodox Church in Montenegro

172 Europe and Russia

Slovenia

Capital	Ljubljana
Land Area	7,780 sq mi; 20,151 sq km
Population	1.9 million
Ethnic Group(s)	Slovene, Croat, Serb, Bosniak, Yugoslav, Hungarian
Religion(s)	Roman Catholic, Protestant, Muslim
Government	parliamentary democratic republic
Currency	tolar
Leading Exports	manufactured goods, machinery and transport equipment, chemicals, food
Language(s)	Slovene (official), Serbo-Croat

Slovenia (sloh VEE nee uh) is located in Central Europe between Austria and Croatia, bordering the Adriatic Sea. The Slovene lands were once part of Austria and the Holy Roman Empire. In the mid-1900s, they became part of Yugoslavia. Since independence in 1991, Slovenia has become a stable democracy with a strong economy and a good relationship with Western Europe. Slovenia has joined the EU and NATO. The country has Eastern Europe's highest standard of living.

Ukraine

Capital	Kiev
Land Area	233,090 sq mi; 603,700 sq km
Population	48.4 million
Ethnic Group(s)	Ukrainian, Russian, Belarusian, Moldovan, Crimea Tartar, Bulgarian, Hungarian, Romanian, Polish
Religion(s)	Eastern Orthodox, Jewish
Government	republic
Currency	hryvnia
Leading Exports	ferrous and nonferrous metals, fuel and petroleum products, machinery and transport equipment, food products
Language(s)	Ukrainian (official), Russian, Tartar

Ukraine (yoo KRAYN) is located between Poland and Russia, bordering the Black Sea. During the 900s and 1000s, Ukraine was the center of the largest and most powerful state in Europe. However, since that time, the region has suffered invasions, occupations, and rebellions. Millions of Ukrainians died under Soviet occupation in the 1920s and 1930s and millions more during World War II. Although Ukraine gained independence from the Soviet Union in 1991, many of its leaders have been slow to encourage political or economic reforms.

SOURCES: CIA World Factbook Online 2002; DK World Desk Reference Online; *The World Almanac*, 2003

Assessment

Comprehension and Critical Thinking

1. Compare and Contrast Compare the physical size and the population of Ukraine to those of Macedonia.

2. Make Generalizations Identify the five countries that were once part of Yugoslavia. What are some characteristics that they share?

3. Categorize Which religions do most people in the region practice?

4. Draw Conclusions The governments of some of these countries are listed as "emerging," or developing democracies. Read about these countries' histories. Why might it be difficult for them to establish democratic governments?

5. Make a Bar Graph Create a bar graph that shows the populations of the countries in the region.

Keeping Current

Access the **DK World Desk Reference Online** at **PHSchool.com** for up-to-date information about the 19 countries in this region.

Go Online
PHSchool.com

Web Code: lde-7500

Assess Progress L1

- Have students create a chart similar to the one you created on the board at the beginning of the lesson. Have them choose any two countries and list their similarities and differences on the chart.

- Ask students to answer the Assessment questions.

Reteach L1

Ask students to create a table on a large piece of poster board that shows the data for all of the countries in the Country Databank. Have them list the categories across the top of the table and the names of the countries along the side. Model filling in the information for one country on the board.

Extend L3

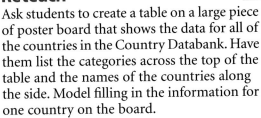

Have students choose one country in the Country Databank. Ask them to research the country, using the DK World Desk Reference Online as a starting point. Then, have them create a paragraph, short story, chart, graph, map, or illustration about the country to add to their portfolios.

Answers

Assessment

1. Ukraine has a much larger area and population size than Macedonia.

2. Bosnia and Herzegovina, Croatia, Macedonia, Serbia and Montenegro, and Slovenia; all have the Serb ethnic group, Muslim and Christian religions, and food as a leading export; all have struggled with instability and are working to improve their economies.

3. Christianity, Islam, and Judaism

4. Most of these countries are struggling to rebuild their government after gaining independence from communist rule.

5. Students' bar graphs should reflect the populations of the countries in the Databank. Use the *Rubric for Assessing a Bar Graph* to evaluate students' work.

All in One Europe and Russia Teaching Resources, *Rubric for Assessing a Bar Graph*, p. 347

Objectives

Social Studies
1. Find out about Polish traditions.
2. Learn about economic changes that have taken place in Poland since the collapse of communism.
3. Understand the future challenges that Poland faces.

Reading/Language Arts
Compare and contrast to help you sort out and analyze information.

Prepare to Read

Build Background Knowledge **L2**
Tell students that in this section they will learn about the country of Poland. Explain that although many changes have affected Poland throughout its history, many Polish traditions have remained. Ask students if they know of any such cultural traditions in their communities. Then have them discuss why they think these traditions have lasted. Conduct a Think-Write-Pair-Share activity (TE, p. T36) to help students generate ideas.

Set a Purpose for Reading **L2**
- Preview the Objectives.

- Read each statement in the *Reading Readiness Guide* aloud. Ask students to mark the statements true or false.

  All in One Europe and Russia Teaching Resources, *Reading Readiness Guide,* p. 314

- Have students discuss the statements in pairs or groups of four, then mark their guides again. Use the Numbered Heads participation strategy (TE, p. T36) to call on students to share their group's perspectives.

Vocabulary Builder
Preview Key Terms **L2**
Pronounce each Key Term, and then ask the students to say the word with you. Provide a simple explanation such as, "An entrepreneur is a person who starts new businesses."

Prepare to Read

Objectives
In this section you will
1. Find out about Polish traditions.
2. Learn about economic changes that have taken place in Poland since the collapse of communism.
3. Understand the future challenges that Poland faces.

Taking Notes
As you read, create an outline of this section. The outline below has been started for you.

```
I. Tradition in Poland
   A. Catholicism
   B.
      1.
      2.
II.
```

Target Reading Skill

Compare and Contrast
When you compare, you look for the similarities between things. When you contrast, you look at the differences. Comparing and contrasting can help you sort out and analyze information. As you read this section, look for similarities and differences in Polish life during and after Soviet domination.

Key Terms
- **shrine** (shryn) *n.* a holy place
- **capitalism** (KAP ut ul iz um) *n.* an economic system in which businesses are privately owned
- **entrepreneur** (ahn truh pruh NOOR) *n.* a person who develops original ideas in order to start new businesses

Dancers at a traditional festival in Mazuka, Poland

In June of 2003, Polish citizens celebrated an event that could not possibly have occurred just two decades earlier. Poland had voted to join the European Union. It was an exciting event for a nation that at one time did not even appear on maps of Europe.

Poland has had a difficult history. In medieval times, it was the largest state in Europe. But by the late 1700s, it had been divided up among its stronger neighbors. For the next two hundred years, Polish territory changed hands many times. Controlled at different times by Russia, Germany, and Austria, Poland became free again at the end of World War I. But after World War II, the Polish government fell under the influence of the Soviet Union. For several decades, Poles lived under a harsh communist government. Poles regained their freedom when that government fell in 1989. Poland then began a long process of reform and rebuilding.

174 Europe and Russia

Target Reading Skill **L2**

Compare and Contrast Point out the Target Reading Skill. Tell students that comparing and contrasting ideas will help them to better understand and organize them.

Model the skill by reading the Capitalism paragraph on p. 177 and comparing and contrasting Poland's economy before and after January 1, 1990. (*After January 1, the government no longer controlled prices, taxes and wages were frozen, and a stock market was set up a year later.*)

Give students *Compare and Contrast.* Have them complete the activity in groups.

All in One Europe and Russia Teaching Resources, *Compare and Contrast,* p. 329

Tradition in Poland

Poland has experienced great change in its long history. Borders have shifted. Rulers have come and gone. Economic systems have changed. But many parts of Polish life have remained the same.

Catholicism in Poland Catholicism has been at the center of Polish tradition for centuries. The communist government tried to discourage Catholicism, but it could not change the devotion many Poles have for the Roman Catholic Church.

Today, about 95 percent of Poles are still Catholic. Poles have their own way of observing Catholic holidays and their own way of prayer. Polish Catholics felt tremendous pride in 1978, when a Pole was selected as pope of the Catholic Church. Pope John Paul II quickly became the most widely traveled Catholic leader in history. He also made the world more aware of Poland and its struggle under communism.

In 1979, the pope visited Poland. About one million joyful and enthusiastic Poles gathered to see him. Mothers held babies over their heads for the pope's blessing. The crowd sang hymns and threw flowers toward the stage on which he sat. For most of these people, the pope stood for traditional Poland.

Orthodoxy in Poland However, not all Poles are Catholic. A minority of Poles are Polish Orthodox. An example of Polish Orthodox religious life can be seen in northeastern Poland, near the forest of Bialowieza (byah woh VYEH zhah). Not far from the forest is the holy hill of Grabarka, with an Orthodox church at the top. In mid-August, visitors climb this hill to visit the church. Each visitor plants a cross in the earth. Among the trees on the hillside are hundreds of crosses. Some are as tall as trees, and others as tiny as flowers. You can see such Orthodox **shrines,** or holy places, all over Poland.

Judaism in Poland A small minority of Poles are Jewish. Today, Poland's Jewish population numbers only in the thousands. However, more than 3 million Jews used to live in Poland. During the Holocaust, about 85 percent of Polish Jews were killed by the German government.

Polish Religious Traditions
Roman Catholic Pope John Paul II, at the top, waves to crowds in his hometown of Wadowice (vah duh VEET seh). Above, Eastern Orthodox worshipers take part in a festival in Bialowieza. **Apply Information** *What role does religion play in the lives of most Poles?*

Vocabulary Builder

Use the information below to teach students this section's high-use words.

High-Use Word	Definition and Sample Sentence
unique, p. 177	*adj.* having no like or equal Each painting the artist created was truly **unique.**
transition, p. 177	*n.* a change from one situation to another Some students find the **transition** from high school to college difficult.
invest, p. 178	*v.* to spend money on something in the hope of making a profit Amanda **invested** her money in stocks of growing companies.

Instruct

Tradition in Poland L2

Guided Instruction

- **Vocabulary Builder** Clarify the high-use word **unique** before reading.

- Read Tradition in Poland, using the Oral Cloze strategy (TE, p. T33).

- Ask students **What is the major religion of Poland?** *(Catholicism)* **How is Polish Catholicism unique?** *(Polish Catholics have their own way of observing holidays and praying.)*

- Have student discuss why Poles felt such pride in Pope John Paul II. *(He stood for traditional Poland, and became the most widely traveled Catholic leader in history, working to make the world more aware of Poland's struggle under communism.)*

- Ask students **What other religion do many Poles practice?** *(Polish Orthodox)* **What is a shrine?** *(a holy place)* **How do you think shrines reflect Polish traditions?** *(They are important to Polish religions, which are a large part of Polish tradition.)*

- Ask students **How does the Polish language link Poles to each other and to other nations?** *(It ties Poles together by making them feel different and special, and because it is a Slavic language, it links Poland with other Slavic nations in Eastern Europe.)*

Independent Practice

Ask students to create the Taking Notes graphic organizer on a blank sheet of paper. Then have them fill in the outline with information they have just learned. Briefly model how to add details using *Transparency B15: Outline.*

📖 **Europe and Russia Transparencies,** *Transparency B15: Outline*

Monitor Progress

As students begin to fill in the graphic organizer, circulate and help individuals understand which details to include. Provide assistance as needed.

Answer

Apply Information Religion is very important to many Poles.

Guided Instruction `L2`

Ask students to study the Country Profile on this page. As a class, answer the Map and Chart Skills questions. Allow students to briefly discuss their responses with a partner before sharing answers.

Independent Practice

- Distribute *Reading a Table*. Have students work in pairs to complete the worksheet.

  All in One **Europe and Russia Teaching Resources,** *Reading a Table*, p. 342

- Turn students' attention to the charts on this page. Ask them to write a few sentences summarizing the information they learned from each chart.

COUNTRY PROFILE
Focus on Government

Poland

A few powerful people had run Poland's communist government. In contrast, as a republic, Poland has a three-branch form of government similar to that of the United States. Poland's economy has also changed. Under communism, the government took control of most privately owned businesses and industries. Poland's republic has encouraged the development of small businesses, as well as foreign trade. Study the map and charts to learn more about Poland's government.

Employment by Sector and Ownership

1989			2001		
Sector	Privately Owned	Government Owned	Sector	Privately Owned	Government Owned
Agriculture	79%	21%	Agriculture	99%	1%
Industry	15%	85%	Industry	77%	23%
Construction	27%	73%	Construction	94%	6%
Transport	6%	94%	Transport	48%	52%
Trade	8%	92%	Trade	98%	2%

SOURCES: Glowny Urzad Statystyczny (GUS), Rocznik Statystyczny

Poland's Government

Executive Branch	Legislative Branch	Judicial Branch
President Elected by the people for a five-year term	**National Assembly** Made up of two houses, the Sejm and the Senate	**Supreme Court** Judges appointed by the president for life
Prime Minister Appointed by the president, and confirmed by the Sejm	**Sejm** Includes 460 members, who are elected to four-year terms	**Constitutional Tribunal** Judges appointed by the Sejm for nine-year terms
Council of Ministers Appointed by the President, and approved by the Sejm	**Senate** Includes 100 members, who are elected to four-year terms	SOURCE: CIA World Factbook Online, 2003

Map and Chart Skills

1. **Locate** Around which Polish cities are the manufacturing industries and trade centered?

2. **Compare** How did the percentage of people employed in privately owned industries change from 1989 to 2001?

3. **Apply Information** How does Poland's government compare to that of the United States?

 Use Web Code **ldp-7521** for **DK Word Desk Reference Online.**

Answers

Map and Chart Skills

1. Warsaw, Katowice, Kraków

2. It increased.

3. Poland has a three-branch government similar to that of the United States.

Go Online PHSchool.com Students can find more information about this topic on the DK World Desk Reference Online.

Differentiated Instruction

For Less Proficient Readers `L1`

To help reinforce students' understanding of the shift from government ownership to private ownership of businesses and industries in Poland, have them choose one of the sectors in the chart and create a pie graph showing the portions that are privately-owned and government-owned. They should create one graph for the sector in 1989 and another for the same sector in 2001. Remind students to label the graphs properly and give each an appropriate title.

The Polish Language The language of the Poles has stood the test of time. In the past, some foreign rulers banned the use of Polish in schools and in the government. Although the communists did not ban Polish, they did force Polish schoolchildren to learn Russian, the official language of the Soviet Union.

Today, Polish is spoken by the majority of the population. The Polish language is a cultural tie that unites Poles, giving them pride in their unique heritage. As a Slavic language, it also links the nation to other Slavic nations in Eastern Europe.

✓ Reading Check What religion do most Poles belong to?

Great Economic Changes

Communism ended in Poland in 1989. After that, Poland underwent rapid change. The greatest of these changes occurred in Poland's economy.

Capitalism Poland has been very successful in making the change from communism to capitalism. **Capitalism** is an economic system in which businesses are privately owned. Most former communist countries made this change gradually. Poland changed almost overnight. On January 1, 1990, Polish leaders made a number of changes. They ended the government's control over prices. They also froze taxes and wages. A year later, Poland set up a stock market. Although these were dramatic changes, they helped Poland successfully make the difficult transition to capitalism.

Learn about life
for Jews in Poland.

Links to
Government

Poland's Solidarity Movement In the 1980s, a radical group formed in Poland. This was a labor union—a group of people seeking workers' rights—called Solidarity. This group was radical because it was the first independent labor union to form in a Soviet-dominated country. Solidarity was formed to protest rising food prices. It organized strikes and demonstrations such as the 1987 march shown in the photo at the left. Solidarity's first leader was an electrician named Lech Walesa. Under Walesa, Solidarity began openly criticizing the communist government, and helped bring about its downfall. Lech Walesa served as president of Poland from 1990 to 1995. Solidarity is still a political party in Poland today.

Show students *Jewish Life in Poland.* Ask **Why did many Jewish people move to Poland in the beginning of the thirteenth century?** *(They were being treated unfairly in some Western European countries. In Poland, they could practice their religion and own property.)*

Great Economic Changes L2

Guided Instruction

■ **Vocabulary Builder** Clarify the high-use words **transition** and **invest** before reading.

■ Read Great Economic Changes with students. As they read, check and make sure that individuals can answer the Reading Check question.

■ Ask students **How did Poland change its economy after January 1, 1990?** *(Polish leaders set up a stock market, ended government control over prices, and froze taxes and wages.)*

■ Ask students **Why do you think that Poles decided to make a rapid change to capitalism?** *(Possible answers: Many Poles had been unhappy under communism and wanted to replace it with another economic system as soon as possible; Poles might have felt that a quick transition would be more effective than a slower one.)*

■ Ask students **What led foreigners to begin investing their money in Poland?** *(the collapse of the communist government)* **What other factors might have encouraged foreign investment?** *(Possible answer: Investors might have been encouraged by the economy's rapid transition to capitalism.)*

Differentiated Instruction

For Special Needs Students L1
Before reading the section, show students *Section Reading Support Transparency ER 48*. Tell them that as they read, they should identify the statements on the completed graphic organizer that match the information in the text.

📖 **Europe and Russia Transparencies**
Section Reading Support Transparency ER 48

For Gifted and Talented L3
Tell students to suppose that they work for Poland's largest newspaper in January 1990. Have each student write a newspaper article about new changes in Poland's economy. Use *Rubric for Assessing a Newspaper Article* to evaluate students' articles.

All in One Europe and Russia Teaching Resources, *Rubric for Assessing a Newspaper Article,* p. 348

Links
Read the **Links to Government** on this page. Ask **Why was Solidarity radical?** *(It was the first independent labor union to form in a Soviet-ruled country.)*

Answer

✓ Reading Check Most Poles are Catholics.

Target Reading Skill L2

Compare and Contrast As a follow up, ask students to do the Target Reading Skill activity in the Student Edition. *(During communist rule, Poland's economy was weak; the government controlled businesses and prices. After the fall of communism, the economy was strengthened due to foreign investment and privatization of businesses.)*

Guided Instruction (continued)

■ Have students describe how small businesses in Poland's cities grew after communism ended. *(At first, traders sold goods in street booths. Eventually they earned enough money to take over stores that had once been owned by the government.)*

■ Ask students **How did the availability of consumer goods in Poland change after the fall of communism?** *(Poles had more access to consumer goods after the fall of communism.)*

■ Ask students **What effect did the transition from communism to capitalism have on farming?** *(Although many farms under communism were privately owned, the government protected farmers by buying their products and ensuring that prices stayed high. After the end of communism, prices dropped and farmers no longer had a guaranteed source of income. As a result, farmers under capitalism have had to be innovative in order to make a living.)*

Independent Practice

Have students continue to fill in their outlines with information from the section.

Monitor Progress

As students fill in their graphic organizers, circulate to make sure they are providing the correct headings and details.

Answers

Chart Skills Compare Slovenia
Generalize Standards of living are higher in Western Europe than in Eastern Europe.

178

Compare and Contrast Describe Poland's economy before and after the fall of communism.

Foreign Investment With the collapse of the communist government, many foreigners began to invest their money in Poland. By 2001, Poland had brought in more foreign investment than had any other Central European country. Foreign investment has greatly strengthened the Polish economy.

Privatization A growth in the number of private businesses has also helped Poland's economy. With the end of communist rule, Poles were free to find new ways of making money. Small businesses soon blossomed in Poland's cities. At first, traders set up booths on the streets. They sold everything they could find, from American blue jeans to old Soviet army uniforms.

Slowly but surely, some traders earned enough money to take over stores that the government had once owned. Now, more than two million businesses are run by entrepreneurs (ahn truh pruh NOORZ). An **entrepreneur** is a person who develops original ideas in order to start new businesses.

Polish industries have also been slowly privatized over the last few years. Poland's most important private industries are food, energy, and mining.

Consumer Goods Poles now have access to more consumer goods than they did under communism. Only half of the homes in Poland had televisions in 1989. Now, almost every home has one. On the streets of cities such as Warsaw, Poland's capital, many people use mobile phones and wear the latest fashions. For these people, the new way of life is good.

■ Chart Skills

Life expectancy and per capita GDP, or the economic output per person, are two factors used to measure a country's standard of living. **Compare** Which Eastern European country has the highest standard of living? **Generalize** Germany is shown as an example of a Western European country. How do standards of living in Western Europe compare to those in Eastern Europe?

Standard of Living Comparison for Selected European Countries

Country	Per Capita GDP	Life Expectancy	
		Male	Female
Bulgaria	$6,600	68.3	75.6
Czech Republic	$15,300	71.7	78.9
Hungary	$13,300	67.8	76.8
Poland	$9,500	69.8	78.3
Slovenia	$18,000	71.7	79.6
Germany (Western Europe)	$26,600	75.5	81.6

178 Europe and Russia

 Skills Mini Lesson

Synthesizing Information L2

1. Tell students that in order to synthesize information, they should analyze each piece of information and then look for connections between them. Finally, they should draw a conclusion based on the connections they found.

2. Have students practice the skill by synthesizing the per capita GDP and life expectancy information in the chart to determine which country has the highest standard of living.

3. Have students apply the skill by synthesizing the information in the chart to compare the standard of living in Hungary and Bulgaria. Tell them to write a few sentences explaining their conclusion.

Changes in Farm Life Unlike many businesses, most farms under communism had remained privately owned. Still, the change to a capitalist economy was harder on farmers than on most other Poles. Under communism, the government always bought produce and meat from farmers, providing them with a reliable income. The government also made sure that prices for farm produce stayed high. After communism, prices dropped, and sales were no longer guaranteed. Farmers learned to be innovative, or creative, to survive.

Some farmers now take on part-time jobs to make extra money. Others invite paying guests from the city to stay on their farms for rural vacations. Some farmers produce organic vegetables, fruits, and meats, which they can sell at higher prices than other farmers' products.

Farmers who cannot find other sources of income often struggle to make a living. Most farms in Poland are small. Many farmers only own about 5 to 12 acres (2 to 5 hectares) of land, which may not produce enough money to live on.

✓ **Reading Check** Why did farmers have a steady income under communism?

A Polish husband and wife use a draft horse to plow a field in Bialowieza.

Future Challenges

Poland has made the change from communism to capitalism with speed and success. It has the strength to compete with other nations as part of the EU. However, the Polish people still face many challenges.

Kraków—A Cultural Treasure
Kraków is Poland's third-largest city. It is also a cultural center with historic architecture, an excellent university, and a marketplace that has existed since the 1200s. **Infer** How have cities such as Kraków changed since the fall of communism in Poland?

Future Challenges L2

Guided Instruction

- Read Future Challenges with students.

- Ask students **What effects did coal-mining and steel production during the communist era have on the environment and people of Poland?** (*They created pollution that killed many of the forests in southern Poland and increased rates of diseases among Poles.*) **What steps has the current government taken to help repair the damage to the environment?** (*The government has closed some polluting factories and has invested in equipment to reduce pollution in others; the use of unleaded gasoline has also reduced pollutants coming from cars.*)

- Ask students **Why are rates of unemployment high across Poland?** (*Under the communist government, people were guaranteed jobs, but under the capitalist system jobs are not guaranteed.*) **What is one way that the unemployment problem might be solved?** (*Many Poles hope that as a result of its membership in the EU, more long-term investment will take place in Poland, creating new jobs.*)

Independent Practice

Have students complete the graphic organizer by adding details about pollution and unemployment.

Monitor Progress

- Show *Section Reading Support Transparency ER 48* and ask students to check their graphic organizers individually. Go over key concepts and clarify key vocabulary as needed.

  📖 **Europe and Russia Transparencies,** *Section Reading Support Transparency ER 48*

- Tell students to fill in the last column of their *Reading Readiness Guides*. Probe for what they learned that confirms or invalidates each statement.

  All in One **Europe and Russia Teaching Resources,** *Reading Readiness Guide,* p. 314

Answers

✓ **Reading Check** The government always bought produce and meat from farmers, which helped keep prices high.

Infer Businesses are now privately owned, and more consumer goods are bought and sold in the marketplaces.

Assess and Reteach

Assess Progress L2

Have students complete the Section Assessment. Then administer the *Section Quiz*.

 Europe and Russia Teaching Resources, *Section Quiz,* p. 316

Reteach L1

If students need more instruction, have them read this section in the Reading and Vocabulary Study Guide.

📖 Chapter 5, Section 1, **Europe and Russia Reading and Vocabulary Study Guide,** pp. 58–60

Extend L3

Divide students into pairs and have them do research in the library and on the Internet to learn more about the events leading to the fall of Poland's communist government in 1989. Then have each pair create a timeline of the major events. Use *Rubric for Assessing a Timeline* to evaluate students' work.

Europe and Russia Teaching Resources, *Rubric for Assessing a Timeline,* p. 349

Answers

✓ Reading Check After the end of communism, some polluting factories were closed, other factories invested in equipment that reduces pollution, and the use of unleaded gasoline reduced pollutants coming from cars. **Conclude** Possible answer: transplanting trees into deforested areas will create new jobs for Poles.

Section 1 Assessment

Key Terms

Students' sentences should reflect an understanding of each Key Term.

🎯 Target Reading Skill

Under communism, most farmers had reliable income because the government bought meat and produce from farmers and kept prices for farm produce high. After the fall of communism, prices dropped and sales were no longer guaranteed. Some farmers still have a steady income, but they must find more creative ways of making money.

Comprehension and Critical Thinking

1. (a) religion and language **(b)** because it was the main language of the Soviet Union, which ruled Poland

---

Bringing Back the Forests
People on a tree farm plant young trees. Once the trees have grown larger, they will be transplanted to regions that were deforested during the communist years. **Conclude** *How can renewed forests strengthen Poland's economy?*

Pollution During the communist era, coal-mining and steel production in southern Poland caused terrible pollution. This pollution destroyed much of the forests in southern Poland and increased rates of diseases, such as cancer.

After the communists left power, Polish leaders began to repair some of the damage to the environment. Old polluting factories were closed. Other factories invested in equipment to reduce pollution. The use of unleaded gasoline reduced the pollutants coming from cars. By 2003, Poland had reduced many forms of pollution by 50 percent.

Unemployment Poland faces other challenges, such as a high unemployment rate. Under communism, people were guaranteed jobs. In the current capitalist system, there is no such guarantee. Many Poles emigrate to other places in Europe to find work. In fact, about one out three Poles today lives outside of Poland. Other Poles hope that membership in the EU will bring more long-term investment into Poland, creating more jobs.

Poles will have to find ways to deal with such challenges, but they are ready to do whatever is needed. For the first time in many years, their future is in their own hands.

✓ **Reading Check** How did Poland reduce its air pollution?

 Section 1 Assessment

Key Terms
Review the key terms at the beginning of this section. Use each term in a sentence that explains its meaning.

🎯 Target Reading Skill
How is farm life in Poland the same as and different from the way it was under communism?

Comprehension and Critical Thinking
1. (a) Identify What parts of Polish life did not change under communism?

(b) Analyze Information Why did the communist government force Polish schoolchildren to learn Russian?
2. (a) Explain What measures did Poland's leaders take to convert the economy to capitalism?
(b) Identify Point of View How might many Polish farmers view the transition to capitalism?
3. (a) Recall What major challenges does Poland still face?
(b) Predict What further changes might membership in the EU bring to Poland?

Writing Activity
Suppose you are a journalist in Poland today. You interview two Poles—a young entrepreneur in Warsaw and an elderly farmer in the countryside. Write a dialogue that gives their views on how capitalism has changed the country.

> **Writing Tip** Be sure to use appropriate language for each of the two people. Also, consider what is important to people of different ages before you begin writing.

---

2. (a) Polish leaders set up a stock market, ended government control over prices, and froze taxes and wages. **(b)** Possible answers: Some Polish farmers might have been unhappy about the transition to capitalism because they no longer had a reliable income from the government. Others may have welcomed the release from government restraints.

3. (a) environmental pollution and a high unemployment rate **(b)** more long-term investment that will create more jobs

Writing Activity
Use the *Rubric for Assessing a Writing Assignment* to evaluate students' dialogues.

Europe and Russia Teaching Resources, *Rubric for Assessing a Writing Assignment,* p. 350

Five Balkan Nations
A Region Tries to Rebuild

Prepare to Read

Objectives
In this section you will
1. Identify the groups of people who live in the Balkans.
2. Understand how Yugoslavia was created and how it broke up.
3. Identify issues that these Balkan nations face in the future.

Taking Notes
As you read this section, look for important events in the history of these five Balkan nations. Copy the timeline below and record the events in the proper places on it.

1918

Target Reading Skill

Make Comparisons
Comparing two or more situations enables you to see how they are alike. This section is about five countries with similar situations. As you read this section, compare the five nations by considering their histories, economies, cultures, and challenges.

Key Terms
- **civil war** (sih vul wawr) *n.* a war between groups of people within the same nation
- **secede** (sih SEED) *v.* to leave a group, especially a political group or a nation
- **embargo** (em BAHR goh) *n.* a ban on trade
- **economic sanctions** (ek uh NAHM ik SANGK shunz) *n.* actions to limit trade with nations that have violated international laws

Objectives
Social Studies
1. Identify the groups of people who live in the Balkans.
2. Understand how Yugoslavia was created and how it broke up.
3. Identify issues that these Balkan nations face in the future.

Reading/Language Arts
Make comparisons to find out how two or more situations are alike.

Prepare to Read

Build Background Knowledge 〔L2〕
Tell students that in this section they will study the history of conflict in the Balkans. Show the video *Rebuilding Kosovo*. Using the Numbered Heads participation strategy (TE, p. T36), ask students how land mines can affect a region after peace has been made. *(Unless land mines are removed, they can continue to injure and kill people years after a war has ended.)*

📼 *Rebuilding Kosovo,* **World Studies Video Program**

Set a Purpose for Reading 〔L2〕
- Preview the Objectives.
- Read each statement in the *Reading Readiness Guide* aloud. Ask students to mark the statements true or false.

  〔All in One〕 **Europe and Russia Teaching Resources,** *Reading Readiness Guide,* p. 318

- Have students discuss the statements in pairs or groups of four, then mark their guides again. Use the Numbered Heads participation strategy (TE, p. T36) to call on students to share their group's perspectives.

In January 1984, the people of the city of Sarajevo (sa ruh YAY voh) were filled with anticipation. They had proudly won the right to host the 1984 Winter Olympics. To prepare for the games, they had built new hotels and restaurants. They had carved ski-racing trails into the mountains and built ski lifts. New bobsled runs and an elegant skating complex awaited the athletes. A shiny new Olympic Village waited to welcome athletes and visitors to the Games.

   Ten years later, most of these facilities lay in ruins. So did much of Sarajevo. How could this have happened? The answer is **civil war,** or a war between groups of people within the same nation. Civil war broke up the nation of Yugoslavia and shattered the grand city.

Scenes of Sarajevo's Olympic Village before and after the war

Chapter 5 Section 2 **181**

🎯 Target Reading Skill 〔L2〕

Make Comparisons Point out the Target Reading Skill. Explain that students can make comparisons to find the similarities between two or more situations.

   Model the skill by reading the second paragraph on p. 183 and identifying a sim-ilarity between the ethnic groups discussed. *(All of the groups speak the same language—Serbo-Croatian.)*

   Give students *Make Comparisons.* Have them complete the activity in groups.

   〔All in One〕 **Europe and Russia Teaching Resources,** *Make Comparisons,* p. 330

Vocabulary Builder
Preview Key Terms 〔L2〕
Pronounce each Key Term, and then ask the students to say the word with you. Provide a simple explanation such as, "During the Civil War, many southern states seceded from the United States."

COUNTRY PROFILE
Focus on Culture

Guided Instruction $\boxed{\text{L2}}$

Ask students to study the Country Profile on this page. As a class, answer the Map and Chart Skills questions. Allow students to briefly discuss their responses with a partner before sharing answers.

Independent Practice

- Distribute *Using a Map Key*. Have students work in pairs to complete the worksheet.

  All in One **Europe and Russia Teaching Resources,** *Using a Map Key,* p. 341

- Tell students that the map of the five Balkan nations in the Student Edition shows the region's ethnic groups. Have them explain what each color in the key stands for. Then ask them to identify what information appears on the map on the worksheet, paying special attention to the map title and key.

Answers

Map and Chart Skills

1. Serbs, Montenegrins, Albanians, Hungarians, Turks, and Roma

2. Most people in the region practice the Eastern Orthodox religion. Most people speak Serbo-Croat.

3. Possible answer: The data shows the religious and ethnic diversity of the region that has led to some of the political unrest—the different groups may have different ideas about politics and government.

Go **Online**
PHSchool.com Students can find more information about this topic on the DK World Desk Reference Online.

COUNTRY PROFILE   Focus on Culture

Five Balkan Nations

Ethnic diversity is one of the most enduring characteristics of the Balkans. In ancient times, the region was occupied by different tribes who often fought among themselves. The arrival of Christianity and then Islam brought more diversity and more ethnic and political differences to the region. Political unrest still continues in modern times. The Balkans occupy an area slightly smaller than the state of Texas. As you study the map and the table, think about what challenges great diversity might present to a small region.

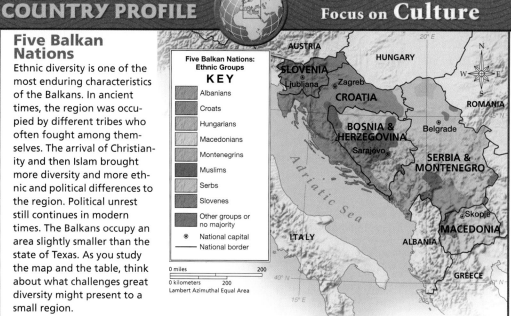

Five Balkan Nations: Ethnic Groups

KEY
- Albanians
- Croats
- Hungarians
- Macedonians
- Montenegrins
- Muslims
- Serbs
- Slovenes
- Other groups or no majority
- ⊛ National capital
- — National border

0 miles 200
0 kilometers 200
Lambert Azimuthal Equal Area

Peoples of Five Balkan Nations

Ethnic Group	Population (millions)	Main Homeland(s)	Language	Main Religion
Croats	5.0	Croatia, Bosnia & Herz.	Serbo-Croat	Roman Catholicism
Serbs	8.4	Serbia & Mont., Bosnia & Herz.	Serbo-Croat	Eastern Orthodox
Slovenes	1.7	Slovenia	Slovenian	Roman Catholicism
Bosniaks	2.0	Bosnia & Herz.	Serbo-Croat	Islam
Montenegrins	0.5	Serbia & Mont.	Serbo-Croat	Eastern Orthodox
Macedonians	1.3	Macedonia	Macedonian	Eastern Orthodox
Albanians	2.3	Serbia & Mont., Macedonia	Albanian	Islam
Hungarians	0.4	Serbia & Mont.	Hungarian	Roman Catholicism
Turks	0.3	Serbia & Mont., Macedonia	Turkish	Islam
Romany	0.2	Serbia & Mont., Macedonia	Romany	Various beliefs

SOURCES: Ethnologue (http://www.ethnologue.org); CIA World Factbook Online, 2003

Map and Chart Skills

1. Identify Which ethnic groups live in Serbia and Montenegro?

2. Analyze Information Which religion do most people in the region practice? What language is spoken by the most people?

3. Apply Information How do the data help explain today's political unrest in the region?

 Use Web Code **Idp-7512** for **DK Word Desk Reference Online.**

Vocabulary Builder

Use the information below to teach students this section's high-use words.

High-Use Word	Definition and Sample Sentence
principle, p. 185	*n.* a basic truth, law, belief, or doctrine One of the **principles** of a democratic government is freedom of speech.
prevent, p. 185	*v.* to keep from happening Using caution can **prevent** forest fires.

Land of Many Peoples

The Balkan Peninsula—also known as the Balkans—is located in southeastern Europe. The Balkans include Serbia and Montenegro, Bosnia and Herzegovina, Macedonia, Croatia, Slovenia, Albania, Romania, Bulgaria, Greece, and European Turkey. This section discusses the first five of these countries, which used to make up the nation of Yugoslavia.

The largest ethnic groups in these five Balkan countries are the Serbs and the Croats (KROH atz), who speak Serbo-Croatian, a Slavic language. Montenegrins (mahnt uh NEE grinz) and Bosniaks, two smaller groups, also speak Serbo-Croatian. Slovenes and Macedonians (mas uh DOH nee unz) speak related Slavic languages.

Although these groups speak related languages, there are important cultural differences among them. For example, both Serbs and Croats speak Serbo-Croatian, but they use different alphabets to write the language.

Religion may be the most important difference, since it separates groups that speak the same language. Most Serbs, Montenegrins, and Macedonians belong to the Eastern Orthodox Church. Croats and Slovenes are mainly Roman Catholic. Bosniaks are mainly Muslim.

In these five countries, there are also groups that speak non-Slavic languages. These groups include Albanians, Hungarians, Roma, and Turks. The Albanians and Turks are mainly Muslim. The Hungarians are mostly Roman Catholic. The Roma have their own unique customs and religious beliefs.

✓ Reading Check **What are the largest ethnic groups in the Balkans?**

The Creation of Yugoslavia

For hundreds of years, the Ottoman Empire, based in Turkey, ruled much of the Balkans. Beginning in the late 1800s, several kingdoms within the empire attempted to form their own states. Sometimes they were supported in their efforts by Russia or western nations, who hoped to gain influence in the region. But none of these groups was successful until World War I ended, and the Ottoman Empire broke up.

A New Nation Is Formed Yugoslavia was the first new Balkan nation to emerge from the old Ottoman Empire. Formed in 1918, the new nation joined together many ethnic and religious groups. From the beginning, these groups disagreed about how the government should be structured.

Faces of the Balkans
Both of the photos above show children of various ethnic groups. The upper photo is from Macedonia, while the lower photo is from Croatia. **Apply Information** *Though these children all live on the Balkan Peninsula, what cultural differences might there be among them?*

Land of Many Peoples 🔲L2

Guided Instruction
- Use the Paragraph Shrinking strategy (TE, p. T34) to read Land of Many Peoples. As students read, circulate and make sure individuals can answer the Reading Check question.

- Ask students **Which Balkan countries share a Slavic heritage?** *(Serbia and Montenegro, Bosnia and Herzegovina, Macedonia, Croatia, and Slovenia)*

- Discuss with students the differences among the Slavic groups in the Balkans. *(People in the Balkans speak different languages, practice different religions, and have different non-Slavic groups within their populations.)*

Independent Practice
Assign *Guided Reading and Review.*

   All in One **Europe and Russia Teaching Resources,** *Guided Reading and Review,* p. 319

Monitor Progress
As students begin the worksheet, circulate to provide assistance as needed.

Answers
Apply Information The children may speak different languages, use different alphabets, and practice different religions.

✓ Reading Check the Serbs and the Croats

Make Comparisons As a follow up, ask students to answer the Target Reading Skill question in the Student Edition. (*In both cases, the people did not always support the government.*)

The Creation of Yugoslavia L2

Guided Instruction

- **Vocabulary Builder** Clarify the high-use word **principle** before reading.

- Read The Creation of Yugoslavia with students.

- Discuss Yugoslavia's government when it was first formed in 1918. (*Yugoslavia was divided into republics. In each republic, one ethnic group held the majority.*)

- Ask students **How did Yugoslavia change after World War II?** (*Tito became head of the government and changed Yugoslavia into a communist state that allied itself with the Soviet Union. Tito also strengthened the economy and unified Yugoslavia.*)

- Ask students **Why did Yugoslavia begin to break up after Tito's death in 1980?** (*Politicians encouraged their followers to identify with their own ethnic group.*)

Independent Practice

Ask students to create the Taking Notes graphic organizer on a blank piece of paper and fill in important dates and events in Yugoslavia's history. Briefly model how to record dates and events on the timeline.

Monitor Progress

As students begin to fill in the timeline, circulate to help individuals understand which details to include.

Answers

MAP MASTER Skills Activity **Explain** The mountainous terrain may have hindered uniting the nation, but the rivers that cross it may have helped. **Predict** Possible answer: by instituting a strong government and allowing little dissension

Go Online PHSchool.com Students may practice their map skills using the interactive online version of this map.

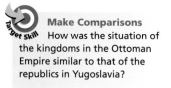

Make Comparisons How was the situation of the kingdoms in the Ottoman Empire similar to that of the republics in Yugoslavia?

Though one nation, Yugoslavia was divided into smaller units called republics. These republics included Serbia, Montenegro, Croatia, Bosnia and Herzegovina, Slovenia, and Macedonia. In each of those republics, one ethnic group held the majority. Yugoslavia's largest republic was Serbia, peopled by Serbs. This republic held the most power, and ran the national government. Other republics, in which Serbs were not the majority, did not always support the government. Resentment against the government grew, along with ethnic conflict among peoples.

The Communist Era During World War II, Germany and Italy occupied Yugoslavia. Josip Broz Tito led the Yugoslav fight against Germany. When the war ended in 1945, Tito became head of the government and changed Yugoslavia into a communist state. Yugoslavia became a firm ally and trade partner of the Soviet Union.

At first, Tito modeled his government after that of the Soviet Union. After a few years, however, he wanted to develop his own government and economic policies. For example, he wanted to maintain trading relations with Western countries in order to strengthen Yugoslavia's economy. This put him in conflict with the Soviet dictator, Joseph Stalin, who broke many ties with Yugoslavia in 1948.

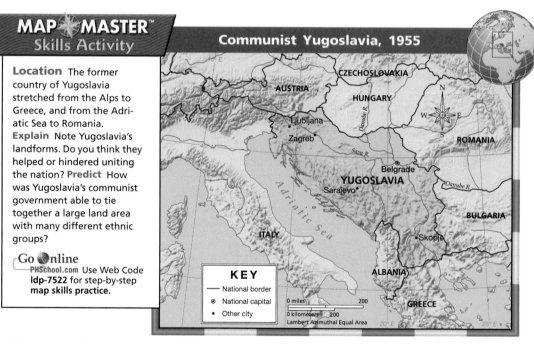

MAP MASTER Skills Activity

Communist Yugoslavia, 1955

Location The former country of Yugoslavia stretched from the Alps to Greece, and from the Adriatic Sea to Romania. **Explain** Note Yugoslavia's landforms. Do you think they helped or hindered uniting the nation? **Predict** How was Yugoslavia's communist government able to tie together a large land area with many different ethnic groups?

Go Online PHSchool.com Use Web Code ldp-7522 for step-by-step map skills practice.

KEY
— National border
⊛ National capital
• Other city

0 miles 200
0 kilometers 200
Lambert Azimuthal Equal Area

184 Europe and Russia

Differentiated Instruction

For Special Needs Students L1
Pair these students with more proficient readers and have them complete the DK Atlas of the World activity *Reading a Political Map*. Then have them use what they learned to help them analyze the map on this page.

All in One **Europe and Russia Teaching Resources,** *DK Compact Atlas of the World Activity: Reading a Political Map*, p. 343

Tito continued to rule Yugoslavia according to communist principles, but he also had good relations with anti-communist nations. For several years, the economy under Tito grew strongly. Tito's strong government also unified Yugoslavia by reducing tensions among ethnic groups. During Tito's time, people began to identify themselves as citizens of a united Yugoslavia.

Yugoslavia Begins to Splinter After Tito's death in 1980, politicians from various ethnic groups struggled for power. They encouraged their followers to once again identify strongly with their own ethnic group. People began to think of themselves less and less as citizens of Yugoslavia.

✓ **Reading Check** What event caused Yugoslavia to splinter?

Yugoslavia Breaks Up

Yugoslavia's problems continued to worsen through the 1980s. In 1989, communism began to crumble in Eastern Europe. Yugoslavia had an unstable government and economy. Many people blamed the Serbs, who still held most of the power in the government. Some republics wanted to govern themselves. In some cases, political change happened almost peacefully. In others, bitter civil wars erupted.

Slovenia and Croatia In 1990, Slovenes and Croats began to pull away from Yugoslavia. That year, the leaders of Slovenia issued a new constitution in which they said they had the right to secede from, or leave, the state of Yugoslavia. Meanwhile, the Yugoslav army threatened to take territory from the republic of Croatia. This alarmed Slovenes and Croats, but also strengthened their desire for independence.

A Croat was elected the new president of Yugoslavia in May 1991. However, Serbia refused to accept the new president. This was the last straw for Slovenia and Croatia. Both republics declared their independence. Serb forces briefly tried to prevent Slovenia from seceding. But soon Serbia recognized the country's independence.

In contrast, war erupted in Croatia. The Serbs attacked Croatian cities. They used terror to drive out the people. This led the United Nations to become involved. In an effort to restore peace, the UN sent peacekeepers to the area and imposed an embargo against Serbia and Montenegro. An embargo is a ban on trade. But peace could not be reached until conflict in neighboring Bosnia and Herzegovina was settled.

Links Across The World

The UN and NATO When World War II ended, many people feared the outbreak of another world war. To help prevent this, several international groups were formed. The United Nations, whose flag is shown below, is an international group founded in 1945. Its member countries work together to bring about peace and cooperation. The UN has 191 member countries, and its headquarters is located in New York City. NATO, or the North Atlantic Treaty Organization, is a group of nations formed in 1949. Its purpose is to provide its members with defense in case of attack.

Links
Read the **Links Across the World** on this page. Ask students **How do the goals of the UN and NATO differ?** *(The UN works to bring about peace, and NATO provides members with defense in case of attack.)*

Yugoslavia Breaks Up L2

Guided Instruction

■ **Vocabulary Builder** Clarify the high-use word **prevent** before reading.

■ Read Yugoslavia Breaks Up with the class.

■ Discuss with students why Slovenia and Croatia seceded from Yugoslavia. *(The Yugoslav army threatened to take territory away from Croatia, and Serbia refused to accept the new Croatian president in 1991, causing resentment in Slovenia and Croatia and leading them to declare independence.)*

■ Ask students **What led to war in Bosnia and Herzegovina?** *(tensions among different ethnic groups)* **Why do you think the United Nations, NATO, and the United States became involved?** *(possible answer: to stop the spread of violence to surrounding areas and to help those who were suffering)*

For English Language Learners L1
Ask students to create lists of nouns and verbs describing the people, things, and actions in each photograph of this section. Have the students write complete sentences describing the events in each picture. If necessary, pair English Language Learners with native speakers for help with writing their sentences.

Answer
✓ **Reading Check** Tito's death in 1980

Show students *Rebuilding Kosovo*. Ask **Why did ethnic Albanians leave Kosovo?** *(The ethnic Albanian majority in Kosovo wanted the province to secede from Serbia because of the increasingly brutal rule of the Serbs, but the Serbs would not relinquish control of Kosovo. Years of guerilla war followed, during which many ethnic Albanians were driven from their homes.)*

Guided Instruction (continued)

■ Ask **Why did tensions increase between Serbs and Albanians in Kosovo?** *(In 1989, Yugoslavian president Slobodan Milosevic took away many freedoms from Albanians in Kosovo.)* **What did Slobodan Milosevic do to try to end the Albanian uprising in Kosovo?** *(He had Serb forces attack Albanians, destroy their homes and villages, and drive thousands of Albanians from their homes.)*

■ Discuss the changes made to Macedonia's constitution. *(The new constitution made Albanian an official language, increased Albanians' access to government jobs, and removed language that had made Albanians second-class citizens.)*

Independent Practice

Have students continue to add dates and events to their timelines.

Monitor Progress

Circulate to make sure students are selecting appropriate dates for their timelines. Provide assistance as needed.

Answer

Infer Possible answer: Tito had helped to unify Yugoslavia and reduced tension among ethnic groups.

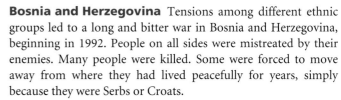

Learn about the rebuilding of Kosovo.

Peace Rally in Sarajevo
Before war broke out in 1992, people in Bosnia and Herzegovina held a peace rally. Some of them displayed a picture of Tito. **Infer** *Why might people have used images of Tito to support their drive for peace?*

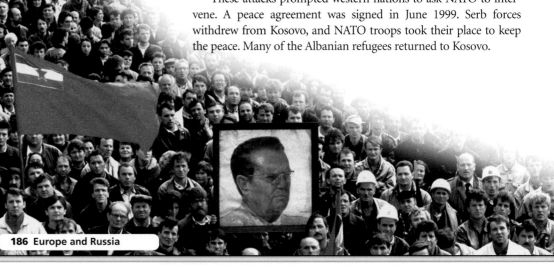

186 Europe and Russia

Bosnia and Herzegovina Tensions among different ethnic groups led to a long and bitter war in Bosnia and Herzegovina, beginning in 1992. People on all sides were mistreated by their enemies. Many people were killed. Some were forced to move away from where they had lived peacefully for years, simply because they were Serbs or Croats.

As you have read, during the war much of Sarajevo, the capital of Bosnia and Herzegovina, was destroyed. Homes and schools were bombed. People were shot as they tried to go about their daily business. Serb armies cut Sarajevo off from the rest of the world. People ran out of food and other necessities.

In 1993, the United Nations began sending troops and supplies to the city. In 1995, NATO forces joined the fighting. Finally, peace talks took place. In 1995, the United States played a key role in getting the Serbs, Croats, and Bosniaks to sign a peace treaty in Dayton, Ohio.

Serbia: Crisis in Kosovo Conflict also broke out in the Serbian province of Kosovo. The population of Kosovo is about 90 percent Albanian. In the old Yugoslavia, Albanians in Kosovo were autonomous, or able to make many decisions for themselves. That situation changed dramatically.

In 1989, Yugoslavian President Slobodan Milosevic (SLOH boh dawn mih LOH suh vich) wanted to increase Serbia's power. He took away Kosovo's freedoms. Tensions between Serbs and Albanians in Kosovo increased, and many Albanians began rebelling against Serbian rule. In the late 1990s, Milosevic tried to end the uprising. Serb forces attacked Albanians in Kosovo. They destroyed homes and villages, forcing thousands of Albanians to become refugees.

These attacks prompted western nations to ask NATO to intervene. A peace agreement was signed in June 1999. Serb forces withdrew from Kosovo, and NATO troops took their place to keep the peace. Many of the Albanian refugees returned to Kosovo.

Background: Biography

Josip Broz Tito (1892–1980) Josip Broz Tito was born in what is now the country of Croatia. While serving in the Austro-Hungarian army during World War I, he was captured by Russians and placed in a prisoner-of-war camp. It was there that Tito was introduced to communism. After he returned to what was then called the Kingdom of the Serbs, Croats, and Slov- enes, he joined the Communist Party of Yugoslavia. As leader of Yugoslavia after World War II, Tito moved the country along an independent path called "non-alignment." He resisted the influence of both the Soviet Union and Western countries during the Cold War.

Macedonia Macedonia declared its independence from Yugoslavia in 1991. From the beginning, ethnic conflict was a problem in the new country. Tensions existed between ethnic Macedonians and ethnic Albanians, who make up a large minority of the population.

Albanians began demanding a number of reforms. The call for reform erupted into violence in 2001. Clashes between ethnic Albanians and the Macedonian military lasted seven months. This prompted fears of another war in the Balkans. A peace agreement was reached after the involvement of NATO.

Soon, Macedonia adopted a new constitution. It made Albanian an official language of the nation. It increased Albanians' access to government jobs. Most important, it removed language in the constitution that had made Albanians second-class citizens.

Ethnic Albanians in Macedonia demand more rights in 2004.

✓ **Reading Check** To which ethnic group do most of the people of Kosovo belong?

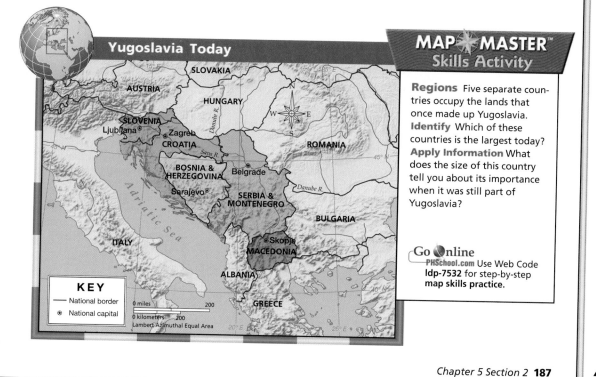

Yugoslavia Today

KEY
— National border
⊛ National capital

0 miles 200
0 kilometers 200
Lambert Azimuthal Equal Area

MAP★MASTER™
Skills Activity

Regions Five separate countries occupy the lands that once made up Yugoslavia.
Identify Which of these countries is the largest today?
Apply Information What does the size of this country tell you about its importance when it was still part of Yugoslavia?

Go Online
PHSchool.com Use Web Code **ldp-7532** for step-by-step map skills practice.

Differentiated Instruction

For Gifted and Talented **L3**
Encourage students to learn more about conflicts among ethnic groups by completing the Internet activity *Genocide in the Balkans*. Have students work in small groups to answer the Analyzing a Reading questions.

Go Online
PHSchool.com **For:** Environmental and Global Issues: *Genocide in the Balkans*
Visit: PHSchool.com
Web Code: ldd-7506

The Region's Future **L2**

Guided Instruction
- Read The Region's Future with the class.
- Ask students **How did the United States and Europe show their disapproval of Slobodan Milosevic?** (*They placed economic sanctions on Yugoslavia.*)
- Ask students **What is the former Yugoslavia now called?** (*Serbia and Montenegro*)
- Discuss with students the problems Balkan nations face in the future. (*They must confront economic problems and overcome a history of ethnic conflict and war.*)

Independent Practice
Have students continue to add dates and events to their timelines.

Monitor Progress
- Show *Section Reading Support Transparency ER 49* and ask students to check their graphic organizers individually. Go over key concepts and clarify key vocabulary as needed. Provide assistance if necessary.

  📖 **Europe and Russia Transparencies,** *Section Reading Support Transparency ER 49*

- Tell students to fill in the last column of their *Reading Readiness Guides*. Probe for what they learned that confirms or invalidates each statement.

  All in One Europe and Russia Teaching Resources, *Reading Readiness Guide,* p. 318

Answers

✓ **Reading Check** Most of the people of Kosovo are Albanians.

MAP★MASTER™ *Skills Activity* **Identify** Serbia and Montenegro **Apply Information** The people of Serbia and Montenegro probably held significant influence when it was part of Yugoslavia.

Go Online
PHSchool.com Students may practice their map skills using the interactive online version of this map.

Assess and Reteach

Assess Progress `L2`

Have students complete the Section Assessment. Administer the *Section Quiz*.

All in One **Europe and Russia Teaching Resources,** *Section Quiz*, p. 320

Reteach `L1`

If students need more instruction, have them read this section in the Reading and Vocabulary Study Guide.

Chapter 5, Section 2, **Europe and Russia Reading and Vocabulary Study Guide,** pp. 61–63

Extend `L3`

Extend students' understanding of conflict in the Balkans by having them complete the *Enrichment* activity about the destruction of Sarajevo. Ask students to work together in small groups to complete the project.

All in One **Europe and Russia Teaching Resources,** *Enrichment,* p. 333

Answer

✔ Reading Check The people of the Balkans are still overcoming ethnic tensions and must resolve economic problems resulting from the conflicts and wars in the region.

Section 2 Assessment

Key Terms
Students' sentences should reflect an understanding of each Key Term.

↻ Target Reading Skill
Answers will vary but should be supported with details from the section.

Comprehension and Critical Thinking
1. (a) Serbia and Montenegro, Bosnia and Herzegovina, Macedonia, Croatia, and Slovenia **(b)** People of these nations speak different languages, practice different religions, and include different ethnic groups.

2. (a) the Ottoman Empire **(b)** Yugoslavia was created in 1918 and turned to communism in 1945 when Tito came to power after World War II. **(c)** The collapse of communism led to an unstable government and economy. People of some republics resented the Serbian-controlled government and wanted to rule themselves.

Business has picked up at markets like this one in Slovenia.

The Region's Future

Although peace treaties were signed and several republics in the region gained independence, trouble did not end. Tensions between different ethnic groups still existed. The United States and Europe held Slobodan Milosevic responsible for the violence that had occurred in the region. To show their disapproval, they placed economic sanctions on Yugoslavia. **Economic sanctions** are actions to limit trade with nations that have violated international laws.

In 2000, Yugoslavia held new presidential elections. Milosevic was defeated, and then arrested by the new government. He was put on trial for war crimes by the court of the United Nations. The United States and European nations promised to lift the sanctions against Yugoslavia. In 2003, the two remaining republics of Yugoslavia—Serbia and Montenegro—decided they would no longer call themselves Yugoslavia. Today, the country is known as Serbia and Montenegro. However, many people in Montenegro want to be independent of Serbia.

What lies ahead for these nations in the Balkans? The destruction that occurred in the 1990s has left the region's population of more than 50 million with deep economic problems. These countries hope to move toward peace and stability, but they will have to overcome a history of ethnic conflict and war.

✔ Reading Check **What problems face people of the Balkans today?**

★ Section 2 Assessment

Key Terms
Review the key terms at the beginning of this section. Use each term in a sentence that explains its meaning.

↻ Target Reading Skill
Compare the histories of these five nations.

Comprehension and Critical Thinking
1. (a) List Which five Balkan nations used to make up the country of Yugoslavia?
(b) Contrast What differences exist among the people of these five nations today?

2. (a) Note Which foreign power ruled the Balkans for hundreds of years?
(b) Sequence When was Yugoslavia created? When did its government turn to communism?
(c) Synthesize Information How did the collapse of communism affect Yugoslavia?
3. (a) Identify Who did the United States and European nations hold responsible for the violence in the Balkans?
(b) Identify Effects How did these nations show their disapproval of Yugoslavia's president?

Writing Activity
Choose one of the Balkan nations discussed in this section. What do you think is the most important challenge facing this nation in the future? Write a paragraph that explains why.

For: An activity on the Dayton peace accord
Visit: PHSchool.com
Web Code: ldd-7502

188 Europe and Russia

---

3. (a) the Yugoslavian president, Slobodan Milosevic **(b)** The nations placed economic sanctions on Yugoslavia. Milosevic was then defeated in the 2000 election and the United Nations tried him for war crimes.

Writing Activity
Use the *Rubric for Assessing a Writing Assignment* to evaluate students' paragraphs.

All in One **Europe and Russia Teaching Resources,** *Rubric for Assessing a Writing Assignment,* p. 350

Go Online PHSchool.com Typing in the Web code when prompted will bring students to detailed instructions for this activity.

Section 3 Ukraine
Independence and Beyond

Prepare to Read

Objectives
In this section you will
1. Understand how Ukraine's history has been shaped by foreign rule.
2. Explain the major issues that Ukrainians have faced since independence.
3. Describe life in Ukraine today.

Taking Notes
As you read this section, look for ways in which the natural resources of Ukraine have shaped its history. Copy the flowchart below and record your findings in it.

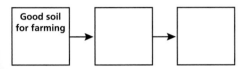

Good soil for farming → ☐ → ☐

Target Reading Skill

Compare and Contrast
One way to understand a nation's history is to compare and contrast different times in its history. When you compare, you look at similarities between things. When you contrast, you look at differences. As you read this section, compare and contrast life in Ukraine before and after independence.

Key Terms
- **chernozem** (CHEHR nuh zem) *n.* rich, black soil
- **collective** (kuh LEK tiv) *n.* a huge government-controlled farm

---

Objectives
Social Studies
1. Understand how Ukraine's history has been shaped by foreign rule.
2. Explain the major issues that Ukrainians have faced since independence.
3. Describe life in Ukraine today.

Reading/Language Arts
Compare and contrast different points in history to understand how a nation has changed over time.

Prepare to Read

Build Background Knowledge ▣L2
Tell students that in this section they will learn about Ukraine, a country that became independent in 1991. Have them preview the section by glancing at headings, Key Terms, and visuals with this question in mind: **How did Ukraine change after gaining independence?** Use the Think-Write-Pair-Share participation strategy (TE, p. T36) to help students brainstorm.

Set a Purpose for Reading ▣L2
- Preview the Objectives.
- Read each statement in the *Reading Readiness Guide* aloud. Ask students to mark the statements true or false.

  All in One Europe and Russia Teaching Resources, *Reading Readiness Guide,* p. 322

- Have students discuss the statements in pairs or groups of four, then mark their guides again. Use the Numbered Heads participation strategy (TE, p. T36) to call on students to share their group's perspectives.

Vocabulary Builder
Preview Key Terms ▣L2
Pronounce each Key Term, then ask the students to say the word with you. Provide a simple explanation such as, "Much of Ukraine is covered with chernozem, a rich soil good for growing crops."

How many people, linked hand-to-hand, would it take to cover 300 miles (483 kilometers)? The people of Ukraine can tell you, because they did it in 1990. It took about 500,000 Ukrainians to make a human chain that long. It stretched from Kiev, Ukraine's capital, to the city of L'viv (luh VEEF). The chain was a symbol of protest against the Soviet Union's control of Ukraine. It also showed that Ukrainians know how to work together to solve their problems. Today, the people of Ukraine are enjoying their independence and are working hard for a better future.

Ukrainians form a human chain.

Target Reading Skill ▣L2

Compare and Contrast Explain that students can compare and contrast different periods in a country's history to see how it has changed over time.

Model the skill by reading Supplying the Soviets on p. 191 and comparing and contrasting industry before and after the Soviet Union took control of Ukraine. *(Industry grew after the Soviet Union took control of Ukraine.)*

Give students *Compare and Contrast*. Have them complete the activity in groups.

All in One Europe and Russia Teaching Resources, *Compare and Contrast,* p. 329

Instruct

COUNTRY PROFILE
Focus on Economics

Guided Instruction · L2
Ask students to study the map and charts on this page. Have students work in pairs to answer the Map and Chart Skills questions and then discuss the answers as a class.

Independent Practice
Have students work with a partner to display the leading import and export partners information in the form of circle graphs. Then have each student write a few sentences explaining which format they think shows the information more clearly and why.

COUNTRY PROFILE   Focus on Economics

Ukraine
When Ukraine became independent in 1991, it faced economic hardship. The Soviet Union had controlled Ukraine's economy. Ukraine's new leaders had no experience with capitalism, and the country had no free markets for its products. After a slow, painful transition, Ukraine's economy began to strengthen. Still, Ukraine's economy relies heavily on Russia as a trade partner. Study the map and graphs to learn more about Ukraine's economy today.

Ukraine: Agricultural Products and Land Use — KEY
- Forestry
- Livestock raising
- Commercial farming
- National border
- National capital
- Other city
- Wheat · Root crops · Sunflowers · Vineyards · Cattle · Sheep · Hogs

0 miles 200 / 0 kilometers 200 / Lambert Azimuthal Equal Area

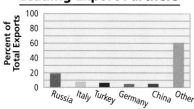
Leading Export Partners
Percent of Total Exports — Russia, Italy, Turkey, Germany, China, Other
Export Partner
SOURCE: CIA World Factbook Online, 2003

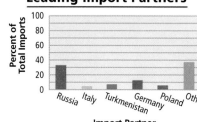
Leading Import Partners
Percent of Total Imports — Russia, Italy, Turkmenistan, Germany, Poland, Other
Import Partner
SOURCE: CIA World Factbook Online, 2003

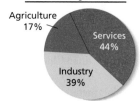
Structure of the Economy, 2002
Agriculture 17%, Services 44%, Industry 39%
SOURCE: The World Bank Group

Map and Chart Skills
1. **Locate** In what regions of Ukraine is land used for forestry?
2. **Synthesize Information** In 2002, what percentage of Ukraine's economy did agriculture make up? How much of Ukraine's land is used for this purpose?
3. **Make Inferences** Why do you think Ukraine exchanges more exports and imports with Russia than with its other trade partners?

 Use Web Code ldp-7513 for DK World Desk Reference Online.

190 Europe and Russia

Answers
Map and Chart Skills
1. in the west and the north
2. 17 percent; nearly all of Ukraine's land
3. because Russia controlled Ukraine's economy prior to 1991

Go Online PHSchool.com Students can find more information about this topic on the DK World Desk Reference Online.

Vocabulary Builder
Use the information below to teach students this section's high-use words.

High-Use Word	Definition and Sample Sentence
consume, p. 191	v. to eat, drink, or use something up. My new car **consumes** less gasoline than my old one.
publish, p. 193	v. to print. Paul was excited that his first book was about to be **published**.
contaminate, p. 194	v. to pollute. The oil spill **contaminated** three miles of beach.
produce, p. 195	n. something grown on a farm, such as fruits or vegetables. The **produce** section has very nice tomatoes today.

190

A History of Occupation

For hundreds of years, Ukraine was ruled by its more powerful neighbors. You can see how this happened if you look at Ukraine's location on the map on page 165. This huge land lies between Russia and the other nations of Europe. In fact, the name Ukraine means "borderland." Look at the political map of Eastern Europe and Russia at the beginning of this chapter. Notice that to the west of Ukraine are Poland, Slovakia, and Hungary. To the east of Ukraine is Russia. The map makes it easy to see why Ukraine has been open to invasion by its neighbors.

Location has been only part of the problem. The other problem has been Ukraine's vast natural resources. These resources have attracted invaders. At one time or another, Poland, Czechoslovakia, and Romania have occupied areas of Ukraine. During World War II, the German army invaded Ukraine to gain access to its natural resources. Russia has been the most difficult neighbor of all, however. Russia, and later the Soviet Union, ruled Ukraine between the late 1700s and 1991.

Supplying the Soviets Under Soviet rule, Ukrainian industries grew. In time, factories in Ukraine were making nearly 20 percent of the Soviet Union's goods. Ukraine produced much of the equipment for the Soviet armed forces. And Ukrainian mines supplied much of the iron ore, coal, and other minerals for Soviet industries.

The Soviets used other Ukrainian resources as well. Ships used Ukraine's ports on the Black Sea to bring goods into and out of the Soviet Union. Several of Ukraine's rivers reach like highways into other countries. The Soviets made use of these rivers to ship goods.

Because Ukraine was one of Europe's largest grain-producing regions, it became known as the breadbasket of Europe. Why is Ukraine's farmland so productive? More than half of the country is covered by a rich, black soil called **chernozem** (CHEHR nuh zem). When the Soviet Union took control of Ukraine in 1922, Ukrainian farmers were forced to supply the rest of the Soviet Union with food. By the end of the 1980s, they were producing one fourth of the grain and meat consumed by the Soviet Union.

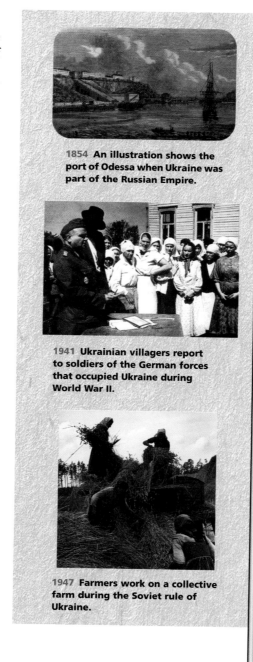

1854 An illustration shows the port of Odessa when Ukraine was part of the Russian Empire.

1941 Ukrainian villagers report to soldiers of the German forces that occupied Ukraine during World War II.

1947 Farmers work on a collective farm during the Soviet rule of Ukraine.

Guided Instruction

- **Vocabulary Builder** Clarify the high-use word **consume** before reading.

- Read A History of Occupation, using the Choral Reading strategy (TE, p. T34).

- Ask students **What are two main reasons Ukraine has been invaded frequently?** (*Ukraine's location between Russia and the countries of Eastern Europe leaves it open to invasion by its neighbors; its rich supply of natural resources also has made it attractive to invading countries.*)

- Ask students **How was the Ukrainian economy affected when it was part of the Soviet Union?** (*Ukrainian farms supplied the rest of the Soviet Union with food; Ukrainian industries grew because they supplied about twenty percent of the Soviet Union's goods. However, the Soviet Union collectivized farmland in Ukraine, causing poverty and starvation in the 1930s.*)

- Have students discuss how Ukrainians might have felt about becoming part of the Soviet Union. (*Answers will vary, but students may note that although the Soviet Union presented Ukraine with a large marketplace for its goods and natural resources, many Ukrainians, especially farmers, probably resented Soviet rule.*)

Independent Practice

Ask students to create the Taking Notes graphic organizer on a blank piece of paper. As students read, have them fill in their flowcharts with information about Ukraine's natural resources. Briefly model how to identify which information to record.

Monitor Progress

Circulate to make sure individuals are filling in their graphic organizers correctly. Provide assistance as needed.

Differentiated Instruction

For English Language Learners L2
Pair English language learners with native English speakers to complete *Guided Reading and Review.* Have Spanish speakers complete *Guided Reading and Review (Spanish)*.

All in One **Europe and Russia Teaching Resources,** *Guided Reading and Review,* p. 323

Guided Reading and Review, **Europe and Russia Spanish Support,** p. 48

For Special Needs Students L1
Have students read the section as they listen to the recorded version on the Student Edition on Audio CD. Check for comprehension by pausing the CD and asking students to share their answers to the Reading Checks.

⊚ Chapter 5, Section 3, **Student Edition on Audio CD**

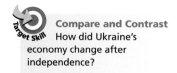

Target Reading Skill [L2]

Compare and Contrast As a follow up, ask students to answer the Target Reading Skill question in the Student Edition. *(Before independence, Ukraine's industries and resources were controlled by the Soviets. Ukrainian farmers were forced to work on collective farms. After independence, Ukrainian farms and businesses were no longer controlled by the government, so people had to start producing consumer goods and redistribute farmland to improve agricultural production.)*

Independence Brings Challenges [L2]

Guided Instruction

- **Vocabulary Builder** Clarify the high-use words **publish** and **contaminate** before reading.

- Read Independence Brings Challenges with students. As students read, circulate and make sure individuals can answer the Reading Check question.

- Ask students **What steps has Ukraine taken to strengthen its economy since independence?** *(Ukrainians had to learn how to start new businesses, produce new goods and keep prices under control, and improve their agricultural production by breaking up Soviet-era collectives.)*

Answers

✓ **Reading Check** The Soviets used Ukraine's ports and rivers to ship goods into and out of the Soviet Union.

Compare and Contrast Similarity—Both pictures show a busy port; difference—the photo shows more industry than the illustration.

192

Compare and Contrast How did Ukraine's economy change after independence?

Odessa—A Thriving Seaport In the 1800s and 1900s, huge quantities of grain were shipped from Odessa to Russia and later the Soviet Union. Today, the city is a major port and a center of Ukrainian industry. **Compare and Contrast** *Compare this photo with the illustration of Odessa on page 191. What similarities and differences do you see?*

192 Europe and Russia

Collectives Bring Starvation To produce all of this grain and meat, Soviet rulers took land away from farmers and created huge government-controlled farms called **collectives.** Most farmers were forced to become workers on these collectives. Other farmers were sent to cities to work in the new factories. All the crops from the collectives went to the government. The people who worked the land were allowed to keep very little of the food they grew. As a result, millions of Ukrainians died of hunger in the 1930s. Over the years, however, life improved on the farms.

✓ **Reading Check** For what purpose did the Soviets use Ukraine's ports and rivers?

Independence Brings Challenges

In 1991, Ukraine won its independence from the Soviet Union. After centuries of foreign rule, the new country now had to decide many important issues for itself.

Building an Independent Economy One of the first issues Ukrainians had to decide was how to build up their economy. Like people in other former Soviet republics, Ukrainians had to learn how to start new businesses. They also needed to learn how to make consumer goods and keep prices under control. Finally, they had to improve their agricultural production by breaking up the inefficient collective farm system put in place by the Soviets.

Differentiated Instruction

For Gifted and Talented [L3]

Have students work in groups to compose a letter to the local power company asking whether the company obtains power from a nuclear plant and, if so, what measures the power company has taken to ensure that the plant does not have an accident similar to the one at Chernobyl.

Choosing a Language Ukrainians also had to restore their culture. Under Soviet rule, the official language of Ukraine was Russian. Books and newspapers were published only in Russian, and schools used Russian textbooks. As a result, many Ukrainians speak only Russian, especially in the cities and in the eastern part of the nation. Russian is also the language of ethnic Russians, who make up about one fifth of the population. The Ukrainian language is widely spoken only in rural areas and in the western part of the nation.

With independence, Ukrainian was made the official language. Many of the people of Ukraine believe that speaking Ukrainian could tie the country together and free Ukraine from its Soviet past. Elementary and secondary schools have begun using Ukrainian, though Russian is also still used in high schools. Most Ukrainians are pleased about the change. One teacher said, "Language is the anchor of our independence."

A Ukrainian Classroom
Elementary school students sit in class on their first day of school. **Analyze Images** *Besides language, what other cultural traditions are important to Ukrainians?*

Guided Instruction (continued)

- Have students explain why Ukrainian became the official language of Ukraine after independence. *(Despite the fact that many Ukrainians spoke only Russian, having Ukrainian as the official language unified the country and distanced it from the Soviet era.)*

- Ask students **How did the disaster at Chernobyl in 1986 affect Ukraine?** *(Many people died or were injured, more than 100,000 people had to move because the area was no longer safe, soil and water were poisoned, and 32,000 acres of farmland were contaminated. Ukraine is still working to repair the damage.)*

- Ask **Which of the three challenges you have just read about—strengthening the economy, establishing a national language, or cleaning up Chernobyl—probably presents the greatest challenge to Ukrainians today? Why?** *(Answers will vary, but opinions should be supported with evidence from the text.)*

Independent Practice
Assign *Guided Reading and Review.*

All in One **Europe and Russia Teaching Resources,** *Guided Reading and Review*, p. 323

Monitor Progress
Provide students with assistance as they fill in the worksheet.

Differentiated Instruction

For Advanced Readers L3
Have students learn more about the Chernobyl disaster by completing the *Small Group Activity: Chernobyl: Report on a Disaster.*

All in One **Europe and Russia Teaching Resources,** *Small Group Activity: Chernobyl: Report on a Disaster*, pp. 335–338

Answers
Analyze Images Students may say that education is important to Ukrainians.

Life in Ukraine L2

Guided Instruction

- **Vocabulary Builder** Clarify the high-use word **produce** before reading.

- Have students read Life in Ukraine.

- Ask students to compare and contrast economic life in Ukraine before and after the transition to independence. *(Before 1991, certain magazines and newspapers did not exist; farmers were not allowed to own their own farms.)*

- Ask students to make a prediction about the future of Ukraine. *(Students may suggest that life in Ukraine will continue to improve due to new freedoms and many natural resources.)*

Independent Practice

Have students complete their graphic organizers.

Monitor Progress

- Show *Section Reading Support Transparency ER 50* and ask students to check their graphic organizers individually.

  📖 **Europe and Russia Transparencies,** *Section Reading Support Transparency ER 50*

- Tell students to fill in the last column of their *Reading Readiness Guides.*

  All in One **Europe and Russia Teaching Resources,** *Reading Readiness Guide,* p. 322

Links

Read the **Links to Science** on this page. Ask students to describe in their own words how nuclear energy is produced. *(Answers will vary, but students should accurately explain the process in their own words.)*

Answers

✓ **Reading Check** Traces of dangerous materials from the explosion were found all over the world; much of Ukraine's soil, water, and farmland is still contaminated.

194

Learn about the after-effects of Chernobyl.

Links to Science

Creating Nuclear Power
Nuclear power is produced from a metal called uranium. The central part of an atom is called the nucleus. To create energy, the uranium nucleus is split in a process called nuclear fission. This splitting releases heat, which turns water into steam. The steam turns large machines called generators, which produce electricity. When nuclear power is made, radioactive waste is produced. The waste must be carefully stored, because radioactive materials are dangerous to people. If the process of making nuclear power is not tightly controlled, too much heat can destroy the reactor and the entire building that contains it, as happened at Chernobyl. Then radioactive materials can escape into the air. The photo at the right shows a town near Chernobyl after the explosion.

194 Europe and Russia

Recovering From Chernobyl Ukraine is still recovering from a terrible event that occurred during the Soviet period. It became one of the most difficult issues Ukraine has had to face since it gained independence.

Under Soviet rule, Ukrainians built five nuclear power plants. These supply about one third of the country's electricity. The Chernobyl (chehr NOH bul) nuclear plant is located 65 miles (105 kilometers) from the city of Kiev. In 1986, an explosion caused by carelessness rocked the Chernobyl plant. Radioactive materials filled the air. Some people died within days or weeks. Others developed serious health problems that killed them slowly or left them suffering. More than 100,000 people had to be moved out of the area. It was no longer safe to live there. In later years, traces of the dangerous materials released at Chernobyl were found all over the world.

Even today, much of Ukraine's soil and water are still poisoned. More than 32,000 square miles of farmland are contaminated. Some towns and farms remain abandoned. With the help of other nations, the Ukrainians are cleaning up the dangerous materials around Chernobyl, but it may take as long as a hundred years to repair the damage.

✓ **Reading Check** **What are the far-reaching effects of Chernobyl?**

Background: Links Across Place

Three Mile Island The most serious nuclear accident in American history occurred on March 28, 1979 just south of Harrisburg, Pennsylvania. At 4:00 AM, a failure in the cooling system at the Three Mile Island nuclear plant caused a minor leak of radioactive gas. Despite the fact that the health risk was small, thousands living near the plant fled. Though much less serious than the Chernobyl disaster in 1986, the accident at Three Mile Island raised the American public's awareness of the danger of nuclear energy. The Three Mile Island accident caused an increasing number of people to oppose the construction of new nuclear plants.

Life in Ukraine

Independence has brought changes to life in Ukraine. For example, the Kreshchatik (kresh CHAH tik), the main street in Kiev, is often jammed with people. Along this street are many parks, stores, and restaurants. People sell ice cream and pyrohy (pih ROH hee), dumplings filled with vegetables, cheese, or fruit. Newsstands are filled with magazines and newspapers, many of which have been published only since independence. At local markets, farmers sell cheese or produce from their own farms.

Other Ukrainian cities are also alive with the new spirit of freedom. East of Kiev is the city of Kharkiv. Located near huge reserves of iron ore and coal, it is the busiest industrial center in the nation. But Kharkiv is not all work. It is also a vibrant cultural area, where people can attend plays or concerts.

Ukraine is in the early stages of an exciting time in its history. The people have always wanted freedom, and now they have it in their grasp. They know that independence is not easy. But with the land's great resources and the people's ability to work together, the Ukrainians have the ability to make independence succeed.

Vendors sell souvenirs in front of a Roman Catholic church in Kiev.

✓ **Reading Check** What is Ukraine's busiest industrial center?

⭐ Section 3 Assessment

Key Terms
Review the key terms at the beginning of this section. Use each term in a sentence that explains its meaning.

🎯 Target Reading Skill
Describe education in Ukraine before and after independence.

Comprehension and Critical Thinking
1. (a) Identify Who controlled Ukraine until 1991?
(b) Find the Main Idea What uses were made of Ukraine's resources?

(c) Predict Now that Ukraine is not supplying another country with its resources, how might that affect its economy?
2. (a) Explain What issues faced Ukraine after independence?
(b) Identify Point of View How might ethnic Russians have reacted when Ukrainian was made the official language?
3. (a) Describe What changes has independence brought to Ukrainian life?
(b) Contrast How was life different in Ukraine before independence?

Writing Activity
Suppose you are a newspaper writer in Ukraine in 1991. Write a short article that describes the views of the people as they start life in an independent country. Be sure to include the views of both Ukrainians and ethnic Russians.

For: An activity on Chernobyl
Visit: PHSchool.com
Web Code: ldd-7503

Assess Progress L2
Have students complete the Section Assessment. Then administer the *Section Quiz*.

📘 **All in One Europe and Russia Teaching Resources,** *Section Quiz,* p. 324

Reteach L1
If students need more instruction, have them read this section in the Reading and Vocabulary Study Guide.

📖 Chapter 5, Section 3, **Europe and Russia Reading and Vocabulary Study Guide,** pp. 64–66

Extend L3
Have students learn more about nuclear power by completing the Internet activity *Using Nuclear Power*. After studying the table, students should answer the questions in pairs or small groups.

Go Online PHSchool.com **For:** Environmental and Global Issues: *Using Nuclear Power*
Visit: PHSchool.com
Web Code: ldd-7507

Answer

✓ **Reading Check** Kharkiv

Writing Activity
Use the *Rubric for Assessing a Newspaper Article* to evaluate students' articles.

📘 **All in One Europe and Russia Teaching Resources,** *Rubric for Assessing a Newspaper Article,* p. 348

Go Online PHSchool.com Typing in the Web code when prompted will bring students to detailed instructions for this activity.

Section 3 Assessment

Key Terms
Students' sentences should reflect an understanding of each Key Term.

🎯 Target Reading Skill
After independence, elementary and secondary schools began teaching in Ukrainian instead of Russian.

Comprehension and Critical Thinking
1. (a) Russia, and later the Soviet Union
(b) The Soviets used Ukraine's natural resources to provide food, goods, minerals, and waterways for transportation.
(c) Answers will vary, but most students will probably suggest that Ukraine's economy will improve because the country now has control over its own resources.

2. (a) After independence, Ukraine needed to build an independent economy and to improve agricultural production. Ukrainians also changed the national language.

(b) Students may suggest that ethnic Russians were fearful that their customs would be forgotten, that they would lose power, or that it would be difficult for them to learn a new language.

3. (a) Ukrainian is now the official language; new magazines and newspapers are being published; farmers at local markets are able to sell produce from their own farms.
(b) Most of Ukraine's resources and farms were controlled by the Soviet Union.

Objective

Learn how to identify frame of reference.

Prepare to Read

Build Background Knowledge L2

Ask students to consider their opinion about the following statement: Students should only have homework two nights a week. Then ask them to consider how teachers would feel about the statement. Explain that the difference in opinion is a matter of frame of reference, or point of view. Tell them that in this lesson they will learn how to identify frame of reference.

Instruct

Identifying Frame of Reference L2

Guided Instruction

■ Read the steps to identifying frame of reference on p. 196 as a class and write them on the board.

■ Complete the Practice the Skill activity on p. 197 together as a class. First identify the main idea of the passage. *(Poland's youth feel it is important for their opinion on the EU to be heard.)* Then discuss the writer's qualifications and experience. *(She is a young woman, so she is part of the Polish youth and may be considered qualified to voice that group's opinion, but we do not know anything about her experience.)*

■ Identify the writer's position *(the opinion of Polish youth on the EU needs to be expressed and heard)*, the tone of the passage *(somewhat forceful and urgent)*, and any emotional language *(words such as demanded)*.

■ Discuss how the writer's age might affect her opinion and why it would be different from the farmer's opinion. *(She is young so her opinion on the EU would probably center around different issues than those of older people who are currently in the workforce. She probably has different concerns than the farmer.)* Finally, put together all

---

> Before Poland joined the European Union, Poles strongly debated the subject. According to 48-year-old Polish farmer Lech Lebedzki, ". . . both of my hands were raised, ready to vote for [it]. . . ." But after hearing that as part of the EU Polish farmers would not receive as much support from the government, he changed his mind. "It's a stab in the back. . . . I will vote against it."

Lebedzki's job as a farmer gave him a certain frame of reference, which influenced his view on EU membership. When you identify a person's frame of reference, you can better understand the influences that shaped his or her position. Writers, for example, may leave information out of an article on purpose to give a stronger argument for their point of view. They may only present one side of the story. Understanding a writer's frame of reference can help you decide whether the writer is a reliable source.

A Polish farmer

Learn the Skill

To identify frame of reference, use the following steps:

1. **Determine the issue.** Read through the passage quickly. What is the main idea?

2. **Look carefully at who the writer is.** What qualifications, if any, does he or she bring to the topic of the passage?

3. **Identify the position taken by the writer.** Look for direct statements of the writer's position. Look also for any emotional language that may give clues to the writer's views. What is the tone, or overall feeling, of the passage? Think about why the writer feels he or she has to write.

4. **Note how the writer's frame of reference may have influenced his or her position on the issue.** Look for connections between who the writer is, the language he or she uses, and the writer's stated position.

5. **Draw a conclusion identifying the writer's position and his or her frame of reference.** Decide whether the writer is giving a reliable picture of the situation.

---

the information that you have learned about Joanna's frame of reference. Write a short paragraph summarizing her frame of reference on the board.

Independent Practice

Assign *Skills for Life* and have students complete it individually.

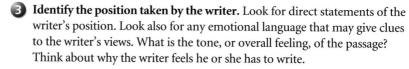 **Europe and Russia Teaching Resources,** *Skills for Life,* p. 334

Monitor Progress

As students are completing *Skills for Life,* circulate to make sure individuals are applying the skill steps effectively. Provide assistance as needed.

Practice the Skill

Use the steps in Learn the Skill to identify frame of reference in the passage at the right.

1. Read through the passage to identify the issue. What main idea does the writer develop in the passage?

2. Look at who the writer is. What qualifications does the writer have that enables her to write the article? Does she have any experience that helps her write the article?

3. What is the writer's position? What is the tone of the passage? Can you find any emotional language in the passage?

4. How might the writer's age affect her viewpoint? Why might her opinion be different from the one expressed by the Polish farmer at the beginning of the previous page?

5. Write a short paragraph explaining the writer's frame of reference.

> Over the months Poland's youth gradually became aware that the issue [of joining the EU] was important to us, because it is we, not our parents, who are going to spend much of our lives in the enlarged EU. Through referenda [votes] and debates in our high schools and universities, we demanded that our voice be heard by those who were longer in the tooth [older]—even though our opinions had no legal value.
>
> —Joanna Margueritte,
> a young Polish woman

The University of Warsaw

> Agricultural production in Poland is now lower than it's been in any time in the last 50 years. . . . The reason is that the European Union and America and other countries have turned Poland into a dumping ground for overproduction. If we are not treated as equals, if the European Union tries to exploit us . . . we will start a propaganda war and make sure that Poles vote No in the referendum. . . .
>
> —Andrzej Lepper, leader of the
> Self Defence Alliance, a Polish
> political party

Apply the Skill

Read the passage at the left. Use the steps above to identify the frame of reference of the writer. Then compare this writer's views with those of the writer at the top of this page. How does the tone differ? How would you compare the writers' purposes? Which of these writers do you think is presenting a more reliable picture of the situation?

Assess Progress   L2

Ask students to do the Apply the Skill activity.

Reteach   L1

If students are having trouble applying the skill steps, have them review the skill using the interactive Social Studies Skills Tutor CD-ROM.

⊙ *Identifying Frame of Reference and Point of View,* **Social Studies Skills Tutor CD-ROM**

Extend   L3

Have students read p. 198 and use the steps they have just learned to determine Yura's frame of reference.

Answers
Apply the Skill

Students should recognize that Lepper's membership in a political party gives him the frame of reference of someone who knows he has the power to influence the vote and is warning that if his terms are not met, he will exercise that power. Lepper's tone is more forceful and threatening than Joanna's. Students may suggest that Lepper is presenting a more reliable picture because he presented a fact at the beginning of his statement and has more political experience.

Differentiated Instruction

For Special Needs Students   L1

Partner special needs students with more proficient readers to do Level 1 of the *Identifying Frame of Reference and Point of View* lesson on the Social Studies Skill Tutor

CD-ROM together. When students feel more confident, they can move onto Level 2 alone.

⊙ *Identifying Frame of Reference and Point of View,* **Social Studies Skills Tutor CD-ROM**

Objectives

Social Studies

1. Investigate the changes that capitalism has brought to Russia.
2. Understand the cultural traditions that have endured throughout Russia.
3. Identify the issues that create challenges for Russians.

Reading/Language Arts

Identify contrasts to find out how two things are different.

Prepare to Read

Build Background Knowledge   L2

Tell students that in this section they will learn about Russia and the changes it underwent when it switched from a communist system to a capitalist one. Show students *Life in the "New" Russia.* Ask students to note the effects a capitalist system has had on Russia's capital city of Moscow. Conduct a Give One, Get One activity (TE, p. T37) to allow students to share their answers.

📼 *Life in the "New" Russia,* **World Studies Video Program**

Set a Purpose for Reading   L2

- Preview the Objectives.

- Read each statement in the *Reading Readiness Guide* aloud. Ask students to mark the statements true or false.

  All in One Europe and Russia Teaching Resources, *Reading Readiness Guide,* p. 326

- Have students discuss the statements in pairs or groups of four, then mark their guides again. Use the Numbered Heads participation strategy (TE, p. T36) to call on students to share their group's perspectives.

Vocabulary Builder

Preview Key Terms   L2

Pronounce each Key Term, then ask the students to say the word with you. Provide a simple explanation such as, "When inflation occurs, things become more expensive."

Prepare to Read

Objectives

In this section you will

1. Investigate the changes that capitalism has brought to Russia.
2. Understand the cultural traditions that have endured throughout Russia.
3. Identify the issues that create challenges for Russians.

Taking Notes

As you read the section, look for details about the changes in Russia since the fall of Soviet communism. Copy the flowchart below and write each detail under the correct heading.

🎯 Target Reading Skill

Identify Contrasts When you contrast two regions, you examine how they are different. In this section you will read about two regions in Russia—Moscow and Siberia. As you read, list the differences between these two regions and ways people live in them.

Key Terms

- **investor** (in VES tur) *n.* someone who spends money on improving a business in the hope of making more money
- **inflation** (in FLAY shun) *n.* an increase in the general level of prices when the amount of goods and services remains the same.

Open-air markets like this one in Perm are a more common sight since the fall of communism.

198 Europe and Russia

In 1991, Yura and Tanya Tabak lived in a tiny one-bedroom apartment in Moscow. Soviet communism had ended. Yura had more freedom to pursue his interest in religious studies. Yet life was difficult for the couple. Their wallpaper was peeling off the walls, and their plumbing didn't always work.

In 2002, the Tabaks had a large, bright apartment filled with goods such as a new television. They had even sent their daughter abroad to study. Yura said, "Sometimes I wake up in the morning and want to pinch myself. . . . Are these things really available to us?"

Yet like many Russians, the Tabaks fear what would happen if one of them were to become ill. Medical care used to be free. Now it is expensive and hard to get. Corruption in business and government is widespread, and the economy is unstable. In Russia, many things have changed—but life is still difficult for most Russians.

🎯 Target Reading Skill   L2

Identify Contrasts Explain that students can contrast two things to find the differences between them.

Model the skill by reading the first two paragraphs on p. 202. Contrast life in Siberia before the fall of the Soviet government with life after the fall. (*Under communist rule, everyone was guaranteed a job, but afterward people had to worry about losing their jobs. Under communist rule people had to live in houses belonging to the state, but afterward people could buy their own homes.*)

Give students *Identify Contrasts.* Have them complete the activity in groups.

All in One Europe and Russia Teaching Resources, *Identify Contrasts,* p. 331

Emerging Capitalism

When the Soviet Union dissolved in 1991, the new Russian Federation—the world's largest country—had to find a new identity for itself. The nation had no experience of democracy, or any laws that supported it. Russian leaders often fought for power within the new government. The new country also struggled to make the transition from communism to a free-market economy.

Moscow, Russia's Capital Moscow is the capital of Russia and the center of its economic activities. It has a population of more than 9 million people. When the Soviet Union first collapsed, business in Moscow boomed. Investors came from many different countries to make money in Moscow. An **investor** is someone who spends money on improving a business in the hope of making more money if the business succeeds.

Some investors became very wealthy. When the first American fast-food chain in Russia opened in Moscow, people lined up in the streets to eat there. The restaurant served 30,000 people on the first day. Ikea, a Swedish furniture store, opened a 250-store mall in Moscow. Russian investors opened 24-hour supermarkets and high-tech companies.

Economic success has not come equally to all Russians. Some Russians have become wealthy because they have influence within the government. For example, a former Soviet official started Russia's largest oil and gas company, Gazprom (GAHS prahm), which is hugely profitable. Other Russians have gained their wealth through corruption.

Explore life in Moscow.

Investment in Moscow
Russia's biggest department store (at the left), built over a hundred years ago in a traditional style, bustles with people and new stores. The modern International Business Center (above) was built in 2001.
Analyze Images *Describe the scene in the department store. Would the scene have been different during Soviet times?*

Show students *Life in the "New" Russia.* Ask **What are the differences between a capitalist and communist system?** *(Possible answer: Under communism, the government controls how goods are produced and how much is produced. Under capitalism, the economy is not controlled by a central authority.)*

Emerging Capitalism L2

Guided Instruction

■ **Vocabulary Builder** Clarify the high-use words **dissolve** and **enforce** before reading.

■ Read Emerging Capitalism using the Paragraph Shrinking strategy (TE, p. T34).

■ Discuss with students the problems Russia faced after the Soviet Union was dissolved in 1991. *(Russia had to find a new identity; its leaders often fought for power; it struggled to make the transition from communism to a free-market economy.)*

■ Ask students **How many people live in Moscow?** *(more than 9 million)* **How did life change in Moscow after the transition to a free-market economy?** *(Many new businesses opened and investors came from everywhere to make money in Moscow. Some investors and former government leaders became very wealthy.)*

Vocabulary Builder

Use the information below to teach students this section's high-use words.

High-Use Word	Definition and Sample Sentence
dissolve, p. 199	*v.* to break up The club **dissolved** after its president quit.
enforce, p. 200	*v.* to cause to be carried out The police help **enforce** our city's laws.
status, p. 203	*n.* the condition of something according to the law His official **status** changed when he became a citizen.
resolve, p. 204	*v.* to find an answer to; to deal with successfully We must **resolve** the disagreement before it leads to a fight.

Answer

Analyze Images The department store is bustling with people; during Soviet times, people probably did not shop at such stores since the government controlled businesses and people did not have access to many goods.

Guided Instruction (continued)

■ Discuss the economic benefits and challenges that ordinary Russians face under capitalism. *(Benefits—Some Russians have been able to start their own businesses, others have opened small factories; some Russians can afford to fix up their apartments and travel abroad. Challenges—Criminal gangs often force money from ordinary business people; in the 1990s bank failures and inflation caused many Russians to lose their life savings.)*

■ Have students describe the region of Siberia. *(It is located in eastern Russia and has rich reserves of coal, gold, iron, oil, and natural gas. During the Soviet era the Trans-Siberian Railroad was built to transport materials from Siberia, and factories and mining operations were started. Much of Siberia is rural, but there are also some large cities.)*

■ Ask students **How has the fall of the Soviet government and the arrival of free enterprise changed life in Siberia?** *(During the Soviet era, mining and factory jobs were guaranteed; farmers were guaranteed certain prices for their crops; now jobs are not guaranteed and people worry about losing their jobs or farms; Siberians can now buy their own homes and make decisions.)*

Independent Practice

Have students create the Taking Notes graphic organizer on a blank piece of paper. Then have them fill it in with details from the section. Briefly model how to identify which details to record using *Transparency B2: Flow Chart.*

📖 **Europe and Russia Transparencies,** *Transparency B2: Flow Chart*

Monitor Progress

Circulate throughout the classroom to ensure that individuals are filling in their flowcharts with the correct information. Provide assistance as needed.

Links

Read the **Links to Art** on this page. Ask **Why do you think Moscow's subway stations are referred to as "underground palaces?"** *(They contain elaborate artwork and architecture similar to what might be found in a palace.)*

200

Links to Art

Art

Moscow's "Underground Palaces" When work on Moscow's subway began in the 1930s, its planners wanted to build more than a comfortable, useful mode of transportation. They also wanted to surround the subway riders with beauty. Architects created palace-like subway stations using more than 20 kinds of marble and other different colored stones. The Kievskaya station, shown below, includes domed ceilings hand-painted by famous artists. Others contain stained-glass windows, murals, and statues. Light reflects off of the colored walls of many stations, filling the halls and brightening the day of many passengers.

200 Europe and Russia

Widespread Corruption Average Russians have been working hard since the collapse of the Soviet government. Many have opened small businesses or factories. Like the Tabaks, more Russians today can afford to fix up their apartments, buy expensive goods, and travel abroad. Yet most Russians still face challenges in their daily lives. Salaries are still low for Russian workers. About 25 percent of all Russians live in poverty.

Corruption is one reason that many Russians have not been able to improve their situations. Criminal gangs often force honest people who own businesses to pay them money. The Russians who own or work in these businesses therefore cannot keep all the money they earn. Laws meant to protect people are often not enforced.

Economic and Health Problems Average Russians also suffer when the economy does not thrive. In the 1990s, large numbers of Russians lost their life savings when banks failed and inflation rose to high levels. **Inflation** is an increase in the general level of prices at a time when the amount of goods and services remains the same. The economy slowly recovered. But some Russians are still working to regain the money they lost years ago.

Finally, as you have read, Russians have major concerns about health care. Life expectancy in Russia is very low for a developed country—just 62 years for men. Hospitals often contain outdated equipment. In some hospitals, patients have to bring their own sheets. Russia's wealthy people can afford better care, but ordinary Russians cannot.

Skills for Life **Skills Mini Lesson**

Recognizing Bias

1. Teach the skill by defining *bias* as a one-sided view. Explain that in determining whether a statement is biased, students should look for false or missing information and for clue words that express emotion instead of fact.

2. Have students practice the skill by determining if the quote by Lech Lebedzki on p. 196 contains bias.

3. Have students apply the skill by analyzing the following statement that could have been made by a former high-ranking Communist party official in the Soviet Union: "We should go back to the way things were before; everything is much worse and nobody is happy."

Russia

As the world's largest country in area, Russia spreads across nearly 180° of latitude. Because of its vast size, the country is divided into eleven separate time zones. While the climate varies from place to place, the summers are generally mild and the winters chilly to bitterly cold. Russia is home to many different landforms, from arctic deserts and tundra to forests, plains, and mountains. Study the map and tables to learn more about Russia's geography.

Russia: Time Zones
KEY

| 4:00 P.M. | Time in zone |
| --- | Other |

- Time in zone
- National border
- ⊛ National capital
- • Other city

Map labels: North Pole, ARCTIC OCEAN, Barents Sea, St. Petersburg, Moscow, Saratov, Volgograd, Novosibirsk, Irkutsk, Yakutsk, Vladivostok, Bering Sea, Sea of Okhotsk, Arctic Circle
Times shown: 3:00 P.M., 4:00 P.M., 5:00 P.M., 6:00 P.M., 7:00 P.M., 8:00 P.M., 9:00 P.M., 10:00 P.M., 11:00 P.M., 12:00 Midnight, 1:00 A.M.

Scale: 0 miles 1,000 / 0 kilometers 1,000
Lambert Azimuthal Equal Area

European Railroads by Length

Country	Total Mileage
Russia	▦▦▦▦▦▦▦▦▦▦▦▦▦▦
Germany	▦▦▦▦▦▦
France	▦▦▦▦▦
Italy	▦▦
Spain	▦▦
Romania	▦▦

 This symbol represents 5,000 miles of railroad track.

SOURCE: *DK World Desk Reference, 2002*

World's Largest Countries

Country	Land Area
Russia	6,562,110 sq mi; 16,995,790 sq km
China	3,600,944 sq mi; 9,326,406 sq km
Canada	3,560,234 sq mi; 9,220,968 sq km
United States	3,536,292 sq mi; 9,158,958 sq km
Brazil	3,265,074 sq mi; 8,456,506 sq km

SOURCE: *The World Almanac, 2004*

Map and Chart Skills

1. **Identify** What time is it in Yakutsk when it is noon in Moscow?
2. **Compare** How does Russia's land area compare to that of the United States?
3. **Analyze Information** Why do you think there are so many more miles of railroad track in Russia than in other European countries?

Go Online PHSchool.com — Use Web Code **ldp-7514** for **DK World Desk Reference Online.**

Differentiated Instruction

For Less Proficient Readers L1
Reinforce students' understanding of Siberia's natural resources by showing them *Color Transparencies ER 13 and ER 15: Northern Eurasia: Natural Resources.* Have students name the resources and identify their locations.

📖 **Europe and Russia Transparencies,** Color Transparency ER 13: Northern Eurasia: Political (Base); Color Transparency ER 15: Northern Eurasia: Natural Resources (overlay)

For Advanced Readers L3
Have students explore the creation of the Trans-Siberian Railroad by completing *Activity Shop Interdisciplinary: Plan a New Railroad Line.*

All in One Europe and Russia Teaching Resources, *Activity Shop Interdisciplinary: Plan a New Railroad Line,* pp. 339–340

Guided Instruction L2
Ask students to study the Country Profile on this page. Have students work in pairs to answer the Map and Chart Skills questions and then discuss the answers as a class.

Independent Practice
Tell students to suppose that they live in Russia. Ask them to write a letter to a friend describing the country's geography. Tell them to include information found in the map and tables on this page.

Answers

Map and Chart Skills

1. 6:00 PM
2. Russia is nearly 2 times larger than the U.S.
3. because Russia is much larger in area than other European countries

Go Online PHSchool.com Students can find more information about this topic on the DK World Desk Reference Online.

Target Reading Skill

Identify Contrasts As a follow up, ask students to answer the Target Reading Skill question in the Student Edition. *(Students may identify two of the following: Siberians worry about losing their jobs or farms; they are able to buy their own homes; they have freedom to make their own decisions.)*

Cultural Traditions Continue

L2

Guided Instruction

- Have students read Cultural Traditions Continue to learn how Russians have continued to preserve their traditions. As they read, circulate and make sure individuals are able to answer the Reading Check question.

- Ask students to compare life in Moscow in Soviet times to life in Moscow today. *(Moscow is still the cultural center of the nation.)*

- Ask students **How do Siberians prepare for winter?** *(Farmers work overtime to harvest crops before the frost, and collect nuts and honey.)* **Would you call these activities examples of cultural traditions? Why or why not?** *(Possible answers: Yes, they are cultural traditions because Siberians have probably been making the same kinds of preparations for centuries.)*

Independent Practice

L2

Have students continue to fill in their graphic organizers with information from the section.

Monitor Progress

Circulate among students and provide assistance to individuals as they add details to their flowcharts.

Answers

✓ **Reading Check** because factory workers and miners are no longer guaranteed jobs, as they were under communism

Generalize Possible answer: Although traditional Russian culture still endures, teenagers may have more freedom and opportunities than they did under Soviet communism.

202

Changes in Siberia Siberia is a region with rich reserves of coal, gold, iron, oil, and natural gas. During the Soviet years, the government built factories, set up mining operations, and built the Trans-Siberian railroad to carry out materials. Although much of Siberia is rural, large cities developed there over time. In fact, four of the ten largest Russian cities are located in Siberia. The city of Novosibirsk (NOH vuh sih BIHRSK) has a population of more than 1.3 million people. Outside of the cities, much of Siberia is agricultural.

Under the Soviet communist system, factory workers and miners were guaranteed jobs, and farmers were guaranteed certain prices for their crops. Now Siberians worry about losing their jobs or their farms. On the other hand, Siberians are able to buy their own homes and make their own decisions.

 Identify Contrasts What are two ways that life has changed for Siberians since the fall of Soviet communism?

✓ **Reading Check** Why are Siberians worried about jobs?

Cultural Traditions Continue

The collapse of Soviet communism brought major changes to the lives of many Russians. But traditional Russian ways endure.

Life in Moscow As it was in Soviet times, Moscow is still the cultural center of the nation. Art, theater, and dance thrive there. The Bolshoi (BOHL shoy) Ballet is based in Moscow. Dancers from this famous Russian school of ballet have performed around the world. And traveling performers, such as folk dancers from northern Russia, come to Moscow.

On Moscow's streets street vendors sell traditional Russian crafts next to vendors selling electronic goods from China. On very cold winter days, some people in Moscow go to the parks to celebrate an old tradition: picnicking in the snow.

Russian Teenagers
Teenagers walk across the square in front of St. Basil's Cathedral in Moscow. **Generalize** *How might teenagers' lives have been the same and different before and after the fall of Soviet communism?*

202 Europe and Russia

Background: Links Across Time

Russia and the Arts Russians are great readers, and many of the books that are favorites of the Russian people were written before the Russian Revolution of 1917. Favorite authors include Leo Tolstoy, Fyodor Dostoyevsky, and Anton Chekhov. Many of the ballets and operas enjoyed by people in Moscow and St. Petersburg were also created before the revolution, with music by Pyotr Ilyich Tchaikovsky and Nikolay Rimsky-Korsakov. Even with this love for tradition, many Russians enjoy today's rock music from the United States. In addition, American movies are shown regularly.

Life in Rural Siberian Villages Much of Siberia's vast expanse is rural. Few people live in these areas, where change comes slowly. Many homes have no running water. Water has to be hauled from wells. Sometimes the wells freeze in the winter. Then people have to drink and cook with melted snow.

Despite problems like these, Siberians have adapted to life in their frigid climate. Farmers work overtime to harvest crops before the frost. Before winter comes, they start collecting nuts and honey. In winter, some families hang huge pieces of meat from their porches. Temperatures in winter are so cold that the meat freezes solid and does not spoil.

During winter, women wearing many layers of clothing leave their log houses to fetch firewood. Inside the log houses, large stoves are used for both cooking and heating. When the nights become bitterly cold, the family may spread a straw mat on top of the still-warm stove and sleep there to stay warm.

√ **Reading Check** What are some cultural traditions in Moscow?

A Nenets mother and child in a reindeer-skin tent in Siberia

Uniting a Vast Nation

Russia is a vast country, covering more than 6 million square miles (17 million square kilometers). Russia has more than 144 million people. The majority of these people are ethnic Russians. However, the nation also includes many different ethnic groups who speak different languages and practice different religions. How can a country with so much land, so many different ethnic groups, and a struggling economy stay united?

War in Chechnya You have read that some Russian republics populated by ethnic minorities have grown tired of Russian rule. One such republic, located in southwestern Russia, is called Chechnya (CHECH nee uh). The people who live in this oil-rich republic are mainly Muslims. In 1991, Chechnya declared its independence from Russia. To prevent the republic from seceding, Russia sent troops into the Chechen capital. For several years during the 1990s, Russian and Chechen troops fought bitterly over the status of the republic. Tens of thousands of people were killed in the struggle. Hundreds of thousands were forced to flee their homes. Although Chechnya remains part of Russia today, conflict still goes on there.

Chechen refugees make a temporary home in a train car.

Uniting a Vast Nation ⬛L2

Guided Instruction

■ **Vocabulary Builder** Clarify the meaning of the high-use words **status** and **resolve** before reading.

■ Have students read Uniting a Vast Nation.

■ Have students describe the events that occurred when Chechnya declared independence from Russia. *(To prevent Chechnya from seceding, Russia sent troops to the Chechen capital. Russian and Chechen troops fought for several years, during which tens of thousands of people were killed and hundreds of thousands were forced to leave their homes; Chechnya remains part of Russia today.)*

■ Ask students **What are some of Russia's major natural resources?** *(oil, natural gas, and metals)* **How could Russia's dependence on the sale of these resources be a problem?** *(When world prices of the materials are low, the Russian economy suffers.)*

■ Ask students **What are some predictions you might make about Russia's future?** *(Possible answers: Russia's economy may improve given its availability of natural resources and a talented workforce. However, economic problems may persist as long as corruption and ethnic tensions remain.)*

Independent Practice
Have students complete their graphic organizers.

Monitor Progress

■ Show *Section Reading Support Transparency ER 51* and ask students to check their graphic organizers individually. Go over key concepts and clarify key vocabulary as needed.

📖 **Europe and Russia Transparencies,** *Section Reading Support Transparency ER 51*

■ Tell students to fill in the last column of the *Reading Readiness Guide*. Probe for what they learned that confirms or invalidates each statement.

⬛All in One **Europe and Russia Teaching Resources,** *Reading Readiness Guide*, p. 326

Answer

√ **Reading Check** The Bolshoi Ballet is in Moscow; folk dancers from the north perform there; street vendors sell traditional Russian crafts.

Assess and Reteach

Assess Progress `L2`

Have students complete the Section Assessment. Administer the *Section Quiz*.

 Europe and Russia Teaching Resources, *Section Quiz,* p. 328

Reteach `L1`

If students need more instruction, have them read this section in the Reading and Vocabulary Study Guide.

📖 Chapter 5, Section 4, **Europe and Russia Reading and Vocabulary Study Guide,** pp. 67–69

Extend `L3`

Have students read the primary source *Housekeeping in Russia Soon After the Revolution* to learn more about another period of change in Russia's history.

 Europe and Russia Teaching Resources, *Housekeeping in Russia Soon After the Revolution,* p. 345

Answers

Infer Answers may vary, but students will probably say that more average Russians are able to buy dachas today because many work hard at successful jobs.

✓ **Reading Check** When world prices for these materials are low, the Russian economy suffers.

Section 4 Assessment

Key Terms

Students' sentences should reflect an understanding of each Key Term.

🔁 Target Reading Skill

After the fall of the Soviet Union, Chechnya tried to secede from Russia and experienced several years of struggle against Russian troops who were sent to prevent the republic from seceding.

Comprehension and Critical Thinking

1. (a) Criminal gangs often force people who own businesses to pay them money. Laws protecting business owners are often not enforced. **(b)** The change to a free-market economy has helped ordinary Russians to start their own businesses or factories and enabled some to fix up their apartments and

---

The Russian Dacha
Country homes called *dachas*, like the one below, were first built by Peter the Great and given to wealthy nobles. In Soviet times, they were usually given to Communist Party officials. **Infer** *Do you think average Russians are able to buy dachas today? Explain why or why not.*

⭐ Section 4 Assessment

Key Terms

Review the key terms at the beginning of this section. Use each term in a sentence that explains its meaning.

🔁 Target Reading Skill

Contrast the situation in Chechnya before and after the fall of the Soviet Union.

Comprehension and Critical Thinking

1. (a) Explain Why have average Russians had difficulty running their own businesses?

(b) Draw Conclusions How has the change to a free-market economy both helped and harmed ordinary Russians?

2. (a) Describe What cultural traditions have endured throughout Russia?

(b) Contrast How does life in rural Siberia differ from life in Moscow?

3. (a) Recall Which Russian republic declared its independence in 1991?

(b) Infer Why did Russia go to war to prevent that republic from seceding?

Writing Activity

Do you live in a city, a small town, or the countryside? Write a paragraph comparing your life with the lives of Russians in one of the places described in this section.

> **Writing Tip** Before you begin, list details about Russian life in the place you have chosen. For each detail, record a detail about your own life that relates to that topic.

204 Europe and Russia

Economic Problems Remain In the early 2000s, Russia's economy shows signs of strengthening. Yet serious economic problems remain. Even one of the country's most important assets—its natural resources—presents problems. For example, Russia has enormous deposits of oil, natural gas, and metals. But Russia depends too heavily on sales of these materials, rather than on creating new jobs. If world prices are low, then Russia's economy suffers.

Corruption is still a problem throughout the country. Laws are still not usually enforced. And banks have never fully recovered from the failures in the 1990s. For these reasons, many Russians distrust the government.

However, Russia is still a powerful nation with many important assets. Besides its natural resources, it has a talented workforce of scientists and engineers. If the country can continue to improve its economy and resolve some of its ethnic tensions, its future should be bright.

✓ **Reading Check** Why is Russia's dependence on its natural resources a problem?

---

travel abroad. Yet many ordinary Russians suffer a lack of job security and have lost money due to bank failures and inflation. There have also been severe food shortages.

2. (a) People from the countryside continue to come to Moscow to buy things; street vendors sell traditional crafts; some people in Moscow still have winter picnics in the snow; traditional art, theater, and dance continue to thrive. **(b)** Life in Siberia is generally rural, and the change to a free-market economy has been slower than in Moscow.

3. (a) Chechnya **(b)** Possible answer: Russia wanted to maintain control of the oil-rich land of Chechnya; it also wanted to discourage other republics from seceding.

Writing Activity

Use the *Rubric for Assessing a Writing Assignment* to evaluate students' comparisons.

 Europe and Russia Teaching Resources, *Rubric for Assessing a Writing Assignment,* p. 350

Review and Assessment

Poland

◆ Chapter Summary

Section 1: Poland
- Despite years of foreign rule, cultural traditions and language have endured in Polish life.
- In 1990, Poland's communist-based economy shifted to capitalism.
- Poland must still overcome environmental problems and unemployment.

Section 2: Five Balkan Nations
- The Balkans is a diverse region of many ethnic groups, religions, and languages.
- Yugoslavia had a troubled history of ethnic conflict from its beginning.
- The countries created upon the breakup of Yugoslavia have faced their own problems of ethnic conflict and political instability.

Section 3: Ukraine
- Ukraine has a long history of occupation by foreign powers.
- Since independence from the Soviet Union, Ukraine has had to face economic and environmental challenges.
- Life in Ukraine is changing as the country embraces its independence.

Section 4: Russia
- Since the fall of the Soviet government, the transition to capitalism has brought some benefits, but also many economic challenges.
- Many cultural traditions have endured throughout Russia.
- Russia's huge size, ethnic diversity, and economic problems have presented challenges to preserving national unity.

◆ Key Terms

Each of the statements below contains a key term from the chapter. If the statement is true, write *true*. If it is false, replace the term to make it true.

1. In the Eastern Orthodox religion, a shrine is a holy place where visitors often plant crosses.

2. An investor is a person who spends money to make more money.

3. Slovenia and Croatia seceded from Yugoslavia in 1990.

4. Capitalism is an economic system in which the government owns the businesses.

5. More than half of Ukraine is covered with a thick, black soil called collectives.

6. After Yugoslavia broke apart, entrepreneurs erupted in Bosnia and Herzegovina.

⌐ Vocabulary Builder

Revisit this chapter's high-use words.

unique
transition
invest
principle
prevent

consume
publish
contaminate
produce

dissolve
enforce
status
resolve

Ask students to review the definitions they recorded on their *Word Knowledge* worksheets.

All in One Europe and Russia Teaching Resources, *Word Knowledge,* p. 332

Consider allowing students to earn extra credit if they use the words in their answers to the questions in the Chapter Review and Assessment. The words must be used correctly and in a natural context to win the extra points.

Review and Assessment
Review Chapter Content

■ Review and revisit the major themes of this chapter by asking students to classify what Guiding Question each bulleted statement in the Chapter Summary answers. Have students work together in groups to classify the sentences. Refer to p. 1 in the Student Edition for the text of the Guiding Questions.

■ Assign *Vocabulary Development* for students to review Key Terms.

All in One Europe and Russia Teaching Resources, *Vocabulary Development,* p. 346

Answers

Key Terms

1. True.

2. True.

3. True.

4. False. Communism is an economic system in which the government owns the businesses.

5. False. More than half of Ukraine is covered with a thick, black soil called chernozem.

6. False. After Yugoslavia broke apart, civil war erupted in Bosnia and Herzegovina.

Comprehension and Critical Thinking

7. (a) Catholicism **(b)** Catholicism in Poland is unique and has been at the center of Polish tradition for centuries; Polish Catholics continued to practice their religion despite discouragement from the communist government; Poles were especially proud when a Pole was selected as pope of the Catholic church.

8. (a) farmers **(b)** It provided them with a reliable income and kept prices high. **(c)** taking on part-time jobs, inviting paying guests to stay with them for vacations, or producing higher-priced organic goods

9. (a) Serbia and Montenegro, Bosnia and Herzegovina, Macedonia, Croatia, Slovenia **(b)** These nations have different languages, practice different religions, and have different non-Slavic ethnic groups. **(c)** After Tito's death and the fall of communism, many people began to support leaders who encouraged them to identify with their own ethnic group, leading many to want to be independent.

10. (a) The nations of this region face economic hardships and must deal with a history of ethnic conflict. **(b)** to help people without food and other supplies, stop conflicts, and create peace treaties

11. (a) The natural resources of Ukraine include rich soil, iron ore, coal, and rivers. **(b)** Ukraine's rich supply of natural resources has made it more likely to be invaded.

12. (a) Some businesses took off and some investors became very wealthy, but ordinary Russians faced challenges in starting new businesses, from bank failures and inflation, and from food shortages. Still, many Russians were able to become successful. **(b)** Capitalism has helped Russians by bringing them new freedoms and opportunities, including the ability to start businesses, fix up their apartments, and travel abroad. However, jobs are no longer guaranteed and corruption and criminal activity affect ordinary Russians' ability to start and maintain profitable businesses.

Skills Practice
Students should identify Havel as a Czech playwright whose tone is persuasive but rational. Students' paragraphs should demonstrate an understanding of the skill.

◆ Comprehension and Critical Thinking

7. (a) Identify What religion do most Poles belong to?
(b) Synthesize Information How has religious belief strengthened the pride Poles feel for their country?

8. (a) Name What group of people in Poland has found it hardest to manage the transition to capitalism?
(b) Analyze Information In what ways did communism help Polish farmers?
(c) Identify Effects What are Polish farmers doing to make extra money?

9. (a) List Which five Balkan nations share a Slavic heritage?
(b) Contrast Discuss the differences among the peoples of these nations.
(c) Summarize How did these differences lead to the breakup of Yugoslavia?

10. (a) Recall What problems are faced by all the nations created by Yugoslavia's breakup?
(b) Identify Cause and Effect Why were UN and NATO forces sent to the Balkans several times?

11. (a) Note What are the natural resources of Ukraine?
(b) Identify the Main Idea How have these resources affected Ukraine's history?

12. (a) Describe What changes did the transition to capitalism bring to Russia?
(b) Evaluate Information How has capitalism both helped and hurt average Russians?

◆ Skills Practice

Identifying Frame of Reference In the Skills for Life activity in this chapter, you learned how to identify frame of reference. Review the steps you followed to learn this skill. Then reread the quotation by Vaclav Havel on page 95. Identify the writer's tone and qualifications for his position. Then use this information to write a paragraph that explains his frame of reference.

◆ Writing Activity: Science

Suppose you are a writer for a science magazine. Your assignment is to write an article about environmental problems in Eastern Europe. Write a short article about the causes and effects of pollution in Poland, or of the Chernobyl accident in Ukraine.

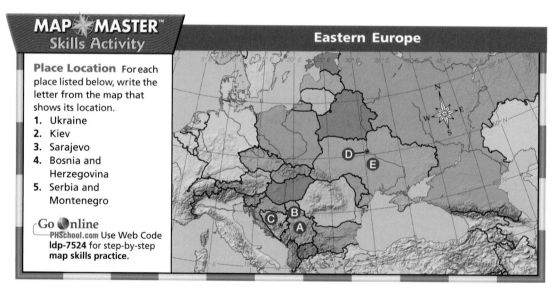

MAP★MASTER™
Skills Activity

Eastern Europe

Place Location For each place listed below, write the letter from the map that shows its location.
1. Ukraine
2. Kiev
3. Sarajevo
4. Bosnia and Herzegovina
5. Serbia and Montenegro

Go **Online**
PHSchool.com Use Web Code **ldp-7524** for step-by-step **map skills practice.**

Writing Activity: Science
Students' articles will vary, but should make clear the connection between causes and effects. Articles about Poland should note the impact of coal mining, steel production, and the use of unleaded gasoline. Articles about Chernobyl should note the cause of the accident and list several of its effects.

Use *Rubric for Assessing a Newspaper Article* to evaluate students' articles. Tell students how many sources you would like them to use, if any, beyond the textbook.

All in One Europe and Russia Teaching Resources, *Rubric for Assessing a Newspaper Article,* pp. 348

Standardized Test Prep

Test-Taking Tips

Some questions on standardized tests ask you to analyze graphic organizers. Study the table below. Then follow the tips to answer the sample question.

Five Balkan Nations: Ethnic Groups

Macedonia	Macedonian (67%) Albanian (23%)
Croatia	Croat (90%) Serb (5%)
Bosnia and Herzegovina	Bosniak (48%) Serb (37%)
Serbia and Montenegro	Serb (63%) Albanian (17%)
Slovenia	Slovene (88%) Croat (3%)

TIP Use what you know about history and geography to help you answer the question.

What is the subject of this chart?

A major ethnic groups of countries that make up Eastern Europe

B major ethnic groups of countries that made up the former Soviet Union

C major ethnic groups of countries that were formed after Yugoslavia broke up

D major ethnic groups of countries that were formed at the end of World War II

TIP Try to answer the question before you look at the answer choices.

Think It Through Each of the names in bold print is a country; to the right of each country is its ethnic makeup. You can eliminate A and B. Eastern Europe includes more than these five countries, and the Soviet Union did not include these countries. You may not know which countries were formed after World War II, but you have probably heard most of these five countries mentioned in reference to Yugoslavia. The answer is C.

Practice Questions

Use the tips above and other tips in this book to help you answer the following questions.

1. Which of the following is NOT an important Polish tradition?
   A communism
   B Polish Orthodoxy
   C Roman Catholicism
   D the Polish language

2. In which country is the republic of Kosovo located?
   A Macedonia
   B Croatia
   C Bosnia and Herzegovina
   D Serbia and Montenegro

3. What led to the growth of towns and cities in Siberia?
   A the collapse of Soviet communism
   B the Trans-Siberian Railroad
   C the transition to capitalism
   D migration from Europe

Use the table below to answer Question 4. Choose the letter of the best answer to the question.

Ukrainian Resources

Resource	Use by Soviet Union
Farmland	Grain, meat
Minerals	Iron ore, coal for industries
	Shipping of goods to and from Soviet Union

4. Which answer would best fit in the blank space on the table?
   A Collectives
   B Seaports and rivers
   C Mines
   D Factories

Go Online PHSchool.com

Use Web Code lda-7504 for a **Chapter 5 self-test**.

Standardized Test Prep
Answers

1. A
2. D
3. B
4. B

Assessment Resources

Teaching Resources
Chapter Tests A and B, pp. 351–356
Final Exams A and B, pp. 363–368

Test Prep Workbook
Europe and Russia Study Sheet, pp. 110–112
Europe and Russia Practice Tests A, B, and C, pp. 37–48

AYP Monitoring Assessments
Europe and Russia Benchmark Test 2, pp. 109–112
Europe and Russia Outcome Tests, pp. 188–193

Technology
⊙ ExamView Test Bank CD-ROM

Projects

- Students can further explore the Guiding Questions by completing hands-on projects.

- Three pages of structured guidance in All-in-One Europe and Russia Teaching Resources support each of the projects described on this page.

   All in One **Europe and Russia Teaching Resources,** *Book Project: Olympic Cities,* pp. 83–85; *Book Project: Folklore Corner,* pp. 86–88

- There are also two additional projects introduced, explained, and supported in the All-in-One Europe and Russia Teaching Resources.

   All in One **Europe and Russia Teaching Resources,** *Book Project: Changing Climates,* pp. 77–79; *Book Project: Tourism in Eastern Europe,* pp. 80–82

- Go over the four project suggestions with students.

- Ask each student to select one of the projects, or design his or her own. Work with students to create a project description and a schedule.

- Post project schedules and monitor student progress by asking for progress reports.

- Assess student projects using rubrics from the All-in-One Europe and Russia Teaching Resources.

   All in One **Europe and Russia Teaching Resources,** *Rubric for Assessing a Student Performance on a Project,* p. 89; *Rubric for Assessing Performance of an Entire Group,* p. 90; *Rubric for Assessing Individual Performance in a Group,* p. 91

    Tell students they can add their completed Book Project as the final item in their portfolios. Assess student portfolios with *Rubric for Assessing a Student Portfolio.*

   All in One **Europe and Russia Teaching Resources,** *Rubric for Assessing a Student Portfolio,* p. 92

Projects

Create your own projects to learn more about Europe and Russia. At the beginning of this book, you were introduced to the **Guiding Questions** for studying the chapters and the special features. You can also find answers to these questions by doing projects on your own or with a group. Use the questions to find topics you want to explore further. Then try the projects described on this page or create your own.

1. **Geography** What are the main physical features of Europe and Russia?

2. **History** How have Europe and Russia been affected by their history?

3. **Culture** How have the people of Europe and Russia been shaped by their cultures?

4. **Government** What types of government have existed in Europe and Russia?

5. **Economics** How have Russian and European economies developed into what they are today?

Project

WRITE A PROPOSAL

Olympic Cities
Plan an Olympic season in a European city. As you read this book, keep track of cities that you find interesting. Research them at the library or on the Internet. After you have gathered your information, choose a city that you think would be a good host of either the summer or winter Olympics. Write a proposal to Olympic officials, explaining what the city has to offer to the Olympics. Include maps or pictures of your city with your proposal.

Project

CREATE A DISPLAY

Folklore Corner
Create a library of folk and fairy tales from countries throughout Europe. As you read about a country in this book, find a traditional tale from that country. Think about how the stories reflect the country's culture. With your classmates, build a Folklore Corner in your classroom. Create a display of books of folk tales. Include objects, drawings, and photographs that represent the culture in these tales. Label each tale with its country of origin.

Table of Contents

The World: Political

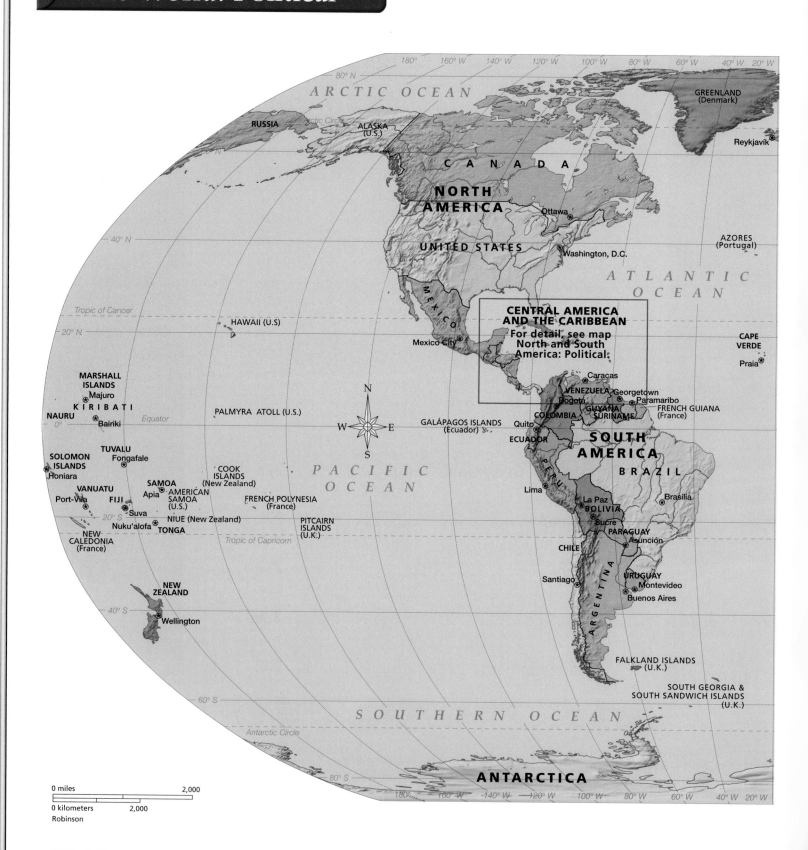

ARCTIC OCEAN

GREENLAND
(Denmark)

RUSSIA

Arctic Circle

ALASKA
(U.S.)

Reykjavík

C A N A D A

NORTH
AMERICA

Ottawa

AZORES
(Portugal)

40° N

UNITED STATES

Washington, D.C.

A T L A N T I C
O C E A N

Tropic of Cancer

HAWAII (U.S)

MEXICO

CENTRAL AMERICA
AND THE CARIBBEAN

20° N

For detail, see map
North and South
America: Political.

CAPE
VERDE

Mexico City

Praia

MARSHALL
ISLANDS
Majuro

Caracas

VENEZUELA Georgetown

K I R I B A T I

PALMYRA ATOLL (U.S.)

Bogotá

Paramaribo

NAURU

GUYANA

FRENCH GUIANA
(France)

Equator

0°

Bairiki

GALÁPAGOS ISLANDS
(Ecuador)

COLOMBIA

SURINAME

Quito

TUVALU

SOUTH
AMERICA

ECUADOR

Fongafale

SOLOMON
ISLANDS

COOK
ISLANDS
(New Zealand)

B R A Z I L

Honiara

PACIFIC
OCEAN

Lima

PERU

Brasília

VANUATU

SAMOA

AMERICAN
SAMOA
(U.S.)

FRENCH POLYNESIA
(France)

La Paz
BOLIVIA

Port-Vila

FIJI

Apia

NIUE (New Zealand)

Sucre

Suva

PITCAIRN
ISLANDS
(U.K.)

PARAGUAY

20° S

Nuku'alofa

TONGA

Asunción

NEW
CALEDONIA
(France)

Tropic of Capricorn

CHILE

ARGENTINA

URUGUAY

NEW
ZEALAND

Santiago

Montevideo
Buenos Aires

40° S

Wellington

FALKLAND ISLANDS
(U.K.)

SOUTH GEORGIA &
SOUTH SANDWICH ISLANDS
(U.K.)

60° S

S O U T H E R N   O C E A N

Antarctic Circle

80° S

ANTARCTICA

0 miles   2,000

0 kilometers   2,000

Robinson

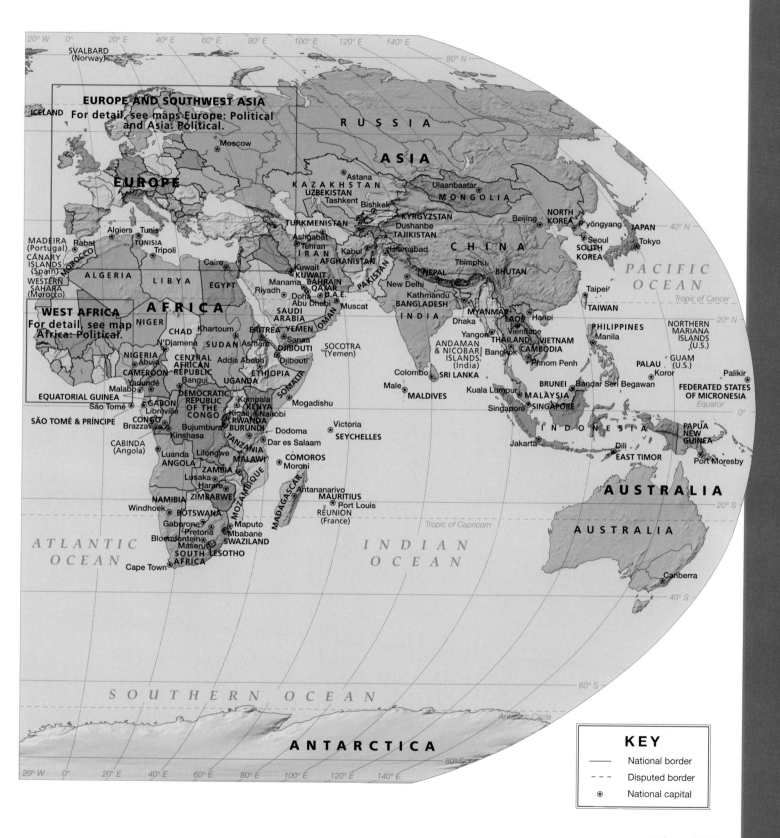

SVALBARD (Norway)

ICELAND

EUROPE AND SOUTHWEST ASIA
For detail, see maps Europe: Political and Asia: Political.

R U S S I A

A S I A

EUROPE

Moscow

Astana
KAZAKHSTAN
UZBEKISTAN
Tashkent Bishkek
KYRGYZSTAN
TURKMENISTAN
Ashgabat Dushanbe
TAJIKISTAN
Ulaanbaatar
M O N G O L I A

Beijing
NORTH
KOREA
P'yŏngyang JAPAN
Seoul Tokyo
SOUTH
KOREA

PACIFIC
OCEAN

40° N

Algiers Tunis
TUNISIA
Tripoli

MADEIRA
(Portugal) Rabat
CANARY
ISLANDS
(Spain)
WESTERN
SAHARA
(Morocco)

ALGERIA   L I B Y A   EGYPT

MOROCCO

Cairo

I R A N
Tehran
Kuwait Kabul
KUWAIT AFGHANISTAN
Manama BAHRAIN
Riyadh Doha QATAR
Abu Dhabi U.A.E.
SAUDI
ARABIA   Muscat
Islamabad

C H I N A

Taipei

TAIWAN

Tropic of Cancer

20° N

WEST AFRICA
For detail, see map
Africa: Political.

A F R I C A
NIGER

CHAD
N'Djamena
NIGERIA SUDAN
Abuja CENTRAL
CAMEROON AFRICAN
Yaundé REPUBLIC
Malabo Bangui
São Tomé GABON UGANDA
SÃO TOMÉ & PRÍNCIPE
Libreville DEMOCRATIC
CONGO REPUBLIC
Brazzaville OF THE
Kinshasa CONGO
CABINDA
(Angola)
Luanda Lilongwe
ANGOLA MALAWI
ZAMBIA
Lusaka
NAMIBIA ZIMBABWE
Windhoek Harare
BOTSWANA
Gaborone Maputo
Pretoria Mbabane
Bloemfontein SWAZILAND
Maseru
SOUTH LESOTHO
Cape Town AFRICA

Khartoum
ERITREA
Asmara
YEMEN
Sanaa
DJIBOUTI
Djibouti
Addis Ababa
ETHIOPIA

OMAN

SOCOTRA
(Yemen)

S O M A L I A

Kampala
KENYA
Kigali Nairobi
RWANDA
Bujumbura BURUNDI
TANZANIA
Dodoma
Dar es Salaam

Mogadishu

New Delhi

I N D I A

Colombo SRI LANKA

NEPAL
Kathmandu
BANGLADESH
Dhaka
Thimphu
BHUTAN

MYANMAR

Yangon

Male
MALDIVES

Victoria
SEYCHELLES

COMOROS
Moroni

MADAGASCAR
Antananarivo
MAURITIUS
Port Louis
RÉUNION
(France)

LAOS Hanoi
Vientiane
THAILAND VIETNAM
Bangkok CAMBODIA
Phnom Penh

PHILIPPINES
Manila

ANDAMAN
& NICOBAR
ISLANDS
(India)

BRUNEI Bandar Seri Begawan
Kuala Lumpur MALAYSIA
Singapore SINGAPORE

I N D O N E S I A

Jakarta

Dili
EAST TIMOR

NORTHERN
MARIANA
ISLANDS
(U.S.)

GUAM
(U.S.)

PALAU
Koror Palikir
FEDERATED STATES
OF MICRONESIA
Equator
0°

PAPUA
NEW
GUINEA
Port Moresby

AUSTRALIA

ATLANTIC
OCEAN

INDIAN
OCEAN

Tropic of Capricorn

A U S T R A L I A

Canberra

20° S

40° S

S O U T H E R N   O C E A N

Antarctic Circle

A N T A R C T I C A

80° S

20° W 0° 20° E 40° E 60° E 80° E 100° E 120° E 140° E

KEY

────── National border

- - - - Disputed border

⊛ National capital

The World: Physical

0 miles   2,000

0 kilometers   2,000

Robinson

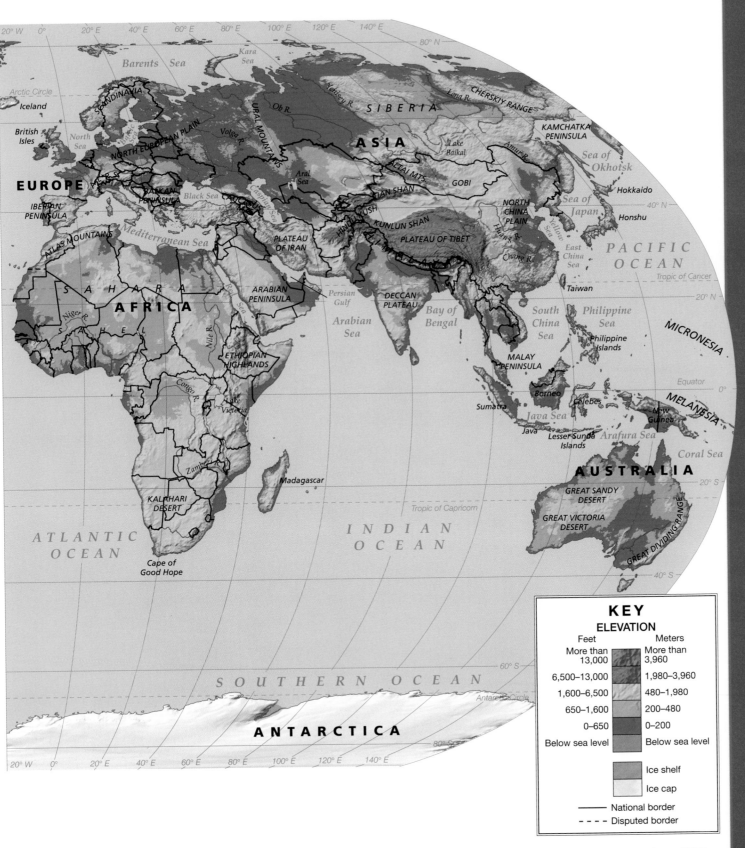

20° W · 0° · 20° E · 40° E · 60° E · 80° E · 100° E · 120° E · 140° E

80° N

Barents Sea

Kara Sea

Arctic Circle

Iceland

SCANDINAVIA

Baltic Sea

Volga R.

URAL MOUNTAINS

Ob R.

Yenisey R.

Lena R.

SIBERIA

CHERSKIY RANGE

British Isles

North Sea

NORTH EUROPEAN PLAIN

ASIA

KAMCHATKA PENINSULA

Amur R.

Sea of Okhotsk

EUROPE

BALKAN PENINSULA

Black Sea

Aral Sea

ALTAI MTS.

Lake Baikal

GOBI

Sea of Japan

Hokkaido

40° N

IBERIAN PENINSULA

CAUCASUS

Caspian Sea

TIAN SHAN

NORTH CHINA PLAIN

Honshu

ATLAS MOUNTAINS

Mediterranean Sea

HINDU KUSH

KUNLUN SHAN

PLATEAU OF TIBET

Huang R.

Yellow Sea

East China Sea

PACIFIC OCEAN

PLATEAU OF IRAN

Tropic of Cancer

SAHARA

Red Sea

ARABIAN PENINSULA

Persian Gulf

DECCAN PLATEAU

Chang R.

Taiwan

20° N

AFRICA

Niger R.

S A H E L

Arabian Sea

Bay of Bengal

South China Sea

Philippine Sea

MICRONESIA

Nile R.

ETHIOPIAN HIGHLANDS

Philippine Islands

Congo R.

Lake Victoria

MALAY PENINSULA

Equator

0°

Sumatra

Borneo

Celebes

MELANESIA

NEW GUINEA

Zambezi R.

Java Sea

Java

Lesser Sunda Islands

Arafura Sea

Coral Sea

Madagascar

AUSTRALIA

20° S

KALAHARI DESERT

GREAT SANDY DESERT

Tropic of Capricorn

GREAT VICTORIA DESERT

GREAT DIVIDING RANGE

ATLANTIC OCEAN

INDIAN OCEAN

Cape of Good Hope

40° S

60° S

SOUTHERN OCEAN

Antarctic Circle

ANTARCTICA

80° S

20° W · 0° · 20° E · 40° E · 60° E · 80° E · 100° E · 120° E · 140° E

KEY

ELEVATION

Feet		Meters
More than 13,000		More than 3,960
6,500–13,000		1,980–3,960
1,600–6,500		480–1,980
650–1,600		200–480
0–650		0–200
Below sea level		Below sea level

Ice shelf

Ice cap

——— National border

- - - Disputed border

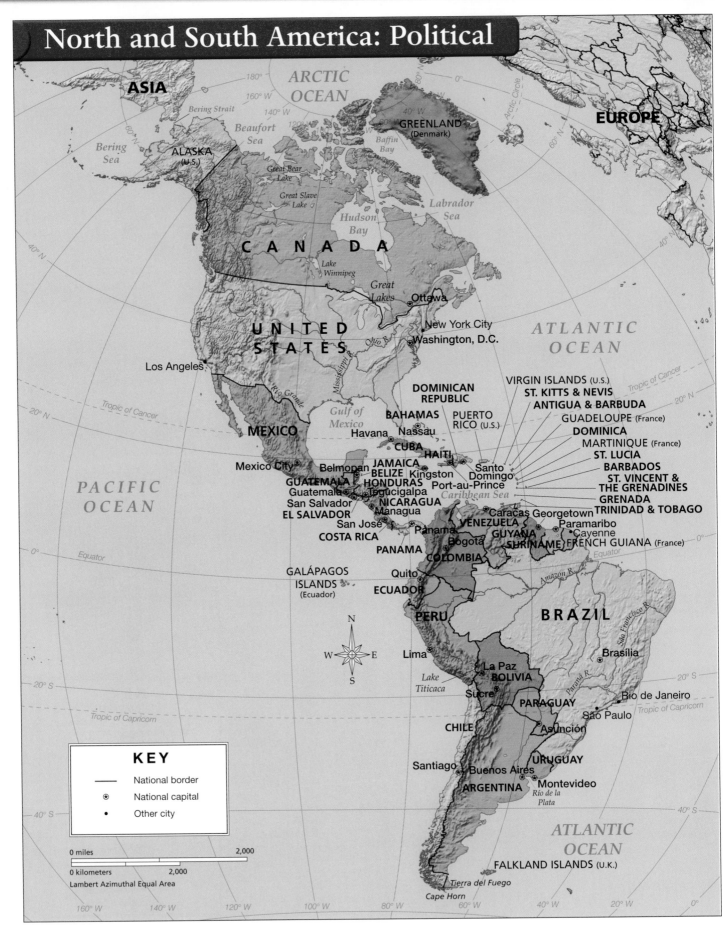

North and South America: Political

ASIA

ARCTIC OCEAN

180°
160° W
140° W
120° W
0°
40° W
60° N
60°

EUROPE

Bering Strait

Beaufort Sea

Bering Sea

ALASKA (U.S.)

GREENLAND (Denmark)

Baffin Bay

Great Bear Lake

Great Slave Lake

Labrador Sea

Hudson Bay

40° N

C A N A D A

Lake Winnipeg

Great Lakes

Ottawa

U N I T E D S T A T E S

New York City
Washington, D.C.

Ohio R.

ATLANTIC OCEAN

Los Angeles

Rio Grande

Mississippi

Tropic of Cancer

20° N

VIRGIN ISLANDS (U.S.)
ST. KITTS & NEVIS
ANTIGUA & BARBUDA

Tropic of Cancer
20° N

DOMINICAN REPUBLIC

Gulf of Mexico

BAHAMAS

PUERTO RICO (U.S.)

GUADELOUPE (France)

MEXICO

Havana

Nassau

DOMINICA

MARTINIQUE (France)

CUBA

HAITI

ST. LUCIA

Mexico City

Belmopan

JAMAICA

Santo

BARBADOS

Kingston

Domingo

ST. VINCENT &

GUATEMALA

BELIZE

THE GRENADINES

Guatemala

HONDURAS

Port-au-Prince

Caribbean Sea

GRENADA

San Salvador

Tegucigalpa

NICARAGUA

TRINIDAD & TOBAGO

EL SALVADOR

Managua

Caracas

Georgetown

PACIFIC OCEAN

San José

VENEZUELA

Paramaribo

COSTA RICA

Panama

GUYANA

Cayenne

PANAMA

Bogotá

SURINAME

FRENCH GUIANA (France)

0°

COLOMBIA

Equator

Equator

GALÁPAGOS ISLANDS (Ecuador)

Quito

Amazon R.

ECUADOR

BRAZIL

PERU

São Francisco R.

N

Brasília

W   E

Lima

S

La Paz

Rio de Janeiro

BOLIVIA

20° S

Lake Titicaca

Paraná R.

20° S

Tropic of Capricorn

Sucre

PARAGUAY

São Paulo

Tropic of Capricorn

CHILE

Asunción

URUGUAY

Santiago

Buenos Aires

Montevideo

ARGENTINA

Río de la Plata

40° S

40° S

ATLANTIC OCEAN

FALKLAND ISLANDS (U.K.)

Tierra del Fuego

Cape Horn

160° W
140° W
120° W
100° W
80° W
60° W
40° W
20° W
0°

KEY

— National border

⊛ National capital

• Other city

0 miles   2,000

0 kilometers   2,000

Lambert Azimuthal Equal Area

North and South America: Physical

ASIA

ARCTIC OCEAN

EUROPE

Bering Strait

Beaufort Sea

Greenland

Bering Sea

Mt. McKinley
20,320 ft
(6,194 m)

Baffin Bay

Aleutian Islands

Alaska Range

Great Bear Lake

Baffin Island

Labrador Sea

Gulf of Alaska

Mackenzie R.

Great Slave Lake

Hudson Bay

CANADIAN SHIELD

Newfoundland

ROCKY MOUNTAINS

GREAT PLAINS

Lake Winnipeg

Great Lakes

Columbia R.

Missouri R.

Mississippi R.

Ohio R.

Appalachian Mts.

ATLANTIC OCEAN

Tropic of Cancer

Tropic of Cancer

Baja California

Sierra Madre Occidental

Sierra Madre Oriental

Río Grande

Gulf of Mexico

PACIFIC OCEAN

Gulf of California

Yucatán Peninsula

Cuba

Greater Antilles

Hispaniola

Lesser Antilles

Caribbean Sea

Isthmus of Panama

Galápagos Islands

Orinoco R.

Guiana Highlands

Equator

Equator

AMAZON BASIN

Amazon R.

ANDES

São Francisco R.

Brazilian Highlands

Lake Titicaca

Paraná R.

20° S

Tropic of Capricorn

ANDES

Gran Chaco

Paraguay R.

Tropic of Capricorn

Aconcagua
22,834 ft
(6,960 m)

Pampas

Río de la Plata

Patagonia

ATLANTIC OCEAN

Falkland Islands

Tierra del Fuego

Cape Horn

KEY
ELEVATION

Feet		Meters
More than 13,000		More than 3,960
6,500–13,000		1,980–3,960
1,600–6,500		480–1,980
650–1,600		200–480
0–650		0–200

Ice cap

—— National border

0 miles 2,000
0 kilometers 2,000
Lambert Azimuthal Equal Area

N W E S

United States: Political

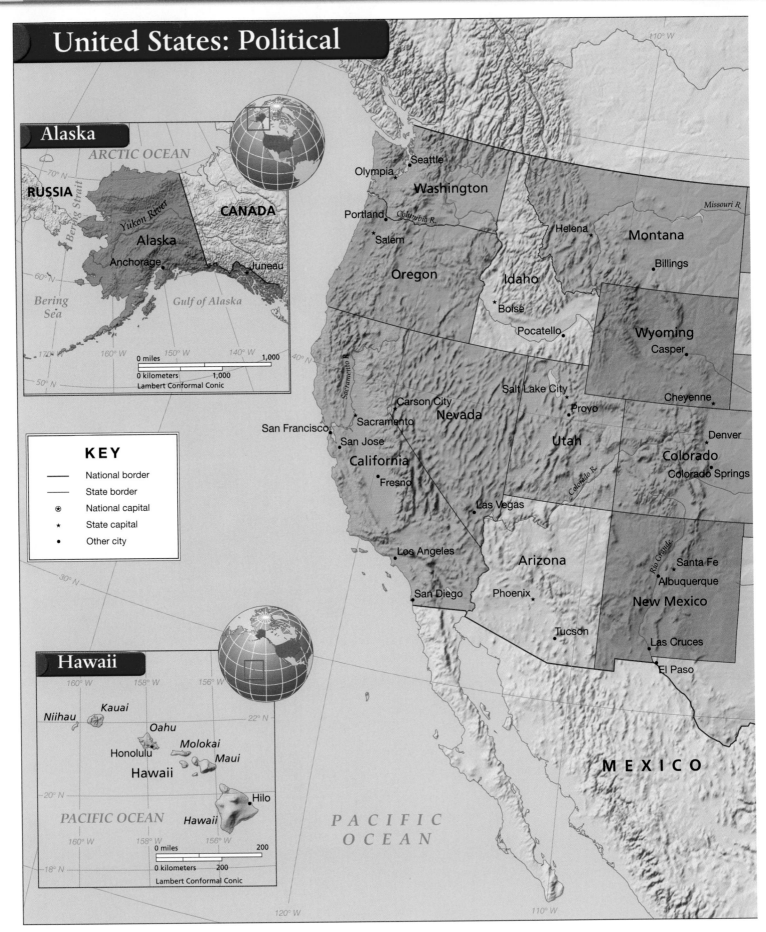

Alaska

ARCTIC OCEAN

RUSSIA

CANADA

Yukon River

Alaska

Anchorage

Juneau

Bering Strait

Arctic Circle

70° N

60° N

Bering Sea

Gulf of Alaska

50° N

170° W   160° W   150° W   140° W

0 miles   1,000
0 kilometers   1,000
Lambert Conformal Conic

KEY

- ——— National border
- ——— State border
- ⊗ National capital
- ★ State capital
- • Other city

Hawaii

160° W   158° W   156° W

Niihau   Kauai
          Oahu
Honolulu   Molokai
          Maui
Hawaii
Hilo

22° N

20° N

18° N

PACIFIC OCEAN   Hawaii

0 miles   200
0 kilometers   200
Lambert Conformal Conic

Seattle
Olympia
Washington
Portland
Columbia R.
Salem
Oregon
Helena
Montana
Billings
Idaho
Boise
Pocatello
Wyoming
Casper
Missouri R.

Sacramento R.
Carson City
Sacramento
Nevada
San Francisco
San Jose
California
Fresno
Salt Lake City
Provo
Utah
Cheyenne
Denver
Colorado
Colorado Springs
Colorado R.

Las Vegas
Los Angeles
Arizona
San Diego
Phoenix
Tucson
New Mexico
Rio Grande
Santa Fe
Albuquerque
Las Cruces
El Paso

40° N
30° N

110° W
120° W
110° W

PACIFIC OCEAN

MEXICO

CANADA

North Dakota
Bismarck ★
Fargo •

Minnesota

South Dakota
Pierre ★
Sioux Falls •

Lake Superior

St. Paul ★
Minneapolis •
Wisconsin

Mississippi R.

Michigan

Lake Huron

Lake Ontario

Maine
Augusta ★
Vermont
Portland •
Montpelier ★
New Hampshire
Concord ★
Boston •
Albany ★
Massachusetts
New York
Buffalo •
Providence
Hartford ★
Rhode Island
Connecticut
New York City

Milwaukee •
Madison ★

Grand Rapids •
Lansing ★
Detroit •

Lake Erie

Cleveland •
Pittsburgh •

Pennsylvania
Harrisburg ★

New Jersey
Trenton ★
Philadelphia
Delaware

Iowa
Des Moines ★

Chicago •
Cedar Rapids •
Fort Wayne •
Ohio
Columbus ★
Indianapolis ★

Nebraska
Omaha •
Lincoln ★

Missouri R.

Illinois
Indiana

Springfield ★
Cincinnati •
Ohio R.

Washington, D.C.
Baltimore •
Dover ★
Annapolis ★
Maryland
District of Columbia

West
Virginia
Charleston ★
Richmond ★
Norfolk •
Virginia

Topeka ★
Kansas City •
Jefferson City ★
St. Louis •

Kansas
Arkansas R.
Wichita •

Missouri

Louisville •
Frankfort ★
Kentucky

Nashville •
Knoxville •

Raleigh ★

North Carolina
Charlotte •

Oklahoma
Tulsa •

Arkansas
Fort Smith •
Little Rock ★

Mississippi R.
Memphis •
Tennessee

Tennessee R.

South Carolina
Columbia ★
Charleston •

ATLANTIC
OCEAN

Oklahoma City ★

Red R.

Mississippi
Jackson ★

Birmingham •
Alabama
Montgomery ★

Atlanta •
Georgia
Columbus •

Savannah •

Fort Worth •
Dallas •
Texas
Austin ★
San Antonio •
Houston •

Shreveport •
Louisiana
Baton Rouge ★
Gulfport •
New Orleans •

Mobile •
Tallahassee ★

Jacksonville •

Florida
Orlando •
Tampa •

Gulf of Mexico

N
W E
S

Miami •

0 miles   250
0 kilometers   250
Lambert Azimuthal Equal Area

50° N
40° N
30° N
100° W   90° W   80° W   70° W
90° W   80° W

Europe: Political

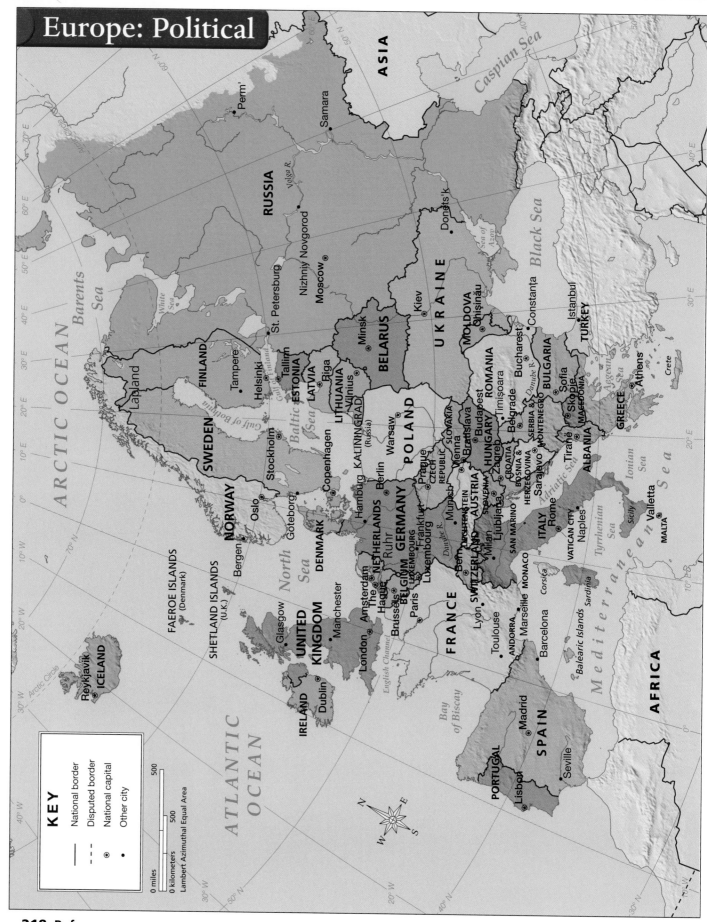

KEY

National border

Disputed border

National capital

Other city

0 miles 500

0 kilometers 500

Lambert Azimuthal Equal Area

ASIA

Caspian Sea

Perm'

Samara

RUSSIA

Volga R.

Nizhniy Novgorod

Moscow

St. Petersburg

Barents Sea

White Sea

ARCTIC OCEAN

Donets'k

Sea of Azov

Black Sea

UKRAINE

Kiev

MOLDOVA

Chişinău

Constanţa

Istanbul

TURKEY

Minsk

BELARUS

FINLAND

Tampere

Helsinki

Gulf of Finland

Tallinn

ESTONIA

Riga

LATVIA

LITHUANIA

Vilnius

KALININGRAD

(Russia)

ROMANIA

Timişoara

Bucharest

Danube R.

BULGARIA

Sofia

Skopje

MACEDONIA

Athens

GREECE

Aegean Sea

Crete

Lapland

SWEDEN

Stockholm

Baltic Sea

Gulf of Bothnia

Warsaw

POLAND

Budapest

HUNGARY

Bratislava

SLOVAKIA

Vienna

Belgrade

SERBIA &

MONTENEGRO

Sarajevo

BOSNIA &

HERZEGOVINA

Tiranë

ALBANIA

Adriatic Sea

Ionian Sea

NORWAY

Oslo

Bergen

Göteborg

Copenhagen

DENMARK

Hamburg

Berlin

GERMANY

Prague

CZECH

REPUBLIC

Munich

AUSTRIA

SLOVENIA

Ljubljana

Zagreb

CROATIA

Milan

SAN MARINO

Rome

ITALY

Naples

VATICAN CITY

Tyrrhenian Sea

Sicily

Valletta

MALTA

North Sea

NETHERLANDS

Amsterdam

The Hague

Ruhr

Frankfurt

LIECHTENSTEIN

Bern

SWITZERLAND

MONACO

Corsica

Sardinia

Mediterranean Sea

AFRICA

FAEROE ISLANDS

(Denmark)

SHETLAND ISLANDS

(U.K.)

Glasgow

Manchester

UNITED

KINGDOM

London

BELGIUM

Brussels

LUXEMBOURG

Luxembourg

Paris

FRANCE

Lyon

Danube R.

Toulouse

Marseille

ANDORRA

Barcelona

Balearic Islands

Reykjavík

ICELAND

Arctic Circle

IRELAND

Dublin

English Channel

Bay of Biscay

Madrid

SPAIN

Seville

PORTUGAL

Lisbon

ATLANTIC OCEAN

N E S W

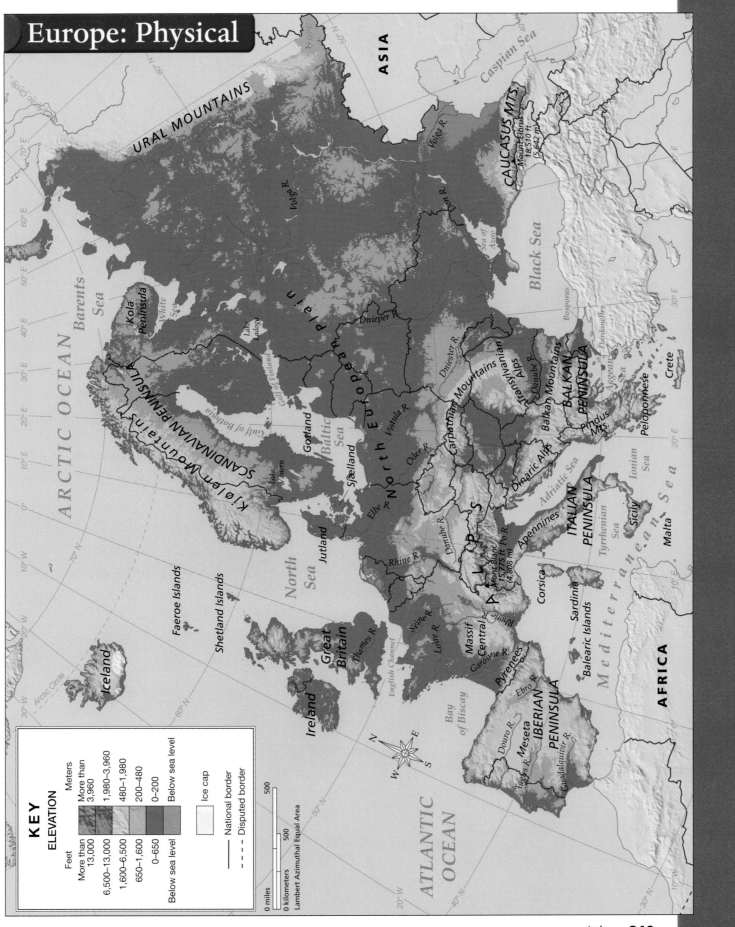

Europe: Physical

ASIA

URAL MOUNTAINS

Caspian Sea

CAUCASUS MTS.

Mount Elbrus
18,510 ft
(5,642 m)

Barents Sea

ARCTIC OCEAN

Kola Peninsula

White Sea

Volga R.

Volga R.

Don R.

Sea of Azov

Black Sea

Lake Ladoga

Dnieper R.

Bosporus

Dardanelles

Crete

North European Plain

SCANDINAVIAN PENINSULA

Kjølen Mountains

Gulf of Bothnia

Lake Vänern

Gulf of Finland

Gotland

Baltic Sea

Sjælland

Dniester R.

Vistula R.

Oder R.

Carpathian Mountains

Transylvanian Alps

Danube R.

Balkan Mountains

BALKAN PENINSULA

Dinaric Alps

Pindus Mts.

Aegean Sea

Peloponnese

Ionian Sea

Elbe R.

Jutland

North Sea

Faeroe Islands

Shetland Islands

Danube R.

Rhine R.

ALPS

Mont Blanc
15,775 ft
(4,808 m)

Po R.

Apennines

Adriatic Sea

ITALIAN PENINSULA

Corsica

Sardinia

Tyrrhenian Sea

Sicily

Mediterranean Sea

Malta

Great Britain

Thames R.

English Channel

Seine R.

Loire R.

Massif Central

Rhône R.

Garonne R.

Pyrenees

Balearic Islands

Ireland

Bay of Biscay

Ebro R.

IBERIAN PENINSULA

Meseta

Douro R.

Tagus R.

Guadalquivir R.

AFRICA

Iceland

Arctic Circle

ATLANTIC OCEAN

KEY

ELEVATION

Feet	Meters
More than 13,000	More than 3,960
6,500–13,000	1,980–3,960
1,600–6,500	480–1,980
650–1,600	200–480
0–650	0–200
Below sea level	Below sea level

Ice cap

—— National border

- - - Disputed border

0 miles 500

0 kilometers 500

Lambert Azimuthal Equal Area

Atlas **219**

Africa: Political

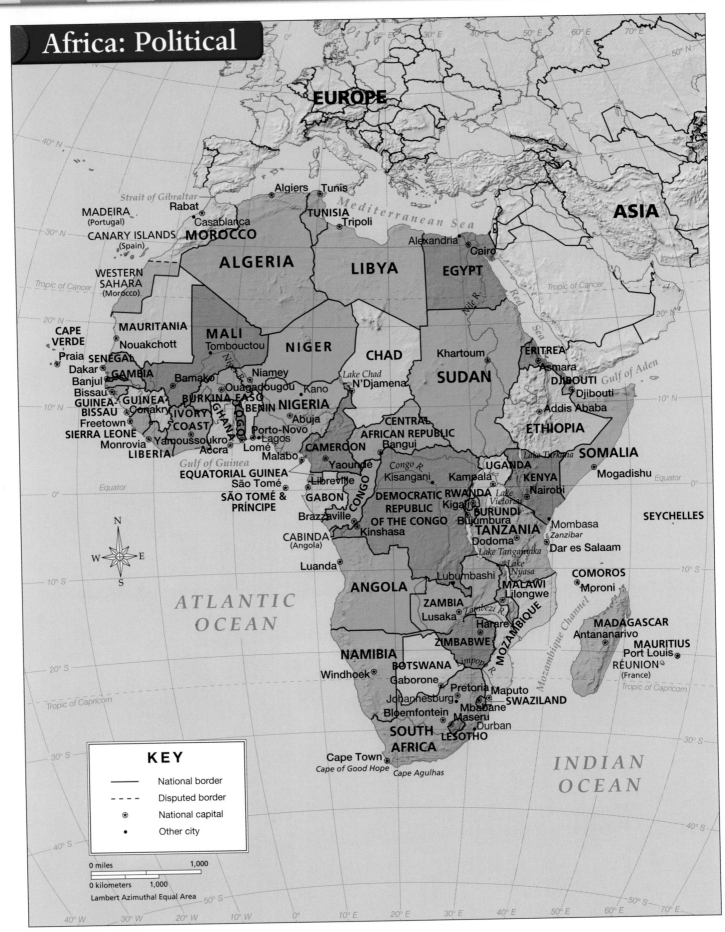

EUROPE

ASIA

Strait of Gibraltar

Mediterranean Sea

Algiers Tunis

MADEIRA
(Portugal) Rabat
Casablanca TUNISIA
Tripoli

CANARY ISLANDS
(Spain) MOROCCO Alexandria
Cairo

Tropic of Cancer WESTERN
SAHARA
(Morocco) ALGERIA LIBYA EGYPT *Tropic of Cancer*

CAPE
VERDE MAURITANIA MALI NIGER CHAD Khartoum ERITREA
Asmara

Nouakchott Tombouctou SUDAN DJIBOUTI
Gulf of Aden

Praia SENEGAL Djibouti

Dakar Niamey *Lake Chad*
N'Djamena

Banjul GAMBIA Bamako Addis Ababa

Bissau Ouagadougou Kano NIGERIA

GUINEA- GUINEA BURKINA FASO ETHIOPIA

BISSAU Conakry IVORY Abuja CENTRAL
AFRICAN REPUBLIC

Freetown COAST Porto-Novo Bangui

SIERRA LEONE Yamoussoukro Lagos CAMEROON *Lake Turkana* SOMALIA

Monrovia Accra Lomé Yaoundé UGANDA

LIBERIA Malabo *Congo R.* Kisangani Kampala KENYA Mogadishu *Equator*

Gulf of Guinea EQUATORIAL GUINEA Libreville DEMOCRATIC RWANDA *Lake
Victoria* Nairobi

Equator São Tomé GABON REPUBLIC Kigali SEYCHELLES

SÃO TOMÉ & OF THE CONGO BURUNDI

PRÍNCIPE Brazzaville Bujumbura Mombasa

Kinshasa TANZANIA Zanzibar

CABINDA Dodoma Dar es Salaam

(Angola) *Lake Tanganyika*

Luanda Lubumbashi *Lake
Nyasa* COMOROS
Moroni

ANGOLA MALAWI *Mozambique Channel*

ZAMBIA Lilongwe

ATLANTIC
OCEAN Lusaka *Zambezi R.* MOZAMBIQUE MADAGASCAR

Harare Antananarivo MAURITIUS

ZIMBABWE Port Louis

NAMIBIA *Limpopo R.* RÉUNION
(France)

BOTSWANA *Tropic of Capricorn*

Windhoek Gaborone Pretoria Maputo

Tropic of Capricorn Johannesburg SWAZILAND

Bloemfontein Mbabane

SOUTH Maseru Durban

AFRICA LESOTHO

Cape Town INDIAN
OCEAN

Cape of Good Hope Cape Agulhas

KEY

——	National border
- - -	Disputed border
⊛	National capital
•	Other city

0 miles   1,000
0 kilometers   1,000
Lambert Azimuthal Equal Area

Africa: Physical

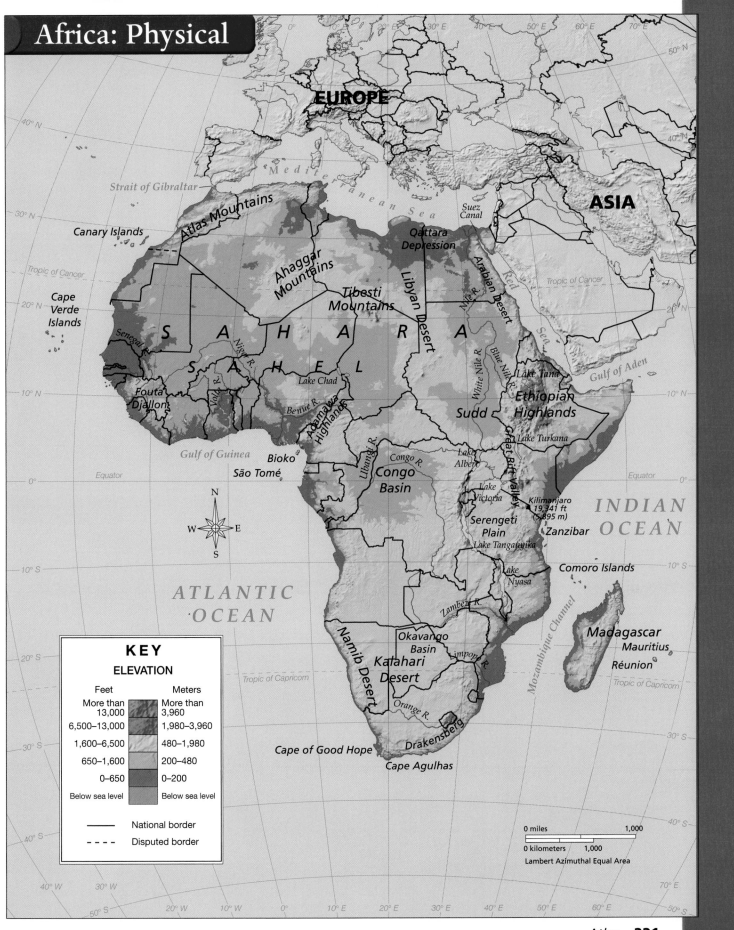

EUROPE

ASIA

Strait of Gibraltar

Atlas Mountains

Canary Islands

Cape Verde Islands

Ahaggar Mountains

Tibesti Mountains

Libyan Desert

Qattara Depression

Suez Canal

Arabian Desert

Red Sea

Gulf of Aden

S A H A R A

Senegal R.

Niger R.

S A H E L

Volta R.

Lake Chad

Benue R.

Fouta Djallon

Adamawa Highlands

Nile R.

White Nile R.

Blue Nile R.

Lake Tana

Ethiopian Highlands

Sudd

Gulf of Guinea

Bioko

São Tomé

Ubangi R.

Congo R.

Congo Basin

Lake Albert

Lake Victoria

Lake Turkana

Great Rift Valley

Kilimanjaro 19,341 ft (5,895 m)

INDIAN OCEAN

Equator

Equator

Serengeti Plain

Zanzibar

Lake Tanganyika

Lake Nyasa

Comoro Islands

ATLANTIC OCEAN

Namib Desert

Okavango Basin

Zambezi R.

Kalahari Desert

Limpopo R.

Mozambique Channel

Madagascar

Mauritius

Réunion

Tropic of Capricorn

Tropic of Capricorn

Orange R.

Drakensberg

Cape of Good Hope

Cape Agulhas

N
W   E
S

Tropic of Cancer

Tropic of Cancer

Mediterranean Sea

KEY

ELEVATION

Feet		Meters
More than 13,000		More than 3,960
6,500–13,000		1,980–3,960
1,600–6,500		480–1,980
650–1,600		200–480
0–650		0–200
Below sea level		Below sea level

——— National border

- - - - Disputed border

0 miles 1,000

0 kilometers 1,000

Lambert Azimuthal Equal Area

Asia: Political

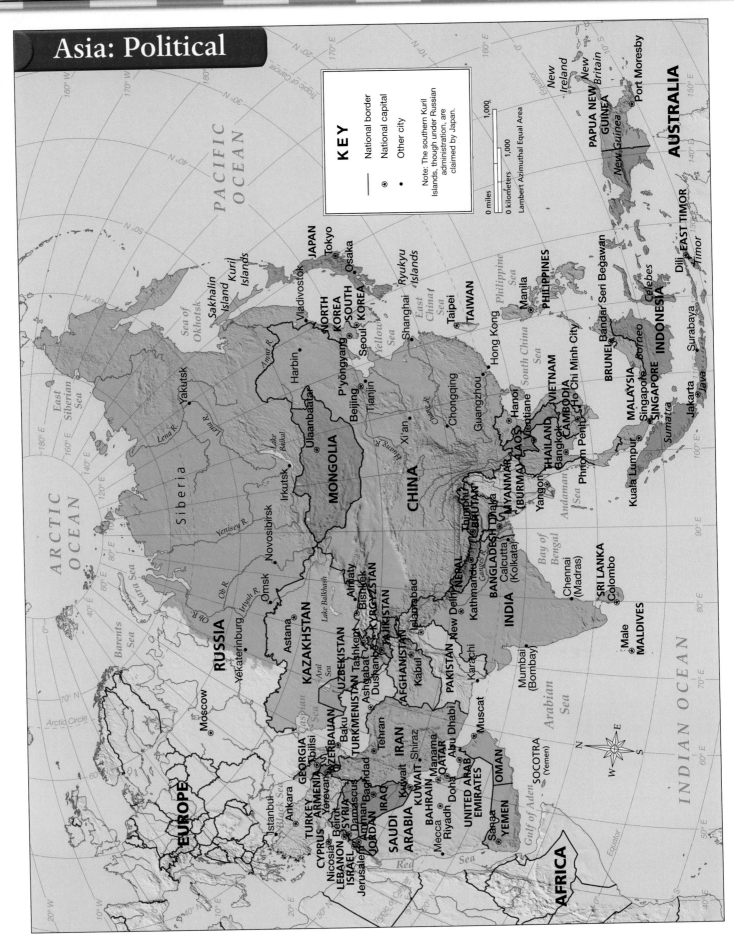

KEY

— National border

⊛ National capital

• Other city

Note: The southern Kuril Islands, though under Russian administration, are claimed by Japan.

0 miles   1,000
0 kilometers   1,000
Lambert Azimuthal Equal Area

ARCTIC OCEAN

PACIFIC OCEAN

INDIAN OCEAN

East Siberian Sea

Sea of Okhotsk

Barents Sea

Kara Sea

Black Sea

Caspian Sea

Aral Sea

Lake Baikal

Lake Balkhash

Yellow Sea

East China Sea

South China Sea

Philippine Sea

Andaman Sea

Bay of Bengal

Arabian Sea

Red Sea

Gulf of Aden

Lena R.

Amur R.

Yenisey R.

Ob R.

Irtysh R.

Huang R.

Chang R.

Ganges R.

Siberia

Sakhalin Island

Kuril Islands

Ryukyu Islands

Sumatra

Java

Borneo

Celebes

New Guinea

New Britain

New Ireland

Socotra (Yemen)

EUROPE

AFRICA

AUSTRALIA

RUSSIA

MONGOLIA

CHINA

JAPAN
- Tokyo
- Osaka

NORTH KOREA ⊛ P'yŏngyang

SOUTH KOREA ⊛ Seoul

TAIWAN ⊛ Taipei

PHILIPPINES ⊛ Manila

PAPUA NEW GUINEA ⊛ Port Moresby

EAST TIMOR ⊛ Dili

INDONESIA ⊛ Jakarta
- Surabaya

BRUNEI ⊛ Bandar Seri Begawan

MALAYSIA ⊛ Kuala Lumpur

SINGAPORE ⊛ Singapore

VIETNAM ⊛ Hanoi
- Ho Chi Minh City

CAMBODIA ⊛ Phnom Penh

LAOS ⊛ Vientiane

THAILAND ⊛ Bangkok

MYANMAR (BURMA) ⊛ Yangon

KAZAKHSTAN ⊛ Astana
- Almaty

UZBEKISTAN ⊛ Tashkent

TURKMENISTAN ⊛ Ashgabat

KYRGYZSTAN ⊛ Bishkek

TAJIKISTAN ⊛ Dushanbe

AFGHANISTAN ⊛ Kabul

PAKISTAN ⊛ Islamabad
- Karachi

INDIA ⊛ New Delhi
- Mumbai (Bombay)
- Calcutta (Kolkata)
- Chennai (Madras)

NEPAL ⊛ Kathmandu

BHUTAN ⊛ Thimphu

BANGLADESH ⊛ Dhaka

SRI LANKA ⊛ Colombo

MALDIVES ⊛ Male

IRAN ⊛ Tehran
- Shiraz

IRAQ ⊛ Baghdad

GEORGIA ⊛ Tbilisi

ARMENIA ⊛ Yerevan

AZERBAIJAN ⊛ Baku

TURKEY ⊛ Ankara
- Istanbul

CYPRUS ⊛ Nicosia

LEBANON ⊛ Beirut

SYRIA ⊛ Damascus

ISRAEL ⊛ Jerusalem

JORDAN ⊛ Amman

SAUDI ARABIA ⊛ Riyadh
- Mecca

KUWAIT ⊛ Kuwait

BAHRAIN ⊛ Manama

QATAR ⊛ Doha

UNITED ARAB EMIRATES ⊛ Abu Dhabi

OMAN ⊛ Muscat

YEMEN ⊛ Sanaa

⊛ Moscow
- Yekaterinburg
- Novosibirsk
- Omsk
- Yakutsk
- Irkutsk
- Vladivostok
- Harbin
- Beijing
- Tianjin
- Shanghai
- Xi'an
- Chongqing
- Guangzhou
- Hong Kong

⊛ Ulaanbaatar

Tropic of Cancer

Equator

Arctic Circle

N E S W

Asia: Physical

KEY

ELEVATION

Feet	Meters
More than 13,000	More than 3,960
6,500–13,000	1,980–3,960
1,600–6,500	480–1,980
650–1,600	200–480
0–650	0–200
Below sea level	Below sea level

—— National border

PACIFIC OCEAN

ARCTIC OCEAN

INDIAN OCEAN

AUSTRALIA

EUROPE

AFRICA

New Ireland
New Britain
New Guinea
Mindanao
Moluccas
Celebes
Borneo
Lesser Sunda Islands
Timor
Java
Sumatra
Luzon
Philippine Sea
Taiwan
South China Sea
Hainan
Malay Peninsula
Strait of Malacca
Indochina Peninsula
Andaman Islands
Andaman Sea
Bay of Bengal
Sri Lanka
Deccan Plateau
Eastern Ghats
Western Ghats
INDIAN PENINSULA
Ganges R.
HIMALAYAS
Mt. Everest 29,035 ft (8,848 m)
Tibetan Plateau
Kunlun Shan
Taklimakan Desert
Tian Shan
Hindu Kush
Thar Desert
Indus R.
Plateau of Iran
Kara Kum Desert
Aral Sea
Lake Balkhash
Arabian Sea
Persian Gulf
Socotra
Gulf of Aden
Rub' al-Khali Desert
ARABIAN PENINSULA
Red Sea
Mediterranean Sea
Cyprus
Plateau of Anatolia
Tigris R.
Euphrates R.
Black Sea
Caspian Sea
CAUCASUS MTS.
URAL MOUNTAINS
Ob R.
Irtysh R.
Ob R.
Yenisey R.
North Siberian Lowland
Central Siberian Plateau
Lena R.
Cherskiy Range
Kolyma Mts
Kamchatka Peninsula
Sea of Okhotsk
Sakhalin Island
Kuril Islands
Hokkaidō
Honshū
Shikoku
Kyūshū
Ryukyu Islands
East China Sea
Yellow Sea
Korean Peninsula
Sea of Japan
Amur R.
Stanovoy Range
Altai Mts
Mongolian Plateau
Lake Baikal
GOBI DESERT
North China Plain
Huang R.
Chang R.
Mekong R.
Salween R.
Irrawaddy R.

Barents Sea
Kara Sea
East Siberian Sea
Arctic Circle

0 miles 1,000
0 kilometers 1,000
Lambert Azimuthal Equal Area

Oceania

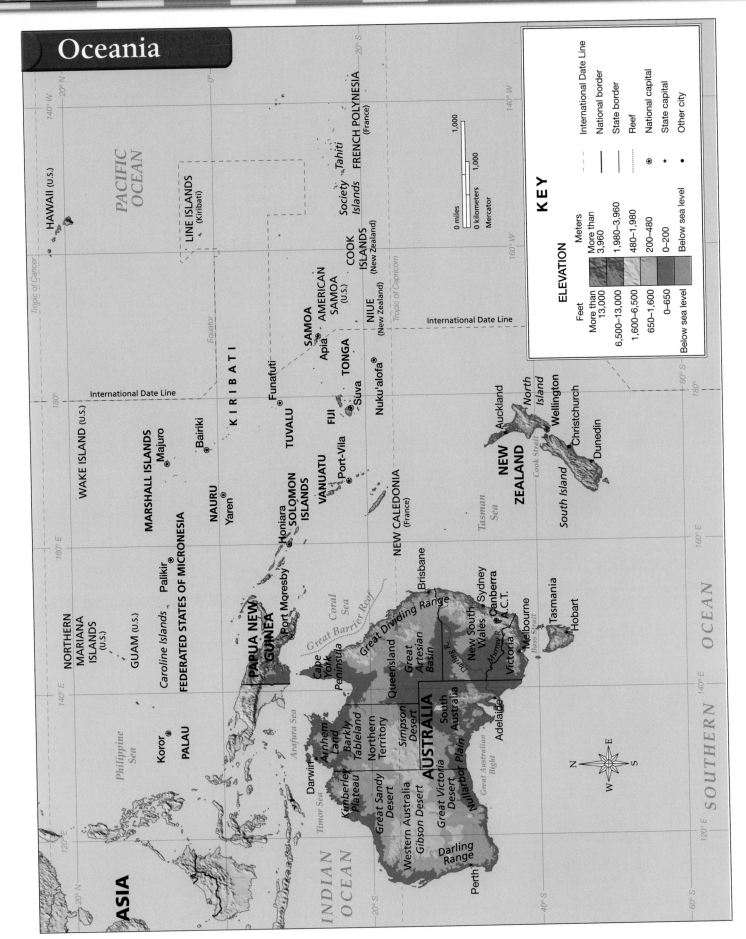

ASIA

HAWAII (U.S.)

PACIFIC OCEAN

Tropic of Cancer

LINE ISLANDS
(Kiribati)

FRENCH POLYNESIA
(France)

Society Tahiti
Islands

COOK
ISLANDS
(New Zealand)

Equator

SAMOA
Apia
AMERICAN
SAMOA
(U.S.)

NIUE
(New Zealand)

TONGA
Nuku'alofa

Tropic of Capricorn

International Date Line

NORTHERN
MARIANA
ISLANDS
(U.S.)

GUAM (U.S.)

Caroline Islands   Palikir
FEDERATED STATES OF MICRONESIA

WAKE ISLAND (U.S.)

MARSHALL ISLANDS
Majuro

Bairiki

K I R I B A T I

Funafuti

TUVALU

FIJI
Suva

International Date Line

Philippine
Sea

Koror
PALAU

NAURU
Yaren

SOLOMON
ISLANDS
Honiara

VANUATU
Port-Vila

NEW CALEDONIA
(France)

Auckland
North
Island
Wellington
Christchurch
Dunedin

NEW
ZEALAND

Cook Strait

South Island

Tasman
Sea

PAPUA NEW
GUINEA
Port Moresby

Great Coral
Sea

Great Barrier Reef

Great Dividing Range

Brisbane

Queensland

Great
Artesian
Basin

New South
Wales
Sydney
Canberra
A.C.T.
Melbourne
Victoria
Bass Strait

Tasmania
Hobart

Arafura Sea

Timor Sea

Darwin

Arnhem
Land

Kimberley
Plateau
Barkly
Tableland

Northern
Territory

Simpson
Desert

AUSTRALIA

South
Australia

Adelaide

Murray R.

Darling R.

Great Sandy
Desert

Western Australia

Gibson Desert

Great Victoria
Desert

Nullarbor Plain

Great Australian
Bight

Darling
Range

Perth

INDIAN
OCEAN

SOUTHERN   OCEAN

N E W S (compass)

224 Reference

KEY

- - -	International Date Line
——	National border
—	State border
····	Reef
⊛	National capital
★	State capital
•	Other city

ELEVATION

Feet	Meters	
More than 13,000	More than 3,960	
6,500–13,000	1,980–3,960	
1,600–6,500	480–1,980	
650–1,600	200–480	
0–650	0–200	
Below sea level	Below sea level	

0 miles   1,000
0 kilometers 1,000
Mercator

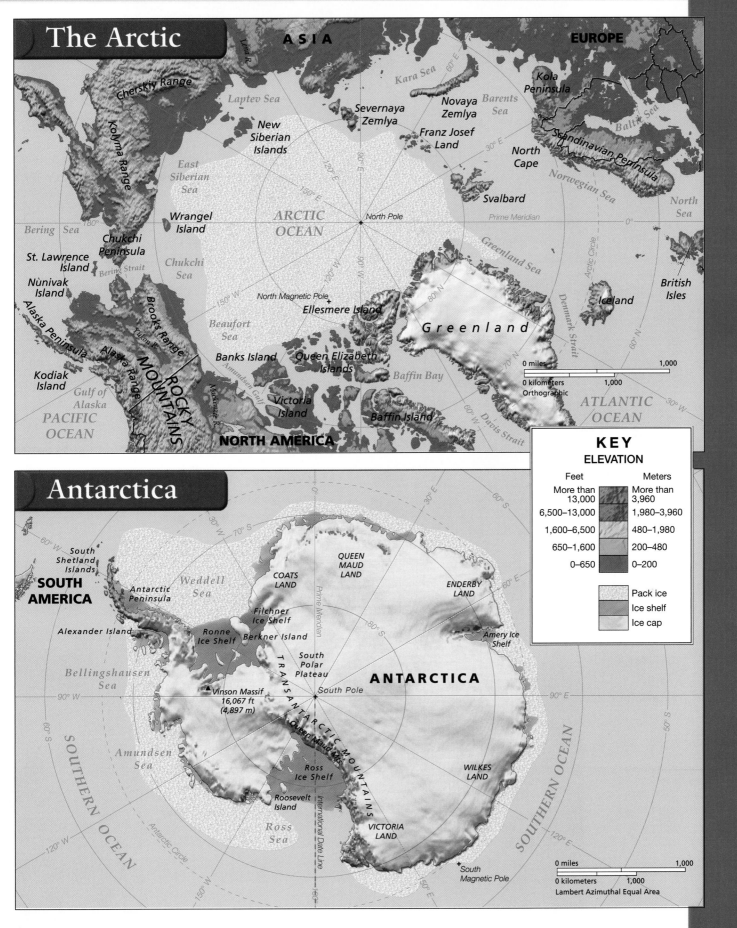

The Arctic

ASIA
EUROPE

Cherskiy Range
Kolyma Range
Lena R.
Laptev Sea
Kara Sea
60° E
Kola Peninsula
Novaya Zemlya
Barents Sea
Severnaya Zemlya
Franz Josef Land
Scandinavian Peninsula
Baltic Sea
New Siberian Islands
North Cape
30° E
East Siberian Sea
ARCTIC OCEAN
90° E
Svalbard
Norwegian Sea
Wrangel Island
North Pole
Prime Meridian
0°
North Sea
Bering Sea
180°
Chukchi Peninsula
Chukchi Sea
120° W
90° W
Greenland Sea
Arctic Circle
Iceland
British Isles
St. Lawrence Island
Bering Strait
150° W
North Magnetic Pole
80° N
Denmark Strait
60° N
Nùnivak Island
Beaufort Sea
Ellesmere Island
Greenland
70° N
Alaska Peninsula
Brooks Range
Yukon R.
Banks Island
Queen Elizabeth Islands
Baffin Bay
30° W
Kodiak Island
Alaska Range
ROCKY MOUNTAINS
Amundsen Gulf
Mackenzie R.
Victoria Island
Baffin Island
Davis Strait
60° W
Gulf of Alaska
PACIFIC OCEAN
NORTH AMERICA
ATLANTIC OCEAN
30° W

0 miles 1,000
0 kilometers 1,000
Orthographic

Antarctica

South Shetland Islands
SOUTH AMERICA
60° W
30° W
70° S
QUEEN MAUD LAND
60° E
Antarctic Peninsula
Weddell Sea
COATS LAND
ENDERBY LAND
Alexander Island
Filchner Ice Shelf
Prime Meridian
60° S
Ronne Ice Shelf
Berkner Island
Amery Ice Shelf
Bellingshausen Sea
TRANSANTARCTIC MOUNTAINS
South Polar Plateau
180° S
ANTARCTICA
90° W
Vinson Massif 16,067 ft (4,897 m)
South Pole
90° E
Queen Maud Mts.
50° S
Amundsen Sea
60° S
Ross Ice Shelf
WILKES LAND
SOUTHERN OCEAN
120° E
Roosevelt Island
International Date Line
120° W
Ross Sea
VICTORIA LAND
Antarctic Circle
South Magnetic Pole
150° W
90° E
180°

SOUTHERN OCEAN

0 miles 1,000
0 kilometers 1,000
Lambert Azimuthal Equal Area

KEY
ELEVATION

Feet		Meters
More than 13,000		More than 3,960
6,500–13,000		1,980–3,960
1,600–6,500		480–1,980
650–1,600		200–480
0–650		0–200

Pack ice
Ice shelf
Ice cap

Glossary of Geographic Terms

basin
an area that is lower than surrounding land areas; some basins are filled with water

bay
a body of water that is partly surrounded by land and that is connected to a larger body of water

butte
a small, high, flat-topped landform with cliff-like sides

▲ **butte**

canyon
a deep, narrow valley with steep sides; often with a stream flowing through it

cataract
a large waterfall or steep rapids

◀ **cataract**

delta
a plain at the mouth of a river, often triangular in shape, formed where sediment is deposited by flowing water

flood plain
a broad plain on either side of a river, formed where sediment settles during floods

glacier
a huge, slow-moving mass of snow and ice

hill
an area that rises above surrounding land and has a rounded top; lower and usually less steep than a mountain

island
an area of land completely surrounded by water

isthmus
a narrow strip of land that connects two larger areas of land

mesa
a high, flat-topped landform with cliff-like sides; larger than a butte

mountain
a landform that rises steeply at least 2,000 feet (610 meters) above surrounding land; usually wide at the bottom and rising to a narrow peak or ridge

▶ **glacier**

◀ delta

mountain pass
a gap between mountains

peninsula
an area of land almost completely surrounded by water but connected to the mainland

plain
a large area of flat or gently rolling land

plateau
a large, flat area that rises above the surrounding land; at least one side has a steep slope

river mouth
the point where a river enters a lake or sea

strait
a narrow stretch of water that connects two larger bodies of water

tributary
a river or stream that flows into a larger river

valley
a low stretch of land between mountains or hills; land that is drained by a river

volcano
an opening in Earth's surface through which molten rock, ashes, and gases escape from the interior

▶ volcano

Gazetteer

A

Alpine Mountain System (46° N, 10° E) a range of mountains that extends through south central Europe; Europe's highest mountain system, p. 13

Athens (37°58' N, 23°43' E) the capital city of modern Greece; the world's most powerful cultural center in the 400s B.C., p. 39

B

Balkan Peninsula (44° N, 23° E) a region in southeastern Europe also known as the Balkans, p. 183

Berlin (52°31' N, 13°24' E) the capital city of Germany; once divided into East Berlin and West Berlin, p. 154

Bosnia and Herzegovina (44° N, 18° E) a country in Eastern Europe, p. 186

C

Central Uplands a region of mountains and plateaus in the center of Southern Europe, p. 13

Chernobyl (51°16' N, 30°14' E) the city in northern Ukraine where a nuclear power station accident occurred in 1986, p. 194

Czechoslovakia a former Central European country that contained the present-day countries of the Czech Republic and Slovakia, p. 95

D

Danube River (45° N, 30° E) a river that flows 1,770 miles (2,850 kilometers) from Germany to the Black Sea, p. 15

E

Eurasia the world's largest landmass; contains the continents of Europe and Asia, p. 11

Europe (50° N, 28° E) the world's second-smallest continent; a peninsula of the Eurasian landmass bordered by the Arctic Ocean, the Atlantic Ocean, the Mediterranean Sea, and Asia, p. 11

F

France (46° N, 2° E) a country in Western Europe, p. 130

Europe's Central Uplands

G

Germany (51° N, 10° E) a country in Western Europe, p. 154

Gulf Stream a warm ocean current in the North Atlantic, flowing northeastward off the North American coast, p. 18

I

Italy (43° N, 13° E) a country in Southern Europe, p. 145

L

London (51°30′ N, 0°10′ W) the capital city of the United Kingdom, p. 19

M

Macedonia (42° N, 22° E) a country in Eastern Europe, p. 187

Mediterranean Sea (35° N, 20° E) the large sea that separates Europe and Africa, p. 18

Moscow (55°45′ N, 37°35′ E) the capital city of modern Russia, p. 63

Tearing down Germany's Berlin Wall

A North Sea oil rig

N

Netherlands, The (52° N, 6° E) a country in Northern Europe, p. 10

North Atlantic Current a warm ocean current in the North Atlantic, flowing northeastward toward Europe, p. 18

North European Plains plains extending from Russia to France; contains Europe and Russia's most productive farmland and largest cities, p. 13

North Sea (56° N, 3° E) an arm of the Atlantic Ocean located between Great Britain and the European mainland, p. 26

Northwestern Highlands a mountainous, forested region in northern Europe, p. 13

Polish folk dancers

P

Paris (48°52′ N, 2°20′ E) the capital city of France, p. 130

Poland (52° N, 19° E) a country in Eastern Europe, p. 174

R

Rhine River (52° N, 6° E) a river that flows about 865 miles (1,392 kilometers) from Switzerland to the Netherlands, p. 15

Rome (41°54′ N, 12°29′ E) the capital of modern Italy; one of the world's greatest ancient civilizations and empires, p. 41

Ruhr (51° N, 7° E) an industrial region in Germany; also the name of a river there, p. 28

Russia (60° N, 80° E) a country in northern Eurasia, p. 198

S

St. Petersburg (59°55′ N, 30°15′ E) a city and important cultural center in Russia, p. 105

Sarajevo (43°52′ N, 18°25′ E) the capital city of Bosnia and Herzegovina, p. 181

Scandinavia a historical region of northern Europe that includes Norway, Finland, Sweden, Denmark, and Iceland, p. 23

Serbia and Montenegro (44° N, 21° E) a country in Eastern Europe, p. 183

Siberia (65° N, 110° E) a resource-rich region of northeastern Russia; contains the West Siberian Plain, the Central Siberian Plateau, and the East Siberian Uplands, p. 14

Silesia (51° N, 17° E) a coal-rich region where Poland, the Czech Republic, and Germany meet, p. 29

Slovenia (46° N, 15° E) a country in Eastern Europe, p. 185

Soviet Union a former communist country that included present-day Russia and several other Eastern European countries, p. 67

Sweden (62° N, 15° E) a country in Northern Europe, p. 138

U

Ukraine (49° N, 32° E) a country in Eastern Europe, p. 189

United Kingdom (54° N, 2° E) a nation in Northern Europe that includes Great Britain and Northern Ireland, p. 122

Ural Mountains (60° N, 60° E) a mountain range in northern Eurasia that forms the border between Europe and Asia, p. 11

V

Vatican City (41°54' N, 12°27' W) a nation-state completely surrounded by Rome, Italy; the seat of the Roman Catholic Church, p. 145

Volga River (46° N, 48° E) Europe's longest river; it flows 2,291 miles (3,687 kilometers) through western Russia to the Caspian Sea, p. 15

Y

Yugoslavia a former Eastern European country that contained the present-day countries of Serbia and Montenegro, Bosnia and Herzegovina, Croatia, Slovenia, and Macedonia, p. 95

Vatican City

Glossary

A

alliance (uh LY uns) *n.* an agreement between countries to protect and defend each other, p. 58

B

basilica (buh SIL ih kuh) *n.* a Roman Catholic church that has a special, high status because of its age or history, p. 146

C

capitalism (KAP ut ul iz um) *n.* an economic system in which businesses are privately owned, p. 177

chernozem (CHEHR nuh zem) *n.* rich, black soil, productive for farming, p. 191

city-state (SIH tee stayt) *n.* a city with its own government that was both a city and an independent state, p. 39

collective (kuh LEK tiv) *n.* a huge government-controlled farm, p. 192

colony (KAHL uh nee) *n.* a territory ruled by another nation, p. 50

communism (KAHM yoo niz um) *n.* a political system in which the central government owns farms, factories, and offices, p. 66

constitution

constitution (kahn stuh TOO shun) *n.* a set of laws that describes how a government works, p. 126

constitutional monarchy (kahn stuh TOO shuh nul MAHN ur kee) *n.* a government in which a monarch is the head of state but has limited powers, p. 127

D

democracy (dih MAHK ruh see) *n.* a kind of government in which citizens govern themselves, p. 39

dialect (DY uh lekt) *n.* a version of a language found only in a certain region, p. 93

E

economic sanctions (ek uh NAHM ik SANGK shunz) *n.* actions to limit trade with nations that have violated international laws, p. 188

embargo (em BAHR goh) *n.* a ban on trade, p. 185

entrepreneur (ahn truh pruh NOOR) *n.* a person who develops original ideas in order to start new businesses, p. 178

ethnic group (ETH nik groop) *n.* a group of people who share the same ancestors, culture, language, or religion, p. 93

euro (YER oh) *n.* the official currency of the European Union, p. 71

Prices for fruit in Spain are shown here in euros and pesetas.

A church in Scotland's highlands

F

feudalism (FYOOD ul iz um) *n.* a system in which land was owned by kinds of lords but held by vassals in return for their loyalty, p. 43

foreign minister (FAWR in MIN is tur) *n.* a government official who is in a charge of a nation's foreign affairs, p. 73

fossil fuel (FAHS ul FYOO ul) *n.* a source of energy that forms from ancient plant and animal remains, p. 28

H

heritage (HEHR uh tij) *n.* the customs and practices passed from one generation to the next, p. 101

Holocaust (HAHL uh kawst) *n.* the mass murder of six million Jews, p. 157

hydroelectric power (hy droh ee LEK trick POW ur) *n.* the power generated by water-driven turbines, p. 28

I

immigrant (IM uh grunt) *n.* a person who moves to one country from another, p. 88

imperialism (im PIHR ee ul iz um) *n.* the political and economic control of one country by another, p. 57

Industrial Revolution (in DUS tree ul rev uh LOO shun) *n.* the life-changing period in the 1800s when products began to be made by machines in factories, p. 53

inflation (in FLAY shun) *n.* an increase in the general level of prices, p. 200

investor (in VES tur) *n.* someone who spends money on improving a business in the hope of making more money if the business succeeds, p. 199

L

land reform (land ree FAWRM) *n.* the process of dividing large properties into smaller ones, p. 150

loess (LOH es) *n.* a type of rich, dustlike soil, p. 27

M

manufacturing (man yoo FAK chur ing) *n.* the process of turning raw materials into finished products, p. 149

Middle Ages (MID ul AY juz) *n.* the time between ancient and modern times, about A.D. 500–1500, p. 38

migration (my GRAY shun) *n.* movement from place to place, p. 91

monarch (MAHN urk) *n.* the ruler of a kingdom or empire, such as a king or queen, p. 48

N

national debt (NASH uh nul det) *n.* the amount of money a government owes, p. 142

nationalism (NASH uh nul iz um) *n.* pride in one's country, p. 58

navigable (NAV ih guh bul) *adj.* wide and deep enough for ships to travel through, p. 15

Alessandro Volta demonstrates his battery.

P

Parliament (PAHR luh munt) *n.* the lawmaking body of the United Kingdom, p. 126

peninsula (puh NIN suh luh) *n.* a land area nearly surrounded by water, p. 12

permafrost (PUR muh frawst) *n.* a permanently frozen layer of ground below the top layer of soil, p. 23

philosophy (fil LAHS uh fee) *n.* a system of ideas and beliefs, p. 131

plateau (pla TOH) *n.* a large raised area of mostly level land bordered on one or more sides by steep slopes or cliffs, p. 13

population density (pahp yuh LAY shun DEN suh tee) *n.* the average number of people living in a square mile or square kilometer, p. 11

propaganda (praph uh GAN duh) *n.* the spread of ideas designed to support a cause, p. 104

R

rain shadow (rayn SHAD oh) *n.* the area on the dry, sheltered side of a mountain, which receives little rainfall, p. 19

Renaissance (REN uh sahns) *n.* a period of European history that was characterized by the rebirth of interest in learning and art, p. 46

representative (rep ruh ZEN tuh tiv) *n.* a person who represents, or stands for, a group of people, p. 126

reunification (ree yoo nih fih KAY shun) *n.* the process of becoming unified again, p. 159

revolution (rev uh LOO shun) *n.* a far-reaching change, p. 50

revolutionary (rev uh LOO shuh neh ree) *adj.* ideas that relate to or cause the overthrow of a government, or other great change, p. 66

A rainy day in St. Petersburg, Russia

S

secede (sih SEED) *v.* to leave a group, especially a political group or a nation, p. 185

shrine (shryn) *n.* a holy place, p. 175

single market (SING ul MAHR ket) *n.* system in which goods, services, and capital move freely with no barriers; used to describe the European Union, p. 72

standard of living (STAN durd uv LIV ing) *n.* the level of comfort in terms of the goods and services that people have, p. 159

steppe (step) *n.* the grassland of fertile soil suitable for farming in Russia, p. 22

T

textile (TEKS tyl) *n.* a cloth product, p. 54

tributary (TRIB yoo tehr ee) *n.* a river or stream that flows into a larger river, p. 15

tsar (zahr) *n.* a Russian emperor, p. 64

tundra (TUN druh) *n.* a cold, dry region covered with snow for more than half the year, p. 23

U

urbanization (ur bun ih ZAY shun) *n.* the movement of populations toward cities, p. 85

W

welfare state (WEL fair stayt) *n.* a country in which many services and benefits are paid for by the government, p. 139

westernization (wes tur nuh ZAY shun) *n.* the adoption of Western culture, p. 62

A Polish Eastern Orthodox church

Index

The *italicized* page numbers refer to illustrations. The *m, g,* or *p* following the number refers to maps *(m)*, charts, diagrams, tables, timelines, or graphs *(g)* or pictures *(p)*.

Blue indicates Teacher's Edition entries.

A

absolute location, M1
absolute monarch, 127
absolute power, 65
Act of Union (1801), 125
Africa, M10*m*, M11*m*, 57, 57*m*, 209*m*, 211*m*, 218*m*, 219*m*
  mountains of, M10
Age of Imperialism, 57, 57*m*
Age of Revolution, 50–51
Agricultural Revolution, 85, 85*g*
agriculture, M16
Akhmatova, Anna, 105, 105*p*
Albania, 3*m*, 6*m*, 187, 216*m*
  culture of, 182, 182*g*, 182*m*
  data about, 166
  ethnic groups in, 93
Alexander II, Tsar of Russia, 65
Alexander III, Tsar of Russia, 65
Alexander the Great, 40, 40*m*, 40*p*
Algeria, 135, 136, 218*m*
alliance, 58, 232
Allied Powers, 58
Alpine Mountain System, 4*m*, 12*m*, 13, 13*p*, 217*m*, 228
Alps, The, 13
American Revolution, 50, 50*p*
Americas, M14, M14*m*, M15*m*, 48
Amsterdam, the Netherlands, 87*p*, 118
Andorra, 3*m*, 6*m*, 112, 112*p*
Andorra la Vella, 112
Apennines, 4*m*, 217*m*
aqueducts, 41

architecture, French, 132, 132*p*
arctic climate, 20
Arctic Ocean, 12, 223*m*
Armenia, 102, 220*m*

art
  Christian, 42*p*
  European Union and, 87–88
  of France, 131
  of Italy, 151, 151*p*
  Renaissance, 46–47, 46*p*, 47*p*
  of Russia, 104, 104*p*, 105, 105*p*, 200, 200*p*
Asia, 209*m*, 211*m*, 220*m*, 221*m*
  borders with Europe, 2
Athens, 38–40, 39*g*, 40*m*, 40*p*, 115, 228
Atlantic Ocean, 20
Atlas Mountains, 219*m*
atomic bomb, 159
Augustus Caesar, 41, 41*p*
Austria, 3*m*, 6*m*, 91, 216*m*
  data about, 113
  labor force in, 85*g*
  natural resources of, 27*m*, 28
Austria-Hungary, 58, 169
automobiles, 144, 144*p*, 149, 149*p*
Axis Powers, 58

B

Balkan Peninsula, 4*m*, 183–188, 183*p*, 184*m*, 186*p*, 187*m*, 187*p*, 188*p*, 217*m*, 228
  culture in, 182, 182*g*, 182*m*, 183
  ethnic groups of, 182, 182*g*, 182*m*, 183
  language in, 183
  population of, 182, 182*g*
  religion in, 182, 182*g*, 183
Barcelona, Spain, 17, 18, 19*g*, 20
Bartók, Béla, 97
basilica, 146, 232
basin, 226
bay, 226
Beefeaters, 122, 122*p*

Belarus, 3*m*, 7*m*, 216*m*
  data about, 166
Belgium, 3*m*, 6*m*, 216*m*
  colonies of, 57, 57*m*
  data about, 113
  in European Coal and Steel Community, 70
Belgrade, 172
Berlin, Germany, 87, 87*p*, 115, 159–160, 228
  division of, 154, 154*p*, 155*m*, 157
Berlin Wall, 154, 154*p*, 157, 158–159, 158*p*, 229*p*
Bern, Switzerland, 120
Bialowieza, Poland, 175, 175*p*, 179*p*
Black Forest, 15
Black Sea, 15, 31
Bloody Sunday, 65
Bon Marché, 133, 133*p*
Bonaparte, Napolean, 64, 64*p*
Bonn, Germany, 157
boreal forest, 21*p*
Boreas (Greek god), 21*p*
Bosnia and Herzegovina, 3*m*, 6*m*, 184, 185, 186, 216*m*, 228
  culture of, 182, 182*g*, 182*m*
  data about, 167
  ethnic groups in, 93*p*
Boston Marathon, 38, 38*p*
Boucicaut, Aristide, 133
bowmen, 80
Boyle, Robert, 51
Bratislava, Slovakia, 172
Brittany, France, 110h
British East India Company, 127
Brussels, Belgium, 113
Bucharest, Romania, 171
Budapest, Hungary, 97, 169
Buddhism, 102, 102*p*
Bulgaria, 3*m*, 7*m*, 216*m*
  data about, 167
  standard of living, 178*g*
Buonarroti, Michelangelo, 36h, 46–47, 46*p*, 146, 146*p*
butte, 226, 226*p*

C

Caesar, Julius, 43
calculus, 52
canals, 10, 15, 110p
canyon, 226
capitalism, 232
  in Poland, 177–179, 180
  in Russia, 199–202
Carême, Marie-Antoine, 133
Carl XVI Gustaf, King of Sweden,
  141p
Carpathian Mountains, 4m, 217m
Caspian Sea, 16, 31
cataract, 226, 226p
Catherine the Great, 62, 62p
Caucasus Mountains, 217m, 221m
Central Siberian Plateau, 14, 221m
Central Uplands, 12m, 13, 228
Chanel, Gabrielle "Coco," 133
Channel Tunnel, the, 110h
Charles I, King of England, 50
Chechen people, 102, 203, 203p
Chechnya, 69, 203, 203p
Chekhov, Anton, 104p
chemistry, 50p, 51
Chernobyl, 194, 194p, 228
chernozem, 191, 232
  in other parts of the world, 164h
Cherskiy Range, 221m
child labor, 53
China, 220m
  Hong Kong and, 128
  in World War II, 58
Chisinau, Moldova, 170
Christianity, 42
  in Middle Ages, 44, 44p
Chukchi people, 14p
Chukchi Sea, 223m
Churchill, Winston, 68
churros, 17
cinema, 104p
cities, 56
citizenship
  Greek, 39

Roman, 41
city-states, 39, 146, 148, 232
civil war
  in England, 50
  in Yugoslavia, 181, 181p
climate, M1
  of France, 19
  of Germany, 19
  of Great Britain, 19
  of Norway, 19, 20
  oceans and, 18–19, 18m
  of Siberia, 17
  of Spain, 17, 20
climate maps, M12m
climate regions, M1, 9m
  of Europe, 20, 20p
  of Russia, 20, 20p
coal, 27m, 28, 29, 29p, 30m, 31
cobalt, 31
Cold War, 68, 68p, 158–159
collectives, 192, 232
colony, 50, 232
Columbus, Christopher, 45, 48, M14
communism, 230
  in Eastern Europe, 94, 95
  in Poland, 174
  in Russia, 198
  in Soviet Union, 66–68, 66p
  in Yugoslavia, 184–185, 184m
compass, M5
compass rose, M8
coniferous forests, 21
Constantine (Roman
  emperor), 42
constitution, 126, 232
Constitution, U.S., 131
constitutional monarchy, 141, 232
consumer goods, 178
Copenhagen, Denmark, 113
Copernicus, Nicolaus, 51
copper, 30m, 31
Council of the European Union, 73
Court of Justice, 73
critical thinking
  analyze, 76, 108
  analyze images, 41

  analyze information, 74, 180, 206
  analyze primary sources, 94
  categorize, 121, 173
  compare, 151
  compare and contrast, 16, 20, 32, 34,
    108, 121, 162, 173
  conclude, 97
  contrast, 34, 44, 76, 129, 188, 195,
    204, 206
  decision making, 143
  define, 34, 52, 69
  describe, 23, 34, 59, 144, 195, 204, 206
  distinguish fact and opinion, 104
  draw conclusions, 16, 23, 32, 34, 44,
    69, 74, 76, 106, 108, 129, 151, 162,
    173, 204
  draw inferences and conclusions, 157
  evaluate, 106
  evaluate information, 206
  explain, 16, 52, 69, 76, 81, 90, 108,
    129, 144, 160, 162, 180, 195, 204
  find main idea, 59, 108, 195
  generalize, 23, 90, 97, 120, 173
  identify, 16, 34, 97, 108, 162, 180,
    188, 195, 206
  identify cause, 69
  identify cause and effect, 34, 48, 59,
    206
  identify effect, 16, 23, 52, 59, 76, 90,
    106, 137, 144, 160, 188, 206
  identify frame of reference, 144
  identify main idea, 73, 206
  identify point of view, 180, 195
  infer, 52, 74, 81, 108, 121, 162, 204
  list, 23, 32, 34, 44, 74, 76, 90, 106,
    108, 137, 151, 162, 188, 206
  locate, 16, 97, 151
  make a bar chart, 173
  make a circle graph, 121
  making valid generalizations, 87
  name, 16, 34, 44, 69, 74, 76, 129, 206
  note, 97, 108, 129, 137, 188, 206
  predict, 34, 52, 59, 74, 81, 106, 108,
    162, 180, 195
  recall, 23, 32, 44, 52, 59, 74, 76, 81,
    90, 106, 108, 129, 137, 151, 160,
    162, 180, 204, 206
  recognize bias, 200
  sequence, 44, 57, 69, 129, 160, 188
  summarize, 23, 32, 34, 44, 52, 69, 76,
    90, 108, 137, 144, 151, 162, 206

interviews, 180
journal entry, 16, 44, 160
language arts, 108
letters, 74, 151
math, 76
newspaper article, 195
paragraph, 23, 32, 59, 69, 97, 129,
   144, 188, 204
postcard, 106
reports, 34
research papers, RW4–RW5
science, 206
short story, 81
social studies, RW2–RW5
television program, 137
travel guide, 108

Y

Yakut people, 102
Yugoslavia, 95, 167, 164g, 170, 172,
   172p, 183–185, 184m, 186m, 188,
   231
   civil war in, 181, 181p

Z

Zagreb, Croatia, 167

Acknowledgments

Cover Design

Pronk&Associates

Staff Credits

The people who made up *World Studies* ©05 team—representing design services, editorial, editorial services, educational technology, marketing, market research, photo research and art development, production services, project office, publishing processes, and rights & permissions—are listed below. Bold type denotes core team members.

Greg Abrom, Ernie Albanese, Rob Aleman, Susan Andariese, **Rachel Avenia-Prol,** Leann Davis Alspaugh, Penny Baker, Barbara Bertell, **Peter Brooks,** Rui Camarinha, John Carle, **Lisa Del Gatto,** Paul Delsignore, Kathy Dempsey, Anne Drowns, Deborah Dukeshire, Marlies Dwyer, **Frederick Fellows,** Paula C. Foye, Lara Fox, Julia Gecha, **Mary Hanisco,** Salena Hastings, Lance Hatch, Kerri Hoar, **Beth Hyslip,** Katharine Ingram, Nancy Jones, John Kingston, Deborah Levheim, Constance J. McCarty, **Kathleen Mercandetti,** Art Mkrtchyan, Ken Myett, **Mark O'Malley,** Jen Paley, Ray Parenteau, **Gabriela Pérez Fiato,** Linda Punskovsky, Kirsten Richert, **Lynn Robbins,** Nancy Rogier, Bruce Rolff, Robin Samper, Mildred Schulte, Siri Schwartzman, **Malti Sharma,** Lisa Smith-Ruvalcaba, Roberta Warshaw, Sarah Yezzi

Additional Credits

Jonathan Ambar, Tom Benfatti, Lisa D. Ferrari, Paul Foster, Florrie Gadson, Phil Gagler, Ella Hanna, Jeffrey LaFountain, Karen Mancinelli, Michael McLaughlin, Lesley Pierson, Debi Taffet

The DK Designs team who contributed to *World Studies* © 05 were as follows: Hilary Bird, Samantha Borland, Marian Broderick, Richard Czapnik, Nigel Duffield, Heather Dunleavy, Cynthia Frazer, James A. Hall, Lucy Heaver, Rose Horridge, Paul Jackson, Heather Jones, Ian Midson, .Marie Ortu, Marie Osborn, Leyla Ostovar, Ralph Pitchford, Ilana Sallick, Pamela Shiels, Andrew Szudek, Amber Tokeley.

Maps

Maps and globes were created by **DK Cartography**. The team consisted of Tony Chambers, Damien Demaj, Julia Lunn, Ed Merritt, David Roberts, Ann Stephenson, Gail Townsley, Iorwerth Watkins.

Illustrations

Kenneth Batelman: **39, 85;** Trevor Johnston: **51;** Jen Paley: **10, 17, 19, 24, 26, 31, 38, 45, 48, 53, 55, 62, 70, 84, 91, 99, 100, 109, 122, 124, 130, 131, 134, 138, 140, 142, 145, 147, 153, 154, 156, 174, 176, 178, 181, 182, 189, 190, 198, 201, 207**

Photos

Cover Photos

tl, Ed Pritchard/Getty Images Inc. **tm,** Jerry Kobalenko/Getty Images Inc. **tr,** Angelo Cavalli/Getty Images Inc. **b,** Mary Liz Austin/Terry Donnelly

Title Page

Mary Liz Austin/Terry Donnelly

Table of Contents

T4, Alain Le Garsmeur/Getty Images, Inc.; **T5 t,** Giraudon/Art Resource, NY; **T5 m,** Thomas Dannenberg/Masterfile Corporation; **T5 b,** Rykoff Collection/Corbis; **T6,** Shaun Egan/Getty Images, Inc.; **T7,** Bettmann/Corbis; **T9,** Laski Diffusion/East News/Liaison/Getty Images Inc.

Professional Development

T35, Royalty-Free/Corbis; **T36,** PhotoDisc/Getty Images, Inc.; **T37,** Comstock.

Learning With Technology

xiii, Discovery Channel School

Reading and Writing Handbook

RW, Michael Newman/PhotoEdit; **RW1,** Walter Hodges/Getty Images, Inc.; **RW2,** Digital Vision/Getty Images, Inc.; **RW3,** Will Hart/PhotoEdit; **RW5,** Jose Luis Pelaez, Inc./Corbis

MapMaster Skills Handbook

M, James Hall/DK Images; **M1,** Mertin Harvey/Gallo Images/Corbis; **M2-3 m,** NASA; **M2-3,** (globes) Planetary Visions: **M5 br,** Barnabas Kindersley/DK Images; **M6 tr,** Mike Dunning/DK Images; **M10 b,** Bernard and Catherine Desjeux/Corbis; **M11,** Hutchinson Library; **M12 b,** Pa Photos; **M13 r,** Panos Pictures; **M14 l,** Macduff Everton/Corbis; **M14 t,** MSCF/NASA; **M15 b,** Ariadne Van Zandbergen/Lonely Planet Images; **M16 l,** Bill Stormont/Corbis; **M16 b,** Pablo Corral/Corbis; **M17 t,** Stone Les/Sygma/Corbis; **M17 b,** W. Perry Conway/Corbis

Guiding Questions

1, Wally McNamee/Corbis

Regional Overview

2, ABC Press-Hofstee/Sygma/Corbis; **3,** Royalty-Free/Corbis; **4,** Roger Antrobus/Corbis; **5 t,** Anders Ryman/Corbis; **5 b,** DK Images; **6 t,** DK Images; **6 b,** Raymond Gehman/Corbis; **7 t,** Jose Fuste Raga/Corbis; **7 b,** Uwe Schmid/Corbis

Chapter One

8f l, Royalty-Free/Corbis; **8f r,** PhotoDisc/Getty Images, Inc.; **8–9,** Derek Croucher/Corbis; **10,** Wolfgang Kaehler/Corbis; **11 t,** The Fringe/Index Stock Imagery, Inc.; **11b,** Konrad Wothe/Minden Pictures; **13 t,** Discovery Channel School; **13 b,** Ray Juno/Corbis; **14,** Natalie Fobes/Getty Images, Inc.; **15,** Zefa Visual Media-Germany/Index Stock Imagery, Inc.; **16,** Gregor Schmid/Corbis; **17 t,** Angela Maynard/Life File/Getty Images, Inc.; **17 b,** Dean Conger/Corbis; **18,** William Manning/Corbis; **20 t,** Dean Conger/Corbis; **20 b,** Mary Rhodes/Animals Animals/Earth Scenes; **23,** Wolfgang Kaehler/Corbis; **24,** Bob Krist/Corbis; **26,** Arnulf Husmo/Getty Images, Inc.; **27,** Paul Thompson; Eye Ubiquitous/Corbis; **28,** Dr. Eric Chalker/Index Stock Imagery, Inc.; **29 t,** Ed Kashi/Corbis; **29 b,** Chris Niedenthal//Time Life Pictures/Getty Images Inc.; **30,** Dave G. Houser/Corbis; **31 l,** Breck P. Kent/Animals Animals/Earth Scenes; **31 m,** Mark Schneider/Visuals Unlimited; **31 r,** Michael St. Maur Sheil/Corbis; **32,** Sovfoto/Eastfoto; **33 t,** Mary Rhodes/Animals Animals/Earth Scenes; **33 b,** Ed Kashi/Corbis

Chapter Two

36h l, Royalty-Free/Corbis; **36h r,** PhotoDisc/Getty Images, Inc.; **36–37,** John Elk III/Lonely Planet Images; **38,** AFP Photo/John Mottern/Corbis; **40,** Scala/Art Resource, NY; **41 t,** ML Sinibaldi/Corbis; **41 b,** Alinari/Art Resource, NY; **42 l,** McRae Books, Srl; **42 r,** Erich Lessing/Art Resource, NY; **43 t,** HIP/Scala/Art Resource, NY; **43 b,** R. G. Ojeda/ Réunion des Musées/Art Resource, NY; **44 t,** Adam Woolfit/Corbis; **44 b,** Owen Franken/Corbis; **45,** Bettmann/Corbis; **46 t,** John Heseltine/Corbis; **46 b,** Bridgeman Art Library; **47 tl,** Musee du Louvre/Philippe Sebert/Dorling Kindersley; **47 tr,** The Granger Collection, New York; **47 bl,** Bettmann/Corbis; **47 br,** James L. Amos/Corbis; **48,** Historical Picture Archive/Corbis; **49 t,** Archivo Iconografico, S.A./Corbis; **49 b,** Art Resource; **50 l,** The Granger Collection; **50 r,** Picture History; **52 t,** Bettmann/Corbis; **52 b,** Sheila Terry/Photo Researchers, Inc.; **53,** Corbis; **54 l,** Dorling Kindersley Media Library; **54 r,** The Granger Collection, New York; **55 l,** Art Resource, NY; **55 m,** Bettmann/Corbis; **55 r,** Scala/Art Resource, NY; **56 t,** Science & Society Picture Library; **56 b,** DK Images; **58 t,** The Granger Collection, NY; **58 b,** Museum of the City of New York; **59,** AP/Wide World Photos; **60,** Giraudon/Art Resource, NY; **61 t,** Roger Wood/Corbis; **61 b,** Christi Graham and Nick Nichols/Dorling Kindersley; **62,** Archivo Iconografico, S.A./Corbis; **64 t,** Discovery Channel School; **64 b,** Christie's Images/Corbis; **65,** Bettmann/Corbis; **66 t,** Hulton-Deutsch Collection/Corbis; **66 b,** Bettmann/Corbis; **67 t,** Yevgeny Khaldei/Getty Images, Inc.; **67 b,** U.S. Army;

68 t, Corbis; **68 b,** PhotoDisc/Getty Images, Inc.; **69,** AFP/Corbis; **70 t,** Time Life Pictures/Getty Images, Inc.; **70 b,** Culver Pictures, Inc.; **72 t,** Thomas Dannenberg/Masterfile Corporation; **72 b,** AP/Wide World Photos; **73,** M. Taner/Masterfile Corporation; **74,** AP/Wide World Photos/Lawrence Jackson; **75,** Thomas Dannenberg/Masterfile Corporation

Literature

79, Giraudon/Art Resource, NY; **80,** Scala/Art Resource, NY

Chapter Three

82f l, Royalty-Free/Corbis; **82f r,** PhotoDisc/Getty Images, Inc.; **82–83,** Holton Collection/SuperStock, Inc.; **84,** Georgina Bowater/Corbis; **86,** Powerstock/Index Stock Imagery, Inc.; **87 t,** Howard Davies/Corbis; **87 b,** Terry Why/Index Stock Imagery, Inc.; **88 t,** SuperStock International; **88 b,** Sion Touhig/Getty Images, Inc.; **89 t,** Discovery Channel School; **89 bl,** Sean Gallup/Getty Images, Inc.; **89 br,** Julio Etchart/The Image Works; **90,** H. Mollenhauer/Masterfile Corporation; **91,** William Miller/University of Texas at Austin; **92,** Chin Allana/Corbis Sygma; **93 l,** AP Photo/Boris Grdanoski; **93 r,** Taner/Masterfile Corporation; **95 t,** Reuters NewMedia Inc./Corbis; **95 b,** Peter Turnle/Corbis; **96,** Anthony Cassidy/Getty Images, Inc.; **97,** Archivo Iconografico, S.A./Corbis; **98,** David Turnley/Corbis; **99,** Richard Haynes; **100,** David Sutherland/Getty Images, Inc.; **101 l,** A. Kuznetsov/Trip Photographic; **101 r,** Dean Conger/Corbis; **102,** James Hill/Getty Images, Inc.; **103 t,** Bettmann/Corbis; **103 m,** DK Images; **103 b,** RIA, Novosti; **104 t,** Laski Diffusion/East News/Liaison/Getty Images Inc.; **104 bl,** Topham/The Image Works; **104 bm,** Bettmann/Corbis; **104 br,** Swim Ink/Corbis; **105 l,** Scala/Art Resource, NY; **105 m,** Liaison/Getty Images, Inc.; **105 r,** Archivo Iconografico, S.A./Corbis; **106,** Gideon Mendel/Corbis; **107 t,** Sion Touhig/Getty Images, Inc.; **107 b,** Laski Diffusion/East News/Liaison/Getty Images Inc.

Chapter Four

110h l, Royalty-Free/Corbis; **110h r,** PhotoDisc/Getty Images, Inc.; **110–111,** Simeone Huber/Getty Images, Inc.; **112 t,** Discovery Channel School; **112 b,** Ric Ergenbright/Corbis; **113,** Willy Thiria/Corbis; **114,** Staffan Widstrand/Corbis; **117,** Swim Ink/Corbis; **118,** Staffan Widstrand/Corbis; **120,** Chris Trotman/Corbis; **122,** TravelPix/Getty Images, Inc.; **123,** Robert Estall/Corbis; **125,** Bridgeman Art Library; **126 t,** Royal Collection Enterprises Ltd.; **126 b,** AP Photo/John Stillwell, Pool; **127 t,** The British Library/Topham-HIP/Image Works; **127 m,** AP/Wide World Photos/Donald McLeod-POOL; **127 b,** Peter Macdiarmid/Reuters NewMedia/Corbis; **128 t,** Topham/The Image Works; **128 b,** Discovery Channel School; **128 m,** Rykoff Collection/Corbis; **129,** Annie Griffiths Belt/Corbis; **130,** Nogues Alain/Corbis Sygma; **131 t,** Stapleton Collection/Corbis; **131 tm,** Elisabeth Louise Vigee-Lebrun/Galleria degli Uffizi, Florence, Italy/Bridgeman Art Library; **131 bm,** National Gallery Collection; by kind permission of the Trustees of the National Gallery, London/Corbis; **131 b,** Christie's Images/Corbis; **132,** K. Yamashita/Mon Tresor/Panoramic Images; **133 t,** Snark/Art Resource, NY; **133 b,** Discovery Channel School; **135 l,** Philippe Desmazes/AFP/Getty Images, Inc.; **135 r,** Stuart Cohen/The Image Works; **136,** EPA/Alfred France Out/AP/Wide World Photos; **137,** C.Garroni Parisi/Das Fotoarchiv/Peter Arnold, Inc.; **138,** Björn Andrén Bilder; **139 t,** Steve Raymer/Corbis; **139 b,** Blaine Harrington; **141 t,** Discovery Channel School; **141 b,** AP/Wide World Photos/Toni Sica; **143,** SuperStock, Inc.; **144,** Macduff Everton/Corbis; **145,** John Miller/Robert Harding World Imagery; **146,** Owen Franken/Corbis; **148 t,** Discovery Channel School; **148 b,** Hulton Archive Photos/Getty Images Inc.; **149 t,** Allsport UK/Getty Images, Inc.; **149 b,** Mimmo Jodice/Corbis; **150,** Shaun Egan/Getty Images, Inc.; **151,** Burstein Collection/Corbis; **152,** Stephen Studd/Getty Images, Inc.; **154,** AP/Wide World Photos; **155,** Hulton-Deutsch Collection/Corbis; **156,** Collection of Stuart S. Corning, Jr. Photo © Rob Huntley /Lightstream; **157 t,** Sovfoto/Eastfoto;

157 b, Bettmann/Corbis; **158,** David Brauchli/Corbis; **159 t,** Bettmann/Corbis; **159 b,** Discovery Channel School; **160,** Ken Straiton/Corbis; **161,** Burstein Collection/Corbis

Chapter Five

164g l, Royalty-Free/Corbis; **164g r,** PhotoDisc/Getty Images, Inc.; **164h l,** GeoStock/Getty Images, Inc.; **164h ml,** Comstock; **164h mr,** PhotoDisc/Getty Images, Inc.; **164h r,** SW Productions/Getty Images, Inc.; **164–165,** Jonathan Blair/Corbis; **166,** Discovery Channel School; **168,** Niall Benvie/Corbis; **170,** Barry Lewis/Corbis; **171 t,** Topham Picturepoint/Image Works; **171 b,** Dave King/Dorling Kindersley; **172,** Tim Thompson/Corbis; **174,** Hideo Haga/The Image Works; **175 t,** AP/Wide World Photos/Rudi Blaha; **175 b,** Raymond Gehman/Corbis; **177 t,** Discovery Channel School; **177 b,** Peter Turnley/Corbis; **179 t,** Raymond Gehman/Corbis; **179 b,** Hicks/Premium/Panoramic Images; **180,** Raymond Gehman/Corbis; **181 t,** David Cannon/Allsport/Getty Images, Inc.; **181 b,** AP/Wide World Photos/Rikard Larma; **183 t,** Jonathan Blair/Corbis; **183 b,** Jim McDonald/Corbis; **185,** Jules Frazier/Getty Images, Inc.; **186 t,** Discovery Channel School; **186 b,** Ron Haviv/VII Photo; **187,** AP/Wide World Photos/EPA/Georgi Licovski; **188,** Janez Skok/Corbis; **189,** Novosti/Sovfoto; **191 t,** Mary Evans Picture Library; **191 m,** TASS/Sovfoto; **191 b,** Robert Capa/Magnum Photo Library; **192–193 b,** TASS/Sovfoto; **193 t,** Ed Kashi/Corbis; **194 t,** Discovery Channel School; **194 b,** Yann Arthus-Bertrand/Corbis; **195,** Sean Sprague/Peter Arnold, Inc.; **196,** Raymond Gehman/Corbis; **197,** Paul Almasy/Corbis; **198,** Peter Turnley/Corbis; **199 t,** Discovery Channel School; **199 m,** TASS/Sovfoto; **199 b,** Demetrio Carrasco/Getty Images, Inc.; **200,** TASS/Sovfoto; **202,** Alain Le Garsmeur/Getty Images, Inc.; **203 t,** B&C Alexander/AgPix; **203 b,** Reuters NewMedia Inc./Corbis; **204;** Marc Garanger/Corbis; **205,** Hideo Haga/The Image Works

Projects

208 t, Andy Crawford/Dorling Kindersley; **208 b,** Wally McNamee/Corbis

Reference

209, Paul A. Souders/Corbis

Glossary of Geographic Terms

226 t, A. & L. Sinibaldi/Getty Images, Inc.; **226 b,** John Beatty/Getty Images, Inc.; **226–227 b,** Spencer Swanger/Tom Stack & Associates; **227 t,** Hans Strand/Getty Images, Inc.; **227 m,** Paul Chesley/Getty Images, Inc.

Gazetteer

228, Ray Juno/Corbis; **229 t,** David Brauchli/Corbis; **229 b,** Arnulf Husmo/Getty Images, Inc.; **230,** Hideo Haga/The Image Works; **231,** John Miller/Robert Harding World Imagery

Glossary

232, AP/Wide World Photos; **233 t,** The Fringe/Index Stock Imagery, Inc.; **233 b,** Scala/Art Resource, NY; **234,** Bob Krist/Corbis; **235,** Raymond Gehman/Corbis

Text

78, Excerpt from *Pearl in the Egg: A Tale of the Thirteenth Century* by Dorothy van Woerkom. Copyright © 1980 by Dorothy van Woerkom.

Note: Every effort has been made to locate the copyright owner of material used in this textbook. Omissions brought to our attention will be corrected in subsequent editions.